www.wadsworth.com

wadsworth.com is the World Wide Web site for
Wadsworth Publishing Company and is your direct
source to dozens of online resources.

At *wadsworth.com* you can find out about
supplements, demonstration software, and
student resources. You can also send e-mail to
many of our authors and preview new publications
and exciting new technologies.

wadsworth.com
Changing the way the world learns®

Aesthetics

Classic Readings from the Western Tradition

SECOND EDITION

Dabney Townsend
Armstrong Atlantic State University

Wadsworth
Thomson Learning™

Australia • Canada • Mexico • Singapore • Spain • United Kingdom • United States

Philosophy Editor: Peter Adams
Assistant Editor: Kerri Abdinoor
Editorial Assistant: Mindy Newfarmer/Mark Andrews
Marketing Manager: Dave Garrison
Print Buyer: Mary Noel
Permissions Editor: Joohee Lee

Production Service: Matrix Productions
Copy Editor: Vicki Nelson
Cover Designer: Ross Carron
Cover Printer: Von Hoffmann/Custom
Compositor: G&S Typesetters, Inc.
Printer/Binder: Von Hoffmann/Custom

For permission to use material from this text, contact
us by
Web: www.thomsonrights.com **Fax:** 1-800-730-2215
Phone: 1-800-730-2214

Library of Congress Cataloging-in-Publication Data
Aesthetics : classic readings from the Western tradition /
   [compiled by] Dabney Townsend—2nd ed.
      p. cm.
   Includes bibliographical references and index.
   ISBN 0-534-55146-7
   1. Aesthetics—History. I. Townsend, Dabney
BH81.A37 2000
111'.85—dc21
                                                99-058562

For more information, contact
Wadsworth/Thomson Learning
10 Davis Drive
Belmont, CA 94002-3098
USA
www.wadsworth.com

International Headquarters
Thomson Learning
290 Harbor Drive, 2nd Floor
Stamford, CT 06902-7477
USA

UK/Europe/Middle East
Thomson Learning
Berkshire House
168-173 High Holborn
London WC1V 7AA
United Kingdom

Asia
Thomson Learning
60 Albert Street #15-01
Albert Complex
Singapore 189969

Canada
Nelson/Thomson Learning
1120 Birchmount Road
Scarborough, Ontario M1K 5G4
Canada

Contents

Preface

The Purpose of This Anthology

This anthology begins with the assumption that our current awareness of art and the aesthetic is such that *aesthetics* is not a familiar term to most students. In approaching the subject for the first time, one needs to keep in mind that students do not really know what aesthetics is or even what the word means. To plunge directly into contemporary philosophical debates about art often leads to confusion and frustration. One effective way to answer the question "What is aesthetics?" is to pay attention to the development of the discipline through key texts in its history. The premise of this anthology, therefore, is that a selection of core historical texts can provide the kind of background that beginning students—undergraduate or graduate—need in order to understand what the issues in aesthetics are. What I have provided is not precisely a history of aesthetics, but the selection of texts does attempt to represent that history as a continuum.

The focus of the texts is limited to the western tradition because that is where philosophical aesthetics has developed. That does not imply that other art traditions should not be considered, nor that there are not interesting philosophical texts from non-western traditions that bear on aesthetics. But the historical and philosophical focus coincide in making the western tradition the most coherent and well developed one in aesthetics. For the introductory student, therefore, it provides the best starting place.

The Major Features of the Text

In this day of expanded electronic resources and convenient copying, one must consider whether an anthology still has a place in the design of an aesthetics course. Most anthologies that are available today seek to be comprehensive. Typically, they try to include something for everyone and a bit of everything. The result is a very large volume whose expense precludes the purchase of any other text. But while that kind of anthology was needed when the only aesthetics books undergraduates would have were the ones that they would buy, today an instructor can place on the Web or in course packets favorite essays and supplement whatever basic texts are assigned quite economically.

In teaching aesthetics to undergraduates and to humanities students outside philosophy through the graduate level, I concluded that a different kind of anthology would be useful. It would focus on those historically significant essays that provide a needed background for the study of philosophical aesthetics and it would be relatively compact. That leaves the instructor free to assign a basic introductory aesthetics textbook or to choose additional contemporary essays for a small course packet while still keeping the cost of the course reasonable.

This anthology is addressed to beginning students in aesthetics. For undergraduates, this will likely be a first course in aesthetics and perhaps even a first course in philosophy. But many students do not encounter aesthetics until they begin some form of graduate study. Aesthetic questions may arise in philosophy courses, in art history and art appreciation courses, or in any area of the humanities. I have tried to provide the kind of selections that can serve as both a beginning and a reference. Thus, the selections in this anthology have been chosen to illustrate a range of approaches in an historical context. I have chosen texts that are obvious and frequently referred to where possible, but I have also included some less well-known selections, such as those from Bonaventure and Dante, in order to show the connections between the ancient and modern worlds.

The selections are classics in aesthetics, but they do not represent my preferred solutions to aesthetic problems. (As with any philosopher, I do not pretend neutrality. I have my own position. I doubt, however, that anyone will be able to infer what it is from these texts.) Many of the positions represented in these texts are incompatible. Philosophy advances by engaging in such disagreements. These theories illustrate not an end but a beginning to an investigation. Aesthetics as a discipline can be regarded as the sum of these possibilities. It remains an open-ended, developing study that will continue to change as art and its audience changes.

Pedagogical Aids

In addition to providing a compact and representative historical selection of texts, I have tried to make the readings as accessible as possible by providing a number of special pedagogical aids.

Introductions. First, a general introduction to each part and section explains the historical setting and provides continuity. Then each selection is introduced individually. The purpose of these introductions is not to provide summaries that students can use in place of reading for themselves but to highlight questions, presuppositions, and context so that the text does not stand in isolation. I have tried to presuppose as little technical philosophical jargon as possible in the introductions. Inevitably, however, basic classical texts do make use of a technical vocabulary. While one can hardly supply a complete discussion of such general terms as *idealism* or *dialectic* in an introduction, some guidance must be provided for the beginner. The introductions serve that purpose.

Annotations. Second, I have annotated each selection. Many of the selections are dense in references to specific facts, works of art, and artists. If one could presume a highly educated audience, those references might be intelligible. For today's student, however, figures from classical history and literature or technical terms from the arts and philosophy are likely to be mysterious. Annotations can dispel some of that mystery.

Questions for Discussion and Review. Third, for each selection I have provided questions for discussion and review. These questions serve two pedagogical purposes.

- They provide a starting point for discussion. Some are intended specifically to get the student to think about alternate applications of the theory in question, for example.
- The questions also provide a kind of reading guide. Sometime the organization of a selection will not be obvious to a student. By providing a set of leading questions, the student can be led to see the key points in the text. I have found that questions are better for this purpose than an outline.

Passages for Discussion. Finally, the very compactness of this anthology presents a problem because innumerable important authors and special formulations could not be included. I have found, for example, that I often need a classic definition such as Aquinas's definition of beauty or Keats's description of "negative capability" in the course of a lecture or discussion. To meet this need, I have provided "Passages for Discussion" that offers some provocative or well-known statements. These passages serve three purposes:

- They suggest further reading.
- They provide needed examples and quotations.
- They can act as starting points for discussion.

These pedagogical aids will, I hope, make this anthology more useful than a simple collection of texts.

New in the Second Edition

As noted, the emphasis of this anthology is upon making available a set of texts from the history of philosophical aesthetics in a form sufficiently compact to allow the instructor some room for additions. For that reason, the first edition stopped with the end of the extended nineteenth century—World War I. The twentieth century is rich in interesting texts. I have my favorites that I always use, and I am sure that other specialists in the field have theirs. But everyone who teaches a course in aesthetics is not a specialist in the field. Comments have indicated that many users would like for this anthology to be the primary text for their course, and for that purpose, an introduction to the twentieth century is needed. This second edition expands Part III to meet that need. In order to retain the original historical orientation and relatively compact size, Part III offers two new features:

A New Introduction. The introduction to this part is more extensive than the other introductions. It surveys the different philosophical approaches to aesthetics in the twentieth century. It also provides footnotes that act as a guide to further reading. While these cannot be comprehensive, they should allow both the student and the instructor to pursue particular topics or approaches on their own as they choose.

New Selections. I have added four representative selections from the mid-twentieth century. The rationale for these selections is slightly different from those of the earlier parts. Because time has done the sorting process for us, it is relatively easy to identify classic texts in the history of aesthetics and representative movements. In the century that we have just completed, that sorting process is still ongoing. I think, however, that some important shifts are obvious. I have chosen four texts that will help students understand those shifts.

- **Walter Benjamin's "Art in the Age of Mechanical Reproduction"** demonstrates the difference in emphasis in continental European and Anglo-American aesthetics. It is more sociological and ideological, and it approaches philosophy from a cultural perspective. It also offers an example of a politically engaged form of philosophy.
- **Morris Weitz's "The Role of Theory in Aesthetics"** was a seminal work in bringing the influence of one of the leading twentieth-century philosophers, Ludwig Wittgenstein, into aesthetics. Wittgenstein's work marks a major shift in the way that Anglo-American philosophy is conceived, and Weitz brings that shift to the fore for aesthetics.
- **George Dickie's "The Myth of the Aesthetic Attitude"** marks a similar shift in the basic presuppositions of twentieth-century aesthetics. It challenges the dominant assumption that aesthetic experience is psychologically unique and that an aesthetic attitude is a necessary condition for aesthetic experience. Dickie also represents a renewed interest in the history of aesthetics as a way to understand contemporary problems.
- **Arthur Danto's "The Artworld"** was an important turning point in the way that aesthetic theory was reconstituted after the challenge of Wittgenstein. If the assumptions about aesthetic experience and an aesthetic attitude are misleading and if the dominant way of philosophizing about aesthetics by a combination of philosophical analysis of definitions and psychological analysis of experience is challenged by the followers of Wittgenstein, then Danto's emphasis on the interaction of theory and the practice of art offers a significant new direction.

These new selections will, I believe, make it possible for this anthology to serve as the primary text for an undergraduate course. While they cannot be considered exhaustive, they suggest the continued development of aesthetics.

I offer this selection of texts as evidence of the deep and perennial interest of aesthetics to philosophers of the first rank. If Plato and Aristotle, David Hume and Immanuel Kant, and a host of other philosophers and critics have written about aesthetics in ways that are central to their philosophy, then we are justified in thinking that aesthetics may continue to be important to us as well.

Acknowledgments

I would like to thank a number of people who have helped in the preparation of this anthology. Gary Hagberg of Bard College read the initial prospectus and a first draft of the whole work. He provided helpful input and encouragement when it was needed. Robert Ginsberg provided a thorough editorial reading of the introductions and many helpful suggestions in addition to early copyediting. I have followed his advice in many places. Arnold Berleant and Arthur Bartlett made useful suggestions. My colleagues at the University of Texas at Arlington, Tim Mahoney and Charles Chiasson, read the classical introductions and notes and saved me from several errors. Tim Mahoney and Sherry Blum of the University of Texas at Austin also provided a new translation of the Plotinus section. Daniel Herwitz, Tom Leddy, Richard Wollheim, Gene Blocker, Anita Silver, and Hilde Hein all read the manuscript and provided useful suggestions as well as specific corrections. For this second edition, readers for Wadsworth have commented on both the organization and the content. It is to them that I owe the impetus for the new selections. I hope that my choices will meet with their approval. Peter Adams, Mindy Newfarmer, and the editorial staff at Wadsworth have been patient and helpful. Billie Hughes typed and retyped the reading selections. Finally, my students in aesthetics have used various versions of this anthology. They have taught me as much as I have taught them. I thank them all.

Needless to say, the individuals named are not responsible for the deficiencies that remain in this anthology. The blame when I have remained stubbornly heedless of their advice is mine alone. Nothing in philosophy can be everything to everyone. I can only hope that using this book will stimulate some of the same excitement that I feel for aesthetics and its history.

PART ONE

Classical and Medieval Aesthetics

*A*ESTHETICS IS A MODERN TERM. It entered our philosophical vocabulary in the eighteenth century. Art and its effects attracted the attention of thinkers virtually from the beginning of Western thought, however. Art is so closely associated with the central cultural and religious forms of life in the classical world that it was inevitably the subject of speculation and comment as soon as philosophers began to write. Moreover, *beauty* was a central philosophical term in a way that we have to recover if we are to understand classical philosophy. In the classical world, art was seldom mere entertainment in our contemporary, escapist sense. Works of art were not valued "for themselves" in the way that our museum-culture promotes. Drama, even in its comic and satiric modes, was a part of cultural and religious festivals. Sculpture and painting provided memorials for the dead and images for the gods. The undoubted and widespread forms of decoration that we know in classical houses and utilitarian objects served to link everyday life to the fabric of myth. Even art that was merely to be looked at served a function; it commemorated events and brought honor and prestige to its owners and patrons. Therefore, art and beauty naturally attracted the comment of philosophers who sought to understand central cultural forms.

Beauty was even more important than art to classical philosophers. Different standards and ideals of beauty prevail in different cultures. The particular natural and artistic forms that are pleasing to me and the way that I describe them need not be the same as they were to the citizens of Athens in the fifth century B.C.E.[1] Some emotional responses seem to be very widespread, however. The pleasure that I take in a sunset or a landscape provides a shared link across cultural boundaries and temporal distance. We are not so different that we do not understand and respond in similar ways. The greatest difference is in the concepts we use to describe our responses. In classical thought, beauty is not understood simply as an emotion. It is a value closely linked

---

[1] Dating inevitably is culturally relative. B.C.E. (Before the Common Era) has the slight advantage of being less theologically arrogant than the older B.C. (Before Christ) though it amounts to the same thing. This style allows dates for our current era to stand without the older A.D. (*Anno Domini*, "year of Our Lord") designation without confusion.

1

with truth and the good. Beauty is understood as a property of the highest forms of being in the world itself. It is associated with harmony and order. When classical writers sought to understand the order of the world, they included beauty in their investigations. They believed that beauty informed the intellect as well as the senses. Beauty must be a topic for consideration for anyone who seeks to understand the place of human beings in the cosmos.

Classical writers lacked a systematic approach to what we call aesthetic phenomena in their own right. Aesthetics was incorporated into discussions of politics, knowledge, religion, and morality. The integration of the aesthetic into larger discussions has the virtue of showing the relevance of art to life. Only rarely was classical aesthetics the province of a small class of "aesthetes" devoted only to the enjoyment of sensation. Consequently, we must look for discussions of aesthetic topics in the context of other issues. Context is always important.

One additional source for classical aesthetics should be considered. The word *art* implies not only the kind of things that we classify as works of art; it also implies craft —knowledge of how to do or make something. Many of the interesting comments on art by classical writers are from the practical standpoint of how to make something that works the way it is supposed to work. This perspective is particularly true of rhetorical works. The art of speaking was a preeminent professional skill in a world without printing. The law, church, court, and tradition all depended on oral performance and rhetorical persuasion. Classical writers studied and employed a detailed array of technical devices. The link between persuasion and aesthetics is often close.

Tradition says that Plato was a poet before turning to philosophy. Discussions of art, poetry, criticism, and rhetoric are scattered throughout the Platonic dialogues. The sustained attention to poetry and the function of the poet in the *Republic* has been one of the most central and influential in the history of philosophy. Aristotle devoted a whole treatise to rhetoric, but his compact discussion of tragedy in the *Poetics* is even more central to aesthetics. It is at once a rhetoric of drama and an analysis of what makes up a poetic imitation. The followers of Plotinus form the school of neo-Platonism.[2] Throughout the Middle Ages and the Renaissance, neo-Platonism provided the framework for a chain of being that was thought to link all elements of the universe into an organic whole. Beauty is taken by neo-Platonists to be a central property of that organism. The discussion of beauty by Plotinus provides the most effective answer in the classical world to Plato's challenge to the arts in the *Republic*.

With the decline of the western Roman empire in the early Middle Ages, art and speculation about it became even more localized in particular institutions. We must always be careful not to project our concepts of "art" and "aesthetic feeling" back onto cultural situations where those concepts and practices did not exist. Art flourished, but it belonged to the church, the court, and special civic institutions. Artists practiced a craft or were scholars, monks or traveling poets. Philosophical treatments of art are found in the context of theology and mystical writings. A medieval "aesthetic" exists in continuity with its classical roots. It is built on harmony and proportion, a love of color and form, and a deep sense that symbols project significance beyond their individual appearance.

---

[2] For a discussion of neo-Platonism, see the introduction to the Plotinus reading selection on p. 44.

Neo-Platonism continued to be influential in a Christianized form through the Middle Ages. It was transmitted through two primary sources and a multitude of influences and unacknowledged references. The two most important sources were the writings of Augustine of Hippo (354–430) and the sixth-century Syrian monk whose work was taken to be by Paul's disciple Dionysius the Areopagite. Augustine incorporated many Platonic elements in his theology. In particular, he was able to use the neo-Platonic concept of spiritual being to solve problems about the existence of evil and the incorporeal nature of God. In aesthetics, this concept made available the hierarchical movement which found harmony in the whole universe and beauty as its object. Pseudo-Dionysius[3] presented parts of earlier neo-Platonists directly in the guise of Christian doctrine. Divine names and a form of dialectical negation opened the hierarchy to speculation. Both Augustine and pseudo-Dionysius distrusted beauty itself, however. It was too pagan. Christian writers throughout the Middle Ages struggled with the competing claims of beauty as the highest value and the tendency of asceticism to distrust anything that was too sensual. Only medieval mysticism was able truly to embrace both at once.

Later medieval philosophers and theologians reintroduced Aristotle's criticisms of Plato. Neo-Platonism remained influential, but it took more concrete, individualistic forms in response to Aristotle's unification of form and sense. In the Renaissance, an increasing emphasis on experience, artistic expression, and individual achievement and skill shifted aesthetics away from beauty as a divine harmony toward beauty as a felt, sensual first step toward a higher consciousness. The aesthetic payoff of art was something that an individual could feel rather than an intellectual union of individual minds with the divine mind. Changes in the philosophy of beauty paralleled a changing status and function of art. No matter how skilled, medieval artists were largely anonymous conduits for a divine inspiration. As first Aristotelianism and then a revised neo-Platonism took hold, artists appeared as individuals whose skill exhibited their own perceptions as well as those communicated to them. Most of the elements remained the same, but artists now produced individual works about individual objects for individual consumers. The aesthetic in its modern sense—a science of feeling as such—became possible.

Based on its strong sense of individualism and humanism, Renaissance art rejected medieval scholasticism. The Aristotelian-Thomist model for philosophy had emphasized logical deduction and an otherworldly subordination of the individual to God's plan. Renaissance writers tended to reject that model (though generalization is suspect in a period of such cultural diversity), but they continued to rely on its more neo-Platonic elements. What was to be put in place of the medieval models was less clear. Many Renaissance theorists and artists thought of themselves as returning to the clarity of classical models, even if their understanding of those models was much different from that of their originators. One of the intramural battles in this struggle for new

---

[3] The works attributed to Dionysius the Aereopagite were in fact probably written or compiled in the sixth century in Syria. They include large sections taken directly from the later neo-Platonist Proclus (410–485). Although the attribution to a disciple of Paul was challenged as early as the twelfth century, these writings retained their influence as near-canonical works through the Middle Ages. Their author is commonly referred to as "pseudo-Dionysius" today.

forms was between the ancients and the moderns. Defenders of the ancients looked back to Greece and Rome for the models of culture. Defenders of the moderns pointed to the new achievements in science and art as improvements on the antique world. One side thought everything new a descent from the standards of a golden age. The other saw itself standing on the shoulders of giants, reaching higher and higher. Writers on art entered into this battle with vigor, but the battle was largely intramural. The aesthetic principles applied by both sides were drawn from classical and medieval sources. Then and now, artistic practice often runs ahead of theory.

The selections in Part I show the principal classical theories of Plato, Aristotle, and Plotinus. Then Bonaventure illustrates briefly the way that neo-Platonism informed the High Middle Ages, and Dante shows how a transformation already had begun to take place by the beginning of the fourteenth century even though medieval theology continued to shape his literary form. The passages for discussion at the end offer additional points of reference from the Renaissance as well as from earlier writers.

Plato

$\cdot \cdot \cdot \cdot \cdot$

Plato (427–347 B.C.E.) reasonably can be claimed as the founder of Western philosophy. Prior to Plato, philosophy was found primarily in traditions of wise teachers and their disciples. It tended to be oracular or prudential in its utterances. Plato made it a rational, argumentative mode of thought. His dialogues are our most important source for the transformation of his teacher Socrates from an oral tradition into a literary and philosophical persona. Socrates was born in 469 B.C.E. and spent his entire life in Athens. He was the center of a considerable circle, but he wrote nothing. We know from other references that there was a tradition of making Socrates the principal character in dialogues, but we have only the dialogues of Plato and Xenophon as examples. In 399, Socrates was tried on charges of impiety and corrupting the youth of Athens. The charges were political in nature, and he was executed when he refused to flee. Plato's use of Socrates and the relation of Plato's teaching to the actual teaching of Socrates are matters of much scholarly debate.

An Athenian, Plato was the son of aristocratic parents. He was born at a time when Athenian culture was still at its height, but the city-state's economic and political stability was declining. War with Athens' great rival, Sparta, had broken out in 431 (the Peloponnesian War), and it led eventually to Athens' defeat in 404. Early in his life, Plato was a poet and intended to become a statesman. Under the influence of Socrates, he turned to philosophy. After the death of Socrates, he traveled widely, especially to Syracuse, the Greek colony in Sicily. Plato returned to Athens, where he established a school known as the Academy. He taught in Athens for the next forty years. His teaching was interrupted by two subsequent trips to Syracuse. He was invited back to try to implement his political ideals when the new ruler of Syracuse, Dionysius II, came to power. The experiment was not a notable success. Plato returned a third time to mediate a political dispute and again failed. His own departure had to be negotiated. Plato died in Athens in 347 B.C.E., but the Academy continued to be an influential school that advanced and preserved his philosophical doctrines.

Plato's works are classified on the basis of their style and content. Dating is very problematic. The "early" dialogues center on Socrates as a character and as an active interlocutor. They make use of a form of irony in which Socrates professes to know nothing positive even as he probes the claims and definitions of his partners in conversation. The "middle" dialogues make much more use of narrative and setting to advance a coherent position. The *Republic* belongs to this middle set. It explores the whole basis

Roman, Imperial Period. *Portrait Head of Marcus Aurelius,* about 170–225. Kimbell Art Museum, Fort Worth, Texas.

for communal life. The discussion of poetry in Book X is only one part of that complex presentation of an ideal state. The theory of forms represented there is different from positions that Plato takes elsewhere. The "late" dialogues become even more expository and make Socrates a subordinate character. These periods should be taken as useful classifications rather than dates. They depend more on style and content than historical fact.

Plato's theory of poetry is scattered throughout his work. He has one dialogue from the early group, *Ion,* which shows Socrates questioning a rhapsode, or reciter of poetry, about what he does and knows. In later dialogues, several references to poetry, inspiration, and alternate theories of imitation appear in the context of other discussions. The discussion in Book X of the *Republic* is a central text because it deals with the major issues directly and presents a challenge that subsequent philosophers have taken up. It is not entirely consistent with Plato's positions elsewhere, however.

◆ ◆ ◆ ◆ ◆ ◆

Classical approaches to the arts can be classified under the general heading "Theories of Imitation." The term *imitation* requires careful consideration, however. It is much more complex than just the idea of making a copy of something else, and it is used in different senses by different philosophers. Plato explored two fundamental aspects of imitation in Book X of his long dialogue on the nature of the ideal state called the *Republic.*

The first topic concerns the nature of imitation itself. Plato approached this point analytically and logically. Given the existence of anything, an observer can discern both its unity or commonality as a type or kind of thing, and its diversity as multiple instances of that thing. Each bed and tree is at least numerically distinct. Yet all beds are identifiable as beds and are different from trees. Logically, Plato argues, there must be a single ideal form that accounts for the unity. Try to imagine two such forms. You will succeed in producing two instances of a single form only if they are both forms of a bed. Nevertheless, instances can be multiplied at will by such simple expedients as holding up a mirror and rotating it. This argument assigns priority to the single form which must come first logically.

The analysis of imitation as a concept results in a threefold distinction in reality. The singular form is original, so whatever follows from it is imitation. But *imitation* itself requires a distinction. The bed that can be slept in differs from the bed made by holding up a mirror. So if the actual beds are imitations, then they are in turn imitated by images and pictures. At first, this seems odd, because concrete objects become the defining instances of imitations. Images and pictures are only imitations of imitations. But the concept of imitation that has emerged is dialectical. *Dialectical* means that we know something in relation to something else; the term designates the relation. The chair in which I sit is at once an imitation in relation to its form and an original in relation to a photograph. When the term *imitation* is applied to some thing, it establishes a hierarchy of imitations. The concrete world is a first-order imitation, at one remove from the unity of forms. Within that concrete world, a secondary class of objects depends on already existing things and thus forms a class of imitations of imitations.

Plato distinguished in a fundamental way between appearance and reality. The relation that he is exploring at this point is between the first- and second-order imitations. Second-order imitations appear to be like first-order imitations and may even be taken for them. Classical literature is full of stories of paintings so like their subjects that they deceive animals and even other painters. Such *trompe l'oeil* effects are obviously only one mode of painting, but they illustrate in the strongest way the inherent deception involved in making one thing in an imitative relation with another. Once a fundamental hierarchy is established, the more levels of imitation that intervene, the farther the last imitation is from the original.

Behind all classical imitation theories is a fundamental organization of space and time into original and repetition. Mythologically, the world is itself a repetition of an original act of creation, and time as it is experienced is a repetition of earlier times in which the acts of gods and heroes provide models and original instances of all subsequent acts. Plato's analysis of imitation fits this pervasive organization. *Reality* here is found not in the immediate present but in an accessible but protected sacred realm that the present imitates. In any such organization of concepts, truth and knowledge depend on the originals. Plato, to a large extent, "demythologizes" this mythological worldview. He derives the structure of forms and imitation from the concepts themselves, but key terms such as *truth, reason,* and *knowledge* presume that reality belongs to the original, not the immediate present. Thus *true* applies not so much to sentences or beliefs but to things. Things are true insofar as they conform to the original. An imitation can be more or less true, therefore, depending on how close it is to the original. Reason is a judge of truth insofar as it is able to judge the likeness to the original. Plato's theory locates the standard for truth in a remote reality that seems to reduce the present to the status of mere appearance. If appearance is achieved at the cost of likeness, then appearance is, to that extent, less true. All of this runs counter to modern analysis, which takes true and false to be incompatible descriptions of sentences, statements, or beliefs and not to be subject to degrees. But the alternative is consistent, and Plato's explication of it is a consequence of a much deeper and more pervasive conceptual organization.

Clearly, painting is an art that will produce only inferior imitative instances on this scheme. Plato shows poetry to belong to the same imitative scheme, so the poet is in no better position than the painter or the naive imitator who holds up a mirror to the world. None of the arts can claim knowledge because of where they stand in the imitative hierarchy. But if this were the only thing wrong, awareness of the limitations of art would be sufficient. As long as no one was deceived, the artist would be a pleasant ornament to the state. Homer would have to give up his pretensions to wisdom, but he might retain his place as entertainer. Unfortunately, Plato argued, this argument is not the end of the story.

Plato turned to a second argument based on the bad effects of imitation itself. We enjoy imitations and imitating other things, but that enjoyment leads us into bad habits. The habits of imitation produce moral weakness. The argument begins by looking at the use to which imitations are put. First-order imitations have an end (a *telos*) of their own. In nature, this end is what they are good for. Some plants are good for food; others are good for building. Others have more obscure uses in the scheme of the world. Likewise some persons are good for one thing, some for another. Things made by those who are skilled at a craft also have uses, and they are good just to the extent that they fulfill their uses and satisfy the needs of their users. But second-order imitations—those at a third remove from reality—lack the ordinary uses. Their use is found in an appeal to the act of imitation itself and to the feelings they produce through their appearance. A painted bed cannot be slept in, though a person may take delight in its appearance and the skill of the artist who painted it.

If those feelings of delight were useful, all still might be well. However, Plato argues that they are not except in the very limited case of education and state propaganda for children and the masses. Appeals to reason and appeals to feeling are fundamentally at odds. One drives out the other. The argument here has to do with the development of habits of mind and with the application of standards of judgment. Feelings are variable and thus provide no standard. Reason is independent of circumstances and thus provides a standard. Its paradigm is measurement. How a thing looks is inferior to how it is measured in determining truth. Feeling varies in the same way that appearance varies and is equally unreliable. So in itself, feeling is not as useful as reason. But even worse, those who rely on feeling will ignore reason because feeling and reason are frequently in conflict and feelings are more pleasurable. Arts, which depend essentially on feeling, appeal to the emotional nature of persons and give priority to that nature. Reason appeals to a different side of a person's being. Since reason is more reliable, it should be developed and emotions should be checked and controlled.

Plato's argument here is more original than his definition of imitation. The classical world was better prepared to accept that reality was to be located "in the beginning" than to accept that reason should reign supreme in the ideal state. In promoting reason and philosophy at the expense of emotion and feeling, Plato argued against the prevailing religious practices, which found contact with the divine in forms of feeling, particularly extreme forms of ecstasy and divine possession mediated by ritual. Elsewhere, Plato was more sympathetic to such claims. In many ways, they are implicit in a hierarchical scheme based on mythological origins. The challenge left open at the end of this part of Book X of the *Republic* indicates the ambivalence of Plato's position. Poetry is invited to reply and show its usefulness. The challenge is ironic, however. It requires a reasonable reply. Such a reply would acknowledge just the rational superiority that forms the basis for the expulsion of poets. Poetry can justify itself only by appealing to philosophy!

The *Republic* is a discussion of the ideal state. It is also a "middle" dialogue that argues more or less straightforwardly toward a single conclusion. Plato's earlier dialogues built more doubts and irony into the arguments themselves. But the *Republic* is not without its own irony. After all, it is not really a dialogue; it is only an imitation of a dialogue. Socrates speaks in this section, but he himself is being instructed. His conclusions cannot be taken without examination. As a statement of the basic theory of imitation, the dialogue is sound. *Imitation* emerges as a complex concept which extends through all levels of a hierarchical scheme. To know what an imitation is requires knowing what it is an imitation of and how this imitation is related to its original. In all but the first instance, the answer will be that another imitation is being imitated. As an argument for the inferiority of poetry and the arts, the dialogue is more ironic. It does not follow from this argument alone that the expulsion of poets and painters should be taken literally in less perfect states. Only if reason can be expected to rule should poets be expelled. Nevertheless, the conclusion to which Glaucon is forced establishes a challenge with which any theory of art as imitation must deal.

From *Republic*, Book X

[THE NARRATOR in the dialogue is Socrates; at this point, Glaucon is responding.]

Of the many excellences which I perceive in the order of our State, there is none which upon reflection pleases me better than the rule about poetry.

To what do you refer?

To the rejection of imitative poetry, which certainly ought not to be received; as I see far more clearly now that the parts of the soul[1] have been distinguished.

What do you mean?

Speaking in confidence, for I should not like to have my words repeated to the tragedians and the rest of the imitative tribe—but I do not mind saying to you, that all poetical imitations are ruinous to the understanding of the hearers, and that the knowledge of their true nature is the only antidote to them.

Explain the purport of your remark.

Well, I will tell you, although I have always from my earliest youth had an awe and love of Homer,[2] which even now makes the words falter on my lips, for he is the great captain and teacher of the whole of that charming tragic company; but a man is not to be reverenced more than the truth, and therefore I will speak out.

Very good, he said.

Listen to me then, or rather, answer me.

Put your question.

Can you tell me what imitation is? for I really do not know.

A likely thing, then, that I should know.

Why not? for the duller eye may often see a thing sooner than the keener.

Very true, he said; but in your presence, even if I had any faint notion, I could not muster courage to utter it. Will you inquire yourself?

Well then, shall we begin the inquiry in our usual manner: Whenever a number of individuals have a common name, we assume them to have also a corresponding idea of form:[3]—do you understand me?

I do.

Let us take any common instance; there are beds and tables in the world—plenty of them, are there not?

Yes.

But there are only two ideas or forms of them —one the idea of a bed, the other of a table.

True.

And the maker of either of them makes a bed or he makes a table for our use, in accordance with the idea—that is our way of speaking in this and similar instances—but no artificer[4] makes the ideas themselves: how could he?

Impossible.

And there is another artist—I should like to know what you would say of him.

Who is he?

One who is the maker of all the works of all other workmen.

What an extraordinary man!

Wait for a little, and there will be more reason for your saying so. For this is he who is able to make not only vessels of every kind, but plants and animals, himself and all other things—the earth and heaven, and the things which are in heaven or under the earth; he makes the gods also.

---

[1] Plato divided the soul into three parts based on the objects of desire: rational, passionate, and appetitive. The rational soul is responsible for understanding and knowledge; the passionate soul for emotions such as ambition, fame, and honor; and the appetitive soul for bodily desires and acquisitiveness.

[2] Homer was the author of the *Iliad* and the *Odyssey,* epic poems that were regarded as the greatest literature of the Greeks. Probably composed sometime between 800 and 700 B.C.E., they would have had canonical status in classical Athens.

[3] Form is the central concept in Plato's philosophy. What Plato meant by form is one of the most difficult issues in understanding his philosophy.

[4] The basic meaning of *art* to Plato is artifice, a skilled making of something. An artificer is a maker of things.

He must be a wizard and no mistake.

Oh! you are incredulous, are you? Do you mean that there is no such maker or creator, or that in one sense there might be a maker of all these things but in another not? Do you see that there is a way in which you could make them all yourself?

What way?

An easy way enough; or rather, there are many ways in which the feat might be quickly and easily accomplished, none quicker than that of turning a mirror around and round—you would soon enough make the sun and the heavens, and the earth and yourself, and other animals and plants, and all the other things of which we were just now speaking, in the mirror.

Yes, he said; but they would be appearances only.

Very good, I said, you are coming to the point now. And the painter too is, as I conceive, just such another—a creator of appearances, is he not?

Of course.

But then I suppose you will say that what he creates is untrue. And yet there is a sense in which the painter also creates a bed?

Yes, he said, but not a real bed.

And what of the maker of the bed? were you not saying that he too makes, not the idea which, according to our view, is the essence of the bed, but only a particular bed?

Yes, I did.

Then if he does not make that which exists he cannot make true existence, but only some semblance of existence; and if any one were to say that the work of the maker of the bed, or of any other workman, has real existence, he could hardly be supposed to be speaking the truth.

At any rate, he replied, philosophers would say that he was not speaking the truth.

No wonder.

Suppose now that by the light of the examples just offered we inquire who this imitator is?

If you please.

Well then, here are three beds: one existing in nature, which is made by God, as I think that we may say—for no one else can be the maker?

No.

There is another which is the work of the carpenter?

Yes.

And the work of the painter is a third?

Yes.

Beds, then, are of three kinds, and there are three artists who superintend them: God, the maker of the bed, and the painter?

Yes, there are three of them.

God, whether from choice or from necessity, made one bed in nature and only one; two or more such ideal beds neither ever have been nor ever will be made by God.

Why is that?

Because even if He had made but two, a third would still appear behind them which both of them would have for their idea, and that would be the ideal bed and not the two others.

Very true, he said.

God knew this, and He desired to be the real maker of a real bed, not a particular maker of a particular bed, and therefore He created a bed which is essentially and by nature one only.

So we believe.

Shall we, then, speak of Him as the natural author or maker of the bed?

Yes, he replied; inasmuch as by the natural process of creation He is the author of this and of all other things.

And what shall we say of the carpenter—is not he also the maker of the bed?

Yes.

But would you call the painter a creator and maker?

Certainly not.

Yet if he is not the maker, what is he in relation to the bed?

I think, he said, that we may fairly designate him as the imitator of that which the others make.

Good, I said; then you call him who is third in the descent from nature an imitator?

Certainly, he said.

And the tragic poet is an imitator, and therefore, like all other imitators, he is thrice removed from the king and from the truth?

That appears to be so.

Then about the imitator we are agreed. And what about the painter?—I would like to know whether he may be thought to imitate that which originally exists in nature, or only the creations of artists?

The latter.

As they are or as they appear? you have still to determine this.

What do you mean?

I mean, that you may look at a bed from different points of view, obliquely or directly or from any other point of view, and the bed will appear different, but there is no difference in reality. And the same of all things.

Yes, he said, the difference is only apparent.

Now let me ask you another question: Which is the art of painting designed to be—an imitation of things as they are, or as they appear—of appearance or of reality?

Of appearance.

Then the imitator, I said, is a long way off the truth, and can do all things because he lightly touches on a small part of them, and that part an image. For example: A painter will paint a cobbler, carpenter, or any other artist, though he knows nothing of their arts; and, if he is a good artist, he may deceive children or simple persons, when he shows them his picture of a carpenter from a distance, and they will fancy that they are looking at a real carpenter.

Certainly.

And whenever any one informs us that he has found a man who knows all the arts, and all things else that anybody knows, and every single thing with a higher degree of accuracy than any other man—whoever tells us this, I think that we can only imagine him to be a simple creature who is likely to have been deceived by some wizard or actor whom he met, and whom he thought all-knowing, because he himself was unable to analyze the nature of knowledge and ignorance and imitation.

Most true.

And so, when we hear persons saying that the tragedians, and Homer, who is at their head,

know all the arts and all things human, virtue as well as vice, and divine things too, for that the good poet can not compose well unless he knows his subject, and that he who has not this knowledge can never be a poet, we ought to consider whether here also there may not be a similar illusion. Perhaps they may have come across imitators and been deceived by them; they may not have remembered when they saw their works that these were but imitations thrice removed from the truth, and could easily be made without any knowledge of the truth, because they are appearances only and not realities? Or, after all, they may be in the right, and poets do really know the things about which they seem to the many to speak so well?

The question, he said, should by all means be considered.

Now do you suppose that if a person were able to make the original as well as the image, he would seriously devote himself to the image-making branch? Would he allow imitation to be the ruling principle of his life, as if he had nothing higher in him?

I should say not.

The real artist, who knew what he was imitating, would be interested in realities and not in imitations; and would desire to leave as memorials of himself works many and fair; and, instead of being the author of encomiums, he would prefer to be the theme of them.

Yes, he said, that would be to him a source of much greater honor and profit.

Then, I said, we must put a question to Homer; not about medicine, or any of the arts to which his poems only incidentally refer: we are not going to ask him, or any other poet, whether he has cured patients like Asclepius,[5] or left behind him a school of medicine such as the Asclepiads were, or whether he only talks about medicine and other arts at second-hand; but we have a right to know respecting military tactics, politics, educa-

---

[5] Asclepius is the hero or god of healing. Note that Plato uses a rhetorical trick to say exactly what he has said he will not discuss.

tion, which are the chiefest and noblest subjects of his poems, and we may fairly ask him about them. "Friend Homer," then we say to him, "if you are only in the second remove from truth in what you say of virtue, and not in the third— not an image maker or imitator—and if you are able to discern what pursuits make men better or worse in private or public life, tell us what State was ever better governed by your help? The good order of Lacedaemon[6] is due to Lycurgus,[7] and many other cities great and small have been similarly benefited by others; but who says that you have been a good legislator to them and have done them any good? Italy and Sicily boast of Charondas,[8] and there is Solon[9] who is renowned among us; but what city has anything to say about you?" Is there any city which he might name?

I think not, said Glaucon; not even the Homerids themselves pretend that he was a legislator.

Well, but is there any war on record which was carried on successfully by him, or aided by his counsels, when he was alive?

There is not.

Or is there any invention of his, applicable to the arts or to human life, such as Thales the Milesian[10] or Anacharsis the Scythian,[11] and other ingenious men have conceived, which attributed to him?

There is absolutely nothing of the kind.

But, if Homer never did any public service, was he privately a guide or teacher of any? Had he in his lifetime friends who loved to associate with him, and who handed down to posterity an Homeric way of life, such as was established by Pythagoras[12] who was so greatly beloved for his wisdom, and whose followers are to this day quite celebrated for the order which was named after him?

Nothing of the kind is recorded of him. For surely, Socrates, Creophylus,[13] the companion of Homer, that child of flesh, whose name always makes us laugh, might be more justly ridiculed for his stupidity, if, as is said, Homer was greatly neglected by him and others in his own day when he was alive?

Yes, I replied, that is the tradition. But can you imagine, Glaucon, that if Homer had really been able to educate and improve mankind—if he had possessed knowledge and not been a mere imitator—can you imagine, I say, that he would not have had many followers, and been honored and loved by them? Protagoras of Abdera,[14] and Prodicus of Ceos,[15] and a host of others, have only to whisper to their contemporaries: "You will never be able to manage either your own house or your own State until you appoint us to be your ministers of education"—and this ingenious device of theirs has such an effect in making men love them that their companions all but carry them about on their shoulders. And is it conceivable that the contemporaries of Homer, or again of Hesiod,[16] would have allowed either of them

---

[6]Lacedaemon was a name for the region ruled by the city-state of Sparta. Sparta was the leading competitor to Athens for dominance in Greece and was well known and much admired for its order and discipline.

[7]Lycurgus was the legendary founder of Sparta's constitution.

[8]Charondas (c. 600 B.C.E.) was the lawgiver of the Greek city-states in Sicily.

[9]Solon (c. 639–559 B.C.E.) was credited with establishing Athenian laws. He was also a poet and reformer.

[10]Thales the Milesian (c. 636–546 B.C.E.) was a natural philosopher who held that water was the primary element out of that everything was made.

[11]Anacharsis the Scythian (fl. c. 600 B.C.E.) was known for maxims as well as being the purported inventor of the anchor. Scythia was a nomadic empire from the eighth to the fourth century B.C.E. that was centered in the Crimea.

[12]Pythagoras (c. 582–507 B.C.E.) was a teacher of wisdom based on harmony and numerical order. His followers formed a secret society into that members had to be initiated.

[13]Creophylus was the stereotype of the fat man in Greek legend. His name means something like "fat head."

[14]Protagoras of Abdera (c. 480–410 B.C.E.) was a famous Sophist best known for his dictum, "Man is the measure of all things." The Sophists were a diverse group of philosophers who claimed special wisdom in some area and who would teach it for a fee. Protagoras taught "virtue." Plato makes Protagoras the object of a Socratic dialogue.

[15]Prodicus of Ceos was another famous fifth century Sophist.

[16]Hesiod was the other great poet (with Homer) of preclassical Greece. His account of the origin of the gods provides the basis for Greek theology. Hesiod is usually taken to come somewhat later than Homer.

to go about as rhapsodists,[17] if they had really been able to make mankind virtuous? Would they not have been as unwilling to part with them as with gold, and have compelled them to stay at home with them? Or, if the master would not stay, then the disciples would have followed him about everywhere, until they had got education enough?

Yes, Socrates, that, I think, is quite true.

Then must we not infer that all these poetical individuals, beginning with Homer, are only imitators; they copy images of virtue and the like, but the truth they never reach? The poet is like a painter who, as we have already observed, will make a likeness of a cobbler though he understands nothing of cobbling; and his picture is good enough for those who know no more than he does, and judge only by colors and figures.

Quite so.

In like manner the poet with his words and phrases may be said to lay on the colors of the several arts, himself understanding their nature only enough to imitate them; and other people, who are as ignorant as he is, and judge only from his words, imagine that if he speaks of cobbling, or of military tactics, or of anything else, in meter and harmony and rhythm, he speaks very well—such is the sweet influence which melody and rhythm by nature have. And I think that you must have observed again and again what a poor appearance the tales of poets make when stripped of the colors which music puts upon them, and recited in simple prose.

Yes, he said.

They are like faces which were never really beautiful, but only blooming; and now the bloom of youth has passed away from them?

Exactly.

Here is another point: The imitator or maker of the image knows nothing of true existence; he knows appearances only. Am I not right?

Yes.

Then let us have a clear understanding, and not be satisfied with half an explanation.

Proceed.

Of the painter we say that he will paint reins, and he will paint a bit?

Yes.

And the worker in leather and brass will make them?

Certainly.

But does the painter know the right form of the bit and reins? Nay, hardly even the workers in brass and leather who make them; only the horseman who knows how to use them—he knows their right form.

Yes.

And the excellence or beauty or truth of every structure, animate or inanimate, and of every action of man, is relative to the use for which nature or the artist has intended them.

True.

Then the user of them must have the greatest experience of them, and he must indicate to the maker the good or bad qualities which develop themselves in use; for example, the flute-player will tell the flute-maker which of his flutes is satisfactory to the performer; he will tell him how he ought to make them, and the other will attend to his instructions?

Of course.

The one knows and therefore speaks with authority about the goodness and badness of flutes, while the other, confiding in him, will do what he is told by him?

True.

The instrument is the same, but about the excellence or badness of it the maker will only attain to a correct belief; and this he will gain from him who knows, by talking to him and being compelled to hear what he has to say, whereas the user will have knowledge?

True.

But will the imitator have either? Will he know from use whether or not his drawing is correct or beautiful? Or will he have right opinion from being compelled to associate with another who knows and gives him instructions about what he should draw?

---

[17]Greece was an essentially oral culture in earlier classical times, but that was beginning to change by the time Plato was writing. Rhapsodists were reciters of poetry, particularly the poetry of Homer and Hesiod.

Neither.

Then he will no more have true opinion than he will have knowledge about the goodness or badness of his imitations?

I suppose not.

The imitative artist will be in a brilliant state of intelligence about his own creations?

Nay, very much the reverse.

And still he will go on imitating without knowing what makes a thing good or bad, and may be expected therefore to imitate only that which appears to be good to the ignorant multitude?

Just so.

Thus far then we are pretty well agreed that the imitator has no knowledge worth mentioning of what he imitates. Imitation is only a kind of play or sport, and the tragic poets, whether they write in Iambic or in Heroic verse,[18] are imitators in the highest degree?

Very true.

And now tell me, I conjure you, has not imitation been shown by us to be concerned with that which is thrice removed from the truth?

Certainly.

And what is the faculty in man to which imitation is addressed?

What do you mean?

I will explain: The body which is large when seen near appears small when seen at a distance?

True.

And the same objects appear straight when looked at out of the water, and crooked when in the water; and the concave becomes convex, owing to the illusion about colors to which the sight is liable. Thus every sort of confusion is revealed within us; and this is that weakness of the human mind on which the art of conjuring and of deceiving by light and shadow and other ingenious devices imposes, having an effect upon us like magic.

True.

And the arts of measuring and numbering and weighing come to the rescue of the human understanding—there is the beauty of them—and the apparent greater or less, or more or heavier, no longer have the mastery over us, but give way before calculation and measure and weight?

Most true.

And this, surely, must be the work of the calculating and rational principle in the soul?

To be sure.

And when this principle measures and certifies that some things are equal, or that some are greater or less than others, there occurs an apparent contradiction?

True.

Then that part of the soul which has an opinion contrary to measure is not the same with that which has an opinion in accordance with measure?

True.

And the better part of the soul is likely to be that which trusts to measure and calculation?

Certainly.

And that which is opposed to them is one of the inferior principles of the soul?

No doubt.

This was the conclusion at which I was seeking to arrive when I said that painting or drawing, and imitation in general, when doing their own proper work, are far removed from truth, and the companions and friends and associates of a principle within us which is equally removed from reason, and that they have no true or healthy aim.

Exactly.

The imitative art is an inferior who marries an inferior, and has inferior offspring.

Very true.

And is this confined to the sight only, or does it extend to the hearing also, relating in fact to what we term poetry?

Probably the same would be true of poetry.

Do not rely, I said, on a probability derived from the analogy of painting; but let us examine further and see whether the faculty with which poetical imitation is concerned is good or bad.

By all means.

We may state the question thus:—Imitation imitates the actions of men, whether voluntary or involuntary, on which, as they imagine, a good or

---

[18]Greek verse structure does not correspond exactly to English; it is based on length of syllables rather than stress. Plato is referring to the kinds of verse typical of drama and epic.

bad result has ensued, and they rejoice or sorrow accordingly. Is there anything more?

No, there is nothing else.

But in all this variety of circumstances is the man at unity with himself—or rather, as in the instance of sight there was confusion and opposition in his opinions about the same things so here also is there not strife and inconsistency in his life? Though I need hardly raise the question again, for I remember that all this has been already admitted; and the soul has been acknowledged by us to be full of these and ten thousand similar oppositions occurring at the same moment?

And we were right, he said.

Yes, I said, thus far we were right; but there was an omission which must now be supplied.

What was the omission?

Were we not saying that a good man, who has the misfortune to lose his son or anything else which is most dear to him, will bear the loss with more equanimity than another?

Yes.

But will he have no sorrow, or shall we say that although he cannot help sorrowing, he will moderate his sorrow?

The latter, he said, is the truer statement.

Tell me: will he be more likely to struggle and hold out against his sorrow when he is seen by his equals, or when he is alone?

It will make a great difference whether he is seen or not.

When he is by himself he will not mind saying or doing many things which he would be ashamed of any one hearing or seeing him do?

True.

There is a principle of law and reason in him which bids him resist, as well as a feeling of his misfortune which is forcing him to indulge his sorrow?

True.

But when a man is drawn in two opposite directions, to and from the same object, this, as we affirm, necessarily implies two distinct principles in him?

Certainly.

One of them is ready to follow the guidance of the law?

How do you mean?

The law would say that to be patient under suffering is best, and that we should not give way to impatience, as there is no knowing whether such things are good or evil; and nothing is gained by impatience; also, because no human thing is of serious importance, and grief stands in the way of that which at the moment is most required.

What is most required? he asked.

That we should take counsel about what has happened, and when the dice have been thrown order our affairs in the way which reason deems best; not, like children who have had a fall, keeping hold of the part struck and wasting time in setting up a howl, but always accustoming the soul forthwith to apply a remedy, raising up that which is sickly and fallen, banishing the cry of sorrow by the healing art.

Yes, he said, that is the true way of meeting the attacks of fortune.

Yes, I said; and the higher principle is ready to follow this suggestion of reason?

Clearly.

And the other principle, which inclines us to recollection of our troubles and to lamentation, and can never have enough of them, we may call irrational, useless, and cowardly?

Indeed, we may.

And does not the latter—I mean the rebellious principle—furnish a great variety of materials for imitation? whereas the wise and calm temperament, being always nearly equable, is not easy to imitate or to appreciate when imitated, especially at a public festival when a promiscuous crowd is assembled in a theatre. For the feeling represented is one to which they are strangers.

Certainly.

Then the imitative poet who aims at being popular is not by nature made, nor is his art intended, to please or to affect the rational principle in the soul; but he will prefer the passionate and fitful temper, which is easily imitated?

Clearly.

And now we may fairly take him and place him by the side of the painter, for he is like him in two ways: first, inasmuch as his creations have an inferior degree of truth—in this, I say, he is like him; and he is also like him in being concerned with an inferior part of the soul; and therefore we shall be right in refusing to admit him into a well-ordered State, because he awakens and nourishes and strengthens the feelings and impairs the reason. As in a city when the evil are permitted to have authority and the good are put out of the way, so in the soul of man, as we maintain, the imitative poet implants an evil constitution, for he indulges the irrational nature which has no discernment of greater and less, but thinks the same thing at one time great and at another small—he is a manufacturer of images and is very far removed from the truth.

Exactly.

But we have not yet brought forward the heaviest count in our accusation:—the power which poetry has of harming even the good (and there are very few who are not harmed), is surely an awful thing?

Yes, certainly, if the effect is what you say.

Hear and judge: The best of us, as I conceive, when we listen to a passage of Homer, or one of the tragedians, in which he represents some pitiful hero who is drawling out his sorrows in a long oration, or weeping, and smiting his breast—the best of us, you know, delight in giving way to sympathy, and are in raptures at the excellence of the poet who stirs our feelings most.

Yes, of course I know.

But when any sorrow of our own happens to us, then you may observe that we pride ourselves on the opposite quality—we would fain be quiet and patient; this is the manly part, and the other which delighted us in the recitation is now deemed to be the part of a woman.[19]

Very true, he said.

Now can we be right in praising and admiring another who is doing that which any one of us would abominate and be ashamed of in his own person?

No, he said, that is certainly not reasonable.

Nay, I said, quite reasonable from one point of view.

What point of view?

If you consider, I said that when in misfortune we feel a natural hunger and desire to relieve our sorrow by weeping and lamentation, and that this feeling which is kept under control in our own calamities is satisfied and delighted by the poets; —the better nature in each of us, not having been sufficiently trained by reason or habit, allows the sympathetic element to break loose because the sorrow is another's; and the spectator fancies that there can be no disgrace to himself in praising and pitying any one who comes telling him what a good man he is, and making a fuss about his troubles; he thinks that the pleasure is a gain, and why should he be supercilious and lose this and the poem too? Few persons ever reflect, as I should imagine, that from the evil of other men something of evil is communicated to themselves. And so the feeling of sorrow which has gathered strength at the sight of the misfortunes of others is with difficulty repressed in our own.

How very true!

And does not the same hold also of the ridiculous? There are jests which you would be ashamed to make yourself, and yet on the comic stage, or indeed in private, when you hear them you are greatly amused by them, and are not at all disgusted at their unseemliness;—the case of pity is repeated;—there is a principle in human nature which is disposed to raise a laugh, and this which you once restrained by reason, because you were afraid of being thought a buffoon, is now let out again; and having stimulated the risible faculty at the theater, you are betrayed unconsciously to yourself into playing the comic poet at home.

And the same may be said of lust and anger and all the other affections, of desire and pain and pleasure, which are held to be inseparable from every action—in all of them poetry feeds and waters the passions instead of drying them up; she lets them rule, although they ought to be controlled, if mankind are ever to increase in happiness and virtue.

---

[19] Plato and his society were undoubtedly patriarchal. That does not change the contrast, however. The good qualities are reason and patience; the bad qualities are emotional and impetuous. If we do not believe that one is especially masculine and the other feminine, the contrast remains intact.

I cannot deny it.

Therefore, Glaucon, I said, whenever you meet with any of the eulogists of Homer declaring that he has been the educator of Hellas,[20] and that he is profitable for education and for the ordering of human things, and that you should take him up again and again and get to know him and regulate your whole life according to him, we may love and honor those who say these things—they are excellent people, as far as their lights extend; and we are ready to acknowledge that Homer is the greatest of poets and first of tragedy writers; but we must remain firm in our conviction that hymns to the gods and praises of famous men are the only poetry which ought to be admitted into our State. For if you go beyond this and allow the honeyed muse to enter, either in epic or lyric verse, not law and the reason of mankind, which by common consent have ever been deemed best, but pleasure and pain will be the rulers in our State.

That is most true, he said.

And now since we have reverted to the subject of poetry, let this our defense serve to show the reasonableness of our former judgment in sending away out of our State an art having the tendencies which we have described; for reason constrained us. But that she may not impute to us any harshness or want of politeness, let us tell her that there is an ancient quarrel between philosophy and poetry; of which there are many proofs, such as the saying of "the yelping hound howling at her lord," or of one "mighty in the vain talk of fools," and "the mob of sages circumventing Zeus," and the "subtle thinkers who are beggars after all"; and there are innumerable other signs of ancient enmity between them. Not withstanding this, let us assure our sweet friend and the sister arts of imitation, that if she will only prove her title to exist in a well-ordered State we shall be delighted to receive her—we are very conscious of her charms; but we may not on that account betray the truth. I dare say, Glaucon, that you are as much charmed by her as I am, especially when she appears in Homer?

Yes, indeed, I am greatly charmed.

Shall I propose, then, that she be allowed to return from exile, but upon this condition only—that she make a defense of herself in lyrical or some other meter?

Certainly.

And we may further grant to those of her defenders who are lovers of poetry and yet not poets the permission to speak in prose on her behalf: let them show not only that she is pleasant but also useful to States and to human life, and we will listen in a kindly spirit; for if this can be proved we shall surely be the gainers—I mean, if there is a use in poetry as well as a delight?

Certainly, he said, we shall be the gainers.

If her defense fails, then, my dear friend, like other persons who are enamored of something, but put a restraint upon themselves when they think their desires are opposed to their interests, so too must we after the manner of lovers give her love of poetry which the education of noble States has implanted in us, and therefore we would have her appear at her best and truest; but so long as she is unable to make good her defense, this argument of ours shall be a charm to us, which we will repeat to ourselves while we listen to her strains; that we may not fall away into the childish love of her which captivates the many. At all events we are well aware that poetry being such as we have described is not to be regarded seriously as attaining to the truth; and he who listens to her, fearing for the safety of the city[21] which is within him, should be on his guard against her seductions and make our words his law.

Yes, he said, I quite agree with you.

Yes, I said, my dear Glaucon, for great is the issue at stake, greater than appears, whether a man is to be good or bad. And what will any one be profited if under the influence of honor or money or power, aye, or under the excitement of poetry he neglected justice and virtue?

---

[20] Hellas is the classical name for Greece.

[21] The *polis* or city-state was fundamental to Greek life and represented all order. The soul of the individual corresponds to the city.

Yes, he said; I have been convinced by the argument, as I believe that anyone else would have been.

Study Questions

1. In this dialogue, how would you characterize Socrates' technique of asking questions?
2. Reconstruct Plato's answer to the question, "Can you tell me what imitation is?"
3. If there is only one bed-form, is there only one poem-form? Is this as plausible for poems as for beds?
4. Why is there more than one artist?
5. What are the uses of poetry? Of painting? Are there uses that might answer some of Socrates' objections?
6. What is the problem about appearances?
7. Here is the final stanza of a poem about a Greek urn. Does it produce the appearance of an urn in the way that a mirror produces an image of an urn? What are the differences?

O Attic shape! Fair attitude! with brede
Of marble men and maidens overwrought,
With forest branches and the trodden weed;
Thou, silent form, dost tease us out of thought
As doth eternity: Cold Pastoral!
When old age shall this generation waste,
Thou shalt remain, in midst of other woe
Than ours, a friend to man, to whom thou
    say'st
"Beauty is truth, truth beauty"—that is all
Ye know on earth, and all ye need to know.
    JOHN KEATS, "Ode on a Grecian Urn"

8. Plato speaks of painting and poetry. Would what he says apply to other arts? How?
9. Socrates objects to artworks on the grounds of their lack of truth and their effects. Do poems claim to be true? Are they ever deceptive in the way that some paintings are deceptive?
10. What are the "parts" of the soul? Which is better?
11. What kinds of poems stir the emotions? How? Is this what Socrates fears?
12. Describe Plato's ideal citizen. How does such a citizen respond to adversity?
13. Which would Plato think less objectionable: a stylized statue of a god or one that looked very natural? Why? What about an abstract painting?

Aristotle
♦ ♦ ♦ ♦ ♦ ♦ ♦

ARISTOTLE (384–322 B.C.E.) was born in the northern part of the Greek peninsula at Stagira. The son of a physician with connections to the Macedonian court,
Aristotle did not go to Athens until he was seventeen. There he joined Plato's Academy,
where he remained until the death of Plato in 347 B.C.E. This kind of apprenticeship under a teacher was not unusual in the classical world. As long as the master remained, his
disciples remained loyal to him. After Plato's death, Aristotle left Athens first for the island of Assos, where he married the niece of his patron. From Assos, he went to nearby
Mytilene. During this period he was engaged in scientific work, particularly zoology.

In 343/342, Aristotle returned to Macedonia at the invitation of Philip of Macedon.
Tradition makes him the tutor of Philip's son, Alexander, who was to become Alexander the Great. Aristotle's exact role is uncertain. At any rate, he did not remain in the position long. Alexander became regent for his father, and at about that time Aristotle returned to Stagira. In 335, he returned to Athens, where he established his own school,
the Lyceum. It included a covered porch or place for walking about, called a *peripatos,*
where Aristotle taught; followers of Aristotle took their name—*Peripatetics*—from this
practice. Aristotle remained in Athens until after the death of Alexander in 323. Again,
tradition has it that Alexander in his conquests had botanical samples collected and
sent to Aristotle. Certainly Aristotle continued to be associated in people's minds with
Macedonian rule. After the death of Alexander, Athens reacted against that association
and Aristotle left the city, "to prevent the Athenians [who had executed Socrates] from
sinning twice against philosophy." He died in 322 in Chalcis on the island of Euboea.

Aristotle's writings include scientific writings, political and ethical theory, metaphysics, and more practical analysis, which includes the *Poetics* and *Rhetoric.* Aristotle
probably wrote dialogues, though none survives. His work is clearly related to that of
Plato. In a fundamental sense, Aristotle retains a theory of forms. He disagreed with
Plato over the independent existence of the forms, however. For Aristotle, forms are always embodied in some way. How they are instantiated may vary considerably. Natural
forms are inherent in objects, though they are not identical with those objects. Other
forms are imposed on matter by some outside agency. Spiritual and intellectual forms
such as number must have suitable intelligible instances. Aristotle also differed from
Plato in method and style. Plato' s work is ironic and dialectical. It is perfectly suited
to the give-and-take of dialogue, even when the dialogues become lectures. Aristotle's

work is much more expository and analytical. Aristotle organized every aspect of his subjects and from that organization deduced conclusions about the essential characteristics of what he investigated. The *Poetics* is typical in this regard. Aristotle's works were probably intended for the students and disciples of his school. The *Poetics* may be a fragment of a larger work.

◆   ◆   ◆   ◆   ◆   ◆

Aristotle and Plato both conceived of art as imitation. *Imitation* can mean many things, however; the term must be considered carefully. Plato's imitation indicated a relation in a hierarchical scheme. Aristotle's imitation picks out a kind of thing. Some things have their form and purpose determined internally. Oak trees, for example, may be pruned and cut for wood, but they grow into their natural shape because they are that kind of tree. But things that have to be made must be given their form according to externally determined patterns and purposes. Thus they follow some other form and are imitations. The fundamental sense of *imitation* for Aristotle, therefore, is "made thing"—something which has its form imposed on it according to some other pattern.

Aristotle can be understood to ask a single fundamental question in the *Poetics*. Confronted with an object, we ask what it is. The question, "What is a tragedy?" organizes the *Poetics*. Aristotle's answer is complex. He can be understood in terms of a fourfold scheme that he developed in detail in another work, the *Metaphysics*. To learn what something is, we ask where it comes from. To that extent, Aristotle agrees with Plato and much of classical thought in believing that the origin of a thing determines what it is. Aristotle answered the question of origins in terms of causes. If we know what causes a thing to be what it is, then we know what it is. But *cause* is much more complex than just our limited sense of a sequence of events. Aristotle described four different kinds of causes that, taken together, determine the nature of an object.

The first is the material cause. It describes the "what" from which a thing is made. In its simplest sense, it is just the stuff that goes into whatever we are trying to understand. The second is the formal cause. Material takes on different shapes. We can have the same stuff and different forms. If we do, we have different things. The third is the efficient cause. The material must be given the shape by some process. Since these are imitations, form has to be imposed on the stuff by someone. Any work of art is thus a material that has a particular shape given to it by some outside agency, making it an imitation. But these three causes are still not enough to explain fully what a thing is. Everything has some purpose, some end toward which it is aimed. This purpose or end is the final cause. To understand it, one must examine the effects of the thing as they are determined by the causal scheme itself. For example, it may be an accidental effect that a poem makes me angry because I dislike the poet. Such an effect is determined by my nature and not by the nature of the poem, so it is not part of the answer to the question "What is this thing?" But if the poem is organized so that its effect is to inspire patriotic fervor, that effect is part of the nature of the poem and must be included in its description. This fourfold causal scheme provides a complex answer to the fundamental question, "What is a tragedy?"

Before we consider how Aristotle answered this question, we should note a further feature of his methodology. The *Poetics* refers at every point to examples. Unfortunately, many of the plays, poems, and paintings mentioned are now lost. This misfortune does not prevent us from seeing how Aristotle worked. He begins with something that has been made by a poet—a maker. He asks then what has been made, and from that response he is able to describe the essential characteristics of that kind of thing. Fortunately, we do have some of Aristotle's most important examples, particularly *Oedipus the King* by Sophocles. So we are able to work in much the same way that Aristotle did, comparing his description to the thing described in order to understand both the thing and the description. But if the description is accurate, it will not be limited to one particular thing, or even to the examples that Aristotle had to work with. In the *Poetics,* tragedy and epic are the objects of the description. The specific examples are instances of those more general kinds, so the description should apply to tragedy and epic wherever they are found. For example, we can apply the Aristotelian descriptions to Elizabethan tragedy or to epic poetry in other cultures far removed from the Greece of Aristotle's time. Thus, while the descriptions in the *Poetics* are concrete and specific, they remain part of an approach to art that tries to give definitions that apply more widely. Aristotle believed that there was some specific kind of imitation that was tragic. Attention to the detail of known examples could disclose that kind in its material, formal, efficient, and final nature.

Early in his analysis, Aristotle offered a definition of *tragedy:* "A tragedy, then, is the imitation of an action that is serious and also, having magnitude, complete in itself; in language with pleasurable accessories, each kind brought in separately in the parts of the work; in a dramatic, not in a narrative form; with incidents arousing pity and fear, wherewith to accomplish its catharsis of such emotions" (Chapter 6). Such a definition is only possible because Aristotle believed tragedy to have an essential nature. The definition summarizes the causal structure. The material of tragedy is language with pleasurable accessories. Its form is that of human actions. Its means are an imitation of those actions played out (not told) by actors. Its ends are the arousal of specific emotions, pity and fear, together with their catharsis. The term *catharsis* is somewhat mysterious. Literally it means "ritual cleansing" or "curing." At the very least, Aristotle is saying that pity and fear are not enough by themselves (as they might be in a modern romantic film or horror film). They must be used for some other final cause if the work is to be tragic. Since this definition is only a summary one, each element of the causal scheme is subject to further description, so that each may in turn have a more detailed causal structure. Fundamentally, however, tragedy is an imitation of actions of a particular kind. Since actions are central, the discussion of tragedy centers on the plot, which is acted out. Human actions are ultimately the material for the imitations (in dramatic language) called tragedy. Tragedy gets its moral seriousness and importance from the nature of tragic actions. We continue to respond to those actions even though they are about situations in a culture very different from ours. Greek tragedy arouses pity and fear in us as it did in the Greeks; we also feel an exhilaration that comes from the way human beings respond within the plot.

While the focus in the *Poetics* is on tragedy and, to a lesser extent, on epic, the descriptions and definitions suggest ways that they could be extended to other forms. Comedy is mentioned in passing as having a different end since it arouses different emotions and deals with actions of a different magnitude. While all of the causal scheme is necessary for a complete understanding of the difference between tragedy and comedy or tragedy and epic, the formal and final causes are most important. Tragedy and epic follow the older, mythological forms. They are expected to resolve deep conflicts about our place in the world. Comedy is less serious. It deals with ordinary events and destroys the pretensions to importance of its protagonists. (Some modern critics think comedy may be as important as tragedy. We need to see through our pretensions and be able to overcome our differences.) Critical judgments follow from this analysis. Tragedies are expected to accomplish some ends by means that they adopt. They are better or worse with respect to how well they achieve the ends that they themselves establish. Thus Aristotle concluded, for example, that the protagonist must be of a particular stature, neither too good nor too bad, for the proper kind of pity and fear to be aroused. For a comedy, a different end is needed. Aristotle's approach takes account of what the drama is trying to achieve in its own terms. It is a good tragedy if it produces pity and fear and changes them into something positive by means of the plot itself. Critically, everything depends on the formal properties of the drama. Plato objected to the act of imitation itself, and Aristotle acknowledges that acts of imitation are pleasurable in themselves. But Aristotle's criticism of an art form is relative to its own kind. We might still conclude that poets are to be expelled from the ideal state that Plato imagined in the *Republic,* but that conclusion would not change the fact that they are good poets who know their craft.

Two quite different theories of poetry and criticism find their justification in Aristotle's *Poetics.* The first is psychological. Since the final cause is emotional (the arousal of pity and fear and their transformation by means of the plot), art is understood in terms of its effects on an audience. A tragedy is a particular kind of emotional instrument on this reading, and other art forms would have different but equally emotional ends. In fact, the common emotion in all art is pleasure because the very act of imitation is pleasurable. Thus the pity and fear of tragedy are compatible with the pleasure the audience feels in the imitation since the fear, for example, is not "real" but only an imitation. We can be both terrified by the fate of a tragic hero and simultaneously pleased because the imitation is well made and works on us. Emotional states that we would never find pleasurable in real life are compatible in the imitations of actions that make up drama. In any case, the psychological states of the audience are the ultimate end toward which the play is aimed on this reading. The *Poetics* provides ample evidence for this approach.

The alternative to a psychological theory is a formalist approach. Formalism concentrates on the way the parts of a play relate to each other rather than on their effect on the audience. In a formalist theory, the actions that take place in the play are the ends of the drama. What happens in the plot is more important than how some member of the audience responds to it. Actions are naturally of certain kinds: they are piteous or fearsome, for example. If the purpose of the play is to arouse pity and fear, then it must provide piteous and fearsome actions. Those actions can only be transformed by the way the plot is put together. Organize the plot differently, and it imitates a different kind of action and thus has different kinds of resolutions. If it is a bad plot, its actions will not be consistent or they will not lead to a resolution. The formalist argues that effects occur in the plot. The arousal of pity and fear takes place internally in the plot, and only secondarily in the audience. The audience may not react properly even if it is a good plot. It would still be a good plot. What makes a drama good or bad is determined by its own organization. A critic should examine that organization, not the effect on the audience. The difference may seem one merely of emphasis. The psychological effect of tragedy could correspond to its formal structure. Psychological criticism and formalism are two very different approaches to art and criticism, however. Different parts of the play appear to be important if we look at the audience first or the internal structure of the play first.

The difference can be seen clearly in the way Aristotle's term *catharsis* is understood. Catharsis seems to be necessary to the definition of tragedy. It is not enough for tragedy to arouse pity and fear; it must also lead to the catharsis of those emotions. On the psychological theory, catharsis is something that can take place only in the audience. Certain emotions are aroused and then transformed by experiencing them in an imitative form where they can do no essential damage. Tragedy is therapeutic. This theory provides a possible answer to Plato's fear of imitation. Perhaps imitation is good for us because it lets us experience emotions like pity and fear without having to experience the real situations that cause them and that would be dangerous to us. A psychological theory also accounts for the relation of tragedy to religious experience. As part of a religious celebration, drama is a way of participating in sacred stories and experiencing their effect without actually being destroyed by contact with the sacred. Crucifixion would be a terrifying event; the crucifixion of a god would be doubly dangerous. In the drama of the mass, the believer can be present at such an event and not be overcome. Tragedy shares that psychological effect.

In contrast, a formalist theory sees catharsis as a matter of the organization of the plot. The emotional actions, which are imitated in the plot, are also changed in the course of the plot itself. Fear and pity, for example, are removed by the course of the actions imitated. What must be comes to pass in such a way that the fearsome and piteous events are changed into positive events associated with accomplishment and order. For example, in Sophocles' play *Oedipus the King*, Oedipus endures one horror after another in spite of his best efforts to avoid them. He learns that he has killed his own father, married his own mother, and that his children are also his brothers and sisters. No wonder Thebes is in a bad state. We see what is happening to Oedipus, often before he recognizes it himself. Such actions are piteous and fearsome, and our response is evidence of that. From the standpoint of the play, however, the pity and fear that Oedipus's fate arouses are instrumental to putting things right in the state of Thebes. Oedipus has cursed whomever is responsible. As the actions turn that curse back on Oedipus himself, the piteous and fearsome events become the means for saving the city at the same time that Oedipus is being destroyed by them.

We can conclude that a tragic plot is different from other kinds of plot with fearsome and piteous events. They are not just piteous and fearsome; they are also a means for setting things right. They are indeed linked to religious ritual on this theory, not as emotional effects but as a way of justifying the presence of suffering and danger in the world. The difference is that on the formalist theory, catharsis is effective and explanatory. On the psychological theory, it is emotional and therapeutic. To the formalist, a psychological explanation seems inadequate because it would be equally effective if the audience could be manipulated into the right emotional state by drugs or electrodes in their brains. Psychological theories counter that only the real effect on the audience can make a difference. The single reference in Aristotle's text is insufficient to decide definitively between the competing theories.

From one perspective, the *Poetics* is a handbook on how to write tragedy. Some critics and dramatists have tried to read it as a set of rules. For Aristotle, the poet is a kind of maker. He or she is guided by the nature of the materials, the form of the object, the ends and means of the process. Art is not inspiration and genius but craft. As such, it is rule-governed. A poet was supposed to follow the rules, and a critic could use them as a way of judging the product. Unfortunately for such critics, poets have shown remarkable ingenuity in violating effectively whatever rules critics formulated. This rule-governed approach violates the spirit and method of the *Poetics*. The poet-maker has a skill, but what is made is judged by its formal and final causes. Only by comparing what has been done to the form imitated and the end that form dictates can we tell whether the result is good or bad. The *Poetics* is fundamentally descriptive rather than prescriptive. The only rule that applies to a poet before the fact is that he or she must be true to the demands of the form, the material, the end, and the means available. Only the results can show whether that rule was followed successfully.

Aristotle's *Poetics* is not a complete theory of poetry. It discusses only tragedy in detail, and its extension of that discussion to other forms, particularly epic, is fragmentary. Yet it is the most methodologically complete treatment of art itself in the classical world. Most classical discussions of art are part of some larger theory such as a theory of beauty or a way to achieve harmony for the soul. Aristotle limits his question to tragedy and asks, "What is it?" He focuses on one thing. As a result, we see it more clearly than we did before. His methods are not limited by his historical place in fourth-century Athens. They invite extension to other forms. We could imagine a poetics of comedy, for example, as Umberto Eco did in his novel, *The Name of the Rose*. Or we might think of how directors and editors work together to craft a film. Even if we are not Aristotelians, we can learn how to analyze as Aristotle did.

From *Poetics*

1. OUR SUBJECT BEING POETRY, I propose to speak not only of the art in general but also of its species and their respective capacities; of the structure of plot required for a good poem; of the number and nature of the constituent parts of a poem; and likewise of any other matters in the same line of inquiry. Let us follow the natural order and begin with the primary facts.

Epic poetry and Tragedy, as also Comedy, Dithyrambic poetry,[1] and most flute-playing and lyre-playing, are all, viewed as a whole, modes of imitation. But at the same time they differ from one another in three ways, either by a difference of kind in their means, or by differences in the objects, or in the manner of their imitations.

Just as color and form are used as means by some, who (whether by art or constant practice) imitate and portray many things by their aid, and the voice is used by others; so also in the above-mentioned group of arts, the means with them as a whole are rhythm, language, and harmony—used, however, either singly or in certain combinations. A combination of harmony and rhythm alone is the means in flute-playing and lyre-playing, and any other arts there may be of the same description, e.g. imitative piping. Rhythm alone, without harmony, is the means in the dancer's imitations; for even he, by the rhythms of his attitudes, may represent men's characters, as well as what they do and suffer. There is further an art which imitates by language alone, without harmony, in prose or in verse, and if in verse, either in some one or in a plurality of meters. This form of imitation is to this day without a name. We have no common name for a mime[2] of Sophron[3] or Xenarchus[4] and a Socratic Conversation;[5] and we should still be without one even if the imitation in the two instances were in trimeters or elegiacs[6] or some other kind of verse—though it is the way with people to tack on 'poet' to the name of a meter, and talk of elegiac-poets and epic-poets, thinking that they call them poets not by reason of the imitative nature of their work, but indiscriminately by reason of the meter they write in. Even if a theory of medicine or physical philosophy be put forth in a metrical form, it is usual to describe the writer in this way; Homer and Empedocles,[7] however, have really nothing in common apart from their meter; so that, if the one is to be called a poet, the other should be termed a physicist rather than a poet. We should be in the same position also, if the imitation in these instances were in all the meters, like the *Centaur* (a rhapsody in a medley of all meters) of Chaeremon;[8] and Chaeremon one has to recognize as a poet. So much, then, as to these arts. There are, lastly, certain other arts, which combine all the means enumerated, rhythm, mel-

---

[1] Dithyrambic poetry was a form of choral poetry associated particularly with the god of wine and revelry, Dionysus. Aristotle's list of kinds of poetry is not meant to be exhaustive. Poetry is thought of as a performance art, however; it is not something read silently, though that custom was becoming more common in Aristotle's time.

[2] Mimes were imitative performances, particularly based on common life.

[3] Sophron was a fifth-century B.C.E. writer from Syracuse in Sicily. He gave literary form to the mime. We have only fragments of his work.

[4] Xenarchus was the son of Sophron.

[5] Plato was not the only writer to compose dialogues based on the Socratic style of conversation. We have a number of dialogues by Xenophon (428–354 B.C.E.) and others are referred to.

[6] Elegiacs were a more complex form of epic hexameter.

[7] Empedocles (493–433 B.C.E.) was one of the leading pre-Socratic philosophers. His philosophy emphasized the dialectical struggle between principles such as love and strife. The pre-Socratic philosophers typically wrote in verse even though their subject matter was speculative or prudential.

[8] Chaeremon was a fourth-century B.C.E. tragic poet. His *Centaur* is lost. His reputation was for plays that were not easily performed and for far-fetched metaphors.

ody, and verse, e.g. Dithyrambic and Nomic[9] poetry, Tragedy and Comedy; with this difference, however, that the three kinds of means are in some of them all employed together, and in others brought in separately, one after the other. These elements of difference in the above arts I term the means of their imitation.

2. The objects the imitator represents are actions, with agents who are necessarily either good men or bad—the diversities of human character being nearly always derivative from this primary distinction, since the line between virtue and vice is one dividing the whole of mankind. It follows, therefore, that the agents represented must be either above our own level of goodness, or beneath it, or just such as we are; in the same way as, with the painters, the personages of Polygnotus[10] are better than we are, those of Pauson[11] worse, and those of Dionysius[12] just like ourselves. It is clear that each of the above-mentioned arts will admit of these differences, and that it will become a separate art by representing objects with this point of difference. Even in dancing, flute-playing, and lyre-playing such diversities are possible; and they are also possible in the nameless art that uses language, prose or verse without harmony, as its means; Homer's personages, for instance, are better than we are; Cleophon's[13] are on our own level; and those of Hegemon of Thasos,[14] the first writer of parodies, and Nicochares,[15] the author of the Dithyramb and the Nome: the personages

may be presented in them with the difference exemplified in the . . . [text incomplete here] . . . and Argas, and in the Cyclopses of Timotheus and Philoxenus.[16] This difference it is that distinguishes Tragedy and Comedy also; the one would make its personages worse, and the other better, than the men of the present day.

3. A third difference in these arts is in the manner in which each kind of object is represented. Given both the same means and the same kind of object for imitation, one may either (1) speak at one moment in narrative and at another in an assumed character, as Homer does; or (2) one may remain the same throughout, without any such change; or (3) the imitators may represent the whole story dramatically, as though they were actually doing the things described.

As we said at the beginning, therefore, the differences in the imitation of these arts come under three heads, their means, their objects, and their manner.

So that as an imitator Sophocles[17] will be on one side akin to Homer, both portraying good men; and on another to Aristophanes,[18] since both present their personages as acting and doing. This in fact, according to some, is the reason for plays being termed dramas, because in a play the personages act the story. . . . So much, then, as to the number and nature of the points of difference in the imitation of these arts.

4. It is clear that the general origin of poetry was due to two causes, each of them part of human nature. *Imitation* is natural to man from childhood, one of his advantages over the lower

---

[9] Nomic poetry combined melody and text.

[10] Polygnotus, a fifth-century B.C.E. painter who came to Athens, was one of the first great Athenian painters. His work was known for idealized figures. Because of its fragile nature, only fragments of Greek painting survive. We know of painters such as Polygnotus primarily from literary descriptions.

[11] Pauson was a fourth-century successor of Polygnotus.

[12] Dionysus was another fourth-century painter. He should not be confused with the god Dionysus.

[13] Cleophon was a tragic poet. Only titles of his work survive.

[14] Hegemon was not the first writer of parodies in classical Greece; he made them an independent form in competitions.

[15] Nicochares was a fourth-century Athenian comic poet; only titles of his works survive. This may not be the person Aristotle had in mind.

[16] In many places, the text of the *Poetics* is a matter of conjecture. Gerald Else reads this passage as "for one can imitate the way Timotheus and Philoxenus did [their] Cyclopses." *Aristotle's Poetics: The Argument* (Cambridge, MA: Harvard University Press, 1967), p. 82. Timotheus and Philoxenus were both poets. Philoxenus was sent to the quarries by Dionysus, the ruler of Syracuse.

[17] Sophocles (496–406 B.C.E.) was one of the three great writers of tragedies whose works survive. His *Oedipus Tyrannus* is the prototype for the kind of tragedy Aristotle is analyzing.

[18] Aristophanes (c. 455–385 B.C.E.) is the greatest of the comic dramatists.

animals being this, that he is the most imitative creature in the world, and learns at first by imitation. And it is also natural for all to delight in works of imitation. The truth of this second point is shown by experience: though the objects themselves may be painful to see, we delight to view the most realistic representations of them in art, the forms for example of the lowest animals and of dead bodies. The explanation is to be found in a further fact: to be learning something is the greatest of pleasures not only to the philosopher but also to the rest of mankind, however small their capacity for it; the reason of the delight in seeing the picture is that one is at the same time learning—gathering the meaning of things, e.g. that the man there is so-and-so; for if one has not seen the thing before, one's pleasure will not be in the picture as an imitation of it, but will be due to the execution or coloring or some similar cause. Imitation, then being natural to us—as also the sense of harmony and rhythm, the meters being obviously species of rhythms—it was through their original aptitude, and by a series of improvements for the most part gradual on their first efforts, that they created poetry out of their improvisations.

Poetry, however, soon broke up into two kinds according to the differences of character in the individual poets; for the graver among them would represent noble actions, and those of noble personages; and the meaner sort the actions of the ignoble. The latter class produced invectives at first, just as others did hymns and panegyrics. We know of no such poem by any of the pre-Homeric poets, though there were probably many such writers among them; instances, however, may be found from Homer downwards, e.g. his *Margites,*[19] and the similar poems of others. In this poetry of invective its natural fitness brought an iambic meter into use; hence our present term 'iambic,' because it was the meter of their 'iambs' or invectives against one another. The result was

that the old poets became some of them writers of heroic and others of iambic verse. Homer's position, however, is peculiar: just as he was in the serious style the poet of poets, standing alone not only through the literary excellence, but also through the dramatic character of his imitations, so too he was the first to outline for us the general forms of Comedy by producing not a dramatic invective, but a dramatic picture of the Ridiculous; his *Margites* in fact stands in the same relation to our comedies as the *Iliad* and *Odyssey* to our tragedies. As soon, however, as Tragedy and Comedy appeared in the field, those naturally drawn to the one line of poetry became writers of comedies instead of iambs,[20] and those naturally drawn to the other, writers of tragedies instead of epics, because these new modes of art were grander and of more esteem than the old.

If it be asked whether Tragedy is now all that need be in its formative elements, to consider that, and decide it theoretically and in relation to the theaters, is a matter for another inquiry. It certainly began in improvisations—as did also Comedy; the one originating with the authors of the Dithyramb, the other with those of the phallic songs,[21] which still survive as institutions in many of our cities. And its advance after that was little by little, through their improving on whatever they had before them at each stage. It was in fact only after a long series of changes that the movement of tragedy stopped on its attaining to its natural form. (1) The number of actors was first increased to two by Aeschylus,[22] who curtailed the business of the Chorus, and made the dialogue, or spoken portion, take the leading part in the play. (2) A third actor and scenery were due to Sophocles. (3) Tragedy acquired also its magnitude. Discarding short stories and a ludicrous diction, through its passing out of its sa-

---

[19] The *Margites* was a comic poem. Aristotle makes Homer the father of all of Greek drama.

[20] Iambs are not simply a metrical form; they are a type of poetry (often satirical).

[21] Greek poetry was sexually uninhibited; the phallus played a significant role in satire and ritual.

[22] With Sophocles and Euripides, Aeschylus (525–456 B.C.E.) was one of the three great writers of tragedy whose works survive.

tyric[23] stage, it assumed, though only at a late point in its progress, a tone of dignity; and its meter changed then from trochaic to iambic.[24] The reason for their original use of the trochaic tetrameter was that their poetry was satyric and more connected with dancing that it now is. As soon, however, as a spoken part came in, nature herself found the appropriate meter. The iambic, we know, is the most speakable of meters, as is shown by the fact that we very often fall into it in conversation, whereas we rarely talk hexameters, and only when we depart from the speaking tone of voice. (4) Another change was a plurality of episodes or acts. As for the remaining matters, the super-added embellishments and the account of their introduction, these must be taken as said, as it would probably be a long piece of work to go through the details.

5. As for Comedy, it is (as has been observed) an imitation of men worse than the average; worse, however, not as regards any and every sort of fault, but only as regards one particular kind, the Ridiculous, which is a species of the Ugly. The Ridiculous may be defined as a mistake or deformity not productive of pain or harm to others; the mask,[25] for instance, that excites laughter, is something ugly and distorted without causing pain.

Though the successive changes in Tragedy and their authors are not unknown, we cannot say the same of Comedy; its early states passed unnoticed, because it was not as yet taken up in a serious way. It was only at a late point in its progress that a chorus of comedians was officially granted by the archon;[26] they used to be mere volunteers. It has also already certain definite forms at the time when the record of those termed comic poets begins. Who it was who supplied it with masks, or prologues, or a plurality of actors and the like, has remained unknown. The invented Fable, or Plot, however, originated in Sicily, with Epicharmus and Phormis;[27] of Athenian poets Crates[28] was the first to drop the Comedy of invective and frame stories of a general and nonpersonal nature, in other words, Fables or Plots.

Epic poetry, then, has been seen to agree with Tragedy to this extent, that of being an imitation of serious subjects in a grand kind of verse. It differs from it, however, (1) in that it is one kind of verse and in narrative form; and (2) in its length —which is due to its action having no fixed limit of time, whereas Tragedy endeavors to keep as far as possible within a single circuit of the sun, or something near that. This, I say, is another point of difference between them, though at first the practice in this respect was just the same in tragedies as in epic poems. They differ also (3) in their constituents, some being common to both and others peculiar to Tragedy—hence a judge of good and bad in Tragedy is a judge of that in epic poetry also. All the parts of an epic are included in Tragedy; but those of Tragedy are not all of them to be found in the Epic.

6. Reserving hexameter poetry and comedy for consideration hereafter,[29] let us proceed now to the discussion of Tragedy; before doing so, however, we must gather up the definition resulting from what has been said. A tragedy, then, is the imitation of an action that is serious and also, as having magnitude, complete in itself; in language with pleasurable accessories, each kind brought in separately in the parts of the work; in a dramatic not in a narrative form; with incidents

---

[23] At festivals, tragedy was performed in sets of three plays. These were followed by a satyr play that was bawdy and inverted the tone of the more solemn tragedies.

[24] A trochaic pattern is long/short while an iambic pattern is short/long. We must remember, however, that Greek poetry does not follow English stress patterns.

[25] Greek drama was performed by actors who wore conventionally stylized masks.

[26] Greek drama was a civic performance, and as such it was supported by public funds. The archon was an elected magistrate.

[27] Epicharmus and Phormis were fifth-century Sicilian comic writers.

[28] Crates won the comic prize in 450 B.C.E. Only titles of his works survive.

[29] The promise of further treatment of poetry and comedy is not fulfilled. Some speculate that the *Poetics* is only a fragment or even notes of one kind or another.

arousing pity and fear, wherewith to accomplish its catharsis of such emotions. Here by 'language with pleasurable accessories' I mean that with rhythm and harmony or song superadded; and by 'the kinds separately' I mean that some portions are worked out with verse only, and others in turn with song.

As they act the stories, it follows that in the first place the Spectacle (or stage-appearance of the actors) must be some part of the whole; and in the second Melody and Diction, these two being the means of their imitation. Here by 'Diction' I mean merely this, the composition of the verses; and by 'Melody,' what is too completely understood to require explanation. But further: the subject represented also is an action; and the action involves agents, who must necessarily have their distinctive qualities both of character and thought, since it is from these that we ascribe certain qualities to their actions. There are in the natural order of things, therefore, two causes, Thought and Character, of their actions, and consequently of their success or failure in their lives. Now the action (that which was done) is represented in the play by the Fable or Plot. The Fable, in our present sense of the term, is simply this, the combination of the incidents, or things done in the story; whereas Character is what makes us ascribe certain moral qualities to the agents; and Thought is shown in all they say when proving a particular point or, it may be enunciating a general truth. There are six parts consequently of every tragedy, as a whole (that is) of such or such quality, viz. a Fable or Plot, Characters, Diction, Thought, Spectacle, and Melody; two of them arising from the means, one from the manner, and three from the objects of the dramatic imitation; and there is nothing else besides these six. Of these, its formative elements, then, not a few of the dramatists have made due use, as every play one may say, admits of Spectacle, Character, Fable, Diction, Melody, and Thought.

The most important of the six is the combination of the incidents of the story. Tragedy is essentially an imitation not of persons but of action and life, of happiness and misery. All human happiness or misery takes the form of action; the end for which we live is a certain kind of activity, not a quality. Character gives us qualities, but it is in our actions—what we do—that we are happy or the reverse. In a play accordingly they do not act in order to portray the Characters; they include the Characters for the sake of the action. So that it is the action in it, i.e. its Fable or Plot, that is the end and purpose of the tragedy; and the end is everywhere the chief thing. Besides this, a tragedy is impossible without action, but there may be one without Character. The tragedies of most of the moderns are characterless—a defect common among poets of all kinds, and with its counterpart in painting in Zeuxis compared with Polygnotus;[30] for whereas the latter is strong in character, the work of Zeuxis is devoid of it. And again: one may string together a series of characteristic speeches of the utmost finish as regards Diction and Thought, and yet fail to produce the true tragic effect; but one will have much better success with a tragedy which, however inferior in these respects, has a Plot, a combination of incidents, in it. And again: the most powerful elements of attraction in Tragedy, the Peripeties and Discoveries, are parts of the Plot. A further proof is in the fact that beginners succeed earlier with the Diction and Characters than with the construction of a story; and the same may be said of nearly all the early dramatists. We maintain, therefore, that the first essential, the life and soul, so to speak, of Tragedy is the Plot; and that the Characters come second—compare the parallel in painting, where the most beautiful colors laid on without order will not give one the same pleasure as a simple black-and-white sketch of a portrait. We maintain that Tragedy is primarily an imitation of action, and that it is mainly for the sake of the action that it imitates the personal agents. Third comes the element of Thought, i.e. the power of saying whatever can be said, or what is appropriate to the occasion. This is what, in

---

[30] Zeuxis was one of the most famous Greek painters of the late fifth and early fourth centuries B.C.E. Anecdotes tell of his paintings looking so realistic that they fooled birds and other painters.

the speeches in Tragedy, falls under the arts of Politics and Rhetoric;[31] for the older poets make their personages discourse like statesmen, and the moderns like rhetoricians. One must not confuse it with Character. Character in a play is that which reveals the moral purpose of the agents, i.e. the sort of thing they seek or avoid, where that is not obvious—hence there is no room for Character in a speech on a purely indifferent subject. Thought, on the other hand, is shown in all they say when proving or disproving some particular point, or enunciating some universal proposition. Fourth among the literary elements is the Diction of the personages, i.e., as before explained, the expression of their thoughts in words, which is practically the same thing with verse as with prose. As for the two remaining parts, the Melody is the greatest of the pleasurable accessories of Tragedy. The Spectacle, though an attraction, is the least artistic of all the parts, and has least to do with the art of poetry. The tragic effect is quite possible without a public performance and actors; and besides, the getting-up of the Spectacle is more a matter for the costumier than the poet.

7. Having thus distinguished the parts, let us now consider the proper construction of the Fable or Plot, as that is at once the first and the most important thing in Tragedy. We have laid it down that a tragedy is an imitation of an action that is complete in itself, as a whole of some magnitude; for a whole may be of no magnitude to speak of. Now a whole is that which has beginning, middle, and end. A beginning is that which is not itself necessarily after anything else, and which has naturally something else after it; an end is that which is naturally after something itself, either as its necessary or usual consequent, and with nothing else after it; and a middle, that which is by nature after one thing and has also another after it. A well-constructed Plot, therefore, cannot either begin or end at any point one likes; beginning and end in it must be of the forms just described. Again: to be beautiful, a living creature, and every whole made up of parts, must not only present a certain order in its arrangement of parts, but also be of a certain definite magnitude. Beauty is a matter of size and order, and therefore impossible either (1) in a very minute creature, since our perception becomes indistinct as it approaches instantaneity; or (2) in a creature of vast size—one, say, 1,000 miles long—as in that case, instead of the object being seen all at once; the unity and wholeness of it is lost to the beholder. Just in the same way, then as a beautiful whole made up of parts, or a beautiful living creature, must be of some size, but a size to be taken in by the eye, so a story or Plot must be of some length, but of a length to be taken in by the memory. As for the limit of its length, so far as that is relative to public performances and spectators, it does not fall within the theory of poetry. If they had to perform a hundred tragedies, they would be timed by water-clocks, as they are said to have been at one period. The limit, however, set by the actual nature of the thing is this: the longer the story, consistently with its being comprehensible as a whole, the finer it is by reason of its magnitude. As a rough general formula, a length which allows of the hero passing by a series of probable or necessary stages from misfortune to happiness, or from happiness to misfortune, may suffice as a limit for the magnitude of the story.

8. The Unity of a Plot does not consist, as some suppose, in its having one man as its subject. An infinity of things befall that one man, some of which it is impossible to reduce to unity; and in like manner there are many actions of one man which cannot be made to form one action. One sees, therefore, the mistake of all the poets who have written a Heracleid, a Theseid,[32] or similar poems; they suppose that, because Heracles was one man, the story also of Heracles must be one story. Homer, however, evidently understood this

---

[31] Note that politics and rhetoric (persuasive public speaking) are classified as arts. *Arts* is an inclusive term for productive skill.

[32] Heracles was the most popular legendary hero of classical Greece; he is renowned for his strength and courage. Theseus was the legendary hero of Athens whose exploits save the city from the Minotaur. Theseus was the friend of Heracles in many stories.

point quite well, whether by art or instinct, just in the same way as he excels the rest in every other respect. In writing an *Odyssey*,[33] he did not make the poem cover all that ever befell his hero—it befell him, for instance, to get wounded on Parnassus[34] and also to feign madness at the time of the call to arms, but the two incidents had no necessary or probable connection with one another—instead of doing that, he took as the subject of the *Odyssey*, as also of the *Iliad*, an action with a Unity of the kind we are describing. The truth is that, just as in the other imitative arts one imitation is always of one thing, so in poetry the story, as an imitation of action, must represent one action, a complete whole, with its several incidents so closely connected that the transposal or withdrawal of any one of them will disjoin and dislocate the whole. For that which makes no perceptible difference by its presence or absence is no real part of the whole.

9. From what we have said it will be seen that the poet's function is to describe, not the thing that has happened, but a kind of thing that might happen, i.e. what is possible as being probable or necessary. The distinction between historian and poet is not in the one writing prose and the other verse—you might put the work of Herodotus into verse, and it would still be a species of history; it consists really in this, that the one describes the thing that has been, and the other a kind of thing that might be. Hence poetry is something more philosophic and of graver import than history, since its statements are of the nature rather of universals, whereas those of history are singulars. By a universal statement I mean one as to what such or such a kind of man will probably or necessarily say or do—which is the aim of poetry, though it affixes proper names to the characters; by a singular statement,[35] one as to what, say, Alci-

biades[36] did or had done to him. In Comedy this has become clear by this time; it is only when their plot is already made up of probable incidents that they give it a basis of proper names, choosing for the purpose any names that may occur to them, instead of writing like the old iambic poets about particular persons. In Tragedy, however, they still adhere to the historic names; and for this reason: what convinces is the possible; now whereas we are not yet sure as to the possibility of that which has not happened, that which has happened is manifestly possible, else it would not have come to pass. Nevertheless even in Tragedy there are some plays with but one or two known names in them, the rest being inventions; and there are some without a single known name, e.g. Agathon's *Antheus*,[37] in which both incidents and names are of the poet's invention; and it is no less delightful on that account. So that one must not aim at a rigid adherence to the traditional stories on which tragedies are based. It would be absurd, in fact, to do so, as even the known stories are only known to a few, though they are a delight none the less to all.

It is evident from the above that the poet must be more the poet of his stories of Plots than of his verses, inasmuch as he is a poet by virtue of the imitative element in his work, and it is actions that he imitates. And if he should come to take a subject from actual history, he is none the less a poet for that; since some historic occurrences may very well be in the probable and possible order of things; and it is in that aspect of them that he is their poet.

---

[33] The *Odyssey* is the "sequel" to Homer's account of the Trojan War, the *Iliad*. The *Odyssey* tells of Odysseus' journey back to his home on Ithaca.

[34] Parnassus is a sacred mountain associated particularly with poetry and the muses.

[35] Aristotelian logic makes extensive use of universal and singular statements. Universal statements have the form "All S is P" or

"No S is P" while singular statements refer to only some individuals: "Some S is (not) P."

[36] Alcibiades was an Athenian of great talent and great notoriety. At the time of the war between Athens and Sparta in the fifth century, Alcibiades was accused of a ritual impiety and fled to the Spartans, who in turn expelled him. Eventually, he found refuge with the Persians.

[37] Agathon was the most famous writer of tragedy after Sophocles, Aeschylus, and Euripides. He is also a major character in Plato's dialogue, the *Symposium*. However, only fragments of his plays survive. His *Antheus* was remarkable in that it was not based on any legendary or heroic figures.

Of simple Plots and actions the episodic are the worst. I call a Plot episodic when there is neither probability not necessity in the sequence of its episodes. Actions of this sort bad poets construct through their own fault, and good ones on account of the players. His work being for public performance, a good poet often stretches out a Plot beyond its capabilities, and is thus obliged to twist the sequence of incident.

Tragedy, however, is an imitation, not only of a complete action, but also of incidents arousing pity and fear. Such incidents have the very greatest effect on the mind when they occur unexpectedly and at the same time in consequence of one another; there is more of the marvelous in them then than if they happened of themselves or by mere chance. Even matters of chance seem most marvelous if there is an appearance of design as it were in them; as for instance the statue of Mitys[38] at Argos killed the author of Mitys' death by falling down on him when a looker-on at a public spectacle; for incidents like that we think to be not without a meaning. A Plot, therefore, of this sort is necessarily finer than others.

10. Plots are either simple or complex, since the actions they represent are naturally of this two-fold description. The action, proceeding in the way defined, as one continuous whole, I call simple, when the change in the hero's fortunes takes place without Peripety or Discovery; and complex, when it involves one or the other, or both. These should each of them arise out of the structure of the Plot itself, so as to be the consequence, necessary or probable, of the antecedents. There is a great difference between a thing happening *propter hoc* and *post hoc*.[39]

A Peripety is the change of the kind described from one state of things within the play to its opposite, and that too in the way we are saying,

in the probable or necessary sequence of events; as it is for instance in *Oedipus:* here the opposite state of things is produced by the Messenger, who, coming to gladden Oedipus and to remove his fears as to his mother, reveals the secret of his birth. And in *Lynceus:* just as he is being led off for execution, with Danaus at his side to put him to death, the incidents preceding this bring it about that he is saved and Danaus put to death.[40] A Discovery is, as the very word implies, a change from ignorance to knowledge, and thus to either love or hate, in the personages marked for good or evil fortune. The finest form of Discovery is one attended by Peripeties, like that which goes with the Discovery in *Oedipus.* There are no doubt other forms of it; what we have said may happen in a way in reference to inanimate things, even things of a very casual kind; and it is also possible to discover whether some one has done or not done something. But the form most directly connected with the Plot and the action of the piece is the first-mentioned. This, with a Peripety, will arouse either piety or fear—actions of that nature being what Tragedy is assumed to represent; and it will also serve to bring about the happy or unhappy ending. The Discovery, then, being of persons, it may be that of one party only to the other, the latter being already known; or both the parties may discover themselves. Iphigenia, for instance, was discovered to Orestes by sending the letter; and another Discovery was required to reveal him to Iphigenia.[41]

Two parts of the Plot, then, Peripety and Discovery, are on matters of this sort. A third part is Suffering; which we may define as an action of a destructive or painful nature, such as murders on

---

[38] The story of Mitys is a typical tale of miraculous intervention. It appears later in classical sources, but Aristotle's reference is the earliest known.

[39] *Post hoc* means "happening after this." *Propter hoc* means "happening because of this." It is a fallacy to think that because something happens after something else, the second event must have happened because of the first event.

[40] The daughter of Danaus was to marry Lynceus, the son of Aegyptus; Danaus opposed the marriage and instructed his daughter to kill Lynceus. She spared him, however, and he founded the royal line at Argos.

[41] Orestes and Iphigenia are the son and daughter of Agamemnon, the great king who led the Greeks in the Trojan War. In older versions of the story, Iphigenia is sacrificed so that the Greek ships may sail to Troy at the beginning of the Trojan War. A later version (in Euripides) has Iphigenia saved at the last minute. Aristotle refers to the later version.

the stage, tortures, woundings, and the like. The other two have been already explained.

12. The parts of Tragedy to be treated as formative elements in the whole were mentioned in a previous Chapter. From the point of view, however, of its quantity, i.e. the separate sections into which it is divided, a tragedy has the following parts: Prologue, Episode, Exode, and a choral portion, distinguished into Parode and Stasimon; these two are common to all tragedies, whereas songs from the stage and *Commoe* are only found in some.[42] The Prologue is all that precedes the Parode of the chorus; an Episode all that comes in between two whole choral songs; the Exode all that follows after the last choral song. In the choral portion the Parode is the whole first statement of the chorus; a Stasimon, a song of the chorus without anapaests or trochees; a Commos, a lamentation sung by chorus and actor in concert. The parts of Tragedy to be used as formative elements in the whole we have already mentioned; the above are its parts from the point of view of its quantity, or the separate sections into which it is divided.

13. The next points after what we have said above will be these: (1) What is the poet to aim at, and what is he to avoid, in constructing his Plots? and (2) What are the conditions on which the tragic effect depends?

We assume that, for the finest form of Tragedy, the Plot must be not simple but complex; and further, that it must imitate actions arousing fear and pity, since that is the distinctive function of this kind of imitation. It follows, therefore, that there are three forms of Plot to be avoided. (1) A good man must not be seen passing from happiness to misery, or (2) a bad man from misery to happiness. The first situation is not fear-inspiring or piteous, but simply odious to us. The second is the most untragic that can be; it has no one of the requisites of Tragedy; it does not appeal either to the human feeling in us, or to our pity, or to our fears. Nor on the other hand, should (3) an

extremely bad man be seen falling from happiness into misery. Such a story may arouse the human feeling in us, but it will not move us to either pity or fear; pity is occasioned by undeserved misfortune, and fear by that of one like ourselves; so that there will be nothing either piteous or fear-inspiring in the situation. There remains, then, the intermediate kind of personage, a man not preeminently virtuous and just, whose misfortune, however, is brought upon him not by vice and depravity but by some error of judgment, of the number of those in the enjoyment of great reputation and prosperity; e.g. Oedipus, Thyestes,[43] and the men of note of similar families. The perfect Plot, accordingly, must have a single, and not (as some tell us a double issue; the change in the hero's fortunes must be not from misery to happiness, but on the contrary from happiness to misery; and the cause of it must lie not in any depravity, but in some great error on his part; the man himself being either such as we have described, or better, not worse, than that. Fact also confirms our theory. Though the poets began by accepting any tragic story that came to hand, in these days the finest tragedies are always on the story of some few houses, on that of Alcmaeon, Oedipus, Orestes, Meleager, Thyestes, Telephus,[44] or any others that may have been involved, as either agents or sufferers, in some deed of horror. The theoretically best tragedy, then, has a Plot of this description. The critics, therefore, are wrong who blame Euripides[45] for taking this line in his tragedies, and giving many of them an unhappy

---

[42] These are technical divisions in tragedy that follow a prescribed order.

[43] Thyestes was deceived by his brother, Atreus, who pretended a reconciliation but served the children of Thyestes to their father at a banquet. Oedipus became king of Thebes but could not resist unraveling the story of his own past that had led him unwittingly to kill his father and marry his mother.

[44] Alcmaeon, like Orestes, avenged his father by killing his mother and was pursued for the murder. Meleager killed the brothers of his mother in a hunting dispute and his mother in turn acted to cause his death. Telephus was separated from his mother at birth and they were to marry but discovered the relation.

[45] Euripides (485–406 B.C.E.) was the third of the great Athenian writers of tragedy. His work was considered more "untraditional" than that of Sophocles and Aeschylus.

ending. It is, as we have said, the right line to take. The best proof is this; on the stage, and in the public performances, such plays, properly worked out, are seen to be the most truly tragic; and Euripides, even if his execution be faulty in every other point, is seen to be nevertheless the most tragic certainly of the dramatists. After this comes the construction of Plot which some rank first, one with a double story (like the *Odyssey*) and an opposite issue for the good and the bad personages. It is ranked as first only through the weakness of the audiences; the poets merely follow their public, writing as its wishes dictate. But the pleasure here is not that of Tragedy. It belongs rather to Comedy, where the bitterest enemies in the piece (e.g. Orestes and Aegisthus[46]) walk off good friends at the end, with no slaying of any one by any one.

14. The tragic fear and pity may be aroused by the Spectacle; but they may also be aroused by the very structure and incidents of the play—which is the better way and shows the better poet. The Plot in fact should be so framed that, even without seeing the things take place, he who simply hears the account of them will be filled with horror and pity at the incidents; which is just the effect that the mere recital of the story in *Oedipus* would have on one. To produce this same effect by means of the Spectacle is less artistic, and requires extraneous aid. Those, however, who make use of the Spectacle to put before us that which is merely monstrous and not productive of fear, are wholly out of touch with Tragedy; not every kind of pleasure should be required of a tragedy, but only its own proper pleasure.

The tragic pleasure is that of pity and fear, and the poet has to produce it by a work of imitation; it is clear, therefore, that the causes should be included in the incidents of his story. Let us see, then, what kinds of incident strike one as horrible, or rather as piteous. In a deed of this description the parties must necessarily be either friends, or enemies, or indifferent to one another. Now when enemy does it on enemy, there is nothing to move us to pity either in his doing or in his meditating the deed, except so far as the actual pain of the sufferer is concerned; and the same is true when the parties are indifferent to one another. Whenever the tragic deed, however is done within the family—when murder or the like is done or meditated by brother on brother, by son on father, by mother on son, or son on mother—these are the situations the poet should seek after. The traditional stories, accordingly, must be kept as they are, e.g. the murder of Clytaemnestra by Orestes and of Eriphyle by Alcmaeon.[47] At the same time even with these there is something left to the poet himself; it is for him to devise the right way of treating them. Let us explain more clearly what we mean by 'the right way.' The deed of horror may be done by the doer knowingly and consciously, as in the old poets, and in Medea's murder of her children[48] in Euripides. Or he may do it, but in ignorance of his relationship, and discover that afterwards, as does the Oedipus in Sophocles. Here the deed is outside the play; but it may be within it, like the act of Alcmaeon in Astydamas,[49] or that of the Telegonus[50] in the *Wounded Odysseus*. A third possibility is for one mediating some deadly injury to another, in ignorance of his relationship, to make the discovery in time to draw back. These exhaust the possibilities, since the deed must necessarily be either done or not done, and either knowingly or unknowingly.

---

[46] Aegisthus was the lover of Clytemnestra. Together they killed Agamemnon. It would take considerable manipulation of the legend to make Orestes and Aegisthus friends at the end.

[47] See note 44 earlier.

[48] Medea had magical powers that she used to aid her lover Jason and to thwart her enemies. When Jason abandoned her, she killed their children as a way of punishing him.

[49] Astydamas was a fourth-century writer of tragedy. He has Alcmaeon kill his mother without knowing her rather than intentionally.

[50] The *Telegonus*, or *Telegonia,* was part of the epic cycle of poems that told of events from the birth of the gods to the end of the events associated with the Trojan War. The *Telegonia* consisted of two books that carried the events of the *Odyssey* to a conclusion. The poems of the epic cycle, except for the *Iliad* and *Odyssey,* are lost.

The worst situation is when the personage is with full knowledge on the point of doing the deed, and leaves it undone. It is odious and also (through the absence of suffering) untragic; hence it is that no one is made to act thus except in some few instances, e.g. Haemon and Creon in *Antigone*.[51] Next after this comes the actual perpetration of the deed mediated. A better situation than that, however, is for the deed to be done in ignorance, and the relationship discovered afterwards, since there is nothing odious in it, and the Discovery will serve to astound us. But the best of all is the last; what we have in *Cresphontes* (by Euripides), for example, where Merope, on the point of slaying her son, recognizes him in time; in *Iphigenia,* where sister and brother are in a like position; and in *Helle,* where the son recognizes his mother, when on the point of giving her up to her enemy.[52]

This will explain why our tragedies are restricted (as we said just now) to such a small number of families. It was accident rather than art that led the poets in quest of subjects to embody this kind of incident in their Plots. They are still obliged, accordingly, to have recourse to the families in which such horrors have occurred.

On the construction of the Plot, and the kind of Plot required for Tragedy, enough has now been said.

15. In the Characters there are four points to aim at. First and foremost, that they shall be good. There will be an element of character in the play, if (as has been observed) what a personage says or does reveals a certain moral purpose; and a good element of character, if the purpose so revealed is good. Such goodness is possible in every type of personage, even in a woman or slave, though the one is perhaps an inferior, and the other a wholly worthless being. The second point is to make them appropriate. The Character before us may be, say, manly; but it is not appropriate in a female Character to be manly, or clever. The third is to make them like the reality, which is not the same as their being good and appropriate, in our sense of the term. The fourth is to make them consistent and the same throughout; even if inconsistency be part of the man before one for imitation as presenting that form of character, he should still be consistently inconsistent. We have an instance of baseness of character, not required for the story, in the Menelaus[53] in *Orestes;* of the incongruous and unbefitting in the lamentation of Odysseus in *Scylla,* and in the (clever) speech of Melanippe,[54] and of inconsistency in *Iphigenia at Aulius,* where Iphigenia the suppliant is utterly unlike other later Iphigenia.[55] The right thing, however, is in the Characters just as in the incidents of the play to endeavor always after the necessary or the probable; so that whenever such-and-such a personage says or does such-and-such a thing, it shall be the necessary or probable outcome of his character; and whenever this incident follows on that, it shall be either the necessary or the probable consequence of it. From this one sees (to digress for a moment) that the Denouement also should arise out of the plot itself, and not depend on a stage-artifice, as in *Medea,*[56] or in the story of the (arrested) departure of the Greeks in the *Iliad.*[57] The artifice must

---

[51] Creon was the brother of Jocasta, the wife-mother of Oedipus, and Haemon was his son. When Haemon sides with Antigone against Creon, Creon turns on his son, but repents.

[52] Aepytus, the son of Cresphontes, fled as a child when his father was killed. When he returns, his mother does not recognize him and almost kills him. Iphigenia similarly fails to recognize Orestes on his return and almost kills him. The legend of Helle (from whom the Hellespont derives its name) has a stepmother plotting against her stepchildren who are saved by their mother.

[53] Menelaus was the brother of Agamemnon and the husband of Helen over whom the Trojan War was fought. In Euripides' play, Menelaus refused to aid Orestes after Orestes avenged Agamemnon.

[54] In a play by Euripides, *Melanippe the Wise* (of which only fragments survive), Melanippe, a descendent of Aeolus, the father of one branch of the Greek ethnic structure, gives a speech in her defense but is condemned anyway.

[55] Euripides' play *Iphigenia in Aulis* presents her first as a young girl and then in an emotional state inconsistent with her earlier appearance.

[56] In Euripides' *Medea,* the appearance of the sun-chariot to provide Medea's escape at the end is a form of *deus ex machina,* a device that the plot has not anticipated.

[57] The Greeks are about to give up the siege of Troy (*Iliad,* Book 2) when the gods intervene.

be reserved for matters outside the play—for past events beyond human knowledge, or events yet to come, which require to be foretold or announced; since it is the privilege of the Gods to know everything. There should be nothing improbable among the actual incidents. If it be unavoidable, however, it should be outside the tragedy, like the improbability in the *Oedipus* of Sophocles.[58] But to return to the Characters. As Tragedy is an imitation of personages better than the ordinary man, we in our way should follow the example of good portrait-painters, who reproduce the distinctive features of a man, and at the same time, without losing the likeness, make him handsomer than he is. The poet in like manner, in portraying men quick or slow to anger, or with similar infirmities of character, must know how to represent them as such, and at the same time as good men, as Agathon[59] and Homer have represented Achilles.[60]

All these rules[61] one must keep in mind throughout, and, further, those also for such points of stage-effect as directly depend on the art of the poet, since in these too one may often make mistakes. Enough, however, has been said on the subject in one of our published writings. . . .

17. At the time when he is constructing his Plots, and engaged on the Diction in which they are worked out, the poet should remember (1) to put the actual scenes as far as possible before his eyes. In this way, seeing everything with the vividness of an eyewitness as it were, he will devise what is appropriate, and be least likely to overlook incongruities. This is shown by what was censured in Carcinus,[62] the return of Amphiaraus

from the sanctuary; it would have passed unnoticed, if it had not been actually seen by the audience; but on the stage his play failed, the incongruity of the incident offending the spectators. (2) As far as may be, too, the poet should even act his story with the very gestures of his personages. Given the same natural qualifications, he who feels the emotions to be described will be the most convincing; distress and anger, for instance, are portrayed most truthfully by one who is feeling them at the moment. Hence it is that poetry demands a man with a special gift for it, or else one with a touch of madness in him; the former can easily assume the required mood, and the latter may be actually beside himself with emotion.[63] (3) His story, again, whether already made or of his own making, he should first simplify and reduce to a universal form, before proceeding to lengthen it out by the insertion of episodes. The following will show how the universal element in *Iphigenia,* for instance, may be reviewed: A certain maiden having been offered in sacrifice, and spirited away from her sacrificers into another land, where the custom was to sacrifice all strangers to the Goddess, she was made there the priestess of this rite. Long after that the brother of the priestess happened to come; the fact, however, of the oracle having for a certain reason bidden him go thither, and his object in going, are outside the Plot of the play. On his coming he was arrested, and about to be sacrificed, when he revealed who he was—either as Euripides puts it, or (as suggested by Polyidus[64]) by the not improbable exclamation, 'So I too am doomed to be sacrificed, and my sister was'; and the disclosure led to his salvation. This done, the next thing, after the proper names have been fixed as a basis for the story, is to work in episodes or accessory incidents. One must mind, however, that the

---

[58] The plot of Oedipus turns on a series of remarkable coincidences, but the actual events presented in the play all follow logically.

[59] See note 37.

[60] The anger of Achilles is the cause of the incidents in the *Iliad,* but Achilles himself remains the greatest of the Greek warriors.

[61] Aristotle's "rules" follow from the analysis of his examples. They are never arbitrary or prescriptive.

[62] Carcinus was a tragic poet in the fourth century B.C.E. who is said to have won eleven victories in the dramatic competitions. Amphiaraus took part in the attack on Thebes by the sons of Oedipus, was driven away, and swallowed up in a cleft opened

by Zeus. The cleft became a sanctuary. The play is lost, so we do not know exactly what Aristotle is referring to.

[63] Aristotle echoes the theory advanced by Plato in Socrates' dialogue with the rhapsodist Ion and elsewhere that poetry is a form of ecstasy or divine madness.

[64] Polyides is known only as a Sophist mentioned by Aristotle. His suggestion may have been that of a critic, not a playwright.

episodes are appropriate, like the fit of madness in Orestes, which led to his arrest, and the purifying, which brought about his salvation. In plays, then the episodes are short; in epic poetry they serve to lengthen out the poem. The argument of the *Odyssey* is not a long one. A certain man has been abroad many years; Poseidon is ever on the watch for him, and he is all alone. Matters at home too have come to this, that his substance is being wasted and his son's death plotted by suitors to his wife. Then he arrives there himself after his grievous sufferings; reveals himself, and falls on his enemies; and the end is his salvation and their death. This being all that is proper to the *Odyssey*, everything else in it is episode.

18. (4) There is a further point to be borne in mind. Every tragedy is in part Complication and in part Denouement; the incidents before the opening scene, and often certain also of those within the play, forming the Complication; and the rest the Denouement. By Complication I mean all from the beginning of the story to the point just before the change in the hero's fortunes; by Denouement, all from the beginning of the change to the end. In the Lynceus of Theodectes,[65] for instance, the complication includes, together with the presupposed incidents, the seizure of the child and that in turn of the parents; and the Denouement all from the indictment for the murder to the end. Now it is right, when one speaks of a tragedy as the same or not the same as another, to do so on the ground before all else of their Plot, i.e. as having the same or not the same Complication and Denouement. Yet there are many dramatists who, after a good Complication, fail in the Denouement. But it is necessary for both points of construction to be always duly mastered. (5) There are four distinct species of Tragedy — that being the number of the constituents also that have been mentioned: first, the complex Tragedy, which is all Peripety and Discovery; second, the

Tragedy of suffering, e.g. the *Ajaxes* and *Ixions;*[66] third, the Tragedy of character, e.g. *The Pythiotides* [*Women of Phthia*] and *Peleus.*[67] The fourth constituent is that of 'Spectacle,' exemplified in *The Phorcides* [*Daughters of Phorcys*],[68] in *Prometheus,*[69] and in all plays with the scene laid in the nether world.[70] The poet's aim, then, should be to combine every element of interest, if possible, or else the more important and the major part of them. This is now especially necessary owing to the unfair criticism to which the poet is subjected in these days. Just because there have been poets before him strong in the several species of tragedy, the critics now expect the one man to surpass that which was the strong point of each one of his predecessors. (6) One should also remember what has been said more than once, and not write a tragedy on an epic body of incident (i.e. one with a plurality of stories in it), by attempting to dramatize, for instance, the entire story of the *Iliad*. In the epic owing to its scale every part is treated at proper length; with a drama, however, on the same story the result is very disappointing. This is shown by the fact that all who have dramatized the fall of Ilium[71] in its entirety, and not part by part, like Euripides, or the whole of the Niobe story,[72] instead of a portion, like

---

[65] Theodectes (375–334 B.C.E.) was a pupil of both Plato and Aristotle. He was both a rhetorician and a writer of tragedies. For Lynceus, see note 38.

[66] Ajax (or Aias) was a major hero in the *Iliad*. His suffering probably refers to the legends around his death; denied the armor of Achilles, he went mad and killed himself. Ixion was the first killer of his own kin; purified by Zeus, he attempted to seduce Hera and was punished on a revolving wheel.

[67] Peleus was banished to Phthia for killing his half-brother. His difficulties in Phthia led to further killing and ritual purification. Eventually, he is given Thetis, a goddess, as his wife; Achilles is their son.

[68] Phorcys was the father of the gorgons and sea monsters.

[69] Prometheus is the god who defies Zeus to bring fire to humans and is punished for his rebellion. At least three plays by Aeschylus are about him.

[70] There may have been tragedies that took the form of conversations in Hades along the lines of the descent of Odysseus into Hades that appears in the *Odyssey*. There Odysseus is allowed to speak to Achilles.

[71] *Ilium* is another name for Troy.

[72] Niobe claimed to be the equal of Leto, the mother of Apollo and Artemis. For this, Apollo and Artemis killed the children of Niobe and Niobe herself was turned into a stone.

Aeschylus, either fail utterly or have but ill success on the stage; for that and that alone was enough to ruin even a play by Agathon. Yet in their Peripeties, as also in their simple plots, the poets I mean show wonderful skill in aiming at the kind of effect they desire—a tragic situation that arouses the human feeling in one, like the clever villain (e.g. Sisyphus[73]) deceived, or the brave wrong-doer worsted. This is probable, however, only in Agathon's sense, when he speaks of the probability of even improbabilities coming to pass. (7) The Chorus too should be regarded as one of the actors; it should be an integral part of the whole, and take a share in the action—that which it has in Sophocles, rather than in Euripides. With the later poets, however, the songs in a play of theirs have no more to do with the Plot of that then of any other tragedy. Hence it is that they are now singing intercalary pieces, a practice first introduced by Agathon.[74] And yet what real difference is there between singing such intercalary pieces, and attempting to fit in a speech, or even a whole act, from one play into another? . . .

23. As for the poetry which merely narrates, or imitates by means of versified language (without action), it is evident that it has several points in common with Tragedy.

The construction of its stories should clearly be like that in a drama; they should be based on a single action, one that is a complete whole in itself, with a beginning, middle, and end, so as to enable the work to produce its own proper pleasure with all the organic unity of a living creature. Nor should one suppose that there is anything like them in our usual histories. A history has to deal not with one action, but with one period and all that happened in that to one or more persons, however disconnected the several events may have been. Just as two events may take place at the same time, e.g. the sea-fight off Salamis and

the battle with the Carthaginians in Sicily,[75] without converging to the same end, so too of two consecutive events one may sometimes come after the other with no one end as their common issue. Nevertheless most of our epic poets, one may say, ignore the distinction.

Herein, then, to repeat what we have said before, we have a further proof of Homer's marvelous superiority to the rest. He did not attempt to deal even with the Trojan war in its entirety, though it was a whole with a definite beginning and end—through a feeling apparently that it was too long a story to be taken in in one view, or if not that, too complicated from the variety of incident in it.[76] As it is, he has singled out one section of the whole; many of the other incidents, however, he brings in as episodes, using the Catalogue of the Ships, for instance, and other episodes to relieve the uniformity of his narrative. As for the other epic poets, they treat one man, or one period; or else of an action which, although one, has a multiplicity of parts in it. This last is what the authors of the *Cypria* and *Little Iliad*[77] have done. And the result is that, whereas the *Iliad* or *Odyssey* supplies materials for only one, or at most two tragedies, the *Cypria* does that for several and *Little Iliad* for more than eight. . . .

24. Besides this, Epic poetry must divide into the same species as Tragedy; it must be either simple or complex, a story of character or one of suffering. Its parts, too, with the exception of Song and spectacle, must be the same, as it

[73] Sisyphus is a son of Aeolus (n. 54) who is condemned in Hades eternally to roll a stone up a hill only to have it role back down. His trickery was legendary.

[74] These were pieces added in as interpolations.

[75] Salamis is an island off the coast of Greece southwest of Athens. In 480 B.C.E. the Persians were defeated there in a naval battle that stopped their advance. Carthage was a maritime empire centered on the city of Carthage in North Africa. Carthagenian expansion was halted when Hamilcar was defeated in Sicily in the same year.

[76] The *Iliad* begins in the tenth year of the Trojan War and ends with the death and burial of the Trojan hero, Hector, before Troy has fallen.

[77] The *Cypria* and the *Little Iliad* were part of the epic cycle. The *Cypria* relates the events leading up to the Trojan War, and the *Little Iliad* tells of what happened after the death of Hector but before the fall of the city. We know of the contents of the poems only through references to them; the poems themselves are lost.

requires Peripeties, Discoveries, and scenes of suffering just like Tragedy. Lastly, the Thought and diction in it must be good in their way. All these elements appear in Homer first; and he has made due use of them. His two poems are each examples of construction, the *Iliad* simple and a story of suffering, the *Odyssey* complex (there is Discovery throughout it) and a story of character. And they are more than this, since in Diction and Thought too they surpass all other poems.

There is, however, a difference in the Epic as compared with Tragedy, (1) in its length, and (2) in its meter. (1) As to its length, the limit already suggested will suffice: it must be possible for the beginning and end of the work to be taken in in one view—a condition which will be fulfilled if the poem be shorter than the old epics, and about as long as the series of tragedies offered for one hearing. For the extension of its length epic poetry has a special advantage, of which it makes large use. In a play one cannot represent an action with a number of parts going on simultaneously; one is limited to the part on the stage and connected with the actors. Whereas in epic poetry the narrative form makes it possible for one to describe a number of simultaneous incidents; and these, if germane to the subject, increase the body of the poem. This then is a gain to the Epic, tending to give it grandeur, and also variety of interest and room for episodes of diverse kinds. Uniformity of incident by the satiety it soon creates is apt to ruin tragedies on the stage. (2) As for its meter, the heroic has been assigned it from experience; were any one to attempt a narrative poem in some one, or in several, of the other meters, the incongruity of the thing would be apparent. The heroic in fact is the gravest and weightiest of meters—which is what makes it more tolerant than the rest of strange words and metaphors, that also being a point in which the narrative form of poetry goes beyond all others. The iambic and trochaic, on the other hand, are meters of movement, the one representing that of life and action, the other that of the dance. Still more unnatural would it appear, if one were to

write an epic in a medley of meters as Chaeremon did. Hence it is that no one has ever written a long story in any but heroic verse; nature herself, as we have said, teaches us to select the meter appropriate to such a story.

Homer, admirable as he is in every other respect, is especially so in this, that he alone among epic poets is not unaware of the part to be played by the poet himself in the poem. The poet should say very little *in propria persona,* as he is no imitator when doing that. Whereas the other poets are perpetually coming forward in person, and say but little, and that only here and there, as imitators, Homer after a brief preface brings in forthwith a man, a woman, or some other Character —no one of them characterless, but each with distinctive characteristics.

The marvelous is certainly required in Tragedy. The Epic, however, affords more opening for the improbable, the chief factor in the marvelous, because in it the agents are not visible before one. The scene of the pursuit of Hector would be ridiculous on the stage—the Greeks halting instead of pursuing him, and Achilles shaking his head to stop them; but in the poem the absurdity is overlooked. The marvelous, however, is a cause of pleasure, as is shown by the fact that we all tell a story with additions, in the belief that we are doing our hearers a pleasure.

Homer more than any other has taught the rest of us the art of framing lies in the right way. I mean the use of paralogism. Whenever, if A is or happens, a consequent, B, is or happens, men's notion is that, if the B is, the A also is—but that is a false conclusion. Accordingly, if A is untrue, but there is something else, B, that on the assumption of its truth follows as its consequent, the right thing then is to add on the B. Just because we know the truth of the antecedent. Here is an instance for the *Bath-story* in the *Odyssey.*[78]

A likely impossibility is always preferable to an unconvincing possibility. The story should never

---

[78] In the *Odyssey*, Odysseus is recognized by a scar when his old nurse bathes him.

be made up of improbable incidents; there should be nothing of the sort in it. If, however, such incidents are unavoidable, they should be outside the piece, like the hero's ignorance in *Oedipus* of the circumstances of Laius' death;[79] not within it, like the report of the Pythian games in *Electra*,[80] or the man's having come to Mysia from Tegea without uttering a word on the way, in *The Mysians*.[81] So that it is ridiculous to say that one's Plot would have been spoilt without them, since it is fundamentally wrong to make up such Plots. If the poet has taken such a Plot, however, and one sees that he might have put in a more probable form, he is guilty of absurdity as well as a fault of art. Even in the *Odyssey* the improbabilities in the setting-ashore of Odysseus would be clearly intolerable in the hands of an inferior poet. As it is, the poet conceals them, his other excellences veiling their absurdity. Elaborate Diction, however, is required only in places where there is no action, and no Character or Thought to be revealed. Where there is Character or Thought, on the other hand, an over-ornate Diction tends to obscure them.

25. As regards Problems and their Solutions, one may see the number and nature of the assumptions on which they proceed by viewing the matter in the following way. (1) The poet being an imitator just like the painter or other maker of likenesses, he must necessarily in all instances represent things in one or other of three aspects, either as they were or are, or as they are said or thought to be or to behave, or as they ought to be. (2) All this he does in language, with an admixture, it may be, of strange words and metaphors, as also of the various modified forms of words, since the use of these is conceded in poetry. (3) It is to be remembered, too, that there

is not the same kind of correctness in poetry as in politics, or indeed any other art. There is, however, within the limits of poetry itself a possibility of two kinds or error, the one directly, the other only accidentally connected with the art. If the poet meant to describe the thing correctly, and failed through lack of power of expression, his art itself is at fault. But if it was through his having meant to describe it in some incorrect way (e.g. to make the horse in movement have both right legs thrown forward) that the technical error (one in a matter of say, medicine or some other special science), or impossibilities of whatever kind they may be, have got into his description, his error in that case is not in the essentials of the poetic art. These, therefore, must be the premises of the solutions in answer to the criticisms involved in the Problems.

As to the criticisms relating to the poet's art itself. Any impossibilities there may be in his descriptions of things are faults. But from another point of view they are justifiable, if they serve the end of poetry itself—if (to assume what we have said of that end) they make the effect of either that very portion of the work or some other portion more astounding. The Pursuit of Hector is an instance in point. If, however, the poetic end might have been as well or better attained without sacrifice of technical correctness in such matters, the impossibility is not to be justified, since the description should be, if it can, entirely free from error. One may ask, too, whether the error is in a matter directly or only accidentally connected with the poetic art; since it is a lesser error in an artist not to know, for instance, that the hind has no horns, than to produce an unrecognizable picture of one.

If the poet's description be criticized as not true to fact, one may urge perhaps the object ought to be as described—an answer like that of Sophocles, who said that he drew men as they ought to be, and Euripides as they were. If the description, however, be neither true nor of the thing as it ought to be, the answer must be then, that it is in accordance with opinion. The tales about Gods,

---

[79] Oedipus killed his father, Laius, but he did not know whom he killed. The play improbably presumes that the circumstances of Laius' death were never discussed before Oedipus begins his inquiry.

[80] *Electra*, l. 680–763.

[81] *The Mysians* is a lost play by Aeschylus. Mysia and Tegea are city-states.

for instance, may be as wrong as Xenophanes[82] thinks, neither true nor the better thing to say; but they are certainly in accordance with opinion. Of other statements in poetry one may perhaps say, not that they are better than the truth, but that the fact was so at the time; e.g. the description of the arms: "their spears stood upright, butt-end upon the ground" for that was the usual way of fixing them then, as it is still with the Illyrians.[83] As for the question whether something said or done in a poem is morally right or not, in dealing with that one should consider not only the intrinsic quality of the actual word or deed, but also the person who says or does it, the person to whom he says or does it, the time, the means, and the motive of the agent—whether he does it to attain a greater good, or to avoid a greater evil. . . .

26. The question may be raised whether the epic or the tragic is the higher form of imitation. It may be argued that, if the less vulgar is the higher, and the less vulgar is always that which addresses the better public, an art addressing any and everyone is of a very vulgar order. It is a belief that their public cannot see the meaning, unless they add something themselves, that causes the perpetual movements of the performers—bad flute-players, for instance, rolling about, if quoit-throwing is to be represented, and pulling at the conductor, if Scylla[84] is the subject of the piece. Tragedy, then, is said to be an art of this order—to be in fact just what the later actors were in the eyes of their predecessors; for Mynniscus used to call Callippides "the ape," because he thought he so overacted his parts; and a similar view was taken of Pindarus also.[85] All Tragedy, however, is said to stand to the Epic as the newer to the older school of actors. The one, accordingly, is said to

address a cultivated audience, which does not need the accompaniment of gesture; the other, an uncultivated one. If, therefore, Tragedy is a vulgar art, it must clearly be lower than the Epic.

The answer to this is twofold. In the first place, one may urge (1) that the censure does not touch the art of the dramatic poet, but only that of his interpreter; for it is quite possible to overdo the gesturing even in an epic recital, as did Sosistratus, and in a singing contest, as did Mnasitheus of Opus.[86] (2) That one should not condemn all movement, unless one means to condemn even the dance, but only that of ignoble people—which is the point of the criticism passed on Callippides and in the present day on others, that their women are not like gentlewomen. (3) That Tragedy may produce its effect even without movement or action in just the same way as Epic poetry; for from the mere reading of a play its quality may be seen. So that, if it be superior in all other respects, this element of its inferiority is no necessary part of it.

In the second place, one must remember (1) that Tragedy has everything that the Epic has (even the epic meter being admissible), together with a not inconsiderable addition in the shape of the Music (a very real factor in the pleasure of the drama) and the Spectacle. (2) That its reality of presentation is felt in the play as read, as well as in the play as acted. (3) That the tragic imitation requires less space for the attainment of its end; which is a great advantage, since the more concentrated effect is more pleasurable than one with a large admixture of time to dilute it—consider the *Oedipus* of Sophocles, for instance, and the effect of expanding it into the number of lines of the *Iliad*. (4) That there is less unity in the imitation of the epic poets, as is proved by the fact that any one work of theirs supplies matter for

---

[82] Xenophanes of Colophon was a sixth-century B.C.E. poet. He was critical of Homer and Hesiod for representing the gods in human form.

[83] To the Greeks, Illyria was an area neighboring Macedonia on the Adriatic coast.

[84] Scylla was a sea monster who snatched men from passing ships.

[85] Mynniscus, Callippides, and Pindarus are probably great actors from the fifth century, some time before Aristotle is writing. Trag-

edy is in decline, in Aristotle's opinion, by the time he is writing in the fourth century.

[86] Sosistratus and Mnasitheus would have been performers. In the fifth century, poetry was still a performance art. By the time Aristotle was writing, it was increasingly something that might be read privately.

several tragedies; the result being that, if they take what is really a single story, it seems curt when briefly told, and thin and waterish when on the scale of length usual with their verse. In saying that there is less unity in an epic, I mean an epic made up of a plurality of actions, in the same way as the *Iliad* and *Odyssey* have many such parts, each one of them in itself of some magnitude; yet the structure of the two Homeric poems is as perfect as can be, and the action in them is nearly as possible one action. If, then, Tragedy is superior in these respects, and also, besides these, in its poetic effect (since the two forms of poetry should give us, not any or every pleasure, but the very special kind we have mentioned), it is clear that, as attaining the poetic effect better than the Epic, it will be the higher form of art.

So much for Tragedy and Epic poetry—for these two arts in general and their species; the number and nature of their constituent parts; the causes of success and failure in them; the Objections of critics, and the Solutions in answer to them.

Study Questions

1. Where does Aristotle begin?
2. What does Aristotle mean by "manner"?
3. How do the six parts of drama—spectacle, melody, diction, thought, character, and plot—correspond to the means, manner, and objects available? Try to give examples of each.
4. In tragedy, what is imitated?
5. How do people learn?
6. Why does Aristotle spend so much of the discussion on plot? Would plot be important if he were discussing lyric poetry?
7. Try to do a parallel analysis of some contemporary art form such as film or television with which you are familiar. Is plot the most important part of a successful contemporary film?
8. Construct a simple plot. Make it complex.
9. What form does the theoretically best plot have?
10. Aristotle prefers traditional stories to original plots. Why?
11. What does Aristotle mean by a "good" character?
12. How would you distinguish a sad ending from a tragic ending to a play?
13. Why would anyone voluntarily go to a play which arouses pity and fear? Why do people go to horror films? Is there more to tragedy than to a horror film?
14. Tragedy seems to have flourished during some periods in history (fifth-century Athens, Elizabethan England) and to have virtually disappeared in others. Why might that be?
15. Is it possible to have an Aristotelian tragedy without some absolute prohibitions like the Greek fear of incest and family murder?
16. Is a Christian tragedy possible? Why or why not?
17. How does epic poetry differ from tragedy?
18. Construct an argument to justify the following statement: "A likely impossibility is always preferable to an unconvincing possibility."
19. Construct an argument that tragedy is the highest form of poetry.
20. Could the *Poetics* as a whole and the final chapter in particular be regarded as an answer to Plato? Try to construct such an answer.

Plotinus
· · · · · · ·

PLOTINUS (204–270 C.E.) was a Greek-speaking Roman citizen born in Egypt. He belonged to the circle of an influential teacher, Ammonias Saccas. Little is known about Saccas's philosophy because he wrote nothing. He may have begun as a Christian but his teaching was Platonist. Saccas had a strong influence on his disciples, who kept his teachings secret. These kinds of philosophical circles approached the level of religious communities. Their teachers inspired loyalty and reverence. Plotinus remained with Ammonias Saccas for eleven years and only after his death asserted his own teaching.

Alexandria in the third century was an intellectual melting pot. The Roman empire met eastern influences, and the city was an intellectual center to rival Rome. Its great library, which had grown up during the Hellenistic period after the death of Alexander the Great, was one of the wonders of the classical world. It was burned in the first century B.C.E., but Alexandria continued to be a center of learning. Christianity, eastern cults, and the Roman civic religion had to compete for followers. In this context, Plotinus was exposed not only to the continued teaching of Platonism but to a whole range of more esoteric beliefs that suggest contact with Hindu sources. In 242–243, Plotinus joined the emperor Gordian in an expedition into Persia. No direct contact with eastern religions need be postulated, however, to explain the hints of eastern influence in Plotinus' philosophy. Everything would have been "in the air" in Alexandria.

After the death of his teacher, Plotinus settled in Rome, where he attracted a circle of wealthy, intellectually inclined followers. We know about this circle and about Plotinus himself from one of his followers, Porphyry, who wrote a life of Plotinus which has survived. Plotinus evidently taught by forming questions and encouraging discussion of them. Only later did he begin to write, and what we have are essentially lectures rather than organized treatises. An esoteric, almost mystical element runs through Plotinus' work. Porphyry was responsible for collecting his writings and giving them the organization they have today. One of the speculative elements had to do with the perfection of numbers. Six and nine were believed to be "perfect" numbers, and Porphyry seized upon that to organize Plotinus' lectures into six groups of nine lectures each. *Ennead* simply means a group of nine.

Plotinus attempted to form a kind of intellectual commune based on the teachings of Plato. His own influence led to the founding of the school we call neo-Platonism.

Neo-Platonism blends elements of Plato's teaching with more mystical doctrines that probably reflect a cult traceable back to the Greek philosopher-mystic Pythagoras in the fifth century B.C.E. Neo-Platonism has many of the characteristics of a religion, but it lacks the ritual and cult apparatus that would make it accessible to a wide audience. As a result, it appealed only to a small intellectual circle that could afford the retirement and leisure of reflection. When neo-Platonism attempted to become more than that on its own, it failed. However, the school was taken up and incorporated into other religions, including Christianity, and it exerted an influence far beyond the scope of its own devotees. Some writings of later neo-Platonists appear disguised in the Christian tradition as the work of early Christian disciples.

◆   ◆   ◆   ◆   ◆   ◆

Plotinus understood himself to be following and clarifying the work of Plato. In the fourth *Ennead,* he says, "Then there is the divine Plato who has so much that is beautiful to say of the soul. . . . Unfortunately, consistency is not his strong point, so it is not easy to catch his meaning" (IV, 8, 1). Centuries of commentators have echoed this sentiment in reference to Plotinus himself.

The first thing to recognize in approaching Plotinus is his introspective method. He begins by asking us to examine our own individual consciousness, which, he believes, we are able to examine without any further concepts. Such self-examination is only the beginning, however. We want to understand the intelligible structure of thought, and from thought we can move to the intelligible structure of the cosmos. Each move brings the mind (or soul, in Plotinus' vocabulary) to a greater perception of an underlying unity. So from sensual perception, each individual moves to a consciousness of ideas that are not unique to that individual, and from ideas we move up an ascending hierarchy toward ever more encompassing ideas until individual thought is lost in an awareness of unity itself. The highest reality is the One, which is beyond all being and thought.

Like Plato, Plotinus understands this movement as dialectical. For Plotinus, the dialectic by which we know ideas and concepts corresponds to a dialectic that is built into the structure of thought and reality. Dialectic is not just a way of knowing; it is a way of being as well. Each step in the ascent is a relation of higher and lower forms. At the lowest is matter, which Plotinus identifies with non-being. The world of sense perception relates matter on one side to individual ideas on the other. Individual ideas in turn form the lower term in a relation to more universal ideas and thus up an ascending ladder of dialectical relations until individuality is left behind and the individual soul is caught up into the intelligible unity which is beyond sense altogether. At the highest levels, consciousness requires neither sense nor individuality.

If this process seems highly speculative and abstract, it often is. Plotinus seeks to evoke a feeling for what the process is about instead of explaining the process. Ultimately his method requires that individuals follow it for themselves. The method is not just about abstract ideas; it is a method of contemplation, a way to wisdom. Plotinus returns us to an earlier form of philosophy that required initiation and participation as well as rational speculation. In this respect, Plotinus shares a great deal with religious movements that required initiation into the mysteries and direct experience. To that end, Plotinus envisaged a community capable of devoting itself to introspection and enlightenment. But unlike his religious counterparts, Plotinus rests his method solely on the intellectual abilities of the individual. His appeal is limited to those who are capable of the rigorous thought and concentration that his philosophy requires.

For all of their esoteric appeal to introspection and their obscure rhetoric of enlightened self-absorption into an extrapersonal ecstasy, the style and method of Plotinus depend on a positive experience. While sense and this world are lower forms that we should finally leave behind, only through sense can the process begin. Only through actually experiencing the higher realms of the neo-Platonic dialectic can one know and understand their appeal. Thus experience is everything, even if experience rapidly loses touch with the ordinary world. His emphasis on experience gives Plotinus' treatment of beauty a special importance to theories of art and the aesthetic. Beauty is one of the primary qualities of a higher consciousness.

Beauty begins with sight. It begins, in other words, with the most important sense, the one that, according to Aristotle, all human beings take delight in. Plotinus analyzed the source of that beauty, and he rejected the most common classical conception of beauty as formal symmetry by appealing to a series of counter-examples. At this point, his argument is not at all esoteric; it is a model of rational philosophical style. Rational arguments allow Plotinus to establish what beauty is not. When he comes to ask where beauty does come from, he turns quickly to communion with ideal forms. A dialectical relation is required for participation in these forms. Beauty depends not on symmetry but on order and harmony between what is experienced and its own orderliness. The relation is one of communion. Each of us is drawn up toward increasing order. At the same time, we are attracted to the less orderly world of sense in which we take delight, because it is more controllable, it is easier, and it provides immediate gratification. We struggle between the attraction of the greater order of ideal forms and our selves, which are trapped in their own sensuality. Philosophy aids us in our struggle if we are capable of the discipline that it demands. Beauty is the reward that it holds out.

The basis for beauty is the greater reality of the ideal. Our bodies are only a starting point. They are ugly in comparison with the purity of the bodiless principles of intellect. Characteristically, neo-Platonic thought identified reality itself not with concrete, ordinary things but with intellectual things which only a mind can grasp. Ideas are more real than what they are ideas of; universal ideas are more real than their individual formulations. Ultimately, only a unitary form can be real. Beyond that, unity itself abandons even the category of being. Beauty is the communication of the higher forms to the lower manifestations of those forms. So physical beauty communicates order and harmony to sensual experience. Intellectual beauty communicates order and harmony to ideas themselves. Higher forms of beauty can be grasped only because our minds ascend from the next lower stage to which beauty has been communicated.

Plotinus described both the process and the experience of beauty in language that is concrete in what it instructs one to do but evocative in its referential content. He cannot describe the end of the process before that end has been experienced. Works of art play no role in the method or descriptions that Plotinus does offer. Art would be one of the sensual elements left behind at the earliest stages. Thinkers and philosophers, not artists and makers of objects, are the seekers of beauty. If Plato expelled artists as dangerous and Aristotle analyzed their products to see what made them so effective, Plotinus simply leaves them behind.

Ironically, of the three (Platonism, Aristotelianism, and neo-Platonism), neo-Platonism has had the greatest effect on subsequent theories of art and justifications of the works of artists. Only a slight twist of Plotinian method turns it into a positive theory of art. The difficulty of practicing neo-Platonism lies in its esoteric, intellectual rigor. It does not provide any useful assistance for ordinary people who want to experience beauty as Plotinus describes it. Unless a person is prepared to withdraw from the world and practice an ascetic, intellectualized philosophy beyond the capabilities of most, neo-Platonism is inaccessible. Yet beauty is fundamentally an experience according to Plotinus. If some way to have that experience were provided, people would be aided in the ascent. Before long, artists claimed to be the ones who could provide that experience. They take the sensual world and turn it into imitations that are not limited by space, time, or decay. Moreover, they make it possible for everyone to have access by lifting perception out of the ordinary and showing us the extraordinary features of order and harmony hidden to the ordinary gaze. Poets and painters become the priests of the neo-Platonic religion.

The alliance between art and neo-Platonic philosophy is uncomfortable. The sensuality of art on its face is just the kind of attraction to sense that Plotinus warns against. To overcome this difficulty, a critical theory developed as a response to the theory of beauty advocated by Plotinus. According to this critical theory, good art is that which transports the soul beyond its own appearance. Artifice and self-conscious style aid that transformation. So higher art is both more abstract and more elevating. At the same time, intensity of experience is valued as a way into ecstasy. Paradoxically, the most sensual art is often the most elevating because the very intensity of the experience is itself extraordinary and thus beyond the realm of everyday sense. On the one hand, this critical theory finds the greatest value in abstraction and high rhetoric; on the other, it favors intensity and sensual expression. The paradox is only apparent, however. As with any dialectical system, works of art both are and are not something at the same time. Art provides its audience with both a presence of higher ideas and a denial that those ideas can be fully expressed within the confines of color, form, and language. The audience is led both to love art and to want more than it can supply.

This neo-Platonic art theory goes beyond the text of Plotinus, who seeks to account for beauty in terms of the ascending hierarchy of his larger system. But through the Renaissance and beyond, Plotinus provided the basis for an answer to Plato's doubts about the dangers of imitation.

Ennead One, Sixth Tractate: On Beauty

Chapter One

Beauty is for the most part in what is seen, but it is also in what is heard, in verbal compositions and also in music of all kinds, since melodies and rhythms are beautiful. And, proceeding upwards from the realm of the senses, there are beautiful ways of life, actions, characters, and crafts, and there is the beauty of virtues. If there is something beautiful higher than these, it will show itself.

What is it, then, that both makes bodies appear to be beautiful, and makes sounds appeal to our hearing because of their beauty? What makes all the things that depend on the soul beautiful? Are all things beautiful due to one and the same beauty, or is there one kind of beauty in bodies and a different kind in other things? Just what are these (if there is more than one kind), or just what is it (if there is only one kind)?

Some things, bodies for example, are not beautiful in virtue of their own substance, but by participation; other things are themselves beautiful, such as the nature of virtue. For since the same bodies sometimes appear to be beautiful, but other times do not, being a body is something different from being beautiful. So what is it that is present in bodies that makes them beautiful? This is the first thing we must investigate.

So what is it that moves the eyes of onlookers, that turns and drags them to itself and makes them enjoy the sight? Once we've discovered this, perhaps we can use it as a ladder to help us see the rest.

It is said by virtually everyone that the proportionality of the parts to one another and to the whole, with the addition of good coloring makes what is visually beautiful beautiful, and, in general, in the case of all other things, that beauty is proportionality and measure. From which it would follow that no simple thing is beautiful, for by necessity only a composite could be beautiful.

And, according to those who maintain this theory, in the case of composites, the whole would be beautiful, but none of the parts would have the property of beauty on their own account. Each part would contribute to the composition of the whole so that the whole would be beautiful. And yet, if the whole is beautiful it must be that the parts are also beautiful. Certainly, a beautiful whole does not come from ugly parts; all of the parts must possess beauty as well.

For those who maintain this theory, colors that are [in fact] beautiful, as well as the light of the sun, because they are simple and do not possess proportionality, would be excluded from what is beautiful. How could gold be beautiful, then? And what would explain the beauty of seeing a lightning flash or stars at night? And similarly, in the case of sounds, what is simple would be lost as a beautiful thing, if their view is correct, and yet in many instances each utterance of a beautiful whole is itself also beautiful. Indeed, when the same face maintains the same proportionality, but the face appears beautiful at one time and not beautiful at another time, don't we have to say that being beautiful is something besides proportion, and that proper proportion is beautiful on account of something else?

And suppose those who maintain this theory move on to ways of life and beautiful speeches, and claim that the beauty of these also is due to their proportionality. What could "proportion" mean in the case of beautiful ways of life, or laws, or fields of learning, or crafts? How could objects of intellectual apprehension be proportionate to one another? If it is because they are harmonious, even bad ones can be in agreement and be harmonious. The claim "justice is simplemindedness with a good pedigree" and the claim "self-composure is the height of folly" are harmonious and resonate and agree with one another. Certainly every virtue of the soul is beautiful and is more genuinely beautiful than those beautiful things discussed earlier; but in what sense is virtue proportioned? It is not proportioned as are magnitudes or number, and assuming that there are many parts of the soul, what sort of principle governs the combination or blending of its parts or objects of contemplation? And what would be the beauty of the intellect taken all by itself?

Chapter Two

Let us resume again, and begin by stating what the primary beauty in bodies really is. For this is what becomes perceptible at the very first glance, and the soul judges it with understanding, and, recognizing a kindred nature, welcomes it. But when confronted with what is ugly, [the soul] recoils and spurns it and turns away from it, finding it discordant and alien to itself. We claim that, because the nature of soul is what it is, in particular because soul is related to the superior kind of beings, [soul] welcomes what it sees as kindred or reminiscent of what is kindred. When it sees such a thing, it is amazed, and, comparing the thing to itself, it recognizes in it itself and its own kind.

What is the similarity, then, between the beautiful things here and those there [in the realm of superior being]? For if there is a similarity, then these things must be similar, but how can these things be similar to those? We claim that the things here participate in form. Whatever is disposed by nature to receive shape and form, but happens to be shapeless, is ugly because it is bereft of reason and form, and outside of divine reason. And this is altogether ugly. Something is also ugly when it is not mastered by shape and reason, because its matter has refused to be entirely shaped according to the form. The form draws near and arranges and composes what will become one thing from many parts and brings it into a single whole and makes it one by the agreement of its parts. Because it [the form] is itself one, what it shapes must also be one as far as this is possible for something composed of many things. So the beauty is established on the thing once

it has been brought together into one and it [beauty] gives itself both to the parts and to the wholes. Whenever it [beauty] gets hold of a unity composed of like parts, it gives the same thing to the whole. For example, a craft might give beauty to a whole house along with its parts, or nature might give beauty to a single stone. Thus, corporeal beauty arises by communion with divine reason.

Chapter Three

The faculty [of the soul] that is assigned to beauty recognizes it, this faculty having the final authority to judge concerning such matters, even when the rest of the soul contributes to the decision. Perhaps this faculty judges by comparing the form within itself to the thing that is being judged, using [the form] as one uses a ruler to determine what is straight. But how can corporeal things accord with what is prior to the corporeal?

How can the builder judge a house external to him to be beautiful by comparing it to the house that he perceives within himself? What the external house is, aside from the stones, is the internal form apportioned over the extension of the outer matter. The internal form is itself indivisible, though it manifests itself in many pieces. So whenever the senses perceive a form in bodies, uniting and overpowering the nature of what is opposite to form, the shapeless, and also perceive a shape, splendidly transcending the other shapes, then, by bringing together into a whole what was scattered, the senses raise the newly created unity up and introduce it into the indivisible interior of the soul and present it to the soul within as something that accords, and harmonizes, and is akin to the soul, just as a trace of virtue in a young person appears pleasant to a good man, because it accords with the true virtue within him. And the simple beauty of color arises from shape, which masters the darkness of the material by means of the presence of incorporeal light, reason and form.

For the same reason, fire is beautiful relative to other bodies, because it has the position of form with respect to the other elements, above them in station, because it is the subtlest of all bodies, and hence the closest to being incorporeal, and also because it alone does not admit the others, but the others receive it. Or it heats them, but they do not cool it; it is the primary thing that is colored, while the other things receive the form of color from it. It shines and glitters as if it were a form. And whatever it does not dominate fades in the light and is no longer beautiful, as if it didn't fully participate in the form of color. And the harmonies in sounds, those that are imperceptible and create the perceptible ones, make the soul perceive beauty in the same way, though it is manifested in another medium. It follows that the perceptible harmonies can be measured numerically, though not by just any formula, but only by those in which the form dominates. So much then for the beauties of perceptible things, which spring up like images and shadows, entering into the matter, embellishing it, and stunning us by their appearance.

Chapter Four

The more distant beauties, which it no longer falls to sensation to see, but which the soul sees and speaks of without [need of] organs, the soul must ascend and contemplate, leaving sensation to remain below. Just as those who have neither seen sensible beauties, nor apprehended them as beautiful (for example, those blind from birth), cannot speak about them, so those who have not accepted the beauty of ways of life and crafts and other such things, cannot speak about them, nor can those who have not imagined how beautiful is the face of justice and self-composure—"neither daybreak nor nightfall is as beautiful"—speak of the brilliance of virtue.

But there must be those who see [the brilliance of virtue] with that by which the soul sees such things, and when they see [the virtues] they must be delighted and flustered and passionately excited much more than they were in the case of those earlier [beauties], because they are now grasping genuine [beauties]. Such should be the

experience of beauty, amazement, pleasant consternation, yearning, ardor, and excitement mixed with pleasure. It is possible to experience such things and virtually all souls also experience them relative to invisible [beauties], especially those who are more in love with these [invisible beauties], just as in the case of bodies everyone sees them, but not everyone is stung as sharply; those who are said to be in love [with the beauty of bodies] are stung most of all.

Chapter Five

We must then ask lovers of the things outside of sense perception: "What is your experience of what are called beautiful ways of life, beautiful habits, well-ordered characters, and, in general, virtuous deeds and dispositions, and the beauty of souls? And when you see beauty within yourselves, what is your experience? And how are you roused and stirred, and how do you long to be united with yourselves, as you assemble away from your bodies?" For this is what genuine lovers experience.

But what is it that causes this experience? It is neither shape, nor color, nor any magnitude that causes this experience. Rather, the cause relates to soul, which has no color, and which possesses self-composure, and the rest of the brilliance of the virtues, none of which have color. This experience arises when you perceive in others or in yourself: greatness of soul, just character, pure self-composure, and a countenance possessing virile courage, donned with dignity and honor in a calm, serene, and unperturbed disposition, with the god-like intellect shining on all this.

We esteem and love these things, but why do we call them beautiful? For they exist and appear and one who sees them can never call them anything but true realities, but the argument still requires that we explain why true realities make the soul beloved. What shines like light on the virtues?

Shall we take for comparison the opposites, the things that are ugly in the soul? Perhaps a consideration of just what ugliness is and its cause is pertinent to what we are investigating. Assume there is an ugly soul, undisciplined and unjust, filled with all kinds of appetites, full of turmoil, beset by fears born from cowardice, jealousies born of pettiness, thinking mortal and base thoughts whenever it thinks, everywhere twisted, loving impure pleasures, living life through the experiences of the body, taking what is ugly as delightful.

Shall we say that this "ugliness" itself arrives in this soul as a kind of alien "beauty," mutilating the soul, making it impure, and blending it with much evil, its life and faculty of sensation no longer pure, having pursued a life mixed with the darkness of evil, having mingled with much death, no longer seeing what soul should see, no longer allowed to remain in itself because it is dragged constantly toward what is external, below and dark? I suppose it is impure because it is dragged in every way toward the things that strike its senses. Having been mingled with much that pertains to the body, associating with much that is material, and accepting an alien form into itself, it is changed for the worse.

When someone gets into clay or slime, he no longer reveals the beauty he had, but what is seen is what has been wiped off from the clay and slime. Ugliness has come to him by the addition of something alien, and his task, if he is to get back his beauty, is to become what he once was by washing himself off and purifying himself. So we would be right to say that a soul is ugly because it is mixed and blended and inclined toward the body and matter.

This is ugliness for the soul: to be neither pure nor unmixed, as for gold [ugliness is] to be filled with earth. If someone removes [the earth], gold remains and is beautiful, separate from other things, alone by itself. It is the same way with the soul. Taken apart from its appetites (which it has through the body to which the soul has clung too much), freed from the rest of its passions, and purified of those things it has as a result of its being embodied, remaining separate [from those things], it puts aside all the ugliness that stems from that other nature.

Chapter Six

As the old adage says, self-composure and courage and every virtue, even wisdom itself, is a purification. This is why the mysteries are right when they cryptically claim that those who are unpurified will lie in the mire of Hades, because those who are not pure are fond of mire on account of their evil, just as pigs, which have impure bodies, revel in mud.

What might genuine self-composure be than not associating with pleasures of the body, fleeing what is impure and what belongs to the impure? Bravery is having no fear of death, and death is separation of the soul from the body; and whoever welcomes that separation would not fear death. Greatness of soul is simply disdain for the things here in the realm of the body. Wisdom is the act of mind turning away from things below and leading the soul to the things above.

Once purified, the soul becomes form and reason, completely incorporeal and intellectual, belonging to the divine, which is the source of beauty and all such things akin to it. Having ascended to intellect, the soul becomes even more beautiful. Intellect and the things pertaining to intellect are the soul's very own beauty, not something alien to it, because only the soul that has ascended is truly soul. That is why it is correct to claim that the soul becomes good and beautiful by being assimilated to god, because beauty and all that pertains to genuine realities come from the divine realm. Or rather the essence of beauty itself is a genuine reality, and the other nature is the ugly, which is itself the primary evil. So for god, goodness and beauty are the same, or the essence of goodness and the essence of beauty are the same. So we should investigate beauty and goodness, and ugliness and evil in similar ways.

We must first determine the essence of beauty, which is also the essence of goodness, from which immediately comes intellect, which is beauty. Soul is beautiful because of intellect. Everything else that is beautiful, including the beauties of actions and beautiful actions and beautiful ways of life, is beautiful because it is shaped by soul. Even bodies that are said to be beautiful are made so by soul.

Chapter Seven

Now we must ascend back again to the good for which every soul yearns. Whoever has seen it understands what I mean by calling it beautiful. It is desirable in so far as it is good and desire is directed at it, and it is attained by those who have ascended above and turned toward it and stripped off all they had put on when they had descended, just as those who go up to the sacred places of the mysteries,[1] after having been purified, put aside their clothes before advancing, naked. The one who ascends passes everything alien to god until, alone by himself, he sees what is itself alone, the unadulterated, completely simple, pure entity on which everything else depends, to which everything looks, and in relation to which everything exists, lives and thinks, for it is the cause of life, intellect and being.

If someone should see this, what powerful love would he experience! How he would long for it, wish to be mingled with it, and how he would be stricken with pleasure! Those who have not yet seen it yearn for it as good, but those who have seen it revel in its beauty, and are filled with astonished delight and struck senseless (but without being harmed), experiencing genuine love and the stings of longing. They mockingly laugh at all other loves and regard with disdain what they had deemed beautiful before. This is the type of experience of those who have seen gods or divinities, and are no longer content with the beauty of other bodies.

What are we to make of someone who contemplates beauty itself, by itself, pure, infected neither by the flesh nor by the body, existing neither on earth nor in heaven on account of its purity? Everything else is adulterated and not primary, but comes from beauty itself which

provides for everything, while remaining in itself, and gives everything while receiving nothing into itself in return. So if someone should see this, remain fixed in the contemplation of it, and welcome his assimilation to it, what other beauty could he want? This itself is beauty most of all, the primary beauty, and it makes those who love it beautiful and worthy of love. Here lies before souls the last and greatest struggle; all our toil is for this, not to be without a share in this vision. Whoever has a share is blessed by viewing a blessed sight; he who has no share fails utterly. For one is not a failure who fails to attain beautiful colors or bodies, power, rule, or even kingship; he is a failure only if he fails to attain this one thing alone. If he must leave behind kingship, and the rule of all the land and sea and heavens, in order to turn toward beauty itself and contemplate this one thing, then he should pass up those things and regard them with contempt.

Chapter Eight

What way leads to it? What means are there of getting there? How might someone see this incomparable beauty that remains within the sacred precincts and never ventures outside, lest it be seen by someone impure? Whoever can should leave visual sights outside and not turn back to the splendors of bodies we encountered earlier, but proceed and follow beauty into the inner sanctuary. When such people perceive corporeal beauties, they must not approach them, but realizing that they are merely images and footprints and shadows, they must flee towards those things of which these are the images.

But should someone take these images to be reality and run after them wanting to grab them, then I think it would be like that story that cryptically depicts someone who, wanting to grab a beautiful image borne on water, plunged down into the flowing water and disappeared.[2] In the same way, one who clings to beautiful bodies, and won't let go, sinks down with his soul (rather than

---

[1] Greek and Roman mystery cults included ceremonies that were known only to those who had been initiated. These religious cults were secret, and our knowledge of their practices comes primarily from allusions such as this one.

---

[2] In the myth of Narcissus, Narcissus sees his own image in the water and, loving himself, is drawn into the water and drowns.

with his body) into the darkness, into depths that are joyless for the mind, there to remain, blind in Hades, keeping company with shadows.

"Let us flee to our beloved fatherland!"—someone might appropriately advise us. What kind of flight is this, and how do we do it? We put out to sea, just like Odysseus who fled from the witch Circe (or Calypso, as the poet says cryptically, I think).[3] He was not content to stay with her even though he enjoyed visual delights and passed his time surrounded by things that were beautiful to his senses. Our fatherland is where we come from and where our father dwells. How then do we accomplish this voyage and this flight? We cannot accomplish this on foot; feet only carry us from one earthly place to another. Neither should we procure a horse-drawn chariot or a sea-going vessel. We must abandon such things, and not even look at them. Rather, we must shut these eyes, exchange them for a different type of eye (a type that everyone has, but which few use), and open these other eyes.

Chapter Nine

And what does the inner eye see? When it has just awakened, it cannot yet see things that are very bright. So the soul must get accustomed to seeing, first of all, beautiful ways of life, then beautiful actions (not those produced by crafts, but those produced by people said to be good), and then the souls of those who produce the beautiful actions. How then might you see the kind of beauty a good soul has? Withdraw into yourself and look. And if you do not yet perceive beauty in yourself, just do what a person in the process of making a statue does. He cuts away, polishes, smoothes and brightens, until he gives the statue a beautiful face. So you, too, cut away what is superfluous, straighten what is bent,

brighten what is dark, making it brilliant, and do not stop crafting your statue until the divine glory of your virtue shines on you and you see self-composure seated on its sacred throne.

If you attain this state, see it within you, and associate with your own purity, and there is no hindrance to becoming unified, nor is anything else mixed with what is within you, then your whole self will be a true light, neither measured by size, nor circumscribed by shape into smallness, nor augmented in size by being without bounds, but unmeasurable in every respect because it is greater than all measure and superior to all magnitude. When you perceive yourself to have become like this, then you have already become an 'eye' in which you might have confidence, and you have already ascended, so that you no longer need someone to show you; just look intently and see for yourself. For this eye alone sees the great beauty.

But, on the other hand, should someone come upon the spectacle bleary-eyed with vice, with an eye that is both unpurified and weak, he will be unable to see what is brilliant because of this weakness. He sees nothing even if someone else shows him what is there to be seen, because what sees must be kindred and similar to what it sees. For there is no way that an eye could see the sun without having become sunlike, nor a soul perceive beauty without having become beautiful. So if the soul intends to behold god and beauty, it must first become wholly godlike and wholly beautiful.

In its ascent, the soul first comes to the realm of intellect, and there it not only recognizes that all the Forms are beautiful, but it also affirms that Beauty itself consists of the Forms. For all things are beautiful because of the Forms, which are the offspring of intellect and being. What is beyond the Forms we call the nature of the good which holds Beauty as a screen before itself. So, in a broad manner of speaking, the first thing, that is, the nature of the good, is beauty. But, if we want to distinguish among intelligible objects, we shall say that intelligible Beauty is the location of the Forms, whereas the Good lies beyond it, and is the source and origin of Beauty. Otherwise, we

---

[3] In Homer's *Odyssey*, Odysseus is trying to return home after the end of the Trojan War. He has angered Poseidon, who opposes him. In one episode, Circe turns the men of Odysseus into pigs. In another, Odysseus is seduced by Calypso and spends seven years with her. She offers to make him immortal, but he rejects her.

will put the Good and primary Beauty on the same level. In any case, Beauty is there in the realm of Intellect.

Study Questions

1. Where is beauty found? What kinds of things are beautiful?
2. Construct the argument that beauty is not proportion.
3. How does symmetry differ from harmony? Give examples.
4. What is the relation of virtue to beauty?
5. What is the basis of the similarity of things?
6. What is the difference between sensible beauty and the beauty of things outside of sense?
7. What does Plotinus mean by *intellect*?
8. What is the difference between material beauty and intellectual beauty? Explain and illustrate.
9. How is the intellectual principle related to individual souls?
10. How is the intellectual principle related to unity?
11. What would an experience of being independent of a body involve? Can individuality survive without a body?
12. What is the relation of beauty to intellect?
13. What is ugliness?
14. What is the difference between a purified soul and one bound to sense?
15. What is the difference between sense and the "inner eye"?
16. How does Plotinus finally define *beauty*?

Bonaventure

GIOVANNI DI FIDANZA was born in Tuscany in central Italy. The traditional date of his birth is 1221, though it has recently been put as early as 1217. He took the name Bonaventure when he entered the Franciscan order in 1243.

Early in the thirteenth century two new monastic orders, the Franciscans and the Dominicans, developed with great rapidity. They differed in important ways from earlier monasticism. They are known as "mendicant" orders because they took as their mission a direct involvement with the outside world and depended on the contributions of others rather than their own work for material support. Earlier monastic orders lived according to a strict rule and separated themselves as much as possible from the world. Their goal was a complete separation and independence from the secular world. Their function was to live and work together piously and to pray, though many of the orders also served an educational role. In contrast to this cloistered monasticism, the mendicant brothers entered actively into the world. The Franciscans and the Dominicans responded to weaknesses in the parish clergy and a widespread demand for greater spirituality in the church with missionary zeal. They preached and conducted sacraments in competition with the local priests, and they took on the task of providing a newly educated priesthood. The Dominicans followed an aggressive military model inspired by their founder, Dominic de Guzman, who was appalled at the heresy spread by uneducated and superstitious people. The Franciscans followed a more spiritual model that emphasized the simplicity and poverty advocated by their founder, John Bernardone, who became known as Francis. Both orders grew very rapidly. They attracted many of the already established scholars of their day. The increasing importance of the universities, particularly at Oxford and Paris, depended on the support and activities of the Dominicans and Franciscans.

Francis died in 1226 while Bonaventure was still a child. Francis's order faced serious problems from its rapid growth and its appeal to an often exuberant spirituality. The order split between those who wanted to maintain a strict, literal version of Francis's simplicity and poverty and those who were committed to the wider educational mission of the order. The former, known as spiritual Franciscans, were attracted to the apocalyptic speculation of Joachim of Fiori (1145–1202), who had prophesied the coming of a new spiritual age in 1260. They were considered heretical by the more orthodox "regular" Franciscans. Bonaventure was educated at the University of Paris, where

Gothic, thirteenth-fourteenth century. *The Barnabus Altarpiece,* about 1250–1350. Kimbell Art Museum, Fort Worth, Texas.

he studied with an outstanding English theologian, Alexander of Hales, who had joined the Franciscan order. In 1243, Bonaventure entered the Franciscan order at Paris, where he continued to study theology. He was known for his humility as well as his learning, and in about 1253, he became the leader of the Franciscan school in Paris.

The Minister-General of the Franciscans, John of Parma, was associated with the spiritual wing of the Franciscan order. Spiritual Franciscans' emphasis on spirituality and speculation about the end of the world seemed to many to encourage an irrational and dangerous form of religion. At the same time, their commitment to poverty brought them into conflict with the secular needs and ambitions of the church. John of Parma was forced by Pope Alexander IV to resign, and Bonaventure was selected to succeed him in 1257. As an intellectual who was also known for his piety and humility, Bonaventure was able to take a middle course and bring the Franciscan order through its crisis. Bonaventure combined the intellectual powers of the University of Paris with the mystical contemplation of his order. As a theologian and philosopher, Bonaventure stands to the Franciscans as Thomas Aquinas stands to the Dominicans—each is the dominant theologian within his order who shaped the thirteenth-century transformation of philosophy.

◆   ◆   ◆   ◆   ◆   ◆

Bonaventure's theological philosophy contains an implicit aesthetic which emerges explicitly at a number of points. He begins with the visible world and individual souls. Individual souls each are little worlds that contain all of the elements of the great world.

By examining our own souls, we have a kind of living mirror that reflects not only the individual but the author. Thus all created beings provide evidence both of God's creative activity and of their own separation from God. We are led by our senses to a greater physical world. That physical world is the product of spiritual causes. So the physical is subordinate to the spiritual, the created to the creator.

Knowledge comes, according to Bonaventure, as a result of the soul's own activity with respect to itself. Reason provides us with guidance and certitude about sensible objects. It can, for example, correct optical illusions. Like most medieval thinkers, however, Bonaventure conceives of sensible knowledge as only a first stage in an ascending ladder of higher forms of knowledge which transcend the senses. Individual reason, which corrects sense, is the lowest form of reason. Eternal reason guides the soul to knowledge of its own place and its own nature. Knowledge that the soul has of itself is a higher knowledge than sensation.

The soul discovers three powers that it possesses. First, it can recall what it has perceived. The ability to recall is not limited to physical perception. The soul can recall and perceive principles given to it as part of its being as well as ideas derived from sense. This ability is the power of memory.

Second, the soul has a power of intellection. It can discover the meaning of terms and draw logical inferences. For Bonaventure, words are not arbitrary or conventional. Terms have their meaning as a result of the significance they have in the greater order of the world. The actual sound or pronunciation may be conventional—a term in Latin differs from a term in Greek in the way it sounds and looks. The real term is an intellectual entity, though, and it is accessible to the soul directly. Logical inference is also a way of reading the order of the world. Modern logic thinks of logic as the result of a system of rules that can be manipulated at will. For a medieval logician such as Bonaventure, logic was a natural part of the intellectual world. So the soul can look to its own order of thought and discover the logic of the greater world as well. The logic of the soul and of the world are the same because there is only one true logic.

Finally, the soul discovers that it is the product of actions and desires and that it can control those actions and desires. This ability is the power of volition or will. It presupposes a knowledge of terms, especially the meaning of *good* and *beautiful*.

Philosophy is the product of the soul's self-reflection on its own powers. As such, philosophy is limited in how far up the ladder it can progress. Rationally, it controls sense perception and can understand its own powers. Philosophy cannot penetrate the highest levels of knowledge, though. There theology and a kind of mystical vision are our only aids. Philosophy can discover the sense in which a single physical cause is an instance of a higher exemplary cause. The pleasure taken in beautiful objects is an instance of the pleasing nature of such objects. Creation itself is exemplary of God's creative act. Philosophy can discover the way that the soul is influenced and influences others. The world follows a pattern of causes which produce effects which act as causes for other effects. The return of the soul to its own source is the product of such a pattern of causes, so philosophy can understand the journey of the soul as it returns to its true place. Philosophy can understand the end toward which the soul is drawn. As the soul sees more and more, one form of light, physical light, is replaced by another form of light, spiritual light or insight. Philosophy can recognize its own ends. Philosophy is limited to those forms of understanding that are directly accessible to the individual soul, however. Beyond lies a higher form of understanding that appears to philosophy as foolishness or ignorance. Learned ignorance is higher than philosophical, rational understanding. Wisdom is not individual understanding but a mystical union. The union of the soul with God takes place not in the light of reason but in the darkness of self-transcendence.

A major influence on Bonaventure was neo-Platonism. The forms of neo-Platonism available had become very complex by the thirteenth century. The problems raised by Aristotle about how sense affects ideas could not be ignored. Bonaventure could not follow the simple introspective path laid down by Plotinus. A gap between the world of sensation and the world of ideas, between the world of the creature and the world of the creator, had opened. No continuity, no pure forms arranged in a neat ascending hierarchy were available to Bonaventure. According to Bonaventure, only the direct activity of God preserves the connections that make the physical world intelligible and the intelligible world accessible to individual beings. From an infinite number of possible worlds, God, in his inscrutable choice, makes one actual. On the one hand, the sensible world becomes more important as a result. Since anything could happen, only what does happen gives us a clue to the divine choice. On the other hand, the seminal nature of what occurs in the divine mind is all that really matters. The sensible world is only the outcome of a potentiality which it does not control.

The key concept for Bonaventure in understanding how knowledge is possible is "illumination." Light is thought of as the means for the soul to understand. The eye and sight are the most basic forms of physical perception; they inform and correct all of the other senses. In order for sight to function, there must be light. Wherever light shines on something, that thing is visible and the eye sees it without any need for thought or practice. For a long tradition of medieval thinkers, illumination seemed to explain how it was possible to see in every sense of the word. At the lowest level, light was physical light. It was thought of as a tangible, physical cause of the sensations that the mind or soul experienced by means of memory and intellect. By extension, as the mind reflected on its own operations, that too required illumination. Light need not be physical. It could be a kind of divine illumination. God chooses one physical world. Part of that choice is where the light will shine. Within the mind, God also chooses which ideas to illuminate so that the mind can see its own powers. Every human who thinks has some illumination. Beyond the universal illumination that God supplies to all human beings, a higher illumination comes only to those who are chosen. The final light is so bright that it blinds the physical eye and appears as darkness. This metaphor of light and illumination operated literally as well. One of the first sciences to be developed in the Middle Ages was optics. By exploring physical light, the higher forms of light also could be understood.

Illumination, in turn, connects us with the fundamental aesthetics of the Middle Ages. Three aspects of aesthetics should be noted in Bonaventure, and they can be observed in different ways in most of the other scattered references to art in medieval philosophy. First, the arts are fundamentally physical activities that involve making something. As such, they follow the creative pattern laid down by God. Fine arts are not distinguished from other forms of making. They are all activities that have a productive, physical function. Cooking, sculpting, architecture, and farming are all forms of producing something that belongs to the world of our senses. Artisans are not creative actors but the means by which some higher form is given a useful physical instance. The distinctions that Bonaventure makes are based on different kinds of activity, not different levels of art. Second, since knowledge requires illumination, the most important aesthetic principle is connected with light. Medieval aesthetics is a manifestation of light and its physical forms. Artisans of the Middle Ages loved color. Like their classical predecessors, they painted their statues in bright colors. Architecture was designed to make light felt and tangible. Stained glass used light and color to exhibit a story to an audience that had a limited level of literacy. It also produced a sensual presence that made the story more immediate. Finally, in medieval aesthetics physical sensation is subordinate to intellectual insight. Beauty begins with the senses, but beauty is also an idea, a higher form perceived by a different form of sight. Bonaventure represents beauty as, above all, a spiritual union so that sense is finally left behind.

The arts remained primarily crafts in the Middle Ages. Painting and sculpture were functions of the church and court. Architecture was public building or religious symbol. A partial exception must be made for poetry and music, however. Music exhibited a harmony that was part of the intellectual nature of the universe—literally, the music of the spheres. In addition, because the classical rhetorical tradition continued to influence the Middle Ages, poetry had an intellectual status closer to philosophy. It involved thought and terms, and it was capable of being understood on many levels at once. The intellect was engaged by poetry in ways that it was not by the more sensuous arts. Sacred scripture required elaborate interpretation to reveal all of its levels of meaning. Underlying all of the arts, however, is the fundamental sense that meaning is both hidden and revealed in everything. Nothing is just what it is; everything is a sign or symbol of the more complex order in which it is embedded and without which it could not exist. This is therefore an aesthetic of significance, not of sense. Bonaventure was concerned to place the arts in their proper perspective with respect to other activities. Only then could the arts be placed properly with respect to theology and the divine lights given to our souls.

Retracing the Arts to Theology

1. *EVERY BEST GIFT and every perfect gift is from above, coming down from the Father of Lights,* James in the first chapter of his Epistle. These words of Sacred Scripture not only reveal the source of all illumination but they likewise point out the generous flow of manifold rays which issue from the Fount of light. Notwithstanding the fact that every illumination of knowledge is within, still, we can with propriety distinguish what we may call the *external* light, or the light of mechanical skill; the *lower* light, or the light of sense perception; the *inner* light, or the light of philosophical knowledge; and the *higher* light, or the light of grace and of Sacred Scripture. The first light illumines the consideration of the *arts and crafts;* the second, in regard to *natural form;* the third, in regard to *intellectual truth;* the fourth and last, in regard to *saving truth.*

2. The first light, then since it enlightens the mind for an appreciation of the *arts and crafts,* which are, as it were, exterior to man and intended to supply the needs of the body, is called the light of *mechanical skill.* Being, in a certain sense, servile and of a lower nature than philosophical knowledge, this light can rightly be termed *external.* It has seven divisions corresponding to the seven mechanical arts enumerated by Hugh in his *Disdascalion,*[1] namely, weaving, armor-making, agriculture, hunting, navigation, medicine, and the dramatic art. That the above mentioned arts *suffice* for all the needs of mankind is shown in the following way: every mechanical art is intended for man's *consolation* or his *comfort;* its purpose, therefore, is to banish either *sorrow* or *want;* it ei-

ther *benefits* or *delights,* according to the words of Horace

> Either to serve or to please is the wish of the poets.

And again:

> He hath gained universal applause who hath combined the profitable with the pleasing.[2]

If its aim is to afford *consolation* and amusement, it is *dramatic art,* or the art of exhibiting plays, which embraces every form of entertainment, be it song, music drama, or pantomime. If, however, it is intended for the *comfort* or betterment of the exterior man, it can accomplish its purpose by providing either *covering* or *food,* or by *serving as an aid in the acquisition of either.* In the matter of *covering,* if it provides a soft and light material, it is weaving; if, a strong and hard material, it is *armor-making* or metal-working, an art which extends to every tool or implement fashioned of iron or of any metal whatsoever, of stone, or of wood.

In the matter of food, mechanical skill may benefit in two ways, for we derive our sustenance from *vegetables* and from *flesh meats.* If it supplies us with *vegetables,* it is *farming;* if it provides us with *flesh meats,* it is *hunting.* Or, again, as regards *food,* mechanical skill has a twofold advantage: either it aids in the *production* and multiplication of crops, in which case it is agriculture, or in various ways of *preparing* food under which aspect it is hunting, an art which extends to every conceivable way of preparing foods, drinks, and delicacies—a task with which bakers, cooks, and innkeepers are concerned. The term "hunting"

---

[1] *Disdascalion,* by Hugh of St. Victor (d. 1141), is a treatise on the order of knowledge of education. Hugh traces the movement from the liberal arts to philosophy and theology and ultimately to contemplation. The Abbey of St. Victor in Paris was an important center of learning in the twelfth century. Hugh was opposing those theologians who maintained that knowledge was dangerous to the soul. Hugh's position was that one should learn everything because nothing is superfluous.

[2] Horace (65–8 B.C.E.) was one of the greatest Latin poets. His *Art of Poetry* is a virtual rhetorical handbook on how to achieve poetic effects.

(*venatio*), however, is derived from one single aspect of the trade, undoubtedly, on account of the excellent nature of game and the popularity of the chase at court.

Furthermore, as an aid in the *acquisition of each of these necessities,* the mechanical arts contribute to the welfare of man in two ways: either by *supplying a want,* and in this case it is *navigation,* which includes all commerce of articles of covering or of food; or by *removing impediments* and ills of the body, under which aspect it is *medicine,* whether it is concerned with the preparation of drugs, potions, or ointments, with the healing of wounds or with the amputation of members, in which latter case it is called surgery. Dramatic art, on the other hand, is in a class by itself. Considered in this light, the classification of the mechanical arts seems adequate.

3. The second light, which enables us to discern *natural forms,* is the light of *sense perception.* Rightly is it called the *lower* light because sense perception begins with a material object and takes place by the aid of corporeal light. It has five divisions corresponding to the five senses. In his third book on Genesis, St. Augustine,[3] in the following way bases the *adequacy* of the senses on the nature of the light present in the elements: if the light or brightness, which makes possible the discernment of things corporeal, exists in a *high degree of its own property* and in a certain purity, it is the sense of *sight; commingled with the air,* it is *hearing; with vapor,* it is smell; *with a fluid* of the body, it is *taste; with a solid earthy substance,* it is *touch.* Now the sensitive life of the body partakes of the nature of light for which reason it thrives in the nerves which are naturally unobstructed and capable of transmitting impressions, and in these five sense it possesses more or less vigor according to the greater or less soundness of the nerves. Therefore, since there are in the world five

simple substances, namely, the four elements and the fifth essence, man has for the perception of all these corporeal forms five senses well adapted to these substances, because, on account of the well-defined nature of each sense, apprehension can take place only when there is a certain conformity and rapport between the faculty and the object. There is another way of determining the adequacy of the senses, but St. Augustine sanctions this method and it seems reasonable since corresponding elements on the part of the faculty, the medium, and the object lend joint support to the proof.

4. The third light which guides man in the investigation of *intelligible truths* is the light of *philosophical knowledge.* It is called *inner* because it inquires into inner and hidden causes through principles of knowledge and natural truth, which are inherent in man. It is a threefold light diffusing itself over the three divisions of philosophy: *rational, natural, and moral,* a classification which seems suitable, since there is truth of *speech,* truth of *things,* and truth of *morals. Rational* philosophy considers the truth of *speech; natural* philosophy, the truth of *things;* and *moral* philosophy, the truth of *conduct.* Or considering it in a different light: just as we believe that the principle of the efficient, the formal or exemplary, and the final cause[4] exists in the Most High God, since "He is the Cause of being the Principle of knowledge, and the Pattern of human life," so do we believe that it is contained in the illumination of philosophy which enlightens the mind to discern the *causes of being* in which case it is physics; or to understand *principles of reasoning* in which case it is *logic;* or to learn the *right way of living* in which case it is *moral* or practical philosophy. Considering it under its third aspect: the light of philosophical knowledge illumines the intellect itself and this enlightenment may be threefold: if it governs the *motive,* it is *moral* philosophy; if it

[3] St. Augustine (354–430) of Hippo in North Africa was one of the most important influences on Bonaventure and the Franciscan tradition. Augustine incorporates many elements of neo-Platonism, but he subordinates them to Christian doctrine in a unique way that proved especially appealing to medieval theologians.

[4] The fourfold scheme of causes is from Aristotle's *Metaphysics.* Bonaventure excludes the material cause here because the material cause is a principle of individuation, and God is not material. The other three causes have their ultimate cause in the mind of God.

sways the *reason,* it is *natural* philosophy; if it directs the *interpretation,* it is *discursive* philosophy. As a result, man is enlightened as regards the truth of life, the truth of knowledge, and the truth of doctrine.

And since one may, through the medium of *speech,* give expression to his thoughts with a threefold purpose in view: namely, to communicate his ideas, to propose something for belief, or to arouse love or hatred, for this reason, *discursive* or rational philosophy has three subdivisions: *grammar, logic,* and *rhetoric.*[5] Of these sciences the first aims to express; the second, to teach; the third, to persuade. The first considers the mind as *apprehending;* the second as *judging;* the third, as *motivating,* and since the mind apprehends by means of *correct* speech, with good reason does this triple science consider these three qualities in speech.

Again, since our intellect must be guided in its judgment by fixed principles, these principles, likewise, must be considered under three aspects: when they pertain to *matter,* they are termed *formal causes;* when they pertain to the *mind,* they are termed *intellectual causes;* and when they pertain to *Divine Wisdom,* they are called *ideal causes;* Natural philosophy, therefore, is subdivided into *physics properly so-called,* into *mathematics,* and *metaphysics.* Physics, accordingly treats of the knowledge of all entities, which leads back to one ultimate Principle from which they proceeded according to ideal causes, that is, to God since He is the *Beginning,* the *End,* and the *Exemplar.* Concerning these ideal causes, however, there has been some controversy among metaphysicists.

Finally, since there are three standards of ethical principles, namely, those governing the *individual,* the *family,* and the *state,* so are there three corresponding divisions of moral philosophy; namely, *ethical, economic,* and *political,* the content of each being clearly indicated by its name.

5. Now the fourth light, which illumines the mind for the understanding of *saving truth,* is the light of *Sacred Scripture.* This light is called *higher*

because it leads to things above by the manifestation of truths which are beyond reason and also because it is not acquired by human research, but comes down by inspiration from the "*Father of lights.*" Although in its literal sense, it is *one,* still, in its spiritual and mystical sense, it is *threefold,* for in all the books of Sacred Scripture, in addition to the *literal* meaning which the words clearly express, there is implied a threefold *spiritual* meaning: namely, the *allegorical,* by which we are taught what to believe concerning the Divinity and humanity; the *moral* by which we are taught how to live; and the *anogogical* by which we are taught how to keep close to God. Hence all of Sacred Scripture teaches these three truths: namely, the eternal generation and Incarnation of Christ, the pattern of human life, and the union of the soul with God. The first regards *faith;* the second, *morals;* the third, the *purpose of both.* To the study of the first, the doctors should devote themselves; on that of the second, the preachers should concentrate; and to the attainment of the third, the contemplatives should aspire. . . .

8. Let us see, therefore, how the other illuminations of knowledge are to be reduced to the light of Sacred Scripture. First of all, let us consider the illumination of *sense* perception, which is concerned exclusively with the cognition of sensible objects, a process in which three phases are to be considered: namely, the *medium* of perception, the *exercise* of perception, and the *delight* of perception. If we consider the *medium* of perception, we shall see therein the Word begotten from all eternity and made man in time. Indeed, a sensible object can make an impression upon a cognitive faculty only through the medium of a likeness which proceeds from the object as an offspring from its parent, and in every sensation, this likeness must be present either generically, specifically, or symbolically. That likeness, however, results in actual sensation only if it is brought into contact with the organ and the faculty, and once that contact is established, there results a new percept, an expressed image by means of which the mind reverts to the object. And even though the object is not always present to the senses, still, the fact remains that perception in its

---

[5] Grammar, logic, and rhetoric formed the first level of the medieval educational curriculum. They became known as the *trivium.*

finished form begets an image. In like manner, know that from the mind of the Most High, Who is knowable by the interior senses of the mind, from all eternity there emanated a Likeness, an Image, and an Offspring; and afterwards, when "the fullness of time had come" he was united to a mind and body and assumed the form of man which He had never been before, and through Him all our minds, which bear the likeness of the Father through faith in our hearts, are brought back to God.

9. To be sure, if we consider the *exercise* of sense perception, we shall see therein the pattern of human life, for each sense applies itself to its own object, shrinks from what may harm it, and does not appropriate the object of any other sense. In like manner, the *spiritual sense* operates in an orderly way, for while applied to its proper object, it opposes *negligence;* while refraining from what is harmful, it combats *concupiscence;* and while respecting the rights of other, it acts in opposition to *pride.* Of a truth, every irregularity springs from negligence, from concupiscence, or from pride. Surely, then, he who lives a prudent, temperate, and submissive life leads a well-ordered life, for thereby he avoids negligence in his duties, concupiscence in his appetites, and pride in his excellence.

10. Furthermore, if we consider the *delight,* we shall see therein the union of the soul with God. Indeed, every sense seeks its proper sensible with longing, finds it with delight, and seeks it again without ceasing, because "the eye is not filled with seeing, neither is the ear filled with hearing." In the same way, our spiritual senses must seek longingly, find joyfully, and seek again without ceasing the beautiful, the harmonious, the fragrant, the sweet, or the delightful to the touch. Behold how the divine Wisdom lies hidden in sense perception and how wonderful is the contemplation of the five spiritual senses in the light of their conformity to the senses of the body.

11. By the same process of reasoning is Divine Wisdom to be found in the illumination of the mechanical arts, the sole purpose of which is the *production of works of art.* In this illumination we can see the *eternal generation and Incarnation of the Word, the pattern of human life, and the union of the soul with God.* And this is true if we consider the *skill of the artist, the quality of the effect produced,* and the *utility of the advantage to be derived therefrom.*

If we consider the *production,* we shall see that the work of art[6] proceeds from the artificer according to a model existing in his mind; this pattern or model the artificer studies carefully before he produces and then he produces as he has predetermined. The artificer, moreover, produces an exterior work bearing the closest possible resemblance to the interior model, and if it were in his power to produce an effect which would know and love him, this he would assuredly do; and if that creature could know its maker, it would be by means of a likeness according to which it came from the hands of the artificer; and if the eyes of the understanding were so darkened that the creature could not be elevated to things above, in order to bring it to a knowledge of its maker, it would be necessary for the likeness according to which the effect was produced to lower itself even to that nature which the creature could grasp and know. In like manner, understand that no creature has proceeded from the Most High Creator except through the Eternal Word, "in Whom He ordered all things," and by which Word He produced creatures bearing not only the nature of His *vestige* but also of His *image* so that through knowledge and love, they might be united to Him. And since by sin the rational creature had dimmed the eye of contemplation, it was most fitting that the Eternal and invisible should become visible and take flesh that He might lead us back to the Father and, indeed, this is what is related in the fourteenth chapter of St. John: "No man cometh to the Father but by Me"; and in the eleventh chapter of St. Matthew: "Neither knoweth any man the Father save the Son, and he to whomsoever the Son will reveal Him." For that reason, then, it is said, "The Word was made flesh." Therefore, considering the illumination of

---

[6]"Work of art" should not be limited to what we call fine art. *Art* in this context means something made with a skill and a vision of the pattern.

mechanical skill as regards the production of the work, we shall see therein the Word begotten and made incarnate, that is, the Divinity and the Humanity and the integrity of all faith.

13. If we consider the *effect,* we shall see therein the *pattern of human life,* for every artificer, indeed, aims to produce a work that is beautiful, useful, and enduring, and only when it possesses these three qualities is the work highly valued and acceptable. Corresponding to the above-mentioned qualities, in the pattern of life there must be found three elements: "knowledge, will, and unaltering and persevering toil." *Knowledge* renders the work beautiful; the *will* renders it useful; *perseverance* renders it lasting. The first resides in the rational, the second in the concupiscible, and the third in the irascible appetite.

14. If we consider the *advantage,* we shall find the union of the soul with God, for every artificer who fashions a work does so that he may derive *praise, benefit,* or *delight* therefrom—a threefold purpose which corresponds to the three formal objects of the appetites: namely, a *noble* good, a *useful* good, and an *agreeable* good. It was for this same threefold reason that God made the soul rational, namely, that of its own accord, it might *praise* Him, *serve* Him, *find delight* in Him, and be at rest; and this takes place through charity. "He that abideth in it, abideth in God and God in him"; in such a way that there is found therein a kind of wondrous union and from that union comes a wondrous delight, for in the Book of Proverbs it is written, "My delights were to be with the children of men." Behold how the illumination of mechanical knowledge is the path to the illumination of Sacred Scripture. There is nothing therein which does not bespeak true wisdom and for this reason Sacred Scripture quite rightly makes frequent use of such similitudes.

15. In the same way is Divine Wisdom to be found in the illumination of *rational philosophy,* the main purpose of which is concerned with *speech.* Here are to be considered three elements corresponding to the threefold consideration of speech itself: namely, as regards the *person speaking,* the *delivery* of the speech, and its final purpose or its effect upon the *hearer.*

16. Considering speech in the light of the *speaker,* we see that all speech is the expression of a *mental concept.* That inner concept is the word of the mind and its offspring which is known to the person conceiving it, but that it may become known to the hearer, it assumes the nature of the voice and clothed in that form, the intelligible word becomes sensible and is heard without; it is received into the ear of the person listening and, still, it does not depart from the mind of the person uttering it. Practically the same procedure is seen in the begatting of the Eternal Word, because the Father conceived Him, begatting Him from all eternity, as it is written in the eighth chapter of the Book of Proverbs. "The depths were not as yet, and I was already conceived." But that He might be known by man who is endowed with senses, He assumed the nature of flesh, and "the Word was made flesh and dwelt amongst us," and yet He remained "in the bosom of His Father."

17. Considering speech in the light of its *delivery,* we shall use therein the *pattern of human life,* for three essential qualities work together for the perfection of speech: namely, *propriety, truth,* and *ornament.* Corresponding to these three qualities, every act of ours should be characterized by *measure, form,* and *order* so that it may be *restrained* by propriety in its outward accomplishment, *rendered beautiful* by purity of affection, *regulated* and adorned by uprightness of intention. For then truly, does one live a correct and well-ordered life which his intention is upright, his affection pure, and his deeds unassuming.

18. Considering speech in the light of its *purpose,* we find that it aims to *express,* to *instruct,* and to *persuade;* but it never *expresses* except by means of a likeness; it never *teaches* except by means of a clear light; and it never *persuades* except by power, and it is evident that these effects are accomplished only by means of an inherent likeness, light, and power intrinsically united to the soul. Therefore, St. Augustine concludes that he alone is a true teacher who can imprint a likeness, shed light, and grant power to the heart of his hearer. Hence it is that "He that teaches within hearts has His throne in heaven." Now, as perfection of speech requires the union of power,

light, and a likeness within the soul, so, too, for the instruction of the soul in the knowledge of God by interior conversation with Him, there is required a union with Him who is "the brightness of glory and the figure of His substance, upholding all things by the word of His power." Hence we see how wondrous is this contemplation by which St. Augustine in his many writings leads soul to Divine Wisdom.

Study Questions

1. What are the four "lights"? Give an example of each.
2. What is the function of mechanical arts?
3. What do a song and a coat have in common? What makes them different?
4. Why is drama included under the mechanical arts?
5. Under which of the four lights would each of the following fall? Why?
   a. Baking a cake
   b. Smelling smoke
   c. The law of gravity
   d. Everyone desires happiness.
   e. God is love.
6. What are the divisions of natural philosophy? If energy is the product of mass times the square of the speed of light, what aspect of that fact corresponds to each of the divisions?
7. To what do the five senses correspond?
8. What is Bonaventure's distinction between an inner and an outer light?
9. Which of the phases of the illumination of sense perception most obviously would suggest aesthetic perception? Why? What is its ultimate source?
10. What is the purpose of the illumination of the mechanical arts? Choose one mechanical art and illustrate the purpose of its illumination.
11. What qualities does someone who makes something strive to attain?
12. What is the role of sense? How many senses are there?
13. What is the threefold function of art?
14. Is speech an art?
15. Distinguish a mental concept from its expression in speech. Give an example.
16. What makes something beautiful? Can you figure out what something ugly would be for Bonaventure? (He does not consider the ugly, but he might have.)

Dante

$\cdot$ $\cdot$ $\cdot$ $\cdot$ $\cdot$

DANTE ALIGHIERI WAS BORN in Florence in 1265. Politically, Italy was a collection of city-states and a network of family alliances. There was no political unity until the nineteenth century. In the thirteenth century, the competing political forces were allied with the Holy Roman Emperor on one side and the papacy on the other. The emperor's power was based in Germany and Austria. The papacy was supported by France. Italy, with all of the symbolic prestige of Rome, was a prize struggled over by everyone. Toward the beginning of the thirteenth century, the parties divided between an aristocratic party known as the Ghibellines, which looked to the emperor and a party called the Guelphs, which at least nominally favored the papacy, though their real interests were more in local control. The results were frequent civil wars complicated by family feuds. In Florence, the Guelphs were successful in expelling the Ghibelline families.

Dante's family was Guelph, and Dante grew up and entered into local civic affairs as a member of an important though not wealthy family. He fought at the decisive battle that repelled a Ghibelline attempt to return, and he assumed public office at a time that turned out to be unfortunate in the history of Florence. The political lines were by no means stable, and feuds between families often split nominal allies. The Guelphs in Florence split into two factions as a result of one such family feud. Dante was a city official at the time the hostilities broke into open fighting. In an attempt to make peace, he agreed to the exile of the leaders of both parties. This decision served only to make him the enemy of both and led ultimately to his own exile in January 1302. Dante never returned to Florence.

While growing up in Florence, at the age of about nine, Dante was introduced to Beatrice Portinari, the daughter of his father's friend. She became the figure of his ideal love and the means to his beatific vision in the *Divine Comedy*. Their actual relation was slight. They were never more than casual acquaintances. Beatrice married someone else and had died by 1290. Dante already had made her the symbol of his ideal love by then. "Love" in the thirteenth century was more than just an emotional attachment. It had little to do with marriage, which was a much more practical affair. (Dante married well, and his wife bore him sons and daughters. After his exile, she remained in Florence and reared his family.) The ideal love that Dante expressed for Beatrice was very different. It had its roots in the twelfth-century cult of courtly love. The beloved served as a ruler and ideal and was the object of a quasireligious devotion. She was explicitly outside of conventional domestic relations. She served as the object of veneration, and if the love-affair became too mundane, it would be destroyed. Dante followed this tradition when he wrote a cycle of love poems for Beatrice. Beatrice supplied for Dante the secular, idealized emotional object that he could transform into a poetic ideal. If she had not existed, Dante would have had to invent her.

The period of Dante's exile saw him move from patron to patron. Among the most important of these patrons was Bartolomeo della Scala, who was head of one of the leading families in Verona. Dante dedicated the third part of his great epic poem to him, and Dante's letters to him are one of our sources of Dante's ideas about poetry and art. As an exile, Dante was temperamentally drawn to some of his aristocratic patrons and shared their sympathies with the more aristocratic Ghibelline faction. He distrusted the secular ambitions of the papacy, and he had little use for the more contentious and less cultured elements of his own party. He longed for a unified Italy and was willing to appeal to the emperor, Henry VII, for political support, though he could not bring himself to join openly the siege of Florence when Henry unsuccessfully tried to take the city. Dante lectured, taught, and served the intellectual and diplomatic needs of his patrons. He maintained a prickly independence, however, which kept him on the move and made reconciliation with Florence impossible. His great epic was written over the years of his exile and had just been completed when he died of a fever in 1321 at the court of Guido Novello in Ravenna. As a poet and scholar, Dante chose to write in Italian rather than the common scholarly language, Latin. His defense of the "vulgar" tongue and the success of his epic poem point in the direction of the Italian Renaissance even as his scholastic knowledge identifies him with the great theologians of the thirteenth century.

◆　◆　◆　◆　◆　◆

At the beginning of the fourteenth century, Italy was already moving out of the medieval synthesis of Latin culture and Christian theology and toward the greater freedom and individuality of the Renaissance. Dante's epic poem, the *Divine Comedy,* sums up a medieval world view and transforms it into a personal history and a prophecy of a new Italy. Dante's aesthetic is also at once medieval and a reflection of what is to come in the Renaissance. In a series of letters to one of his patrons, Dante attempted to explain and justify his poetic methods. The tenth letter in this series is a remarkable combination of philosophical explication and self-critical commentary.

The most important background for Dante is the metaphysics of Aristotle as it was reinterpreted in a Christian context by Thomas Aquinas (1226–1274). The rediscovery in the thirteenth century of Aristotle's metaphysical writings proved to be a necessary step in changing the way philosophers thought about the importance of the individual in relation to the world. Metaphysics is the science of being, of what there is and how it exists. By making metaphysics more concrete and this-worldly, the new metaphysics of the medieval Aristotelians also changed the older metaphysics of Plotinus and Augustine and opened the way for new forms of painting and poetry. Aquinas adopted the Aristotelian categories for explaining the most basic levels of what makes up the universe. The fundamental categories for Aquinas are substance and accidents, substantial form and prime matter, act and potency, and essence and existence. Each of these pairs of terms was given a special meaning by Aristotle and taken over by Aquinas to redescribe reality.

"Substance" is a subject, whatever exists as a thing itself. Its "accidents" are those aspects of it that can change without a thing ceasing to be itself. So, for example, an oak tree consists of a substance that makes it an oak tree and accidents that include the number of leaves on the tree. When a leaf falls, the tree does not cease to be an oak tree. "Substantial form" is whatever determines a particular substance. "Form" is a basic term for all of classical and medieval metaphysics. It is the principle that gives reality to things. Aristotle made form substantial rather than independent as it was for Plato or intellectual (ideal) as it was for Plotinus. Substantial forms are what determine all of the natural kinds of things in the universe—oak trees, humans, dogs, and stars. For there to be a kind of thing, it must have a substantial form. When that substantial form is combined with prime matter, an individual instance of the thing appears. A single oak tree is a combination of the substantial form of an oak tree with prime matter to produce *this* oak tree. The metaphysics of Aquinas becomes very concrete in this way.

The move from the possibility represented by substantial form to its realization takes us from potency to act. Everything is both something actual and potentially something else. An oak tree actualizes a potential to be an oak tree, but it also remains potentially a piece of firewood or a pile of ashes, neither of which is any longer an oak tree. Everything combines some actuality and potentiality. Only God is pure act with no unrealized potentiality.

Finally, the move to actuality is a move to existence—to being something at some time and place. In order for existence to be possible, there must be some defining characteristics that identify what exists. Nothing exists "in general." Everything that exists exists as some essential being, but its essence is not its existence. On this view, I am defined by who *I* am, not by my particular existence as one time and place. Essence defines a thing; existence merely locates it. This thumbnail sketch of the metaphysics of Aristotle and Aquinas is elaborated upon extensively in the thirteenth and fourteenth centuries by theologians and philosophers until it becomes the basis for a new way of looking at the world. It is more concrete and specific than any of the other theological and philosophical systems available.

Dante took this metaphysic and shaped it into a way of constructing a poetic world. Hell, purgatory, and heaven are formed according to the picture drawn by Aquinas. Everything has an ordered place; its nature is determined by its true form while its concrete existence exhibits that form for all to see. The difference from the ordinary world is that in the poetic world the true nature of people is shown rather than concealed by their accidents. Dante strips away appearances to show each individual in his or her precise circle of hell, purgatory, or heaven. Art is able to define and disclose the essence of individuals and their place in an eternal order in an exemplary way.

Dante's great epic poem consists of three parts: hell, purgatory, and heaven. The poet, Dante himself, is lost at the beginning. He must be guided by the greatest poet of Italy, Virgil, the author of Rome's epic poem, the *Aeneid,* not directly to his goal but indirectly by way of a route that requires him to descend into hell and climb the mountain of purgatory before being allowed a vision of paradise. Each part of Dante's journey is divided into precise circles which characterize some aspect of reality and are peopled by the symbolic and historical figures who belong to them. The poem is called a comedy because, though it begins with a lost soul wandering alone, it ends with a vision of unification with God and the poet's beloved. The final result is achieved by a joining together.

Dante is maddeningly specific in the details of his poem. To understand it, we need to know a great deal of obscure history. Dante got even with all of his enemies by placing them in the appropriate circles of hell, and he praised his friends and patrons by putting them higher up. At the same time, the structure of the poem represents a universal picture. Its historical and mythological characters are not just individuals. They represent the kind of metaphysical choices that make up a universe. Each has a multi-layered interpretation, worked out in great detail by Dante. He tried to explain the way to interpret his poem to his patron in the letters we have.

Aquinas did not simply adopt Aristotle's metaphysics. He transformed it and combined it with elements from neo-Platonism[1] that were also a part of the medieval worldview. We might take medieval neo-Platonism to be characterized by the thesis that the form of things is essentially intellectual and the task of the mind or soul is to become as much a part of the intellectual forms as possible. To the neo-Platonist, the individual, concrete instances of forms were less important than their ideal, intellectual perfection. Individual minds or intellects sought to return to their source in the forms. Neo-Platonism tended to be otherworldly. This version of neo-Platonism was very much a part of the thinking of Aquinas. Aristotle's metaphysics made it more concrete but did not change the essential importance of the forms.

Neo-Platonism remained very important to Dante as well. It provided an essential element in early Renaissance poetics and art theory. In some fundamental ways, however, the influence of Aristotle changed neo-Platonism so that the version developed by Dante and the Renaissance differed from the medieval version. Renaissance aesthetics is thoroughly neo-Platonic, but it is a new neo-Platonism transformed by the more concrete metaphysics of Aristotle and Aquinas. For Dante and for other Renaissance poets, the soul must undertake a journey to reach its goal of purification. Neo-Platonism had always used this metaphor, and it is prominent in medieval mysticism. The difference is that for Dante, the individual soul must make the journey by itself and remains itself throughout. Dante remains himself through his entire trip down into the inferno of hell, up the mount of purgatory, and into the vision of paradise. A second metaphor reinforces this individuality. The goal of Dante's journey, and implicitly of poetry and art in general, is to reach his beloved. Love, too, is a medieval metaphor. It had been developed as a secular alternative to religion in the cults of courtly love and in troubadour poetry, and it was the metaphor for union with God in much mystical theology. But Dante and his contemporaries made love both specific and individual. Beatrice is Dante's beloved, not just an idealized symbol. She is an object of real passion which undergoes symbolic transformation in the poetry.

As aesthetic philosophy became more and more concrete and individualistic in the Renaissance, it became more important to understand allegorical meaning. Allegorical theory is a staple of biblical interpretation throughout the late classical and medieval periods. But there allegory is essentially a way of understanding what God had already

---

[1] For a discussion of neo-Platonism, see the introduction to the Plotinus reading selection, p. 44.

done. It is a way of reading the signs that have been built into the natural and histori-cal world by a God who controls everything and destines it for a specific end. Dante's allegory retains the same structure. The literal meaning of a text is "what happens," and the allegorical meaning is its significance. Significance can be broken down into sym-bolic, moral, and finally universal or "anagogical" meaning. But Dante's allegory works differently from the medieval allegory of Bonaventure less than a hundred years earlier. It is an historical allegory. Real people and real political events are figured in the *Divine Comedy*. Instead of turning history back into a single divine plan, Dante turns the di-vine plan into a way of understanding history. In the process, art becomes individual expression. It depends on individual emotions. Medieval allegory led to contemplation that dissolved the individual into the universal form of God, but Dante's beatific vision is specifically of Beatrice. This new concreteness and individuality exploded into a fas-cination with perspective, color, and individuality for their own sakes in the painting and sculpture of the fifteenth and sixteenth centuries. Art and aesthetics were redirected toward the individual, toward feeling and emotion, and toward personal expression. Dante, who still belonged to the medieval world, can be regarded as the first step in that new aesthetic.

Letter Ten

TO THE MAGNIFICENT *and most victorious Lord, the Lord Can Grande della Scala, Vicar-General of the most holy principality of Caesar in the city of Verona, and town of Vicenza, his most devoted servant, Dante Alighieri, a Florentine by birth, not by disposition, prayeth a long and happy life, and perpetual increase of the glory of his name. . . .*

§5. As the Philosopher[2] says in the second book of the *Metaphysics,* "as a thing is in respect of being, so is it in respect of truth"; the reason of which is, that the truth concerning a thing, which consists in the truth as in its subject, is the perfect likeness of the thing as it is. Now of things which exist, some are such as to have absolute being in themselves; while others are such as to have their being dependent upon something else, by virtue of a certain relation, as being in existence at the same time, or having respect to some other thing, as in the case of correlatives, such as father and son, master and servant, double and half, the whole and part, and other similar things, in so far as they are related. Inasmuch, then, as the being of such things depends upon something else, it follows that the truth of these things likewise depends upon something else; for if the half is unknown, its double cannot be known; and so of the rest.

§6. If anyone, therefore, is desirous of offering any sort of introduction to part of a work, it behooves him to furnish some notion of the whole of which it is a part. Wherefore I, too, being desirous of offering something by way of introduction to the above-mentioned part of the whole *Comedy,* thought it incumbent on me in the first place to say something concerning the work as a whole, in order that access to the part might be the easier and the more perfect. There are six points, then, as to which inquiry must be made at the beginning of every didactic work; namely,

the subject, the author, the form, the aim, the title of the book, and the branch of philosophy to which it belongs. Now of these six points there are three in respect of which the part which I have had in mind to address to you differs from the whole work; namely, the subject, the form, and the title; whereas in respect of the others there is no difference, as is obvious to any one who considers the matter. Consequently, in an examination of the whole, these three points must be made the subject of a separate inquiry; which being done, the way will be sufficiently clear for the introduction to the part. Later we will examine the other three points, not only with reference to the whole work, but also with reference to the particular part which is offered to you.

§7. For the elucidation, therefore, of what we have to say, it must be understood that the meaning of this work is not of one kind only; rather the work may be described as "polysemous," that is, having several meanings; for the first meaning is that which is conveyed by the letter, and the next is that which is conveyed by what the letter signifies; the former of which is called literal, while the latter is called allegorical, or mystical. And for the better illustration of this method of exposition we may apply it to the following verses: "When Israel went out of Egypt, the house of Jacob from a people of strange language; Judah was his sanctuary, and Israel his dominion." For if we consider the letter alone, the thing signified to us is the going out of the children of Israel from Egypt in the time of Moses; if the allegory, our redemption through Christ is signified; if the moral sense, the conversion of the soul from the sorrow and misery of sin to a state of grace is signified; if the anagogical, the passing of the sanctified soul from the bondage of the corruption of this world to the liberty of everlasting glory is signified. And although these mystical meanings are called by various names, they may one and all in a general sense be termed allegorical, inasmuch as they are

---

[2] "The Philosopher" was a common way of referring to Aristotle in the thirteenth and fourteenth centuries.

different (*diversii*) from the literal or historical; for the word "allegory" is so called from the Greek *alleon,* which in Latin is *alienum* (strange) or *diversum* (different).

§8. This being understood, it is clear that the subject, with regard to which the alternative meanings are brought into play, must be twofold. And therefore the subject of this work must be considered in the first place from the point of view of the literal meaning, and next from that of the allegorical interpretation. The subject, then, of the whole work, taken in the literal sense only, is the state of souls after death, pure and simple. For on and about that the argument of the whole work turns. If, however, the work be regarded from the allegorical point of view, the subject is man according as by his merits or demerits in the exercise of his free will he is deserving of reward or punishment by justice.

§9. And the form is twofold—the form of the treatise, and the form of the treatment. The form of the treatise is threefold, according to the threefold division. The first division is that whereby the whole work is divided into three cantiche; the second, whereby each cantica is divided into cantos; and the third, whereby each canto is divided into rhymed lines.[3] The form or manner of treatment is poetic, fictive, descriptive, digressive, and figurative; and further, it is definitive, analytical, probative, refutative, and exemplificative.

§10. The title of the book is "Here begins the *Comedy* of Dante Alighieri, a Florentine by birth, not by disposition." For the understanding of which it must be noted that "comedy" is so called from *comos,* a village, and *oda,* a song; whence comedy is as it were a "rustic song." Now comedy is a certain kind of poetical narration which differs from all others. It differs, then, from tragedy

in its subject-matter, in that tragedy at the beginning is admirable and placid, but at the end or issue is foul and horrible. And tragedy is so called from *tragos,* a goat, and *ola;* as it were a "goat-song," that is to say foul like a goat, as appears from the tragedies of Seneca.[4] Whereas comedy begins with sundry adverse conditions, but ends happily, as appears from the comedies of Terence.[5] And for this reason it is the custom of some writers in their salutation to say by way of greeting: "a tragic beginning and a comic ending to you!" Tragedy and comedy differ likewise in their style of language; for that of tragedy is high-flown and sublime, while that of comedy is unstudied and lowly. And this is implied by Horace in the *Art of Poetry,*[6] where he grants that the comedian may on occasion use the language of tragedy and vice versa:

> Yet sometimes comedy her voice will rise,
> And angry Chremes scold with swelling
>   phrase;
> And prosy periods oft our ears assail
> When Telephus and Peleus tell their tragic tale.

And from this it is clear that the present work is to be described as a comedy. For if we consider the subject matter, at the beginning it is horrible and foul as being *Hell;* but at the close it is happy, desirable, and pleasing, as being *Paradise.* As regards the style of language, the style is unstudied and lowly, as being in the vulgar tongue,[7] in which even women-folk hold their talk. And hence it is evident why the work is called a comedy. And there are other kinds of poetical narration, such as the pastoral poem, the elegy, the sat-

---

[3] The *Divine Comedy* is divided into three parts: *Inferno, Purgatorio,* and *Paradiso.* Each canto is a separate segment. The poem is composed in a triple rhyme scheme—in each three-line stanza, the first and third lines rhyme, while the second line rhymes with the first and third lines of the next stanza. The result is an interlocking unit of three-line stanzas that ends with a single line to complete the rhyme scheme.

[4] Seneca (3 B.C.E.–65) was a Roman rhetorician, Stoic philosopher, and playwright. He wrote tragedies probably intended for recitation rather than stage performance.

[5] Terence was a second-century B.C.E. Roman playwright. A freed slave, he based his comedies on Greek models.

[6] Horace (65–8 B.C.E.) wrote satires and odes as well as a rhetorical treatise on poetry.

[7] The "vulgar tongue" was Italian; Latin was the "educated" language.

ire, and the votive song,[8] as may also be gathered from Horace in the *Art of Poetry;* but of these we need say nothing at present.

§11. It can now be shown in what manner the subject of the part offered to you is to be determined. For if the subject of the whole work taken in the literal sense is the state of souls after death, pure and simple, without limitation; it is evident that in this part the same state is the subject, but with a limitation, namely the state of blessed souls after death. And if the subject of the whole work from the allegorical point of view is man according as by his merits or demerits in the exercise of his free will he is deserving of reward or punishment by justice, it is evident that in this part this subject has a limitation, and that it is man according as by his merits he is deserving of reward by justice.

§12. In like manner the form of the part is determined by that of the whole work. For if the form of the treatise as a whole is threefold, in this part it is twofold only, the division being that of the cantica and of the cantos. The first division (into cantiche) cannot be applicable to the form of the part, since the cantica is itself a part under the first division.

§13. The title of the book also is clear. For the title of the whole book is "Here begins the *Comedy,*" &c., as above; but the title of the part is "Here begins the third cantica of the *Comedy* of Dante, which is called *Paradise.*"

§14. These three points, in which the part differs from the whole, having been examined, we may now turn our attention to the other three, in respect of which there is no difference between the part and the whole. The author, then, of the whole and of the part is the person mentioned above, who is seen to be such throughout.

§15. The aim of the whole and of the part might be manifold; as, for instance, immediate and remote. But leaving aside any minute examination of this question, it may be stated briefly that the aim of the whole and of the part is to re-move those living in this life from a state of misery, and to bring them to a state of happiness.

§16. The branch of philosophy to which the work is subject, in the whole as in the part, is that of morals or ethics; inasmuch as the whole as well as the part was conceived, not for speculation, but with a practical object. For if in certain parts or passages the treatment is after the manner of speculative philosophy, that is not for the sake of speculation, but for a practical purpose; since, as the Philosopher says in the second book of the *Metaphysics:* "practical men occasionally speculate on things in their particular and temporal relations".

§17. Having therefore premised these matters, we may now apply ourselves to the exposition of the literal meaning, by way of sample; as to which it must first be understood that the exposition of the letter is in effect but a demonstration of the form of the work. . . .

§23. He[9] says well, then, when he says that the divine ray, or divine glory, "penetrates and shines through the universe"; penetrates, as to essence; shines forth, as to being. And what he adds as to "more and less" is manifestly true, since we see that one essence exists in a more excellent degree, and another in a less; as is clearly the case with regard to the heaven and the elements, the former being incorruptible, while the latter are corruptible.

§24. And having premised this truth, he next goes on to indicate Paradise by a circumlocution; and says that he was in that heaven which receives the glory of God, or his light, in most bountiful measure. As to which it must be understood that that heaven is the highest heaven, which contains all the bodies of the universe, and is contained by none, within which all bodies move (itself remaining everlastingly at rest), and which receives virtue from no corporeal substance. And it is called the Empyrean, which is as much as to say, the heaven glowing with fire or heat; not that

---

[8] A votive song is a hymn to a god.

[9] Dante refers to himself in third person as "the author." He has become his own commentator.

there is material fire or heat therein, but spiritual, which is holy love, or charity.

§25. Now that this heaven receives more of the divine light than any other can be proved by two things. Firstly, by its containing all things, and being contained by none; secondly, by its state of everlasting rest or peace. As to the first the proof is as follows: The containing body stands in the same relation to the content in natural position as the formative does to the formable, as we are told in the fourth book of the *Physics*. But in the natural position of the whole universe the first heaven is the heaven which contains all things; consequently it is related to all things as the formative to the formable, which is to be in the relation of cause to effect. And since every causative force is in the nature of a ray emanating from the first cause, which is God, it is manifest that that heaven which is in the highest degree causative receives most of the divine light.

§26. As to the second the proof is this: Everything which has motion moves because of something which it has not, and which is the terminus of its motion. The heaven of the moon,[10] for instance, moves because of some part of itself which has not attained the station towards which it is moving; and because no part whatsoever of it has attained any terminus whatsoever (as indeed it never can), it moves to another station, and thus is always in motion, and is never at rest, which is what it desires. And what I say of the heaven of the moon applies to all the other heavens, except the first. Everything, then, which has motion is in some respect defective, and has not its whole being complete. That heaven, therefore, which is subject to no movement, in itself and in every part whatsoever of itself has whatever it is capable of having in perfect measure, so that it has no need of motion for its perfection. And since every perfection is a ray of the Primal One, inasmuch as He is perfection in the highest degree, it is manifest that the first heaven receives more than any other of the light of the Primal One,

which is God. This reasoning, however, has the appearance of an argument based on the denial of the antecedent,[11] in that it is not a direct proof and according to syllogistic form. But if we consider its content it is a good proof, because it deals with a thing eternal, and assumes it to be capable of being eternally defective; so that, if God did not give that heaven motion, it is evident that He did not give it material in any respect defective. And on this supposition the argument holds good by reason of the content; and this form of argument is much the same as though we should reason: "if he is man, he is able to laugh"; for in every convertible proposition a like reasoning holds good by virtue of the content. Hence it is clear that when the author says "in that heaven which receives more of the light of God," he intends by a circumlocution to indicate Paradise, or the heaven of the Empyrean.

§27. And in agreement with the foregoing is what the Philosopher says in the first book *On Heaven,* namely that "a heaven has so much the more honourable material than those below it as it is the further removed from terrestrial things." In addition to which might be adduced what the Apostle[12] says to the Ephesians of Christ: "Who ascended up far above all heavens, that He might fill all things." This is the heaven of the delights of the Lord; of which delights it is said by Ezekiel against Lucifer: "Thou, the seal of similitude, full of wisdom, beautiful in perfection, wast in the delights of the Paradise of God."

§28. And after he has said that he was in that place of Paradise which he describes by circumlocution, he goes on to say that he saw certain things which he who descends therefrom is powerless to relate. And he gives the reason, saying that "the intellect plunges itself to such depth" in its very longing, which is for God, "that the

---

[10] In Dante's cosmology, each heavenly body moves in a separate sphere or heaven of its own.

[11] The denial of the antecedent is a logical fallacy. It has the form "If *P*, then *Q*" and "not *P*"; therefore, "not *Q*." It is shown to be a fallacy by examples such as, "If that is a dog, it is a mammal" and "It is not a dog"; therefore, "It is not a mammal." Obviously just because dogs are mammals and "it" is not a dog, one should not conclude that "it" is not a mammal.

[12] Paul.

memory cannot follow." For the understanding of which it must be noted that the human intellect in this life, by reason of its connaturality and affinity to the separate intellectual substance, when in exaltation, reaches such a height of exaltation that after its return to itself memory fails, since it has transcended the range of human faculty. And this is conveyed to us by the Apostle where he says, addressing the Corinthians: "I know a man (whether in the body, or out of the body, I cannot tell; God knoweth) how that he was caught up to the third heaven, and heard unspeakable words, which it is not lawful for a man to utter." Behold, after the intellect had passed beyond the bounds of human faculty in its exaltation, it could not recall what took place outside of its range. This again is conveyed to us in Matthew, where we read that the three disciples fell on their faces, and record nothing thereafter, as though memory had failed them. And in Ezekiel it is written: "And when I saw it, I fell upon my face." And should these not satisfy the cavillers, let them read Richard of St. Victor[13] in his book *On Contemplation;* let them read Bernard[14] in his book *On the Consideration;* let them read Augustine[15] in his book *On the Capacity of the Soul;* and they will cease from their caviling. But if on account of the sinfulness of the speaker they should cry out against his claim to have reached such a height of exaltation, let them read Daniel, where they will find that even Nebuchadnezzar by divine permission beheld certain things as a warning to sinners, and straightway forgot them. For He "who maketh his sun to shine on the good and on the evil, and sendeth rain on the just and on the unjust," sometimes in compassion for their conversion, sometimes in wrath for their chastisement, in greater or lesser measure, according as He wills, manifests his glory to evil-doers, be they never so evil.

§29. He saw, then, as he says, certain things "which he who returns has neither knowledge nor power to relate." Now it must be carefully noted that he says "has neither knowledge nor power"—knowledge he has not because he has forgotten; power he has not, because even if he remembers, and retains it thereafter, nevertheless speech fails him. For we perceive many things by the intellect for which language has no terms—a fact which Plato indicates plainly enough in his books by his employment of metaphors; for he perceived many things by the light of the intellect which his everyday language was inadequate to express.

Study Questions

1. What makes something true?
2. Give an example of something that has its being, and therefore its truth, in itself.
3. What are the different meanings of Dante's work?
4. Select another passage from the Bible and try to give Dante's fourfold explication—literal, allegorical, moral, and anagogical.
5. Does it make any difference that Dante says that the literal meaning refers to something we might consider false—the existence of a physical place such as the inferno he describes?
6. Why does Dante call his work a comedy?
6. Can a comedy end unhappily? Can a tragedy end happily? Why would anyone go to a tragedy?
7. What is the aim of Dante's work?
8. Dante classifies the *Divine Comedy* as moral philosophy. Why?
9. What is the divine light?
10. Give an example of something "formative" that is related to something "formable."
11. Dante claims that we perceive many things by the intellect for which we have

---

[13] Richard of St. Victor (d. 1173) was prior of the Abbey of St. Victor in Paris. He is known for combining a kind of Platonic philosophy with Christian mysticism.

[14] Bernard of Clairveaux (d. 1153) was a Cistercian monk whose persuasive preaching and reputation for moral authority made him one of the most powerful figures in the twelfth century.

[15] Augustine of Hippo (354–430) was the most influential of the Latin Church Fathers. His theological works provided the foundation for much of medieval theology.

no terms. How, then, can those things be expressed?

12. Why is Dante "powerless to relate" what he saw in paradise? How does this relate to his allegorical method?

13. Medieval art tended to be anonymous. Dante builds his own personal history into his work and his commentary on it. What is the significance of this self-identification and self-assertion?

The gift which you possess of speaking excellently about Homer is not an art, but, as I was just saying, an inspiration; there is a divinity moving you, like that contained in the stone which Euripides calls a magnet, but which is commonly known as the stone of Heraclea. This stone not only attracts iron rings, but also imparts to them a similar power of attracting other rings; and sometimes you may see a number of pieces of iron and rings suspended from one another so as to form quite a long chain; and all of them derive their power from the original stone. In like manner the Muse first of all inspires men herself; and from these inspired persons a chain of other persons is suspended, who take the inspiration. For all good poets, epic as well as lyric, compose their beautiful poems not by art, but because they are inspired and possessed.

PLATO, *Ion*

He who, ascending from these earthly things under the influence of true love, begins to perceive that beauty, is not far from the end. And the true order of going, or being led by another, to the things of love, is to begin from the beauties of earth and mount upwards for the sake of that other beauty, using these as steps only, and form one going on to two, and from two to all fair bodily forms, and from fair bodily forms to fair practices, and from fair practices to fair sciences, until from fair sciences he arrives at the science of which I have spoken, the science which has no other object than absolute beauty.

PLATO, *Symposium*

The third kind is the madness of those who are possessed by the Muses; which taking hold of a delicate and virgin soul, and there inspiring frenzy, awakens lyrical and all other numbers; with these adorning the myriad actions of ancient heroes for the instruction of posterity. But he who, having no touch of the Muses' madness in his soul, comes to the door and thinks that he will get into the temple by the help of art—he, I say, and his poetry are not admitted; the sane man disappears and is nowhere when he enters into rivalry with the madman.

PLATO, *Phaedrus*

The chief kinds of beauty are order, symmetry, and definition, which the discipline of mathematics demonstrates to a special degree.

ARISTOTLE, *Metaphysics*

To speak, generally, you should consider that to be truly beautiful and sublime which pleases all people at all times. For when men who differ in their habits, their lives, their tastes, their ages, their dates, all agree together in holding one and the same view about the same writings, then the unanimous verdict, as it were, of such discordant judges makes our faith in the admired passages strong and indisputable.

LONGINUS (first century B.C.E.?), *On the Sublime*

The poet wants either to profit or please, or at the same time to speak both delightfully and usefully. Whatever you teach, be brief, so that the mind may easily and faithfully perceive it. . . . Poetry is like painting. One piece is viewed properly if looked at closely, another if from a greater distance. This one needs a dim light, that one needs a strong light and cannot be judged without critical skill. This one charms only once; that will please if repeated ten times.

HORACE (65–8 B.C.E.), *Art of Poetry*

Clearly no one loves what disgusts the eye, that is, sheer repulsiveness. Proportion makes beautiful things pleasing. As we have shown, equality is found not only in sounds heard by the ear and in movement of the body, but also in visible forms, in which hitherto equality has been identified with beauty even more frequently than in sounds.

AUGUSTINE (354–430), *De Musica*

I am the living and fiery essence of the divine substance that glows in the beauty of the fields. I shine in the water, I burn in the sun and the moon and the stars.

HILDEGARD OF BINGEN (1098–1179)

Beauty includes three conditions, integrity or perfection, since those things which are incomplete are by that very fact ugly; due proportion or harmony; and lastly, brightness, or clarity, according to which things are called beautiful that have a bright color.

THOMAS AQUINAS (1226–1274), *Summa Theologica* (Q. 39, Art. 8)

[Painting] calls for imagination to discover things that are not visible, hiding themselves beneath the shadow of natural objects, and manual skill, to fix them by hand, presenting to plain sight what does not exist in actuality. Painting deserves to be enthroned next to theory and to be crowned with poetry.

CENNINO CENNINI (1370–1440), *Libro dell' arte*

How much painting contributes to the legitimate pleasures of the soul and to the dignified beauty of things can be seen clearly . . . especially from this: one can conceive of almost nothing so precious that painting does not make it richer and more beautiful. . . . Painting has this virtue that any master painter who sees his works adored will feel as if he were another God.

LEON BATTISTA ALBERTI (1404–1472), *On Painting*

Sculpture is not a science but a mechanical art, because it causes the sculptor to sweat and to experience bodily fatigue. A sculptor need know only the simple measurements of the limbs and the nature of movements and postures. With this knowledge he can finish his works. The spectator is given no other cause to admire the work than the likeness of what it represents to the eye, unlike painting, which uses science to show on a flat surface the greatest landscapes with their distant horizons.

LEONARDO DA VINCI (1452–1519), *On Painting*

No painter should ever imitate the style of another painter because he will be called a nephew and not a child of nature with respect to art. Because nature provides so many things, we ought rather to rely on nature than on those masters who have learned from her. And I am not speaking of those who wish to become wealthy through art but of those who seek honor and renown through art.

LEONARDO DA VINCI (1452–1519), On Painting

Nature never set forth the earth in so rich tapestry as divers poets have done—neither with pleasant rivers, fruitful trees, sweet-smelling flowers, nor whatsoever else may make the too much loved earth more lovely. Her world is brazen, the poets only deliver a golden.

SIR PHILIP SIDNEY (1554–1586), An Apology for Poetry

For suppose it be granted (that which I suppose with great reason may be denied) that the philosopher, in respect of his methodical proceeding, doth teach more perfectly than the poet, yet do I think that no man is so much *Philophilosophos* as to compare the philosopher, in moving, with the poet.

And that moving is of a higher degree than teaching, it may by this appear, that it is well-nigh the cause and effect of teaching. For who will be taught, if he be not moved with desire to be taught, and what so much good doth that teaching bring forth (I speak still of moral doctrine) as that it moveth one to do that which it doth teach?

SIR PHILIP SIDNEY (1554–1586), An Apology for Poetry

PART TWO

Modern Aesthetics

BY THE MODERN WORLD, we mean to include all post-Renaissance, postscientific revolution western history. *Modernism* is a complex term with different meanings for different people. It may be more or less inclusive. In its broadest interpretation, modernism signifies the world as perceived by western individualistic culture. Perhaps that perception of the world has lost its dominance. Perhaps we now belong to a *postmodern* world. No matter. We will define the *modern world* for our purposes as the western world from the Renaissance to the end of World War I. Whatever else it means, that period shaped aesthetics.

No clear historical line need be drawn between classical aesthetics and the modern world. The medieval world still operated with essentially classical assumptions about beauty, harmony, and order. The Renaissance declared itself a rebirth of classical values out of a medieval "darkness" as Renaissance writers characterized their own past. Certainly the visual arts exploded into new forms and new aesthetic attitudes. However, much of Renaissance thinking continued the tradition of reinterpretation of Plato and Aristotle begun by Plotinus and continued throughout the Middle Ages. The very idea of a Renaissance cannot be precisely defined historically. As early as the fourteenth century in Italy, many of the elements of a break with medieval thought already were evident. As late as the seventeenth century in England and Germany, some of the same elements were just being acknowledged.

As far as aesthetics is concerned, the decisive change began with the late seventeenth- and eighteenth-century acknowledgment of sense as the basis of judgment and appreciation. The neo-Platonic hierarchy of being was finally replaced with a more immediate dependence on experience. Artists, writers, and critics already had changed practically. Philosophy followed. For our purposes, no sharp division need be drawn, however. We acknowledge that "modern" culture and philosophy emerges gradually from the medieval and Renaissance world. Aesthetics should be no different.

The development and explication of these modern beginnings require us to hypothesize a long, extended nineteenth century. We might think of the nineteenth century as reaching all the way to the battlefields of World War I. The destruction and death brought by that war surpassed all expectations of its participants. In a literal sense, it changed the world, and art changed with it. Therefore, we will take the Great War as a convenient, though not absolute, ending to that extended century. Modern art and modern aesthetics were marked by a sense of optimism, of progress, of new developments and new movement. Feeling gained a legitimacy that made art and aesthetics central to philosophy in a new way. That optimism ended on the battlefields of France. The aesthetics of sense and sensibility have faced new challenges in the twentieth century. Our responses are built on the modernist aesthetics of the seventeenth through the nineteenth centuries, but we are still very much a part of a new, emerging world culture with its diversity and nonwestern, nonmale reorientation. For the purposes of this anthology, we will draw the line around 1914.

The Seventeenth and
Eighteenth Centuries

SOMEWHERE IN THE COURSE OF the sixteenth and seventeenth centuries, we can locate a decisive shift in the theoretical principles applied to aesthetics. New artistic practices such as the use of perspective and attention to human form, which developed in the earlier Renaissance, demanded new theories. The social and cultural role of art shifted. Patronage passed from church and court to middle-class city dwellers and independent-minded country landowners. The new aristocracy and the rising middle class had money to spend, leisure time, and a higher level of literacy. New art forms appeared. The invention of printing created an audience and an insatiable demand for writers to supply new tastes not just for poetry and fiction but for comment and criticism. Literature, in particular, saw the rise of a new form of fiction, the novel, in the seventeenth and eighteenth centuries. Out of this ferment emerged a strikingly different aesthetic.

The metaphysics of Aristotle and neo-Platonic theories of knowledge and reality made the empirical world only a first stage to a higher, spiritual understanding. The seventeenth and eighteenth centuries marked a shift away from neo-Platonism and medieval scholastic theories. Perhaps the most important element in this shift was the new science of Kepler, Galileo, Descartes, and Newton. The rise of the new science created a different standard, empirical evidence, and a new focus of attention, the individual experience of an observer. In philosophy, both the empiricists, led by John Locke, and the rationalists, led by Gottfried Leibniz and René Descartes, agreed in turning inward to the individual mind as the arbiter of knowledge. Such shifts in philosophical direction are never clear-cut or simple, of course. Neo-Platonism remained influential. Aristotelianism, particularly in the form that Aristotle's works had been interpreted by Thomas Aquinas, continued to contest the field. But by the latter half of the seventeenth century, the intellectual world had changed, though many did not recognize the change. Within that context, new theories of art and the aesthetic took shape.

Modern aesthetics is, first of all, an aesthetics of individual experiences of discrete objects. Observers have experiences through their senses. So thinkers such as Anthony Ashley Cooper, the third Earl of Shaftesbury, turned to an aesthetic sense as the source of aesthetic experience. The five ordinary senses were supplemented by the postulation of a sense of beauty and a moral sense that responds to aesthetic and moral qualities in what is observed. In its early forms, claims for the existence of an aesthetic and moral sense were tentative. Neo-Platonic language about order, harmony, and beauty continued to be the more common mode of description of the experience of art, beauty, and the good. Increasingly, however, that language was turned to more individualistic purposes.

Joshua Reynolds, English, 1723–1792. *Lady Frances Warren* (?),
1759. Kimbell Art Museum, Fort Worth, Texas.

The model for aesthetic sense is not the eye, as usually was the case in the classical world, but the tongue. *Taste* was transformed into an aesthetic term; foremost among the reasons for this shift is the analogy that taste offers for the diversity, privacy, and immediacy of the kinds of experience that art and beauty produce. When I taste something, I experience that taste without having to think about it. It is my taste in a way that cannot be denied. If something tastes salty to me, no one can make me believe that it doesn't. Yet someone else may have a different experience. Tastes that one person finds pleasant may not please another, and nothing that I can say or do will change that situation. The experience of art and beauty seemed to many early modern philosophers and critics to be exactly like that.

Modern writers on aesthetics struggled to overcome the evident subjectivity of their starting point. Once individual ideas became the criteria, as they did for Locke, or the individual thinking subject took precedence, as it did for Descartes, each person's experience stood on an equal footing. Aesthetic response is the most variable form of experience. It seemingly is unchecked by any failures of prediction or practical consequences. Science and morality are corrected by their results. If what scientists predict will happen does not happen, their theories are refuted. If a moral theory leads to suffering, it is a bad theory. In contrast, experiences of art and beauty are personal and matters of taste, so they need no correction. But then they provide no principles, either. To the early modern writers on aesthetics, taste seemed the perfect way to describe this situation. What one's taste approved could not be questioned.

In addition to taste itself, the problems of aesthetics were multiplied by the chaos of new forms, which created new demands in art and literature during the period known by historians as the Enlightenment. One way to control taste would be to have a reasonably homogeneous art world. As long as most consumers of art think more or less alike, differences in taste will be minimized. But in the seventeenth and eighteenth centuries, many new consumers of art expressed their preferences and tastes, and they did not think alike. Artists and writers struggled to find rules that would guide their practice, but many of the most successful artists were the ones who broke the rules. So a struggle ensued in aesthetics between the quest for guiding rules within an empirical context and the constant push for new forms. Creativity eventually became a value in itself.

Beauty was a function of the order and harmony of the cosmos in classical and medieval theories. Nature could exemplify beauty because it reflected the greater cosmological order. When modern writers spoke of natural beauty, they began to associate it with sensual experiences of nature. Those experiences could be enhanced by arrangement and by associations with art. Modern theories replaced the clear priority that nature had over art in classical theories of imitation with expectations about nature that often make it difficult to tell which comes first, art or nature. Nowhere is this ambiguity clearer than in the seventeenth- and eighteenth-century taste for landscape and the picturesque. Painters looked for views that met aesthetic standards. A subgenre of literature, the travel narrative, arose to provide vicariously the experience of the picturesque. Nature came to be envisioned as it was depicted in art. It was not long before the obvious step was taken to make nature conform to aesthetic principles. Landscape gardening joined the fine arts. Nature had to be made to look like the pictures painted by artists and the imagined landscapes of writers. If no romantic ruins were available, they could be built.

Theories of taste gradually merged into theories of an aesthetic attitude. Taste tended toward a passive response on the model of perception laid down by Locke. The properties of the object were thought of as acting upon the sensory organs; by analogy, natural beauty and works of art were thought to act on a complex inner sense to produce the characteristic experiences of aesthetic taste. But once authority was ceded to the observer and beauty was no longer conceived of as a property of the organism of the cosmos or of transcendent forms, thinkers began to suggest that the observer could convert external sensory data into aesthetic forms by modifying the way the world is perceived. At that point, the analogy of taste was abandoned and replaced with an active mind whose imaginative powers transform and express both what is perceived and its own powers. The aesthetic became, in a phrase common to a number of later eighteenth-century thinkers, an expression of the powers of the mind itself.

Two characteristics mark the shift to modern aesthetics. The first is the idea of aesthetic experience itself. Aesthetic experience is different and valuable for its own sake. Art and nature alike can supply the means, and the audience participates in converting them to the right "kind" of experience. The second characteristic identifies aesthetic experience with a particular emotion, pleasure. Modern aesthetics becomes fundamentally hedonistic, separating emotional response from the intellect. A number of thinkers, including Immanuel Kant, tried to reunite the intellect and aesthetic judgment, but once Humpty Dumpty has fallen, he cannot be put back together again.

The eighteenth century gave us the modern word *aesthetics*. The term is usually credited to the German philosopher Alexander Baumgarten. Baumgarten was a part of the continental philosophical movement known as rationalism. The rationalists tried to reconcile experience and science with an overarching rational principle that assured order and certainty. Baumgarten's task was to fit the immediate experiences of sense into that rationalist scheme. He coined the word *aesthetics* for the independent realm of feeling that had its own reasons and science. Baumgarten remained a rationalist, but the master of modern aesthetics, Immanuel Kant, adopted his term and made it central to our philosophical vocabulary. The term *aesthetics* captures perfectly an area of feeling, the peculiar pleasures of art and nature that are studied and valued for their own sake. For both rationalists and empiricists, experience became fundamental to the ability to know anything. Since aesthetics appealed directly to sense, it also could be understood as a new form of knowledge. Sense and knowledge, rules for producing art and ways of experiencing it, and the quest for standards in a chaotic new field dominated modern aesthetics.

The selections in this section focus on the formative stages of modern aesthetics. Because of the way aesthetics develops, one would certainly be justified in looking to poetry, literary criticism, and art history for alternative selections. But the central achievement of early modern aesthetics was to give a philosophical form to aesthetics as a discipline within philosophy. Francis Hutcheson began that systematic task; David Hume confronted the problems that the increasing subjectivism of aesthetics raised; and Immanuel Kant took up Hume's challenge and laid down the foundations that Hegel, the German Idealists, and the Romantics each developed.

Francis Hutcheson

· · · · · · · · · · · · · · · · · ·

Francis Hutcheson (1694–1746) was born at Drumalig in Ireland. His grandfather and father were Presbyterian ministers from Scotland who had moved to Northern Ireland to establish and maintain the Protestant religion. Hutcheson was educated by his grandfather and, as was the common practice for Irish Calvinists at that time, at the University of Glasgow in Scotland. At Glasgow, Hutcheson was exposed to a more liberal Calvinism, the new light theology. When he returned to Ireland as a minister, his preaching seemed too liberal for his congregation, and he soon moved to Dublin, where he taught school. While in Dublin, Hutcheson formed a philosophical society and began to write about ethics and philosophy.

In 1730, Hutcheson was appointed to a chair at Glasgow University. His philosophical writings were already well known. During the eighteenth century, conformity to the articles of faith of the Church of England was a requirement for government office and education in England. Scotland had its own established church, however, and offered an alternative to English dissenters. Glasgow was an important institution not only for Scottish Calvinist students but also for English students excluded from Oxford and Cambridge because of their religion. When Hutcheson first arrived at Glasgow, some of these students asserted themselves to insist that Hutcheson teach them moral philosophy. He continued to appeal to a wide range of students and influenced the more "enlightened" circles of Scottish Presbyterian ecclesiastical politics. Hutcheson remained at Glasgow teaching moral philosophy for the remainder of his life. He exerted considerable influence on the educational organization of the university. As a professor of philosophy, he was able to stay clear of the more serious theological controversies that plagued Scottish Calvinism. His own moderate positions were not so unorthodox as to provoke extreme attacks, but they were sufficiently forward looking to attract intellectual admiration from a wide circle of his students and contemporaries.

Hutcheson's writings can be divided into two groups. At Glasgow, he wrote careful, pedagogically sound academic treatises on moral philosophy and educational reforms. These works, in Latin, were addressed to a strictly academic audience. While he was still in Dublin, he already had begun to write for a wider audience, however. He entered into the philosophical and literary controversies of his day, particularly in opposition to the position of Thomas Hobbes who held that all moral actions were self-interested. *An Inquiry into the Original of Our Ideas of Beauty and Virtue* was written while Hutcheson lived in Dublin. It was first published anonymously in London in 1725.

◆   ◆   ◆   ◆   ◆   ◆

In the course of the seventeenth century, a major change in our way of thinking about objects in the world emerged. For Aristotle, experience was the end product of sense, memory, and thought. It was a complex that only the human mind could achieve. For modern philosophers, experience is the starting point; it is equivalent to sense and observation. Nothing else is needed, and no knowledge is possible without experience. That position is called *empiricism*. A more pervasive shift whose roots reach back into the nominalism of the fourteenth century helped produce the change. Nominalists acknowledged that only individuals can be known directly. Empiricism agrees and takes its starting point from individual objects rather than universals. A view of the world is built up from what is immediately evident rather than being derived from what must be or what was always present. Temporally, the present comes to be considered more important than the time of the beginning. The advocates of this new worldview included Descartes and Galileo on the continent and Locke and Newton in Britain. The changes are gradual and complex, but they affect theories of art and what comes in the course of the eighteenth century to be known as the aesthetic along with every other aspect of philosophy.

The third Earl of Shaftesbury was instrumental in applying this new perspective to art. John Locke was closely associated with Shaftesbury's grandfather, the first Earl, and the third Earl learned from Locke while retaining much of the older neo-Platonic language and structure for talking about art. Francis Hutcheson, in turn, attributed the inspiration for his essay on beauty to Shaftesbury. Consequently, a clear line runs from Locke through Shaftesbury to Hutcheson, whom we may take as the first systematic thinker about art and beauty in the new empiricist tradition.

The most important statement of early empiricist philosophy is found in John Locke's *Essay Concerning Human Understanding*. Locke argued that all of our knowledge comes from simple ideas supplied by sense and combined into complex ideas in the mind. Hutcheson began with a description of ideas and their relation to sense that is based very closely on Locke's description. Hutcheson's treatment differs in detail from Locke's, but Hutcheson took himself to be following Locke closely. All knowledge, on Hutcheson's view, begins with simple ideas provided by sense. The senses are distinguished by their fundamental differences and correspond, except for touch, to different organs. Locke allowed a second source of ideas which he called ideas of reflection and which came from the mind's awareness of its own abilities with respect to simple ideas. For example, I can be aware not only of a color, red, but of my ability to remember what red looked like. The idea that I have of my own power to remember is an idea of reflection. I could not have it without the original idea provided by sense, but my idea of memory is not the same idea as what I remember. From these two sources, all experience and knowledge arise. This theory is a significant break with the past because it eliminates any ideas which are innate. As a result, nothing is implanted in us except abilities. The classical quest for origins and for universal ideas, such as Plato's forms which must be present to everyone, is abandoned as superstition and error. Hutcheson accepted Locke's simple ideas but avoided ideas from reflection. Thus he has an even more restricted empirical base than Locke.

Hutcheson's major contribution was to identify an additional source of ideas in the areas of morals and beauty. This source is also a sense, but it applies to other ideas and complexes of ideas to produce a distinct, immediate response. At some points, Hutcheson treats this response as a new idea in its own right and speaks of beauty as a separate idea. In other places, he treats beauty as the complex of ideas to which one responds. In either case, beauty is not a substantive relation between objects like the classical harmony but a relation between the mind and the causes of the mind's ideas. Hutcheson was careful to claim only that his account applies to human beings. The internal sense might be constituted differently in other beings.

The idea of an internal sense is not new in itself. It appears in the writings of St. Augustine of Hippo at the beginning of the fifth century, for example. There, however, it is merely a check on the mind's application of its operations. God gives all human beings certain ideas. Inner sense lets us perceive them. The internal sense began to be recast by the Earl of Shaftesbury in the seventeenth century. Shaftesbury made it the source of our knowledge of virtue. For Hutcheson, it became the sole source of ideas in the areas of morals and beauty. Thus the internal sense joined the external senses as a source of ideas. Like them, it is immediate and, appropriately understood, beyond doubt. Anyone's internal sense might be mistaken or corrupted in various ways, just as the external senses can be. But we cannot deny the immediate content of our senses. The external senses are right or wrong depending on how the world is. Inner sense refers only to feelings that cannot be doubted, so inner sense cannot be wrong about beauty. It may be confused or obscured. I do not always know clearly exactly what I feel. But when I do know, I know directly.

The internal sense differs from the external senses in two fundamental respects. Hutcheson had to argue carefully that it should be considered a sense at all as a consequence. First, no organ is identified with an internal sense. Touch, too, is "diffused" in its source, but even touch can be localized. The internal sense cannot be. It belongs to the mind, not to the body. Second, an internal sense applies not directly to things but to the ideas of things that already are available to the mind. It is a response primarily to complexes of other ideas supplied by the external senses. In this respect it plays somewhat the same role as Locke's ideas of reflection, but it differs from them in that the internal sense is "about" the other ideas and not about the powers of the mind. Thus, the internal sense operates authoritatively just as external sense does. It is subject to the same kinds of error and has the same kind of evidential weight.

The result of Hutcheson's claims about an internal sense was to place discussions of beauty and art on the same footing as discussions in the sciences. During the eighteenth century, Sir Isaac Newton exercised tremendous influence not just as a scientist but also as a thinker who provided a model for all knowledge. In theology, one result was deism, a theological movement that adopted the idea that the world itself is a machine. Scientific investigations were having great successes. These successes produced a widespread sense of optimism that the Newtonian model could solve all problems. Hutcheson sought the same kind of authority for beauty that experimental science found in the senses by trying to fit the experience of beauty to an internal sense.

The scheme that Hutcheson produced is significant not so much for the results it produced as for the shift in thinking that it fixed. After Hutcheson, only with difficulty can beauty be thought of as a substantial relation built into the structure of the cosmos. Hutcheson concluded that beauty is some feeling raised in us, and that it is traceable, at least as our senses are constructed, to certain causal uniformities in our perception of objects. In the latter respect, Hutcheson proposed the formula of "uniformity amidst variety." Neither uniformity nor variety are unique to Hutcheson. They were used long before in classical formulas. Hutcheson adapted the formula in a new way, however. He understood it as a complex relation of ideas themselves to which we are particularly suited to respond. Thus our response is the real test. That the combination of uniformity and variety is instrumental in producing the response of beauty by means of an internal sense is merely an empirical generalization. If we observe and experiment, our response turns out that way.

The response of beauty is identified with a feeling of pleasure. Thus, the empirical basis for our knowledge of beauty is the feeling itself that each individual has, and that feeling is characterized by pleasure. Hutcheson admitted that some objects or—speaking more carefully—some complexes of ideas might produce no feeling at all, so that the internal sense would produce only indifference to them, but he denied that the internal sense of beauty could produce anything painful. Implicitly, beauty is the feeling of pleasure which is traceable to internal sense. If we have a separate "idea of beauty," it must be constantly conjoined to the characteristic pleasure associated with it. Some of Hutcheson's empirical observations about what produces beauty are more than a little problematic. His empirical method is more important than his results. We are unlikely to accept the comparisons of the beauty of simple figures that Hutcheson laid down. He hoped to develop a kind of mechanics of beauty like Newton's mechanics of objects. That hope proved illusory. But his insistence that the experience provided by sense forms the basis for hypotheses fundamentally changed the basis for aesthetics.

On that empiricist basis, Hutcheson worked out a theory of beauty founded on the individual responder. The feeling produced by sense is the starting point for all reasoning about beauty or art. Whatever produces that feeling is secondary. Nature and art are on the same footing, therefore. They are distinguished on the basis of a prior distinction between absolute beauty, which is traceable directly to a sense response to something, and secondary beauty, which requires comparison. Art can imitate and thus initiate comparison; nature cannot. Art can provide a further source of pleasure and thus a relative beauty that may exceed the absolute beauty produced by a direct response. However, art itself is only one among many possible causes of such responses. Hutcheson included the beauty of theorems, for example. The aesthetics that Hutcheson began subordinates theories of art to theories of aesthetic response. At bottom, art and nature are only alternate means to the same end. Both are equally sources for our internal sense.

Many complications remain for Hutcheson. He appealed to the association of ideas to explain why there is not more unanimity in human aesthetic response. Association was the dominant psychological theory in the mid-eighteenth century. It held that either some subsensory physical connection linked ideas or the similarity of ideas themselves produced similar responses. Either way, ideas could stimulate other ideas. If we have internal senses, then they should produce the same uniformity of responses in aesthetics as external senses do in color perception, for example. But they do not, and the differences are attributed to the differences in the way our experiences are built up and in the associations that overlay the internal sense response.

Hutcheson was not prepared for the relativism that can result from his shifting of authority to individual responses. He was a Calvinist with a strong sense that the world was ordered in a deterministic way. According to his beliefs, we, as human beings, are the beneficiaries of a fortunate overall plan that directs us toward a predetermined end. God's plan assures uniformity except in cases of depravity or predestined damnation. At this early stage in the development of modern aesthetics, a deep optimism about the progressive disappearance of disagreement and error prevailed. Not all later writers shared that optimism, and the relativity of aesthetic response either removed taste from the realm of knowledge or led to more complex attempts to find a standard. But that was in the future. Hutcheson made "taste" in aesthetics more than a metaphor. It is an empirical foundation for what he hoped would be a new science.

From *An Inquiry into the Original of Our Ideas of Beauty and Virtue:* An Inquiry Concerning Beauty, Order, Etc.

Sect. I: *Concerning some Powers of Perception, distinct from what is generally understood by Sensation.*

To make the following observations understood, it may be necessary to premise some definitions, and observations either universally acknowledged, or sufficiently proved by many writers both ancient and modern,[1] concerning our perceptions, called sensations, and the actions of the mind consequent upon them.

Art. 1. Those ideas that are raised in the mind upon the presence of external objects, and their acting upon our bodies, are called sensations. We find that the mind in such cases is passive, and has not power directly to prevent the perception or idea or to vary it at its reception, as long as we continue our bodies in a state fit to be acted upon by the external object.

2. When two perceptions are entirely different from each other, or agree in nothing but the general idea of sensation, we call the powers of receiving those different perceptions, different senses. Thus seeing and hearing denote the different powers of receiving the ideas of colors and sounds. And altho colors have vast differences among themselves, as also have sounds; yet there is a greater agreement about the most opposite colors, than between any color and a sound: Hence we call all colors perceptions of the same sense. All the several senses seem to have their distinct organs, except feeling, which is in some degree diffused over the whole body.

3. The mind has a power of compounding ideas that were received separately, of comparing their objects by means of the ideas, and of observing their relations and proportions; of enlarging and diminishing its ideas at pleasure, or in any certain ration, or degree; and of considering separately each of the simple ideas, which might perhaps have been impressed jointly in the sensation. This last operation we commonly call abstraction.

4. The ideas of substances are compounded of the various simple ideas jointly impressed, when they presented themselves to our senses. We define substances[2] only by enumerating these sensible ideas: And such definitions may raise an idea clear enough of the substance in the mind of one who never immediately perceived the substance; provided he has separately received by his senses all the simple ideas that are in the composition of the complex one of the substance defined: But if he has not received any of these ideas, or wants the senses necessary for the perception of them, no definition can ever raise in him any idea of that sense in which he is deficient.

5. Many of our sensitive perceptions are pleasant, and many painful, immediately, and that without any knowledge of the cause of this pleasure or pain, or how the objects excite it, or are the occasions of it; or without seeing to what further advantage or detriment the use of such objects might tend: Nor would the most accurate knowledge of these things vary either the pleasure or pain of the perception, however it might give a rational pleasure distinct from the sensible; or might raise a distinct joy, from prospect of

---

[1] The most prominent ancient writer on this subject was Aristotle. John Locke was Hutcheson's modern source.

[2] Substance was a basic category in medieval metaphysics. It was the underlying "stuff" that took on essential form. Locke and the empiricists denied that we have any idea of substance apart from the ideas provided by particular senses.

further advantage in the object, or aversion, from apprehension of evil.

6. Hence it follows, that when instruction, education, or prejudice of any kind raise any desire or aversion toward an object, this desire or aversion must be founded upon an opinion of some perfection, or some deficiency in those qualities for perception, of which we have the proper senses. Thus if beauty be desired by one who has not the sense of sight, the desire must be raised by some apprehended regularity of figure, sweetness of voice, smoothness or softness, or some other quality perceivable by the other senses, without relation to the ideas of color. . . .

8. The only pleasure of sense, that our philosophers seem to consider, is that which accompanies the simple ideas of sensation: But there are vastly greater pleasures in those complex ideas of objects, which obtain the names of beautiful, regular, harmonious. Thus every one acknowledges he is more delighted with a fine face, a just picture, than with the view of any one color, were it as strong and lively as possible; and more pleased with a prospect of the sun rising among settled clouds and coloring their edges, with a starry hemisphere, a fine landscape, a regular building; than with a clear blue sky, a smooth sea, or a large open plain, not diversifyed by woods, hills, waters, buildings: And yet even these latter appearances are not quite simple. So in music, the pleasure of fine composition is incomparably greater than that of any one note, how sweet, full, or swelling soever.

9. Let it be observed, that in the following papers, the word beauty is taken for the idea raised in us, and a sense of beauty for our power of receiving this idea. Harmony also denotes our pleasant ideas arising from composition of sounds, and a good ear (as it is generally taken) a power of perceiving this pleasure. In the following sections, an attempt is made to discover what is the immediate occasion of these pleasant ideas, or what real quality in the objects ordinarily excites them.

10. It is of no consequence whether we call these ideas of beauty and harmony, perceptions of the external senses of seeing and hearing, or not. I should rather choose to call our power of perceiving these ideas, an *Internal sense,* were it only for the convenience of distinguishing them from other sensations of seeing and hearing, which men may have without perception of beauty and harmony. It is plain from experience, that many men have, in the common meaning, the senses of seeing and hearing perfect enough; they perceive all the simple ideas separately, and have their pleasures; they distinguish them from each other, such as one color from another, either quite different, or the stronger or fainter of the same color; they can tell in separate notes, the higher, lower, sharper or flatter, when separately sounded; in figures they discern the length, breadth, wideness, of each line, surface, angle; and may be as capable of hearing and seeing at great distances as any men whatsoever: And yet perhaps they shall relish no pleasure in musical compositions, in painting, architecture, natural landscape; or but a very weak one in comparison of what others enjoy from the same objects. This greater capacity of receiving such pleasant ideas we commonly call a fine genius or taste: In music we seem universally to acknowledge something like a distinct sense from the external one of hearing, and call it a good ear; and the like distinction we would probably acknowledge in other affairs, had we also got distinct names to denote these powers of perception by.

11. There will appear another reason perhaps afterwards, for calling this power of perceiving the ideas of beauty, an *Internal Sense,* from this, that in some other affairs, where our external senses are not much concerned, we discern a sort of beauty, very like, in many respects, to that observed in sensible objects, and accompanyed with like pleasure: Such is that beauty perceived in theorems, or universal truths, in general causes, and in some extensive principles of action.

12. Let every one here consider, how different we must suppose the perception to be, with which a poet is transported upon the prospect of any of those objects of natural beauty, which ravish us even in his description; from that cold lifeless conception which we imagine to be in a dull

critic, or one of the virtuosi, without what we call a fine taste. This latter class of men may have greater perfection in that knowledge, which is derived from external sensation; they can tell all the specific differences of trees, herbs, minerals, metals; they know the form of every leaf, stalk, root, flower, and seed of all the species, about which the poet is often very ignorant: And yet the poet shall have a vastly more delightful perception of the whole; and not only the poet, but any man of fine taste. Our external sense may by measuring teach us all the proportions of architecture to the tenth of an inch, and the situation of every muscle in the human body; and a good memory may retain these; and yet there is still something further necessary, not only to make a compleat master in architecture, painting, or statuary, but even a tolerable judge in these works; or to receive the highest pleasure in contemplating them. Since then there are such different powers of perception, where what are commonly called the external senses are the same; since the most accurate knowledge of what the external senses discover, often does not give the pleasure of beauty or harmony, which yet one of a good taste will enjoy at once without much knowledge; we may mostly use another name for these higher and more delightful perceptions of beauty and harmony, and call the power of receiving such impressions, an *Internal Sense*. The difference of the perceptions seems sufficient to vindicate the use of a different name.

13. This superior power of perception is justly called *a sense,* because of its affinity to the other senses in this, that pleasure does not arise from any knowledge of principles, proportions, causes, or of the usefulness of the object; but strikes us at first with the idea of beauty: nor does the most accurate knowledge increase this pleasure of beauty, however it may super-add a distinct rational pleasure from prospects of advantage, or from the increase of knowledge.

14. And further, the ideas of beauty and harmony, like other sensible ideas, are necessarily pleasant to us, as well as immediately so; neither can any resolution of our own, nor any prospect of advantage or disadvantage, vary the beauty or

deformity of an object: For as in the external sensations, no view of interest will make an object grateful, nor detriment, distinct from immediate pain in the perception, make it disagreeable to the sense; so propose the whole world as a reward, or threaten the greatest evil, to make us approve a deformed object, or disapprove a beautiful one; dissimulation may be procured by rewards or threatenings, or we may in external conduct abstain from any pursuit of the beautiful, and pursue the deformed; but our sentiments of the forms, and our perceptions, would continue invariably the same.

15. Hence it plainly appears, that some objects are immediately the occasions of this pleasure of beauty, and that we have senses fitted for perceiving it; and that it is distinct from that joy which arises from self-love upon prospect of advantage: Nay, do not we often see convenience and use neglected to obtain beauty, without any other prospect of advantage in the beautiful form, than the suggesting the pleasant ideas of beauty? [3] Now this shows us, that however we may pursue beautiful objects from self-love, with a view to obtain the pleasures of beauty, as in architecture, gardening, and many other affairs; yet there must be a sense of beauty, antecedent to prospects of this advantage, without which sense, these objects would not be thus advantageous, nor excite in us this pleasure which constitutes them advantageous. Our sense of beauty from objects, by which they are constituted good to us, is very distinct from our desire of them when they are thus constituted: Our desire of beauty may be counter-balanced by rewards or threatenings, but never our sense of it; even as fear of death, or love of life, may make us choose and desire a bitter potion, or neglect those meats which the sense of taste would recommend as pleasant; and yet no prospect of advantage, or fear of evil, can make that potion agreeable to the sense, or meats disagreeable to it, that were not so antecedently to this prospect. Just in the same manner as to the sense of beauty and harmony; that the pursuit of

---

[3] Thomas Hobbes attributed all moral judgments to self-interest. Hutcheson is among many who opposed Hobbes on this point.

such objects is frequently neglected, from prospects of advantage, aversion to labour, or any other motive of self-love, does not prove that we have no sense of beauty, but only that our desire of it may be counter-balanced by a stronger desire: So gold out-weighing silver, is never adduced as a proof that the latter is void of gravity. . . .

17. Beauty is either original, or comparative; or if any like the terms better, absolute, or relative: Only let it be noted, that by absolute or original beauty, is not understood any quality supposed to be in the object, that should of itself be beautiful, without relation to any mind which perceives it: For beauty, like other names of sensible ideas, properly denotes the perception of some mind; so cold, heat, sweet, bitter, denote the sensations in our minds, to which perhaps there is not resemblance in the objects that excite these ideas in us, however we generally imagine that there is something in the object just like our perception. The ideas of beauty and harmony being excited upon our perception of some primary quality, and having relation to figure and time, may indeed have a nearer resemblance to objects, than these sensations that seem not so much any pictures of objects, as modifications of the perceiving mind; and yet were there no mind with a sense of beauty to contemplate objects, I see not how they could be called beautiful. We therefore by absolute beauty understand only that beauty, which we perceive in objects without comparison to any thing external, of which the object is supposed an imitation, or picture; such as that beauty perceived from the works of nature, artificial forms, figures, theorems. Comparative or relative beauty is that which we perceive in objects, commonly considered as imitations or resemblances of something else. . . .

Section II: *Of Original or Absolute Beauty*

1. Since it is certain that we have ideas of beauty and harmony, let us examine what quality in objects excites these ideas, or is the occasion of them. And let it be here observed, that our in-

quiry is only about the qualities that are beautiful to men, or about the foundation of their sense of beauty; for, as was above hinted, beauty has always relation to the sense of some mind; and when we afterwards show how generally the objects that occur to us, are beautiful, we mean agreeable to the sense of men: for as there are not a few objects, which seem no way beautiful to men, so we see a variety of other animals who seem delighted with them; they may have senses otherwise constituted than those of men, and may have the ideas of beauty excited by objects of a quite different form. We see animals fitted for every place; and what to men appears rude and shapeless, or loathsome, may be to them a paradise.

2. That we may more distinctly discover the general foundation or occasion of the ideas of beauty among men, it will be necessary to considered it first in its simpler kinds, such as occurs to us in regular figures; and we may perhaps find that the same foundation extends to all the more complex species of it.

3. Figures that excite in us the ideas of beauty, seem to be those in which there is *uniformity amidst variety*. There are many conceptions of objects that are agreeable upon other accounts, such as grandeur, novelty, sanctity, and some others, that shall be touched at afterwards. But what we call beautiful in objects, to speak in the mathematical style, seems to be in a compound ratio of uniformity and variety; so that where the uniformity of bodies is equal, the beauty is as the variety; and where the variety is equal, the beauty is as the uniformity. This will be plain from examples.

First, the variety increases the beauty in equal uniformity. The beauty of an equilateral triangle is less than that of the square; which is less than that of a pentagon; and this again is surpassed by the hexagon. When indeed the number of sides is much increased, the proportion of them to the radius, or diameter of the figure, is so much lost to our observation, that the beauty does not always increase with the number of sides; and the want of parallelism in the sides of heptagons, and other figures of odd numbers, may also diminish their beauty. So in solids, the icosahedron sur-passes the dodecahedron,[4] and this the octa-hedron, which is still more beautiful than the cube; and this again surpasses the regular pyra-mid: The obvious ground of this, is greater vari-ety with equal uniformity.

The greater uniformity increases the beauty amidst equal variety, in these instances: an equi-lateral triangle, or even an isosceles, surpasses the scalenuum; a square surpasses the rhombus or lozenge, and this again the rhomboides, which yet is still more beautiful than the trapezium, or any figure with irregularly curved sides. So the regular solids vastly surpasses all other solids of equal number of plain surfaces: And the same is observable not only in the five perfectly regular solids, but in all those which have any consider-able uniformity, as cylinders, prisms, pyramids, obelisks; which please every eye more than any rude figures, where there is not unity or resem-blance among the parts. . . .

5. It is the same foundation which we have for our sense of beauty in the works of nature; in every part of the world which we call beautiful, there is vast uniformity amidst almost infinite va-riety. Many parts of the universe seem not at all designed for the use of man; nay, it is but a very small spot with which we have any acquaintance. The figures and motions of the great bodies are not obvious to our senses, but found out by rea-soning and reflection, upon many long obser-vations; and yet as far as we can by sense dis-cover, or by reasoning enlarge our knowledge, and extend our imagination, we generally find the structure, and order, and motion, agreeable to our sense of beauty. Every particular object in nature does not indeed appear beautiful to us; but there is a vast profusion of beauty over most of the objects which occur either to our senses or reasonings upon observation. . . .

14. But in all these instances of beauty let it be observed, that the pleasure is communicated to those who never reflected on this general foun-dation; and that all here alleged is this, that the pleasant sensation arises only from objects, in which there is uniformity amidst variety: We may have the sensation without knowing what is the occasion of it; as a man's taste may suggest ideas of sweets, acids, bitters, though he be igno-rant of the forms of the small bodies, or their mo-tions, which excite these perceptions in him. . . .

Section IV: *Of Relative or Comparative Beauty*

1. If the preceding thoughts concerning the foun-dation of absolute beauty be just, we may easily understand wherein relative beauty consists. All beauty is relative to the sense of some mind per-ceiving it; but what we call relative is that which is apprehended in any object, commonly consid-ered as an imitation of some original: And this beauty is founded on a conformity, or a kind of unity between the original and the copy. The original may be either some object in nature, or some established idea; for if there be any known idea as a standard, and rules to fix this image or idea by, we may make a beautiful imitation. Thus a statuary, painter, or poet, may please us with an Hercules,[5] if his piece retains that grandeur, and those marks of strength, and courage, which we imagine in that hero. And farther, to obtain com-parative beauty alone, it is not necessary that there be any beauty in the original; the imitation of absolute beauty may indeed in the whole make a more lovely piece, and yet an exact imitation shall still be beautiful, though the original were entirely void of it: Thus the deformities of old age in a picture, the rudest rocks or mountains in a landscape, if well represented, shall have abun-dant beauty, though perhaps not so great as if the original were absolutely beautiful, and as well represented. . . .

---

[4] An icosahedron is a solid with twenty faces; a dodecahedron has twelve faces.

[5] In Greek and Roman mythology, Hercules is known primarily for his strength.

5. Concerning that kind of comparative beauty which has a necessary relation to some established idea, we may observe that some works of art acquire a distinct beauty by their correspondence to some universally supposed intention in the artificer, or the persons who employed him: and to obtain this beauty, some times they do not form their works so as to attain the highest perfection of original beauty separately considered; because a composition of this relative beauty, along with some degree of the original kind, may give more pleasure, than a more perfect original beauty separately. Thus we see that strict regularity in laying out gardens in parterres,[6] vistas, parallel walks, is often neglected to obtain an imitation of nature even in some of its wildnesses. And we are more pleased with this imitation especially when the scene is large and spacious, than with the more confined exactness of regular work. So likewise in the monuments erected in honor of deceased heroes, although a cylinder, or prism, or regular solid, may have more original beauty than a very acute pyramid or obelisk, yet the latter pleases more, by answering better the supposed intentions of stability, and being conspicuous. For the same reason cubes, or square prisms, are generally chosen for the pedestals of statues, and not any of the more beautiful solids, which do not seem so secure from rolling. This may be the reason too why columns or pillars look best when made a little taper from the middle, or a third from the bottom, that they may not seem top-heavy and in danger of falling.

6. The like reason may influence artists, in many other instances, to depart from the rules of original beauty, as above laid down. And yet this is not argument against our sense of beauty being founded as was above explained, on uniformity amidst variety, but only an evidence that our sense of beauty of the original kind may be varied and over balanced by another kind of beauty. . . .

---

[6] *Parterres* are patterned walks and beds in a garden. Landscape gardening was included among the fine arts by most eighteenth-century writers concerned with aesthetics.

Section VI: *Of the Universality of the Sense of Beauty among Men*

1. We before insinuated that all beauty has a relation to some perceiving power; and consequently since we know not the variety of senses which may be among animals, there is no form of nature concerning which we can pronounce that it has no beauty; for it may still please some perceiving power. But our Inquiry is confined to men; and before we examine the universality of this sense of beauty, or agreement in approving uniformity, it may be proper to consider, if as the other senses which give us pleasure do also give us pain, so this sense of beauty does make some objects disagreeable to us, and the occasion of pain. That many objects give no pleasure to our sense is obvious, many are certainly void of beauty: but then there is no form which seems necessarily disagreeable of itself, when we dread no other evil from it, and compare it with nothing better of the kind. Many objects are naturally displeasing, and distasteful to our external senses, as well as others pleasing and agreeable; as smells, tastes, and some separate sounds: but for our sense of beauty, no decomposition of objects which give not unpleasant simple ideas, seems positively unpleasant or painful of itself, had we never observed any thing better of the kind. Deformity is only the absence of beauty, or deficient in the beauty expected in any species: Thus bad music pleases rustics who never heard any better, and the finest ear is not offended with tuning the instruments if it be not too tedious, where no harmony is expected; and yet much smaller dissonancy shall offend amidst the performance, where harmony is expected. A rude heap of stones is no way offensive to one who shall be displeased with irregularity in architecture, where beauty was expected. And had there been a species of that form which we call now ugly or deformed, and had we never seen or expected greater beauty, we should have received no disgust from it, although the pleasure would not have been so great in this form as in those we now admire. Our sense of beauty seems designed to give us positive pleasure, but

not positive pain or disgust, any further than what arises from disappointment. . . .

3. We shall see afterwards, that association of ideas make objects pleasant, and delightful, which are not naturally apt to give any such pleasures; and the same way the casual conjunctions of ideas may give a disgust, where there is nothing disagreeable in the form itself. And this is the occasion of many fantastic aversions to figures of some animals, and to some other forms: Thus swine, serpents of all kinds, and some insects really beautiful enough, are beheld with aversion by many people, who have got some accidental ideas associated to them. And for distastes of this kind, there is no other account can be given.

4. But as to the universal agreement of mankind in their sense of beauty from uniformity amidst variety, we must consult experience; and as we allow all men reason, since all men are capable of understanding simple arguments, tho few are capable of complex demonstrations; so in this case it must be sufficient to prove this sense of beauty universal, if all men are better pleased with uniformity in the simpler instances than the contrary, even when there is no advantage observed attending it; and likewise if all men according as their capacity enlarges, so as to receive and compare more complex ideas, do further extend their delight in uniformity, and are pleased with its more complex kinds, both original and relative. . . .

11. The association of ideas above hinted at, is one great cause of the apparent diversity of fancies in the sense of beauty, as well as in the external senses; and often makes men have an aversion to objects of beauty, and a liking of others void of it, but under different conceptions than those of beauty or deformity. And here it may not be improper to give some instances of some of these associations. The beauty of trees, their cool shades, and their aptness to conceal from observation, have made groves and woods the usual retreat to those who love solitude, especially to the religious, the pensive, the melancholy, and the amorous. And do not we find that we have so joined the ideas of these dispositions of mind

with those external objects, that they always recur to us along with them? The cunning of the heathen priests might make such obscure places the scene of the fictitious appearances of their deities; and hence we join ideas of something divine to them. We know the like effect in the ideas of our churches, from the perpetual use of them only in religious exercises. The faint light in Gothic buildings has had the same association of a very foreign idea, which our poet[7] shews in his epithet:

—A Dim religious Light.

In like manner it is known, that often all the circumstances of actions or places, or dresses of persons, or voice or song, which have occurred at any time together, when we were strongly affected by any passion, will be so connected that any one of these will make all the rest recur. And this is often the occasion both of great pleasure and pain, delight and aversion to many objects, which of themselves might have been perfectly indifferent to us; but these approbations, or distastes are remote from the ideas of beauty, being plainly different ideas.

Study Questions

1. What are sensations? What is the role of the mind with respect to sensations?
2. What pleasures accompany ideas?
3. What is Hutcheson's definition of *beauty*?
4. What does Hutcheson mean by *internal sense*? Why is it called a sense?
5. Hutcheson argues that the universality of an internal sense of beauty is demonstrated by the uniformity of responses to simple figures. Try comparing some nongeometrical figures with respect to their uniformity and variety. What complications arise?
6. What kind of objects stimulate the sense of beauty?

---

[7]John Milton (1608–1674), *Il Penseroso*.

7. What is the difference between original and comparative beauty? Give examples.

8. Does Hutcheson's analogy of an internal sense to sight and taste work equally well for literary and visual examples?

9. Construct Hutcheson's argument that the sense of beauty does not give us pain.

10. What can cause disagreements about the beauty of an object? Explain each potential cause of disagreement.

11. Assume that you do not have the same responses as Hutcheson to theorems. How would the association of ideas explain the differences?

12. Does the fact that we are mistaken about some aesthetic matters refute Hutcheson? Why or why not?

13. Hutcheson distinguishes beauty from ugliness. They do not work the same way. What is the distinction?

David Hume

· · · · · · · · · ·

DAVID HUME (1711–1776) was a major figure in the Scottish Enlightenment and one of the greatest philosophers to write in English. He was born in 1711 in Edinburgh. The family name, Home, was pronounced Hume, and David changed the spelling while attending Edinburgh University. His elder brother retained the older spelling. Hume entered Edinburgh University at the age of twelve, which was not uncommon at that time. His father had died when he was an infant, and his mother's influence remained strong as long as she lived. Hume was educated in the law, but he was drawn to books and philosophy at an early age. In 1729, he underwent some kind of mental crisis that remains a matter of conjecture. It produced both a mental depression and a remarkable physical change. Hume went from being lean and raw-boned to quite heavy in a short period. He sought to escape from his depressed mental state first by turning to business in Bristol, and then by withdrawing to France.

During this first period in France, Hume wrote his great philosophical work, *A Treatise of Human Nature*. It was written while Hume was still in his twenties and published in 1739–1740. Hume was ambitious for philosophical and literary fame. John Locke had transformed English philosophy with his *Essay Concerning Human Understanding*. Hume hoped to do no less. Instead, his *Treatise* met with a little hostility and considerable indifference. Hume was forced to look elsewhere to establish his reputation.

As the second son of a landed Scottish family, Hume belonged to the gentry, but he did not have the money to support the literary life to which he aspired. He held a number of positions as a tutor, military lawyer, and diplomatic secretary before he was able to establish his literary reputation. He finally gained financial independence not as a result of his philosophical work but as a diplomat and historian. His *History of England* was composed in a series of volumes and achieved a great success. It earned him the money to set himself up in Edinburgh, and, equally importantly, it established his reputation as one of the leading intellectuals and popular writers of the mid-eighteenth century. While he served as the secretary to the English ambassador to France, Hume was lionized by the French salons. He achieved a popularity that he thoroughly enjoyed, and he maintained strong ties with France throughout his life. With the success of the *History of England,* he was able to continue writing literary essays and to recast the *Treatise* in a more accessible form as *An Enquiry Concerning Human Understanding* and *An Enquiry*

Concerning the Principles of Morals. The essay "Of the Standard of Taste" first appeared in 1757 and belongs to this period of literary productivity.

Hume developed a circle of friends in Edinburgh, and though he was drawn to London from time to time, particularly by his publishers, he belonged to the Scottish Enlightenment more than to London society. Hume's reputation was that of a skeptic and atheist. He was widely attacked and deplored by the religious establishment of his day. He held a post for a time as librarian to the advocates' (lawyers) library in Edinburgh, but he was denied appointment to the university by ecclesiastical opposition. Hume managed to disarm all but the most conservative of his opponents by his personal manner, however. Those who abhorred his positions enjoyed his company. Even a famous incident in which the French philosopher-writer Jean-Jacques Rousseau accused Hume of persecuting him after Hume had extended his hospitality to Rousseau, who was exiled in England, could not seriously damage Hume's reputation for goodwill and personal virtue. Hume continued to lead a literary life in Edinburgh until his death in 1776. His last major work, *Dialogues Concerning Natural Religion,* could not be published until after his death because of its skepticism about revealed religion. James Boswell, whose life of Samuel Johnson is one of the great biographical works of English literature, visited Hume, who was dying. Boswell was appalled that Hume, even facing death, retained his skeptical positions and seemed unaffected by fear of dying.

Perception does not vary much from one individual to another. Each of us sees very much what anyone else in a similar position would see. Perspective varies, of course, and the vision of some people is sharper than that of others. By and large, however, we rely on our senses because our responses are relatively uniform. The empiricist theory of knowledge depends on what the senses initially supply. So the reliability of the senses is one of the intuitive supports for the claim that all knowledge is ultimately traceable to sense experience. Locke cast this empiricism in terms of "ideas." Experience produces individual ideas, and those ideas are the basis of all knowledge. David Hume saw the theoretical weakness in the early empiricist way of ideas, however. If everything is traced back to ideas, the contingency of those ideas is inescapable. The only thing individuals have access to are their own ideas. Both the external world and other minds appear only as ideas to an individual mind. Empiricism is threatened with solipsism and skepticism. Solipsism arises when everything is reduced to a single point of view or a single observer. It says, in effect, "I am all that I can know." Its counterpart with respect to the external world is skepticism. Skeptics doubt that any belief can be confirmed. Everything is reduced to uncertainty. Hume knew that we never act as if we believe in either solipsism or skepticism, but if empiricism leads to those conclusions, that would be a strong reason to reject the empiricist thesis.

In his major works, *A Treatise of Human Nature* and the *Enquiries Concerning Human Understanding and Concerning the Principles of Morals,* Hume explored the difficulties of earlier empiricism in detail. He did not conclude that it was wrong. Hume remained firmly within the empiricist camp because he could find no starting point other than experience. But he raised questions indicating that the claim that ideas alone are sufficient for certainty of knowledge is exaggerated. More modest claims about the extent of knowledge are all that can be sustained. We have a working knowledge of the world and other minds, and we can know and respect the limits of human knowledge. We are guided by our feelings even in the arguments that we take seriously. Those limits, in themselves, should make us more tolerant and less prone to exaggerated claims. Hume remained optimistic about the ability of science to guide progress in human knowledge. But knowledge itself will stop short of certainty, and emotion and feeling have a place even in reasoning.

In the area of morals, and especially in the area of the arts, the whole empiricist model seemed to a careful thinker like Hume to be in danger of breaking down. The key aesthetic term for Hume is *taste*. It indicates that in the arts, we rely on a faculty that operates as the senses do. Taste supplies ideas of the same kind as the other senses. If that were all, taste would be subject to the same limits on certainty as sight or hearing. Individual taste might be mistaken, and perspective and perceptual acuity would introduce minor variations. Since taste supplies ideas, those ideas would have the same empirical limits imposed on all ideas by the necessity of their belonging to some individual mind. In itself, that would be only a limitation on certainty just as the conclusions of scientists are limited to probable rather than certain results.

Unfortunately, the faculty of taste as it applies to aesthetics differs from our natural senses. Unlike Hutcheson, Hume did not believe that the faculty of taste constituted a full internal sense like the other senses. Hume sometimes speaks of an internal sense, but it is not reliable. Human beings do not agree in their taste for beauty to nearly the same degree that they do in sight or hearing or touch or physical taste. Virtually everyone can tell the white powder salt from the visually similar white powder sugar by their taste. If someone is unable to distinguish sweet from salty, a physiological or psychological explanation is always available in principle. But two paintings that follow all of the same rules may produce radically different responses, and the same painting may seem beautiful to the taste of one observer and indifferent or ugly to another. No corresponding explanation is available. Each observer finds his or her own taste satisfactory. Such disagreement is the rule, not the exception.

Variation of taste is not the sole cause of the problem. After all, we could just be tolerant and grant people their own taste. But such variations make it doubtful that the empiricist's claims for knowledge based on sense can be extended to the realm of the aesthetic. According to Hume, the relation of cause and effect itself depends on regularity. The idea of a cause arises only from the constant, regular appearance of a succession of ideas. Without that regularity, no inference from the idea to the object as the cause of the idea is possible. A taste so variable that it produces no regularities would be no different from random ideas which cannot be traced back to a cause. Beauty cannot be assigned to a painting unless the effects of the painting are regular. Hutcheson had concluded that beauty was only an idea raised in us. Even then, we do not respond uniformly. The movie I like today may seem boring the next time that I see it. At best, taste appears highly individual and idiosyncratic. At worst, it is no different from daydreams.

Thus, when Hume took up the question of critical standards, he was not just considering a minor problem about why people disagree. A standard of taste is needed not just to produce critical conformity. Unless some standard of taste is available, the whole concept of taste is in jeopardy. Hume's reasoning is straightforward. The empirical fact is that people disagree widely in matters of taste. If taste is a sense, people should not disagree so widely. Empirically, we know that people do maintain standards. At the same time that they grant the subjectivity of taste, they hold fast to judgments based on taste. So unless there is a standard of taste, a hopeless confusion arises—we act as if we have a standard while admitting that we do not! The only honest thing to do would be to give up judgments of taste altogether. Taste would be reduced to nothing more than personal preference—chocolate or vanilla. But even that would not be the end. Such personal preference would be only about an individual's state of mind, so aesthetic experiences would have nothing to do with knowledge at all. As judgments, they would be impossible. A good part of the language we use about art and nature would have to be given up as nonsense.

The criticism of taste is an empiricist criticism. The facts are that people disagree and make judgments. The solution must be equally empirical. It cannot appeal to the ideas of taste directly (as Hutcheson implicitly did with his standard of uniformity amidst variety) because everyone's taste is equal as far as its ability to produce ideas is concerned. If someone finds something beautiful, that person cannot be convinced that the object should not be called beautiful; to be so convinced would directly contradict the person's immediate experience that the object is beautiful. The idea by itself cannot refute itself. If ideas are the basis of knowledge, only ideas provide a standard. So if there is a standard, some way must be found to appeal to ideas without appealing solely to one's own ideas.

Hume's solution is to set up an empirical standard for those who have ideas. Judge the qualifications of judges. Such qualifications are judged by their ability to exhibit the regularity that other scientific judgments exhibit. Uniformities are found in judgments of taste that are exhibited by critics and artists. They come in two ways. One is over time: while the immediate art world is chaotic, the past has sorted itself to a much greater degree. The second is in standards: one may disagree whether a particular object satisfies some standard or other, but some standards themselves are very widely held. Those works that I find beautiful, harmonious, and profound are also good. We may disagree about whether x is beautiful, but we agree that being beautiful is a desirable property for x to produce. Taken together, these two areas of regularity are sufficient for us to be able to test the kinds of qualifications that judges must have to perceive aesthetically and report accurately on their taste.

Hume thus arrives at a list of qualifications, not of judgments of taste but of the judges. Such judges must be of good sense and delicate imagination, free of prejudice, of wide education and practiced experience for their judgments to have standing. These qualifications are established by examining the judges. Some judges have produced judgments that exhibit regularities over time and generality of standards. We recognize their judgments as uniform. Those judges are the ones who can be relied upon. Whether a judge has these qualifications can be empirically investigated, as illustrated by Hume's famous story of Sancho Panza's kinsmen who taste iron and leather in a barrel of wine. Their taste is confirmed when the barrel is emptied and an iron key with a leather thong is found. A trustworthy wine taster's palate is confirmed by subsequent experience, but the only basis for the wine taster's judgment is how the wine tasted. The existence of such judges, in turn, confirms that taste is indeed the foundation for aesthetic knowledge.

Having shifted the ground, Hume was content to let the matter rest. Two further points deserve attention, however. First, judgments of taste remain intuitive. *Judgment* in this context does not mean just saying that something is good or bad, beautiful or ugly. That is only a part of judgment. A judgment of taste is primarily the production of an idea about an object understood in some way. Someone who looks at a painting and only sees color on canvas lacks judgment. But if someone sees a painting, taste is engaged. Whether the painting is liked or disliked, a judgment has been made by the act of exercising the faculty of taste itself. So judgments of taste are immediate. I do not say that *x* is beautiful and then decide that I like it. Liking and finding something beautiful are the same act. As soon as taste is active, it is judging. Second, rules play a role, but they are empirical rules. Eighteenth-century writers and artists such as William Hogarth and Sir Joshua Reynolds agreed on the need for rules in art. Such rules could be taken as prescriptive, and they were by lesser artists. But Hume's approach to rules makes it clear that they are only rules because empirical investigation discloses that they are what works. Such rules come close to the universal validity of Newton's laws of motion. Like those laws, they are essentially empirical generalizations. Anyone is free to modify the rules, just as anyone is free to try to fly. If they succeed, then they will have discovered a more basic understanding of how the world is structured. Rules are only rules because our experience verifies them.

Hume shifted the ground for modern aesthetics. On the one hand, he confirmed the empirical hypothesis that beauty could be located only in the experience of an observer. Even ideas and forms are known only in experience. On the other hand, taste becomes a much more complex, subjective, and tenuous basis for aesthetic judgments than it at first appeared to be. Initially, empiricists thought that taste could be just another sense. Hume recognized the problems that sense and ideas raised if they are made the starting point for all knowledge. His solution was practical. Limit the claims, and judge the judges. Later writers find that advice hard to follow.

Of the Standard of Taste

THE GREAT VARIETY OF TASTE, as well as of opinion, which prevails in the world, is too obvious not to have fallen under every one's observation. Men of the most confined knowledge are able to remark a difference of taste in the narrow circle of their acquaintance, even where the persons have been educated under the same government, and have early imbibed the same prejudices. But those, who can enlarge their view to contemplate distant nations and remote ages, are still more surprized at the great inconsistency and contrariety. We are apt to call *barbarous* whatever departs widely from our own taste and apprehension: But soon find the epithet of reproach retorted on us. And the highest arrogance and self-conceit is at last startled, on observing an equal assurance on all sides, and scruples, amidst such a contest of sentiment, to pronounce positively in its own favour.

As this variety of taste is obvious to the most careless enquirer; so will it be found, on examination, to be still greater in reality than in appearance. The sentiments of men often differ with regard to beauty and deformity of all kinds, even while their general discourse is the same. There are certain terms in every language, which import blame, and others praise; and all men, who use the same tongue, must agree in their application of them. Every voice is united in applauding elegance, propriety, simplicity, spirit in writing; and in blaming fustian,[1] affectation, coldness, and a false brilliancy: But when critics come to particulars, this seeming unanimity vanishes; and it is found, that they had affixed a very different meaning to their expressions. In all matters of opinion and science, the case is opposite: The difference among men is there oftener found to lie in generals than in particulars; and to be less in reality than in appearance. An explanation of the terms commonly ends the controversy; and the disputants are surprized to find, that they had been quarreling, while at bottom they agreed in their judgment.

Those who found morality on sentiment, more than on reason, are inclined to comprehend ethics under the former observation, and to maintain, that, in all questions which regard conduct and manners, the difference among men is really greater than at first sight it appears. It is indeed obvious, that writers of all nations and all ages concur in applauding justice, humanity, magnanimity, prudence, veracity; and in blaming the opposite qualities. Even poets and other authors, whose compositions are chiefly calculated to please the imagination, are yet found, from Homer[2] down to Fenelon,[3] to inculcate the same moral percepts, and to bestow their applause and blame on the same virtues and vices. This great unanimity is usually ascribed to the influence of plain reason; which, in all these cases, maintains similar sentiments in all men, and prevents those controversies, to which the abstract sciences are so much exposed. So far as the unanimity is real, this account may be admitted as satisfactory: But we must also allow that some part of the seeming harmony in morals may be accounted for from the very nature of language. The word *virtue,* with its equivalent in every tongue, implies praise; as that of *vice* does blame: And no one, without the most obvious and grossest impropriety, could affix reproach to a term, which in general acceptation is understood in a good sense; or bestow applause, where the idiom requires disapprobation. Homer's general percepts, where he delivers any such, will never be controverted; but it is obvious, that, when he draws particular pictures of

---

[1] Fustian is a pompous, ridiculous, overwritten style.

[2] Homer is the Greek epic poet, author of the *Iliad* and the *Odyssey.*
[3] Fenelon (1651–1715) was a French theologian, archbishop, and writer. His poem *Telemaque* treats the relation of Odysseus and his son, Telemachus, as a moral fable.

manners and represents heroism in Achilles[4] and prudence in Ulysses,[5] he intermixes a much greater degree of ferocity in the former, and of cunning and fraud in the latter, than Fenelon would admit of. The sage Ulysses in the Greek poet seems to delight in lies and fictions, and often employs them without any necessity or even advantage: But his more scrupulous son, in the French epic writer, exposes himself to the most imminent perils, rather than depart from the most exact line of truth and veracity.

The admirers and followers of the Alcoran[6] insist on the excellent moral percepts interspersed throughout that wild and absurd performance. But it is to be supposed, that the Arabic words, which correspond to the English, equity, justice, temperance, meekness, charity, were such as, from the constant use of that tongue, must always be taken in a good sense; and it would have argued the greatest ignorance, not of morals, but of language, to have mentioned them with any epithets, besides those of applause and approbation. But would we know, whether the pretended prophet had really attained a just sentiment of morals? Let us attend to his narration; and we shall soon find, that he bestows praise on such instances of treachery, inhumanity, cruelty, revenge, bigotry, as are utterly incompatible with civilized society. No steady rule of right seems there to be attended to; and every action is blamed or praised, so far only as it is beneficial or hurtful to the true believers.

The merit of delivering true general percepts in ethics is indeed very small. Whoever recommends any moral virtues, really does no more than is implied in the terms themselves. That people, who invented the word *charity*, and used it in a good sense, inculcated more clearly and much more efficaciously, the precept, *be chari-*

table, than any pretended legislator or prophet, who should insert such a *maxim* in his writings. Of all expressions, those, which, together with their other meaning, imply a degree either of blame or approbation, are the least liable to be perverted or mistaken.

It is natural for us to seek a *Standard of Taste;* a rule, by which the various sentiments of men may be reconciled; at least, a decision, afforded, confirming one sentiment, and condemning another.

There is a species of philosophy, which cuts off all hopes of success in such an attempt, and represents the impossibility of ever attaining any standard of taste. The difference, it is said, is very wide between judgment and sentiment.[7] All sentiment is right; because sentiment has a reference to nothing beyond itself, and is always real, wherever a man is conscious of it. But all determinations of the understanding are not right; because they have a reference to something beyond themselves, to wit, real matter of fact; and are not always conformable to that standard. Among a thousand different opinions which different men may entertain of the same subject, there is one, and but one, that is just and true; and the only difficulty is to fix and ascertain it. On the contrary, a thousand different sentiments, excited by the same object, are all right: Because no sentiment represents what is really in the object. It only marks a certain conformity or relation between the object and the organs or faculties of the mind; and if that conformity did not really exist, the sentiment could never possibly have being. Beauty is no quality in things themselves: It exists merely in the mind which contemplates them; and each mind perceives a different beauty. One person may even perceive deformity, where another is sensible of beauty; and every individual ought to acquiesce in his own sentiment, without pretending to regulate those of others. To seek the real beauty, or real deformity, is as fruitless an enquiry, as to pretend to ascertain the real sweet or real bitter. According to the disposition of the organs, the same object may be both sweet and

---

[4] Achilles is the greatest of the Greek warriors in the Trojan War. His anger sets the events of the *Iliad* in motion.

[5] Hume uses the Latin form for the name of Odysseus. Odysseus' greatest characteristics were his cunning and his ability to lie.

[6] The Alcoran is the Qur'an (Koran), the scriptural text delivered to Muhammad and sacred to Islam. Hume shares the eighteenth-century European disdain for religions other than Christianity, but his irony extends to Christianity as well.

[7] Hume means by *sentiment* the whole range of passions, emotions, and feelings that we have whether we choose to or not.

bitter; and the proverb has justly determined it to be fruitless to dispute concerning tastes. It is very natural, and even quite necessary, to extend this axiom to mental, as well as bodily taste; and thus common sense, which is so often at variance with philosophy, especially with the sceptical kind, is found, in one instance at least, to agree in pronouncing the same decision.

But though this axiom, by passing into a proverb, seems to have attained the sanction of common sense; there is certainly a species of common sense which opposes it, at least serves to modify and restrain it. Whoever would assert an equality of genius and elegance between Ogilby[8] and Milton,[9] or Bunyan[10] and Addison,[11] would be thought to defend no less an extravagance, than if he had maintained a mole-hill to be as high as Teneriffe,[12] or a pond as extensive as the ocean. Though there may be found persons, who give the preference to the former authors; no one pays attention to such a taste; and we pronounce with scruple the sentiment of these pretended critics to be absurd and ridiculous. The principle of the natural equality of tastes is then totally forgot and while we admit it on some occasions, where the objects seem near an equality, it appears an extravagant paradox, or rather a palpable absurdity, where objects so disproportioned are compared together.

It is evident that none of the rules of composition are fixed by reasonings *a priori*,[13] or can be esteemed abstract conclusions of the understanding, from comparing those habitudes and rela-

tions of ideas which are eternal and immutable. Their foundation is the same with that of all the practical sciences, experience; nor are they any thing but general observations, concerning what has been universally found to please in all countries and in all ages. Many of the beauties of poetry and even of eloquence are founded on falsehood and fiction, on hyperboles, metaphors, and an abuse or perversion of terms from their natural meaning. To check the sallies of the imagination, and to reduce every expression to geometrical truth and exactness, would be the most contrary to the laws of criticism; because it would produce a work, which, by universal experience, has been found the most insipid and disagreeable. But though poetry can never submit to exact truth, it must be confined by rules of art, discovered to the author either by genius or observation. If some negligent or irregular writers have pleased, they have not pleased by their transgressions of rule or order, but in spite of these transgressions: They have possessed other beauties, which were conformable to just criticism; and the force of these beauties has been able to overpower censure, and give the mind a satisfaction superior to the disgust arising from the blemishes. Ariosto[14] pleases; but not by his monstrous and improbable fictions, by his bizarre mixture of the serious and comic styles, by the want of coherence in his stories, or by the continual interruptions of his narration. He charms by the force and clearness of his expression, by the readiness and variety of his inventions, and by his natural pictures of the passions, especially those of the gay and amorous kind: And however his faults may diminish our satisfaction, they are not able entirely to destroy it. Did our pleasure really arise from those parts of his poem, which we denominate faults, this would be no objection to criticism in general: It would only be an objection to those particular rules of criticism, which would establish such circumstances to be faults, and would represent them as universally blameable.

---

[8] John Ogilby (1600–1676) was a minor poet and translator.

[9] John Milton (1608–1674) was, after Shakespeare, acknowledged as the greatest English poet. His *Paradise Lost* and *Paradise Regained* aspire to be the English equivalent of the *Iliad* and *Odyssey*.

[10] John Bunyan (1628–1688) was the author of *Pilgrim's Progress* and other works in the Puritan tradition. His style is intentionally simple and plain and therefore not to the taste of authors like Hume, who would also have disdained his religiosity.

[11] Joseph Addison (1672–1719) was an essayist and poet whose periodical *The Spectator* was considered a model of prose style.

[12] Tenerife (formerly Teneriffe) is a volcanic peak in the Canary Islands.

[13] *A priori* reasoning is based on deductions from given premises or definitions. It requires no reference to empirical facts.

---

[14] Ariosto (1474–1533) was an Italian poet whose epic *Orlando Furioso* continues the story of Roland, the Christian hero who fought against the Moors in Spain.

If they are found to please, they cannot be faults, let the pleasure, which they produce, be ever so unexpected and unaccountable.

But though all the general rules of art are founded only on experience and on the observation of the common sentiments of human nature, we must not imagine, that, on every occasion, the feelings of men will be conformable to the rules. Those finer emotions of the mind are of a very tender and delicate nature, and require the concurrence of many favourable circumstances to make them play with facility and exactness, according to their general and established principles. The least exterior hindrance to such small springs, or the least internal disorder, disturbs their motion, and confounds the operation of the whole machine. When we would make an experiment of this nature, and would try the force of any beauty or deformity, we must choose with care a proper time and place, and bring the fancy to a suitable situation and disposition. A perfect serenity of mind, a recollection of thought, a due attention to the object; if any of these circumstances be wanting, our experiment will be fallacious, and we shall be unable to judge of the catholic and universal beauty. The relation, which nature has placed between the form and the sentiment, will at least be more obscure; and it will require greater accuracy to trace and discern it. We shall be able to ascertain its influence not so much from the operation of each particular beauty, as from the durable admiration, which attends those works, that have survived all the caprices of mode and fashion, all the mistakes of ignorance and envy.

The same Homer, who pleased at Athens and Rome two thousand years ago, is still admired at Paris and London. All the changes of climate,[15] government, religion, and language, have not been able to obscure his glory. Authority or prejudice may give a temporary vogue to a bad poet or orator; but his reputation will never be durable or general. When his compositions are examined by posterity or by foreigners, the enchantment is dissipated, and his faults appear in their true colours. On the contrary, a real genius, the longer his works endure, and the more wide they are spread, the more sincere is the admiration which he meets with. Envy and jealousy have too much place in a narrow circle; and even familiar acquaintance with his person may diminish the applause due to his performances: But when these obstructions are removed, the beauties, which are naturally fitted to excite agreeable sentiments, immediately display their energy; and while the world endures, they maintain their authority over the minds of men.

It appears then, that, amidst all the variety and caprice of taste, there are certain general principles of approbation or blame, whose influence a careful eye may trace in all operations of the mind. Some particular forms or qualities, from the original structure of the internal fabric, are calculated to please, and others to displease; and if they fail of their effect in any particular instance, it is from some apparent defect or imperfection in the organ. A man in a fever would not insist on his palate as able to decide concerning flavours; nor would one, affected with the jaundice, pretend to give a verdict with regard to colours. In each creature, there is a sound and a defective state; and the former alone can be supposed to afford us a true standard of taste and sentiment. If, in the sound state of the organ, there be an entire or a considerable uniformity of sentiment among men, we may thence derive an idea of the perfect beauty; in like manner as the appearance of objects in day-light, to the eye of a man in health, is denominated their true and real colour, even while colour is allowed to be merely a phantasm of the senses.

Many and frequent are the defects in the internal organs, which prevent or weaken the influence of those general principles, on which depends our sentiment of beauty or deformity. Though some objects, by the structure of the mind, be naturally calculated to give pleasure, it

---

[15] Some critics, most notably the Abbe Jean Baptiste Dubos, argued that differences in taste were due to differences in climate: literally, the air we breathe was believed to affect what we find pleasing.

is not to be expected, that in every individual the pleasure will be equally felt. Particular incidents and situations occur, which either throw a false light on the objects, or hinder the true from conveying to the imagination the proper sentiment and perception.

One obvious cause, why many feel not the proper sentiment of beauty, is the want of that *delicacy* of imagination, which is requisite to convey a sensibility of those finer emotions. This delicacy every one pretends to: Every one talks of it; and would reduce every kind of taste or sentiment to its standard. But as our intention in this essay is to mingle some light of the understanding with the feelings of sentiment, it will be proper to give a more accurate definition of delicacy, than has hitherto been attempted. And not to draw our philosophy from too profound a source, we shall have recourse to a noted story in Don Quixote.[16]

It is a good reason, says Sancho to the squire with the great nose, that I pretend to have a judgment in wine: This is a quality hereditary in our family. Two of my Kinsmen were once called to give their opinion of a hogshead, which was supposed to be excellent, being old and of a good vintage. One of them tastes it, considers it; and after mature reflection pronounces the wine to be good, were it not for a small taste of leather, which he perceived in it. The other, after using the same precautions, gives also his verdict in favour of the wine; but with the reserve of a taste of iron, which he could easily distinguish. You cannot imagine how much they were both ridiculed for their judgment. But who laughed in the end? On emptying the hogshead, there was found at the bottom, an old key with a leathern thong tied to it.

The great resemblance between mental and bodily taste will easily teach us to apply this story. Though it be certain, that beauty and deformity,

more than sweet and bitter, are not qualities in objects, but belong entirely to the sentiment, internal or external; it must be allowed, that there are certain qualities in objects, which are fitted by nature to produce those particular feelings. Now as these qualities may be found in a small degree, or may be mixed and confounded with each other, it often happens, that the taste is not affected with such minute qualities, or is not able to distinguish all the particular flavours, amidst the disorder, in which they are presented. Where the organs are so fine, as to allow nothing to escape them; and at the same time so exact as to perceive every ingredient in the composition: This we call delicacy of taste, whether we employ these terms in the literal or metaphorical sense. Here then the general rules of beauty are of use; being drawn from established models, and from the observation of what pleases or displeases, when presented singly and in a high degree: And if the same qualities, in a continued composition and in a smaller degree, affect not the organs with a sensible delight or uneasiness, we exclude the person from all pretensions to this delicacy. To produce these general rules or avowed patterns of composition is like finding the key with the leathern thong; which justified the verdict of Sancho's kinsmen, and confounded those pretended judges who had condemned them. Though the hogshead had never been emptied, the taste of the one was still equally delicate, and that of the other equally dull and languid: But it would have been more difficult to have proved the superiority of the former, to the conviction of every bystander. In like manner, though the beauties of writing had never been methodized, or reduced to general principles; though no excellent models had ever been acknowledged; the different degrees of taste would still have subsisted, and the judgment of one man been preferable to that of another; but it would not have been so easy to silence the bad critic, who might always insist upon his particular sentiment, and refuse to submit to his antagonist. But when we show him an avowed principle of art; when we illustrate this principle by examples, whose operation, from his

---

[16] Miguel de Cervantes' (1547–1616) novel tells of the comic adventures of a knight and his squire, Sancho. Sancho, in turn, relates a story about some kinsmen of his. The story is found in *Don Quixote*, part 2, chapter 13. Hume changes the story somewhat for his own purposes.

own particular taste, he acknowledges to be conformable to the principle; when we prove, that the same principle may be applied to the present case, where he did not perceive or feel its influence: He must conclude, upon the whole, that the faults lies in himself, and that he wants the delicacy, which is requisite to make him sensible of every beauty and every blemish, in any composition or discourse.

It is acknowledged to be the perfection of every sense or faculty, to perceive with exactness its most minute objects, and allow nothing to escape its notice and observation. The smaller the objects are, which become sensible to the eye, the finer is that organ, and the more elaborate its make and composition. A good palate is not tried by strong flavours; but by a mixture of small ingredients, where we are still sensible of each part, notwithstanding its minuteness and its confusion with the rest. In like manner, a quick and acute perception of beauty and deformity must be the perfection of our mental taste; nor can a man be satisfied with himself while he suspects, that any excellence or blemish in a discourse has passed him unobserved. In this case, the perfection of the man, and the perfection of the sense or feeling, are found to be united. A very delicate palate, on many occasions, may be a great inconvenience both to a man himself and to his friends: But a delicate taste of wit or beauty must always be a desirable quality; because it is the source of all the finest and most innocent enjoyments, of which human nature is susceptible. In this decision the sentiments of all mankind are agreed. Whenever you can ascertain a delicacy of taste, it is sure to meet with approbation; and the best way of ascertaining it is to appeal to those models and principles, which have been established by the uniform consent and experience of nations and ages.

But though there be naturally a wide difference in point of delicacy between one person and another, nothing tends further to increase and improve this talent, than *practice* in a particular art, and the frequent survey or contemplation of a particular species of beauty. When objects of any kind are first presented to the eye or imagination, the sentiment, which attends them, is obscure and confused; and the mind is, in a great measure, incapable of pronouncing concerning their merits or defects. The taste cannot perceive the several excellences of the performance; much less distinguish the particular character of each excellency, and ascertain its quality and degree. If it pronounce the whole in general to be beautiful or deformed, it is the utmost that can be expected; and even this judgment, a person, so unpractised, will be apt to deliver with great hesitation and reserve. But allow him to acquire experience in those objects, his feeling becomes more exact and nice: He not only perceives the beauties and defects of each part, but marks the distinguishing species of each quality, and assigns it suitable praise or blame. A clear and distinct sentiment attends him through the whole survey of the objects; and he discerns that very degree and kind of approbation or displeasure, which each part is naturally fitted to produce. The mist dissipates, which seemed formerly to hang over the object: The organ acquires greater perfection in its operations; and can pronounce, without danger of mistake, concerning the merits of every performance. In a word, the same address and dexterity, which practice gives to the execution of any work, is also acquired by the same means, in the judging of it.

So advantageous is practice to the discernment of beauty, that, before we can give judgment on any work of importance, it will even be requisite, that that very individual performance be more than once perused by us, and be surveyed in different lights with attention and deliberation. There is a flutter or hurry of thought which attends the first perusal of any piece, and which confounds the genuine sentiment of beauty. The relation of the parts is not discerned: The true characters of style are little distinguished: The several perfections and defects seem wrapped up in a species of confusion, and present themselves indistinctly to the imagination. Not to mention, that there is a species of beauty, which, as it is florid and superficial, pleases at first; but being found incompatible with a just expression either of reason or passion, soon palls upon the taste, and is then rejected with disdain, at least rated at a much lower value.

It is impossible to continue in the practice of contemplating any order of beauty, without being frequently obliged to form *comparisons* between the several species and degrees of excellence, and estimating their proportion to each other. A man, who has had no opportunity of comparing the different kinds of beauty, is indeed totally unqualified to pronounce an opinion with regard to any object presented to him. By comparison alone we fix the epithets of praise or blame, and learn how to assign the due degree of each. The coarsest daubing contains a certain lustre of colours and exactness of imitation, which are so far beauties, and would affect the mind of a peasant or Indian with the highest admiration. The most vulgar ballads are not entirely destitute of harmony or nature; and none but a person, familiarized to superior beauties, would pronounce their numbers harsh, or narration uninteresting. A great inferiority of beauty gives pain to a person conversant in the highest excellence of the kind, and is far that reason pronounced a deformity: As the most finished object, with which we are acquainted, is naturally supposed to have reached the pinnacle of perfection, and to be entitled to the highest applause. One accustomed to see, and examine, and weigh the several performances, admired in different ages and nations, can only rate the merits of a work exhibited to his view, and assign its proper rank among the productions of genius.

But to enable a critic the more fully to execute this undertaking, he must preserve his mind free from all *prejudice,* and allow nothing to enter into his consideration, but the very object which is submitted to his examination. We may observe, that every work of art, in order to produce its due effect on the mind, must be surveyed in a certain point of view, and cannot be fully relished by persons, whose situation, real or imaginary, is not conformable to that which is required by the performance. An orator addresses himself to a particular audience, and must have a regard to their particular genius, interests, opinions, passions, and prejudices; otherwise he hopes in vain to govern their resolutions, and inflame their affections. Should they even have entertained some prepossessions against him, however unreasonable, he must not overlook this disadvantage; but, before he enters upon the subject, must endeavour to conciliate their affection, and acquire their good graces. A critic of a different age or nation, who should peruse this discourse, must have all these circumstances in his eye, and must place himself in the same situation as the audience, in order to form a true judgment of the oration. In like manner, when any work is addressed to the public, though I should have a friendship or enmity with the author, I must depart from this situation; and considering myself as a man in general, forget, if possible, my individual being and my peculiar circumstances. A person influenced by prejudice, complies not with this condition; but obstinately maintains his natural position, without placing himself in that point of view, which the performance supposes. If the work be addressed to persons of a different age or nation, he makes no allowance for their peculiar views and prejudices; but, full of the manners of his own age and country, rashly condemns what seemed admirable in the eyes of those for whom alone the discourse was calculated. If the work be executed for the public, he never sufficiently enlarges his comprehension, or forgets his interest as a friend or enemy, as a rival or commentator. By this means, his sentiments are perverted; not have the same beauties and blemishes the same influence upon him, as if he had imposed a proper violence on his imagination, and had forgotten himself for a moment. So far his taste evidently departs from the true standard; and of consequence loses all credit and authority.

It is well known, that in all questions, submitted to the understanding, prejudice is destructive of sound judgment, and perverts all operations of the intellectual faculties: It is no less contrary to good taste; nor has it less influence to corrupt our sentiment of beauty. It belongs to *good sense* to check its influence in both cases; and in this respect, as well as in many others, reason, if not an essential part of taste, is at least requisite to the operations of this latter faculty. In all the nobler productions of genius, there is a mutual relation and correspondence of parts; nor can either the beauties or blemishes be perceived by him, whose thought is not capacious enough to comprehend all those parts, and compare them with each other, in order to perceive the consistence and uniformity of the whole. Every work of art has also a certain end or purpose, for which it is calculated; and is to be deemed more or less perfect, as it is more or less fitted to attain this end. The object of eloquence is to persuade, of history to instruct, of poetry to please by means of the passions and the imagination. These ends we must carry constantly in our view, when we peruse any performance; and we must be able to judge how far the means employed are adapted to their respective purposes. Besides, every kind of composition, even the most poetical, is nothing but a chain of propositions and reasonings; not always, indeed, the justest and most exact, but still plausible and specious, however disguised by the colouring of the imagination. The persons introduced in tragedy and epic poetry, must be represented as reasoning, and thinking, and concluding, and acting, suitably to their character and circumstances; and without judgment, as well as taste and invention, a poet can never hope to succeed in so delicate an undertaking. Not to mention, that the same excellence of faculties which contributes to the improvement of reason, the same clearness of conception, the same exactness of distinction, the same vivacity of apprehension, are essential to the operations of true taste, and are its infallible concomitants. It seldom, or never happens, that a man of sense, who has experience in any art, cannot judge of its beauty; and it is no less rare to meet with a man who has a just taste without a sound understanding.

Thus, though the principles of taste be universal, and, nearly, if not entirely the same in all men; yet few are qualified to give judgment on any work of art, or establish their own sentiment

as the standard of beauty. The organs of internal sensation are seldom so perfect as to allow the general principles their full play, and produce a feeling correspondent to those principles. They either labour under some defect, or are vitiated by some disorder; and by that means, excite a sentiment, which may be pronounced erroneous. When the critic has no delicacy, he judges without any distinction, and is only affected by the grosser and more palpable qualities of the object: The finer touches pass unnoticed and disregarded. Where he is not aided by practice, his verdict is attended with confusion and hesitation. Where no comparison has been employed, the most frivolous beauties, such as rather merit the name of defects, are the object of his admiration. Where he lies under the influence of prejudice, all his natural sentiments are perverted. Where good sense is wanting, he is not qualified to discern the beauties of design and reasoning, which are the highest and most excellent. Under some or other of these imperfections, the generality of men labour; and hence a true judge in the finer arts is observed, even during the most polished ages, to be so rare a character: Strong sense, united to delicate sentiment, improved by practice, perfected by comparison, and cleared of all prejudice, can alone entitle critics to this valuable character; and the joint verdict of such, wherever they are to be found, is the true standard of taste and beauty.

But where are such critics to be found? By what marks are they to be known? How distinguish them from pretenders? These questions are embarrassing; and seem to throw us back into the same uncertainty, from which, during the course of this essay, we have endeavoured to extricate ourselves.

But if we consider the matter aright, these are questions of fact, not of sentiment. Whether any particular person be endowed with good sense and a delicate imagination, free from prejudice, may often be the subject of dispute, and be liable to great discussion and enquiry: But that such a character is valuable and estimable will be agreed in by all mankind. Where these doubts occur, men can do no more than in other disputable questions, which are submitted to the under-standing: They must produce the best arguments, that their invention suggests to them; they must acknowledge a true and decisive standard to ex-ist somewhere, to wit, real existence and matter of fact; and they must have indulgence to such as differ from them in their appeals to this standard. It is sufficient for our present purpose, if we have proved, that the taste of all individuals is not upon an equal footing, and that some men in general, however difficult to be particularly pitched upon, will be acknowledged by universal sentiment to have a preference above others.

But in reality the difficulty of finding, even in particulars, the standard of taste, is not so great as it is represented. Though in speculation, we may readily avow a certain criterion in science and deny it is sentiment, the matter is found in prac-tice to be much more hard to ascertain in the for-mer case than in the latter. Theories of abstract philosophy, systems of profound theology, have prevailed during one age: In a successive period, these have been universally exploded: Their ab-surdity has been detected: Other theories and sys-tems have supplied their place, which again gave place to their successors: And nothing has been experienced more liable to the revolutions of chance and fashion than these pretended deci-sions of science. The case is not the same with the beauties of eloquence and poetry. Just expres-sions of passion and nature are sure, after a little time, to gain public applause, which they main-tain for ever. Aristotle, and Plato, and Epicurus,[17] and Descartes,[18] may successively yield to each other: But Terence[19] and Virgil[20] maintain an uni-versal, undisputed empire over the minds of men. The abstract philosophy of Cicero[21] has lost its credit: The vehemence of his oratory is still the object of our admiration.

Though men of delicate taste be rare, they are easily to be distinguished in society, by the sound-ness of their understanding and the superiority of their faculties above the rest of mankind. The ascendant, which they acquire, gives a prevalence to that lively approbation, with which they re-ceive any productions of genius, and renders it generally predominant. Many men, when left to themselves, have but a faint and dubious percep-tion of beauty, who yet are capable of relishing any fine stroke, which is pointed out to them. Every convert to the admiration of the real poet or orator is the cause of some new conversion. And though prejudices may prevail for a time, they never unite in celebrating any rival to the true genius, but yield at last to the force of nature and just sentiment. Thus, though a civilized na-tion may easily be mistaken in the choice of their admired philosopher, they never have been found long to err, in their affection for a favorite epic or tragic author.

But notwithstanding all our endeavours to fix a standard of taste, and reconcile the discor-dant apprehensions of men, there still remain two sources of variation, which are not sufficient indeed to confound all the boundaries of beauty and deformity, but will often serve to produce a difference in the degrees of our approbation or blame. The one is the different humours of par-ticular men; the other, the particular manners and opinions of our age and country. The general principles of taste are uniform in human nature: Where men vary in their judgments, some de-fect or perversion in the faculties may commonly be remarked; proceeding either from prejudice, from want of practice, or want of delicacy; and there is just reason for approving one taste, and condemning another. But where there is such a

---

[17] Epicurus (341–270 B.C.E.) was the founder of the philosophi-cal school known by his name, Epicureanism. It is popularly characterized as holding that the object of life is happiness, but Epicurus defined happiness as the avoidance of pain, so his phi-losophy is significantly different from its modern reputation.

[18] René Descartes (1596–1650) was a French philosopher and mathematician, one of the founders of rationalism. His ideal was a deductive method that would avoid all error.

[19] Terence was a second-century B.C.E. Roman writer of comedies.

[20] Virgil was the author of the Latin epic the *Aeneid,* which tells of the founding of Rome by Aeneas after his escape from Troy.

[21] Cicero (106–43 B.C.E.) was an orator, politician, and Stoic philosopher. Cicero's philosophical works are largely derivative, but his orations became the model for Latin style.

diversity in the internal frame or external situation as is entirely blameless on both sides, and leaves no room to give one the preference above the other; in that case a certain degree of diversity in judgment is unavoidable, and we seek in vain for a standard, by which we can reconcile the contrary sentiments.

A young man, whose passions are warm, will be more sensibly touched with wise, philosophical reflections concerning the conduct of life and moderation of the passions. At twenty, Ovid[22] may be the favourite author; Horace[23] at forty; and perhaps Tacitus[24] at fifty. Vainly would we, in such cases, endeavour to enter into the sentiments of others, and divest ourselves of those propensities, which are natural to us. We choose our favourite author as we do our friend, from a conformity of humour and disposition. Mirth or passion, sentiment or reflection; whichever of these most predominates in our temper, it gives us a peculiar sympathy with the writer who resembles us.

One person is more pleased with the sublime; another with the tender; a third with raillery.[25] One has a strong sensibility to blemishes, and is extremely studious of correctness: Another has a more lively feeling of beauties, and pardons twenty absurdities and defects for one elevated or pathetic stroke. The ear of man is entirely turned towards conciseness and energy; that man is delighted with a copious, rich, and harmonious expression. Simplicity is affected by one; ornament by another. Comedy, tragedy, satire, odes, have each its partisans, who prefer that particular species of writing to all others. It is plainly an error in a critic, to confine his approbation to one species or style of writing, and condemn all the rest. But it is almost impossible not to feel a predilection for that which suits our particular turn and disposition. Such preferences are innocent and unavoidable, and can never reasonably be the object of dispute, because there is no standard, by which they can be decided.

For a like reason, we are more pleased, in the course of our reading, with pictures and characters, that resembles objects which are found in our own age or country, than with those which describe a different set of customs. It is not without some effort, that we reconcile ourselves to the man, who can boast of great constancy and uniformity in this particular. Whatever speculative errors may be found in the polite writings of any age or country, they detract but little from the value of those compositions. There needs but a certain turn of thought or imagination to make us enter into all the opinions, which then prevailed, and relish the sentiments or conclusions derived from them. But a very violent effort is requisite to change our judgment of manners, and excite sentiments of approbation or blame, love or hatred, different from those to which the mind from long custom has been familiarized. And where a man is confident of the rectitude of that moral standard, by which he judges, he is justly jealous of it, and will not pervert the sentiments of his heart for a moment, in complaisance to any writer whatsoever.

Of all speculative errors, those, which regard religion, are the most excusable in compositions of genius; nor is it ever permitted to judge of the civility or wisdom of any people, or even of single persons, by the grossness or refinement of their theological principles. The same good sense, that directs men in the ordinary occurrences of life, is not hearkened to in religious matters, which are supposed to be placed altogether above the cognizance of human reason. On this account, all the absurdities of the pagan system of theology must be overlooked by every critic, who would pretend to form a just notion of ancient poetry; and our posterity, in their turn, must have the same indulgence to their forefathers. No religious principles can ever be imputed as a fault to any poet, while they remain merely principles, and take not such strong possession of his heart, as to lay him

---

[22] Ovid (43 B.C.E.–18) was a Roman poet, particularly known for passionate lyrics.

[23] Horace (65–8 B.C.E.) was a Roman poet known for satire and criticism.

[24] Tacitus (55–117 C.E.) was a Roman historian whose works praised the moral virtues of the Roman Republic.

[25] Raillery is ridicule; the Earl of Shaftesbury had advocated raillery as a form of criticism that would expose truth and overcome pretension.

under the imputation of *bigotry* or *superstition.* Where that happens, they confound the sentiments of morality, and alter the natural boundaries of vice and virtue. They are therefore eternal blemishes, according to the principle above mentioned; nor are the prejudices and false opinions of the age sufficient to justify them.

It is essential to the Roman catholic religion to inspire a violent hatred of every other worship, and to represent all pagans, mahometans, and heretics as the objects of divine wrath and vengeance. Such sentiments, though they are in reality very blameable, are considered as virtues by the zealots of that communion, and are represented in their tragedies and epic poems as a kind of divine heroism. This bigotry has disfigured two very fine tragedies of the French theatre, *Polieucte*[26] and *Athalia;*[27] where an intemperate zeal for particular modes of worship is set off with all the pomp imaginable, and forms the predominant character of the heroes. "What is this," says the sublime Joad to Josabet, finding her in discourse with Mathan, the priest of Baal. "Does the daughter of David speak to this traitor? Are you not afraid, lest the earth should open and pour forth flames to devour you both? Or lest these holy walls should fall and crush you together? What is his purpose? Why comes that enemy of God hither to poison the air, which we breathe, with his horrid presence?" Such sentiments are received with great applause on the theatre of Paris; but at London the spectators would be full as much pleased to hear Achilles tell Agamemnon,[28] that he was a dog in his forehead, and a deer in his heart, or Jupiter threaten Juno[29] with a sound drubbing, if she will not be quiet.

Religious principles are also a blemish in any polite composition, when they rise up to superstition, and intrude themselves into every sentiment, however remote from any connection with religion. It is no excuse for the poet, that the customs of his country had burthened life with so many religious ceremonies and observances, that no part of it was exempt from that yoke. It must for ever be ridiculous in Petrarch to compare his mistress Laura,[30] to Jesus Christ. Nor is it less ridiculous in that agreeable libertine, Boccace,[31] very seriously to give thanks to God Almighty and the ladies, for their assistance in defending him against his enemies.

Study Questions

1. Do people agree about works of art? What do they agree about?
2. Do people act as if there is no disputing about taste?
3. Why is a standard of taste needed? Why not just let everyone go their own way?
4. Hume says that "beauty is no quality in things themselves" and "sentiment has a reference to nothing beyond itself." What is beauty, then? How does Hume's theory compare to classical theories of beauty found in Plato, Aristotle, and Plotinus?
5. Give examples of disagreements in judgments of taste from contemporary arts. Are any of them as obvious as Hume thinks the comparison of Ogilby to Milton would be?
6. Does Hume share the prejudices of his age? What are they? Do they affect his argument?
7. What does Hume mean by *sentiment?*
8. What would rules of composition be? Why can't a single set of rules be

---

[26] *Polyeucte,* a tragedy by Pierre Corneille (1606–1684), tells a story of conversion and martyrdom.

[27] *Athalia* is a tragedy by Jean Racine ((1639–1699) based on the Old Testament stories found in 2 Kings 11 and 2 Chronicles 22–23. They tell of the triumph of the priests of Yahweh over Athalia and the priests of Baal. The plot elements that Hume mentions are from *Athalia.*

[28] The dispute between the leading Greek warrior, Achilles, and the Greek war king, Agamemnon, is a central plot element of the *Iliad.*

[29] Jupiter is the Roman name for Zeus, the king of the gods; Juno is Hera, his queen.

---

[30] Petrarch (1304–1374) was a Renaissance Italian poet who composed an extended cycle of poems to his beloved, Laura. The poems are both sensual and allegorical.

[31] Giovanni Boccaccio (1313–1375) was a contemporary of Petrarch. His *Decameron* is a collection of witty but licentious tales set against the background of the great plague that swept Europe in the fourteenth century.

determined? Does Hume conclude that there are no rules?

9. In what sense does Hume conduct "experiments"?

10. What is the point of the story of Sancho's kinsmen?

11. Supply examples from contemporary arts (including, for example, movies) for
    a. strong sense
    b. delicacy of sentiment
    c. practice
    d. comparison
    e. freedom from prejudice
    as Hume intends these criteria. How does strong sense differ from delicacy? How does practice differ from comparison? What kind of prejudices are particularly dangerous for a critic?

12. Name one true judge of movies. If you have difficulty, is that a difficulty for Hume's argument?

13. Why are there so few good critics, according to Hume's criteria?

14. Give contemporary examples of differences in taste among people at the ages of twenty, forty, and fifty.

15. Hume obviously does not think highly of religion, especially in art and criticism. Why isn't that a prejudice on his part (as he uses the term *prejudice*)?

16. Construct Hume's argument that over time the public is right.

17. What are the sources of disagreement about taste?

Immanuel Kant

• • • • • • • • • • •

IMMANUEL KANT (1724–1804) was born in Königsberg in East Prussia. His parents were poor but devout pietists. Pietism was a Lutheran reform movement which stressed individual religious experience, devotional sincerity, biblical study, and practical as opposed to dogmatic Christianity. Kant was educated in a pietist school. He reacted against the forced and artificial emotion of the school, but his talent attracted support. He entered the university at Königsberg in 1740 at the age of sixteen. At that time, the University of Königsberg was divided between pietist theology and the rationalism of Christian Wolff, who was a follower of Leibniz. His view of religion was similar to that of deism: God was a first cause and orderer of the universe but not a direct intervener through miracles. Wolff and the rationalists attempted to establish a set of first principles through cosmological and ontological proofs of God's existence. From those principles, a theoretical and deductive apparatus could be applied to all subsequent phenomena. Kant was attracted to the order and logical rigor of this philosophical movement. He turned from the theology he was intended to study to science, mathematics, and philosophy.

After graduation, Kant taught as a private tutor before securing an appointment at the university as a lecturer in 1755. He lectured to large classes on logic, mathematics, metaphysics, natural science, and physical geography. During this period, Kant's writings were conventional examples of Wolffian rationalism. He continued as a lecturer for fifteen years, twice failing to receive an appointment as a professor. Finally, in 1770, Kant was appointed professor of logic and metaphysics. He credits his reading of David Hume with wakening him from his "dogmatic slumber." Kant began to question the possibility of obtaining the kind of certainty about foundations rationalism required. He was led to a unique position that took account of Hume's empirical critique of any metaphysical assumptions. This position is known as Kant's *critical philosophy*. It retained the order and deductive rigor of rationalism, but it applied them only to what was presented to the mind by sense together with the mind's own necessary structuring of its perceptions.

The result was a series of "critiques"—the *Critique of Pure Reason* (1781), the *Critique of Practical Reason* (1788) and the *Critique of Judgment* (1790)—that changed the course of modern philosophy. Prior to Kant, empiricism and rationalism offered competing philosophies. Both rejected the traditional metaphysics of the medieval and Renaissance schools. Empiricism went a step farther and rejected metaphysics altogether. Rationalism replaced it with its own metaphysical system based on the I-centered philosophy of Descartes and Leibniz. Kant made that competition obsolete. His philosophy was at once ordered and autonomous, skeptical about our ability to penetrate to the heart of the cosmos or religion and yet confident of its deductions within the sphere of the mind's own competence. Kant united the individualism of empiricism and pietism with the mathematical and scientific systems of Leibniz and the new science. Kant's influence continues to be felt today.

Kant spent his entire life in Königsberg. He was known as a solitary man, hard working to the point of exhaustion in spite of frail health, forgetful yet a friend to be valued. He died in 1804 as the Napoleonic wars were just beginning to change the face of modern Europe. Kant already had changed its philosophical face.

◆   ◆   ◆   ◆   ◆   ◆

Immanuel Kant turned to a consideration of aesthetics in his third *Critique* only after completing two prior "Critiques"—the *Critique of Pure Reason* (1781) and the *Critique of Practical Reason* (1788). The *Critique of Judgment* (1790) thus belongs to a complex scheme of philosophy that attempted to organize all areas of our ability to know and judge. The first *Critique* describes the conditions of knowledge itself. The second *Critique* analyzes the conditions of knowledge as it leads to some form of action. Thus, these two critiques cover pure knowing (theory) and active knowing (morality). The third *Critique* can be regarded as moving backward to discover the beginnings of knowledge, what makes knowledge possible at all. Feeling, intuition, and sense present themselves affectively. They do not have to be "thought"; they are simply present to us without our being able to "decide" one way or the other to engage them. They provide a starting point for the mind. Kant's overall scheme of theory and practice is completed by what he calls *pure intuition*—the direct encounter of a being that is conscious with its environment. For animals, intuition does not go much further than instinct. But for humans, it leads to thought, theory, and considered action. For theory, perception (pure intuition) must be shaped into conceptual patterns. For considered action, perception must be linked to goals and purposes. Our theoretical concepts give us science; practical concepts are the realm of moral and economic life. Neither would be possible without the pure intuition provided by sense experience. That experience can be understood either scientifically (theoretically) or practically only if it is already given in some way. The prior givenness of intuition itself produces feelings and even consequences. This is the realm of judgments that already must be a part of experience before experience can become higher ordered forms of knowledge. Thus, while Kant's *Critique of Judgment* comes third in the series of critiques, logically it deals with the prior conditions which the first two critiques have disclosed as necessary.

The aesthetic belongs to this logically prior realm. The term *aesthetic,* which Kant adopted from an earlier German writer, Alexander Baumgarten, is a transliteration of a Greek word for *feeling.* (The same word is the root for our term *anesthetic*—"not feeling.") After Kant's *Critique of Judgment,* the aesthetic becomes the principle term in modern discussions of the whole realm of beauty and art. The use of *aesthetic* prior to Baumgarten is an anachronism, and only in Kant's work does the term achieve its dominance. After Kant, modern writers on art and beauty can take it as established that they are dealing with a special area of "feeling" arising from the encounter of the mind with the world. Only recently has this assumption begun to be questioned. A number of contemporary writers in the field of aesthetics doubt that feeling alone is sufficient as a basis for understanding what we know as art.[1]

Kant presents the aesthetic as the realm of pure intuition which is logically prior to any practical or conceptual formulation. Because of that intuition, the mind can go on to shape theories and make practical judgments according to certain *a priori* categories such as "space" and "time." Kant's idea is that the input that we receive from the world is organized in ways that are characteristic of human judgment. We think by fitting our raw perception into logical categories, and without those categories, we would not be able to make sense of the world. The categories themselves are not ideas or part of the perception. Thinking is empirical, but it is not just the random collection of simple ideas and associations.

Thinking leads to knowledge and action. However, the initial perception has its own qualities. We are never purely indifferent to the realm of intuitions as we encounter the world. Intuitions are also feelings; we experience them as pleasures and pains. Pure intuitions, together with their attendant pleasures and pains, form the basis for our purely aesthetic judgments. *Judgment* here can be misleading. It means more than just a voluntary preference or passing judgment on something as good or bad, right or wrong. A theoretical judgment is an experience of something as organized in a certain way, according to a theory. All theoretical grasp of an object must have some organization or other, and what that organization consists of is given in a judgment. For example, I judge that objects naturally fall when dropped, implicitly organizing them according to the law of gravity. Similarly, practical judgment is an experience of something as having some purpose or end. To grasp something as purposeful is to make a judgment as well. For example, deciding to eat ice cream is to judge that it will satisfy an appetite or desire that I have. Fundamentally, then, *judging* is organizing mentally. It need not involve terms like good or bad. Aesthetic judgments are those that belong to pure intuition itself. They rest on the feelings that we have as a result of an intuition that is immediately present. They too are organizations of the mind, but they are more immediate and basic than either theoretical or practical judgments. Their foundation is feeling itself and the pleasure or pain that that feeling includes.

Kant brought together all of the different strands of eighteenth-century philosophy of art and beauty. He identified taste as the feeling that belongs to aesthetic intuition. Thus taste is purely subjective. Its subjectivity is a consequence of where it comes in the overall scheme about knowing that Kant is describing. Thus, taste belongs to sense. It is not limited to any particular sense, but at the same time it is not itself a separate sense. Taste is about as far back as we can go in tracing our own experiences. Even before I have any understanding of thunder or enough sense to get out of the rain, I have an immediate feeling about the sensation I experience—the awe or fear that the thunder can produce, for example. Awe may be pleasant; I enjoy thunder storms. Fear is unpleasant; I do not enjoy them. So taste must be my own; it cannot be learned or acquired from others, and it cannot be questioned. What I feel, I feel, regardless of how it comes to be understood later or to what use I put that knowledge.

---

[1] See George Dickie's essay, "The Myth of The Aesthetic Attitude," in Part III, for example.

Kant took up another key eighteenth-century term, *disinterest*,[2] to further distinguish the aesthetic. *Disinterestedness* had already been used to describe moral actions that were benevolent rather than selfish. It becomes one of the characteristic aesthetic terms because of the way Kant made it central to his description of aesthetic intuitions. *Interest* is what an individual or group gets or hopes to get from some object or action. It is used in the sense of possession or benefit, not curiosity. If I have an interest in a piece of property in this sense, I own some part of the property. I am not expressing my curiosity about what the property is like. Thus interest involves desire, and it includes a desire for the existence of the object. It makes no sense to say that I could own or benefit from something that does not exist. The aesthetic is prior to all practical concern, however, so the aesthetic is "disinterested." For someone to be disinterested means that neither desires nor even the existence of the object matters in the judgment. We are all "interested" in this sense as soon as we start to project our wishes, and that is very soon, of course. But contemplating nature or art does not require such interest. It does not even require that the object be there. Just to have the experience, regardless of its source, is enough.

Disinterested judgment belongs to the subject, not the object. A subject is an experiencer. Because disinterested judgments are "about" a subject's experience, they belong to the subject. To be a subject, to be conscious, is to have such judgments. If a disinterested judgment were "about" the object, it already would have to have placed the object in some conceptual scheme. Thus, to be disinterested, a judgment must be free of concepts as well as of any end, goal, or desire.

Kant distinguished three different forms that feeling can take: (1) Gratification refers to some desire; so it is a feeling which accompanies practical judgments. I am satisfied if I want something and then receive it. (2) Goodness likewise implies some standard. If I think something is good, I believe it corresponds to the way it ought to be. (The standard might be an objective standard, so it need not be linked to my desire.) So judgments that something is good are theoretical or practical. (3) But the pleasure someone takes in an intuition itself is free of desire or approval. It is just pleasing for itself, and we call that feeling beauty. Thus, Kant links beauty and taste. Beauty is disinterested pleasure; taste is the ability to experience beauty. The way to have taste is to cultivate disinterestedness.

Judgments of taste are not simple. Subjectively, they tell us only about the individual who formed them, but they have a form and function of their own. Although they are based solely on subjective feeling, formally their content refers to an object, not the subject. All pleasures are not the same. Moreover, I never identify beauty as simply "mine." I take pleasure in the object unconditionally, so it "should" please anyone. The form of judgments about beauty extends the judgment without restriction, so they are universal. Thus judgments of beauty are subjective but universal. The universality follows from their form alone. Free of both concepts and interest, nothing binds the judgment to the individual except its subjective origin. Such judgments are not responses to some fixed standard. They form their own standards and extend them to everyone. That subjectivity is the basis for universality. It is not controlled by the person who

---

[2] *Disinterested* should not be confused with *uninterested*, which implies a lack of attention.

forms it. My judgments belong to me, but they do not depend on any concepts that are peculiar to me, nor on any interests that distinguish me from anyone else.

In order to account for the combination of subjectivity and universality in the same judgment, Kant had recourse to another term that was in use in the eighteenth century and had roots in classical and medieval sources. He speaks of a "common sense," which he identifies as a *sensus communis*. On the one hand, the aesthetic rests on sense alone. On the other, sense produces a universal form, beauty, which is free of the particular identity of the person who experiences it. Sense must be common to all. Kant's claim here is not based on psychological or empirical observation of such a sense. The empirical observation is that the aesthetic intuition has a universal form and functions as if it had a purpose even though it is prior to all interest and purpose. For there to be such a form, sense must have a common as well as an individual form. Thus the medieval notion of *sensus communis* is given new life. Since we have empirical knowledge even at the aesthetic level, but we do not depend on theories or concepts at that level, some means of grasping things must be available that is sense but not an idea. A common sense must operate even before we know what sense is—in effect, before we have the experience to become individuals. That means that the *sensus communis* is *a priori*—known independently of having to learn it by experience—because we would never be able to learn by experience unless we could get started.

Kant's location of the aesthetic prior to rational control by formulated concepts makes the actual production of art problematic. Eighteenth-century artists and writers derived rules for art and criticism from classical rhetoric. That produced a movement called neoclassicism which tried to follow classical rules. Kant inherited the neoclassical concern with rules as the basis for making works of art. Neoclassicism tends to produce highly ordered, artificial, and imitative art. But great art is not like anything else. It breaks the rules.

Kant adapted still another eighteenth-century term to account for the fact that some artists are able to produce actual works of art which go beyond anything previously created. Production requires knowing what one is doing and fitting material and means to an end. But if the aesthetic is independent of concepts and ends, rules cannot guide production. Kant appealed to the concept of *genius* to resolve this difficulty. When actual works appear, they have some form and thus obey some ordering principles—rules. No work is random and chaotic. If it were, no one would be able to understand it. But such rules cannot precede the work if it is part of the aesthetic. The genius goes ahead of the formulation of rules to produce works that have the form that rules would have given them without the work having been produced according to a rule. The genius is the one who gives the rule to art. After Kant, genius and imagination played much larger roles than they ever had before in the art world. The nineteenth-century romantics identified imagination as the creative faculty and genius as the state of mind that transforms aesthetic intuition into art. Implicitly, the separation between the audience and the artist was complete. An audience can experience art but cannot produce it. Geniuses are bound by no prior rule; they can transform what is present to their own minds into art.

Kant confronted Hume's paradox that judgments of taste are both subjective and treated as if they are objectively true. In Kant's formulation, this produces what is called an *antinomy*. Two apparently opposite and contradictory statements are juxtaposed. The antinomy of taste arises from these statements: "A judgment of taste cannot be based on any concept," but "judgments of taste must be determined by concepts if they are objectively true." The key word is *concept*. The antinomy arises because we seem to need concepts as a standard for objective, universal judgments, but the subjectivity of taste does not allow concepts into those judgments. Kant resolved this antinomy by arguing that *concept* is used in two different senses. In the first sense, a judgment of taste cannot be based on or appeal to concepts. Freedom from concepts distinguishes taste from science. If judgments of taste were based on concepts, we would be able to tell if something were beautiful by pointing out the specific features that satisfied the concepts. We cannot make those inferences. Instead, we consult our feelings directly. If concepts told us that some features were always beauty-making, knowing the presence of those features would be sufficient for us to know that the object was beautiful. We could know that something was beautiful without any direct experience of it. No such set of features exists. All attempts to supply something like uniformity amidst variety or the classical golden section[3] fail because some things that have those qualities are not experienced as beautiful by many people, and things without those qualities are experienced as beautiful. In the second sense, *concept* refers not to an external standard but to a part of the judgment. We experience beauty as something that is not limited to our own existence. So we believe our judgments of taste to be universally valid, and we must use the form of a concept to express our experience of beauty accurately. Saying that something is beautiful is just not the same as saying that I like it. The universality of judgments of taste requires that they must be intelligible, in principle, to everyone. No one can have someone else's experience. If the judgment that "*x* is beautiful" appealed to no concept, it would be private and unintelligible and thus could not be universal. It would collapse back into "I like *x*." So our judgments must be "conceptual" in the sense that our experience of beauty incorporates some common element.

Kant calls the conceptual element built into experience *supersensible*, an obscure and difficult appeal. Concepts that are independent of individual sensible things organize sensible experience. They cannot be appealed to in a judgment of taste. But a judgment of taste itself has order. Its order is not from a prior concept, but it nevertheless is experienced as order. This ordered judgment is supersensible. In classical sources, it would have been a realm of ideas. But Kant is not able to appeal to neo-Platonic ideas, because they are also conceptual in his terms. For example, Aristotle appealed to metaphysical "categories" like *quantity*. I have an idea of quantity because I can distinguish *all* from *some*. To Kant, that kind of appeal required experience of many things that were identified already. So I cannot use metaphysical categories unless I have already organized experience of individual things. The supersensible has to be a different kind of concept altogether. So the supersensible is referred to only in the formulation of the sensible. In effect, it is the fortunate fact that we find the world intelligible. The world might have remained a confusion of sensory input to us or our response might not have risen above the level of instinct and habit. Since we know more than that, we know of an order *in* our experience that is different from the orderliness of *what* we experience

---

[3] The golden section was regarded as a law of the beauty of proportions in both art and nature. The proportion of a line or size that is divided so that length *A* is to length *B* as *B* is to *A* + *B* was believed to be universally beautiful.

that is abstracted by science. Put another way, not only does the mind discover an order to the input it receives; it also discovers that it is itself part of that order and attuned
to it. The latter is not a sensible but a supersensible fact. Taste is able to function only
because of concepts which are supersensible in order to produce the ground for sensible concepts.

Kant drew together all of the various strands of eighteenth-century aesthetics and
fitted them into his larger philosophical scheme. He made the aesthetic the cornerstone
of that philosophy. Kant is the inventor of modern aesthetics. His outline guided aesthetic philosophy in one way or another for the next one hundred and fifty years. During that period, aesthetics was understood to be about a special realm of disinterested
pleasure. Its object was the subjective experience of a perceiver. Art and nature were
equally aesthetic sources. Both the work and the artist are understood in relation to the
experience that they made possible. So aesthetics as a philosophical discipline in its
Kantian form is about our experience and its sources. Kant gave aesthetic feeling its
modern form. Kant's own treatment of all of the details of this new branch of philosophy is immensely complicated, but it is the pivot upon which all else rests until it is
finally challenged in contemporary aesthetics.

From *Critique of Judgment*

FIRST DIVISION
Analytic of the Aesthetical Judgment

FIRST BOOK
Analytic of the Beautiful

FIRST MOMENT
of the Judgment of Taste, According to Quality

1. The Judgment of Taste Is Aesthetical

In order to distinguish whether anything is beautiful or not, we refer the representation, not by the understanding to the object for cognition, but by the imagination (perhaps in conjunction with the understanding) to the subject and its feeling of pleasure or pain. The judgment of taste is therefore not a judgment of cognition, and is consequently not logical but aesthetical, by which we understand that whose determining ground can be no *other than subjective*. Every reference of representations, even that of sensations, may be objective (and then it signifies the real [element] of an empirical representation), save only the reference to the feeling of pleasure and pain, by which nothing in the object is signified, but through which there is a feeling in the subject as it is affected by the representation.

To apprehend a regular, purposive building by means of one's cognitive faculty (whether in a clear or a confused way of representation) is something quite different from being conscious of this representation as connected with the sensation of satisfaction. Here the representation is altogether referred to the subject and to its feeling of life, under the name of the feeling of pleasure or pain. This establishes a quite separate faculty of distinction and of judgment, adding nothing to cognition, but only comparing the given representation in the subject with the whole faculty of representations, of which the mind is conscious in the feeling of its state. Given representations in a judgment can be empirical (consequently, aesthetical); but the judgment which is formed by means of them is logical, provided they are referred in the judgment to the object. Conversely, if the given representations are rational, but are referred in a judgment simply to the subject (to its feeling), the judgment is so far always aesthetical.

2. The Satisfaction which Determines the Judgment of Taste is Disinterested

The satisfaction which we combine with the representation of the existence of an object is called "interest." Such satisfaction always has reference to the faculty of desire, either as its determining ground or as necessarily connected with its determining ground. Now when the question is if a thing is beautiful, we do not want to know whether anything depends or can depend on the existence of the thing, either for myself or for anyone else, but how we judge it by mere observation (intuition or reflection). If anyone asks me if I find that palace beautiful which I see before me, I may answer: I do not like things of that kind which are made merely to be stared at. Or I can answer like that Iroquois Sachem, who was pleased in Paris by nothing more than by the cook shops. Or again, after the manner of Rousseau,[4] I may rebuke the vanity of the great who waste the sweat of the people on such superfluous things.

---

[4] Jean-Jacques Rousseau (1712–1778), a French philosopher and political theorist, argued that humans are corrupted by society and that goodness is to be found in a natural state.

In fine, I could easily convince myself that if I found myself on an uninhabited island without the hope of ever again coming among men, and could conjure up just such a splendid building by my mere wish, I should not even give myself the trouble if I had a sufficiently comfortable hut. This may all be admitted and approved, but we are not now talking of this. We wish only to know if this mere representation of the object is accompanied in me with satisfaction, however indifferent I may be as regards the existence of the object of this representation. We easily see that, in saying it is *beautiful* and in showing that I have taste, I am concerned, not with that in which I depend on the existence of the object, but with that which I make out of this representation in myself. Everyone must admit that a judgment about beauty, in which the least interest mingles, is very partial and is not a pure judgment of taste. We must not be in the least prejudiced in favor of the existence of the things, but be quite indifferent in this respect, in order to play the judge in things of taste.

We cannot, however, better elucidate this proposition, which is of capital importance, than by contrasting the pure disinterested satisfaction in judgments of taste with that which is bound up with an interest, especially if we can at the same time be certain that there are no other kinds of interest than those which are to be now specified.

3. The Satisfaction in the Pleasant Is Bound Up with Interest

That which pleases the senses in sensation is "pleasant." Here the opportunity presents itself of censuring a very common confusion of the double sense which the word "sensation" can have, and of calling attention to it. All satisfaction (it is said or thought) is itself sensation (of a pleasure). Consequently everything that pleases is pleasant because it pleases (and according to its different degrees or its relations to other pleasant sensations it is *agreeable, lovely, delightful, enjoyable*, etc.) But if this be admitted, then impressions of sense which determine the inclination, fundamental propositions of reason which determine the will, mere reflective forms of intuition which determine the judgment, are quite the same as regards the effect upon the feeling of pleasure. For this would be pleasantness in the sensation of one's state; and since in the end all the operations of our faculties must issue in the practical and unite in it as their goal, we could suppose no other way of estimating things and their worth than that which consists in the gratification that they promise. It is of no consequence at all how this is attained, and since then the choice of means alone could make a difference, men could indeed blame one another for stupidity and indiscretion, but never for baseness and wickedness. For thus they all, each according to his own way of seeing things, seek one goal, that is, gratification.

If a determination of the feeling of pleasure or pain is called sensation, this expression signifies something quite different from what I mean when I call the representation of a thing (by sense, as a receptivity belonging to the cognitive faculty) sensation. For in the latter case the representation is referred to the object, in the former simply to the subject, and is available for no cognition whatever, not even for that by which the subject *cognizes* itself.

In the above elucidation we understand by the word "sensation" an objective representation of sense; and, in order to avoid misinterpretation, we shall call that which must always remain merely subjective and can constitute absolutely no representation of an object by the ordinary term "feeling." The green color of the meadows belongs to *objective* sensation, as a perception of an object of sense; the pleasantness of this belongs to *subjective* sensation by which no object is represented, i.e. to feeling, by which the object is considered as an object of satisfaction (which does not furnish a cognition of it).

Now that a judgment about an object by which I describe it as pleasant expresses an interest in it, is plain from the fact that by sensation it excites a desire for objects of that kind; consequently the satisfaction presupposes, not the mere judgment about it, but the relation of its existence to my state, so far as this is affected by such an object. Hence we do not merely say of the pleasant, *it pleases,* but, *it gratifies.* I give it no mere assent, but inclination is aroused by it; and in the case of what is pleasant in the most lively fashion there is no judgment at all upon the character of the object, for those [persons] who always lay themselves out for enjoyment (for that is the word describing intense gratification) would fain dispense with all judgment.

4. The Satisfaction in the Good Is Bound Up with Interest

Whatever by means of reason pleases through the mere concept is *good.* That which pleases only as a means we call *good for something* (the useful), but that which pleases for itself is *good in itself.* In both there is always involved the concept of a purpose, and consequently the relation of reason to the (at least possible) volition, and thus a satisfaction in the *presence* of an object or an action, i.e. some kind of interest.

In order to find anything good, I must always know what sort of a thing the object ought to be, i.e. I must have a concept of it. But there is no need of this to find a thing beautiful. Flowers, free delineations, outlines intertwined with one another without design and called [conventional] foliage, have no meaning, depend on no definite concept, and yet they please. The satisfaction in the beautiful must depend on the reflection upon an object, leading to any concept (however indefinite), and it is thus distinguished from the pleasant, which rests entirely upon sensation.

It is true, the pleasant seems in many cases to be the same as the good. Thus people are accustomed to say that all gratification (especially if it lasts) is good in itself, which is very much the same as to say that lasting pleasure and the good are the same. But we can soon see that this is merely a confusion of words, for the concepts which properly belong to these expressions can

in no way be interchanged. The pleasant, which, as such, represents the object simply in relation to sense, must first be brought by the concept of a purpose under principles of reason, in order to call it good, as an object of the will. But there is [involved] a quite different relation to satisfaction in calling that which gratifies at the same time *good* may be seen from the fact that, in the case of the good, the question always is whether it is mediately or immediately good (useful or good in itself); but on the contrary in the case of the pleasant, there can be no question about this at all, for the word always signifies something which pleases immediately. (The same is applicable to what I call beautiful.)

Even in common speech men distinguish the pleasant from the good. Of a dish which stimulates the taste by spices and other condiments we may say unhesitatingly that it is pleasant, though it is at the same time admitted not to be good; for though it immediately *delights* the senses, yet mediately, i.e. considered by reason which looks to the after results, it displeases. Even in the judging of health we may notice this distinction. It is immediately pleasant to everyone possessing it (at least negatively, i.e. as the absence of all bodily pains). But in order to say that it is good, it must be considered by reason with reference to purpose, viz. that it is a state which makes us fit for all business. Finally, in respect of happiness, everyone believes himself entitled to describe the greatest sum of the pleasantness of life (as regards both their number and their duration) as a true, even as the highest, good. However, reason is opposed to this. Pleasantness is enjoyment. And if we were concerned with this alone, it would be foolish to be scrupulous as regards the means which procure it for us, or [to care] whether it is obtained passively by the bounty of nature or by our own activity and work. But reason can never be persuaded that the existence of a man who merely lives for *enjoyment* (however busy he may be in this point of view) has a worth in itself, even if he at the same time is conducive a means to the beat enjoyment of others and shares in all their gratifications by sympathy. Only what he does, without reference to enjoyment, in full freedom and independently of what nature can procure for him passively, gives an [absolute] worth to his presence [in the world] as the existence of a person; and happiness, with the whole abundance of its pleasures, is far from being an unconditioned good.

However, notwithstanding all this difference between the pleasant and the good, they both agree in this that they are always bound up with an interest in their object; so are not only the pleasant (para. 3), and the mediate good (the useful) which is pleasing as a means toward pleasantness somewhere, but also that which is good absolutely and in every aspect, viz. moral good, which brings with it the highest interest. For the good is the object of will (i.e. of a faculty of desire determined by reason). But to wish for something and to have a satisfaction in its existence, i.e. to take an interest in it, are identical.

5. Comparison of the Three Specifically Different Kinds of Satisfaction

The pleasant and the good have both a reference to the faculty of desire, and they bring with them, the former a satisfaction pathologically conditioned (by impulses, *stimuli*), the latter a pure practical satisfaction which is determined not merely by the representation of the object but also by the represented connection of the subject with the existence of the object. [It is not merely the object that pleases, but also its existence.] On the other hand, the judgment of taste is merely *contemplative;* i.e., it is a judgment which, indifferent as regards the existence of an object, compares its character with the feeling of pleasure and pain. But this contemplation itself is not directed to concepts; for the judgment of taste is not a cognitive judgment (either theoretical or practical), and thus is not *based* on concepts, nor has it concepts as its *purpose.*

The pleasant, the beautiful, and the good designate then three different relations of representations to the feeling of pleasure and pain, in reference to which we distinguish from one another objects or methods of representing them. And the expressions corresponding to each, by which we mark our complacency in them, are not the same. That which *gratifies* a man is called *pleasant;* that which merely *pleases* him is *beautiful;* that which is *esteemed* [or *approved*] by him, i.e. that to which he accords an objective worth, is *good.* Pleasantness concerns irrational animals also, but beauty only concerns men, i.e. animals, but still rational, beings—not merely *qua* rational (e.g. spirits), but *qua* animal also—and the good concerns every rational being in general. This is a proposition which can only be completely established and explained in the sequel. We may say that, of all these three kinds of satisfaction, that of taste in the beautiful is alone a disinterested and *free* satisfaction; for no interest, either of sense or of reason, here forces our assent. Hence we may say of satisfaction that it is related in the three aforesaid cases to *inclination,* to *favor,* or to *respect.* Now *favor* is the only free satisfaction. An object of inclination and one that is proposed to our desire by a law of reason leave us no freedom in forming for ourselves anywhere an object of pleasure. All interest presupposes or generates a want, and, as the determining ground of assent, it leaves the judgment about the object no longer free.

As regards the interest of inclination in the case of the pleasant, everyone says that hunger is the best sauce, and everything that is eatable is relished by people with a healthy appetite; and thus a satisfaction of this sort shows no choice directed by taste. It is only when the want is appeased that we can distinguish which of many men has or has not taste. In the same way there may be manners (conduct) without virtue, politeness without good will, decorum without modesty, etc. For where the moral law speaks there is no longer, objectively, a free choice as regards what is to be done; and to display taste in its fulfillment (or in judging of another's fulfillment of it) is something quite different from manifesting the moral attitude of thought. For this involves a command and generates a want, while moral tastes only plays with the objects of satisfaction, without attaching itself to one of them.

Explanation of the Beautiful Resulting from the First Moment

Taste is the faculty of judging of an object or a method of representing it by an *entirely disinterested* satisfaction or dissatisfaction. The object of such satisfaction is called *beautiful*.

SECOND MOMENT
Of the Judgment of Taste, According to Quantity

6. The Beautiful Is That Which Apart from Concepts Is Represented as the Object of a Universal Satisfaction

This explanation of the beautiful can be derived from the preceding explanation of it as the object of an entirely disinterested satisfaction. For the fact of which everyone is conscious, that the satisfaction is for him quite disinterested, implies in his judgment a ground of satisfaction for all men. For since it does not rest on any inclination of the subject (nor upon any other premeditated interest), but since the person who judges feels himself quite *free* as regards the satisfaction which he attaches to the object, he cannot find the ground of this satisfaction in any private conditions connected with his own subject, and hence it must be regarded as grounded on what he can presuppose in every other person. Consequently he must believe that he has reason for attributing a similar satisfaction to everyone. He will therefore speak of the beautiful as if beauty were a characteristic of the object and the judgment logical (constituting a cognition of the object by means

of concepts of it), although it is only aesthetical and involves merely a reference of the representation of the object to the subject. For it has this similarity to a logical judgment that we can presuppose its validity for all men. But this universality cannot arise from concepts; for from concepts there is no transition to the feeling of pleasure or pain (except in pure practical laws, which bring an interest with them such as is not bound up with the pure judgment of taste). Consequently the judgment of taste, accompanied with the consciousness of separation from all interest, must claim validity for every man, without this universality depending on objects. That is, there must be bound up with it a title to subjective universality.

7. Comparison of the Beautiful with the Pleasant and the Good By Means of the Above Characteristic

As regards the pleasant, everyone is content that his judgment, which he bases upon private feeling and by which he says of an object that it pleases him, should be limited merely to his own person. Thus he is quite contented that if he says, "Canary wine[5] is pleasant," another man may correct his expression and remind him that he ought to say, "It is pleasant *to me.*" And this is the case not only as regards the taste of the tongue, the palate, and the throat, but for whatever is pleasant to anyone's eyes and ears. To one, violet color is soft and lovely; to another, it is washed out and dead. One man likes the tone of wind instruments, another that of strings. To strive here with the design of reproving as incorrect another man's judgment which is different from our own, as if the judgments were logically opposed, would be folly. As regards the pleasant, therefore, the fundamental proposition is valid: *everyone has his own taste* (the taste of sense).

---

[5] Canary wine is a sweet wine similar to Madeira but from the Canary Islands.

The case is quite different with the beautiful. It would (on the contrary) be laughable if a man who imagined anything to his own taste thought to justify himself by saying: "This object (the house we see, the coat that person wears, the concert we hear, the poem submitted to our judgment) is beautiful *for me*." For he must not call it *beautiful* if it merely pleases him. Many things may have for him charm and pleasantness—no one troubles himself at that—but if he gives out anything as beautiful, he supposes in others the same satisfaction; he judges not merely for himself, but for everyone, and speaks of beauty as if it were a property of things. Hence he says "the *thing* is beautiful"; and he does not count on the agreement of others with this his judgment of satisfaction, because he has found this agreement several times before, but he *demands* it of them. He blames them if they judge otherwise and he denies them taste, which he nevertheless requires from them. Here, then, we cannot say that each man has his own particular taste. For this would be as much as to say that there is no taste whatever, i.e. no aesthetical judgment which can make a rightful claim upon everyone's assent.

At the same time we find as regards the pleasant that there is an agreement among men in their judgments upon it in regard to which we deny taste to some and attribute it to others, by this not meaning one of our organic senses, but a faculty of judging in respect of the pleasant generally. Thus we say of a man who knows how to entertain his guests with pleasures (of enjoyment for all the senses), so that they are all pleased, "he has taste." But here the universality is only taken comparatively; and there emerge rules which are only *general* (like all empirical ones), and not *universal,* which latter the judgment of taste upon the beautiful undertakes or lays claim to. It is a judgment in reference to sociability, so far as this rests on empirical rules. In respect of the good it is true that judgments make rightful claim to validity for everyone; but the good is represented only *by means of a concept* as the object of a universal satisfaction, which is the case neither with the pleasant nor with the beautiful.

8. The Universality of the Satisfaction Is Represented in a Judgment of Taste Only as Subjective

This particular determination of the universality of an aesthetical judgment, which is to be met with in a judgment of taste, is noteworthy, not indeed for the logician, but for the transcendental philosopher.[6] It requires no small trouble to discover its origin, but we thus detect a property of our cognitive faculty which without this analysis would remain unknown.

First, we must be fully convinced of the fact that in a judgment of taste (about the beautiful) the satisfaction in the object is imputed to *everyone,* without being based on a concept (for then it would be the good). Further, this claim to universal validity so essentially belongs to a judgment by which we describe anything as *beautiful* that, if this were not thought in it, it would never come into our thoughts to use the expression at all, but everything which pleases without a concept would be counted as pleasant. In respect of the latter, everyone has his own opinion; and no one assumes in another agreement with his judgment of taste, which is always the case in a judgment of taste about beauty. I may call the first the taste of sense, the second the taste of reflection, so far as the first lays down mere private judgments and the second judgments supposed to be generally valid (public), but in both cases aesthetical (not practical) judgments about an object merely in respect of the relation of its representation to the feeling of pleasure and pain. Now here is something strange. As regards the taste of sense, not only does experience show that its judgment (of pleasure or pain connected with anything) is not valid universally, but everyone is content not

---

[6] Kant's philosophy is sometimes called *transcendental idealism* because like idealism it locates reality in ideas, but it does not make ideas either purely subjective (in an individual's mind) or transcendent (realities independent of their being thought.) In Kant's usage, *transcendental* means independent of human experience but not of human minds.

to impute agreement with it to others (although actually there is often found a very extended concurrence in these judgments). On the other hand, the taste of reflection has its claim to the universal validity of its judgments (about the beautiful) rejected often enough, as experience teaches, although it may find it possible (as it actually does) to represent judgments which can demand this universal agreement. In fact it imputes this to everyone for each of its judgments of taste, without the persons that judge disputing as to the possibility of such a claim, although in particular cases they cannot agree as to the correct application of this faculty.

Here we must, in the first place, remark that a universality which does not rest on concepts of objects (not even on empirical ones) is not logical but aesthetical;[7] i.e. it involves no objective quantity of the judgment, but only that which is subjective. For this I use the expression *general validity,* which signifies the validity of the reference of a representation, not to the cognitive faculty, but to the feeling of pleasure and pain for every subject. (We can avail ourselves also of the same expression for the logical quantity of the judgment, if only we prefix "objective" to "universal validity," to distinguish it from that which is merely subjective and aesthetical.)

A judgment with *objective universal validity* is also always valid subjectively; i.e. if the judgment holds for everything contained under a given concept, it holds also for everyone who represents an object by means of this concept. But from a *subjective universal validity,* i.e. aesthetical and resting on no concept, we cannot infer that which is logical because that kind of judgment does not extend to the object. But, therefore, the aesthetical universality which is ascribed to a judgment must be of a particular kind, because it does not unite the predicate of beauty with the concept of the object, considered in its whole logical sphere, and yet extends it to the whole sphere of judging persons.

In respect of logical quantity, all judgments of taste are *singular* judgments. For because I must refer the object immediately to my feeling of pleasure and pain, and that not by means of concepts, they cannot have the quantity of objective generally valid judgments. Nevertheless, if the singular representation of the object of judgment of taste in accordance with the conditions determining the latter, were transformed by comparison into a concept, a logically universal judgment could result therefrom. E.g., I describe by a judgment of taste the rose that I see as beautiful. But the judgment which results from the comparison of several singular judgments, "Roses in general are beautiful," is no longer described simply as aesthetical, but as a logical judgment based on an aesthetical one. Again the judgment, "The rose is pleasant" (to use) is, although aesthetical and singular, not a judgment of taste but of sense. It is distinguished from the former by the fact that the judgment of taste carries with it an *aesthetic quantity* of universality, i.e. of validity for everyone, which cannot be found in a judgment about the pleasant. It is only judgments about the good which, although they also determine satisfaction in an object, have logical and not merely aesthetical universality, for they are valid of the object as cognitive of it, and thus are valid for everyone.

If we judge objects merely according to concepts, then all representation of beauty is lost. Thus there can be no rule according to which anyone is to be forced to recognize anything as beautiful. We cannot press [upon others] by the aid of any reasons or fundamental propositions our judgment that a coat, a house, or a flower is beautiful. People wish to submit the object to their own eyes, as if the satisfaction in it depended on sensation; and yet, if we then call the object beautiful, we believe that we speak with a universal voice, and we claim the assent of everyone, although on the contrary all private sensation can only decide for the observer himself and his satisfaction.

We may see now that in the judgment of taste nothing is postulated but such a *universal voice,* in respect of the satisfaction without the interven-

---

[7] Logic can be thought and reasoned about in the same way by everyone; the *aesthetical* can only be felt.

tion of concepts, and thus the *possibility* of an aesthetical judgment that can, at the same time, be regarded as valid for everyone. The judgment of taste itself does not *postulate* the agreement of everyone (for that can only be done by a logically universal judgment because it can adduce reasons); it only *imputes* this agreement to everyone, as a case of the rule in respect of which it expects, not confirmation by concepts, but assent from others. The universal voice is, therefore, only an idea (we do not yet inquire upon what it rests). It may be uncertain whether or not the man who believes that he is laying down a judgment of taste is, as a matter of fact, judging in conformity with that idea; but that he refers his judgment thereto, and consequently that it is intended to be a judgment of taste, he announces by the expression "beauty." He can be quite certain of this for himself by the mere consciousness of the separating of everything belonging to the pleasant and the good from the satisfaction which is left; and this is all for which he promises himself the agreement of everyone—a claim which would be justifiable under these conditions, provided only he did not often make mistakes, and thus lay down an erroneous judgment of taste.

9. Investigation of the Question Whether in the Judgment of Taste the Feeling of Pleasure Precedes or Follows the Judging of the Object

The solution of this question is the key to the critique of taste, and so is worthy of all attention.

If the pleasure in the given object precedes, and it is only its universal communicability that is to be acknowledged in the judgment of taste about the representation of the object, there would be a contradiction. For such pleasure would be nothing different from the mere pleasantness in the sensation, and so in accordance with its nature could have only private validity, because it is immediately dependent on the representation through which the object *is given.*

Hence it is the universal capability of communication of the mental state in the given representation which, as the subjective condition of the judgment of taste, must be fundamental and must have the pleasure in the object as its consequent. But nothing can be universally communicated except cognition and representation, so far as it belongs to cognition. For it is only thus that this latter can be objective, and only through this has it a universal point of reference, with which the representative power of everyone is compelled to harmonize. If the determining ground of our judgment as to this universal communicability of the representation is to be merely subjective, i.e. is conceived independently of any concept of the object, it can be nothing else than the state of mind, which is to be met with in the relation of our representative powers to each other, so far as they refer a given representation to *cognition in general.*

The cognitive powers, which are involved by this representation, are here in free play, because no definite concept limits them to a definite rule of cognition. Hence the state of mind in this representation must be a feeling of the free play of the representative powers in a given representation with reference to a cognition in general. Now a representation by which an object is given that is to become a cognition in general requires *imagination* for the gathering together the manifold of intuition, and *understanding* for the unity of the concept uniting the representations. This state of *free play* of the cognitive faculties in a representation by which an object is given must be universally communicable, because cognition, as the determination of the object with which given representations (in whatever subject) are to agree, is the only kind of representation which is valid for everyone.

The subjective universal communicability of the mode of representation in a judgment of taste, since it is to be possible without presupposing a definite concept, can refer to nothing else than the state of mind in the free play of the imagination and the understanding (so far as they agree with each other, as is requisites for *cognition in general*). We are conscious that this subjective relation, suitable for cognition in general, must be valid for everyone, and thus must be universally communicable, just as if it were a definite cognition, resting always on that relation as its subjective condition.

This merely subjective (aesthetical) judging of the object, or of the representation by which it is given, precedes the pleasure in the same and is the ground of this pleasure in the harmony of the cognitive faculties; but on that universality of the subjective conditions for judging of objects is alone based the universal subjective validity of the satisfaction bound up by us with the representation of the object that we call beautiful.

That the power of communicating one's state of mind, even though only in respect of the cognitive faculties, carries a pleasure with it, this we can easily show from the natural propension of man toward sociability (empirical and psychological). But this is not enough for our design. The pleasure that we feel is, in a judgment of taste, necessarily imputed by us to everyone else, as if, when we call a thing beautiful, it is to be regarded as a characteristic of the object which is determined in it according to concepts, though beauty, without a reference to the feeling of the subject, is nothing by itself. But we must reserve the examination of this question until we have answered that other—if and how aesthetical judgments are possible *a priori*.

We now occupy ourselves with the easier question, in what way we are conscious of a mutual subjective harmony of the cognitive powers with one another in the judgment of taste—is it aesthetically by mere internal sense and sensation, or is it intellectually by the consciousness of our designed activity, by which we bring them into play?

If the given representation which occasions the judgment of taste were a concept uniting understanding and imagination in the judging of the object, into a cognition of the object, the consciousness of this relation would be intellectual (as in the objective schematism of the judgment of which the *Critique* treats). But then the judgment would not be laid down in reference to pleasure and pain, and consequently would not be a judgment of taste. But the judgment of taste, independently of concepts, determines the object in respect of satisfaction and of the predicate of beauty. Therefore that subjective unity of relation can only make itself known by means of sensation. The excitement of both faculties (imagination and understanding) to indeterminate but yet, through the stimulus of the given sensation, harmonious activity, viz. that which belongs to cognition in general, is the sensation whose universal communicability is postulated by the judgment of taste. An objective relation can only be thought, but yet, so far as it is subjective according to its conditions, can be felt in its effect on the mind; and, of a relation based on no concept (like the relation of the representative powers to a cognitive faculty in general), no other consciousness is possible than that through the sensation of the effect, which consists in the more lively play of both mental powers (the imagination and the understanding) when animated by mutual agreement. A representation which, as individual and apart from comparison with others, yet has an agreement with the conditions of universality which it is the business of the understanding to supply, brings the cognitive faculties into that proportionate accord which we require for all cognition, and so regard as holding for everyone who is determined to judge by means of understanding and sense in combination (i.e. for every man).

Explanation of the Beautiful Resulting from the Second Moment

The *beautiful* is that which pleases universally without [requiring] a concept. . . .

40. Of Taste as a Kind of *Sensus Communis*

We often give to the judgment, if we are considering the result rather than the act of its reflection, the name of a sense, and we speak of a sense of truth, or of a sense of decorum, of justice, etc. And yet we know, or at least we ought to know, that these concepts cannot have their place in sense, and further, that sense has not the least capacity for expressing universal rules; but that no representation of truth, fitness, beauty, or justice, and so forth could come into our thoughts if we could not rise beyond sense to higher faculties of cognition. *The common understanding of men,* which, as the mere healthy (not yet cultivated) understanding, we regard as the least to be expected from anyone claiming the name of man, has therefore the doubtful honor of being given the name of "common sense" (*sensus communis*); and in such a way that, by the name "common" (not merely in our language, where the word actually has a double signification, but in many others), we understand "vulgar," that which is everywhere met with, the possession of which indicates absolutely no merit or superiority.

But under the *sensus communis* we must include the idea of a sense *common to all,* i.e. of a faculty of judgment which, in its reflection, takes account (*a priori*) of the mode of representation of all other men in thought, in order, as it were, to compare its judgment with the collective reason of humanity, and thus to escape the illusion arising from the private conditions that could be so easily taken for objective, which would injuriously affect the judgment. This is done by comparing our judgment with the possible rather than the actual judgments of others, and by putting ourselves in the place of any other man, by abstracting from the limitations which contingently attach to our own judgment. This again is brought about by leaving aside as much as possible the matter of our representative state, i.e. sensation, and simply having respect to the formal peculiarities of our representation or representative state. Now this operation of reflection seems perhaps too artificial to be attributed to the faculty called *common sense,* but it only appears so when expressed in abstract formulae. In itself there is nothing more natural than to abstract from charm or emotion if we are seeking a judgment that is to serve as a universal rule.

The following maxims of common human understanding do not properly come in here, as parts of the Critique of Taste, but yet they may serve to elucidate its fundamental propositions. They are: (1) to think for oneself; (2) to put ourselves in thought in the place of everyone else; (3) always to think consistently. The first is the maxim of *unprejudiced* thought; the second of *enlarged* thought; the third of *consecutive* thought. The first is the maxim of a never *passive* reason. The tendency to such passivity, and therefore to heteronomy of the reason, is called *prejudice;* and the greatest prejudice of all is to represent nature as not subject to the rules that the understanding places at its basis by means of its own essential law, i.e. is *superstition.* Deliverance from superstition is called *enlightenment,* because, although this name belongs to deliverance from prejudices in general, yet superstition specially (*in sensu eminenti*[8]) deserves to be called a prejudice. For the blindness in which superstition places us, which it even imposes on us as an obligation, makes the need of being guided by others, and the consequent passive state of our reason, peculiarly noticeable. As regards the second maxim of the mind, we are otherwise wont to call him limited (*borne,* the opposite of *enlarged*) whose talents attain to no great use (especially as regards intensity). But here we are not speaking of the faculty of cognition, but of the *mode of thought* which makes a purposive use thereof. However small may be the area or the degree to which a man's natural gifts reach, yet it indicates a man of *enlarged thought* if he disregards the subjective private conditions of his own judgment, by which so many others are confined, and reflects upon it from a *universal standpoint* (which he can only determine by placing himself at the standpoint of others). The third maxim, viz. that of *consecutive thought,* is the most difficult to attain, and can only be attained by the combination of both the former and after the constant observance of them has grown into a habit. We may say that the first of

---

[8]*In sensu eminenti* means "in the primary sense of the term."

these maxims is the maxim of understanding, the second of judgment, and the third of reason.

I take up again the threads interrupted by this digression, and I say that taste can be called *sensus communis* with more justice than sound understanding can, and that the aesthetical judgment rather than the intellectual may bear the name of a sense common to all, if we are willing to use the word "sense" of an effect of mere reflection upon the mind, for then we understand by sense the feeling of pleasure. We could even define taste as the faculty of judging of that which makes *universally communicable,* without the mediation of a concept, our feeling in a given representation.

The skill that men have in communicating their thoughts requires also a relation between the imagination and the understanding in order to associate intuitions with concepts, and concepts again with those concepts, which then combine in a cognition. But in that case the agreement of the two mental powers is *according to law,* under the constraint of definite concepts. Only where the imagination in its freedom awakens the understanding and is put by it into regular play, without the aid of concepts, does the representation communicate itself not as a thought, but as an internal feeling of a purposive state of mind.

Taste is then the faculty of judging *a priori* of the communicability of feelings that are bound up with a given representation (without the mediation of a concept).

If we could assume that the mere universal communicability of a feeling must carry in itself an interest for us with it (which, however, we are not justified in concluding from the character of a merely reflective judgment), we should be able to explain why the feeling in the judgment of taste comes to be imputed to everyone, so to speak, as a duty. . . .

44. Of Beautiful Art

There is no science of the beautiful,[9] but only a critique of it; and there is no such thing as beautiful science, but only beautiful art. For as regards the first point, if it could be decided scientifically, i.e. by proofs, whether a thing was to be regarded as beautiful or not, the judgment upon beauty would belong to science and would not be a judgment of taste. And as far as the second point is concerned, a science which should be beautiful as such is a nonentity. For if in such a science we were to ask for grounds and proofs, we would be put off with tasteful phrases (*bon-mots*). The source of the common expression, *beautiful science,* is without doubt nothing else than this, as it has been rightly remarked, that for beautiful art in its entire completeness much science is requisite, e.g. a knowledge of ancient languages, a learned familiarity with classical authors, history, a knowledge of antiquities, etc. And hence these historical sciences, because they form the necessary preparation and basis for beautiful art, and also partly because under them is included the knowledge of the products of beautiful art (rhetoric and poetry), have come to be called beautiful sciences by a transposition of words.

If art which is adequate to the *cognition* of a possible object performs the actions requisite therefor merely in order to make it actual, it is *mechanical* art; but if it has for its immediate design the feeling of pleasure, it is called *aesthetical* art. This is again either *pleasant* or *beautiful.* It is the first if its purpose is that the pleasure should accompany the representations [of the object] regarded as mere *sensations;* it is the second if they are regarded as *modes of cognition.*

Pleasant arts are those that are directed merely to enjoyment. Of this class are all those charming arts that can gratify a company at table, e.g. the art of telling stories in an entertaining way, of starting the company in frank and lively conversation, of raising them by jest and laugh to a certain pitch of merriment; when, as people say, there may be a great deal of gossip at the feast, but no one will be answerable for what he says, because they are only concerned with momentary entertainment, and not with any permanent material for reflection or subsequent discussion. (Among these are also to be reckoned the way of arranging the table for enjoyment and, at great feasts, the management of the music. This latter

---

[9] A science has to have rules, theories, and concepts.

is a wonderful thing. It is meant to dispose to gaiety the minds of the guests, regarded solely as a pleasant noise, without anyone paying the least attention to its composition; and it favors the free conversation of each with his neighbor.) Again, to this class belong all games which bring with them no further interest than that of making the time pass imperceptibly.

On the other hand, beautiful art is a mode of representation which is purposive for itself and which, although devoid of [definite] purpose, yet furthers the culture of the mental powers in reference to social communication.

The universal communicability of a pleasure carries with it in its very concept that the pleasure is not one of enjoyment, from mere sensation, but must be derived from reflection; and thus aesthetical art, as the art of beauty, has for standard the reflective judgment and not sensation. . . .

46. Beautiful Art Is the Art of Genius

Genius [10] is the talent (or natural gift) which gives the rule to art. Since talent, as the innate productive faculty of the artist, belongs itself to nature, we may express the matter thus: Genius is the innate mental disposition (*ingenium*) *through which* nature gives the rule to art.

Whatever may be thought of this definition, whether it is merely arbitrary or whether it is adequate to the concept that we are accustomed to combine with the word *genius* (which is to be examined in the following paragraphs), we can prove already beforehand that, according to the signification of the word here adopted, beautiful arts must necessarily be considered as arts of *genius*.

For every art presupposes rules by means of which in the first instance a product, if it is to be called artistic, is represented as possible. But the concept of beautiful art does not permit the judgment upon the beauty of a product to be derived from any rule which has a *concept* as its determining ground, and therefore has at its basis a concept of the way in which the product is possible. Therefore beautiful art cannot itself devise the rule according to which it can bring about its product. But since at the same time a product can never be called art without some precedent rule, nature in the subject must (by the harmony of its faculties) give the rule to art; i.e. beautiful art is only possible as a product of genius.

We thus see (1) that genius is a *talent* for producing that for which no definite rule can be given; it is not a mere aptitude for what can be learned by a rule. Hence *originality* must be its first property. (2) But since it also can produce original nonsense, its products must be models, i.e. *exemplary,* and they consequently ought not to spring from imitation, but must serve as a standard or rule of judgment for others. (3) It cannot describe or indicate scientifically how it brings about its products, but it gives the rule just as nature does. Hence the author of a product for which he is indebted to his genius does not know himself how he has come by his ideas; and he has not the power to devise the like at pleasure or in accordance with a plan, and to communicate it to others in percepts that will enable them to produce similar products. (Hence it is probable that the word "genius" is derived from *genius,* that peculiar guiding and guardian spirit given to a man at his birth, from whose suggestion these original ideas proceed.) (4) Nature, by the medium of genius, does not prescribe rules to science but to art, and to it only in so far as it is to be beautiful art.

47. Elucidation and Confirmation of the Above Explanation of Genius

Everyone is agreed that genius is entirely opposed to the *spirit of imitation*. Now since learning is nothing but imitation, it follows that the greatest ability and teachableness (capacity) regarded *qua* teachableness cannot avail for genius. Even if a

---

[10] Prior to Kant, the primary meaning of *genius* was a kind of individual spirit, character, or talent—"his genius was for making money." Kant gives it a special meaning more in line with its later usage, when genius becomes a capacity for individual creative production without any model.

man thinks or composes for himself and does not merely take in what others have taught, even if he discovers many things in art and science, this is not the right ground for calling such a (perhaps great) *head* a genius (as opposed to him who, because he can only learn and imitate, is called a *shallowpate*). For even these things could be learned; they lie in the natural path of him who investigates and reflects according to rules, and they do not differ specifically from what can be acquired by industry through imitation. Thus we can readily learn all that Newton has set forth in his immortal work on the *Principles of Natural Philosophy,* however great a head was required to discover it, but we cannot learn to write spirited poetry, however express may be the precepts of the art and however excellent its models. The reason is that Newton could make all his steps, from the first elements of geometry to his own great and profound discoveries, intuitively plain and definite as regards consequence, not only to himself but to everyone else. But a Homer [11] or a Wieland [12] cannot show how his ideas, so rich in fancy and yet so full of thought, come together in his head, simply because he does not know and therefore cannot teach others. In science, then, the greatest discoverer only differs in degree from his laborious imitator and pupil, but he differs specifically from him whom nature has gifted for beautiful art. For in the fact that the former talent is directed to the ever advancing greater perfection of knowledge and every advantage depending on it, and at the same time to the imparting this same knowledge to others—in this it has a great superiority over [the talent of] those who deserve the honor of being called geniuses. For art stands still at a certain point; a boundary is set to it beyond which it cannot go, which presumably has been reached long ago and cannot be extended further. Again, artistic skill cannot be communicated; it is imparted to every artist immediately by the hand of nature; and so it dies

with him, until nature endows another in the same way, so that he only needs an example in order to put in operation in a similar fashion the talent of which he is conscious.

If now it is a natural gift which must prescribe its rule to art (as beautiful art), of what kind is this rule? It cannot be reduced to a formula and serve as a precept, for then the judgment upon the beautiful would be determinable according to concepts; but the rule must be abstracted from the fact, i.e. from the product, on which others may try their own talent by using it as a model, not to be *copied* but to be *imitated.* How this is possible is hard to explain. The ideas of the artist excite like ideas in his pupils if nature has endowed them with a like proportion of their mental powers. Hence models of beautiful art are the only means of handing down these ideas to posterity. This cannot be done by mere descriptions, especially not in the case of the arts of speech; and in this latter classical models are only to be had in the old dead languages, now preserved only as "the learned languages."

Although mechanical and beautiful art are very different, the first being a mere art of industry and learning and the second of genius, yet there is no beautiful art in which there is not a mechanical element that can be comprehended by rules and followed accordingly, and in which therefore there must be something *scholastic* [13] as an essential condition. For [in every art] some purpose must be conceived; otherwise we could not ascribe the product to art at all; it would be a mere product of chance. But in order to accomplish a purpose, definite rules from which we cannot dispense ourselves are requisite. Now since the originality of the talent constitutes an essential (though not the only) element in the character of genius, shallow heads believe that they cannot better show themselves to be full-blown geniuses than by throwing off the constraint of all rules; they believe, in effect, that one could make a braver show on the back of a wild horse than on

---

[11] Homer was the seventh- or eighth-century B.C.E. Greek composer of the epic poems the *Iliad* and the *Odyssey.*
[12] Christoph Martin Wieland (1733–1813) was a German poet and novelist whose subjects included classical stories.

[13] Scholasticism was the medieval philosophical technique that depended on logical syllogisms and classical authorities, particularly Aristotle.

the back of a trained animal. Genius can only furnish rich *material* for products of beautiful art: its execution and its *form* require talent cultivated in the schools, in order to make such a use of this material as will stand examination by the judgment. But it is quite ridiculous for a man to speak and decide like a genius in things which require the most careful investigation by reason. One does not know whether to laugh more at the impostor who spreads such a mist around him that we cannot clearly use our judgment, and so use our imagination the more, or at the public which naively imagines that his inability to cognize clearly and to comprehend the masterpiece before him arises from new truths crowding in on him in such abundance that details (duly weighed definitions and accurate examination of fundamental propositions) seem but clumsy work.

48. Of the Relation of Genius to Taste

For *judging* of beautiful objects as such, *taste* is requisite; but for beautiful art, i.e. for the *production* of such objects, *genius* is requisite.

If we consider genius as the talent for beautiful art (which the special meaning of the word implies) and in this point of view analyze it into the faculties which must concur to constitute such a talent, it is necessary in the first instance to determine exactly the difference between natural beauty, the judging of which requires only taste, and artificial beauty, the possibility of which (to which reference must be made in judging such an object) requires genius.

A natural beauty is a *beautiful thing;* artificial beauty is a *beautiful representation* of a thing.

In order to judge of a natural beauty as such, I need not have beforehand a concept of what sort of thing the object is to be; i.e. I need not know its material purposiveness (the purpose), but its mere form pleases by itself in the act of judging it without any knowledge of the purpose. But if the object is given as a product of art and as such is to be declared beautiful, then, because art always supposes a purpose in the cause (and its causal-

ity), there must be at bottom in the first instance a concept of what the thing is to be. And as the agreement of the manifold in a thing with its inner destination, its purpose, constitutes the perfection of the thing, it follows that in judging of artificial beauty the perfection of the thing must be taken into account; but in judging of natural beauty (*as such*) there is no question at all about this. It is true that in judging of objects of nature, especially objects endowed with life, e.g. a man or a horse, their objective purposiveness also is commonly taken into consideration in judging of their beauty; but then the judgment is no longer purely aesthetical, i.e. a mere judgment of taste. Nature is no longer judged inasmuch as it appears like art, but in so far as it *is* actual (although superhuman) art; and the teleological judgment serves as the basis and condition of the aesthetical, as a condition to which the latter must have respect. In such a case, e.g. if it is said "That is a beautiful woman," we think nothing else than this: nature represents in her figure the purposes in view in the shape of a woman's figure. For we must look beyond the mere form to a concept, if the object is to be thought in such a way by means of a logically conditioned aesthetical judgment.

Beautiful art shows its superiority in this, that it describes as beautiful things which may be in nature ugly or displeasing. The Furies,[14] diseases, the devastations of war, etc., may [even regarded as calamitous] be described as very beautiful, as they are represented in a picture. There is only one kind of ugliness which cannot be represented in accordance with nature without destroying all aesthetical satisfaction, and consequently artificial beauty, viz. that which excites *disgust.* For in this singular sensation, which rests on mere imagination, the object is represented as it were obtruding itself for our enjoyment, while we strive against it with all our might. And the artistic representation of the object is no longer distinguished

---

[14]The Furies belonged to the older generation of Greek gods. Their function was to pursue those guilty of some blood crime such as incest or patricide.

from the nature of the object itself in our sensation, and thus it is impossible that it can be regarded as beautiful. The art of sculpture again, because in its products art is almost interchangeable with nature, excludes from its creations the immediate representation of ugly objects; e.g. it represents death by a beautiful genius, the warlike spirit by Mars,[15] and permits [all such things] to be represented only by an allegory or attribute that has a pleasing effect, and thus only indirectly by the aid of the interpretation of reason, and not for the mere aesthetical judgment.

So much for the beautiful representation of an object, which is properly only the form of the presentation of a concept, by means of which this latter is communicated universally. But to give this form to the product of beautiful art, mere taste is requisite. By taste the artist estimates his work after he has exercised and corrected it by manifold examples from art or nature, and after many, often toilsome, attempts to content himself he finds that form which satisfies him. Hence this form is not, as it were, a thing of inspiration or the result of a free swing of the mental powers, but of a slow and even painful process of improvement, by which he seeks to render it adequate to his thought, without detriment to the freedom of the play of his powers.

But tastes is merely a judging and not a productive faculty, and what is appropriate to it is therefore not a work of beautiful art. It can only be a product belonging to useful and mechanical art or even to science, produced according to definite rules that can be learned and must be exactly followed. But the pleasing form that is given to it is only the vehicle of communication and a mode, as it were, of presenting it, in respect of which we remain free to a certain extent, although it is combined with a definite purpose. Thus we desire that table appointments, a moral treatise, even a sermon, should have in themselves this form of beautiful art, without it seeming to be *sought;* but we do not therefore call these things works of beautiful art. Under the latter class are reckoned a poem, a piece of music, a picture gallery, etc.; and in some works of this kind asserted to be works of beautiful art we find genius without taste, while in others we find taste without genius. . . .

50. Of the Combination of Taste with Genius in the Products of Beautiful Art

To ask whether it is more important for the things of beautiful art that genius or taste should be displayed is the same as to ask whether in it more depends on imagination or on judgment. Now since in respect of the first an art is rather said to be *full of spirit,* but only deserves to be called a *beautiful* art on account of the second, this latter is at least, as its indispensable condition (*conditio sine qua non*), the most important thing to which one has to look in the judging of art as beautiful art. Abundance and originality of ideas are less necessary to beauty than the accordance of the imagination in its freedom with the conformity to law of the understanding. For all the abundance of the former produces in lawless freedom nothing but nonsense; on the other hand, the judgment is the faculty by which it is adjusted to the understanding.

Taste, like the judgment in general, is the discipline (or training) of genius; it clips its wings, it makes it cultured and polished; but, at the same time, it gives guidance as to where and how far it may extend itself if it is to remain purposive. And while it brings clearness and order into the multitude of the thoughts [of genius], it makes the ideas susceptible of being permanently and, at the same time, universally assented to, and capable of being followed by others, and of an ever progressive culture. If, then, in the conflict of these two properties in a product something must be sacrificed, it should be rather on the side of genius; and the judgment, which in the things of beautiful art gives its decision from its own proper principles, will rather sacrifice the freedom and wealth of the imagination than permit anything prejudicial to the understanding.

---

[15] Mars was the Roman god of war.

For beautiful art, therefore, *imagination, understanding, spirit,* and *taste* are requisite. . . .

56. Representation of the Antinomy of Taste [16]

The first commonplace of taste is contained in the proposition, with which every tasteless person proposes to avoid blame: *everyone has his own taste.* That is as much as to say that the determining ground of this judgment is merely subjective (gratification or grief), and that the judgment has no right to the necessary assent of others.

The second commonplace invoked even by those who admit for judgments of taste the right to speak with validity for everyone is: *there is no disputing about taste.* That is as much as to say that the determining ground of a judgment of taste may indeed be objective, but that it cannot be reduced to definite concepts; and that consequently about the judgment itself can be *decided* by proofs, although much may rightly be *contested.* For *contesting* [quarreling] and *disputing* [controversy] are doubtless the same in this, that, by means of the mutual opposition of judgments they seek to produce their accordance, but different in that the latter hopes to bring this about according to definite concepts as determining grounds, and consequently assumes *objective concepts* as grounds of the judgment. But where this is regarded as impracticable, controversy is regarded as alike impracticable.

We easily see that, between these two commonplaces, there is a proposition wanting which, though it has not passed into a proverb, is yet familiar to everyone, viz. *there may be a quarrel about taste* (although there can be no controversy). But this proposition involves the contradictory of the former one. For wherever quarreling is permissible, there must be a hope of mutual reconciliation; and consequently we can count on grounds of our judgment that have not merely private validity, and therefore are not merely subjective.

And to this the proposition, *everyone has his own taste,* is directly opposed.

There emerges therefore in respect of the principle of taste the following antinomy:

1. *Thesis.* The judgment of taste is not based upon concepts, for otherwise it would admit of controversy (would be determinable by proofs).
2. *Antithesis.* The judgment of taste is based on concepts, for otherwise, despite its diversity, we could not quarrel about it (we could not claim for our judgment the necessary assent of others).

57. Solution of the Antinomy of Taste

There is no possibility of removing the conflict between these principles that underlie every judgment of taste (which are nothing else than the two peculiarities of the judgment of taste exhibited above in the Analytic), except by showing that the concept to which we refer the object in this kind of judgment is not taken in the same sense in both maxims of the aesthetical judgment. This twofold sense or twofold point of view is necessary to our transcendental judgment, but also the illusion which arises from the confusion of one with the other is natural and unavoidable.

The judgment of taste must refer to some concept; otherwise it could make absolutely no claim to be necessarily valid for everyone. But it is not therefore capable of being proved *from* a concept, because a concept may be either determinable or in itself undetermined and undeterminable. The concepts of the understanding are of the former kind; they are determinable through predicates of sensible intuition which can correspond to them. But the transcendental rational concept of the supersensibles, which lies at the basis of all sensibles intuition, is of the latter kind, and therefore cannot be theoretically determined further.

Now the judgment of taste is applied to objects of sense, but not with a view of determining a *concept* of them for the understanding; for it is

---

[16] An *antinomy* is a contradiction between two laws (from *antinomian*), each of which seems reasonable or obvious.

not a cognitive judgment. It is thus only a private judgment, in which a singular representation intuitively perceived is referred to the feeling of pleasure, and so far would be limited as regards its validity to the individual judging. The object is *for me* an object of satisfaction; by others it may be regarded quite differently—everyone has his own taste.

Nevertheless there is undoubtedly contained in the judgment of taste a wider reference of the representation of the object (as well as of the subject), whereon we base an extension of judgments of this kind as necessary for everyone. At the basis of this there must necessarily be a concept somewhere, though a concept which cannot be determined through intuition. But through a concept of this sort we know nothing, and consequently it can *supply no proof* for the judgment of taste. Such a concept is the mere pure rational concept of the supersensible which underlies the object (and also the subject judging it), regarded as an object of sense and thus as phenomenal. For if we do not admit such a reference, the claim of the judgment of taste to universal validity would not hold good. If the concept on which it is based were only a mere confused concept of the understanding, like that of perfection, with which we could bring the sensible intuition of the beautiful into correspondence, it would be at least possible in itself to base the judgment of taste on proofs, which contradicts the thesis.

But all contradiction disappears if I say: the judgment of taste is based on a concept (viz. the concept of the general ground of the subjective purposiveness of nature for the judgment); from which, however, nothing can be known and proved in respects of the object, because it is in itself undeterminable and useless for knowledge. Yet at the same time and on that very account the judgment has validity for everyone (though, of course, for each only as a singular judgment immediately accompanying his intuition), because its determining ground lies perhaps in the concept of that which may be regarded as the supersensible substrata of humanity.

The solution of an antinomy only depends on the possibility of showing that two apparently contradictory propositions do not contradict each other in fact, but that they may be consistent, although the explanation of the possibility of their concept may transcend our cognitive faculties. That this illusion is natural and unavoidable by human reason, and also why it is so and remains so, although it ceases to deceive after the analysis of the apparent contradiction, may be thus explained.

In the two contradictory judgments we take the concept on which the universal validity of a judgment must be based in the same sense, and yet we apply to it two opposite predicates. In the thesis we mean that the judgment of taste is not based upon *determinate* concepts, and in the antithesis that the judgment of taste is based upon a concept, but an *indeterminate* one (viz. of the supersensible substrata of phenomena). Between these two there is no contradiction.

We can do nothing more than remove this conflict between the claims and counterclaims of taste. It is absolutely impossible to give a definite objective principle of taste in accordance with which its judgments could be derived, examined, and established, for then the judgment would not be one of taste at all. The subjective principle, viz. the indefinite idea of the supersensibles in us, can only be put forward as the sole key to the puzzle of this faculty whose sources are hidden from us; it can be made no further intelligible.

The proper concept of taste, that is of a merely reflective aesthetical judgment, lies at the basis of the antinomy here exhibited and adjusted. Thus the two apparently contradictory principles are reconciled—*both can be true,* which is sufficient. If, on the other hand, we assume as some do, *pleasantness* as the determining ground of taste (on account of the singularity of the representation which lies at the basis of the judgment of taste) or, as others will have it, the principle of perfection (on account of the universality of the same), and settle the definition of taste accordingly, then there arises an antinomy which it is absolutely impossible to adjust except by showing that *both* the contrary[17] (not merely contradictory) *propositions are false.* And this would prove that the concept on which they are based is self-contradictory. Hence we see that the removal of the antinomy of the aesthetical judgment takes a course similar to that pursued by the critique in the solution of the antinomies of pure theoretical reason. And thus here, as also in the *Critique of Practical Reason,* the antinomies force us against our will to look beyond the sensible and to seek in the supersensible the point of union for all our *a priori* faculties, because no other expedient is left to make our reason harmonious with itself.

Study Questions

1. What does Kant mean by *aesthetical?* Give an example of an aesthetical judgment.
2. What is the difference between pleasure and delight? Between being pleased and being gratified?

---

[17] In Aristotelian logic, contraries cannot both be true, but they may both be false; for example, "All dogs are spotted" and "No dogs are spotted" cannot both be true, but they can both be false.

3. Why isn't art morally good (or bad)?
4. What does it mean to say that judgments of taste are contemplative?
5. What distinguishes the beautiful from the pleasant and the good?
6. What kind of judgments are literally "for me"?
7. Kant was notorious for the ordinariness of his taste. What kind of examples does he give for beauty?
8. If beauty and taste are free of all concepts, what is the basis for a judgment that one painting is better than another?
9. Genius "gives the rule to art." Can there be genius that does not produce anything?
10. Kant identifies taste with a pure delight. What, then, is bad taste? What is ugliness?
11. Give specific examples of the antinomy of taste from (a) popular music, (b) film, and (c) television.
12. How is the antinomy of taste resolved?
13. What role does "imagination" play in Kant's theory?
14. Does the existence of a "common sense" mean that everyone thinks alike? Explain.

Section 1 Passages for Discussion

♦ ♦

To philosophise, in a just signification, is but to carry good-breeding a step higher. For the accomplishment of breeding is, to learn whatever is decent in company or beautiful in arts; and the use of philosophy is, to learn what is just in society and beautiful in Nature and the order of the world.

'Tis not wit merely, but a temper which must form the well-bred man. In the same manner, 'tis not a head merely, but a heart and resolution which must complete the real philosopher. Both characters aim at what is excellent, aspire to a just taste, and carry in view the model of what is beautiful and becoming. Accordingly, the respective conduct and distinct manners of each party are regulated; the one according to the perfectest ease and good entertainment of company, the other according to the strictest interest of mankind and society; the one according to a man's rank and quality in his private station, the other according to his rank and dignity in nature.

. . . Thus, according to our author, the taste of beauty and the relish of what is decent, just, and amiable perfects the character of the gentleman and the philosopher. And the study of such a taste or relish will, as we suppose, be ever the great employment and concern of him who covets as well to be wise and good as agreeable and polite.

ANTHONY, EARL OF SHAFTESBURY (1671–1713),
Characteristics of Men, Manners, Opinions, Times

First follow Nature, and your judgment frame
By her just standard, which is still the same:
Unerring Nature! still divinely bright,
One clear, unchang'd, and universal light,
Life, force and beauty, must to all impart,
At once the source, and end, and test of art.

ALEXANDER POPE (1688–1744), *An Essay on Criticism*

This Secondary Pleasure of the Imagination proceeds from that Action of the Mind, which compares the ideas arising from the Original Objects, with the Ideas we receive from the Statue, Picture, Description, or Sound that represents them. It is impossible for us to give the necessary Reason, why this Operation of the Mind is attended with so much Pleasure, as I have before observed on the same Occasion; but we find a great variety of Entertainments derived from this single Principle.

JOSEPH ADDISON (1672–1719), *The Pleasures of the Imagination*

Taste consists chiefly in the improvement of those principles, which are commonly called the powers of imagination, and are considered by modern philosophers as internal or reflex senses, supplying us with finer and more delicate perceptions, than any which can be properly referred to our external organs. These are reducible to the following principles: the senses of novelty, of sublimity, of beauty, of imitation, of harmony, of ridicule, and of virtue.

ALEXANDER GERARD (1728–1795), *An Essay on Taste*

The business of a poet is to examine, not the individual, but the species; to remark general properties and large appearances; he does not number the streaks of the tulip, or describe the different shades in the verdure of the forest. He is to exhibit in his portraits of nature such prominent and striking features, as recall the original to every mind; and must neglect the minuter discriminations, which one may have remarked, and another have neglected, for those characteristics which are alike obvious to vigilance and carelessness.

SAMUEL JOHNSON (1709–1784), Rasselas

What we now call genius begins, not where rules, abstractedly taken, end; but where known vulgar and trite rules have no longer any place. It must of necessity be that even works of genius, like every other effect, as they must have their cause, must likewise have their rules; it cannot be by chance that excellences are produced with any constancy or any certainty, for this is not the nature of chance; but the rules by which men of extraordinary parts, and such as are called men of genius, work, are either such as they discover by their own peculiar observations, or of such a nice texture as not easily to admit being expressed in words; especially as artists are not very frequently skilful in that mode of communicating ideas.

SIR JOSHUA REYNOLDS (1723–1792), Discourse VI

Art has taken in much greater territory in modern times. Its imitations extend over the whole of nature of which beauty is only a small part. Truth and expression are its first law; and just as nature itself sacrifices beauty to higher purposes, so the artist must subordinate beauty also to his greater purpose and pursue it no further than truth and expression allow. Enough that through truth and expression the ugliness of nature is changed into a beauty of art.

G. E. LESSING (1729–1781), Laocoön

If it is true that painting uses a completely different kind of sign for its imitations than poetry—painting using figures and colors in space, poetry using articulate tones in time, as unquestionably signs must have a sequential relation to what they signify— then signs ordered next to each other can represent only objects or parts of objects which exist next to one another while signs which follow one another can express object or their parts which follow one another.

Objects that are next to one another or whose parts are next to one another are called bodies. Consequently, bodies, with their visible properties, are the proper object of painting.

Objects that follow one another, or whose parts parts follow one another in time, are actions. Consequently actions are the proper subjects of poetry.

G. E. LESSING, Laocoön

"I do not wish to influence Mr. Rushworth," he [Edmund] continued, "but had I a place to new fashion, I should not put myself into the hands of an improver. I would rather have an inferior degree of beauty, of my own choice, and acquired progressively. I would rather abide by my own blunders than by his."

"You would know that you were about of course—but that would not suit me. I have no eye or ingenuity for such matters, but as they are before me; and had I a place of my own in the country, I should be most thankful to any Mr. Repton who would undertake it, and give me as much beauty as he could for my money; and I should never look at it, till it was complete."

"It would be delightful to me to see the progress of it all," said Fanny.

"Ay—you have been brought up to it. It was no part of my education; and the only dose I ever had, being administered by not the first favourite in the world, has made me consider improvements in hand as the greatest nuisances. . . . I would have every thing as complete as possible in the country, shrubberies and flower gardens, and rustic seats innumerable; but it must be all done without my care."

JANE AUSTEN (1775–1817), *Mansfield Park*

The object of the sensuous instinct, expressed in a universal conception, is named Life in the widest acceptation: a conception that expresses all material existence and all that is immediately present in the senses. The object of the formal instinct, expressed in a universal conception, is called shape or form, as well in an exact as in an inexact acceptation; a conception that embraces all formal qualities of things and all relations of the same to the thinking powers. The object of the play instinct, represented in a general statement, may therefore bear the name of living form; a term that serves to describe all aesthetic qualities of phenomena, and what people style, in the widest sense, beauty.

FRIEDRICH SCHILLER (1759–1805), *Aesthetical Letters XV*

The Nineteenth Century <u>Section 2</u>

ONE WAY TO REGARD AESTHETICS in the nineteenth century is to see it as the heritage of Immanuel Kant. Kant had brought together the empiricist and rationalist traditions from the eighteenth century in a single, massive synthesis. Empiricism had emphasized that sense was at the basis of knowledge and that aesthetics was the most immediate form of sense. Rationalism did not ignore sense, but rationalists insisted that sense without order and coherence was meaningless. Kant found the order for sense in the mind itself and gave sense a place at the foundation of knowledge. The aesthetic was understood as the preconceptual basis for both moral practice and theoretical concepts. G. W. F. Hegel developed the mental side of Kant's insight into a logical and historical system. Hegel's followers gave aesthetics an increasing role in his system. In the other direction, romanticism developed Kant's aesthetic intuition and his concepts of genius and imagination into a poetics of sense and feeling. This development was not all due to Kant, of course, but Kant provides a convenient point of reference for the developments that followed.

One of the most important changes in aesthetics was the Kantian separation of the aesthetic from concepts and theory. Increasingly after Kant, aesthetics was understood as an autonomous realm either independent of or opposed to conceptual thought. Feeling did not need reason as a faculty or reasons as justification. In some versions of an autonomous aesthetics, it was believed that reliance on concepts would repress feelings and make aesthetic experience impossible. One consequence of such theories was that aesthetics was treated as something isolated culturally from the everyday world. Art existed for art's sake, and an aesthete sought to live for art's sake. The rising industrial world had appalled many toward the end of the eighteenth century. In the nineteenth century, many felt that beauty could be found only in art which opposed the commercial world. The unreality of art was felt not as a disadvantage but as its virtue. The danger, of course, was that aesthetics would become as unreal as its advocates wanted it to be.

One way to avoid that danger was to recognize a close relation between aesthetics and religion. If aesthetics was unworldly, so was religion. If aesthetic feeling did not depend on reasons or justification, neither did faith. Religious piety had long depended on feeling as its essence. Revelation was inward. Aesthetic feeling and religious feeling could easily be associated with each other. Both were ways out of an unacceptable and, to the religious thinker, an ungodly world. If the identification between religious and aesthetic feeling could be sustained, then the aesthetic was not less real but more real than the ordinary world. Inspiration frequently was used in aesthetics in ways that parallel earlier doctrines of divine inspiration. In the nineteenth century, the emphasis of such inspiration was on the feeling it produced.

Frederic Leighton, English, 1830–1896. *Miss May Sartoris,* about
1860. Kimbell Art Museum, Fort Worth, Texas.

A second important Kantian legacy was the identification of aesthetics with knowledge. A basic problem for aesthetics, particularly among rationalists, had been that feeling seemed opposed to reason. Feeling and knowing were so different that they had
nothing in common. Knowing something was a rational process that no longer depended on feeling. Aesthetics would then be nothing more than a first step to be left
behind as soon as rational people could acquire more accurate ways of knowing. Kant

showed that that version of rationalism could not be correct. Aesthetic intuition was indeed the first step, but instead of leaving it behind, the mind transformed it into action and concepts. Accordingly, aesthetics was always a part of knowledge. Hegel took these possibilities seriously, and a whole tradition of German philosophy after Hegel tried to turn aesthetics into systematic philosophy. How far could the mind shape reality? Perhaps the mind itself was the model for reality and for history. Artists, particularly poets, found themselves in the role of philosophers. If what was required for knowledge was imagination and genius, then the arts were the place to look.

In many ways, the development of this theme was at odds with the doctrine of aesthetic feeling. The movement in the arts and philosophy known as romanticism incorporated elements of both. "Romanticism" is difficult to pin down to a single doctrine or movement. Its very nature was to defy rational examination and appeal directly to an intuition of the self. It might be regarded as an inward movement that is then projected outward onto the world. But romanticism also was productive. It did not stop with aesthetic feeling but turned that feeling into a creative force. In the words of the poet Samuel Taylor Coleridge, the creative mind of the poet repeats the creative act of the infinite I AM. According to Percy Bysshe Shelley, poets are the unacknowledged legislators of the world. Much of the romantic argument was taken quite literally, and romantics such as the poet Lord Byron acted out their theory in their lives. Byron died in Greece, where he had gone to join the Greeks fighting for independence from Turkey. From romantic theory emerged a belief in a creative imagination and a view of the artist as a personality and a hero. Romantic artists tried to be at once above the world and against it. They knew, but they also felt, and their knowing was a product of the intensity with which they feel.

Kantian aesthetics and its developments in Hegel and his followers as well as in romanticism produced a philosophical reaction. Instead of the mind shaping the world, the world may shape the mind. Materialism and determinism reject the mental priority of the mind and ideas. One important form of deterministic philosophy was based on the biological and zoological work of Charles Darwin. Darwin's interpreters and followers seized on his theories as a natural account of history that needed no human intervention. Darwinism had two forms. Its biological form emphasized that life evolved according to a process of competition and selection. Those life forms best equipped to survive were the future; choice and will had nothing to do with it. From this biological theory, a corresponding social theory developed. Those people who were best equipped to survive in a society would do best and be most successful. So success was a sign of ability, and poor and unsuccessful people deserved their place because they were not equipped to do better.

Darwinism had its aesthetic counterparts. Art and beauty have limited survival value, but they are economic forces. A materialist, Ludwig Feuerbach, reminded philosophers that we are what we eat. Karl Marx located art as a support to the class that made it possible. These and other materialist theories can be thought of as a direct inversion of Hegel's elevation of Kant's theories into a theory of history. Matter, not mind, is what has a history, according to this view. To understand what takes place in history, including art, we must look for what does the work and who pays.

An even more radical inversion of the Hegelian movement extended to romanticism and picked up the connection between religious feeling and art. Romanticism, with all its revolutionary fervor, is essentially positive about what the artist can do and the effects that art can have. Creative imagination is a good thing, and the self and personality are positive goods if they can be freed of their bondage to the ordinary. But the self also can be felt as a burden, and its isolation can be a cause of anxiety and fear. Thinkers who inverted romanticism and Hegel's positive history discovered an abyss that only faith can overcome. Individuals are thrown back upon the negative side of their personalities and feel a darkness in the soul. The Danish writer Søren Kierkegaard explored that inversion and located the aesthetic as a stage in the soul's confrontation with its own dread. A century later, Kierkegaard's aesthetics found its echoes in the post–World War I despair that produced the movement known as existentialism. Existentialism insists that the optimism about historical progress was only an illusion. The destruction of World War I seemed to bear that out. Aesthetics could be a freedom only without hope or absolutes of any kind. An even more radical inversion of Hegel's idealism is found in the work of Friedrich Nietzsche. For Nietzsche, only a complete dialectical inversion offers any historical hope. Rather than framing aesthetics as a religious feeling, Nietzsche contrasted the aesthetics of light with the aesthetics of descent and denial. Apollo, the god of light, dialectically opposes Dionysus, the god of ecstatic self-destruction. An aesthetics of reason and clarity opposes an aesthetics of rebellion and denial. God must die in order for anyone to be free, but freedom is terrible as well as joyful. These radical inversions incorporate the aesthetic into their picture, but they do not produce the kind of concrete relations between productivity and theory in their own time that one finds in romanticism. The romantics were poets first and theorists second. Kierkegaard, Nietzsche, and their followers tried to turn theory into poetry. Both Kierkegaard and Nietzsche provide inspiration in the twentieth century to new movements in art and philosophy that may or may not be accurate reflections of their nineteenth-century contexts.

A much more significant problem for aesthetics in the nineteenth century is its social and political transformation. The extended century we have identified, running from the French Revolution to World War I, is marked by significant cultural turns. In France, the Revolution degenerated into the Terror. A revolution that began as an attempt to throw off aristocratic domination in favor of social freedom turned on itself and slaughtered not only aristocrats but its own intellectuals. The eighteenth century Enlightenment thinkers had been very optimistic about the direction of history. The American Revolution bore out that optimism for many, but the Terror undermined it. In aesthetics and the arts as well, the degeneration of what had seemed an act of human freedom into a bloodbath deeply influenced philosophers and artists alike. It became much more difficult to believe that the self and its sensations were essentially good. In England, in particular, the combination of industrial society and empire building came into conflict with the finer feelings for art and the aesthetic. Critics like Thomas Carlyle and John Ruskin looked at history and tried to find some meaning in it. Art, they believed, had a social responsibility. They were pulled in opposing directions. They wanted to save art from the madness of an increasingly coarse society, but they also expected art to elevate at least some parts of that society and counteract the evil influences of money and power.

At the end of the century, the battlefields of World War I raised slaughter to unprecedented levels, and the established social and cultural fabric of Europe was changed irrevocably. In between, philosophers of art and theoretically aware artists sought ways to reconcile their art with the industrial age and its grim side-effects. Aesthetic autonomy had to compete with social responsibility. Realism and naturalism challenged romanticism. The freedom of artists was difficult to reconcile with theories of scientific and economic determinism. The fundamental problem of nineteenth-century aesthetics was how to reconcile its reliance on aesthetic feeling and experience with the realities of economic struggle and social disruption. The problem was not so much solved as abolished on the battlefields of France.

Nineteenth-century aesthetics defies systematic reduction. The different theories are interwoven in complex mixes. A massive academic literature grew up, particularly in Germany, but it is far less important than the eccentric but seminal writers such as Nietzsche and Kierkegaard, who went their own way. Nietzsche and Kierkegaard were to have their major influence only much later, however. Much of the significant aesthetic writing in the nineteenth century is also criticism or art theory by practicing artists and critics. The nineteenth century was a century of movements in painting, poetry, the novel, and music. Romanticism, realism, and impressionism influenced each other as theory and as practice. For a century devoted to systematic philosophies, all of these movements create an impression of difference and diversity.

The readings in this section begin with Hegel, who, no matter how difficult his prose, was the philosophical master of the century. Schopenhauer rejected Hegel's historical dialectic and saw himself as the true inheritor of Kant and Plato. Friedrich Nietzsche followed Schopenhauer; his philosophy anticipated the breakdown of order and confidence that we have experienced in the twentieth century. John Ruskin represented the critic as well as the connoisseur and brings us into direct contact with art history. Count Leo Tolstoy, one of the great novelists of the century, appears here as a theoretician.

G. W. F. Hegel

GEORG WILHELM FRIEDRICH HEGEL (1770–1831) was born in Stuttgart, Germany. He studied theology at Tübingen, and from 1793 until 1800 was a private tutor to aristocratic families. He then lectured at the University at Jena until 1807. For a time, he edited a newspaper in Bavaria and was a schoolmaster in Nuremberg. He became professor of philosophy at Heidelberg in 1816 and moved to the University of Berlin in 1818, where he remained until his death of cholera in 1831.

Hegel belonged to the first generation of scholars after Kant. His contemporaries included Friedrich Schelling (1775–1854) and the poet Friedrich Hölderlin. Schelling preceded Hegel at Jena and succeeded him to the chair at Berlin after Hegel's death. Schelling was the first to write a philosophy of art, but Hegel came to dominate the systematization and idealization of Kantian philosophy. Basically, the new generation of thinkers argued that Kant had not gone far enough in analyzing the possibilities of the mind. By the time they had finished, those possibilities extended to everything in the universe which they characterized as a single absolute mind. Religion was their other major emphasis. After the theological disputes of the seventeenth and eighteenth centuries—between deism and its variations with orthodox Lutheranism on the one hand and pietism on the other—Hegel and his contemporaries and followers sought to defend Christianity in a positive way by incorporating it into an historical development. They assigned to religion a preeminent place in the development of civilization and to Christianity a preeminent place in the development of religion. This universalization fit into the nineteenth-century's confident expansion of Western hegemony.

Hegel's writings are voluminous. They include *The Phenomenology of Mind* (1807), *The Science of Logic* (1812–1816), *The Encyclopedia of the Philosophical Sciences in Outline* (1817), and *The Philosophy of Right* (1821). After his death, his friends and students at Berlin published eighteen volumes of his works and lectures, and more have been added from work unpublished during his lifetime.

◆　◆　◆　◆　◆　◆

G. W. F. Hegel was the great philosophical systematizer of the early nineteenth century. His philosophy sought to describe all that could be thought; literally everything would be placed in relation to everything else. The means for doing this was a form of what is called *philosophical idealism*.[1] According to idealism, the totality of worlds includes both things and ideas, minds and objects. Idealism accounts for objects in terms of ideas and ideas in terms of minds. The ultimate principles of description and expla-

---

[1] Idealism in philosophy is the theory that includes minds and ideas as real. It should not be confused with idealism in the sense of "high ideals." The opposite of idealism is materialism—the thesis that everything, including minds, can be reduced to some material form.

nation are mental, not physical. This argument in no way prevents us from talking about physical objects; they are part of the world. But physical objects are only one manifestation of a totality that also has mental characteristics. Those mental characteristics are the ultimate ordering principles, so it is mind, not material objects, that determine both what there is and what we can know.

Hegel's form of idealism is dialectical. What we know is a product of relations between what is and what logically can be. We can discover those relations only by thinking through a fundamental opposition between what is and what is not. In order to know what something is, I must also know what it is not—what its form of being excludes and what it is excluded from. For example, a vase has a physical presence and a form. Logically, its form can be known and can become the basis for a painting of the vase. The painting as well as the physical object manifests the form of the vase, and its ideal form is dialectically known in both and yet is neither. The form is excluded from the individuality of the painting and vase. The painting is excluded from the practical use of the vase. To know the form is to know that it is present in the vase, but also that it is not present there alone.

Hegel understood this dialectical relation both logically and historically. Logically, it accounts for the ultimately ideal forms and arranges them in an ascending hierarchy until absolute mind is reached as the ultimate principle of explanation and understanding. Historically, since time and history are themselves part of the world, they are also part of the ideal, and their manifestations express the ideal forms as well. How the vase is painted will depend on where in history it is seen. Consequently, particular cultures and historical periods have the same kind of dialectical relation to past and future as the vase has to its painting. Art and religion are forms of historical realization of the possibilities of minds and ideas. Through art and religion, Hegel hoped to penetrate the relations of ideas to understand the whole structure of history and ultimately of reality. If this hope seems to us grandiose and doomed to failure, it nevertheless inspired a century of investigation which both followed Hegel's methods and reacted against them by looking either to alternative principles (materialism, for example) or to mystery (radical faith) to accomplish the desired end.

To penetrate Hegel's difficult, complex style and language, we must try to understand his starting point. Immanuel Kant had brought about what he called a "Copernican revolution" in philosophy. Instead of the view that the earth was the center of the universe, Copernicus recognized that the earth moves around the sun. Human existence was no longer regarded as the center; we became part of a cosmos. Today, we go one step farther and think of the entire universe as a single system in which solar systems move and in which the idea of a center is relative to the expanding whole. Kant claimed to recognize that reality was no external, fixed point that minds observed; instead, the mind itself could only observe what its powers shaped and formed. In effect, the mind moved rather than occupying a fixed point at the center of things. Nothing could be said about reality that was not mentally shaped. For Kant, that fact implied only a limitation on our powers and a new source of certainty about what we could observe by means of them. The categories of our minds that allow us to perceive are not themselves part of what we perceive. They have to be built in from the beginning. They are not ideas, however. The categories limit what can be known so that we never know things in themselves. But we can be certain about the categories themselves because they are the mind's own realm. For example, space and time are not absolute things to be measured but mental categories which shape what we perceive. We can be certain about the categories even if we can never be certain about what they are applied to. Thus Kant, in effect, took the same position as Copernicus. He shifted the center from a fixed point to the system in which an observer exists. That system is defined by the conditions of space and time and thought.

Hegel took Kant's revolution a step farther. If the mind can only observe what it shapes and forms, then the absolute nature of reality itself can only be mental. One cannot "found" any observation on anything but mind itself. Hegel is like a modern cosmologist who thinks not just of a solar system but of the universe as a whole. Its "center" is relative to the whole, not to any one part. This fact is essentially a logical requirement. The argument might go as follows: (1) If anything nonmental were part of what is observable, there would be some nonmental observation. (2) But all observation is itself mental. (3) Therefore, nothing nonmental is part of what is observable. (4) Yet everything that is known is observable. (We are not limited to examining our own navels or our own powers.) (5) Therefore, everything is mental. In effect, no nonmental absolute point from which the universe could be defined exists. This argument is why we call Hegel an idealist.

Hegel's version of idealism differs from some earlier seventeenth- and eighteenth-century versions because it is not limited to what we know but extends to what there is. It differs from seventeenth- and eighteenth-century Platonism in affirming the importance of history. What Hegel calls spirit or mind, and what we might more comfortably call consciousness, is reality. It has individual forms and manifestations, but those forms and manifestations can exist only as particularizations of a single absolute mind—the cosmos of mental observables. Anything else would lead to the logical absurdity of multiple minds that are known but exist somewhere that is not mental. From within this system, much of what Hegel claims seems logical and necessary. However, for an individual thinker, it is difficult not to slip out of the larger context into particularized occurrences which, from Hegel's position, are only false absolutes—back into a situation in which I try to be the center of the universe again rather than acknowledging that absolute mind is the universe and that it must center itself.

Hegel writes of God, Absolute Mind, Spirit, and other abstract objects that are hard to grasp. We should not put too much weight on this terminology. Hegel's God is not some theological being but the referent of ideas that his system makes necessary. Hegel probably thought that practical religion as he knew it was one very imprecise way of explaining God and religion as they really were, but we need not accept those connections, nor will they help much in understanding what Hegel meant by God or Spirit or Religion. They must be understood as only part of his complex system. At the same time, for all his abstraction, Hegel is remarkably concrete. Each of us can try to anchor what we say in our own experience, and when Hegel talks of art, it is helpful to think of particular artists and poets who might fit his descriptions. Hegel's aesthetics, consequently, is a useful introduction not only to his system to but to subsequent forms of idealist aesthetics.

Art and religion provide the highest forms of the ideal that we can experience. Thus they stand at the top of Hegel's system. Hegel sums up their role in his *Encyclopedia*. The context is the mind, but the notion of a mind is itself mental. The absolute idea should not be thought of as some external, existent object. To do so would make no sense to a reality that is itself mental. So if reality is to be grasped at all as idea, consciousness must be free of any other grounds. Hegel's language may be obscure, but the basic idea is clear enough: absolute idea cannot be contingent on anything else, so Kant's Copernican revolution is completed. One does not need some unreachable *noumena*[2] (things in themselves) when examining mind, consciousness, and "spirit."

Religion is not the worship of some transcendent being but the communal nature of absolute spirit. "God," like absolute spirit, is both subjective and objective. Hegel wished to emphasize both. He rejected the developing romantic subjectivism that placed God wholly within the realm of feeling and interior experience because romantic subjectivism loses the absolute nature of God, but he acknowledged that romanticism was partially correct. Without a subjective side, religion would only be dogma. If God is both subjective and objective at once, then access to God (by faith or belief) must be both a feeling and a rational certainty.

The clearest and most comprehensive manifestations of mind are in art and religion. Hegel understood art as a system of fine arts that are the cultural products of a people. They are a manifestation of a collective spirit. But art is only a first step and leads finally to a transcendent form in religion. Hegel identifies three cultural stages of art: classical art, symbolic art, and romantic art. All three are concrete manifestations of absolute mind by individuals under the conditions made possible by history and culture. As art takes shape, it divides consciousness between a productive and appreciative mental direction. Artists produce art for an audience, and an audience appreciates what artists produce. Artist and audience are not independent of each other. Hegel consequently can link particular styles of painting and poetry to stages in the historical manifestation of consciousness. They are never merely accidental; they follow from the ways that the mind can actualize itself.

Art is limited to an expression of individual minds rather than being a direct expression of mind itself. Works of art are made by an artist. That implies technical activity and the separation of the work from the maker. At the same time, something in the making and the product is greater than the individual artist. For example, artists have a style that is common to a school such as abstract expressionism. Consequently, part of the power of an artist is not individual but is a product of that style. This power is a kind of force, and it is greater than artists themselves. Art requires enthusiasm and genius. The artist is master, but only in transmitting the immediacy of form to something made. Hegel's artist is a part of the dialectic of spirit, not an independent producer of things. The artist's work is always more than what the artist intends it to be. When art works, it brings together self-consciousness and form without the sense of opposition between the idea and its expression. Hegel called that *classical art.* Symbolic art, on the other hand, divides thought or idea and expression. We must think about such art and grasp its symbolic meaning in order to appreciate it. The immediacy of classical art is a way of transcending the limitations imposed by art's specificity. It is the difference between being caught up by the art and led directly to the idea and having to think about the work of art and decipher it as is the case with symbolic art.

---

[2] Kantian philosophy distinguishes between *phenomena,* which we experience, and *noumena,* which are the presumed causes of the experience but cannot be experienced themselves. There is no way to grasp the *noumena* in themselves because any such grasp would itself be an experience—that is, phenomenal. Nevertheless, *noumena* can be known as necessary conditions of *phenomena.*

When a person turns inward to discover ideas, a third kind of art becomes possible. Hegel calls it romantic art. Romantic art subordinates anything external such as the appearance of an object and an object's beauty to the significance that can be understood only by an inward turn of the spirit. When this inward turn is complete, religion replaces art. Thus, romantic art is a move toward a higher manifestation of absolute mind. That movement is what Hegel meant by religion. Philosophy of religion identifies the way that the absolute is expressed in self-consciousness and national life. The creation of the absolute is history. Romantic art is concrete; therefore it is not yet absolute. As an idea is manifested in religion, religion loses its dependence on beautiful art. It does not need the imaginative visibility of art any longer. Romantic art is more successful than symbolic art—it makes whatever is natural into an expression of spirit. Romantic art then transcends the kind of religion that depends on idols and images. But religion that depends on art is moving in the wrong direction; it is declining. Ultimately, religion must replace art. For Hegel, romantic art and beauty are superior to the kind of religion that is itself a concrete form and depends on ritual and dogma. But religion itself is the higher form because it is the manifestation of spirit itself. Art is never as free as religion in that sense. Romantic art has its future in true religion. Hegel's romantic successors would understand religion in this sense. Their problem was how to achieve this liberation. For some, it could come only from a form of denial, a radical rejection of reason or a declaration that God himself had died. For Hegel, however, it was the end to an intellectual odyssey where the mind would be liberated from its own limitations.

Hegel began with absolute mind, a mental context. From that he derived the necessity of subjective expression in two directions—toward an object and toward the contemplation of the object. Art is thus the result of the subjective immediacy of consciousness, mind, or spirit. Art serves a positive function in giving concrete, immediate expression to mental life. Beauty is the form of that expression. In classical art, the expression of beauty is successful; its immediacy is experienced as a unity of pure form. If it remains divided so that sensuality and expression are separated, it is symbolic art. When it attempts to realize the idea itself rather than the form of beauty and turns inward toward self-realization, it is romantic art. Art is an expression of sensuality and thus of the historical form of a people or culture's ideal reality. As such, however, art is only a means to religion, which is the historical realization of spirit in a people or culture. Beautiful art can play the role of philosophy by freeing spirit, but it is limited by its sensuality. Any religion that depends only on art is in decline—it is idolatrous and bound to sensuality. Ultimately, pure religion transcends art into revelation. It no longer needs the sensuous, and the self embodies the idea in a community and a history.

Hegel's thinking is undoubtedly abstract, difficult, and often obscure. He turns nouns into objects and then refers to those objects as if they were perceivable while denying the primacy of perception. If we can penetrate his language by following the logic of his reasoning, however, we are led to a comprehensive system that makes art an essential expression of culture. Hegel's influence was pervasive, perhaps even greater than Kant's, through the nineteenth century. Even Hegel's enemies worked within his overall vision of the role of art. It was not until twentieth-century philosophers returned to a different form of empiricism that Hegel's influence began to wane.

From *The Encyclopedia of the Philosophical Sciences*

Absolute Mind

Para. 553

The *notion*[3] of mind has its *reality* in the mind. If this reality in identity with that notion is to exist as the consciousness of the absolute Idea, then the necessary aspect is that the *implicitly* free intelligence be in its actuality liberated to its notion, if that actuality is to be a vehicle worthy of it. The subjective and the objective spirit are to be looked on as the road on which this aspect of *reality* or existence rises to maturity.

Para. 554

The absolute mind, while it is self-centered *identity,* is always also identity returning and ever returned into itself: if it is the one and universal *substance* it is so as a spirit, discerning itself into a self and a consciousness, for which it is as substance. *Religion,* as this supreme sphere may be in general designated, if it has on one hand to be studied as issuing from the subject and having its home in the subject, must no less be regarded as objectively issuing from the absolute spirit which as spirit is in its community.

That here, as always, belief or faith is not opposite to consciousness or knowledge, but rather to a sort of knowledge, and that belief is only a particular form of the latter, has been remarked already. If nowadays[4] there is so little consciousness of God, and his objective essence is so little dwelt upon, while people speak so much more of the subjective side of religion, i.e. of God's indwelling in us, and if that and not the truth as such is called for in this there is at least the correct principle that God must be apprehended as spirit in his community.

Para. 555

The subjective consciousness of the absolute spirit is essentially and intrinsically a process, the immediate and substantial unity of which is the *Belief* in the witness of the spirit as the *certainty* of objective truth. Belief, at once this immediate unity and containing it as a reciprocal dependence of these different terms, has in *devotion* —the implicit or more explicit act of worship (*cultus*)—passed over into the process of superseding the contrast till it becomes spiritual liberation, the process of authenticating that first certainty by this intermediation, and of gaining its concrete determination, viz. reconciliation, the actuality of the spirit.

Art

Para. 556

As this consciousness of the Absolute first takes shape, its immediacy produces the factor of finitude in Art. On the one hand, that is, it breaks up into a work of external common existence, into the subject which produces that work, and the subject which contemplates and worships it. But, on the other hand, it is the concrete *contemplation* and mental picture of implicitly absolute spirit as the *Ideal*. In this ideal, or the concrete shape born of the subjective spirit, its natural immediacy, which is only a *sign* of the Idea, is so transfigured by the informing spirit in order to express the Idea, that the figure shows it and it alone—the shape or form of *Beauty*.

---

[3] *Notion* is a technical term for an individual, conscious act. Because *idea* and *spirit* refer to mental realities that are independent of any one individual, Hegel needs a different term for the individual conscious act.

[4] In the early nineteenth century, German religion included a strong pietist element that emphasized God's felt presence.

Para. 557

The sensuous externality attaching to the beautiful—the *form of immediacy* as such—at the same time *qualifies* what it *embodies:* and the God (of art) has with his spirituality at the same time the stamp upon him of a natural medium or natural phase of existence—He contains the so-called *unity* of nature and spirit—*i.e.* the immediate unity in sensuously intuitional form—hence not the spiritual unity, in which the natural would be put only as 'ideal,' as superseded in spirit, and the spiritual content would be only in self-relation. It is not the absolute spirit which enters this consciousness. On the subjective side the community has of course an ethical life, aware, as it is, of the spirituality of its essence: and its self-consciousness and actuality are in it elevated to substantial liberty. But with the stigma of immediacy upon it, the subject's liberty is only a *manner of life,* without the infinite self-reflection and the subjective inwardness of *conscience.* These considerations govern in their further developments the devotion and the worship in the religion of fine art.

Para. 558

For the objects of contemplation it has to produce, Art requires not only an external given material—(under which are also included subjective images and ideas), but—for the expression of spiritual truth—must use the given forms of nature with a significance which art must divine and possess. Of all such forms the human is the highest and the true, because only in it can the spirit have its corporeity and thus its visible expression.

This disposes of the principle of the *imitation of nature* in art: a point on which it is impossible to come to an understanding while a distinction is left thus abstract—in other words, so long as the natural is only taken in its externality, not as the 'characteristic' meaningful nature-form which is significant of spirit.

Para. 559

In such single shapes the 'absolute' mind cannot be made explicit: in and to art therefore the spirit is a limited natural spirit whose implicit universality, when steps are taken to specify its fullness in detail, breaks up into an indeterminate polytheism. With the essential restrictedness of its content, Beauty in general goes no further than a penetration of the vision or image by the spiritual principle—something formal, so that the thought embodied, or the idea, can, like the material which it uses to work in, be of the most diverse and unessential kind, and still the work be something beautiful and a work of art.

Para. 560

The one-sidedness of *immediacy* on the part of the Ideal involves the opposite one-sidedness that it is something *made* by the artist. The subject or agent is the mere technical activity: and the work of art is only then an expression of the God, when there is no sign of subjective particularity in it, and the net power of the indwelling spirit is conceived and born into the world, without admixture and unspotted from its contingency. But as liberty only goes as far as there is thought, the action inspired with the fullness of this indwelling power, the artist's *enthusiasm,* is like a foreign force under which he is bound and passive; the artistic *production* has on its part the form of natural immediacy, it belongs to the *genius* or particular endowment of the artist—and is at the same time a labour concerned with technical cleverness and mechanical externalities. The work of art therefore is just as much a work due to free option, and the artist is the master of the God.

Para. 561

In work so inspired the reconciliation appears so obvious in its initial stage that it is without more ado accomplished in the subjective self-consciousness, which is thus self-confident and of good cheer, without the depth and without the sense of its antithesis to the absolute essence. On the further side of the perfection (which is reached in such reconciliation, in the beauty of *classical art*) lies the art of sublimity—*symbolic art,* in which the figuration suitable to the Idea is not yet found, and the thought as going forth and wrestling with the figure is exhibited as a negative attitude to it, and yet all the while toiling to work itself into it. The meaning or theme thus shows it has not yet reached the infinite form, is not yet known, not yet conscious of itself, as free spirit. The artist's theme only is as the abstract God of pure thought, or an effort towards him— a restless and unappeased effort which throws itself into shape after shape as it vainly tries to find its goal.

Para. 562

In another way the Idea and the sensuous figure it appears in are incompatible; and that is where the infinite form, subjectivity, is not as in the first extreme a mere superficial personality, but its inmost depth, and God is known not as only seeking his form or satisfying himself in an external form, but as only finding himself in himself, and thus giving himself his adequate figure in the spiritual world alone. *Romantic art* gives up the task of showing him as such in external form and by means of beauty: it presents him as only condescending to appearance, and the divine as the heart of hearts in an externality from which it always disengages itself. Thus the external can here appear as contingent towards its significance.

The Philosophy of Religion has to discover the logical necessity in the progress by which the Being, known as the Absolute, assumes fuller and firmer features; it has to note to what particular feature the kind of cultus corresponds—and then to see how the secular self-consciousness, the consciousness of what is the supreme vocation of man—in short how the nature of a nation's moral life, the principle of its law, of its ac-tual liberty, and of its constitution, as well as of its art and science, corresponds to the principle which constitutes the substance of a religion. That all these elements of a nation's actuality constitute one systematic totality, that one spirit creates and informs them, is a truth on which follows the further truth that the history of religion coincides with the world-history.

As regards the close connection of art with the various religions it may be specially noted that *beautiful* art can only belong to those religions in which the spiritual principle, though concrete and intrinsically free, is not yet absolute. In religions where the Idea has not yet been revealed and known in its free character, though the craving for art is felt in order to bring in imaginative visibility to consciousness the idea of the supreme being, and though art is the sole organ in which the abstract and radically indistinct content—a mixture from natural and spiritual sources—can try to bring itself to consciousness; —still this art is defective; its form is defective because its subject-matter and theme is so—for the defect in subject-matter comes from the form not being immanent in it. The representations of this symbolic art keep a certain tastelessness and stolidity—for the principle it embodies is itself stolid and dull, and hence has not the power freely to transmute the external to significance and shape. Beautiful art, on the contrary, has for its condition the self-consciousness of the free spirit—the consciousness that compared with it the natural and sensuous has no standing of its own: it makes the natural wholly into the mere expression of spirit, which is thus the inner form that gives utterance to itself alone.

But with a further and deeper study, we see that the advent of art, in a religion still in the bonds of sensuous externality, shows that such religion is on the decline. At the very time it seems to give religion the supreme glorification, expression, and brilliancy, it has lifted the religion away over its limitation. In the sublime divinity to which the work of art succeeds in giving expression the artistic genius and the spectator find themselves at home, with their personal sense and feeling, satisfied and liberated: to them the vision and the consciousness of free spirit has been vouchsafed and attained. Beautiful art, from its side, has thus performed the same service as philosophy: it has purified the spirit from its thraldom. The older religion in which the need of fine art, and just for that reason, is first generated, looks up in its principle to an other world which is sensuous and unmeaning: the images adored by its devotees are hideous idols regarded as wonder-working talismans, which point to the unspiritual objectivity of that other world—and bones perform a similar or even a better service than such images. But even fine art is only a grade of liberation, not the supreme liberation itself.—The genuine objectivity, which is only in the medium of thought—the medium in which alone the pure spirit is for the spirit, and where the liberation is accompanied with reverence— is still absent in the sensuous beauty of the work of art, still more in that external, unbeautiful sensuousness.

Para. 563

Beautiful Art, like the religion peculiar to it, has its future in true religion. The restricted value of the Idea passes utterly and naturally into the universality identical with the infinite form;—the vision in which consciousness has to depend upon the senses passes into a self-mediating knowledge, into an existence which is itself knowledge into *revelation*. Thus the principle which gives the Idea its content is that it embody free intelligence, and as 'absolute' *spirit it is for the spirit.*

Study Questions

1. Is "absolute mind" one thing among others? Explain.
2. What is a "concrete determination" of absolute spirit?
3. How would Hegel define *beauty*?
4. What would the "religion of fine art" be?
5. Why does religion rank above the aesthetic and philosophy above religion in Hegel's system?
6. Give examples of classical art. What makes them "classical"?
7. Give examples of symbolic art. What makes them "symbolic"?
8. Give examples of romantic art. What makes them "romantic"?
9. How does the ideal contrast with what an artist makes?
10. How is romantic art related to absolute spirit?
11. What is Hegel's view of the history of art? Of culture?
12. Try to apply Hegel's historical scheme to twentieth-century arts such as movies.

Arthur Schopenhauer

· · · · · · · · · · · · · · · · · ·

ARTHUR SCHOPENHAUER (1788–1860) was born in Danzig. He left Danzig when it became part of Poland, eventually taking his doctorate at Jena with a thesis on *The Quadruple Root of the Principle of Sufficient Reason.* He had a brief academic career in which he tried to compete directly with Hegel as a lecturer, but he retired to private life, where he lived on a pension from his estranged mother, who was a popular novelist, and the income from family property. His principle work, *The World as Will and Idea,* was published in 1818 when he was only 29. It received little notice at the time. He added to it extensively in 1844. Schopenhauer was reclusive and apparently somewhat misanthropic. His lack of acceptance by the academic world, which was dominated by Hegel and his followers, evidently rankled. Only during the last ten years of his life did Schopenhauer achieve the recognition that he sought from a new generation that found in his work the rejection of convention. He never married and died alone.

♦ ♦ ♦ ♦ ♦ ♦

Schopenhauer's work stands outside the main line of systematizing German idealism represented by Hegel. His influence is strongest on the Danish philosopher-theologian Søren Kierkegaard and Friedrich Nietzsche, who share his opposition to Hegel. Nevertheless, Schopenhauer remains a part of the German idealist tradition. He acknowledges two major, and seemingly contradictory, sources: Immanuel Kant and Plato. From Kant, he gets the separation between phenomena and the "thing in itself." Like Kant, Schopenhauer accepts that the mind implicitly shapes the only knowable world to its categories of thought. Any other reality remains beyond our grasp. But Schopenhauer rejects Kant's way of building a system of knowledge. When Kant limits the mind to phenomena, he strictly limits knowledge itself. Both our practical and theoretical knowledge are matters of conditions that the mind must accept, but within those conditions, practical and theoretical knowledge alike are informed by perception. Aesthetic perception is precognitive and disinterested, but it is not different from the practical ethical knowledge and the theoretical knowledge of reason and science except in the way that the mind knows it. Schopenhauer, instead, sharply distinguishes knowledge from perception in the manner of Plato. He appeals to a form of contemplation as a way of going beyond the limits of perceptual knowledge.

For Schopenhauer, the Idea is independent of the particular. In this, he remains a firm idealist. Ideas, not physical things, are the reality, and ideas sustain all individual instances. Science and perception depend on the individual, as does history. But art can present the Idea in itself. Thus, for Schopenhauer, true art is always concerned with the universal. The individual characteristics are unimportant. This is a view of art that contrasts sharply with the increasing individualism of romantic art and with the materialism of the other forms of anti-Hegelian philosophy represented by Ludwig Feuerbach and Karl Marx. At the same time, Schopenhauer's form of Platonic idealism raises art to the status of knowledge in direct contradiction to Plato's view of art as imitation. Schopenhauer's idealism is an idealism of contemplative purity and rejection of the increasingly industrialized state of Europe that appeals, ironically, to just those rebellious and late romantic thinkers who seek to return to a preindustrialized worldview.

Another way in which Schopenhauer's philosophy remains a part of the German idealist tradition is in its use of a dialectical relation of concepts. Kant introduced this dialectic as a basic condition of knowledge, but it remained essentially analytical. Hegel transformed dialectic into an historical movement as well. Ideas are embodied in the world as thought, and they are realized in historical forms according to the culture of a people. So art and religion define stages in the realization of ideas that are formed in opposition to each other. Schopenhauer rejects the historicizing tendency in Hegel's dialectic, but he introduces his own dialectical opposition at the heart of his philosophy The will is the actualizing drive that produces objects. All individual objectification is really a matter of will, on this account. A particular thing or a particular mind are alike in that they are singled out and separated from everything else by the will.

Will in this sense is not a psychological motivation, though psychological phenomena are products of the will. Will might be understood as objectifying thought. In order to think in terms of particulars, thought must be about something, some object. Thought might be said to have a direction toward an object, even if that object is its own existence. In order to have that kind of direction, thought must be directed toward its object; that is the sense in which all individual, objective thought can be said to be willed. So will is one pole of a necessary dialectical relation.

The other pole is "idea" or "representation." The object of will has a content, something that makes it that object and not some other object. As long as that content is individual and objective, it is dependent on the will for its existence. But equally, there cannot be a will without the content of the object, what that object is about or what makes it what it is. So will and idea are related to each other in the kind of dialectical relation that Hegel before him and Nietzsche after him also depend on.

What makes Schopenhauer different is his return to a form of Platonism. For Plato, reality is essentially other. It is the unchangeable, unitary idea as opposed to the changeable individual forms that ideas take in our perception and experience. For Plato, that otherness of ideas can take a form that shares much with religion. The ideas sustain the objects, without which objects would not exist. The world is a shadow of the ideas, and one must look to ideas for knowledge, which is necessary to avoid chaos. Religion depends on ritual to maintain that connection. Plato hoped to find it in knowledge. Schopenhauer cannot appeal to religion in the same way for support for his notion of ideas. His dialectic of will and idea is thus much more tenuous than Plato's. It shares the negative interpretation that Plato places on the individual object, however. For

Hegel, the dialectic is just a necessary condition for any thing. There is no good or bad to the opposition. For Schopenhauer, the will produces all pain and suffering; the idea is the form of peace. So Schopenhauer's dialectic is not just an opposition that produces reality as we know it. It is a contest between good and bad, pain and contentment.

Every idea is essentially singular because will distinguishes only individuals in their multiple appearances. As long as one remains bound to the will, one can know only individual forms of objects, all of which will differ as the basis of their individuality. These forms are governed by what Schopenhauer calls the *principle of sufficient reason.* Sufficient reason has four governing principles. Each corresponds to a form of representation, that is, to one of the ways that particulars can be known. Sense is only one form of representation. It provides perceptual input and form. Judgment is another. It places a value on a representation, or better, represents something as valuable. Intuition is a third principle of reason. Intuition differs from sense in not requiring empirical representation. The mathematician, for example, depends on intuition to understand mathematical objects. Finally, will, in the sense of voluntary action or motivation, is a principle of reason. When one raises one's arm, that individual act is an act of will. It is singled out as an action, which is an object of thought, by the voluntary nature of the will. Taken together, these principles make up sufficient reason, which determines all specific knowledge and science. We know something scientifically when we know the sufficient reasons for all of the representations that are referred to in the knowledge.

In order to know ideas themselves, one must be free of the principle of sufficient reason and its dependence on will. One cannot know an idea in its singularity as long as what one knows is a particular individual object. Every individual object implies an idea, but as long as the principle of sufficient reason is the basis of what one knows, one will know according to the forms of the will that makes individual objects available. The only way to escape that limitation is to escape the will.

Schopenhauer turns to aesthetic contemplation as the means for escaping one's own individual objectivity and thus the objectivity imposed by the will. Through art and aesthetic contemplation, the object as idea replaces the object as object of will. Unlike Kant, therefore, Schopenhauer believes that one can follow Plato and participate in the idea of an object independently of the individuality of the object. There are two ways of knowing. One is determined by the principle of sufficient reason. The other is available as aesthetic contemplation. This separation of knowing into two kinds parallels Kant's division between pure reason and practical reason, and *aesthetic* in both cases is logically prior to the division. But where Kant divides knowledge only on the basis of the kind of a priori conditions it implies, Schopenhauer makes a real distinction between two forms of knowledge.

One result of his division is that Schopenhauer becomes essentially pessimistic about the conditions of knowledge. As long as one remains in the world, the controlling force is will and knowledge is limited by the principle of sufficient reason. That knowledge cannot satisfy us, and we are condemned to live in a world that must, on the whole, be painful because of its separateness and the inadequacy to its own ideas. The highest form of poetry is tragedy, and music, which is nonrepresentational, is the only form of transcending art itself.

At the same time, Schopenhauer lays down the basic principles of an aesthetic contemplation and aesthetic attitude. We do have a way out of the pain and suffering of the world through art, at least momentarily. The conditions for knowing an idea independently of the will are essentially the conditions for aesthetic contemplation. The role of art and genius is to realize that contemplative state, both as state and as means to the state. Art shows us the idea in the particular object. Genius recognizes the idea in the object and frees it in art for those who are not geniuses. Schopenhauer takes the view of genius as the productive side of aesthetic contemplation from Kant, but he raises genius to the level of world hero. Schopenhauer shares with romanticism, which was developing at the same time, a kind of religion of art, or a replacement of religion by art in which genius plays the role of priest. But Schopenhauer does not believe that art can save us in the way that romanticism did. For the romantic, the individual is all. For Schopenhauer, as long as the individual is present, so is the will. They are two parts of a necessary dialectic. So there can be no individual salvation either through art or religion. The expectation that there could be is weakness and delusion. The result of tragedy, therefore, is to bring one to the point of rejecting life.

Schopenhauer's philosophy finds its culmination in Friedrich Nietzsche's more radical dialectic that leads to an affirmation of the individual through negation and in existentialism's dialectic of being and nonbeing that finds the individual's freedom precisely in its nonbeing. Schopenhauer remains closer to Plato, however. The individual is lost, and art is art only to the extent that it is a universal in a particular. That conclusion is too negative to produce many immediate followers.

At the same time, Schopenhauer finally frees aesthetics from its role as mere founding intuition or historical force to be subsumed into a higher form of knowledge. His description of aesthetic contemplation and how it may be achieved lays the foundation for later nineteenth- and twentieth-century versions of an aesthetic attitude. If one drops the idealist metaphysics, Schopenhauer's aesthetic contemplation leaves art as a free, autonomous way to an alternative form of knowledge. Such knowledge cannot be expressed in terms of principles such as sufficient reason. It must be experienced, and to experience it is to enter into a disinterested, almost ecstatic mode of experience where one's individuality and the existence of the object alike play no role. Schopenhauer's formulations finally break with those of both Kant and Hegel. System is replaced by contemplation. The object of aesthetics is experience of a different kind, not ordinary, everyday knowledge. If there is aesthetic knowledge, it is a different kind of knowledge. And one can achieve that knowledge through art or, if one is accomplished enough, directly from any object. That is essentially the basis of modern aesthetics.

From *The World as Will and Idea*

§36. HISTORY FOLLOWS THE thread of events; it is pragmatic so far as it deduces them in accordance with the law of motivation, a law that determines the self-manifesting will wherever it is enlightened by knowledge. At the lowest grades of its objectivity, where it still acts without knowledge, natural science, in the form of etiology,[1] treats of the laws of the changes of its phenomena, and, in the form of morphology,[2] of what is permanent in them. This almost endless task is lightened by the aid of concepts, which comprehend what is general in order that we may deduce what is particular from it. Lastly, mathematics treats of the mere forms, time and space, in which the Ideas, broken up into multiplicity, appear for the knowledge of the subject as individual. All these, of which the common name is science, proceed according to the principle of sufficient reason[3] in its different forms, and their theme is always the phenomenon, its laws, connections, and the relations which result from them. But what kind of knowledge is concerned with that which is outside and independent of all relations, that which alone is really essential to the world, the true content of its phenomena, that which is subject to no chance, and therefore is known with equal truth for all time, in a word, the *Ideas,* which are the direct and adequate objectivity of the thing-in-itself, the will? . . . We answer, *Art,* the work of genius. It repeats or reproduces the eternal Ideas grasped through pure contemplation, the essential and abiding in all the phenomena of the world; and according to what the material is in which it reproduces, it is

sculpture or painting, poetry or music. Its one source is the knowledge of Ideas; its one aim the communication of this knowledge. While science, following the unresting and inconstant stream of the fourfold forms of reason and consequent, with each end attained sees further, and can never reach a final goal nor attain full satisfaction, any more than by running we can reach the place where the clouds touch the horizon; art, on the contrary, is everywhere at its goal. For it plucks the object of its contemplation out of the stream of the world's course, and has it isolated before it. And this particular thing, which in that stream was a small perishing part, becomes to art the representative of the whole, an equivalent of the endless multitude in space and time. It therefore pauses at this particular thing; the course of time stops; the relations vanish for it; only the essential, the Idea, is its object. We may, therefore, accurately define it as the *way of viewing things independent of the principle of sufficient reason,* in opposition to the way of viewing them which proceeds in accordance with that principle, and which is the method of experience and of science. This last method of considering things may be compared to a line infinitely extended in a horizontal direction, and the former to a vertical line which cuts it at any point. The method of viewing things which proceeds in accordance with the principle of sufficient reason is the rational method, and it alone is valid and of use in practical life and in science. The method which looks away from the content of this principle is the method of genius, which is only valid and of use in art. The first is the method of Aristotle,[4] the second is, on the whole, that of Plato.[5] The first is like the mighty storm, that rushes along

---

[1] Study of the origin, source, or cause of something.

[2] The formal characteristics of something.

[3] Schopenhauer's first work was his doctoral dissertation on the fourfold principle of sufficient reason—sense, judgment, intuition, and will or motivation. This principle provides the complete scientific explanation of what something is, though for Schopenhauer, the *what* is a representation. See the introduction to this reading.

[4] See the introduction and the preceding selection, pp. 20ff. Aristotle's method is to divide according to the "causes" of a thing.

[5] See the introduction and the preceding selection, pp. 5ff. Plato's method is to seek essential definitions through questioning.

without beginning and without aim, bending, agitating, and canting away everything before it; the second is like the silent sunbeam, that pierces through the storm quite unaffected by it. The first is like the innumerable showering drop of the waterfall, which, constantly changing, never rest for an instant; the second is like the rainbow, quietly resting on this raging torrent. Only through the pure contemplation described above, which ends entirely in the object, can Ideas be comprehended; and the nature of *genius* consists in [a] preeminent capacity for such contemplation. Now, as this requires that a man should entirely forget himself and the relations in which he stands, *genius* is simply the completest *objectivity, i.e.,* the objective tendency of the mind, as opposed to the subjective, which is directed to one's own self—in other words, to the will. Thus genius is the faculty of continuing in the state of pure perception, of losing oneself in perception, and of enlisting in this service the knowledge which originally existed only for the service of the will—that is to say, genius is the power of leaving one's own interests, wishes, and aims entirely out of sight, thus of entirely renouncing one's own personality for a time, so as to remain *pure knowing subject,* clear vision of the world; and this not merely at moments, but for a sufficient length of time, and with sufficient consciousness, to enable one to reproduce by deliberate art what has thus been apprehended, and "to fix in lasting thoughts the wavering images that float before the mind." It is as if, when genius appears in an individual, a far larger measure of the power of knowledge falls to his lot than is necessary for the service of an individual will; and this superfluity of knowledge, being free, now becomes subject purified from will, a clear mirror of the inner nature of the world. This explains the activity, amounting even to disquietude, of men of genius, for the present can seldom satisfy them, because it does not fill their consciousness. This gives them that restless aspiration, that unceasing desire for new things, and for the contemplation of lofty things, and also that longing that is hardly ever satisfied, for men of similar

nature and of like stature, to whom they might communicate themselves; whilst the common mortal, entirely filled and satisfied by the common present, ends in it, and finding everywhere his like, enjoys that peculiar satisfaction in daily life that is denied to genius.

Imagination has rightly been recognised as an essential element of genius; it has sometimes even been regarded as identical with it; but this is a mistake. As the objects of genius are the eternal Ideas, the permanent, essential forms of the world and all its phenomena, and as the knowledge of the Idea is necessarily knowledge through perception, is not abstract, the knowledge of the genius would be limited to the Ideas of the objects actually present to his person, and dependent upon the chain of circumstances that brought these objects to him, if his imagination did not extend his horizon far beyond the limits of his actual personal existence, and thus enable him to construct the whole out of the little that comes into his own actual apperception, and so to let almost all possible scenes of life pass before him in his own consciousness. Further, the actual objects are almost always very imperfect copies of the Ideas expressed in them; therefore the man of genius requires imagination in order to see in things, not that which Nature has actually made, but that which she endeavored to make, yet could not because of that conflict of her forms among themselves which we referred to in the last book. We shall return to this farther on in treating of sculpture. The imagination then extends the intellectual horizon of the man of genius beyond the objects which actually present themselves to him, both as regards quality and quantity. Therefore extraordinary strength of imagination accompanies, and is indeed a necessary condition of genius. But the converse does not hold, for strength of imagination does not indicate genius; on the contrary, men who have no touch of genius may have much imagination. For as it is possible to consider a real object in two opposite ways, purely objectively, the way of genius grasping its Idea, or in the common way, merely in the relations in which it stands to other objects and to one's own will, in accordance with the principle of sufficient reason, it is also possible to perceive an imaginary object in both of these ways. Regarded in the first way, it is a means to the knowledge of the Idea, the communication of which is the work of art; in the second case, the imaginary object is used to build castles in the air congenial to egotism and the individual humour, and which for the moment delude and gratify; thus only the relations of the phantasies so linked together are known. The man who indulges in such an amusement is a dreamer; he will easily mingle those fancies that delight his solitude with reality, and so unfit himself for real life: perhaps he will write them down, and then we shall have the ordinary novel of every description, which entertains those who are like him and the public at large, for the readers imagine themselves in the place of the hero, and then find the story very agreeable.

The common mortal, that manufacture of Nature which she, produces by the thousand every day, is, as we have said, not capable, at least not continuously so, of observation that in every sense is wholly disinterested, as sensuous contemplation, strictly so called, is. He can turn his attention to things only so far as they have some relation to his will, however indirect it may be. Since in this respect, which never demands anything but the knowledge of relations, the abstract conception of the thing is sufficient, and for the most part even better adapted for use; the ordinary man does not linger long over the mere perception, does not fix his attention long on one object, but in all that is presented to him hastily seeks merely the concept under which it is to be brought, as the lazy man seeks a chair, and then it interests him no further. This is why he is so soon done with everything, with works of art, objects of natural beauty, and indeed everywhere with the truly significant contemplation of all the scenes of life. He does not linger; only seeks to know his own way in life, together with all that might at any time become his way. Thus he makes topographical notes in the widest sense; over the consideration of life itself as such he wastes no

time. The man of genius, on the other hand, whose excessive power of knowledge frees it at times from the service of will, dwells on the consideration of life itself, strives to comprehend the Idea of each thing, not its relations to other things; and in doing this he often forgets to consider his own path in life, and therefore for the most part pursues it awkwardly enough. While to the ordinary man his faculty of knowledge is a lamp to lighten his path, to the man of genius it is the sun which reveals the world. This great diversity in their way of looking at life soon becomes visible in the outward appearance both of the man of genius and of the ordinary mortal. The man in whom genius lives and works is easily distinguished by his glance, which is both keen and steady, and bears the stamp of perception, of contemplation. This is easily seen from the likenesses of the few men of genius whom Nature has produced here and there among countless millions. On the other hand, in the case of an ordinary man, the true object of his contemplation, what he is prying into, can be easily seen from his glance, if indeed it is not quite stupid and vacant, as is generally the case. Therefore the expression of genius in a face consists in this, that in it a decided predominance of knowledge over will is visible, and consequently there also shows itself in it a knowledge that is entirely devoid of relation to will, *i.e., pure knowing.* On the contrary, in ordinary countenances there is a predominant expression of will; and we see that knowledge only comes into activity under the impulse of will, and thus is directed merely by motives.

§37. Genius, then, consists, according to our explanation, in the capacity for knowing, independently of the principle of sufficient reason, not individual things, which have their existence only in their relations, but the Ideas of such things, and of being oneself the correlative of the idea—and thus no longer an individual, but the pure subject of knowledge. Yet this faculty must exist in all men in a smaller and different degree; for if not, they would be just as incapable of enjoying works of art as of producing them; they would have no susceptibility for the beautiful or the sublime; indeed, these words could have no meaning for them. We must therefore assume that there exists in all men this power of knowing the Ideas in things, and consequently of transcending their personality for the moment, unless indeed there are some men who are capable of no aesthetic pleasure at all. The man of genius excels ordinary men only by possessing this kind of knowledge in a far higher degree and more continuously. Thus, while under its influence he retains the presence of mind which is necessary to enable him to repeat in a voluntary and intentional work what he has learned in this manner; and this repetition is the work of art. Through this he communicates to others the Idea he has grasped. This Idea remains unchanged and the same, so that aesthetic pleasure is one and the same whether it is called forth by a work of art or directly by the contemplation of nature and life. The work of art is only a means of facilitating the knowledge in which this pleasure consists. That the Idea comes to us more easily from the work of art than directly from nature and the real world, arises from the fact that the artist, who knew only the Idea, no longer the actual, has reproduced in his work the pure Idea, has abstracted it from the actual, omitting all disturbing accidents. The artist lets us see the world through his eyes. That he has these eyes, that he knows the inner nature of things apart from all their relations, is the gift of genius, is inborn; but that he is able to lend us this gift, to let us see with his eyes, is acquired, and is the technical side of art. . . .

§41. The course of the discussion has made it necessary to insert at this point the treatment of the sublime, though we have only half done with the beautiful, as we have considered its subjective side only. For it was merely a special modification of this subjective side that distinguished the beautiful from the sublime. This difference was found to depend upon whether the state of pure will-less knowing, which is presupposed and demanded by all aesthetic contemplation, was reached without opposition by the mere disappearance of the will from consciousness, be-

cause the object invited and drew us towards it; or whether it was only attained through the free, conscious transcending of the will, to which the object contemplated had an unfavorable and even hostile relation, which would destroy contemplation altogether, if we were to give ourselves up to it. This is the distinction between the beautiful and the sublime. In the object they are not essentially different, for in every case the object of aesthetical contemplation is not the individual thing, but the Idea in it which is striving to reveal itself; that is to say, adequate objectivity of will at a particular grade. Its necessary correlative, independent, like itself, of the principle of sufficient reason, is the pure subject of knowing; just as the correlative of the particular thing is the knowing individual, both of which lie within the province of the principle of sufficient reason.

When we say that a thing is *beautiful,* we thereby assert that it is an object of our aesthetic contemplation, and this has a double meaning; on the one hand, it means that the sight of the thing makes us *objective,* that is to say, that in contemplating it we are no longer conscious of ourselves as individuals, but as pure will-less subjects of knowledge; and on the other hand, it means that we recognize in the object, not the particular thing. But an Idea, and this can only happen, so far as our contemplation of it is not subordinated to the principle of sufficient reason, does not follow the relation of the object to anything outside it (which is always ultimately connected with relations to our own will), but rests in the object itself. For the Idea and the pure subject of knowledge always appear at once in consciousness as necessary correlatives, and on their appearance all distinction of time vanishes, for they are both entirely foreign to the principle of sufficient reason in all its forms, and lie outside the relations which are imposed by it; they may be compared to the rainbow and the sun, which have no part in the constant movement and succession of the falling drops. Therefore, if, for example, I contemplate a tree aesthetically, *i.e.,* with artistic eyes, and thus recognize not it, but its Idea, it becomes at once of no consequence whether it is this tree or its predecessor which flourished a thousand years ago, and whether the observer is this individual or any other that lived anywhere and at any time; the particular thing and the knowing individual are abolished with the principle of sufficient reason, and there remains nothing but the Idea and the pure subject of knowing, which together constitute the adequate objectivity of will at this grade. And the Idea dispenses not only with time, but also with space, for the Idea proper is not this special form which appears before me but its expression, its pure significance, its inner being, which discloses itself to me and appeals to me, and which may be quite the same though the spatial relations of its form be very different.

Since, on the one hand, every given thing may be observed in a purely objective manner and apart from all relations; and since, on the other hand, the will manifests itself in everything at some grade of its objectivity, so that everything is the expression of an Idea; it follows that everything is also *beautiful*. That even the most insignificant things admit of pure objective and will-less contemplation, and thus prove that they are beautiful, is shown by what was said above in this reference about the Dutch pictures of still life (§38).[6] But one thing is more beautiful than another, because it makes this pure objective contemplation easier, it lends itself to it, and, so to speak, even compels it, and then we call it very beautiful. This is the case sometimes because, as an individual thing, it expresses in its purity the Idea of its species by the very distinct, clearly defined, and significant relation of its parts, and also fully reveals that Idea through the completeness of all the possible expressions of its species united in it, so that it makes the transition from the individual thing to the Idea, and therefore also the condition of pure contemplation, very easy for the beholder. Sometimes this possession of spe-

cial beauty in an object lies in the fact that the Idea itself which appeals to us in it is a high grade of the objectivity of will, and therefore very significant and expressive. Therefore it is that man is more beautiful than all other objects, and the revelation of his nature is the highest aim of art. Human form and expression are the most important objects of plastic art, and human action the most important object of poetry. Yet each thing has its own peculiar beauty, not only every organism which expresses itself in the unity of an individual being, but also everything unorganized and formless, and even every manufactured article. For all these reveal the Ideas through which the will objectifies itself at its lowest grades; they give, as it were, the deepest resounding bass notes of nature. Gravity, rigidity, fluidity, light, and so forth, are the Ideas which express themselves in rocks, in buildings, in waters. Landscape gardening or architecture can do no more than assist them to unfold their qualities distinctly, fully, and variously; they can only give them the opportunity of expressing themselves purely, so that they lend themselves to aesthetic contemplation and make it easier. Inferior buildings or ill-favored localities, on the contrary, which nature has neglected or art has spoiled, perform this task in a very slight degree or not at all; yet even from them these universal, fundamental Ideas of nature cannot altogether disappear. To the careful observer they present themselves here also, and even bad buildings and the like are capable of being aesthetically considered; the Ideas of the most universal properties of their materials are still recognizable in them, only the artificial form which has been given them does not assist but hinders aesthetic contemplation. Manufactured articles also serve to express Ideas, only it is not the Idea of the manufactured article which speaks in them, but the Idea of the material to which this artificial form has been given. This may be very conveniently expressed in two words, in the language of the schoolmen,[7] thus

---

[6] In the seventeenth century, Dutch painters began to paint realistic pictures of common objects such as fruit and flowers rather than the religious subjects that were considered suitable for painting in the Renaissance.

[7] The medieval philosophers and theologians who followed the methods and logic of Aristotle.

—the manufactured article expresses the Idea of its *forma substantialis*[8] *but not that of* its *forma accidentalis;*[9] the latter leading to no Idea, but only to a human conception of which it is the result. It is needless to say that by manufactured article, no work of plastic art is meant. The schoolmen understand, in fact, by *forma substantialis* that which I call the grade of the objectification of will in a thing. . . .

§42. 1 return to the exposition of the aesthetic impression. The knowledge of the beautiful always supposes at once and inseparably the pure knowing subject and the known Idea as object. Yet the source of aesthetic satisfaction will sometimes lie more in the comprehension of the known idea, sometimes more in the blessedness and spiritual peace of the pure knowing subject freed from all willing, and therefore from all individuality, and the pain that proceeds from it. And, indeed, this predominance of one or the other constituent part of aesthetic feeling will depend upon whether the intuitively grasped Idea is a higher or a lower grade of the objectivity of will. Thus in aesthetic contemplation (in the real, or through the medium of art) of the beauty of nature in the inorganic and vegetable worlds, or in works of architecture, the pleasure of pure will-less knowing will predominate, because the Ideas which are here apprehended are only low grades of the objectivity of will, and are therefore not manifestations of deep significance and rich content. On the other hand, if animals and man are the objects of aesthetic contemplation or representation, the pleasure will consist rather in the comprehension of these Ideas, which are the most distinct revelation of will; for they exhibit the greatest multiplicity of forms, the greatest

richness and deep significance of phenomena, and reveal to us most completely the nature of will, whether in its violence, its terribleness, its satisfaction or its aberration (the latter in tragic situations), or finally in its change and self-surrender, which is the peculiar theme of Christian painting; as the Idea of the will enlightened by full knowledge is the object of historical painting in general, and of the drama. . . .

§45 . . . One would suppose that art achieved the beautiful by imitating nature. But how is the artist to recognize the perfect work which is to be imitated, and distinguish it from the failures, if he does not anticipate the beautiful *before experience?* And besides this, has nature ever produced a human being perfectly beautiful in all his parts? It has accordingly been thought that the artist must seek out the beautiful parts, distributed among a number of different human beings, and out of them construct a beautiful whole; a perverse and foolish opinion. For it will be asked, how is he to know that just these forms and not others are beautiful? We also see what kind of success attended the efforts of the old German painters to achieve the beautiful by imitating nature. Observe their naked figures. No knowledge of the beautiful is possible purely *a posteriori,*[10] and from mere experience; it is always, at least in part, *a priori,*[11] although quite different in kind, from the forms of the principle of sufficient reason, of which we are conscious *a priori.* These concern the universal form of phenomena as such, as it constitutes the possibility of knowledge in general, the universal how of all phenomena, and from this knowledge proceed mathematics and pure natural science. But this other kind of knowledge *a priori,* which makes it possible to express the beautiful, concerns, not the form but the content of phenomena, not the how but the

---

[8] Substantial form: that which makes a thing what it is and not something else. A change in substantial form means a change in the identity of the thing. If a tree is cut down and burned, it is no longer a tree. The substantial form of a tree is not the same as the substantial form of ashes.

[9] Accidental form: may change without changing the thing's identity. When a tree loses its leaves, it does not cease to be that tree, so having those leaves is only an accidental form of the tree.

[10] The form of knowledge that follows from experience. Something is known *a posteriori* when one must first experience it to know it.

[11] The form of knowledge that is independent of experience. Something is known *a priori* when knowledge of it can be gained simply from examining the concept.

what of the phenomenon. That we all recognize human beauty when we see it, but that in the true artist this takes place with such clearness that he shows it as he has never seen it, and surpasses nature in his representation; this is only possible because *we ourselves are* the will whose adequate objectification at its highest grade is here to be judged and discovered. Thus alone have we in fact an anticipation of that which nature (which is just the will that constitutes our own being) strives to express. And in the true genius this anticipation is accompanied by so great a degree of intelligence that he recognizes the Idea in the particular thing, and thus, as it were, *understands the half-uttered speech of nature,* and articulates clearly what she only stammered forth. He expresses in the hard marble that beauty of form which in a thousand attempts she failed to produce; he presents it to Nature, saying, as it were, to her, "That is what you wanted to say!" And whoever is able to judge replies, "Yes that is it." Only in this way was it possible for the genius of the Greeks to find the type of human beauty and establish it as a canon for the school of sculpture; and only by virtue of such an anticipation is it possible for all of us to recognize beauty, when it has actually been achieved by nature in the particular case. This anticipation is the *Ideal.* It is the *Idea* so far as it is known *a priori,* at least half, and it becomes practical for art, because it corresponds to and completes what is given *a posteriori* through nature. The possibility of such an anticipation of the beautiful *a priori* in the artist, and of its recognition *a posteriori* by the critic, lies in the fact that the artist and the critic are themselves the "in-itself" of nature, the will which objectifies itself. . . .

. . . As the merely spatial manifestation of will can objectify it fully or defectively at each definite grade, and it is this which constitutes beauty or ugliness—so the temporal objectification of will, *i.e.,* the action, and indeed the direct action, the movement, may correspond to the will, which objectifies itself in it, purely and fully without foreign admixture, without superfluity, without de-

fect, only expressing exactly the act of will determined in each case;—or the converse of all this may occur. In the first case the movement is made with *grace,* in the second case without it. Thus as beauty is the adequate representation of will generally, through its merely spatial manifestation; *grace* is the adequate representation of will through its temporal manifestation, that is to say, the perfectly accurate and fitting expression of each act of will, through the movement and position which objectify it. . . .

§51. . . . Ideas are essentially perceptible; if, therefore, in poetry only abstract conceptions are directly communicated through words, it is yet clearly the intention to make the hearer perceive the Ideas of life in the representatives of these conceptions, and this can only take place through the assistance of his own imagination. But in order to set the imagination to work for the accomplishment of this end, the abstract conceptions, which are the immediate material of poetry as of dry prose, must be so arranged that their spheres intersect each other in such a way that none of them can remain in its abstract universality; but, instead of it, a perceptible representative appears to the imagination; and this is always further modified by the words of the poet according to what his intention may be. . . .

From the general nature of the material, that is, the concepts, which poetry uses to communicate the Ideas, the extent of its province is very great. The whole of nature, the Ideas of all grades, can be represented by means of it, for it proceeds according to the Idea it has to impart, so that its representations are sometimes descriptive, sometimes narrative and sometimes directly dramatic. If, in the representation of the lower grades of the objectivity of will, plastic and pictorial art generally surpass it, because lifeless nature, and even brute nature, reveals almost its whole being in a single well-chosen moment; man, on the contrary, so far as he does not express himself by the mere form and expression of his person, but through a series of actions and the accompanying thoughts and emotions, is the principal object of Poetry, in which no other art can compete with it, for here the progress or movement which cannot be represented in plastic or pictorial art just suits its purpose.

. . . Our own experience is the indispensable condition of understanding poetry as of understanding history; for it is, so to speak, the dictionary of the language that both speak. But history is related to poetry as portrait painting is related to historical painting; the one gives us the true in the individual, the other the true in the universal; the one has the truth of the phenomenon, and can therefore verify it from the phenomenal, the other has the truth of the Idea, which can be found in no particular phenomenon, but yet speaks to us from them all. The poet from deliberate choice represents significant characters in significant situations; the historian takes both as they come. Indeed, he must regard and select the circumstances and the persons, not with reference to their inward and true significance, which expresses the Idea, but according to the outward, apparent, and relatively important significance with regard to the connection and the consequences. He must consider nothing in and for itself in its essential character and expression, but must look at everything in its relations, in its connection, in its influence upon what follows, and especially upon its own age. Therefore he will not overlook an action of a king, though of little significance, and in itself quite common, because it has results and influence. And, on the other hand, actions of the highest significance of particular and very eminent individuals are not to be recorded by him if they have no consequences. For his treatment follows the principle of sufficient reason, and apprehends the phenomenon, of which this principle is the form. But the poet comprehends the Idea, the inner nature of man apart from all relations, outside all time, the adequate objectivity of the thing-in-itself, at its highest grade. Even in that method of treatment which is necessary for the historian, the inner nature and significance of the phenomena, the kernel of all these shells, can never be entirely lost. He who seeks for it, at any rate, may find it and recognize

it. Yet that which is significant in itself, not in its relations, the real unfolding of the Idea, will be found far more accurately and distinctly in poetry than in history, and, therefore, however paradoxical it may sound, far more really genuine inner truth is to be attributed to poetry than to history. For the historian must accurately follow the particular event according to life, as it develops itself in time in the manifold tangled chains of causes and effects. It is, however, impossible that he can have all the data for this; he cannot have seen all and discovered all. He is forsaken at every moment by the original of his picture, or a false one substitutes itself for it, and this so constantly that I think I may assume that in all history the false outweighs the true. The poet, on the contrary, has comprehended the Idea of man from some definite side which is to be represented; thus it is the nature of his own self that objectifies itself in it for him. His knowledge, as we explained above when speaking of sculpture, is half *a priori;* his ideal stands before his mind firm, distinct, brightly illuminated, and cannot forsake him; therefore he shows us, in the mirror of his mind, the Idea pure and distinct, and his delineation of it down to the minutest particular is true as life itself. The great ancient historians are, therefore, in those particulars in which their data fail them, for example, in the speeches of their heroes—poets; indeed their whole manner of handling their material approaches to the epic. But this gives their representations unity, and enables them to retain inner truth, even when outward truth was not accessible, or indeed was falsified. . . .

The representation of the Idea of man, which is the Work of the poet, may be performed, so that what is represented is also the representer. This is the case in lyrical poetry, in songs, properly so called, in which the poet only perceives vividly his own state and describes it. Thus a certain subjectivity is essential to this kind of poetry from the nature of its object. Again, what is to be represented may be entirely different from him who represents it, as is the case in all other kinds of poetry, in which the poet more or less conceals himself behind his representation, and at last disappears altogether. In the ballad the poet still expresses to some extent his own state through the tone and proportion of the whole; therefore, though much more objective than the lyric, it has yet something subjective. This becomes less in the idyll, still less in the romantic poem, almost entirely disappears in the true epic, and even to the last vestige in the drama, which is the most objective and, in more than one respect, the completest and most difficult form of poetry. The lyrical form of poetry is consequently the easiest, and although art, as a whole, belongs only to the true man of genius, who so rarely appears, even a man who is not in general very remarkable may produce a beautiful song if by actual strong excitement from without, some inspiration raises his mental powers; for all that is required for this is a lively perception of his own state at a moment of emotional excitement. . . .

In the more objective kinds of poetry, especially in the romance, the epic, and the drama, the end, the revelation of man, is principally attained by two means, by true and profound representation of significant characters, and by the invention of pregnant situations in which they disclose themselves. For as it is incumbent upon the chemist not only to exhibit the simple elements, pure and genuine, and their principal compounds, but also to expose them to the influence of such reagents as will clearly and strikingly bring out their peculiar qualities, so is it incumbent on the poet not only to present to us significant characters truly and faithfully as nature itself; but, in order that we may get to know them, he must place them in those situations in which their peculiar qualities will fully unfold themselves, and appear distinctly in sharp outline; situations which are therefore called significant. In real life, and in history, situations of this kind are rarely brought about by chance, and they stand alone, lost and concealed in the multitude of those which are insignificant. The complete significance of the situations ought to distinguish the romance, the epic, and the drama from real life as completely as the arrangement

and selection of significant characters. In both, however, absolute truth is a necessary condition of their effect, and want of unity in the characters, contradiction either of themselves or of the nature of humanity in general, as well as impossibility, or very great improbability in the events, even in mere accessories, offend just as much in poetry as badly drawn figures, false perspective, or wrong lighting in painting. For both in poetry and painting we, demand the faithful mirror of life, of man, of the world, only made more clear by the representation, and more significant by the arrangement. For there is only one end of all the arts, the representation of the Ideas; and their essential difference lies simply in the different grades of the objectification of will to which the Ideas that are to be represented belong. . . .

Tragedy is to be regarded, and is recognised as the summit of poetical art, both on account of the greatness of its effect and the difficulty of its achievement. It is very significant for our whole system, and well worthy of observation, that the end of this highest poetical achievement is the representation of the terrible side of life. The unspeakable pain, the wail of humanity, the triumph of evil, the scornful mastery of chance, and the irretrievable fall of the just and innocent, is here presented to us; and in this lies a significant hint of the nature of the world and of existence. It is the strife of will with itself, which here, completely unfolded at the highest grade of its objectivity, comes into fearful prominence. It becomes visible in the suffering of men, which is now introduced, partly through chance and error, which appear as the rulers of the world, personified as fate, on account of their insidiousness, which even reaches the appearance of design; partly it proceeds from man himself, through the self-mortifying efforts of a few, through the wickedness and perversity of most. It is one and the same will that lives and appears in them all, but whose phenomena fight against each other and destroy each other. In one individual it appears powerfully, in another more weakly; in one more subject to reason, and softened by the light of knowledge, in another less so, till at last, in some single case, this knowledge, purified and heightened by suffering itself, reaches the point at which the phenomenon, the veil of Maya,[12] no longer deceives it. It sees through the form of the phenomenon, the *principium individuationis.*[13] The egoism which rests on this perishes with it, so that now *the motives* that were so powerful before have lost their might, and instead of them the complete knowledge of the nature of the world, which has a *quieting* effect on the will, produces resignation, the surrender not merely of life, but of the very will to live. Thus we see in tragedies the noblest men, after long conflict and suffering, at last renounce the ends they have so keenly followed, and all the pleasures of life for ever, or else freely and joyfully surrender life itself. . . . On the other hand, the demand for so-called poetical justice rests on [an] entire misconception of the nature of tragedy, and, indeed, of the nature of the world itself. It boldly appears in all its dullness in the criticisms which Dr. Samuel Johnson[14] made on particular plays of Shakespeare, for he very naively laments its entire absence. And its absence is certainly obvious, for in what has Ophelia,[15] Desdemona,[16] or Cordelia[17] offended? But only the dull, optimistic, Protestant-rationalistic, or peculiarly Jewish view of life will make the demand for poetical justice, and find satisfaction in it. The true sense of tragedy is the deeper insight, that it is not his own individual sins that the hero atones for, but original sin, *i.e.,* the crime of existence itself.

Study Questions

1. What is the difference between scientific knowledge and knowledge of ideas? Give examples of each.
2. How does art grasp ideas? How does it present them?
3. How is art defined?
4. What is genius? What would a nongenius be?
5. What does genius produce? How?
6. Why is the lot of genius not a happy one?
7. Why does genius require imagination?
8. Why is imagination not limited to genius?
9. Who will pay more attention to things as they are in themselves—the common mortal or the artist? Why?
10. How is the common mortal related to the man of genius?
11. What is the difference between the abstraction performed by an artist and the abstract conceptualization of the common mortal?
12. How does a beautiful object differ from a sublime object?
13. How does aesthetic contemplation differ from ordinary perception?
14. What kind of things can be contemplated aesthetically? How?
15. How is grace distinguished from beauty?
16. What is the difference between poetry and history?
17. How does Schopenhauer rank the kinds of poetry? What explains his ranking?
18. Why is tragedy the "summit of poetical art"?

---

[12] In Hindu philosophy, illusion is often portrayed as Maya, a veiled goddess.

[13] The principle of individuation is that which allows one to distinguish one object of a kind from another of the same kind.

[14] Samuel Johnson's (1709–1784) edition of Shakespeare with critical prefaces is one of the outstanding works of eighteenth-century criticism. Johnson was highly moral, but his criticism of Shakespeare is not naive in the way that Schopenhauer depicts it.

[15] In Shakespeare's *Hamlet,* Ophelia loves Hamlet. When he seems to reject her, she goes mad and drowns in a stream.

[16] In Shakespeare's *Othello,* Desdemona is the wife of Othello. Deceived by Iago, Othello kills Desdemona.

[17] In Shakespeare's *King Lear,* Cordelia is the one of Lear's daughters who will not flatter him. As a result, he rejects her and she dies.

Friedrich Nietzsche
• • • • • • • • • • • • • •

WILHELM FRIEDRICH NIETZSCHE was born in Prussia in 1844. His father was a Lutheran pastor who died when Nietzsche was five. Nietzsche was raised by his mother and aunts in a family dominated by women. He was educated at the universities at Bonn and Leipzig, where he was the student of the most prominent classical philologist of the time, Friedrich Ritschl. Ritschl was instrumental in gaining for Nietzsche an appointment as professor of classical philology at Basel in 1869 before Nietzsche had completed his residency requirements for his doctorate at Leipzig. Such an appointment was very unusual and signaled the high expectations Nietzsche had aroused. Nietzsche undertook a heavy load of teaching and writing at Basel, and his health, which had suffered from his volunteer service in the Prussian army during the Franco-Prussian War of 1870, was not good. At Basel, he published *The Birth of Tragedy* in 1872, but its approach to classical culture proved too extreme to be understood by his colleagues. Nietzsche became increasingly dissatisfied with the conventional academicism of philology. He was influenced by Arthur Schopenhauer (1788–1860) and particularly by the composer Richard Wagner (1813–1883), with whom he became friendly. His vocation as a philosopher led him to reject the strictly academic life. He pleaded ill health and resigned his professorship in 1879.

The next phase of Nietzsche's life saw his major literary/philosophical production. His style had become increasingly aphoristic and paradoxical. *Thus Spake Zarathustra* attempts to present his new vision, but it defies summary. *Beyond Good and Evil* and *The Genealogy of Morals* complete the break with both conventional morality and conventional literary and philosophical form. Nietzsche was forging a highly idiosyncratic style of philosophy that was frequently misunderstood in his own day. He broke with Wagner and continued to live a largely solitary existence in Switzerland and Italy. In 1889, only two weeks after the completion of *Nietzsche Contra Wagner,* he collapsed into insanity and never recovered. His insanity is usually attributed to syphilis, though speculation about where and when he might have acquired it is fruitless. He lived until 1900. By that time, his reputation had greatly expanded, and his work was the subject of considerable debate and interpretation.

Nietzsche's subsequent reputation has fluctuated. His iconoclasm, style, and lack of systematic consistency have contributed to a great deal of misunderstanding. His sister edited and published many of his notes after his insanity. She had her own agenda, and the result was a distorted picture both of Nietzsche and his philosophy. His work was adopted by German fascists, who found in his Dionysian impulses echoes of their own mythology. Nothing in Nietzsche would warrant the authoritarian and simple-minded version produced by Hitler, however. Nevertheless, Nietzsche was clearly a product of his nineteenth-century European background, and that culture tolerated outrageous anti-Semitic and gender-specific prejudices. It is pointless to try to explain away some of Nietzsche's less palatable aphorisms. They are a part of the extreme cultural rebellion that he felt necessary for his philosophy. We should remember, however, that Nietzsche is never simplistic or dogmatic. His whole style is designed to free forces that he could not control. The power of those forces has continued to make Nietzsche important to twentieth-century philosophical movements, such as existentialism, which he could not have anticipated.

◆ ◆ ◆ ◆ ◆ ◆

Paradoxically, one kind of religion can produce its religious vision only by denying the orthodoxies of conventional religion. To replace the old gods with new gods appears as blasphemy. Religion that has become established appears as law. A new religious vision is unlawful. Only by being irreligious can the new religious vision present itself. A countermovement sometimes appears as the negation of the gods and the sacred itself. If the gods are above, "in heaven," but have become too distant, then the only way to return may be downward through the affirmation of the underworld and the denial of the gods. From time to time, such movements have appeared in the history of religions and in forms of religious mysticism. Nietzsche's work suggests such a movement.

By announcing the death of God in *Thus Spake Zarathustra,* Nietzsche makes it possible to experience the naked power of the sacred. By rejecting Christianity with all of its historical forms, Nietzsche hoped to return to an older source of being. By opposing the self-sacrificing aspects of Christianity and affirming the power of the self, Nietzsche hoped to bring the self back into contact with its origins. Psychologically, Nietzsche returns us to the period before we became rational, intellectually controlled beings. His philosophy proposes that that return is also a vision of the way things really are.

Nietzsche was prepared for this paradoxical way of thinking by his training as a classicist. In the Greeks, he found an older vision of a world before civilization and a classical vision of Greek civilization as an order emerging from chaos. In the eighteenth and nineteenth centuries, German scholarship had led the way in classical scholarship. The Greeks were held up as the models of artistic control, rational order, and ideal citizenship. The beauty of their civilization was contrasted to the disorder of the Middle Ages and the mercenary nature of the emerging middle-class culture in Europe. The tendency was to idealize classical culture as orderly, rational, and restrained. Emotion was controlled by the mind. Nietzsche began in this tradition, but he rebelled against its values and saw more accurately and deeply that the vitality of the Greeks owed much to their darker psychological attraction to the old gods of violence and intoxication. Nietzsche's philosophy grows out of his increasing frustration with both the conventionality of European society and of classical scholarship.

Nietzsche was also prepared for his radical rejection of conventional philosophy by the tradition of Hegel and particularly Arthur Schopenhauer (1788–1860). After Hegel,

German philosophy sought various forms of the "spirit" within the movement of history. Initially, this movement was optimistic. The human spirit was viewed as moving toward a greater consciousness which its own absolute spirit embodied. European culture was viewed as the embodiment of this higher spirit, particularly in the arts. With Schopenhauer, however, pessimism intruded. The progress of human culture was checked by the isolation of the individual spirit. The will was not so much a control of ideas as a manifestation of desires that could not be fulfilled. A deep sense of being alone was felt. Nietzsche shared that pessimism, at least about the majority of humans. The only way forward was by finding the spirit in its most primitive forms. The music of Richard Wagner and the philosophy of Schopenhauer influenced Nietzsche, but his own willingness to follow the path as far as it led proved more radical than either Wagner or Schopenhauer was prepared for.

Finally, Nietzsche was able to draw on another aspect of nineteenth-century culture. Religion and art became more closely allied after the romantic movements of the late eighteenth and earlier nineteenth centuries. Romanticism was not a single, unified movement; it took many forms. A common feature, however, was the promotion of feeling to a new importance. Feeling was like religious experience, and religious experience depended on feeling. The most direct and effective way to stimulate that kind of feeling was art, or at least the new, personal art of the romantics. Another common feature of romanticism was the promotion of individual artists as creators and prophets. Artists had to actually experience what they expressed in their art. Artists were an avant garde who saw new visions before everyone else and opened the way to experiences and feelings closed off by the mundane world. Aesthetic feeling was embraced as one way to that vision. The result was to break down the differences between art and philosophy. Philosophy as a form of discourse had to become poetry. Poetry as a form of discourse had to play the role of philosophy. Nietzsche was attracted to the Greek philosophers before Socrates whose writings have come down to us as poetic fragments and aphorisms. This union of philosophy and poetry, particularly in an aphoristic form, shaped Nietzsche's approach. It fits his paradoxical style and frees his writing from the conventions of rationalism, logic, and Hegelian systems.

Nietzsche inverted the classical way of thinking to reestablish a genuinely classical vision of art against the "dead" art of science and cultural control. Consider thought as a push and pull of thinker and thing thought. In the classical world, that tension subordinated the individual to the universal, the present to the eternal, the singular to the type. Nietzsche reversed the order while accepting the structure. He thought that the only way that a mechanistic world could establish the full dialectic of humans and gods was by denying modern rationalism. In the second half of the nineteenth century, the influence of Hegel continued to focus aesthetics on the mind's ability to project itself onto reality and find itself in an answering movement. Consciousness, will, and ideas formed reality. Nietzsche agreed to the extent that mind and reality are intermingled. However, the self cannot exert rational control nor can it lose itself in a system. Nietzsche found that only by reasserting the self can thought overcome its own limitations and contingency. The result is a philosophy that denies large, impersonal systems and takes paradox to be constructive.

Nietzsche belongs to a long tradition of philologists and classical scholars who found in classical Greece the model for an artistic temperament. Throughout the eighteenth century, the arts were compared on the basis of presumed classical models. Classical art was understood to have been intellectual and restrained compared to the wildness and lack of control of later periods of art such as Gothic art. "Naturalism"—particularly the expression of emotion—was considered a lesser form of art compared to an idealized vision of classical art. Art forms were judged on their comparative ability to achieve classical ideals of control and restraint. The relative superiority of poetry over sculpture or painting was argued based on the ability of poetry to utilize motion in its form. We read one line after another, so that our thoughts move through time as we read or hear a poem. Painting and sculpture can show only a single pregnant moment, frozen in time. The three-dimensionality of sculpture made it superior to painting in the eyes of some, while others argued that painting, with its ability to use color and perspective for emotional purposes, was superior to sculpture. As a trained classicist and philologist, Nietzsche inherited these disputes and continued to pursue them. At the same time, he rejected the cool indifference of the scholar to the emotional appeal of art. Aesthetics had turned to sensation in the eighteenth century, and Nietzsche continued that tradition. But aesthetics also sought art in disinterested emotion, and Nietzsche denied that possibility. He sought a return to classicism, but he inverted the classical ideal.

Nietzsche transformed earlier debates over the relation of different art forms into a comparison of different cultural tendencies reflected in art. Two competing cultural impulses are reflected in art. The first is cool and distanced. It appeals to the plastic arts for its models because they offer complete visions of coherent, identifiable objects. Painting and sculpture show their objects as if they were real. They also freeze them at a single moment in time. This vision is one mark of what Nietzsche calls Apollonian form after the god Apollo, who was both the lawgiver of the new order of gods and a jealous protector of the gods from the pretensions of lesser beings. Apollo played the lyre, and those who presumed to produce a comparable music, he destroyed. The opposite of Apollo's control and order is the intoxication and ecstasy of Dionysus—the god associated with mystery and disorder. Music can also be wild and unrestrained, emotional and passionate in its appeal. Nonvisual and musical arts seem to present emotion directly without appeal to images or the intellect. They swallow everyone in an ecstasy that blurs the distinction between god and human. Dionysian art appeals to this untamed, emotional side of the self and culture.

Neither Dionysus nor Apollo should be considered as historical phases, however. Nietzsche uses them to describe tendencies in culture, tendencies in art, and psychological tendencies in individuals. Culture is torn between its Apollonian and Dionysian sides. Art is the product of the struggle between the exuberance and ecstasy of Dionysus and the controlled harmony of Apollo. Individuals have two sides to their personalities. They are both rational and irrational, controlled and impulsive. Nietzsche sees the necessity of both, but ultimately it is Dionysus to whom he turns as the older, more powerful side of our natures.

Nietzsche draws upon the deepest psychological appeals of religion and art to return to our subconscious desires and fears. Both Dionysian and Apollonian elements are involved. The world of dreams and intoxication requires interpretation. It is illusion—especially its art forms, which literally depend on deceiving the eye—but we need to be able to distinguish illusion from reality. Apollonian art helps make that distinction. Interpretation points back to an older, pre-Apollonian impulse, however. For illusion requires an image of reality; interpretation of dreams requires a dream world unconstrained by the newer gods. The pre-Apollonian is the realm of Dionysus. Art must appeal to both. Apollo represents order and creative expression; Dionysus represents the disorder and chaos necessary to creation, the older order without which the Apollonian images and illusions would not be possible.

Like the ancient gods, Nietzsche rejects intellectual control and conceptual limits. Images and illusions are free compared to the constraints of reason. Nietzsche's vision is anarchic and anticultural. The individual is nothing. Culture is convention. But where classical artists thought to find the universal through abstraction and reasoned control, Nietzsche hoped to recreate them by a return to older forms through a process of negation. Science and logic, reason, and knowledge are all the enemies of art because they limit and control the urgent Dionysian needs for losing self-awareness by becoming a single awareness of the world. Nietzsche may lose his self-consciousness, but he does so only by a heightened awareness of self that takes in everything else as well. Nietzsche denied conventional religion in order to reach the same deep creativity that original religion appealed to.

Hegel and many of his followers saw the movement of art as an historical movement. Nietzsche is close enough to later Hegelians to take history seriously as a form of cultural expression. But Nietzsche rejects the abstraction of Hegelian history. We are not interested in absolute spirit for its own sake; we want our own history. Nietzsche's art is neither the externally illusory art of images and stories nor the self-indulgent self-expression of the romantics. Nietzsche's self asserts its reality against the illusion of art, but it is only interested in real, concrete expressions of its artistic vision.

By rejecting the disinterested, detached emotion of modern aesthetics, Nietzsche's inclusion of Dionysus in art appeals to the creative, avant-garde distrust of aesthetic classicism. To take Nietzsche as the exponent of an anticivilized naturalism is to see only one part of his aesthetic, however. The other side of Nietzsche's work seeks a way back to the full classical heritage that includes both Apollo and Dionysus. Nietzsche objects to the whole modern empiricist assertion of the self and its ideas as supreme. From that point of view, Nietzsche is really conservative rather than avant garde. His way back is through negation and denial, but it is a genuine quest for an art that is in contact with the deepest psychological desires of every individual and culture.

It is impossible to select or anthologize Nietzsche without distorting him. *The Birth of Tragedy* is one of Nietzsche's earlier, more coherently argued works. It is still full of paradox and contradiction, however. In selecting sections that bear most directly on aesthetics, I do violence to Nietzsche's thought by reducing its paradoxical nature. I make Nietzsche more "Socratic" and rational than he is. I also shift the emphasis of the work. *The Birth of Tragedy* is also about the death of tragedy. According to Nietzsche, tragedy is born from the irrational depths of pre-Socratic philosophy and the mysteries of Dionysus. Nietzsche found the expression of that emotion in the music of Wagner. But Nietzsche also shows us the death of tragedy. The rationality of Socrates and Plato make tragedy impossible because they control and rationalize the emotional power that tragedy expressed. Tragedy is born in music that appeals directly to the soul. It dies when music becomes intellectualized and conventional. When Wagner appeared to Nietzsche to have succumbed to Christian values in his opera *Parsifal,* Nietzsche broke with him. When Schopenhauer moved in the direction of eastern mysticism as a way to overcome the alienation of the will, Nietzsche understood this as an abandonment of the full paradox of existence. Both appeared to Nietzsche as a failure of nerve. We must be very careful not to domesticate Nietzsche.

Increasingly in his later works, Nietzsche played on the full power of paradox. We should not expect from him the kind of logical arguments found in Hegel or the empiricists. Each fragment in the later works stands alone and qualifies every other fragment as well. Art is the perfect form for this philosophy, and it is a blending of philosophical and creative form that defies the conventions of both. If we think of aesthetic feeling as pure, disinterested intuition, Nietzsche radically rejects such feeling. But if we think of aesthetics as the integration of philosophy and art, Nietzsche is a model for aesthetics. Feeling replaces reason; art replaces philosophy. Both are transformed.

From *The Birth of Tragedy from the Spirit of Music*

MUCH WILL HAVE BEEN GAINED for aesthetics once we have succeeded in apprehending directly—rather than merely *ascertaining*—that art owes its continuous evolution to the Apollonian-Dionysiac duality, even as the propagation of the species depends on the duality of the sexes, their constant conflicts and periodic acts of reconciliation. I have borrowed my adjectives from the Greeks, who developed their mystical doctrines of art through plausible *embodiments,* not through purely conceptual means. It is by those two art-sponsoring deities, Apollo and Dionysus, that we are made to recognize the tremendous split, as regards both origins and objectives, between the plastic, Apollonian arts and the non-visual art of music inspired by Dionysus. The two creative tendencies developed alongside one another, usually in fierce opposition, each by its taunts forcing the other to more energetic production, both perpetuating in a discordant concord that agon[1] which the term *art* but feebly denominates: until at last, by the thaumaturgy[2] of an Hellenic[3] act of will, the pair accepted the yoke of marriage and, in this condition, begot Attic tragedy,[4] which exhibits the salient features of both parents.

To reach a closer understanding of both these tendencies, let us begin by reviewing them as the separate art realms of *dream* and *intoxication,* two physiological phenomena standing toward one another in much the same relationship as the Apollonian and Dionysiac.

♦　♦　♦　♦　♦　♦

The fair illusion of the dream sphere, in the production of which every man proves himself an accomplished artist, is a precondition not only of all plastic art, but even, as we shall see presently, of a wide range of poetry. Here we enjoy an immediate apprehension of form, all shapes speak to us directly, nothing seems indifferent or redundant. Despite the high intensity with which these dream realities exist for us, we still have a residual sensation that they are illusions; at least such has been my experience—and the frequency, not to say normality, of the experience is borne out in many passages of the poets. Men of philosophical disposition are known for their constant premonition that our everyday reality, too, is an illusion, hiding another, totally different kind of reality.

♦　♦　♦　♦　♦　♦

We can learn something about that naive artist through the analogy of dream. We can imagine the dreamer as he calls out to himself, still caught in the illusion of his dream and without disturbing it, "This is a dream, and I want to go on dreaming," and we can infer, on the one hand, that he takes deep delight in the contemplation of his dream, and, on the other, that he must have forgotten the day, with its horrible importunity, so to enjoy his dream. Apollo, the interpreter of dreams, will furnish the clue to what is happening here. Although of the two halves of life—the waking and the dreaming—the former is generally considered not only the more important but the only one which is truly lived, I would, at the risk of sounding paradoxical, propose the opposite view. The more I have come to realize in nature those omnipotent formative tendencies and, with them, an intense longing for illusion, the more I feel inclined to the hypothesis that the original Oneness, the ground of being, ever-suffering and contradictory, time and again has need of rapt vision and delightful illusion to redeem itself. Since we ourselves are the very stuff of such illusions, we must view ourselves as the truly non-existent, that is to say, as a perpetual

---

[1] Conflict, particularly of characters in a drama.
[2] Magic or miracle.
[3] Synonymous with *Greek.*
[4] Attica is the part of the Greek peninsula centered on Athens.

unfolding in time, space, and causality—what we label "empiric reality." But if, for the moment, we abstract from our own reality, viewing our empiric existence, as well as the existence of the world at large, as the idea of the original Oneness, produced anew each instant, then our dreams will appear to us as illusions of illusions, hence as a still higher form of satisfaction of the original desire for illusion. It is for this reason that the very core of nature takes such a deep delight in the naive artist and the naive work of art, which likewise is merely the illusion of an illusion. Raphael,[5] himself one of those immortal "naive" artists, in a symbolic canvas has illustrated that reduction of illusion to further illusion which is the original act of the naive artist and at the same time of all Apollonian culture. In the lower half of his "Transfiguration," through the figures of the possessed boy, the despairing bearers, the helpless, terrified disciples, we see a reflection of original pain, the sole ground of being: "illusion" here is a reflection of eternal contradiction, begetter of all things. From this illusion there rises, like the fragrance of ambrosia, a new illusory world, invisible to those enmeshed in the first: a radiant vision of pure delight, a rapt seeing through wide-open eyes. Here we have, in a great symbol of art, both the fair world of Apollo and its substratum, the terrible wisdom of Silenus,[6] and we can comprehend intuitively how they mutually require one another. But Apollo appears to us once again as the apotheosis[7] of the *principium individuationis,* in whom the eternal goal of the original Oneness, namely its redemption through illusion, accomplishes itself. With august gesture the god shows us how there is need for a whole world of torment in order for the individual to

produce the redemptive vision and to sit quietly in his rocking rowboat in mid-sea, absorbed in contemplation.

If this apotheosis of individuation is to be ready in normative terms, we may infer that there is one norm only: the individual—or, more precisely the observance of the limits of the individual: *sophrosyne.*[8] As a moral deity Apollo demands self-control from his people and, in order to observe such self-control, a knowledge of self. And so we find that the aesthetic necessity of beauty is accompanied by the imperatives, "Know thyself," and "Nothing too much."[9] Conversely, excess and *hubris*[10] come to be regarded as the hostile spirits of the non-Apollonian sphere, hence as properties of the pre-Apollonian era— the age of Titans[11]—and the extra-Apollonian world, that is to say the world of the barbarians. It was because of his Titanic love of man that Prometheus[12] had to be devoured by vultures; it was because of his extravagant wisdom which succeeded in solving the riddle of the Sphinx that Oedipus[13] had to be cast into a whirlpool of crime: in this fashion does the Delphic god[14] interpret the Greek past.

The effects of the Dionysiac spirit struck the Apollonian Greeks as titanic and barbaric; yet they could not disguise from themselves the fact

---

[5] Raphael Sanzio (1483–1520) was a major painter of the Italian Renaissance. His *Transfiguration* depicts Christ raised from the dead and changed into his form as a god.

[6] Silenus was a satyr, a half-human, half-bestial creature associated with drunkenness and revelry. Silenus was the companion and tutor of Dionysus.

[7] *Apotheosis* is transformation into a god. Apollo is the god who corresponds to the perfection of the individual, the transformation of the principle of individuation itself into a divine model.

[8] The Greek word *sophrosyne* means rationality, also moderation or prudence.

[9] The motto "Know thyself" is associated with Socrates; "Nothing too much" is associated with Aristotle. Both are demands for rational self-control and self-knowledge.

[10] *Hubris* means "pride" in the sense of excessive trust in oneself rather than the gods.

[11] The Titans were a race of gods who preceded the Olympian deities. They were overthrown by Zeus, the king of the new gods, in part for their actions against Dionysus. In one myth, humans are born from the ashes of the Titans.

[12] Prometheus was a Titan who aided humans and was punished by Zeus for his rebellion.

[13] Oedipus became king of Thebes by solving the riddle posed by the monster—the Sphinx—who was demanding tribute from the city. The riddle was, "What walks on four legs in the morning, two legs at noon, and three legs in the evening?" The answer was a man: first he crawls, then he walks upright, then he must walk with the aid of a stick.

[14] Delphi was famous as the site of an oracle sacred to Apollo.

that they were essentially akin to those deposed Titans and heroes. They felt more than that: their whole existence, with its temperate beauty, rested upon a base of suffering and *knowledge* which had been hidden from them until the reinstatement of Dionysus uncovered it once more. And lo and behold! Apollo found it impossible to live without Dionysus. The elements of Titanism and barbarism turned out to be quite as fundamental as the Apollonian element. And now let us imagine how the ecstatic sounds of the Dionysiac rites penetrated ever more enticingly into that artificially restrained and discrete world of illusion, how this clamor expressed the whole outrageous gamut of nature—delight, grief, knowledge—even to the most piercing cry; and then let us imagine how the Apollonian artist with his thin, monotonous harp music must have sounded beside the demoniac chant of the multitude! The muses presiding over the illusory arts paled before an art which enthusiastically told the truth, and the wisdom of Silenus cried "Woe!" against the serene Olympians. The individual, with his limits and moderations, forgot himself in the Dionysiac vortex and became oblivious to the laws of Apollo. Indiscreet extravagance revealed itself as truth, and contradiction, a delight born of pain, spoke out of the bosom of nature. Wherever the Dionysiac voice was heard, the Apollonian norm seemed suspended or destroyed. Yet it is equally true that, in those places where the first assault was withstood, the prestige and majesty of the Delphic god appeared more rigid and threatening than before. The only way I am able to view Doric art and the Doric state [15] is as a perpetual military encampment of the Apollonian forces. An art so defiantly austere, so ringed about with fortifications—an education so military and exacting—a polity so ruthlessly cruel—could endure only in a continual state of resistance against the titanic and barbaric menace of Dionysus.

◆　◆　◆　◆　◆　◆

---

[15] The Dorians were a group that migrated into preclassical Greece. Their simple art began the classical style.

Our scholarly ideas of elementary artistic process are likely to be offended by the primitive events which I have adduced here to explain the tragic chorus. And yet nothing can be more evident than the fact that the poet is poet only insofar as he sees himself surrounded by living, acting shapes into whose innermost being he penetrates. It is our peculiar modern weakness to see all primitive aesthetic phenomena in too complicated and abstract a way. Metaphor, for the authentic poet, is not a figure of rhetoric but a representative image standing concretely before him in lieu of a concept. A character, to him, is not an assemblage of individual traits laboriously pieced together, but a personage beheld as insistently living before his eyes, differing from the image of the painter only in its capacity to continue living and acting. What is it that makes Homer so much more vivid and concrete in his descriptions than any other poet? His lively eye, with which he discerns so much more. We all talk about poetry so abstractly because we all tend to be indifferent poets. At bottom the aesthetic phenomenon is quite simple: all one needs in order to be a poet is the ability to have a lively action going on before one continually, to live surrounded by hosts of spirits. To be a dramatist all one needs is the urge to transform oneself and speak out of strange bodies and souls.

Dionysic excitation is capable of communicating to a whole multitude this artistic power to feel itself surrounded by, and one with, a host of spirits. What happens in the dramatic chorus is the primary *dramatic* phenomenon: projecting oneself outside oneself and then acting as though one had really entered another body, another character. This constitutes the first step in the evolution of drama. This art is no longer that of the rhapsodist, who does not merge with his images but, like the painter, contemplates them as something outside himself; what we have here is the individual effacing himself through entering a strange being. It should be made clear that this phenomenon is not singular but epidemic: a whole crowd becomes rapt in this manner.

◆　◆　◆　◆　◆　◆

Having now recognized that Euripides[16] failed in founding the drama solely on Apollonian elements and that, instead, his anti-Dionysiac tendency led him towards inartistic naturalism, we are ready to deal with the phenomenon of aesthetic Socraticism. Its supreme law may be stated as follows: "Whatever is to be beautiful must also be sensible"—a parallel to the Socratic notion that knowledge alone makes men virtuous.

◆　◆　◆　◆　◆　◆

Euripides set out, as Plato was to do, to show the world the opposite of the "irrational" poet; his aesthetic axiom, "whatever is to be beautiful must be conscious" is strictly parallel to the Socratic "whatever is to be god must be conscious." We can hardly go wrong then in calling Euripides the poet of aesthetic Socraticism. But Socrates was precisely that *second spectator,* incapable of understanding the older tragedy and therefore scorning it, and it was in his company that Euripides dared to usher in a new era of poetic activity. If the old tragedy was wrecked, aesthetic Socraticism is to blame, and to the extent that the target of the innovators was the Dionysiac principle of the older art we may call Socrates the god's chief opponent, the new Orpheus[17] who, though destined to be torn to pieces by the maenads[18] of Athenian judgment, succeeded in putting the overmastering god to flight. The latter, as before, when he fled from Lycurgus, king of the Edoni, took refuge in the depths of the sea;[19] that

is to say, in the flood of a mystery cult that was soon to encompass the world.

◆　◆　◆　◆　◆　◆

Once we have fully realized how, after Socrates, the mystagogue of science, one school of philosophers after another came upon the scene and departed; how generation after generation of inquirers, spurred by an insatiable thirst for knowledge, explored every aspect of the universe; and how by that ecumenical concern a common net of knowledge was spread over the whole globe, affording glimpses into the workings of an entire solar system—once we have realized all this, and the monumental pyramid of present-day knowledge, we cannot help viewing Socrates as the vortex and turning point of Western civilization. For if we imagine that immense store of energy used, not for the purposes of knowledge, but for the practical, egotistical ends of individuals and nations, we may readily see the consequence: universal wars of extermination and constant migrations of peoples would have weakened man's instinctive zest for life to such an extent that, suicide having become a matter of course, duty might have commanded the son to kill his parents, the friend his friend, as among the Fiji islanders. We know that such wholesale slaughter prevails wherever art in some form or other—especially as religion or science—has not served as antidote to barbarism.

◆　◆　◆　◆　◆　◆

Whoever has tasted the delight of a Socratic perception, experienced how it moves to encompass the whole world of phenomena in ever widening circles, knows no sharper incentive to life than his desire to complete the conquest, to weave the net absolutely tight. To such a person the Platonic Socrates appears as the teacher of an entirely new form of "Greek serenity" and affirmation. This positive attitude toward existence must release itself in actions for the most part pedagogic, exercised upon noble youths, to the

---

[16] Euripides was the last of the great Athenian dramatists. Nietzsche accepts the characterization of him as too "naturalistic," though Euripides might also be thought of as more emotional than Aeschylus and Sophocles.

[17] Orpheus descended into the underworld but failed in his attempt to recover his wife, Eurydice. The cult of Orpheus both resembles and is opposed to that of Dionysus.

[18] The maenads were female followers of Dionysus. In their ecstasy, they sometimes tore apart human victims. This was the fate Orpheus met.

[19] Lycurgus (not to be confused with the founder of Sparta) attacked the followers of Dionysus. The god himself fled and jumped into the sea, where he was protected by Thetis, the sea nymph and mother of Achilles.

end of producing genius. But science, spurred on by its energetic notions, approaches irresistibly those outer limits where the optimism implicit in logic must collapse. For the periphery of science has an infinite number of points. Every noble and gifted man has, before reaching the mid-point of his career, come up against some point of the periphery that defied his understanding, quite apart from the fact that we have no way of knowing how the area of the circle is ever to be fully charted. When the inquirer, having pushed to the circumference, realizes how logic in that place curls about itself and bites its own tail, he is struck with a new kind of perception: a tragic perception, which requires, to make it tolerable, the remedy of art.

◆　◆　◆　◆　◆　◆

We have tried to illustrate by this historical example how tragedy, being a product of the spirit of music, must surely perish by the destruction of that spirit. In order to moderate the strangeness of such an assertion and at the same time to demonstrate how we arrived at it, we must now frankly confront certain analogues of our own day. We must step resolutely into the thick of those struggles which are being waged right now between the insatiable thirst for knowledge and man's tragic dependency on art. I will not speak in this connection of those lesser destructive instincts which have at all times opposed art and especially tragedy, and which in our own day seem to triumph to such an extent that of all the theatrical arts only the farce and the ballet can be said to thrive, with a luxuriance which not all find pleasing. I shall deal here only with the distinguished enemies of the tragic view, that is to say with the exponents of science, all dyed-in-the-wool optimists like their archetype, Socrates. And presently I shall name those forces which seem to promise a rebirth of tragedy and who knows what other fair hopes for the German genius.

Before rushing headlong into the fight let us put on the armor of such perceptions as we have already won. In opposition to all who would de-

rive the arts from a single vital principle, I wish to keep before me those two artistic deities of the Greeks, Apollo and Dionysus. They represent to me, most vividly and concretely, two radically dissimilar realms of art. Apollo embodies the transcendent genius of the *principium individuationis;* through him alone is it possible to achieve redemption in illusion. The mystical jubilation of Dionysus, on the other hand, breaks the spell of individuation and opens a path to the maternal womb of being. Among the great thinkers there is only one who has fully realized the immense discrepancy between the plastic Apollonian art and the Dionysiac art of music. Independently of Greek religious symbols, Schopenhauer[20] assigned to music a totally different character and origin from all the other arts, because it does not, like all the others, represent appearance, but the will directly. It is the metaphysical complement to everything that is physical in the world; the thing-in-itself where all else is appearance (*The World as Will and Idea,* I). Richard Wagner[21] set his seal of approval on this key notion of all aesthetics when he wrote in his book on Beethoven that music obeys aesthetic principles quite unlike those governing the visual arts and that the category of beauty is altogether inapplicable to it— although a wrongheaded aesthetic based on a misguided and decadent art has attempted to make music answer to criteria of beauty proper only to the plastic arts, expecting it to generate *pleasure in beautiful forms.* Once I had become aware of this antinomy I felt strongly moved to explore the nature of Greek tragedy, the profoundest manifestation of Hellenic genius. For the first time I seemed to possess the key enabling me to inspect the problem of tragedy in terms that were no longer derived from conventional aesthetics. I was given such a strange and unfamiliar glimpse into the essence of Hellenism that it seemed to

---

[20] Arthur Schopenhauer treats the will as an impersonal force. See p. 160.
[21] Richard Wagner wrote operas based on the Germanic myths. His music appeals to power rather than beauty.

me that our classical philology, for all its air of triumphant achievement, had only dealt with phantasmagorias and externals.

We might approach this fundamental problem by posing the following question: what aesthetic effect is produced when the Apollonian and Dionysiac forces of art, usually separate, are made to work alongside each other? Or, to put it more succinctly, in what relation does music stand to image and concept?

◆　◆　◆　◆　◆　◆

In accordance with Schopenhauer's doctrine, interpret music as the immediate language of the will, and our imaginations are stimulated to embody that immaterial world, which speaks to us with lively motion and yet remains invisible. Image and concept, on the other hand, gain a heightened significance under the influence of truly appropriate music. Dionysiac art, then, affects the Apollonian talent in a twofold manner; first, music incites us to a symbolic intuition of the Dionysiac universality; second, it endows that symbolic image with supreme significance. From these facts, perfectly plausible once we have pondered them well, we deduce that music is capable of giving birth to myth, the most significant of similitudes; and above all, to the tragic myth, which is a parable of Dionysiac knowledge. When I spoke earlier of the lyric poet I demonstrated how, through him, music strives to account for its own essence in Apollonian images. Once we grant that music raised to its highest power must similarly try to find an adequate embodiment, it stands to reason that it will also succeed in discovering a symbolic expression for its proper Dionysiac wisdom. And where should we look for that expression if not in tragedy and the tragic spirit?

It is vain to try to deduce the tragic spirit from the commonly accepted categories of art: illusion and beauty. Music alone allows us to understand the delight felt at the annihilation of the individual. Each single instance of such annihilation will clarify for us the abiding phenomenon of Dionysiac art, which expresses the omnipotent will behind individuation, eternal life continuing beyond all appearance and in spite of destruction. The metaphysical delight in tragedy is a translation of instinctive Dionysiac wisdom into images. The hero, the highest manifestation of the will, is destroyed, and we assent, since he too is merely a phenomenon, and the eternal life of the will remains unaffected. Tragedy cries, "We believe that life is eternal!" and music is the direct expression of that life. The aims of plastic art are very different: here Apollo overcomes individual suffering by the glorious apotheosis of what is eternal in appearance: here beauty vanquishes the suffering that inheres in all existence, and pain is, in a certain sense, glossed away from nature's countenance. That same nature addresses us through Dionysiac art and its tragic symbolism, in a voice that rings authentic: "Be like me, the Original Mother, who, constantly creating, finds satisfaction in the turbulent flux of appearances!"

◆　◆　◆　◆　◆　◆

Dionysiac art, too, wishes to convince us of the eternal delight of existence, but it insists that we look for this delight not in the phenomena but behind them. It makes us realize that everything that is generated must be prepared to face its painful dissolution. It forces us to gaze into the horror of individual existence, yet without being turned to stone by the vision: a metaphysical solace momentarily lifts us above the whirl of shifting phenomena. For a brief moment we become, ourselves, the primal Being, and we experience its insatiable hunger for existence. Now we see the struggle, the pain, the destruction of appearances, as necessary, because of the constant proliferation of forms pushing into life, because of the extravagant fecundity of the world will. We feel the furious prodding of this travail in the very moment in which we become one with the immense lust for life and are made aware of the eternity and indestructibility of that lust. Piety and terror notwithstanding, we realize our great good fortune in having life—not as individuals, but as part of the life force with whose procreative lust we have become one.

♦   ♦   ♦   ♦   ♦   ♦

Thus the Apollonian spirit rescues us from the Dionysiac universality and makes us attend, delightedly, to individual forms. It focuses our piety on these forms and so satisfies our instinct for beauty, which longs for great and noble embodiments. It parades the images of life before us and incites us to seize their ideational essence. Through the massive impact of image, concept, ethical doctrine, and sympathy, the Apollonian spirit wrests man from his Dionysiac self-destruction and deceives him as to the universality of the Dionysiac event. It pretends that he sees only the particular image, e.g., Tristan and Isolde,[22] and that the music serves only to make him see it more intensely. What could possibly be immune from the salutary Apollonian charm, if it is able to create in us the illusion that Dionysus may be an aid to Apollo and further enhance his effects? that music is at bottom a vehicle for Apollonian representations? In the pre-established harmony obtaining between the consummate drama and its music, that drama reaches an acme of visual power unobtainable to the drama of words merely. As we watch the rhythmically moving characters of the stage merge with the independently moving lines of melody into a single curving line of motion, we experience the most delicate harmony of sound and visual movement. The relationships of things thus become directly available to the senses, and we realize that in these relationships the essence of a character and of a melodic line are simultaneously made manifest. And as music forces us to see more, and more inwardly than usual, and spreads before us like a delicate tissue the curtain of the scene, our spiritualized vision beholds the world of the stage at once infinitely expanded and illuminated from within. What analogue could the verbal poet possibly furnish—he who tries to bring about that inward expansion of the visible stage world, its inner illumination, by much more indirect and imperfect means, namely word and concept? But, once musical tragedy has appropriated the word, it can at the same time present the birthplace and subsoil of the word and illuminate the genesis of the word from within. And yet it must be emphatically stated that the process I have described is only a marvelous illusion, by whose effects we are delivered from the Dionysiac extravagance and onrush. For, at bottom, music and drama stand in the opposite relation: music is the true idea of the cosmos, drama but a reflection of that idea. The identity between the melodic line and the dramatic character, between relations of harmony and character, obtains in an opposite sense from what we experience when we witness a musical tragedy. However concretely we move, enliven, and illuminate the characters from within, they will always remain mere appearance, from which there is no gateway leading to the true heart of reality. But music addresses us from that center; and though countless appearances were to file past that same music, they would never exhaust its nature but remain external replicas only. Nothing is gained for the understanding of either music or drama by resorting to that popular and utterly false pair of opposites, body and soul. Yet this contrast, crude and unphilosophical as it is, seems to have developed among our aestheticians into an article of faith. About the contrast between the phenomenon and the thing-in-itself, on the other hand, they have never learned anything nor, for some obscure reason, wanted to learn.

If our analysis has shown that the Apollonian element in tragedy has utterly triumphed over the Dionysiac quintessence of music, bending the latter to its own purposes—which are to define the drama completely—still an important reservation must be made. At the point that matters most the Apollonian illusion has been broken

---

[22] In Arthurian legend, Tristan is sent to bring Isolde back to King Mark. Instead, he himself drinks the magic potion and they fall in love. Tristan is torn between his love and loyalty. Wagner based an opera on this legend.

through and destroyed. This drama which deploys before us, having all its movements and characters illumined from within by the aid of music—as though we witnessed the coming and going of the shuttle as it weaves the tissue—this drama achieves a total effect quite beyond the scope of any Apollonian artifice. In the final effect of tragedy the Dionysiac element triumphs once again: its closing sounds are such as were never heard in the Apollonian realm. The Apollonian illusion reveals its identity as the veil thrown over the Dionysiac meanings for the duration of the play, and yet the illusion is so potent that at its close the Apollonian drama is projected into a sphere where it begins to speak with Dionysiac wisdom, thereby denying itself and its Apollonian concreteness. The difficult relations between the two elements in tragedy may be symbolized by a fraternal union between the two deities: Dionysus speaks the language of Apollo, but Apollo, finally, the language of Dionysus; thereby the highest goal of tragedy and of art in general is reached.

◆   ◆   ◆   ◆   ◆   ◆

Art is not an imitation of nature but its metaphysical supplement, raised up beside it in order to overcome it. Insofar as tragic myth belongs to art, it fully shares its transcendent intentions. Yet what is transcended by myth when it presents the world of phenomena under the figure of the suffering hero? Certainly not the "reality" of that phenomenal world, for myth tells us on the contrary: "Just look! Look closely! This is your life. This is the hour hand on the clock of your existence." Is this the life that myth shows us in order to transcend it? And if not, how are we to account for the delight we feel in viewing these images? I am speaking of *aesthetic* delight, being at the same time fully aware that many of these images yield a moral delight as well, in the form of compassion or ethical triumph. But whoever tries to trace the tragic effect solely to these moral sources, as has been the custom among aestheticians for so long, need not think that he is doing art a service. Art must insist on interpretations

that are germane to its essence. In examining the peculiar delight arising from tragedy, we must look for it in the aesthetic sphere, without trespassing on the areas of pity, terror, or moral grandeur. How can ugliness and disharmony, which are the content of tragic myth, inspire an aesthetic delight?

At this point we must take a leap into the metaphysics of art by reiterating our earlier contention that this world can be justified only as an aesthetic phenomenon. On this view, tragic myth has convinced us that even the ugly and discordant are merely an aesthetic game which the will, in its utter exuberance, plays with itself. In order to understand the difficult phenomenon of Dionysiac art directly, we must now attend to the supreme significance of *musical dissonance*. The delight created by tragic myth has the same origin as the delight dissonance in music creates. That primal Dionysiac delight, experienced even in the presence of pain, is the source common to both music and tragic myth.

◆   ◆   ◆   ◆   ◆   ◆

Music and tragic myth are equally expressive of the Dionysiac talent of a nation and cannot be divorced from one another. Both have their origin in a realm of art which lies beyond the Apollonian; both shed their transfiguring light on a region in whose rapt harmony dissonance and the horror of existence fade away in enchantment. Confident of their supreme powers, they both toy with the sting of displeasure, and by their toying they both justify the existence of even the "worst possible world." Thus the Dionysiac element, as against the Apollonian, proves itself to be the eternal and original power of art, since it calls into being the entire world of phenomena. Yet in the midst of that world a new transfiguring light is needed to catch and hold in life the stream of individual forms. If we could imagine an incarnation of dissonance—and what is man if not that?—that dissonance, in order to endure life, would need a marvelous illusion to cover it with a veil of beauty. This is the proper artistic intention of Apollo, in whose name are gathered together all those countless illusions of fair semblance which at any moment make life worth living and whet our appetite for the next moment.

But only so much of the Dionysiac substratum of the universe may enter an individual consciousness as can be dealt with by that Apollonian transfiguration; so that these two prime agencies must develop in strictest proportion, conformable to the laws of eternal justice. Whenever the Dionysiac forces become too obstreperous, as is the case today, we are safe in assuming that Apollo is close at hand, though wrapped in a cloud, and that the rich effects of his beauty will be witnessed by a later generation.

Study Questions

1. How are the Apollonian and Dionysian elements in anything described? Find contemporary examples of each.
2. What kind of art does Apollo sponsor? Dionysus? Describe an example of each.
3. Nietzsche describes tragedy as a combination of both Dionysian and Apollonian elements. Describe each part for a particular Greek tragedy.
4. What is the relation between our everyday reality and dreams?
5. Which is more important—waking or dreaming? Why?
6. If Apollo is considered a perfect form, what does that say about the Greek idea of perfection?
7. Does the idealization of the male form indicate something about the place of the female in Greek culture? In Nietzsche's philosophy?
8. How does tragedy expose the Dionysian elements that underlie the "temperate art" of the Greeks?
9. How does Nietzsche describe the aesthetic phenomenon? How is it related to Dionysus and Apollo?
10. What is the law of aesthetic Socraticism? Apply it to a description of some work of art.
11. What is the argument that leads to the conclusion that Socraticism destroys tragedy?
12. Why does Nietzsche equate Socrates with Orpheus?
13. What are the limits of optimism?
14. What is the relation of knowledge and art?
15. Which is the greater form—music or painting? Why?
16. What is Nietzsche's view of the "self"?
17. Which "wins" in a tragedy—Dionysus or Apollo? Is Nietzsche consistent about this?
18. What justifies this world? Why and how?
19. What is the role of dissonance in music? How is that role related to Dionysus?

John Ruskin

J OHN RUSKIN (1819–1900) was the son of a wine merchant in Edinburgh. His father was part of the rising English middle class whose entrepreneurial spirit changed cultural expectations in nineteenth-century England. Art and culture were no longer the exclusive property of the upper classes. Changes in taste followed the change in audience. The arts became more sentimental and more socially conscious. Ruskin exhibits both tendencies. He came from devout parents and at first intended to enter the ministry. His interests in books, art, and writing were encouraged, and at Oxford he won a poetry prize which finally determined him against the ministry. At seventeen, he had written a critical defense of the painter J. M. W. Turner (1775–1851), which he sent to the artist. It was not published, but by his second year at Oxford, Ruskin was publishing critical articles on architecture in magazines. He returned to his defense of Turner in the first volume of *Modern Painters,* which was published in 1843 when Ruskin was only twenty-four. Its success established him as a major art critic.

As a critic, Ruskin became acquainted with the pre-Raphaelite school of artists. This group of poets and painters took their inspiration and name from what they considered the simplicity of style of early Renaissance painting that preceded the symbolic complexity and mannerism of Raphael. In painting, the leading figures were William Holman Hunt, John Millais, and Dante Gabriel Rosetti. Edward Burne-Jones was also associated with them for a time. Their style was simple and sentimental with a strong emphasis on narrative elements and clarity of drawing and color. In poetry, Christina Rosetti was the best known. Ruskin became their critical defender. He was attracted to their rejection of the elaborate style of painting known as mannerism and their accessibility. The materialism and vulgarity of industrial England appalled both Ruskin and the pre-Raphaelites, but they rejected the social elitism of upper-class patronage. The result was a kind of romantic nostalgia combined with an evangelical view of art and its ability to transform the souls of those it touched. Ruskin advocated this position in the continuing volumes of *Modern Painters,* and in his attempt to relate architecture to its cultural surrounding in *The Seven Lamps of Architecture* (1849) and *The Stones of Venice* (1851–53). Ruskin had no training as an architect. Instead, he approached architecture as he approached painting, in terms of its cultural and physical setting and its aesthetic impact. In the mid-nineteenth century, Ruskin achieved the status of an artistic and critical arbiter of taste with immense popular influence.

Ruskin's life was not altogether happy. His father was wealthy, and he never lacked the opportunity to pursue his critical and intellectual career. However, as early as 1840, as he was finishing at Oxford, his health deteriorated. Driven by the nineteenth-century Protestant work ethic and by a social consciousness that would not allow him to rest, he pushed himself constantly. He was an executor of the estate of Turner and undertook to catalogue Turner's bequest of paintings to the National Gallery. He lectured and published widely. In addition to his critical writing, he exerted himself on various schemes for social reform including education and labor organization. Ruskin found the effects of industry ugly, but he could not turn away from the bourgeois class. In 1854, his marriage was annulled and his wife immediately married his pre-Raphaelite friend John Millais. In 1870, Ruskin became the first professor of art at a British University when he was named Slade Professor of Fine Art at Oxford. At the time, he was involved in a complex love affair with a woman thirty years younger than he. He suffered a mental breakdown about this time and was forced to withdraw to some extent.

As Ruskin spent an increasing amount of time at his country estate and in Oxford, he founded a kind of feudal society of his own, the Company of St. George. In 1878, he was sued by the impressionist painter James McNeill Whistler in one of the most famous artistic controversies of the century. Ruskin had been critical of Whistler's painting *Falling Rocket: Nocturne in Black and Gold,* which Ruskin found offensive because of what he considered its lack of painterly skill and because of Whistler's antisocial aesthetic doctrine of art for art's sake which Ruskin found irresponsible. Ruskin said that Whistler asked "two hundred guineas for flinging a pot of paint in the public's face." The jury found for Whistler but awarded him no significant damages. Ruskin the defender of Turner had become Ruskin, the critical reactionary, though Ruskin's social theory played a large role in his critical reaction. Ruskin suffered another mental breakdown, though he continued to write, including his autobiography, *Praeterita* (1885–89). After 1889, his mental state deteriorated further until his death in 1900.

♦   ♦   ♦   ♦   ♦   ♦

John Ruskin was arguably the most influential art critic of the nineteenth century. He has been variously dismissed as an example of upper-class British prejudice and Victorian sentimentality and praised as the only original British thinker of his day.[1] His work is related to romanticism in complex ways, but he was both a practicing art critic and a prolific writer who tried to place his criticism in a theoretical context that would support his judgments. Ruskin offers one of the best available examples of how nineteenth-century aesthetic theory was being assimilated and applied. His judgments may seem wrongheaded, but they are provocative, well-documented, and buttressed by a formidable intelligence.

As a critic, Ruskin was both a connoisseur of painting and an elitist in his judgments. But his elitism was essentially intellectual rather than social. This perspective grows directly out of his aesthetic theory. Understanding and appreciation, he believed, are based on a mental union between artists and those who are capable of appreciating

---

[1] The praise came from John Stuart Mill. Mill excepted his own group from the implied criticism of others. Cited by Katherine Gilbert and Helmut Kuhn, *A History of Esthetics* (New York: Dover, 1953), p. 414.

them. The greater and more advanced the artist, the more the work will require greatness and mental ability on the part of its audience. It follows that only a few will be capable of truly appreciating great art. Ruskin's argument is virtually counterinductive. Widely popular art is unlikely to be great because, if it appeals to many, it must be too easy. So unpopular art is most likely to be great art! At the same time, only what is supported by evidence and is in fact great can survive, so while only a few will be able to appreciate great art, their judgments will survive over time. Popularity will fade. In time, the cumulative judgments of the few will become the established judgments of history. Ruskin believed that history is essentially a positive movement. What emerges over time cannot help but be what is supported by evidence.

As a practicing critic, however, this test of time left Ruskin with a problem. New work is going to appeal to only a few. The popular work that imitates past greatness will tend to overwhelm the truly outstanding art of the present. The task of the critic must be to offer judgments in advance of history. The art critic is a kind of prophet crying in the wilderness, preparing the way for new artists to be received. For that task, the critic must have principles and evidence. Nothing that can be said on the basis of taste alone will convince because popular taste is no guide. Without evidence, one cannot tell true critics from popular taste (except perhaps by the sophistication and uniqueness of their judgments). To obtain principles, Ruskin looked to past greatness; the critic also must be an art historian, therefore. In this respect, Ruskin expressed a distinct preference for what he called the true greatness of the Renaissance (broadly defined) and a distaste for what he called the "old masters," by which he meant the landscapes and still life of the seventeenth and eighteenth centuries. Ruskin's significance as an aesthetic theorist rests on his unification of art history and aesthetics. His justification for his art-historical preferences more than the specific judgments that he produced in his role as a Victorian arbiter of taste make Ruskin worth paying attention to.

At the beginning of *Modern Painters,* Ruskin provides two arguments for aesthetic principles. The first is based on an analogy between painting and language; the second arises from a definition of greatness in art in terms of the quantity of what Ruskin called great ideas. The analogy between painting and language leads in two directions. By identifying painting as a form of language, Ruskin can adopt a theory of art as expressive of ideas and oppose imitation theories. For art to be expressive at all, it must have a means of expression. In that respect, all art is poetry, and pictorial art has a language of forms, colors, lines, space, and design that allows it to express ideas and emotions. However, Ruskin also distinguished the means of expression from its content. As language, art is a system of signs. As poetry, it is an expression of ideas. This distinction does not find much favor with more recent philosophers of language. It seems to imply that one can have ideas without a means of expressing those ideas. Many would hold that thought requires some form of language; without language, there is no thought. Clearly Ruskin disagreed. However, one should not be too quick to reject Ruskin's point in its context. Ruskin never says that language is not necessary for expression. Language that is expressive serves the ideas that it expresses. Language that aims merely to please is ornamentation or decoration. Ruskin's distinction between language and thought or ideas is intended to hold to the position that what is expressed is more important than the manner of its expression. He is undoubtedly influenced here by his interest in art history. Manner or style could become ease and elaboration. Ruskin held, with both Hegel and the romantic poets, that the movement of emotion and intellect rather than elaboration and manner should be served by the style. His distinction is more practical than theoretical.

The more important part of Ruskin's argument about painting as language links ideas and sense. Even sense itself qualifies as an idea in the fundamental sense of ideas as the units of thought. So when Ruskin distinguishes language as a means of expression from what is expressed, he does not separate ideas from sense and feeling; sense and feeling *are* ideas. This union is Ruskin's way of solving a fundamental problem in modern aesthetics. On one hand, aesthetics is a felt pleasure; as such it is sensual. On the other hand, the highest forms of experience are universal. They are not limited by mere sense. Kant had united aesthetic feeling and the universal by making aesthetic feeling the intuition prior to thought. Hegel shifted the emphasis by incorporating the aesthetic, in art, into mind. Ruskin is more concrete and commonsensical. He simply goes back to basic experience and holds that sense is itself a form of idea. Thus, we have ideas independently of language. The problem is to find a language adequate to sensibility. Artists create that language, but they do not depend on it. In this respect, Ruskin is clearly at one with the romantic poets such as Coleridge and Keats, according to whom art is a creative force prior to language.

Once art in its pictorial forms is identified with poetry as a form of creation and distinguished from the skills and elaboration that are used to express it, Ruskin is led to a definition of art in terms of the greatness of ideas: "The art is greatest, which conveys to the mind of the spectator, by any means whatsoever, the greatest number of the greatest ideas." An idea is great "in proportion as it is received by a higher faculty of the mind, and as it more fully occupies, and in occupying, exercises and exalts, the faculty by which it is received." Although framed as a definition of great art, this is actually a definition of all art since the difference between great and lesser art is merely the quantitative number of ideas and the qualitative greatness of the ideas themselves. So we know something is art if it conveys ideas to the mind of the spectator, and it is great art depending on what kind of ideas it conveys. Ideas that are presented only to the senses will be less than those that engage the mind on a moral or emotional plane. Ruskin still holds to what is called a *faculty psychology:* perception is a lower faculty than imagination, which is creative. Morality or conscience is a higher faculty still. Ideas of love and mortality carry more moral weight than ideas of color and form by themselves. They are thought to depend on separate faculties of the mind. Contemporary psychology is more holistic. It links feelings and ideas in a single complex. It is also more physicalist, holding that the psychology of a being is a function of its physical makeup. However, Ruskin's argument does not depend on his outdated psychology. Even without separate faculties, he could still hold that different kinds of ideas distinguish the qualities of art and that those ideas range from the purely sensual (say, the pleasure of a favorite color) to the moral or intellectual (say, the moral complexity of *King Lear*).

In fact, Ruskin goes on to distinguish five kinds of ideas that divide roughly into two classes. The kinds are power, imitation, truth, beauty, and relation. Power and imitation are basically mechanical ideas that contribute to skill. Truth, beauty, and relation are intellectual ideas, and they form the higher ideas that produce greatness in art. The description of these five ideas constitutes Ruskin's second major argument. It may be a bit difficult to think of power, imitation, truth, beauty, and relation as ideas. Ruskin is close enough to idealism to have a very broad sense of idea. He is also close enough to earlier empiricists to think of every mental event as an idea. When he speaks of truth as an idea, therefore, he means that whatever is true is understood in an ideational form. Art is made up of the expression of such ideas.

Power is described as the overcoming of difficulty, and imitation requires a combination of resemblance and difference. Both range from simple physical levels to more elaborate skills. For example, at its simplest, overcoming difficulties requires physical ability; however, we also might think of one aspect of plot as the overcoming of difficulties. Imitation retains a simple physical copying (like Plato's example of an image in a mirror), but Ruskin also describes it as a kind of juggling. An audience is given simultaneously enough to recognize what is being imitated while being made aware that the thing is not present. Simple illusion does not produce ideas of imitation. Elaborate effects in which paint is made to seem three dimensional, even though touch tells us that it is two dimensional, require great skill, and that skill is evident only if a viewer sees what is depicted but is not fooled. These ideas are limited. Ruskin does not regard them as having no value in art, but they belong to the elaboration of the language.

In contrast to imitation, truth presents ideas that are directly present. In imitation, the presentation is what is important. We marvel at the skill of the poet or the painter in presenting images. True ideas present not the image but the thing itself, and we marvel at what it is, not at the skill of its presentation. Ruskin treats truth as a quality of ideas that are transparent to objects or emotions. Imitation only partially presents its objects; as imitation, it must also partially conceal them so that the difference as well as the resemblance is maintained. But true ideas let one feel exactly what the idea expresses. When these ideas are sensual and pleasurable, beauty is present. Beauty is thus a direct contemplation by means of sense. It is pleasurable. But beauty is still sensual. Feeling that is understood surpasses mere sense. Taste is replaced with judgment, beauty with relation, the senses with the intellect. Aesthetic judgments may still appeal to felt emotion, but the emotions imply moral and social relations. The highest forms of art express just such ideas of relation.

Ruskin's aesthetics was related to romanticism by his idealism and his emotionalism. Unlike some romantics, however, he understood feeling as more than sensual indulgence. One fundamental tension in nineteenth-century aesthetics was between the tendency to regard aesthetic experience as so singular and different that to feel it was an end in itself and the desire to see art as a higher social form. The isolation of the aesthetic produced a kind of aestheticism that was unworldly either in a religious sense or in a sensual concentration. The alternative produced the kind of social art represented by realism in both domestic drama and painting. Ruskin's position is closer to the latter mode: art has a social function. Yet his feeling for the history of art and his view of ideas as greater in proportion to their rarity keeps him from presenting art and aesthetic feeling as a form of social action. In trying to balance the social tensions in his theory, his critical judgments sometimes become erratic. What Ruskin saw in the pre-Raphaelite painters was their idealism; he overlooked the easy, sentimental appeal of their subject matter. He was unprepared to recognize the power of impressionism because its appeal to vision itself lacked the intellectual content his theory demanded. However, his theory is a very powerful attempt to combine history and sensibility, romantic idealism and the empiricism of Locke and Hume. If Hegel is quintessentially German in his tendency to abstraction, Ruskin is quintessentially British in his tendency to hold to a middle course.

From *Modern Painters*

The Definition of Greatness in Art

In the 15th Lecture of Sir Joshua Reynolds,[2] incidental notice is taken of the distinction between those excellencies in the painter which belong to him *as such,* and those which belong to him in common with all men of intellect, the general and exalted powers of which art is the evidence and expression, not the subject. But the distinction is not there dwelt upon as it should be, for it is owing to the slight attention ordinarily paid to it, that criticism is open to every form of coxcombry, and liable to every phase of error. It is a distinction on which depend all sound judgment of the rank of the artist, and all just appreciation of the dignity of art.

Painting, or art generally, as such, with all its technicalities, difficulties, and particular ends, is nothing but a noble and expressive language, invaluable as the vehicle of thought, but by itself nothing. He who has learned what is commonly considered the whole art of painting, that is, the art of representing any natural object faithfully, has as yet only learned the language by which his thoughts are to be expressed. He has done just as much towards being that which we ought to respect as a great painter, as a man who has learned how to express himself grammatically and melodiously has towards being a great poet. The language is, indeed, more difficult of acquirement in the one case than in the other, and possesses more power of delighting the sense, while it speaks to the intellect, but it is, nevertheless, nothing more than language, and all those excellences which are peculiar to the painter as such, are merely what rhythm, melody, precision and force are in the words of the orator and the poet, necessary to their greatness, but not the tests of their greatness. It is not by the mode of representing and saying, but by what is represented and said, that the respective greatness either of the painter or the writer is to be finally determined.

Speaking with strict propriety, therefore, we should call a man a great painter only as he excelled in precision and force in the language of lines, and a great versifier, as he excelled in precision or force in the language of words. A great poet would then be a term strictly, and in precisely the same sense applicable to both, if warranted by the character of the images or thoughts which each in their respective languages convey. . . .

It is not, however, always easy, either in painting or literature, to determine where the influence of language stops, and where that of thought begins. Many thoughts are so dependent upon the language in which they are clothed, that they would lose half their beauty if otherwise expressed. But the highest thoughts are those which are least dependent on language, and the dignity of any composition and praise to which it is entitled, are in exact proportion to its independency of language or expression. A composition is indeed usually most perfect, when to such intrinsic dignity is added all that expression can do to attract and adorn; but in every case of supreme excellence this all becomes as nothing. We are more gratified by the simplest lines or words which can suggest the idea in its own naked beauty, than by the robe or the gem which conceal while they decorate; we are better pleased to feel by their absence how little they could bestow, than by their presence how much they can destroy.

There is therefore a distinction to be made between what is ornamental in language and what is expressive. That part of it which is necessary

---

[2] Sir Joshua Reynolds (1723–1792) was one of the leading English painters of the eighteenth century. As the first president of the Royal Academy of the Arts, he delivered each year a discourse on art. These discourses were collected and published. They are among the most important pieces of eighteenth-century art theory by a practicing artist.

to the embodying and conveying the thought is worthy of respect and attention as necessary to excellence, though not the test of it. But that part of it which is decorative has little more to do with the intrinsic excellence of the picture than the frame or the varnishing of it. And this caution in distinguishing between the ornamental and the expressive is peculiarly necessary in painting; for in the language of words it is nearly impossible for that which is not expressive to be beautiful, except by mere rhythm or melody, any sacrifice to which is immediately stigmatized as error. But the beauty of mere language in painting is not only very attractive and entertaining to the spectator, but requires for its attainment no small exertion of mind and devotion of time by the artist. Hence, in art, men have frequently fancied that they were becoming rhetoricians and poets when they were only learning to speak melodiously, and the judge has over and over again advanced to the honor of authors those who were never more than ornamental writing-masters. . . .

Yet although in all our speculations on art, language is thus to be distinguished from, and held subordinate to, that which it conveys, we must still remember that there are certain ideas inherent in language itself, and that strictly speaking, every pleasure connected with art has in it some reference to the intellect. The mere sensual pleasure of the eye, received from the most brilliant piece of coloring, is as nothing to that which it receives from a crystal prism, except as it depends on our perception of a certain meaning and intended arrangement of color, which has been the subject of intellect. Nay, the term idea, according to Locke's[3] definition of it, will extend even to the sensual impressions themselves as far as they are "things which the mind occupies itself about in thinking," that is, not as they are felt by the eye only, but as they are received by the mind through the eye. So that, if I say that the greatest picture is the greatest number of the greatest ideas, I have a definition which will include as subjects of comparison every pleasure which art is capable of conveying. If I were to say, on the contrary, that the best picture was that which most closely imitated nature, I should assume that art could only please by imitating nature, and I should cast out of the pale of criticism those parts of works of art which are not imitative, that is to say, intrinsic beauties of color and form, and those works of art wholly, which, like the arabesques[4] of Raffaelle[5] in the Loggias,[6] are not imitative at all. Now I want a definition of art wide enough to include all its varieties of aim: I do not say therefore that the art is greatest which gives most pleasure, because perhaps there is some art whose end is to teach, and not to please. I do not say that the art is greatest which teaches us most, because perhaps there is some art whose send is to please, and not to teach. I do not say that the art is greatest which teaches us most, because perhaps there is some art whose end is to please, and not to teach. I do not say that the art is greatest which imitates best, because perhaps there is some art whose end is to create, and not to imitate. But I say that the art is greatest, which conveys to the mind of the spectator, by any means whatsoever, the greatest number of the greatest ideas, and I call an idea great in proportion as it is received by a higher faculty of the mind, and as it more fully occupies, and in occupying, exercises and exalts, the faculty by which it is received.

If this then be the definition of great art, that of a great artist naturally follows. He is the greatest artist who has embodied, in the sum of his works, the greatest number of the greatest ideas.

Of Ideas of Power

The definition of art which I have just given, requires me to determine what kinds of ideas can be received from works of art, and which of these

---

[3] John Locke (1632–1704) was the first great British exponent of empiricism. His *Essay Concerning Human Understanding* traces all knowledge back to ideas that we have from experience. Locke uses the notion of *idea* in the widest possible sense.

[4] In painting, arabesques are intertwined patterns of leaves, scrollwork, and other ornamental figures.

[5] Sanzio Raphael (1483–1520) was a major Italian Renaissance painter. His style of religious painting combined perspective and color.

[6] Porches or window openings.

are the greatest, before proceeding to any practical application of the test.

I think that all the sources of pleasure, or any other good, to be derived from works of art, may be referred to five distinct heads.

I. Ideas of Power.—The perception or conception of the mental or bodily powers by which the work has been produced.

II. Ideas of Imitation.—The perception that the thing produced resembles something else.

III. Ideas of Truth.—The perception of faithfulness in a statement of facts by the thing produced.

IV. Ideas of Beauty.—The perception of beauty, either in the thing produced, or in what it suggests or resembles.

V. Ideas of Relation.—The perception of intellectual relations, in the thing produced, or in what it suggests or resembles.

I shall briefly distinguish the nature and effects of each of these classes of ideas.

I. Ideas of Power.—These are the simple perception of the mental or bodily powers exerted in the production of any work of art. According to the dignity and degree of the power perceived is the dignity of the idea; but the whole class of ideas is received by the intellect, and they excite the best of the moral feelings, veneration, and the desire of exertion. As a species, therefore, they are one of the noblest connected with art; but the differences in degree of dignity among themselves are infinite, being correspondent with every order of power—from that of the fingers to that of the most exalted intellect. Thus, when we see an Indian's paddle carved from the handle to the blade, we have a conception of prolonged manual labor, and are gratified in proportion to the supposed expenditure of time and exertion. These are, indeed, powers of a low order, yet the pleasure arising from the conception of them enters very largely indeed into our admiration of all elaborate ornament, architectural decoration, etc. The delight with which we look on the fretted front of Rouen Cathedral depends in no small degree on

the simple perception of time employed and labor expended in its production. But it is a right, that is, an ennobling pleasure, even in this its lowest phase; and even the pleasure felt by those persons who praise a drawing for its "finish," or its "work," which is one precisely of the same kind, would be right, if it did not imply a want of perception of the higher powers which render work unnecessary. If to the evidence of labor be added that of strength or dexterity, the sensation of power is yet increased, if to strength and dexterity be added that of ingenuity and judgment, it is multiplied tenfold, and so on, through all the subjects of action of body or mind, we receive the more exalted pleasure from the more exalted power.

So far the nature and effects of ideas of power cannot but be admitted by all. But the circumstance which I wish especially to insist upon, with respect to them, is one which may not, perhaps, be so readily allowed, namely, that they are independent of the nature of worthiness of the object from which they are received, and that whatever has been the subject of a great power, whether there be intrinsic and apparent worthiness in itself or not, bears with it the evidence of having been so, and is capable of giving the ideas of power, and the consequent pleasures, in their full degree. For observe, that a power, on which only some part of that power has been expended. A nut may be cracked by a steam-engine, but it has not, in being so, been the subject of the power of the engine. And thus it is falsely said of great men, that they waste their lofty powers on unworthy objects: the object may be dangerous or useless, but, as far as the phrase has reference to difficulty of performance, it cannot be unworthy of the power which it brings into exertion, because nothing can become a subject of action to a greater power which can be accomplished by a less, any more than bodily strength can be exerted where there is nothing to resist it.

So then, men may let their great powers lie dormant, while they employ their mean and petty powers on mean and petty objects; but it is physically impossible to employ a great power, except on a great object. Consequently, wherever power of any kind or degree has been exerted, the marks and evidence of it are stamped upon its results: it is impossible that it should be lost or wasted, or without record, even in the "estimation of a hair:" and therefore, whatever has been the subject of a great power bears about with it the image of that which created it, and is what is commonly called "excellent." And this is the true meaning of the word excellent, as distinguished from the terms, "beautiful," "useful," "good," etc.; and we shall always, in future, use the word excellent, as signifying that the thing to which it is applied required a great power for its production.

The faculty of perceiving what powers are required for the production of a thing, is the faculty of perceiving excellence. It is this faculty in which men, even of the most cultivated taste, must always be wanting, unless they have added practice to reflection; because none can estimate the power manifested in victory, unless they have personally measured the strength to be overcome. Though, therefore, it is possible, by the cultivation of sensibility and judgment, to become capable of distinguishing what is beautiful, it is totally impossible, without practice and knowledge, to distinguish or feel what is excellent. The beauty or the truth of Titian's flesh-tint may be appreciated by all; but it is only to the artist, whose multiplied hours of toil have not reached the slightest resemblance of one of its tones, that its *excellence* is manifest.

Wherever, then, difficulty has been overcome, there is excellence: and therefore, in order to prove a work excellent, we have only to prove the difficulty of its production: whether it be useful or beautiful is another question; its excellence depends on its difficulty alone. Nor is it a false or diseased taste which looks for the overcoming of difficulties, and has pleasure in it, even without any view to resultant good. It has been made part of our moral nature that we should have a pleasure in encountering and conquering opposition, for the sake of the struggle and the victory, not for the sake of any after result; and not only our own victory, but the perception of that of another, is in all cases the source of pure and ennobling pleasure. And if we often hear it said,

and truly said, that an artist has erred by seeking rather to show his skill in overcoming technical difficulties, than to reach a great end, be it observed that he is only blamed because he has sought to conquer an inferior difficulty rather than a great one; for it is much easier to overcome technical difficulties than to reach a great end. Whenever the visible victory over difficulties is found painful or in false taste, it is owning to the preference of an inferior to a great difficulty, or to the false estimate of what is difficult and what is not. It is far more difficult to be simple than to be complicated; far more difficult to sacrifice skill and cease exertion in the proper place, than to expend both indiscriminately. We shall find, in the course of our investigation, that beauty and difficulty go together; and that they are only mean and paltry difficulties which it is wrong or contemptible to wrestle with. Be it remembered then —Power is never wasted. Whatever power has been employed, produces excellence in proportion to its own dignity and exertion; and the faculty of perceiving this exertion, and appreciating this dignity, is the faculty of perceiving excellence.

Of Ideas of Imitation

Fusseli,[7] in his lectures, and many other persons of equally just and accurate habits of thought, (among others, S. T. Coleridge,[8]) make a distinction between imitation and copying, representing the first as the legitimate function of art—the latter as its corruption; but as such a distinction is by no means warranted, or explained by the common meaning of the words themselves, it is not easy to comprehend exactly in what sense they are used by those writers. And though, reasoning from the context, I can understand what ideas those words stand for in their minds, I cannot

---

[7] Henry Fuseli (1741–1825) was a painter whose style is fantastic and mystical. Born in Zurich, he moved to England, where he became a professor at the Royal Academy.

[8] Samuel Taylor Coleridge (1772–1834) was a romantic poet and literary theorist. His *Biographia Literaria* is one of the most important works of romantic theory.

allow the terms to be properly used as symbols of those ideas, which (especially in the case of the word Imitation) are exceedingly complex, and totally different from what most people would understand by the term. And by men of less accurate thought, the word is used still more vaguely or falsely. For instance, Burke[9] (*Treatise on the Sublime,* part i. sec. 16) says, "When the object represented in poetry or painting is such as we could have no desire of seeing in the reality, then we may be sure that its power in poetry or painting is owing to the power of *imitation.*" In which case the real pleasure may be in what we have been just speaking of, the dexterity of the artist's hand; or it may be in a beautiful or singular arrangement of colors, or a thoughtful chiaroscuro,[10] or in the pure beauty of certain forms which art forces on our notice, though we should not have observed them in the reality; and I conceive that none of these sources of pleasure are in any way expressed or intimated by the term "imitation."

But there is one source of pleasure in works of art totally different from all these, which I conceive to be properly and accurately expressed by the word "imitation": one which, though constantly confused in reasoning, because it is always associated in fact, with other means of pleasure, is totally separated from them in its nature, and is the real basis of whatever complicated or various meaning may be afterwards attached to the word in the minds of men.

I wish to point out this distinct sources of pleasure clearly at once, and only to use the word "imitation" in reference to it. Whenever anything looks like what it is not, the resemblance being so great as *nearly* to deceive, we feel a kind of pleasurable surprise, an agreeable excitement of mind, exactly the same in its nature as that which we receive from juggling. Whenever we perceive

this in something produced by art, that is to say, whenever the work is seen to resemble something which we know it is not, we receive what I call an idea of imitation. *Why* such ideas are pleasing, it would be out of our present purpose to inquire; we only know that there is no man who does not feel pleasure in his animal nature from gentle surprise, and that such surprise can be excited in no more distinct manner than by the evidence that thing is not what it appears to be. Now two things are requisite to our complete and more pleasurable perception of this: first, that the resemblance be so perfect as to amount to a deception; secondly, that there be some means of proving at the same moment that it is a deception. The most perfect ideas and pleasures of imitation are, therefore, when one sense is contradicted by another, both bearing as positive evidence on the subject as each is capable of alone; as when the eye says a thing is round, and the finger says it is flat; they are, therefore, never felt in so high a degree as in painting, where appearance of projection, roughness, hair, velvet, etc., are given with a smooth surface, or in wax-work, where the first evidence of the senses is perpetually contradicted by their experience; but the moment we come to marble, our definition checks us, for a marble figure does not look like what it is not: it looks like marble, and like the form of a man, but then it is marble, and it is the form of a man. It does not look like a man, which it is not but like the form of a man, which it is. Form is form, *bona fide* and actual, whether in marble or in flesh—not an imitation or resemblance of form, but real form. The chalk outline of the bough of a tree on paper, is not an imitation; it looks like chalk and paper —not like wood, and that which it suggests to the mind is not properly said to be *like* the form of a bough, it is the form of a bough. Now, then, we see the limits of an idea of imitation; it extends only to the sensation of trickery and deception occasioned by a thing's intentionally seeming different from what it is; and the degree of the pleasure depends on the degree of difference and the perfection of the resemblance of the resemblance, not on the nature of the thing resembled. The simple pleasure in the imitation would be

---

[9] Edmund Burke (1729–1797) was primarily a political theorist and practical politician. His *Philosophical Enquiry into the Origin of Our Ideas of the Sublime and Beautiful* (1756) is his only significant work on aesthetics. It is important because of its psychology of the sublime as a combination of fear and pleasure.

[10] The technique in painting of contrasting light and shade to produce highlights and contrasts.

precisely of the same degree (if the accuracy could be equal) whether the subject of it were the hero or his horse. There are other collateral sources of pleasure, which are necessarily associated with this, but that part of the pleasure which depends on the imitation is the same in both.

Ideas of imitation, then, act by producing the simple pleasure of surprise, and that not of surprise in its higher sense and function, but of the mean and paltry surprise which is felt in jugglery. These ideas and pleasures are the most contemptible which can be received from art; first, because it is necessary to their enjoyment that the mind should reject the impression and address of the thing represented, and fix itself only upon the reflection that it is not what it seems to be. All high or noble emotion or thought are thus rendered physically impossible, while the mind exults in what is very like a strictly sensual pleasure. We may consider tears as a result of agony or of art, whichever we please, but not of both at the same moment. If we are surprised by them as an attainment of the one, it is impossible we can be moved by them as a sign of the other.

Ideas of imitation are contemptible in the second place, because not only do they preclude the spectator from enjoying inherent beauty in the subject, but they can only be received from mean and paltry subjects, because it is impossible to imitate anything really great. We can "paint a cat or a fiddle, so that they look as if we could take them up;" but we cannot imitate the ocean, or the Alps. We can imitate fruit, but not a tree; flowers, but not a pasture; cut-glass, but not the rainbow. All pictures in which deceptive powers of imitation are displayed are therefore either of contemptible subjects, or have the imitation shown in contemptible parts of them, bits of dress, jewels, furniture, etc.

Thirdly, these ideas are contemptible, because no ideas of power are associated with them; to the ignorant, imitation, indeed, seems difficult, and its success praiseworthy, but even they can by no possibility see more in the artist than they do in a juggler, who arrives at a strange end by means with which they are unacquainted. To the instructed, the juggler is by far the more respectable artist of the two, for they know sleight of hand to be an art of immensely more difficult acquirement, and to imply more ingenuity in the artist than a power of deceptive imitation in painting, which requires nothing more for its attainment than a true eye, a steady hand, and moderate industry—qualities which in no degree separate the imitative artist from a watch-maker, pin-maker, or any other neat-handed artificer. These remarks do not apply to the art of the Diorama,[11] or the stage, where the pleasure is not dependent on the imitation, but is the same which we should receive from nature herself, only far inferior in degree. It is a noble pleasure; but we shall see in the course of our investigation, both that it is inferior to that which we receive when there is no deception at all, and why it is so.

Whenever then in future, I speak of ideas of imitation, I wish to be understood to mean the immediate and present perception that something produced by art is not what it seems to be. I prefer saying "that it is not what it seems to be," to saying "that it seems to be what it is not," because we perceive at once what it seems to be, and the idea of imitation, and the consequent pleasure, result from the subsequent perception of its being something else—flat, for instance, when we thought it was round.

Of Ideas of Truth

The word truth, as applied to art, signifies the faithful statement, either to the mind or senses, of any fact of nature.

We receive an idea of truth, then, when we perceive the faithfulness of such a statement.

The difference between ideas of truth and of imitation lies chiefly in the following points.

First—Imitation can only be of something material, but truth as reference to statements both of

---

[11] A device popular in the nineteenth century for producing special effects. A painting was arranged in such a way that when it was viewed through an aperture, three-dimensional illusions and other effects were achieved.

the qualities of material things, and of emotions, impressions, and thoughts. There is a moral as well as material truth—a truth of impression as well as of form—of thought as well as of matter; and the truth of impression and thought is a thousand times the more important of the two. Hence, truth is a term of universal application, but imitation is limited to that narrow field of art which takes cognizance only of material things.

Secondly—Truth may be stated by any signs or symbols which have a definite signification in the minds of those to whom they are addressed, although such signs be themselves no image nor likeness of anything. Whatever can excite in the mind the conception of certain facts, can give ideas of truth, though it be in no degree the imitation or resemblance of those facts. If there be— we do not say there is—but if there be in painting anything which operates, as words do, not by resembling anything, but by being taken as a symbol and substitute for it, and thus inducing the effect of it, then this channel of communication can convey uncorrupted truth, though it do not in any degree resemble the facts whose conception it induces. But ideas of imitation, of course, require the likeness of the object. They speak to the perceptive faculties only: truth to the conceptive.

Thirdly—And in consequence of what is above stated, an idea of truth exists in the statement of one attribute of anything, but an idea of imitation requires the resemblance of as many attributes as we are usually cognizant of in its real presence. A pencil outline of the bough of a tree on white paper is a statement of a certain number of fact of form. It does not yet amount to the imitation of anything. The idea of that form is not given in nature by lines at all, still less by black lines with a white space between them. But those lines convey to the mind a distinct impression of a certain number of facts, which it recognizes as agreeable with its previous impressions of the bough of a tree; and it receives, therefore, an idea of truth. If, instead of two lines, we give a dark form with the brush, we convey information of a certain relation of shade between the bough and

sky, recognizable for another idea of truth; but we have still no imitation, for the white paper is not the least like air, nor the black shadow like wood. It is not until after a certain number of ideas of truth have been collected together, that we arrive at an idea of imitation.

Hence it might at first sight appear, that an idea of imitation, inasmuch as several ideas of truth were united in it, was nobler than a simple idea of truth. And if it were necessary that the ideas of truth should be perfect, or should be subjects of contemplation *as such,* it would be so. But, observe, we require to produce the effect of imitation only so many and such ideas of truth as the *senses* are usually cognizant of. Now the senses are not usually, nor unless they be especially devoted to the service, cognizant, with accuracy, of any truths but those of space and projection. It requires long study and attention before they give certain evidence of even the simplest truths of form. . . .

We shall see, in the course of our investigation of ideas of truth, that ideas of imitation not only do not imply their presence, but even are inconsistent with it; and that pictures which imitate so as to deceive, are never true. But this is not the place for the proof of this; at present we have only to insist on the last and greatest distinction between ideas of truth and of imitation—that the mind, in receiving one of the former, dwells upon its own conception of the fact, or form, or feeling stated, and is occupied only with the qualities and character of that fact or form, considering it as real and existing, being all the while totally regardless of the signs or symbols by which the notion of it has been conveyed. These signs have no pretense, nor hypocrisy, nor legerdemain about them;—they bear their message simply and clearly, and it is that message which the mind takes from them and dwells upon, regardless of the language in which it is delivered. But the mind, in receiving an idea of imitation, is wholly occupied in finding out that what has been suggested to it is not what it appears to be: it does not dwell on the suggestion, but on the perception that it is a false suggestion: it derives its pleasure, not from the contemplation of a truth, but from the discovery of a falsehood. So that the moment ideas of truth are grouped together, so as to give rise to an idea of imitation, they change their very nature—lose their essence as ideas of truth—and are corrupted and degraded, so as to share in the treachery of what they have produced. Hence, finally, ideas of truth are the foundation, and ideas of imitation the destruction, of all art. We shall be better able to appreciate their relative dignity after the investigation which we propose of the functions of the former; but we may as well now express the conclusion to which we shall then be led—that no picture can be good which deceives by its imitation, for the very reason that nothing can be beautiful which is not true.

Of Ideas of Beauty

Any material object which can give us pleasure in the simple contemplation of its outward qualities without any direct and definite exertion of the intellect, I call in some way, or in some degree, beautiful. Why we receive pleasure from some forms and colors, and not from others, is no more to be asked or answered than why we like sugar and dislike wormwood. The utmost subtlety of investigation will only lead us to ultimate instincts and principles of human nature, for which no farther reason can be given than the simple will of the Deity that we should be so created. We may, indeed, perceive as far as we are acquainted with His nature, that we have been so constructed as, when in a healthy and cultivated state of mind, to derive pleasure from whatever things are illustrative of that nature; but we do not receive pleasure from them *because* they are illustrative of it, nor from any perception that they are illustrative of it, but instinctively and necessarily, as we derive sensual pleasure from the scent of a rose. On these primary principles of our nature, education and accident operate to an unlimited extend; they may be cultivated or checked, directed or diverted, gifted by right guidance with the most acute and faultless sense, or subjected by neglect

to every phase of error and disease. He who has followed up these natural laws of aversion and desire, rendering them more and more authoritative by constant obedience, so as to derive pleasure always from that which God originally intended should give him pleasure, and who derives the greatest possible sum of pleasure from any given object, is a man of taste.

This, then, is the real meaning of this disputed word. Perfect taste is the faculty of receiving the greatest possible pleasure from those material sources which are attractive to our moral nature in its purity and perfection. He who receives little pleasure from these sources, wants taste; he who receives pleasure from any other sources, has false or bad taste.

And it is thus that the term "taste" is to be distinguished from that of "judgment," with which it is constantly confounded. Judgment is a general term, expressing definite action of the intellect, and applicable to every kind of subject which can be submitted to it. There may be judgment of congruity, judgment of truth, judgment of justice, and judgment of difficulty and excellence. But all these exertions of the intellect are totally distinct from taste, properly so called, which is the instinctive and instant preferring of one material object to another without any obvious reason, except that it is proper to human nature in its perfection so to do.

Observe, however, I do not mean by excluding direct exertion of the intellect from ideas of beauty, to assert that beauty has no effect upon nor connection with the intellect. All our moral feelings are so inwoven with our intellectual powers, that we cannot affect the one without in some degree addressing the other; and in all high ideas of beauty, it is more than probable that much of the pleasure depends on delicate and untraceable perceptions of fitness, propriety, and relation, which are purely intellectual, and through which we arrive at our noblest ideas of what is commonly and rightly called "intellectual beauty." But there is yet no immediate *exertion* of the intellect; that is to say, if a person receiving even the noblest ideas of simple beauty be asked *why* he likes the object exciting them, he will not be able to give any distinct reason, nor to trace in his mind any formed thought, to which he can appeal as a source of pleasure. He will say that the thing gratifies, fills, hallows, exalts his mind, but he will not be able to say why, or how. If he can, and if he can show that he perceives in the object any expression of distinct thought, he has received more than an idea of beauty—it is an idea of relation.

Ideas of beauty are among the noblest which can be presented to the human mind, invariably exalting and purifying it according to their degree; and it would appear that we are intended by the Deity to be constantly under their influence, because there is not one single object in nature which is not capable of conveying them, and which, to the rightly perceiving mind, does not present an incalculably greater number of beautiful than of deformed parts; there being in fact scarcely anything, in pure, undiseased nature, like positive deformity, but only degrees of beauty, or such slight and rare points of permitted contrast as may render all around them more valuable by their opposition, spots of blackness in creation, to make its colors felt.

But although everything in nature is more or less beautiful, every species of object has its own kind and degree of beauty; some being in their own nature more beautiful than others, and few, if any, individuals possessing the utmost degree of beauty of which the species is capable. This utmost degree of specific beauty, necessarily coexistent with the utmost perfection of the object in other respects, is the ideal of the object.

Ideas of beauty, then, be it remembered, are the subjects of moral, but not of intellectual perception. By the investigation of them we shall be led to the knowledge of the ideal subjects of art.

Of Ideas of Relation

I use this term rather as one of convenience than as adequately expressive of the vast class of ideas which I wish to be comprehended under it, namely, all those conveyable by art, which are the subjects of distinct intellectual perception and action, and which are therefore worthy of the name of thoughts. But as every thought, or definite exertion of intellect, implies two subjects, and some connection or relation inferred between them the term "ideas of relation" is not incorrect, though it is inexpressive.

Under this head must be arranged everything productive of expression, sentiment, and character, whether in figures or landscapes (for there may be as much definite expression and marked carrying out of particular thoughts in the treatment of inanimate as of animate nature), everything relating to the conception of the subject and to the congruity and relation of its parts; not as they enhance each other's beauty by known and constant laws of composition, but as they give each other expression and meaning, by particular application, requiring distinct thought to discover or to enjoy: the choice, for instance, of a particular lurid or appalling light, to illustrate an incident in itself terrible, or of a particular tone of pure color to prepare the mind for the expression of refined and delicate feeling; and, in a still higher sense, the invention of such incidents and thoughts as can be expressed in words as well as on canvas, and are totally independent of any means of art but such as may serve for the bare suggestion of them. The principal object in the foreground of Turner's[12] "Building of Carthage" is a group of children sailing toy boats. The exquisite choice of this incident, as expressive of the ruling passion, which was to be the source of future greatness, in preference to the tumult of busy stone-masons or arming soldiers, is quite as appreciable when it is told as when it is seen—it has nothing to do with the technicalities of painting; a scratch of the pen would have conveyed the idea and spoken to the intellect as much as the elaborate realizations of color. Such a thought as this is something far above all art; it is epic

----

[12] J. M. W. Turner (1775–1851) was one of the most important English painters. His landscapes and seascapes became increasingly abstract, emphasizing color and light.

poetry of the highest order. Claude,[13] in subjects of the same kind, commonly introduces people carrying red trunks with iron locks about, and dwells, with infantine delight, on the lustre of the leather and the ornaments of the iron. The intellect can have no occupation here; we must look to the imitation or to nothing. Consequently, Turner rises above Claude in the very first instant of the conception of his picture, and acquires an intellectual superiority which no powers of the draughtsman or the artist (supposing that such existed in his antagonist) could ever wrest from him.

Such are the function and force of ideas of relation. They are what I have asserted in the second chapter of this section to be the noblest subjects of art. Dependent upon it only for expression, they cause all the rest of its complicated sources of pleasure to take, in comparison with them, the place of mere language or decoration; nay, even the noblest ideas of beauty sink at once beside these into subordination and subjection. It would add little to the influence of Landseer's [14] picture . . . that the form of the dog should be conceived with every perfection of curve and color which its nature was capable of, and that the ideal lines should be carried out with the science of a Praxiteles; [15] nay, the instant that the beauty so obtained interfered with the impression of agony and desolation, and drew the mind away from the feeling of the animal to its outward form, that instant would the picture become monstrous and degraded. The utmost glory of the human body is a mean subject of contemplation, compared to the emotion, exertion and character of that which animates it; the lustre of the limbs of the Aphrodite is faint beside that of the brow of the Madonna; and the divine form of the Greek god, except as it is the incarnation and expression of divine mind, is degraded beside the passion and the prophecy of the vaults of the Sistine. [16]

Ideas of relation are of course, with respect to art generally, the most extensive as the most important source of pleasure; and if we proposed entering upon the criticism of historical works, it would be absurd to attempt to do so without further subdivision and arrangement. But the old landscape painters got over so much canvas without either exercise of, or appeal to, the intellect, that we shall be little troubled with the subject as far as they are concerned; and whatever subdivision we may adopt, as it will therefore have particular reference to the works of modern artists, will be better understood when we have obtained some knowledge of them in less important points.

By the term "ideas of relation," then, I mean in future to express all those sources of pleasure, which involve and require, at the instant of their perception, active exertion of the intellectual powers.

Study Questions

1. According to Ruskin, what should painters paint?
2. What do language and painting have in common?
3. What is the difference between language and thought that Ruskin is trying to capture?
4. What would a thought without language be like?
5. Find examples of each of the five kinds of ideas that Ruskin discusses.
6. What does Ruskin mean by *experience*?

---

[13] Claude Lorrain (1600–1682) was a French neoclassical painter whose landscapes, in particular, emphasize light and a distinctive sky.

[14] Edwin Landseer (1802–1873) was an extremely popular naturalistic English painter of grandiloquent animals and sentimental scenes. One of his most famous paintings is of a dog grieving for its dead master.

[15] Praxiteles (c. 370–c. 330) was one of the most important late classical sculptors. His style is naturalistic.

---

[16] Among the most famous examples of Renaissance painting are scenes by Michelangelo on the Sistine Chapel ceiling in the Vatican.

7. How does Ruskin define *art?*

8. When are imitations art?

9. Is truth limited to language?

10. How does Ruskin define *beauty?*

11. How is beauty related to taste?

12. Does Ruskin treat taste as a form of judgment? Give his argument.

13. What is the relation of moral feeling to aesthetic feeling?

14. How does the intellect relate to artistic skill?

15. If great art has a greater quantity of ideas, what measure of quantity would you use?

16. Ruskin likes the work of both Turner and Landseer. Why? (If possible, compare a work by Turner with one by Landseer. Do they have anything in common?)

Leo Tolstoy

T HE LIFE OF COUNT LEO TOLSTOY (1828–1910) is a study in contradictions. His family was aristocratic. They owned a vast estate, Yasnaya Polyana, in Russia. Russia in the nineteenth century was still feudal in many ways. Serfdom bound peasants to an estate or to a landowner. The institution was not abolished in Russia until 1861. Even afterward, the distance between peasants and landowners remained extreme. The industrialization that changed most of Europe in the nineteenth century moved much more slowly in Russia. The czar remained an absolute ruler long after his cousins had ceded much power to constitutional bodies. The Russian Orthodox Church exerted a strong conservative religious influence. In this situation, Tolstoy was torn in two directions. He entered the university at Kazan but did not graduate. He briefly tried to educate the peasants on his family estate and failed. Then he turned in a different direction. He served in the army and lived the life of a rich Russian nobleman. He also was part of a literary group and began to write largely autobiographical stories. In 1859, he tried a second time to found a school for peasants and to free his serfs but failed in this attempt as well.

After traveling in western Europe, Tolstoy married in 1862 and returned to Yasnaya Polyana. He had a large family and devoted himself to writing. His great novels, *War and Peace* (1865–69) and *Anna Karenina* (1875–77) belong to this period. Tolstoy's view of history is somewhat Hegelian—history is a movement with its own force. But the sensibility that had led to his early attempts to reform the conditions of his own estates and his doubts about the purpose and style of his own earlier life continued to haunt him. Late in the 1870s, Tolstoy underwent a religious conversion. He embraced a form of Christianity based on love, nonviolence, and simplicity. His literary style underwent a corresponding change. His work took on a mystical quality and social relations, particularly within the family, became central. Only through human sympathy and communication, Tolstoy came to believe, can we find meaning. A virtual cult grew up around him. His unorthodox beliefs and their social consequences led to his excommunication from the Russian Orthodox Church in 1901.

The contradictions go even deeper. Tolstoy tried to impose his new beliefs on his own estate and people. He wanted to give away all his earthly possessions and live a simple life free from material concerns. The unreality of this program was evident. The demands he made on others were both difficult and intolerant. His family life deteriorated, and Tolstoy was not blameless. He made the lives of those dependent on him as unpleasant as their lack of understanding of him made his own life frustrating. During this period, Tolstoy rejected all of the literary and artistic achievements that he felt belonged to an unspiritual and inhuman civilization. He did not hesitate to include his own work in this condemnation. *What Is Art?* belongs to this late period of questioning and radical rejection.

Tolstoy's death was as paradoxical as his life. A novel by Feodor Dostoevsky, *The Possessed,* ends with one of the main characters leaving his home alone in his old age after he feels humiliated and rejected. Tolstoy emulated the character of Stephan Trofimovich. In 1910, he simply left home without provisions or preparation. He got as far as a railway station, where he died. His last words, reportedly repeated over and over were "I do not understand what it is I have to do."

◆   ◆   ◆   ◆   ◆   ◆

Count Leo Tolstoy's investigation of the nature of art should be understood in the light of what it opposed as well as what it argued for. In the course of the eighteenth and nineteenth centuries, art was increasingly identified as a system of the fine arts. Painting, dance, sculpture, poetry, and fiction all appealed to an audience that was able to appreciate the "higher" forms of art and, incidentally, to pay for them and support them. The older systems of patronage and public performance were replaced by a bourgeois and aristocratic taste. An increasing division was perceptible between popular arts and entertainment on the one hand and "serious" and "difficult" art on the other. Tolstoy's own novels were successful primarily in their appeal to a middle-class readership. Tolstoy, late in his life, attempted to overcome that division. His religious identification with Russia and its people was translated into a theory of art as the bearer of a new religious perception. At the same time, Tolstoy was very much a part of the nineteenth century in two respects. First, he understood aesthetic experience as a singular form based on a deep, quasireligious feeling. Second, he understood history as moving toward a higher end, and art as the embodiment of the spirit of a culture and age. *What Is Art?* attempts to reconcile Tolstoy's aesthetic feeling with his social and religious consciousness.

In place of the distinction between fine art and popular art or entertainment, Tolstoy differentiates art from counterfeit art. He understood aesthetic experience as a form of feeling. As such, it is a mental condition, a state of mind. Counterfeit art plays on the mind to excite it and provide diversion. Such diversion is only momentary, however, and leads nowhere. It must be contrasted with true art, which unites and moves individuals from their personal isolation to a communal feeling. Aesthetic feeling is thus contrasted to the momentary and individual feeling of counterfeit art. Tolstoy had in mind by this contrast the difference between an audience that goes to something like a ballet in order to marvel at the skill of the dancers and an audience that, perhaps at a folk dance or festival, shares a history and attachment to each other. The former gets only excitement and diversion. The latter experiences aesthetic emotion. Most of what is identified as fine art will turn out to be counterfeit, according to Tolstoy's analysis.

The distinction between art and its counterfeits requires that we have criteria so that we can know the difference. Tolstoy claimed that all true art is "infectious" and that counterfeit art is not. By the infectiousness of art, Tolstoy seems to mean a kind of common feeling, a shared emotion. Not all shared emotion would qualify, however. Excessive patriotism, such as that aroused by military bands, is not what Tolstoy meant. Just because everyone in a crowd is raised to a state of excitement at the same time does not make something art. The feelings shared must have their origin in some initial feeling of the artist. They are not manipulative but deeply personal. Tolstoy means by infectiousness the connection of one personality to another by means of some object or performance. Without that root in personality reaching out to other persons, only imitations of art can result.

Infectiousness thus leads to more specific criteria. To have aesthetic feeling, an individual must experience another as a unique person. That individuality must be clear and sincere. Tolstoy defines art as an expression of individuality, therefore, just as the romantics did. However, Tolstoy's individuality reaches out to overcome its isolation. When that reaching out takes a clear form and is a sincere expression of its source, then art is infectious. When it is not, someone may have intense feelings, but they will not achieve the interpersonal communication required for art. Ultimately, these criteria have to be internal. Art has no external rules. I must feel what the other feels and we must come to a union of souls. The height of personal expression is to transcend personality into a felt union. Art is better the more infectious it is, and it is more infectious as it is more individual, clear, and sincere. Counterfeit art leaves individuals alone with their own feelings; true art unites individuals. It is at once intensely personal and intensely communal.

We can recognize several themes in Tolstoy's aesthetics that come from earlier theories. Immanuel Kant's "common sense" required that aesthetic intuition be more than just private feeling. Later nineteenth-century theories that developed an aesthetic attitude and sensibility find their echoes in Tolstoy's claim that art produces a special feeling that must be experienced to be understood. Like Kant and the romantics, Tolstoy thought of the artist as having special abilities, a genius, that cannot be covered by rules or skill. Tolstoy developed this idea in a different way, however. He rejected fine art and aesthetic feeling "for itself" and demanded that art justify itself by its results in creating community and advancing the religious spirit that he identified with Russia. Tolstoy's aesthetic feeling is a special experience, but it is never an autonomous experience for its own sake.

Art is more than momentary experience, therefore. Tolstoy believed in an historical movement toward a higher perfection. Aesthetic feeling and religious feeling were understood and described in very similar terms throughout the nineteenth century: both were regarded as personal and more than personal at once, both as ways of being taken out of oneself and united to others or to God. Christian religion combined that feeling with a sense of direction toward greater perfection. Tolstoy shared that vision of religion and considered it Russia's greatest virtue. Thus the feeling of art is a means to religious feeling, and the subject matter of art is good whenever it moves toward unity and the ends of perfection. Every age has its potential for a degree of perfection. Its art expresses that vision and contributes to achieving that unity. Therefore, we can tell good art by what it communicates as well as the fact that it communicates. Certain feelings are positive. They are what human beings need to live and experience each other as human. Feelings of love and kindness contribute to the religious perception of an age. In the example of military bands, however, no individual feeling is being communicated;

what feeling exists is warlike and divisive. Such feelings cannot be the subject matter of art. The subject matter of aesthetic feeling, therefore, has two criteria. It must move humanity forward, and it must express the fundamental character of human nature. Art that tries to hold onto past forms becomes mannered. It concentrates on style and more and more elaborate exhibitions of skill. It is neither forward looking nor humane.

Tolstoy was not optimistic about the state of art at the end of the nineteenth century. It had all of the mannered, elitist characteristics that he condemned. Instead, he looked for a future art that would break decisively with the past and return to its roots in human expression. He hoped to find that art in peasant art, folk art, and the genuine, sincere expression of feeling. Anything that divided artists from their audiences belonged to the past. An artist on a pedestal or treated as a cultural ornament would be out of touch with true feeling. It follows that artists should not be supported by the state or patronage. They should be "of the people." If that meant that their work could not be so elaborate and difficult, so much the better. Simplicity and common feeling are more important than skill and elaborate forms.

Tolstoy's arguments are extreme, but they sum up several important tendencies in nineteenth-century aesthetics. Feelings are a defining characteristic of art, but which feelings? Tolstoy's answer is both practical and theoretical. Practically, they are the feelings that communicate, unify, and contribute to the fellow feeling of people. Theoretically, they are the class of feelings that are at once personal and communal. By taking feelings as a starting point, aesthetics turns inward. It becomes intensely personal, but it is in danger of losing its outward, productive, and social forms. Tolstoy counters that tendency by identifying aesthetics with those feelings that create community by communicating common needs, hopes, and desires. This kind of feeling moves aesthetics back into a social context, and it makes aesthetic feeling much closer to religious feeling. Tolstoy ultimately identified the two as a single experience.

Tolstoy's ideas are easily parodied. His specific judgments were the product both of his theory and of his passionate rejection of what he saw as the disintegration of the modern world. So most of what we take as exemplary instances of art were, to Tolstoy, counterfeit art or even worse. Symphonies that required extended rehearsals and state- or community-supported musicians and that could be appreciated only by an audience of a few elite or would-be-elite patrons were anathema to Tolstoy. If the drama of Shakespeare no longer spoke to everyone, so much the worse for Shakespeare. We must keep in mind that Tolstoy was not so wrong in what he saw. The nineteenth century had become stratified into classes that exploited workers and peasants. It was still ruled by an aristocracy allied with an industrial class, and it was moving toward a catastrophic breakdown in World War I. Among European nations, Tolstoy's Russia was in nearly the worst situation in that respect. Tolstoy hoped to draw on the country's religious strengths to offer a different future. The result was undoubtedly naive and misleading in its particulars. However, his philosophy captured much of the complexity of nineteenth-century idealism and gave it a clearer, more concrete form than its speculative German cousins. For Tolstoy, art was social and aesthetic, historically motivated and religiously transcendent. His theory singles out some of the most important themes of romantic and idealist art: sincerity, personality, religious feeling, and a spirit of the age. It deserves to be taken seriously.

From *What Is Art?*

Chapter Fifteen

Art, in our society, has been so perverted that not only has bad art come to be considered good, but even the very perception of what art really is has been lost. In order to be able to speak about the art of our society, it is, therefore, first of all necessary to distinguish art from counterfeit art.

There is one indubitable indication distinguishing real art from its counterfeit, namely, the infectiousness of art. If a man, without exercising effort and without altering his standpoint on reading, hearing, or seeing another man's work, experiences a mental condition which unites him with that man and with other people who also partake of that work of art, then the object evoking that condition is a work of art. And however poetical, realistic, effectful, or interesting a work may be, it is not a work of art if it does not evoke that feeling (quite distinct from all other feelings) of joy and of spiritual union with another (the author) and with others (those who are also infected by it).

It is true that this indication is an *internal* one, and that there are people who have forgotten what the action of real art is, who expect something else from art (in our society the great majority are in this state), and that therefore such people may mistake for this aesthetic feeling the feeling of diversion and a certain excitement which they receive from counterfeits of art. But though it is impossible to undeceive these people, just as it is impossible to convince a man suffering from "Daltonism"[1] that green is not red, yet, for all that, this indication remains perfectly definite to those whose feeling for art is neither perverted nor atrophied, and it clearly distinguishes the feeling produced by art from all other feelings.

The chief peculiarity of this feeling is that the receiver of a true artistic impression is so united to the artist that he feels as if the work were his own and not someone else's—as if what it expresses were just what he had long been wishing to express. A real work of art destroys, in the consciousness of the receiver, the separation between himself and the artist—not that alone, but also between himself and all whose minds receive this work of art. In this freeing of our personality from its separation and isolation, in this uniting of it with others, lies the chief characteristic and the great attractive force of art.

If a man is infected by the author's condition of soul, if he feels this emotion and this union with others, then the object which has effected this is art; but if there be no such infection, if there be not this union with the author and with others who are moved by the same work—then it is not art. And not only is infection a sure sign of art, but the degree of infectiousness is also the sole measure of excellence in art.

The stronger the infection, the better is the art as art, speaking now apart from its subject matter, i.e., not considering the quality of the feelings it transmits.

And the degree of the infectiousness of art depends on three conditions:

1. On the greater or lesser individuality of the feeling transmitted;
2. on the greater or lesser clearness with which the feeling is transmitted;
3. on the sincerity of the artist, i.e., on the greater or lesser force with which the artist himself feels the emotion he transmits.

The more individual the feeling transmitted the more strongly does it act on the receiver; the

---

[1] Daltonism is a form of color blindness. It is named for the English scientist John Dalton (1766–1844), who suffered from it and studied it.

more individual the state of soul into which he is transferred, the more pleasure does the receiver obtain, and therefore the more readily and strongly does he join in it.

The clearness of expression assists infection because the receiver, who mingles in consciousness with the author, is the better satisfied the more clearly the feeling is transmitted, which, as it seems to him, he has long known and felt, and for which he has only now found expression.

But most of all is the degree of infectiousness of art increased by the degree of sincerity in the artist. As soon as the spectator, hearer, or reader feels that the artist is infected by his own production, and writes, sings, or plays for himself, and not merely to act on others, this mental condition of the artist infects the receiver; and contrariwise, as soon as the spectator, reader, or hearer feels that the author is not writing, singing, or playing for his own satisfaction—does not himself feel what he wishes to express—but is doing it for him, the receiver, a resistance immediately springs up, and the most individual and the newest feelings and the cleverest technique not only fail to produce any infection but actually repel.

I have mentioned three conditions of contagiousness in art, but they may be all summed up into one, the 1st, sincerity, i.e., that the artist should be impelled by an inner need to express his feeling. That condition includes the first; for if the artist is sincere he will express the feeling as he experienced it. And as each man is different from everyone else, his feeling will be individual for everyone else; and the more individual it is— the more the artist has drawn it from the depths of his nature—the more sympathetic and sincere will it be. And this same sincerity will impel the artist to find a clear expression of the feeling which he wishes to transmit.

Therefore this third condition—sincerity—is the most important of the three. It is always complied with in peasant art, and this explains why such art always acts so powerfully; but it is a condition almost entirely absent from our upper-class art, which is continually produced by art-

ists actuated by personal aims of covetousness or vanity.

Such are the three conditions which divide art from its counterfeits, and which also decide the quality of every work of art apart from its subject matter.

The absence of any one of these conditions excludes a work from the category of art and relegates it to that of art's counterfeits. If the work does not transmit the artist's peculiarity of feeling and is therefore not individual, if it is unintelligibly expressed, or if it has not proceeded from the author's inner need for expression—it is not a work of art. If all these conditions are present, even in the smallest degree, then the work, even if a weak one, is yet a work of art.

The presence in various degrees of these three conditions—individuality, clearness, and sincerity—decides the merit of a work of art as art, apart from subject matter. All works of art take rank of merit according to the degree in which they fulfill the first, the second, and the third of these conditions. In one the individuality of the feeling transmitted may predominate; in another, clearness of expression; in a third, sincerity; while a fourth may have sincerity and individuality but be deficient in clearness; a fifth, individuality and clearness but less sincerity; and so forth, in all possible degrees and combinations.

Thus is art divided from that which is not art, and thus is the quality of art as art decided, independently of its subject matter, i.e., apart from whether the feelings it transmits are good or bad.

But how are we to define good and bad art with reference to its subject matter?

Chapter Sixteen

How are we to decide what is good or bad in the subject matter of art?

Art, like speech, is a means of communication, and therefore of progress, i.e., of the movement of humanity forward toward perfection. Speech renders accessible to men of the latest generations all the knowledge discovered by the experience and reflection, both of preceding generations and of the best and foremost men of their own times; art renders accessible to men of the latest generations all the feelings experienced by their predecessors, and those also which are being felt by their best and foremost contemporaries. And as the evolution of knowledge proceeds by truer and more necessary knowledge, dislodging and replacing what is mistaken and unnecessary, so the evolution of feeling proceeds through art—feelings less kind and less needful for the well-being of mankind are replaced by others kinder and more needful for that end. That is the purpose of art. And, speaking now of its subject matter, the more art fulfills that purpose the better the art, and the less it fulfills it, the worse the art.

And the appraisement of feelings (i.e., the acknowledgment of these or those feelings as being more or less good, more or less necessary for the well-being of mankind) is made by the religious perception of the age.

In every period of history, and in every human society, there exists an understanding of the meaning of life which represents the highest level to which men of that society have attained, an understanding defining the highest good at which that society aims. And this understanding is the religious perception of the given time and society. And this religious perception is always clearly expressed by some advanced men, and more or less vividly perceived by all the members of the society. Such a religious perception and its corresponding expression exists always in every society. If it appears to us that in our society there is no religious perception, this is not because there really is none, but only because we do not want to see it. And we often wish not to see it because it exposes the fact that our life is inconsistent with that religious perception.

Religious perception in a society is like the direction of a flowing river. If the river flows at all, it must have a direction. If a society lives, there must be a religious perception indicating the direction in which, more or less consciously, all its members tend.

And so there always has been, and there is, a religious perception in every society. And it is by the standard of this religious perception that the feelings transmitted by art have always been estimated. Only on the basis of this religious perception of their age have men always chosen from the endlessly varied spheres of art that art which transmitted feelings making religious perception operative in actual life. And such art has always been highly valued and encouraged, while art transmitting feelings already outlived, flowing from the antiquated religious perceptions of a former age, has always been condemned and despised. All the rest of art, transmitting those more diverse feelings by means of which people commune together, was not condemned, and was tolerated, if only it did not transmit feelings contrary to religious perception. Thus, for instance, among the Greeks art transmitting the feeling of beauty, strength, and courage (Hesiod, Homer, Phidias[2]) was chosen, approved, and encouraged, while art transmitting feelings of rude sensuality, despondency, and effeminacy was condemned and despised. Among the Jews, art transmitting feelings of devotion and submission to the God of the Hebrews and to His will (the epic of Genesis, the prophets, the Psalms) was chosen and encouraged, while art transmitting feelings of idolatry (the golden calf[3]) was condemned and despised. All the rest of art—stories, songs, dances, ornamentation of houses, of utensils, and of clothes—which was not contrary to religious perception was neither distinguished nor discussed. Thus, in regard to its subject matter, has art been appraised always and everywhere, and thus it should be appraised; for this attitude toward art proceeds from the fundamental characteristics of human nature, and those characteristics do not change. . . .

---

[2] Hesiod and Homer are the epic poets of classical Greece. Phidias (c. 500–432 B.C.E.) was one of the greatest sculptors of classical Athens.

[3] Aaron, the brother of Moses, made a golden calf for the Israelites to worship. It was destroyed by an angry Moses (Exodus 32).

Chapter Nineteen

People talk of the art of the future, meaning by "art of the future" some especially refined, new art, which, as they imagine, will be developed out of that exclusive art of one class which is now considered the highest art. But no such new art of the future can or will be found. Our exclusive art, that of the upper classes of Christendom, has found its way into a blind alley. The direction in which it has been going leads nowhere. Having once let go of that which is most essential for art (namely, the guidance given by religious perception), that art has become ever more and more exclusive and therefore ever more and more perverted, until finally it has come to nothing. The art of the future, that which is really coming, will not be a development of present-day art but will arise on completely other and new foundations, having nothing in common with those by which our present art of the upper classes is guided.

Art of the future, that is to say, such part of art as will be chosen from among all the art diffused among mankind, will consist not in transmitting feelings accessible only to members of the rich classes, as is the case today, but in transmitting such feelings as embody the highest religious perception of our times. Only those productions will be considered art which transmit feelings drawing men together in brotherly union, or such universal feelings as can unite all men. Only such art will be chosen, tolerated, approved, and diffused. But art transmitting feelings flowing from antiquated, worn-out religious teaching—Church art, patriotic art, voluptuous art, transmitting feelings of superstitious fear, of pride, of vanity, of ecstatic admiration of national heroes—art exciting either exclusive love of one's own people or sensuality—will be considered bad, harmful art and will be censured and despised by public opinion. All the rest of art, transmitting feelings accessible only to a section of people, will be considered unimportant and will be neither blamed nor praised. And the appraisement of art in general will devolve, not, as is now the case, on a separate class of rich people, but on the whole people; so that for a work to be esteemed good and to be approved of and diffused, it will have to satisfy the demands, not of a few people living in identical and often unnatural conditions, but it will have to satisfy the demands of all those great masses of people who are situated in the natural conditions of laborious life.

And the artists producing art will also not be, as now, merely a few people selected from a small section of the nation, members of the upper classes or their hangers-on, but will consist of all those gifted members of the whole people who prove capable of, and are inclined toward, artistic activity.

Artistic activity will then be accessible to all men. It will become accessible to the whole people because, in the first place, in the art of the future not only will that complex technique which deforms the productions of the art of today and requires so great an effort and expenditure of time not be demanded, but, on the contrary, the demand will be for clearness, simplicity, and brevity—conditions mastered not by mechanical exercises but by the education of taste. And secondly, artistic activity will become accessible to all men of the people because, instead of the present professional schools which only some can enter, all will learn music and depictive art (singing and drawing) equally with letters in the elementary schools, and in such a way that every man, having received the first principles of drawing and music and feeling a capacity for, and a call to, one or other of the arts, will be able to perfect himself in it.

People think that if there are no special art schools the technique of art will deteriorate. Undoubtedly, if by technique we understand those complications of art which are now considered an excellence, it will deteriorate; but if by technique is understood clearness, beauty, simplicity, and compression in works of art, then, even if the elements of drawing and music were not to be taught in the national schools, the technique will not only not deteriorate but, as is shown by all peasant art, will be a hundred times better. It will be improved, because all the artists of genius now hidden among the masses will become producers of art and will give models of excellence, which (as has always been the case) will be the best schools of technique for their successors. For every true artist even now learns his technique chiefly not in the schools, but in life, from the examples of the great masters; then—when the producers of art will be the best artists of the whole nation, and there will be more such examples, and they will be more accessible—such part of the school training as the future artist will lose will be a hundredfold compensated for by the training he will receive from the numerous examples of good art diffused in society.

Such will be one difference between present and future art. Another difference will be that art will not be produced by professional artists receiving payment for their work and engaged on nothing else besides their art. The art of the future will be produced by all the members of the community who feel the need of such activity, but they will occupy themselves with art only when they feel such need.

In our society people think that an artist will work better and produce more if he has a secured maintenance. And this opinion would serve once more to show clearly, were such demonstration still needed, that what among us is considered art is not art but only its counterfeit. It is quite true that for the production of boots or loaves division of labor is very advantageous, and that the bootmaker or baker who need not prepare his own dinner or fetch his own fuel will make more boots or loaves than if he had to busy himself about these matters. But art is not a handicraft; it is the transmission of feeling the artist has experienced. And sound feeling can only be engendered in a man when he is living on all its sides the life natural and proper to mankind. And therefore security of maintenance is a condition most harmful to an artist's true productiveness since it removes him from the condition natural to all men —that of struggle with nature for the maintenance of both his own life and that of others— and thus deprives him of opportunity and possibility to experience the most important and natural feelings of man. There is no position more injurious to an artist's productiveness than that position of complete security and luxury in which artists usually live in our society.

The artist of the future will live the common life of man, earning his subsistence by some kind of labor. The fruits of that highest spiritual strength which passes through him he will try to share with the greatest possible number of people, for in such transmission to others of the feelings that have arisen in him he will find his happiness and his reward. The artist of the future will be unable to understand how an artist, whose chief delight is in the wide diffusion of his works, could give them only in exchange for a certain payment.

Until the dealers are driven out, the temple of art will not be a temple. But the art of the future will drive them out. . . .

The art of the future will thus be completely distinct, both in subject matter and in form, from what is now called art. The only subject matter of the art of the future will be either feelings drawing men toward union, or such as already unite them; and the forms of art will be such as will be open to everyone. And therefore, the ideal of excellence in the future will not be the exclusiveness of feeling, accessible only to some, but, on the contrary, its universality. And not bulkiness, obscurity, and complexity of form, as is now esteemed, but, on the contrary, brevity, clearness, and simplicity of expression. Only when art has attained to that, will art neither divert nor deprave men as it does now, calling on them to expend their best strength on it, but be what it should be—a vehicle wherewith to transmit religious, Christian perception from the realm of reason and intellect into that of feeling, and really drawing people in actual life nearer to that perfection and unity indicated to them by their religious perception.

Study Questions

1. What kind of emotions are good? What kind are bad?
2. How is art distinguished from counterfeit art?
3. Can aesthetic emotion be distinguished from ordinary emotions?
4. How is the "infection" of art spread?
5. What are the characteristics of good art?
6. Does "sincerity" imply that artists must believe everything they write or paint? Would that be possible?
7. What is the subject matter of art?
8. Are some art forms better than other art forms? Why or why not?
9. Must religious art have religious subject matter? Give examples of religious art.
10. What would Tolstoy think was the religious spirit of our age? What kind of art would exhibit its perfection? Give examples.
11. How is art related to culture? To history?
12. Italians are enthusiastic about opera. Does that make opera an infectious form and therefore art?
13. What would Tolstoy think the future of art would be now?
14. Is all popular art good art?
15. Give Tolstoy's argument against state-supported art.
16. How does Tolstoy's argument about art compare to Ruskin's claim that only a few can understand the ideas of great art?

Section 2   Passages for Discussion

◆ ◆

I have said that poetry is the spontaneous overflow of powerful feelings: it takes its origin from emotion recollected in tranquillity: the emotion is contemplated till, by a species of reaction, the tranquillity gradually disappears, and an emotion, kindred to that which was before the subject of contemplation, is gradually produced, and does itself actually exist in the Mind.

WILLIAM WORDSWORTH (1770–1850), Preface to *Lyrical Ballads*

The excellence of every art is its intensity, capable of making all disagreeables evaporate, from their being in close relationship with Beauty and Truth. . . . Several things dovetailed in my mind, and at once it struck me what quality went to form a Man of Achievement, especially in Literature, and which Shakespeare possessed so enormously—I mean *Negative Capability,* that is, when a man is capable of being in uncertainties, mysteries, doubts, without any irritable reaching after fact and reason. . . . This pursued through volumes would perhaps take us no further than this, that with a great poet the sense of Beauty overcomes every other consideration, or rather obliterates all consideration.

JOHN KEATS (1795–1821), Letter of Dec. 21, 1817

The IMAGINATION then, I consider either as primary, or secondary. The primary IMAGINATION I hold to be the living Power and prime Agent of all human Perception, and as a repetition in the finite mind of the eternal act of creation in the infinite I AM. The secondary Imagination I consider as an echo of the former, co-existing with the conscious will, yet still as identical with the primary in the kind of its agency, and differing only in degree, and in the mode of its operation. . . . Fancy, on the contrary, has no other counters to play with, but fixities and definites. The Fancy is indeed no other than a mode of Memory emancipated from the order of time and space.

S. T. COLERIDGE (1772–1834), *Biographia Literaria*

When composition begins, inspiration is already on the decline, and the most glorious poetry that has ever been communicated to the world is probably a feeble shadow of the original conceptions of the poet.

PERCY BYSSHE SHELLEY (1792–1822), *A Defence of Poetry*

Poets are the hierophants of an unapprehended inspiration; the mirrors of the gigantic shadows which futurity casts upon the present; the words which express what they understand not; the trumpets which sing to battle, and feel not what they inspire; the influence which is moved not, but moves. Poets are the unacknowledged legislators of the world.

PERCY BYSSHE SHELLEY, *A Defence of Poetry*

Life imitates Art far more than Art imitates Life. This results not merely from Life's imitative instinct, but from the fact that the self-conscious aim of Life is to find expression, and that Art offers it certain beautiful forms through which it may realize that energy. It is a theory that has ever been put forward before, but it is extremely fruitful, and throws an entirely new light upon the history of Art.

OSCAR WILDE (1856–1900), "The Decay of Lying" in *Intentions and the Soul of Man*

How it is that music may, nevertheless, awaken feelings . . . such as sadness and joy we shall try to explain hereafter when we come to examine music from a subjective point of view. At this stage of our inquiry it is enough to determine whether music is capable of representing any definite emotion whatever. To this question only a negative answer can be given, the definiteness of an emotion being inseparably connected with concrete notions and conceptions, and to reduce these to a material form is altogether beyond the power of music. . . . The beautiful in music would not depend on the accurate representation of feelings even if such a representation were possible.

EDUARD HANSLICK (1825–1904), *The Beautiful in Music*

Section 3 *The Turn of the Century*

AESTHETICS IN THE FIRST PART of the twentieth century, prior to World War I, continued to be based on the principles laid down by Immanuel Kant at the end of the eighteenth century and developed throughout the nineteenth century by both artists and philosophers. These principles include the following: the aesthetic is a unique emotional sphere, characterized by its own form of pleasure; the aesthetic is fundamentally experiential and subjective; art and artists play a special role in providing aesthetic experience, but having the right kind of experience is all that is necessary for it to be aesthetic; and intellectual and practical judgments are distinct and even alien forms that interfere with aesthetic perception. As we shift to contemporary concerns, a number of new and interesting formulations of these basic principles emerge. Two shifts should be noted. First, the idealism that dominated the nineteenth century was under attack at the beginning of the twentieth century. The alliance between aesthetics and a philosophy of the mind must be reexamined, therefore. Second, psychology was emerging as a separate discipline at the turn of the century. Thus a psychological aesthetics must be distinguished from its conceptual counterpart.

A central aesthetic problem has to do with where and how the aesthetic is to be experienced. Aesthetic theory was influenced in this sphere by the emergence, around the turn of the century, of psychology as a discipline distinct from the philosophy of mind. New empirical approaches to the study of mental phenomena influenced aesthetic theory. In the course of the nineteenth century, the concept of an aesthetic attitude appeared as a fully developed theory of how people could have aesthetic experiences. But an aesthetic attitude was a part of an idealist theory of knowledge. The mind and mental phenomena had significance as mirrors of the world. The world itself was thought of as essentially mental. The new psychology suggested ways that aesthetic experience could be studied without appeal to romantic and idealist philosophy. An aesthetic attitude could be part of a theory of perception, for example. The emphasis shifted from a comprehensive system in which the aesthetic is one part to a more pragmatic exploration of how the mind might adopt different states and control its emotional and perceptual input. A number of theories along these lines occupied philosophers and artists as well as psychologists.

A different link between aesthetics and philosophy—religion—assumed increasing importance. Modernism includes a strong secular, naturalistic thesis. Under the pressure of scientific theory and a wider knowledge of the world, supernaturalism increasingly was untenable within the sphere of ordinary life. Scientists did not need God to explain natural phenomena. The immense variety of religious beliefs challenged the primacy of any one religion. Natural disasters were harder to fit into a divine plan when viewed from a global perspective. Very early, aesthetic experience was seen as an alter-

Edvard Munch, Norwegian, 1863–1944. *Girls on the Jetty,* about 1904. Kimbell Art Museum, Fort Worth, Texas.

native source of religious explanation. The similarities between religious and aesthetic experience were offered during the eighteenth and nineteenth centuries as ways of retaining religious experience without the intrusion of the supernatural into the sphere of science: both religious and aesthetic experience could claim direct, subjective verification. Both offered a form of significance independent of ordinary consequences. Both appealed to contemplation and intrinsic rewards. In the eighteenth century, for example, the German Protestant theologian Friedrich Schleiermacher (1768–1834) suggested that cultured unbelievers could approach religious experience through nature and art. Religion, which remained culturally central, could be supported by appeals to art, which was more accessible and not subject to so many doctrinal and metaphysical doubts. Gradually, however, the alliance between aesthetics and religious feeling was pulled apart and became a competition.

In the later nineteenth century and continuing into the prewar twentieth century, the roles began to reverse. Aesthetic experience now offered an independent alternative to religious belief. It had all of the immediate subjective characteristics without any of the metaphysical baggage modern aesthetes find unacceptable. Art no longer was viewed as supporting religion; instead, religion was viewed as an earlier form of aesthetic experience that could now be replaced in a more enlightened age. Someone who found religion problematic could continue to appreciate religious forms without having to take seriously their metaphysical or doctrinal content. In many theories, the interrelation is subtle. As more and more of the explanatory power shifted to other forms of theory, aesthetics offered a refuge. At the same time, art and nature perceived aesthetically offered powerful solace. Religion did not need to be explicitly repudiated by someone who finds aesthetic significance the most attractive alternative to a modern secular isolation. Only in extreme forms was the dehumanization of art understood as an avant-garde reaction against all that modernism came to represent.

Several possibilities were explored in the years preceding World War I. First, one form of early twentieth-century aesthetics embraced the difference between aesthetic experience and ordinary or scientific perception. An aesthetic attitude is a practical version of older theories of aesthetic sense and taste. Second, some critics and philosophers then elevate aesthetic experience into an alternative metaphysics. That elevation gives us the alternative religion of art and the aesthetic to replace supernatural forms. A third possibility exists, however. Hegelianism and systematic idealism gradually lost out to the critiques by analytic and phenomenological philosophers. As different as these complex philosophical movements are, they shared an essentially analytical, this-worldly approach to phenomena. They professed not to know what to do with abstract entities such as Hegel's absolute being. An alternative, non-Hegelian form of Kantianism arose that sought to retain a more empirical and culturally significant theory. These "neo-Kantians" looked for ordering principles in cultural phenomena such as language. Thought, language, and art were recognized as the embodiment of knowledge. Language and culture can be studied with the tools of linguistics and anthropology. Rather than isolating the aesthetic from scientific and practical concerns, neo-Kantians sought to reunite them by looking for common roots. Some found them in language itself, others in culture, myth, and reconceived theories of perception and experience. Together these new theories connected aesthetics to a theory of knowledge that is less abstract and speculative than the idealism of Hegel and the nineteenth century.

Finally, a trend in early twentieth-century aesthetics abandoned altogether both the system building of the nineteenth century and the complex epistemology of analysis. The focus shifted to specific forms of art. Theory of any kind was suspect. Music, painting, and literary theory came in for specific attention. The result was what we call critical and aesthetic formalism. In reaction to the sometimes grandiose claims of a quasi-

religious aesthetics and the complications of idealist and neo-Kantian theories, attention was focused on the forms of art. Formalism offered a way to talk about the specifics
of art forms without appealing to the intersubjectively unavailable data of personal
experience, though many formalists were quite ingenious in retaining the emotional
roots of traditional modern aesthetics while they described essentially formal relations
in works of art. Formalism did not so much deny theory as give it up in disgust. Concrete criticism could do without too much theory. All that was really needed, according to a critic like Clive Bell, was sensitivity to spatial form and color, unimpeded by
cultural prejudice. Similar ideas were voiced in music criticism and literary theory.

The reading selections in this section illustrate three different methodologies: psychological exploration, formalist criticism, and a more modest idealist-epistemological
theory. All three grew directly out of the cultural changes that were taking place at the
beginning of the twentieth century. They also illustrate the complex and interactive
nature of early twentieth-century aesthetics and how it is built on eighteenth- and
nineteenth-century foundations.

Benedetto Croce

$\cdot$ $\cdot$ $\cdot$ $\cdot$ $\cdot$ $\cdot$ $\cdot$ $\cdot$ $\cdot$ $\cdot$ $\cdot$ $\cdot$ $\cdot$ $\cdot$

BENEDETTO CROCE (1866–1952) was born in Pescassaeroli in the Abruzzi region of Italy. When he was seventeen, his parents and sister were killed and he was buried for hours by an earthquake while the family was on holiday. Afterward, he lived for a time in Rome before settling in Naples and entering upon a literary career. Croce was influenced by nineteenth-century Hegelianism and by the Italian philosopher Giambattista Vico (1668–1774). In particular, Vico argued for a view of history that included the study of languages and mythology. Vico's philosophy of history is less prone to the rigid progression of stages that Hegelians adopted and shares much with other neo-Kantian forms of philosophy. Croce combined many of the elements of Vico's philosophy into his own form of idealism, which emphasized expression and language as historically contingent forms of mental formation.

Together with Giovanni Gentile (1875–1944), Croce founded the influential journal *Critica,* which he edited from 1903 to 1944. This journal included literary criticism, history, and philosophy. It represented the range of Croce's intellectual activity. Croce also was active politically. He became a senator in 1910 and served as minister of education from 1920 to 1921. Croce was strongly antifascist. He broke with Gentile, who supported the fascists, and retired to Naples, where he remained until 1943, living on the island of Capri. With the fall of fascism in Italy, Croce helped negotiate the armistice with the Allies. As a leader in the Liberal Party, he was active in the postwar reconstruction of Italy.

Croce's philosophy is always historically informed and influenced by his practical critical involvement. His later work takes on an increasingly moral quality, but he consistently held to his own form of idealism and to the basic distinction between art defined as expression and nonart that is only a form of imitation. Croce's philosophy of art and history was further developed by the Oxford philosopher R. G. Collingwood.

$\blacklozenge$ $\blacklozenge$ $\blacklozenge$ $\blacklozenge$ $\blacklozenge$ $\blacklozenge$

Benedetto Croce's philosophy combines the emphasis on aesthetic experience and expression characteristic of early twentieth-century aesthetics with theories of an active, world-shaping mind that reach back to Kant and neo-Kantian philosophy in the nineteenth century. The tradition that individual aesthetic response is the empirical foundation for a philosophy of art is strong. Croce incorporates that empiricism into a form of idealism. For Croce, experience is possible only because our minds can "express" what sense begins to apprehend. When expression takes concrete form, we know the world and its contents. Until then, we have only undifferentiated, intuitive input. Art might be defined for Croce as the mediation between the world as experienced and the mind. Art is not the imitation of an already formed world. It is the expression of a world being formed.

At the foundation of Croce's thought is a division between what he called logical knowledge and intuitive knowledge. Logical knowledge is relational and conceptual. It includes and is modeled on the reasoning of formal logic, but it includes more—all of theoretical science, for example. Arithmetic would be logical knowledge, but so would predictions of an eclipse or knowing how to build a house. Logical knowledge is useful, but it is not the only kind of knowledge. Croce defends an alternative, intuitive knowledge. He rejects the view that aesthetics is a realm of pure feeling and thus independent of knowledge claims. Croce argued that our intuitive grasp of the world has an equal claim to be taken as knowledge. Thus art and the aesthetic involve knowing something, though what they know is not "logical." They operate differently than logical knowledge. Intuitive knowledge depends on imagination to create form. Logical knowledge depends on reason to demonstrate truths. Both are equally knowledge though, if pressed, Croce would maintain that intuitive knowledge is closer to the real world.

A key term for Croce is *expression*. On one side, sensations provide a kind of raw input to the mind. But by itself, sensation would produce nothing more than a stimulus for instinctual response. On the other side, abstract categories like space and time, the real and unreal, divide the world into theoretical forms. In between are intuition and perceptual form, the realm of expression. Croce argues vigorously that expression is not something in addition to form or sensation. It is how one senses something as a form. "Pure sensation" is as much an abstraction in one direction as pure logical form is in the other. Neither is possible by itself. The mind does not just respond to the world; it gives form to that world.

Croce was aware of some of the problems of an idealist aesthetic of this type. They had arisen repeatedly in the course of the nineteenth century. In particular, if the creative act is mental, then the physical work of art might not be really necessary. The way is open for unacknowledged poets who never write a word. Croce rejected that kind of idealism as a misconception. What is expressed is presented in concrete forms of expression such as language and images, not in some mental shadow. So the expression of a poem takes place in the formation of words; a painting is formed of colors and shapes. The creative work may take place in the mind of the artist, but expression must be given an appropriate form that can be shared publicly. Just imagining that I am an artist is not enough; if I am really an artist, my imagination must express what is imagined.

For Croce, art is continuous with the ordinary world of forms rather than sharply separated from ordinary objects. Art and nonart differ only in the degree of their expression. Expression is the essential artistic activity; art just is expressive activity. It is no different in kind from perception or memory or practical expression. However, art is quantitatively different from the small expressive acts of which everyone is capable. Everyone expresses something just by coming to grips with the world. How much we know of the world is a function of how much we are capable of expressing. Art and artists express more than ordinary folk. No qualitative marks of art and the aesthetic distinguish it from other objects or kinds of knowledge, but artists are more creative, more perceptive, and more open to new experiences than ordinary people. Expression is not a different kind of activity. It is the only formative activity. Art is not a different kind of object. It is any expressive object. Because forming any object is an expressive act, everything we know belongs to art.

Obviously everything is not art in the ordinary sense of the word *art,* and Croce never thought that it was. The difference between what we typically call art and Croce's inclusive sense of the word is quantitative and organic. The artist's ability to express things exceeds the ordinary. So while most of us make do with expressions already formed and our own little achievements, the artist opens new worlds and shapes new experiences. Our everyday worlds are quite restricted. We know only the small sphere of our expression as it surrounds us with familiar objects. Art is extensive; it reaches out to the possible as well as the actual. It belongs to a whole. Croce used the imagery of organic wholes to explain the difference between a piecemeal grasp of the world available to everyone and the artistic completion of a world. Unity and uniformity amidst diversity are important not as special qualities of art but as characteristics of the holistic movement that artistic expression implies.

Nevertheless, a universally present aesthetic experience follows from Croce's arguments. If art is just what is produced as a result of aesthetic experience, everything is art. Croce's epistemological claims for intuitive knowledge would not produce a philosophy of art because they would fail to distinguish art from its contrary. Croce was aware of this danger. The aesthetic is indeed universal, according to Croce, but art is distinguishable from aesthetic experience. Art is distinguished by its value. The value that identifies art is found in the activity of production. Everything expressive is beautiful. Art is also productive of something. Ugliness is an inexpressive failure of the mind's activity. Unfortunately, such failure is possible, both in the ordinary world and in attempts at art. Thus Croce resurrects the distinction between art and nonart as a distinction between successful expression and failed expression or, as he points out, between expression and failures in attempting expression, since all expression is, by definition, successful.

What we are left with, then, is a threefold equation: art equals expression equals beauty. *Expression* is the key term. It is defined as giving form to impressions that come from whatever is other than mind. But expression cannot be understood as a two-stage process in which impressions are first apprehended and then interpreted by expression. Expression must be understood as the single act of formation by which the impressions are grasped. Expression is intuitive knowledge and as much a form of knowledge as its logical counterpart. In fact, as in Kant's work, logical knowledge would not be possible without the prior activity of expression. Unlike Kant, however, Croce did not believe that categories such as space and time were independent of experience. Intuition is not limited to spatiotemporal categories. Expression is already conceptual in its own imaginative way. The aesthetic is expressive activity, and art is successful expression that quantitatively exceeds what has already been expressed. Croce inherited and incorporated the romantic values of originality and poetic creativity without the romantic promotion of genius as a specially informed being. Croce's artist works methodologically in the same way that we all work, only more so.

Croce's work bridges a gap between the earlier quests for empirical marks of art and a twentieth-century emphasis on art as an activity. By linking aesthetics to knowledge, Croce sought to counter the increasing subjectivity of an aesthetic theory that emphasized feeling as an end in itself. Croce's aesthetics was socially and culturally engaged in a way that had been lost to much of idealist aesthetics in the course of the nineteenth century. But Croce's aesthetics remained idealist. Aesthetic expression, he believed, is an activity of independent minds. If *mind* or *spirit* become problematic theoretical terms, Croce's synthesis is in trouble. In spite of his attempts to avoid a purely mental art with its attendant problems of concreteness, Croce's aesthetics could easily be taken to mean that only the work of art in the mind is important, a conclusion that leads back to the very subjectivism that Croce sought to avoid.

From *Aesthetic*

Theory of Aesthetic

Intuition and Expression

Knowledge has two forms: it is either *intuitive* knowledge or *logical* knowledge; knowledge obtained through the *imagination* or knowledge obtained through the *intellect;* of *individual things* or of the *relations* between them: it is, in fact productive either of *images* or of *concepts*.

In ordinary life, constant appeal is made to intuitive knowledge. It is said that we cannot give definitions of certain truths; that they are not demonstrable by syllogisms; that they must be learned intuitively. The politician finds fault with the abstract reasoner, who possesses no lively intuition of actual conditions; the educational theorist insists upon the necessity of developing the intuitive faculty in the pupil before everything else; the critic in judging a work of art makes it a point of honor to set aside theory and abstractions, and to judge it by direct intuition; the practical man professes to live rather by intuition than by reason.

But this ample acknowledgment granted to intuitive knowledge in ordinary life, does not correspond to an equal and adequate acknowledgment in the field of theory and of philosophy. There exists a very ancient science of intellectual knowledge, admitted by all without discussion, namely, Logic; but a science of intuitive knowledge is timidly and with difficulty asserted by but a few. Logical knowledge has appropriated the lion's share; and if she does not slay and devour her companion outright, yet yields to her but grudgingly the humble place of maid-servant or doorkeeper.—What can intuitive knowledge be without the light of intellectual knowledge? It is a servant without a master; and though a master find a servant useful, the master is a necessity to the servant, since he enables him to gain his livelihood. Intuition is blind; intellect lends her eyes.

Now, the first point to be firmly fixed in the mind is that intuitive knowledge has no need of a master, nor to lean upon any one; she does not need to borrow the eyes of others, for she has excellent eyes of her own. Doubtless it is possible to find concepts mingled with intuitions. But in many other intuitions there is no trace of such a mixture, which proves that it is not necessary. The impression of a moonlight scene by a painter; the outline of a country drawn by a cartographer; a musical motive, tender or energetic; the words of a sighing lyric, or those with which we ask, command and lament in ordinary life, may well all be intuitive facts without a shadow of intellectual relation. But, think what one may of these instances, and admitting further the contention that the greater part of the intuitions of civilized man are impregnated with concepts, there yet remains to be observed something more important and more conclusive. Those concepts which are found mingled and fused with the intuitions are no longer concepts, in so far as they are really mingled and fused, for they have lost all independence and autonomy. They have been concepts, but have now become simple elements of intuition. The philosophical maxims placed in the mouth of a personage of tragedy or of comedy, perform there the function, not of concepts but of characteristics of such personage; in the same way as the red in a painted face does not there represent the red color of the physicists, but is a characteristic element of the portrait. The whole is that which determines the quality of the parts. A work of art may be full of philosophical concepts; it may contain them in greater abundance and they may there be even more profound than in a philosophical dissertation, which in its turn may be rich to overflowing with descriptions and intuitions. But notwithstanding all these concepts the total effect of the work of art is an intuition; and not withstanding all those intuitions, the total effect of the philosophical dissertation is a concept. The *Promessi Sposi*[1] contains copious ethical observations and distinctions, but does not for that reason lose as a whole its character of simple story or intuition. In like manner the anecdotes and satirical effusions to be found in the works of a philosopher like Schopenhauer[2] do not deprive those works of their character of intellectual treatises. The difference between a scientific work and a work of art, that is, between an intellectual fact and an intuitive fact, lies in the difference of the total effect aimed at by their respective authors. This it is that determines and rules over the several parts of each not these parts separated and considered abstractly in themselves.

But to admit the independence of intuition as regards concept does not suffice to give a true and precise idea of intuition. Another error arises among those who recognize this, or who at any rate do not explicitly make intuition dependent upon the intellect, to obscure and confuse the real nature of intuition. By intuition is frequently understood *perception,* or the knowledge of actual reality, the apprehension of something as *real.*

Certainly perception is intuition: the perceptions of the room in which I am writing, of the ink-bottle and paper that are before me, of the pen I am using, of the objects that I touch and make use of as instruments of my person, which, if it write, therefore exists;—these are all intuitions. But the image that is now passing through my brain of a me writing in another room, in another town, with different paper, pen and ink, is also an intuition. This means that the distinction between reality and non-reality is extraneous,

secondary, to the true nature of intuition. If we imagine a human mind having intuitions for the first time, it would seem that it could have intuitions of actual reality only, that is to say, that it could have perceptions of nothing but the real. But since knowledge of reality is based upon the distinction between real images and unreal images, and since this distinction does not at the first moment exist, these intuition would in truth not be intuitions either of the real or of the unreal, not perceptions, but pure intuitions. Where all is real, nothing is real. The child, with its difficulty of distinguishing true from false, history from fable, which are all one to childhood, can furnish us with a sort of very vague and only remotely approximate idea of this ingenuous state. Intuition is the undifferentiated unity of the perception of the real and of the simple image of the possible. In our intuitions we do not oppose ourselves as empirical beings to external reality, but we simply objectify our impressions, whatever they be.

Those, therefore, who look upon intuition as sensation formed and arranged simply according to the categories of space and time, would seem to approximate more nearly to the truth. Space and time (they say) are the forms of intuition; to have an intuition is to place it in space and in temporal sequence. Intuitive activity would then consist in this double and concurrent function of spatiality and temporality. But for these two categories must be repeated what was said of intellectual distinctions, when found mingled with intuitions. We have intuitions without space and without time: the color of a sky, the color of a feeling, a cry of pain and an effort of will, objectified in consciousness: these are intuitions which we possess, and with their making space and time have nothing to do. In some intuitions, spatiality may be found without temporality, in others, vice versa; and even where both are found, they are perceived by later reflection; they can be fused with the intuition in like manner with all its other elements: That is, they are in it *materialiter* and not *formaliter*, as ingredients and not as arrangement. Who, without an act of reflection which

---

[1] *I Promessi Sposi* (*The Betrothed*) is an historical novel of Milan by Alessandro Manzoni (1785–1873). The novel was published in 1826 and is influenced by Sir Walter Scott. It is among the most popular novels in Italy. Manzoni is sometimes called simply *Il Grande,* and is credited with transforming Italian prose style.

[2] Arthur Schopenhauer (1788–1860) was a German philosopher. Schopenhauer was influenced by Kant. His *The World as Will and Idea* emphasizes the struggle of the will to find satisfaction and expression in an alien world. See the selection from Schopenhauer in part II, pp. 163–172.

for a moment breaks in upon his contemplation, can think of space while looking at a drawing or a view? Who is conscious of temporal sequence while listening to a story or a piece of music without breaking into it with a similar act of reflection? What intuition reveals in a work of art is not space and time, but *character, individual physiognomy*. The view here maintained is confirmed in several quarters of modern philosophy. Space and time, far from being simple and primitive functions, are nowadays conceived as intellectual constructions of great complexity. And further, even in some of those who do not altogether deny to space and time the quality of formative principles, categories and functions, one observes an effort to unite them and to regard them in a different manner from that in which these categories are generally conceived. Some limit intuition to the sole category of spatiality, maintaining that even time can only be intuited in terms of space. Others abandon the three dimensions of space as not philosophically necessary, and conceive the function of spatiality as void of all particular spatial determination. But what could such a spatial function be, a simple arrangement that should arrange even time? It represents, surely, all that criticism and refutation have left standing—the bare demand for the affirmation of some intuitive activity in general. And is not this activity truly determined, when one single function is attributed to it, not spatializing nor temporalizing, but characterizing? Or rather, when it is conceived as itself a category or function which gives us knowledge of things in their concreteness and individuality?

Having thus freed intuitive knowledge from any suggestion of intellectualism and from every later and external addition, we must now explain it and determine its limits from another side and defend it from a different kind of invasion and confusion. On the hither side of the lower limit is sensation, formless matter, which the spirit can never apprehend in itself as simple matter. This it can only possess with form and in form, but postulates the notion of it as a mere limit. Matter, in its abstraction, is mechanism, passivity; it is what

the spirit of man suffers, but does not produce. Without it no human knowledge or activity is possible; but mere matter produces animality, whatever is brutal and impulsive in man, not the spiritual communion, which is humanity. How often we strive to understand clearly what is passing within us! We do catch a glimpse of something, but this does not appear to the mind as objectified and formed. It is in such moments as these that we best perceive the profound difference between matter and form. These are not two acts of ours, opposed to one another; but the one is outside us and assaults and sweeps us off our feet, while the other inside us tends to absorb and identify itself with that which is outside. Matter, clothed and conquered by form, produces concrete form. It is the matter, the content, which differentiates one of our intuitions from another: the form is constant; it is spiritual activity, while matter is changeable. Without matter spiritual activity would not forsake its abstractness to become concrete and real activity, this or that spiritual content, this or that definite intuition.

It is a curious fact, characteristic of our times, that this very form, this very activity of the spirit, which is essentially ourselves, is so often ignored or denied. Some confound the spiritual activity of man with the metaphorical and mythological activity of what is called nature which is mechanism and has no resemblance to human activity, save when we imagine, with Aesop, that *"arbores loquuntur non tantum ferae."*[3] Some affirm that they have never observed in themselves this "miraculous" activity, as though there were no difference, or only one of quantity, between sweating and thinking, feeling cold and the energy of the will. Others, certainly with greater reason, would unify activity and mechanism in a more general concept, though they are specifically distinct. Let us, however, refrain for the moment from examining if such a final unification be possible, and in what sense, but admitting that the attempt may be made, it is clear that to unify two

---

[3] "Not only animals but trees can talk." Aesop's fables, moral tales with animals that talk, are traced back to the sixth century B.C.E.

concepts in a third implies to begin with the admission of a difference between the two first. Here it is this difference that concerns us and we set it in relief.

Intuition has sometimes been confused with simple sensation. But since this confusion ends by being offensive to common sense, it has more frequently been attenuated or concealed with a phraseology apparently designed at once to confuse and to distinguish them. Thus, it has been asserted that intuition is sensation, but not so much simple sensation as association of sensations. Here a double meaning is concealed in the word "association." Association is understood, either as memory, mnemonic association, conscious recollection, and in that case the claim to unite in memory elements which are not intuited, distinguished, possessed in some way by the spirit and produced by consciousness, seems inconceivable: or it is understood as association of unconscious elements, in which case we remain in the world of sensation and of nature. But if with certain associationists we speak of an association which is neither memory not flux of sensations, but a *productive* association (formative, constructive, distinguishing); then our contention is admitted and only its name is denied to it. For productive association is no longer association in the sense of the sensationalists, but synthesis, that is to say, spiritual activity. Synthesis may be called association; but with the concept of productivity is already posited the distinction between passivity and activity, between sensation and intuition.

Other psychologists are disposed to distinguish from sensation something which is sensation no longer, but is not yet intellectual concept: the representation or image. What is the difference between their representation or image and our intuitive knowledge? Everything and nothing: for "representation" is a very equivocal word. If by representation be understood something cut off and standing out from the psychic basis of the sensations, then representation is intuition. If, on the other hand, it be conceived as complex sensation we are back once more in crude sensa-

tion, which does not vary in quality according to its richness or poverty, or according to whether the organism in which it appears is rudimentary or highly developed and full of traces of past sensations. Nor is the ambiguity remedied by defining representation as a psychic product or secondary degree in relation to sensation, defined as occupying the first place? What does secondary degree mean here? Does it mean a qualitative, formal difference? If so, representation is an elaboration of sensation and therefore intuition. Or does it mean greater complexity and complication, a quantitative, material difference? In that case intuition is once more confused with simple sensation.

And yet there is a sure method of distinguishing true intuition, true representation, from that which is inferior to it: the spiritual fact from the mechanical, passive, natural fact. Every true intuition or representation is also expression. That which does not objectify itself in expression is not intuition or representation, but sensation and mere natural fact. The spirit only intuits in making, forming, expressing. He who separates intuition from expression never succeeds in reuniting them.

Intuitive activity *possesses intuitions to the extent that it expresses them.* Should this proposition sound paradoxical, that is partly because, as a general rule, a too restricted meaning is given to the word "expression." It is generally restricted to what are called verbal expressions alone. But there exist also non-verbal expressions, such as those of line, color and sound, and to all of these must be extended our affirmation, which embraces therefore every sort of manifestation of the man, as orator, musician, painter, or anything else. But be it pictorial, or verbal, or musical, or in whatever other form it appear, to no intuition can expression in one of its forms be wanting; it is, in fact, an inseparable part of intuition. How can we really possess an intuition of geometrical figure, unless we possess so accurate an image of it as to be able to trace it immediately upon paper or on the blackboard? How can we really have an intuition of the contour of a region, for example of the island of Sicily, if we are not able to draw it as it is in all its meanderings? Everyone can experience the internal illumination which follows upon his success in formulating to himself his impressions and feelings, but only so far as he is able to formulate them. Feelings or impressions, then pass by means of words from the obscure region of the soul into the clarity of the contemplative spirit. It is impossible to distinguish intuition from expression in this cognitive process. The one appears with the other at the same instant, because they are not two, but one.

The principal reason which makes our view appear paradoxical as we maintain it, is the illusion or prejudice that we possess a more complete intuition of reality than we really do. One often hears people say that they have many great thoughts in their minds, but that they are not able to express them. But if they really had them, they would have coined them into just so many beautiful, sounding words, and thus have expressed them. If these thoughts seem to vanish or to become few and meagre in the act of expressing them, the reason is that they did not exist or really were few and meagre. People think that all of us ordinary men image and intuit countries, figures and scenes like painters, and bodies like sculptors; save that painters and sculptors know how to paint and carve such images, while we bear them unexpressed in our souls. They believe that any one could have imagined a Madonna of Raphael;[4] but that Raphael was Raphael owing to this technical ability in putting the Madonna upon canvas. Nothing can be more false than this view. The world which as a rule we intuit is a small thing. It consists of little expressions, which gradually become greater and wider with the increasing spiritual concentration of certain moments. They are the words we say to ourselves, our silent judgments: "Here is a man, here is a horse, this is heavy, this is sharp, this pleases me," etc. It is medley of light and color, with no greater

pictorial value than would be expressed by a haphazard splash of colors, from among which one could barely make out a few special, distinctive traits. This and nothing else is what we possess in our ordinary life; this is the basis of our ordinary action. It is the index of a book. The labels tied to things (it has been said) take the place of the things themselves. This index and these labels (themselves expressions) suffice for small needs and small actions. From time to time we pass from the index to the book, from the label to the thing, or from the slight to the greater intuitions, and from these to the greatest and most lofty. This passage is sometimes far from easy. It has been observed by those who have best studied the psychology of artists that when, after having given a rapid glance at any one, they attempt to obtain a real intuition of him in order, for example, to paint his portrait, then this ordinary vision, that seemed so precise, so lively, reveals itself as little better than nothing. What remains is found to be at the most some superficial trait, which would not even suffice for a caricature. The person to be painted stands before the artist like a world to discover. Michael Angelo[5] said, "One paints, not with the hands, but with the brain." Leonardo[6] shocked the prior of the Convent of the Graces by standing for days together gazing at the "Last Supper," without touching it with the brush. He remarked of this attitude: "The minds of men of lofty genius are most active in invention when they are doing the least external work." The painter is a painter, because he sees what others only feel or catch a glimpse of, but do not see. We think we see a smile, but in reality we have only a vague impression of it, we do not perceive all the characteristics traits of which it is the sum, as the painter discovers them after he has worked upon them and is thus able to fix them on the canvas. We do not intuitively possess more even

---

[4] Sanzio Raphael (1483–1520) was an Italian Renaissance painter whose paintings of the Virgin Mary with Jesus combine a strong sense of color with spiritual sensibility, imagination, and elaboration.

[5] Michelangelo Buonarroti (1475–1564) was a sculptor, painter, architect, and poet.
[6] Leonardo da Vinci (1452–1519) was an engineer and inventor as well as an artist. His fresco (a painting on a plastered wall) of *The Last Supper* is one of the most famous paintings of the Renaissance.

of our intimate friend, who is with us every day and at all hours, than at most certain traits of physiognomy which enable us to distinguish him from others. The illusion is less easy as regards musical expression; because it would seem strange to every one to say that the composer had added or attached notes to a motive which was already in the mind of him who is not the composer; as if Beethoven's Ninth Symphony[7] were not his own intuition and his intuition the Ninth Symphony. Now, just as one who is deluded as to the amount of his material wealth is confuted by arithmetic, which states its exact amount, so he who nourishes delusions as to the wealth of this own thoughts and images is brought back to reality, when he is obliged to cross the *Pons Asinorum*[8] of expression. Let us say to the former, count; to the latter, speak; or here is a pencil, draw, express yourself.

Each of us, as a matter of fact, has in him a little of the poet, of the sculptor, of the musician, of the painter, of the prose writer: but how little, as compared with those who bear those names, just because they possess the most universal dispositions and energies of human nature in so lofty a degree! How little too does a painter possess of the intuitions of a poet! And how little does one painter possess those of another painter! Nevertheless, that little is all our actual patrimony of intuitions or representations. Beyond these are only impressions, sensations, feelings, impulses, emotions, or whatever else one may term what still falls short of the spirit and is not assimilated by man; something postulated for the convenience of exposition, while actually non-existent, since to exist also is a fact of the spirit.

We may thus add this to the various verbal descriptions of intuition, noted at the beginning: intuitive knowledge is expressive knowledge. Independent and autonomous in respect to intellectual function; indifferent to later empirical discriminations, to reality and to unreality, to formations and apperceptions, of space and time, which are also later: intuition or representation is distinguished as form from what is felt and suffered, from the flux or wave of sensation, or from psychic matter; and this form, this taking possession, is expression. To intuit is to express; and nothing else (nothing more, but nothing less) than to express.

Intuition and Art

Before proceeding further, it may be well to draw certain consequences from what has been established and to add some explanations.

We have frankly identified intuitive or expressive knowledge with the aesthetic or artistic fact, taking works, of art as examples of intuitive knowledge and attributing to them the characteristics of intuition, and *vice versa*. But our identification is combated by a view held even by many philosophers, who consider art to be an intuition of an altogether special sort. "Let us admit" (they say) "that art is intuition; but intuition is not always art: artistic intuition is a distinct species differing from intuition in general by something *more*."

But no one has ever been able to indicate of what this something more consists. It has sometimes been thought that art is not a simple intuition, but an intuition of an intuition, in the same way as the concept of science has been defined, not as the ordinary concept, but as the concept of a concept. Thus man would attain to art by objectifying, not his sensations, as happens with ordinary intuition, but intuition itself. But this process of raising to a second power does not exist; and the comparison of it with the ordinary and scientific concept does not prove what is intended, for the good reason that it is not true that the scientific concept is the concept of a concept. If this comparison proves anything, it proves just the opposite. The ordinary concept, if it be really a concept and not a simple representation, is a perfect concept, however poor and limited. Science substitutes concepts for representations; for

---

[7] Ludwig van Beethoven (1770–1827) was a German composer. His *Ninth Symphony* was composed between 1817 and 1823.

[8] Literally, "the bridge of asses"; metaphorically, it means anything hard for beginners or the unintelligent to accomplish. In geometry, the *Pons Asinorum* is Euclid's theorem that the base angles of an isosceles triangle are equal—the point in learning plain geometry that stumps beginning students.

those concepts that are poor and limited it substitutes others, larger and more comprehensive;
it is ever discovering new relations. But its method
does not differ from that by which is formed the
smallest universal in the brain of the humblest of
men. What is generally called *par excellence* art,
collects intuitions that are wider and more complex than those which we generally experience,
but these intuitions are always of sensations and
impressions.

Art is expression of impressions, not expression of expression.

For the same reason, it cannot be asserted that
the intuition, which is generally called artistic,
differs from ordinary intuition as intensive intuition. This would be the case if it were to operate
differently on the same matter. But since the artistic function is extended to wider fields, yet does
not differ in method from ordinary intuition, the
difference between them is not intensive but
extensive. The intuition of the simplest popular
love-song, which says the same thing, or very
nearly, as any declaration of love that issues at
every moment from the lips of thousands of ordinary men, may be intensively perfect in its poor
simplicity, although it be extensively so much
more limited than the complex intuition of a
love-song by Leopardi.[9]

The whole difference, then, is quantitative, and
as such is indifferent to philosophy, *scientia quali-
tatum*.[10] Certain men have a greater aptitude, a
more frequent inclination fully to express certain
complex states of the soul. These men are known
in ordinary language as artists. Some very complicated and difficult expressions are not often
achieved, and these are called works of art. The
limits of the expression-intuitions that are called
art, as opposed to those that are vulgarly called
non-art, are empirical and impossible to define.
If an epigram be art, why not a simple word? If
a story, why not the news-jottings of the jour-

nalist? If a landscape, why not a topographical
sketch? The teacher of philosophy in Moliere's
comedy was right: "whenever we speak, we create prose."[11] But there will always be scholars like
Monsieur Jourdain, astonished at having spoken
prose for forty years without knowing it, who
will have difficulty in persuading themselves that
when they call their servant John to bring their
slippers, they have spoken nothing less than—
prose.

We must hold firmly to our identification, because among the principal reasons which have
prevented Aesthetic, the science of art, from revealing the true nature of art, its roots in human
nature, has been its separation from the general
spiritual life, the having made of it a sort of special function or aristocratic club. No one is astonished when he learns from physiology that
every cell is an organism and every organism a
cell or synthesis of cells. No one is astonished at
finding in a lofty mountain the same chemical
elements that compose a small stone fragment.
There is not one physiology of small animals and
one of large animals; nor is there a special chemical theory of stones as distinct from mountains.
In the same way, there is not a science of lesser
intuition as distinct from a science of greater intuition, nor one of ordinary intuition as distinct
from artistic intuition. There is but one Aesthetic,
the science of intuitive or expressive knowledge,
which is the aesthetic or artistic fact. And this
Aesthetic is the true analog of Logic, which includes, as facts of the same nature, the formation
of the smallest and most ordinary concept and
the most complicated scientific and philosophical system.

Nor can we admit that the word *genius* or artistic genius, as distinct from the non-genius of
the ordinary man, possesses more than a quantitative signification. Great artists are said to reveal
us to ourselves. But how could this be possible,
unless there were identity of nature between their

---

[9] Count Giacomo Leopardi (1798–1837) was an outstanding
nineteenth-century lyric poet of Italy.

[10] Philosophy is the "science of qualities." Arithmetic is the science of quantities.

[11] Jean-Baptiste Molière (1622–1673) was a French dramatist and
actor whose comedies and farces ridicule social types such as the
intellectual, the miser, and the doctor.

imagination and ours, and unless the difference were only one of quantity? It were better to change *poeta nascitur* into *homo nascitur poeta:* some men are born great poets, some small.[12] The cult of the genius with all its attendant superstitions has arisen from this quantitative difference having been taken as a difference of quality. It has been forgotten that genius is not something that has fallen from heaven, but humanity itself. The man of genius who poses or is represented as remote from humanity finds his punishment in becoming or appearing somewhat ridiculous. Examples of this are the *genius* of the romantic period and the *superman* of our time.

But it is well to note here, that those who claim unconsciousness as the chief quality of an artistic genius, hurl him from the eminence far above humanity to a position far below it. Intuitive or artistic genius, like every form of human activity, is always conscious; otherwise it would be blind mechanism. The only thing that can be wanting to artistic genius is the reflective consciousness, the superadded consciousness of the historian or critic, which is not essential to it.

The relation between matter and form, or between *content* and *form,* as is generally said, is one of the most disputed questions in Aesthetic. Does the aesthetic fact consist of content alone, or of form alone, or of both together? This question has taken on various meanings, which we shall mention, each in its place. But when these words are taken as signifying what we have above defined, and matter is understood as emotionality not aesthetically elaborated, or impressions, and form as intellectual activity and expression, then our view cannot be in doubt. We must, that is to say, reject both the thesis that makes the aesthetic fact to consist of the content alone (that is, the simple impressions), and the thesis which makes it to consist of a junction between form and content, that is, of impressions plus expressions. In the aesthetic fact, expressive activity is not added to the fact of the impressions, but these latter are formed and elaborated by it. The impressions re-

appear as it were in expression, like water put into a filter, which reappears the same and yet different on the other side. The aesthetic fact, therefore, is form, and nothing but form.

From this was inferred not that the content is something superfluous (it is, on the contrary, the necessary point or departure for the expressive fact); but that *there is no passage* from the qualities of the content to those of the form. It has sometimes been thought that the content, in order to be aesthetic, that is to say, transformable into form, should possess some determined or determinable qualities. But were that so, then form and content, expression and impression, would be the same thing. It is true that the content is that which is convertible into form, but it has no determinable qualities until this transformation takes place. We know nothing about it. It does not become aesthetic content before, but only after it has been actually transformed. The aesthetic content has also been defined as the *interesting.* That is not an untrue statement; it is merely void of meaning. Interesting to what? To the expressive activity? Certainly the expressive activity would not have raised the content to the dignity of form, had it not been interested in it. Being interested is precisely the raising of the content to the dignity of form. But the word "interesting" has also been employed in another and an illegitimate sense, which we shall explain further on.

The proposition that art is imitation of nature has also several meanings. Sometimes truths have been expressed or at least shadowed forth in these words, sometimes errors have been promulgated. More frequently, no definite thought has been expressed at all. One of the scientifically legitimate meanings occurs when "imitation" is understood as representation or intuition of nature, a form of knowledge. And when the phrase is used with this intention, and in order to emphasize the spiritual character of the process, another proposition becomes legitimate also: namely, that art is the *idealization or idealizing* imitation of nature. But if by imitation of nature be understood that art gives mechanical reproductions, more or less

---

[12] Croce is playing on the saying that poets are born, not made.

perfect duplicates of natural objects, in the presence of which is renewed the same tumult of impressions as that caused by natural objects, then the proposition is evidently false. The colored waxen effigies that imitate the life, before which we stand astonished in the museums where such things are shown, do not give aesthetic intuitions. Illusion and hallucination have nothing to do with the calm domain of artistic intuition. But on the other hand if an artist paint the interior of wax-work museum, or if an actor give a burlesque portrait of a man-statue on the stage, we have work of the spirit and artistic intuition. Finally, if photography have in it anything artistic, it will be to the extent that it transmits the intuition of the photographer, his point of view, the pose and grouping which he has striven to attain. And if photography be not quite art, that is precisely because the element of nature in it remains more or less unconquered and ineradicable. Do we ever, indeed, feel complete satisfaction before even the best of photographs? Would not an artist vary and touch up much or little, remove or add something to all of them?

The statements repeated so often, that art is not knowledge, that it does not tell the truth, that it does not belong to the world of theory, but to the world of feeling, and so forth, arise from the failure to realize exactly the theoretic character of simple intuition. This simple intuition is quite distinct from intellectual knowledge, as it is distinct from perception of the real; and the statements quoted above arise from the belief that only intellectual cognition is knowledge. We have seen that intuition is knowledge, free from concepts and more simple than the so-called perception of the real. Therefore art is knowledge, form; it does not belong to the world of feeling or to psychic matter. The reason why so many aestheticians have so often insisted that art is *appearance* (Schein), is precisely that they have felt the necessity of distinguishing it from the more complex fact of perception, by maintaining its pure intuitiveness. And if for the same reason it has been claimed that art is *feeling* the reason is the same. For if the concept as content of art, and historical

reality as such, be excluded from the sphere of art, there remains no other content than reality apprehended in all its ingenuousness and immediacy in the vital impulse, in its *feeling,* that is to say again, pure intuition.

The theory of the *aesthetic senses* has also arisen from the failure to establish, or from having lost to view, the character of expression as distinct from impression, of form as distinct from matter.

This theory can be reduced to the error just indicated of wishing to find a passage from the qualities of the content to those of the form. To ask, in fact, what the aesthetic senses are, implies asking what sensible impressions are able to enter into aesthetic expressions, and which must of necessity do so. To this we must at once reply, that all impressions can enter into aesthetic expressions or formations, but that none are bound to do so of necessity. Dante[13] raised to the dignity of form not only the "sweet color of the oriental sapphire" (visual impressions), but also tactual or thermic impressions, such as the "dense air" and the "fresh rivulets" which "parch the more" the throat of the thirsty. The belief that a picture yields only visual impressions is a curious illusion. The bloom on a cheek, the warmth of a youthful body, the sweetness and freshness of a fruit, the edge of a sharp knife, are not these, too, impressions obtainable from a picture? Are they visual? What would a picture mean to an imaginary man, lacking all or many of his senses, who should in an instant acquire the organ of sight alone? The picture we are looking at and believe we see only with our eyes would seem to his eyes to be little more than an artist's paint-smeared palette.

Some who hold firmly to the aesthetic character of certain groups of impressions (for example, the visual and auditive), and exclude others, are nevertheless ready to admit that if visual and auditive impressions enter *directly* into the aesthetic

---

[13] Dante Alighieri (1265–1321) was the author of the *Divine Comedy*—a journey through hell and purgatory to a beatific vision of paradise. He is the epic poet of the Italian language. See the selection from Dante's Letters in Part I, pp. 71–76.

fact, those of the other senses also enter into it, but only as associated. But this distinction is altogether arbitrary. Aesthetic expression is synthesis, in which it is impossible to distinguish direct and indirect. All impressions are placed by it on a level, in so far as they are aestheticized. A man who absorbs the subject of a picture or poem does not have it before him as a series of impressions, some of which have prerogatives and precedence over the others. He knows nothing as to what has happened prior to having absorbed it, just as, on the other hand, distinctions made after reflection have nothing whatever to do with art as such.

The theory of the aesthetic senses has also been presented in another way; as an attempt to establish what physiological organs are necessary for the aesthetic fact. The physiological organ or apparatus is nothing but a group of cells, constituted and disposed in a particular manner; that is to say, it is a merely physical and natural fact or concept. But expression does not know physiological facts. Expression has its point of departure in the impressions, and the physiological path by which these have found their way to the mind is to it altogether indifferent. One way or another comes to the same thing: it suffices that they should be impressions.

It is true the want of given organs, that is of certain groups of cells, prevents the formation of certain impressions (when these are not otherwise obtained through a kind of organic compensation). The man born blind cannot intuit and express light. But the impressions are not conditioned solely by the organ, but also by the stimuli which operate upon the organ. One who has never had the impression of the sea will never be able to express it, in the same way as one who has never had the impression of the life of high society or of the political arena will never express either. This, however, does not prove the dependence of the expressive function on the stimulus or on the organ. It merely repeats what we know already: expression presupposes impression, and particular expressions particular impressions. For the rest, every impression excludes other impressions during the moment in which it dominates; and so does every expression.

Another corollary of the conception of expression as activity is the *indivisibility* of the work of art. Every expression is a single expression. Activity is a fusion of the impressions in an organic whole. A desire to express this has always prompted the affirmation that the work of art should have *unity,* or what amounts to the same thing, *unity in variety.* Expression is a synthesis of the various, or multiple, in the one.

The fact that we divide a work of art into parts, a poem into single figures and objects, background, foreground, etc., may seem opposed to this affirmation. But such division annihilates the work, as dividing the organism into heart, brain, nerves, muscles and so on, turns the living being into a corpse. It is true that there exist organisms in which division gives rise to other living beings, but in such a case we must conclude, maintaining the analogy between the organism and the work of art, that in the latter case too there are numerous germs of life each ready to grow, in a moment, into a single complete expression.

It may be said that expression sometimes arises from other expressions. There are simple and there are *compound* expressions. One must surely admit some difference between the *eureka,* with which Archimedes[14] expressed all his joy at his discovery, and the expressive act (indeed all the five acts) of a regular tragedy.—Not in the least: expression always arises directly from impressions. He who conceives a tragedy puts into a crucible a great quantity, so to say, of impressions: expressions themselves, conceived on other occasions, are fused together with the new in a single mass, in the same way as we can cast into a melting furnace formless pieces of bronze and choicest statuettes. Those choicest statuettes must be melted just like the pieces of bronze, before there can be a new statue. The old expressions must

---

[14]Legend has it that the Greek scientist Archimedes (287–212 B.C.E.) shouted "Eureka!" ("I have found it!") when he discovered the relation between the density of an object and the weight of water it would displace by noting the overflow from his bath.

descend again to the level of impressions, in order to be synthesized in a new single expression.

By elaborating his impressions, man *frees* himself from them. By objectifying them, he removes them from him and makes himself their superior. The liberating and purifying function of art is another aspect and another formula of its character as activity. Activity is the deliverer, just because it drives away passivity.

This also explains why it is usual to attribute to artists both the maximum of sensibility of *passion,* and the maximum of insensibility of Olympian *serenity* . The two characters are compatible, for they do not refer to the same object. The sensibility or passion relates to the rich material which the artist absorbs into his psychic organism; the insensibility or serenity to the form with which he subdues and dominates the tumult of the sensations and passions.

◆   ◆   ◆   ◆   ◆   ◆

Value is activity that unfolds itself freely: disvalue is its contrary.

We will content ourselves with this definition of the two terms, without entering into the problem of the relation between value and disvalue, that is, the problem of contraries (that is to say, whether they are to be thought of dualistically, as two beings or two orders of beings, like Ormuzd and Ahriman,[15] angels and devils, enemies to one another; or as a unity, which is also contrariety). This definition of the two terms will be sufficient for our purpose, which is to make clear the nature of aesthetic activity, and at this particular point one of the most obscure and disputed concepts of Aesthetic: the concept of the *Beautiful.*

Aesthetic, intellectual, economic and ethical values and disvalues are variously denominated in current speech: *beautiful, true, good, useful, expedient, just, right* and so on—thus designating the free development of spiritual activity, action, scientific research, artistic production, when they

are successful; *ugly, false, bad, useless, inexpedient, unjust, wrong* designating embarrassed activity, the product that is a failure. In linguistic usage, these denominations are being continually shifted from one order of facts to another. Beautiful, for instance, is said not only of a successful expression, but also of a scientific truth, of an action successfully achieved, and of a moral action: thus we talk of an *intellectual beauty,* of a *beautiful action,* of a *moral beauty.* The attempt to keep up with these infinitely varying usages leads into a trackless labyrinth of verbalism in which many philosophers and students of art have lost their way. For this reason we have thought it best studiously to avoid the use of the word "beautiful" to indicate successful expression in its positive value. But after all the explanations that we have given, all danger of misunderstanding being now dissipated, and since on the other hand we cannot fail to recognize that the prevailing tendency, both in current speech and in philosophy, is to limit the meaning of the word "beautiful" precisely to the aesthetic value, it seems now both permissible and advisable to define beauty as *successful expression,* or rather, as *expression* and nothing more, because expression when it is not successful is not expression.

Consequently, the ugly is unsuccessful expression. The paradox is true, for works of art that are failures, that the beautiful presents itself as *unity,* the ugly as multiplicity. Hence we hear of *merits* in relation to works of art that are more or less failures, that is to say, of *those parts of them that are beautiful,* which is not the case with perfect works. It is in fact impossible to enumerate the merits or to point out what parts of the latter are beautiful, because being a complete fusion they have but one value. Life circulates in the whole organism: it is not withdrawn into the several parts.

Unsuccessful works may have merit in various degrees, even the greatest. The beautiful does not possess degrees, for there is no conceiving a more beautiful, that is, an expressive that is more expressive, an adequate that is more than adequate. Ugliness, on the other hand, does possess degrees, from the rather ugly (or almost beautiful) to

---

[15] Zoroastrianism was a dualistic religion centered in Persia. Ormuzd was the principle or god of good; Ahriman was the principle or god of evil.

the extremely ugly. But if the ugly were complete, that is to say, without any element of beauty, it would for that very reason cease to be ugly, because it would be without the contradiction in which is the reason of its existence. The disvalue would become non-value; activity would give place to passivity, with which it is not at war, save when activity is really present to oppose it.

And because the distinctive consciousness of the beautiful and of the ugly is based on the conflicts and contradictions in which aesthetic activity is developed, it is evident that this consciousness becomes attenuated to the point of disappearing altogether, as we descend from the more complicated to the more simple and to the simplest instances of expression. Hence the illusion that there are expressions neither beautiful nor ugly, those which are obtained without sensible effort and appear easy and natural being considered such.

The whole mystery of the *beautiful* and the *ugly* is reduced to these henceforth most easy definitions. Should any one object that there exist perfect aesthetic expressions before which no pleasure is felt, and others, perhaps even failures, which give him the greatest pleasure, we must recommend him to concentrate his attention in the aesthetic fact, upon that which is truly aesthetic pleasure. Aesthetic pleasure is sometimes reinforced or rather complicated by pleasures arising from extraneous facts, which are only accidentally found united with it. The poet or any other artist affords an instance of purely aesthetic pleasure at the moment when he sees (or intuits) his work for the first time; that is to say, when his impressions take form and his countenance is irradiated with the divine joy of the creator. On the other hand, a mixed pleasure is experienced by one who goes to the theater, after a day's work, to witness a comedy: when the pleasure of rest and amusement, or that of laughingly snatching a nail from his coffin, accompanies the moment of true aesthetic pleasure in the art of the dramatist and actors. The same may be said of the artist who looks upon his labor with pleasure when it is finished, experiencing, in addition to the aesthetic

pleasure, that very different one which arises from the thought of self-complacency satisfied, or even of the economic gain which will come to him from his work. Instances could be multiplied.

A category of *apparent* aesthetic feelings has been formed in modern Aesthetic, not arising from the form, that is to say, from the works of art as such, but from their content. It has been remarked that artistic representations arouse pleasure and pain in their infinite shades of variety. We tremble with anxiety, we rejoice, we fear, we laugh, we weep, we desire, with the personages of a drama or of a romance, with the figures in a picture and with the melody of music. But these feelings are not such as would be aroused by the real fact outside art; or rather, they are the same in quality, but are quantitatively an attenuation of real things. Aesthetic and *apparent* pleasure and pain show themselves to be light, shallow, mobile. We have no need to treat here of these *apparent* feelings, for the good reason that we have already amply discussed them; indeed, we have hitherto treated of nothing but them. What are these apparent or manifested feelings, but feelings objectified, intuited, expressed? And it is natural that they do not trouble and afflict us as passionately as those of real life, because those were matter, these are form and activity; those true and proper feelings, these intuitions and expressions. The formula of *apparent feelings* is therefore for us nothing but a tautology, through which we can run the pen without scruple.

Study Questions

1. How is intuitive knowledge related to ordinary life?
2. What is the proper relation of intuitive knowledge to logic? Why?
3. Is it possible to give examples of "intuitions" without using logical concepts? Try. What do you end up doing?
4. How is perception related to intuition?
5. How is true intuition distinguished from mechanical fact?
6. What kinds of things can be experiences?

7. What makes expressions art?
8. Does Croce accept a form of aesthetic experience separated from life? Give his argument.
9. What is the relation of form and matter?
10. How is a genius distinguished from ordinary people?
11. How does Croce define *beautiful* and *ugly?*
12. Give examples of a failed attempt at expression. How can you know that the expression itself failed instead of your failing to understand what was expressed?
13. What might the prior of the convent say in reply to Leonardo da Vinci?
14. What is the relation between aesthetic intuition and pleasure?
15. Why does aesthetic intuition qualify as knowledge and not just feeling?

Edward Bullough

. . . .

Edward Bullough (1880–1934) was born in Switzerland. His mother was German, his father English. He was educated at Cambridge, where he studied medieval and modern languages, and he remained at Cambridge for his entire career except for a period of naval service during the World War I. Bullough's academic career was distinguished. He was a lecturer in German and then University Lecturer in Italian at Cambridge and finally Professor of Italian at the university. He served on numerous educational boards, including the Faculty Board of Architecture, and was an honorary Associate of the Royal Institute of British Architects. His published output was modest: a number of articles in scholarly journals, an anthology of Italian literature, and several translations and published lectures. One of those journal articles, " 'Psychical Distance' as a Factor in Art and as an Aesthetic Principle" (1912) has achieved the status of a classic and has made Bullough's name known widely in the field of aesthetics.

When Bullough began to lecture on aesthetics at Cambridge in 1907, he was the first to do so. At about the same time, psychology was being established as a scientific discipline separate from philosophy of mind. Bullough knew and worked with the founding members of the British Psychological Society. He studied physiology and conducted experiments at the Cambridge Psychological Laboratories. A number of his publications appeared in the *British Journal of Psychology,* particularly a series concerning experiments on color that he carried out. Bullough's methods remained introspective; he rejected statistical methods in aesthetics. He was committed to a psychological understanding of aesthetic experience. He accepted as an empirical given an "aesthetic consciousness" and on that basis proposed to examine its characteristics by psychological means. He held that "this consciousness, as a mental state *sui generis,* is the level of psychic life which must be reached and maintained, if aesthetic appreciation is to be realized."[1] This psychological thesis alone is sufficient to establish Bullough's importance in aesthetics at the beginning of the twentieth century.

◆   ◆   ◆   ◆   ◆   ◆

---

[1] Edward Bullough, "Recent Work in Experimental Aesthetics," *British Journal of Psychology* 12, 1 (1921): 99. Quoted by Elizabeth M. Wilkinson, ed., *Aesthetics: Lectures and Essays by Edward Bullough* (Stanford, CA: Stanford University Press, 1957), p. xxix.

Edward Bullough approached aesthetic experience as a psychological fact that can be explicated in terms of a metaphor of "distance." He develops this metaphor first with respect to the experience of a spectator. Then he extends it to kinds of art that are productive of aesthetic experience.

Bullough's initial distinction is one common to the history of modern aesthetics. Practical experience produces actions and consequences. A purely "phenomenal" experience is limited to the immediate impression made upon the senses. A phenomenon is just an immediate experience as it occurs before anything else results. Phenomenal experience is "objective"; it concerns only the phenomenal object—the object as it appears in perception—and not the uses or causes of that object. Phenomenal experience is also "subjective"; it belongs directly to the experience of a subject and does not concern the status of the thing experienced. This purely phenomenal experience is the one Bullough identifies as "aesthetic." He claims that the concept of "distance," applied metaphorically to the relation of a spectator to the content of an experience, will clarify many of the basic aesthetic relations. For example, distance distinguishes the senses of *objective* and *subjective* which apply to aesthetic terms. A distanced experience is intensely subjective because the perceiver's experience is both strong and immediate. But it does not involve the subject's own personality. Only the content from the object is attended to, so the experience is also intensely objective. Furthermore, distance provides a criterion for the beautiful as opposed to the merely agreeable. Distanced experience produces a pleasure that arises from the experience of the object as such; the agreeableness of the same object depends on what it can be used for. Therefore, distanced experience forms the aesthetic consciousness.

In Bullough's basic sense of *distance* the focus is on the relation of the spectator and the object, whether that object is a work of art or a natural object. Bullough tries to give a description of what a distanced experience is like. He claims that an immediate state characterized as distanced is sufficiently distinct from ordinary modes of experience to justify treating it separately. Moreover, such experience is uniquely aesthetic. Part of Bullough's case rests on the evocation of the experience. He suggests in an example which has become famous that it is like the experience of a fog at sea. The fog can be experienced immediately as a sensory impression of isolation, heightened awareness of the senses themselves, and a feeling of awe and pleasure. The fog also can be experienced in terms of its consequences as annoying, frightening because the ship might run into something, and unpleasant. He also gives other evocative descriptions which allow us to identify areas of our own experience as similar to the fog at sea and thus to understand directly what distanced experience is. At the same time, Bullough can be read as providing instructions on how to achieve such experience. Our experience of an object must be "put out of gear" with our everyday ways of responding, for example. Distanced experience is something we can learn to achieve. In either case, aesthetic experience is a personal state described as a distanced experience of an object.

Distance in this basic sense is a state of mind or an attitude, not a quantitative measure. There are no units of aesthetic distance as there are units of physical distance. Distanced experience can occur in almost any situation and with respect to almost any object, given a sufficient ability of a spectator for such experience. Bullough is careful to qualify claims for distance so as not to lose the personal involvement that aesthetic experience requires. Distance does not imply lack of involvement at all; it indicates a *type* of involvement. The need to combine distance with involvement led Bullough to formulate what he called "the antinomy of distance": one should maximize involvement without the loss of distance. In this regard, distance is best understood as a state of mind achieved by the proper kind of attitude or attention. Distance is like an on-off switch; either an experience is distanced or it is not, though Bullough claims as one advantage of the term *distance* that distance implies degrees. We can be more or less distanced in the sense that we are more or less free of the practical concerns that impede distance. Bullough's descriptions suggest that the temporal extent of the experience might shift quite rapidly as an individual's attention shifted from practical to distanced attention. I may have a distanced experience of a storm for only a brief instant before its danger forces my attention back into practical modes, for example. Some approaches to objects are not appropriate for distanced attention. Critics and intellectuals, in particular, have difficulty achieving distance. Those who are too emotionally involved or too cool and personally detached are not able to distance most experiences. A scientific attitude is not conducive to the production of distance in the required sense.

Bullough's terms shift in a subtle way. He speaks of experience as either over-distanced or under-distanced. Under-distancing increases the personal and emotional involvement at the expense of the objective qualities of the immediate experience. Over-distancing assumes an analytical approach to the content of an experience. It detaches spectators in such a way that they become uninvolved observers. They lack the intensity needed for aesthetic experience. However, over-distancing and under-distancing are not degrees of distance; they describe methodological tendencies and abilities. Some individuals tend to under-distance, for example. In so doing, they produce something other than distanced experience along a continuum of degrees of under-distancing. As under-distancing increases, it becomes increasingly difficult to discover any distanced experience in immediate perception. Whatever phenomenally distanced experience remains is aesthetic. It is not a lesser kind of aesthetic experience by virtue of being under-distanced. Similarly, over-distancing also inhibits distanced experience, but it is not a lesser kind or degree of that experience.

Thus *under-distanced* and *over-distanced* are different kinds of terms than *distanced*. 'Distance' applies directly to the immediate, psychological state of a spectator. *Over-distanced* and *under-distanced* can apply to the spectator as a subject or to works of art as objects. Objects do not have experiences. Properly speaking, only an experience is distanced. Since a person or a work of art may be under- or over-distanced, these terms describe stages in learning how to approach objects, not experiences. For example, Bullough argues that "idealistic" art, by which he means art that presents scenes, objects, or forms that are not recognizably ordinary and everyday—idealized landscapes or abstract art, for example—tends to be over-distanced. He does not mean, however, that no one can have a properly distanced experience of such works. It only means that idealistic works have properties that tend to inhibit the formation of such experience for all but a minority of spectators. That tendency has degrees that could, in principle, be measured by psychological investigations of the effects of the works on normal spectators. Under-distancing and over-distancing must be kept distinct from "distance." Distance is defined descriptively and investigated introspectively. If the experience has degrees, they are degrees of intensity, not of distance. Under-distancing and over-distancing have degrees within each kind. How under-distanced or over-distanced an object is can be investigated empirically in terms of its ability to produce or inhibit the formation of distanced experience in normal observers.

Such psychological investigation led Bullough to posit what he calls a *distance-limit* for both spectators and producers. The primary focus of Bullough's work is on the spectator-object relation. The artist comes into the theory only as someone who has an extended distance-limit. The distance-limit determines a spectator's ability to have distanced experiences. It will vary from individual to individual and from time to time and subject to subject for the same individual. Sometimes Bullough seems to say that a distance-limit is a function of the spectator's psychological makeup, but at other times he makes it depend on the nature of the subject matter. Artists have characteristically high distance-limits. They are able to distance a wider variety of objects (e.g., horrific experiences) under a wider variety of conditions (e.g., greater personal danger). Ordinary spectators have relatively low distance-limits and tend to return quickly to practical, ordinary modes of experience.

Bullough is able to move from a basic metaphor to a form of cultural analysis because the conditions that determine anyone's ability to distance experiences vary. They are relative to the cultural presuppositions that we bring to art. In fact, what can and cannot be distanced determines the forms of a particular culture. Bullough was not simply an "attitude" theorist; he does not make aesthetic experience depend solely on an attitude that can be voluntarily adopted by anyone at any time. Conditions of time and space, style, political status, and ability all enter into the determination of what will be distanced by a typical spectator. Moreover, something that is easily distanced at one time may be virtually impossible to distance at another. Thus some things will appear as art in one culture and not as art in others. Censorship, for example, would be pointless if everyone were equally capable of distancing the same things at all times. But, Bullough argues, some objects that are perfectly distanced in one time and culture may be so under-distanced at other times that they will give rise to censorship to prevent quite different responses.

Bullough's argument moves from a single state—distanced experience—to an assessment of the conditions that tend to produce that state—underdistancing and over-distancing—and then to a cultural analysis of the conditions that tend to produce under-distancing and over-distancing. The three levels of analysis are different, and they involve terms used in different ways. Degrees of under- and over-distancing are not the same as distance, and Bullough's conclusions about cultural phenomena are not the same as his theory of distance. The metaphor of distance provides one of the most powerful descriptions of the modern sense of aesthetic experience. But *distance* is an elusive term just because it remains metaphorical. Bullough suggests that psychological data should be collected about how distance works. With respect to distance itself, however, the state is only introspectively available. Because it is based on a metaphor, the description of distanced experience is not precise enough for the kind of psychological investigation that Bullough hoped for. Nevertheless, *distance* has become part of the aesthetic vocabulary of the twentieth century.

From *"Psychical Distance" as a Factor in Art and as an Aesthetic Principle*

I.

1. The conception of "Distance" suggests, in connection with Art, certain trains of thought by no means devoid of interest or of speculative importance. Perhaps the most obvious suggestion is that of *actual spatial* distance, i.e. the distance of a work of Art from the spectator, or that of *represented spatial* distance, i.e. the distance represented within the work. Less obvious, more metaphorical, is the meaning of *temporal* distance. The first was noticed already by Aristotle in his *Poetics;* the second has played a great part in the history of painting in the form of perspective; the distinction between these two kinds of distance assumes special importance theoretically in the differentiation between sculpture in the round, and relief-sculpture. Temporal distance, remoteness from us in point of time, though often a cause of misconceptions, has been declared to be a factor of considerable weight in our appreciation.

It is not, however, in any of these meaning that "Distance" is put forward here, though it will be clear in the course of this essay that the above mentioned kinds of distance are rather special forms of the conception of Distance as advocated here, and derive whatever *aesthetic* qualities they may possess from Distance in its general connotation is 'psychical distance.'

A short illustration will explain what is meant by 'Psychical Distance.' Imagine a fog at sea: for most people it is an experience of acute unpleasantness. Apart from the physical annoyance and remoter forms of discomfort such as delays, it is apt to produce feelings of peculiar anxiety, fears of invisible dangers, strains of watching and listening for distant and unlocalized signals. The listless movements of the ship and her warning calls soon tell upon the nerves of the passengers; and that special, expectant, tacit anxiety and nervousness, always associated with this experience, make a fog the dreaded terror of the sea (all the more terrifying because of its very silence and gentleness) for the expert seafarer no less that for the ignorant landsman.

Nevertheless, a fog at sea can be a source of intense relish and enjoyment. Abstract from the experience of the sea fog, for the moment, its danger and practical unpleasantness, just as every one in the enjoyment of a mountain-climb disregards its physical labor and its danger (though, it is not denied, that these may incidentally enter into the enjoyment and enhance it); direct the attention to the features "objectively" constituting the phenomenon—the veil surrounding you with an opaqueness as of transparent milk, blurring the outline of things and distorting their shapes into weird grotesqueness; observe the carrying-power of the air, producing the impression as if you could touch some far-off siren by merely putting out your hand and letting it lose itself behind that white wall; note the curious creamy smoothness of the water, hypocritically denying as it were any suggestion of danger; and, above all, the strange solitude and remoteness from the world, as it can be found only on the highest mountain-tops: and the experience may acquire, in its uncanny mingling of repose and terror, a flavor of such concentrated poignancy and delight as to contrast sharply with the blind and distempered anxiety of its other aspects. This contrast, often emerging with startling suddenness, is like a momentary switching on of some new current, or the passing ray of a brighter light, illuminating the outlook upon perhaps the most ordinary and familiar objects—an impression which we experience sometimes in instants of direct extremity, when our practical interest snaps like a wire from sheer over-tension, and we watch the consummation of some impending catastrophe with the marveling unconcern of a mere spectator.

It is a difference of outlook, due—if such a metaphor is permissible—to the insertion of Distance. This Distance appears to lie between our own self and its affections, using the latter term in its broadest sense as anything which affects our being, bodily or spiritually, e.g. as sensation, perception, emotional state or idea. Usually, though not always, it amounts to the same thing to say that the Distance lies between our own self and such objects as are the sources or vehicles of such affections.

Thus, in the fog, the transformation by Distance is produced in the first instance by putting the phenomenon, so to speak, out of gear with our practical, actual self; by allowing it to stand outside the context of our personal needs and ends—in short, by looking at it "objectively," as it has often been called, by permitting only such reactions on our part as emphasize the "objective" features of the experience, and by interpreting even our "subjective" affections not as modes of our being but rather as characteristics of the phenomenon.

The working of Distance is, accordingly, not simple, but highly complex. It has a *negative, inhibitory* aspect—the cutting-out of the practical sides of things and of our practical attitude to them—and a *positive* side—the elaboration of the experience on the new basis created by the inhibitory action of distance.

2. Consequently, this distanced view of things is not, and cannot be, our normal outlook. As a rule, experiences constantly turn the same side towards us, namely, that which has the strongest practical force of appeal. We are not ordinarily aware of those aspects of things which do not touch us immediately and practically, nor are we generally conscious of impressions apart from our own self which is impressed. The sudden view of things from their reverse, usually unnoticed, side, comes upon us as a revelation, and such revelations are precisely those of Art. In this most general sense, Distance is a factor in all Art.

3. It is, for this very reason, also an aesthetic principle. The aesthetic contemplation and the aesthetic outlook have often been described as "objective." We speak of "objective" artists as Shakespeare or Velasquez,[2] of "objective" works or art-forms as Homer's *Iliad* or the drama. It is a term constantly occurring in discussions and criticisms, though its sense, if pressed at all, becomes very questionable. For certain forms of Art, such as lyrical poetry, are said to be "subjective"; Shelley,[3] for example, would usually be considered a "subjective" writer. On the other hand, no work of Art can be genuinely "objective" in the sense in which this term might be applied to work on history or to a scientific treatise; nor can it be "subjective" in the ordinary acceptance of that term, as a personal feeling, a direct statement of a wish or belief, or a cry of passion is subjective. "Objectivity" and "subjectivity" are a pair of opposites which in their mutual exclusiveness when applied to Art soon lead to confusion.

Nor are they the only pair of opposites. Art has with equal vigor been declared alternately "idealistic" and "realistic," "sensual" and "spiritual," "individualistic" and "typical." Between the defence of either terms of such antitheses most aesthetic theories have vacillated. It is one of the contentions of this essay that such opposites find their synthesis in the more fundamental conception of Distance.

Distance further provides the much needed criterion of the beautiful as distinct from the agreeable.

Again, it marks one of the most important steps in the process of artistic creation and serves as a distinguishing feature of what is commonly so loosely described as the "artistic temperament."

Finally, it may claim to be considered as one of the essential characteristics of the "aesthetic consciousness," if I may describe by this term

---

[2] Diego Rodriguez de Silva y Velasquez (1599–1660) was court painter to the King of Spain. His paintings combine intellectual coolness with compassion and detail.
[3] Percy Bysshe Shelley (1792–1822) was one of the leading English romantic poets of the nineteenth century.

that special mental attitude towards, and outlook upon, experience, which finds its most pregnant expression in the various forms of Art.

II

Distance, as I said before, is obtained by separating the object and its appeal from one's own self, by putting it out of gear with practical needs and ends. Thereby the "contemplation" of the object becomes alone possible. But it does not mean that the relation between the self and the object is broken to the extent of becoming "impersonal." Of the alternatives "personal" and "impersonal" the latter surely comes nearer to the truth; but here, as elsewhere, we meet the difficulty of having to express certain facts in terms coined for entirely different uses. To do so usually results in paradoxes, which are nowhere more inevitable than in discussions upon Art. "Personal" and "impersonal," "subjective" and "objective" are such terms, devised for purposes other than aesthetic speculation, and becoming loose and ambiguous as soon as applied outside the sphere of their special meanings. In giving preference therefore to the term "impersonal" to describe the relation between the spectator and a work of Art, it is to be noticed that it is not impersonal in the sense in which we speak of the "impersonal" character of Science, for instance. In order to obtain "objectively valid" results the scientist excludes the "personal factor," *i.e.* his personal wishes as to the validity of his results, his predilection for any particular system to be proved or disproved by his research. It goes without saying that all experiments and investigations are undertaken out of personal interest in the science, for the ultimate support of a definite assumption, and involve personal hopes of success but this does not affect the "dispassionate" attitude of the investigator, under pain of being accused of "manufacturing his evidence."

1. Distance does not imply an impersonal, purely intellectually interested relation of such a kind. On the contrary, it describes a *personal* relation, often highly emotionally colored, but of a *peculiar character*. Its peculiarity lies in that the personal character of the relation has been, so to speak, filtered. It has been cleared of the practical, concrete nature of its appeal, without, however, thereby losing its original constitution. One of the best-known examples is be found in our attitude towards the events and characters of the drama: they appeal to us like persons and incidents of normal experience, except that that side of their appeal, which would usually affect us in a directly personal manner, is held in abeyance. This difference, so well known as to be almost trivial, is generally explained by reference to the knowledge that the characters and situations are "unreal," imaginary. In this sense Witasek[4] operating with Meinong's theory of *Annahmen*,[5] has described the emotions involved in witnessing a drama as *Scheingefuhle*,[6] a term which has so frequently been misunderstood in discussions of his theories. But, as a matter of fact, the "assumption" upon which the imaginative emotional reaction is based is not necessarily the condition, but often the consequence, of Distance; that is to say, the converse of the reason usually stated would then be true: *viz.* that Distance, by changing our relation to the characters, renders them seemingly fictitious, not that the fictitiousness of the characters alters our feelings toward them. It is, of course, to be granted that the actual and admitted unreality of the dramatic action reinforces the effect of Distance. But surely the proverbial unsophisticated yokel, whose chivalrous interference in the play on behalf of the hapless heroine can only be prevented by impressing upon him that "they are only pretending," is not the ideal type of theatrical audience. The proof of the seeming paradox that it is Distance which primarily gives to dramatic action the appearance of

---

[4] S. Witasek was a nineteenth-century German academic philosopher. His theory distinguishes two parallel mental tracks, one real and one imagined.

[5] Alexius Meinong (1853–1920) was a German philosopher and psychologist in the idealist tradition. He is best known for holding that there are nonexistent objects. His theory of *Annahmen* concerns *supposition*.

[6] *Scheingefuhle* means illusional feeling.

unreality and not *vice versa,* is the observation that the same filtration of our sentiments and the same seeming "unreality" of *actual* men and things occur, when at times, by a sudden change of inward perspective, we are overcome by the feeling that "all the world's a stage."

2. This personal, but "distanced" relation (as I will venture to call this nameless character of our view) directs attention to a strange fact which appears to be one of the fundamental paradoxes of Art: it is what I propose to call "the antinomy of Distance."

It will be readily admitted that a work of art has the more chance of appealing to us the better it finds us prepared for its particular kind of appeal. Indeed, without some degree of predisposition on our part, if must necessarily remain incomprehensible, and to that extent unappreciated. The success and intensity of its appeal would seem, therefore, to stand in direct proportion to the completeness with which it corresponds with our intellectual and emotional peculiarities and the idiosyncrasies of our experience. The absence of such a concordance between the characters of a work and of the spectator is, of course, the most general explanation for differences of "tastes."

At the same time, such a principle of concordance requires a qualification, which leads at once to the antinomy of distance.

Suppose a man, who believes that he has cause to be jealous about his wife, witnesses a performance of *Othello.*[7] He will the more perfectly appreciate the situation, conduct and character of Othello, the more exactly the feelings and experiences of Othello coincide with his own—at least he ought to on the above principle of concordance. In point of fact, he will probably do anything but appreciate the play. In reality, the concordance will merely render him acutely conscious of his own jealousy; by a sudden reversal of perspective he will no longer see Othello apparently betrayed by Desdemona, but himself in an analogous situation with his own wife. This

reversal of perspective is the consequence of the loss of Distance.

If this be taken as a typical case, if follows that the qualification required is that the coincidence should be as complete as is compatible with maintaining Distance. The jealous spectator of *Othello* will indeed appreciate and enter into the play the more keenly, the greater the resemblance with his own experience—*provided* that he succeeds in keeping the Distance between the action of the play and his personal feelings: a very difficult performance in the circumstance. It is on account of the same difficulty that the expert and the professional critic make a bad audience, since their expertness and critical professionalism are *practical* activities, involving their concrete personality and constantly endangering their Distance. (It is, bye the way, one of the reasons why Criticism is an art, for it requires the constant interchange from the practical to the distanced attitude and *vice versa,* which is characteristic of artists.)

The same qualification applies to the artist. He will prove artistically most effective in the formulation of an intensely *personal* experience, but he can formulate it artistically only on condition of a detachment from the experience *qua personal.* Hence the statement of so many artists that artistic formulation was to them a kind of catharsis, a means of ridding themselves of feelings and ideas the acuteness of which they felt almost as a kind of obsession. Hence, on the other hand, the failure of the average man to convey to others at all adequately the impression of an overwhelming joy or sorrow. His personal implication in the event renders it impossible for him to formulate and present it in such a way as to make other, like himself, feel all the meaning and fullness which it possesses for him.

What is therefore, both in appreciation and production, most desirable is the *utmost decrease of Distance without its disappearance.*

3. Closely related, in fact a presupposition to the "antinomy," is the *variability of Distance.* Herein especially lies the advantage of Distance compared with such terms as "objectivity" and "detachment." Neither of them implies a *per-*

---

[7] In Shakespeare's tragedy *Othello,* Othello's jealousy leads him to believe the lies of Iago and to kill his wife, Desdemona.

sonal relaxation—indeed both actually preclude it; and the mere inflexibility and exclusiveness of their opposites render their application generally meaningless.

Distance, on the contrary, admits naturally of degrees, and differs not only according to the nature of the *object,* which may impose a greater or smaller degree of Distance, but varies also according to the *individual's capacity* for maintaining a greater or lesser degree. And here on my remark that not only do *persons differ from each other* in their habitual measure of Distance, but that the *same individual differs* in his ability to maintain it in the face of different objects and different arts.

There exist, therefore, two different sets of conditions affecting the degree of Distance in any given case: those offered by the object and those realized by the subject. In their interplay they afford one of the most extensive explanations for varieties of aesthetic experience, since loss of Distance, whether due to the one or the other, means loss of aesthetic appreciation.

In short, Distance may be said to be *variable both according to the distancing-power of the individual, and according to the character of the object.*

There are two ways of losing Distance: either to "under-distance" or to "over-distance." "Under-distancing" is the commonest failing of the *subject,* an excess of Distance is a frequent failing of Art, especially in the past. Historically it looks almost as if Art had attempted to meet the deficiency of Distance on the part of the subject and had overshot the mark in this endeavor. It will be seen later that this is actually true, for it appears that over-distanced Art is specially designed for a class of appreciation which has difficulty to rise spontaneously to any degree of Distance. The consequence of a loss of Distance through one or other cause is familiar: the verdict in the case of under-distancing is that the work is "crudely naturalistic," "harrowing," "repulsive in its realism." An excess of Distance produces the impression of improbability, artificiality, emptiness or absurdity.

The individual tends, as I just stated, to under-distance rather than to lose Distance by over-

distancing. *Theoretically* there is no limit to the decrease of Distance. In theory, therefore, not only the usual subjects of Art, but even the most personal affections, whether ideas, percepts or emotions, can be sufficiently distanced to be aesthetically appreciable. Especially artists are gifted in this direction to a remarkable extent. The average individual, on the contrary, very rapidly reaches his limit of decreasing Distance, his "Distance-limit," *i.e.* that point at which Distance is lost and appreciation either disappears or changes its character.

In the *practice,* therefore, of the average person, a limit does exist which marks the minimum at which his appreciation can maintain itself in the aesthetic field, and this average minimum lies considerably higher that the Distance-limit of the artist. It is practically impossible to fix this average limit, in the absence of data, and on account of the wide fluctuations from person to person to which this limit is subject. But it is safe to infer that, in art practice, explicit references to organic affections, to the material existence of the body, especially to sexual matters, lie normally below the Distance-limit, and can be touched upon by Art only with special precautions. Allusions to social institutions of any degree of personal importance—in particular, allusions implying any doubt as to their validity—the questioning of some generally recognized ethical sanctions, references to topical subjects occupying public attention at the moment, and such like, are all dangerously near the average limit and may at any time fall below it, arousing, instead of aesthetic appreciation, concrete hostility or mere amusement.

This difference in the Distance-limit between artists and the public has been the source of much misunderstanding and injustice. Many an artist has seen his work condemned and himself ostracized for the sake of so-called "immoralities" which to him were *bona fide* aesthetic objects. His power of distancing, nay, the necessity of distancing feelings, sensations, situations which for the average person are to intimately bound up with his concrete existence to be regarded in that light, have often quite unjustly earned for him accusations of cynicism, sensualism, morbidness, or frivolity. The same misconception has arisen over many "problem plays" and "problem novels" in which the public have persisted in seeing nothing but a supposed "problem" of the moment, whereas the author may have been—and often has demonstrably been—able to distance the subject matter sufficiently to rise above its practical problematic import and to regard it simply as a dramatically and humanly interesting situation.

The variability of Distance in respect to Art, disregarding for the moment the subjective complication, appears both as a general feature in Art, and in the differences between the special arts.

It has been an old problem why the "arts of the eye and of the ear" should have reached the practically exclusive predominance over arts of other senses. Attempts to raise "culinary art" to the level of a Fine Art have failed in spite of all propaganda, as completely as the creation of scent or liqueur "symphonies." There is little doubt that, apart from other excellent reasons of a partly psycho-physical, partly technical nature, the actual, *spatial distance* separating objects of sight and hearing from the subject has contributed strongly to the development of this monopoly. In a similar manner *temporal remoteness* produces Distance, and objects removed from us in point of time are *ipso facto* distanced to an extent which was impossible for their contemporaries. Many pictures, plays and poems had, as a matter of fact, rather an expository or illustrative significance— as for instance much ecclesiastical Art—or the force of a direct practical appeal—as the invectives of many satires or comedies—which seem to us nowadays irreconcilable with their aesthetic claims. Such works have consequently profited greatly by lapse of time and have reached the level of Art only with the help of temporal distance, while others, on the contrary, often for the same reason have suffered a loss of Distance, through *over*-distancing.

Special mention must be made of a group of artistic conceptions which present excessive Distance in their form of appeal rather than in their actual presentation—a point illustrating the necessity of distinguishing between distancing an object and distancing the appeal of which it is the source. I mean here what is often rather loosely termed "idealistic Art," that is, Art springing from abstract conceptions, expressing allegorical meanings, or illustrating general truths. Generalizations and abstractions suffer under this disadvantage that they have too much applicability to invite a personal interest in them, and to little individual concreteness to prevent them applying to us in all their force. They appeal to everybody and therefore to none. An axiom of Euclid[8] belongs to nobody, just because it compels everyone's assent; general conceptions like Patriotism, Friendship, Love, Hope, Life, Death, concern as much Dick, Tom, and Harry as myself, and I, therefore, either feel unable to get into any kind of personal relation to them, or, if I do so, they become at once, emphatically and concretely, *my* Patriotism, *my* Friendship, *my* Love, *my* Hope, *my* Life and Death. By mere force of generalization, a general truth or a universal ideal is so far distanced from myself that I fail to realize it concretely at all, or, when I do so, I can realize it only as part of my *practical actual being, i.e.* it falls below the Distance-limit altogether. "Idealistic Art" suffers consequently under the peculiar difficulty that its excess of Distance turns generally into an under-distance appeal—all the more easily, as it is the usual failing of the subject to *under*- rather than to *over*-distance.

The different special arts show at the present time very marked variations in the degree of Distance which they usually impose or require for their appreciation. Unfortunately here again the absence of data makes itself felt and indicates the necessity of conducting observations, possibly experiments, so as to place these suggestions upon a securer basis. In one single art, *viz.* the *theater,* a small amount of information is available, from an unexpected source, namely the pro-

---

[8] Euclid was the third-century B.C.E. Greek mathematician whose *Elements of Geometry* became the standard textbook for plane geometry.

ceedings of the censorship committee, which on closer examination might be made to yield evidence of interest to the psychologist. In fact, the whole censorship problem, as far as it does not turn upon purely economic questions, may be said to hinge upon Distance; if every member of the public could be trusted to keep it, there would be no sense whatever in the existence of a censor of plays. There is, of course, no doubt that, speaking generally theatrical performances *eo ipso* run a special risk of a loss of Distance owing to the material presentment of its subject-matter. The physical presence of living human beings as vehicles of dramatic art is a difficulty which no art has to face in the same way. A similar, in many ways even greater, risk confronts dancing: though attracting perhaps a less widely spread human interest, its animal spirits are frequently quite unrelieved by any glimmer of spirituality and consequently form a proportionately stronger lure to under-distancing. In the higher forms of dancing technical execution of the most wearing kind makes up a great deal for its intrinsic tendency towards a loss of Distance, and as a popular performance, at least in southern Europe, it has retained much of its ancient artistic glamour, producing a peculiarly subtle balancing of Distance between the pure delight of bodily movement and high technical accomplishment. In passing, it is interesting to observe (as bearing upon the development of Distance) that this art, once as much a fine art as music and considered by the Greeks as a particularly valuable educational exercise, should—except in sporadic cases—have fallen so low from the pedestal it once occupied. Next to the theater and dancing stands *sculpture*. Though not using a *living* bodily medium, yet the human form in its full spatial materiality constitutes a similar threat to Distance. Our northern habits of dress and ignorance of the human body have enormously increased the difficulty of distancing Sculpture, in part through the gross misconceptions to which it is exposed, in part owing to complete lack of standards of bodily perfection, and an inability to realize the distinction between sculptural form and bodily

shape, which is the only but fundamental point distinguishing a statue from a cast taken from life. In *painting* it is apparently the form of its presentment and the usual reduction in scale which would explain why this art can venture to approach more closely than sculpture to the normal Distance-limit. As this matter will be discussed later in a special connection this simple reference may suffice here. *Music* and *architecture* have a curious position. These two most abstract of all arts show a remarkable fluctuation in their Distances. Certain kinds of music, especially "pure" music, or "classical" or "heavy" music, appear for many people over-distanced; light, "catchy" tunes, on the contrary, easily reach that degree of decreasing Distance below which they cease to be Art and become a pure amusement. In spite of its strange abstractness which to many philosophers has made it comparable to architecture and mathematics, music possesses a sensuous, frequently sensual, character: the undoubted physiological and muscular stimulus of its melodies and harmonies, no less than its rhythmic aspects, would seem to account for the occasional disappearance of Distance. To this might be added its strong tendency, especially in unmusical people, to stimulate trains of thought quite disconnected with itself, following channels of subjective inclinations—day-dreams of a more or less directly personal character. *Architecture* requires almost uniformly a very great Distance; that is to say, the majority of persons derive no aesthetic appreciation from architecture as such, apart from the incidental impression of its decorative features and its associations. The causes are numerous, but prominent among them are the confusion of building with architecture and the predominance of utilitarian purposes, which overshadow the architectural claims upon the attention.

4. That all art requires a Distance-limit beyond which, and a Distance within which only, aesthetic appreciation becomes possible, is the *psychological formulation of a general characteristic of Art, viz. its anti-realistic nature*. Though seemingly paradoxical, this applies as much to "naturalistic" as to "idealistic" Art. The difference commonly

expressed by these epithets is at bottom merely the difference in the degree of Distance; and this produces, so far as "naturalism" and "idealism" in Art are not meaningless labels, the usual result that what appears obnoxiously "naturalistic" to one person, may be "idealistic" to another. To say that Art is anti-realistic simply insists upon the fact that Art is not nature, never pretends to be nature and strongly resists any confusion with nature. It emphasizes the *art*-character of Art: "artistic" is synonymous with "anti-realistic"; it explains even sometimes a very marked degree of artificiality.

"Art is an imitation of nature," was the current art-conception in the eighteenth century. It is the fundamental axiom of the standard work of that time upon aesthetic theory by the Abbe Du Bos, *Reflexions critiques sur la poesie et la peinture,* 1719;[9] the idea received strong support from the literal acceptance of Aristotle's theory of *mimesis* and produced echoes everywhere, in Lessing's *Laocöon*[10] no less that in Burke's famous statement that "all Art is great as it Deceives."[11] Though it may be assumed that since the time of Kant and of the Romanticists this notion has died out, it still lives in unsophisticated minds. Even when formally denied, it persists, for instance, in the belief that "Art idealized nature," which means after all only that Art copies nature with certain improvements and revisions. Artists themselves are unfortunately often responsible for the spreading of this conception. Whistler[12] indeed said that to produce Art by imitating nature would be like trying to produce music by sitting upon the piano, but the selective, idealizing imitation of nature finds merely another support in such a saying. Naturalism, pleinairism, impressionism, even the guileless enthusiasm of the artist for the works of nature, her wealth of suggestion, her delicacy of workmanship, for the steadfastness of her guidance, only produce upon the public the impression that Art is, after all, an imitation of nature. Then how can it be anti-realistic?: The antithesis, Art *versus* nature, seems to break down. Yet if it does, what is the sense of Art?

Here the conception of Distance comes to the rescue. The solution of the dilemma lies in the "antinomy of Distance" with its demand: utmost decrease of distance without its disappearance. The simple observation that Art is the more effective, the more it falls into line with our predispositions which are inevitably moulded on general experience and nature, has always been the original motive for "naturalism." "Naturalism," "impressionism" is no new thing; it is only a new name for an innate leaning of Art, from the time of the Chaldeans and Egyptians down to the present day. Even the Apollo of Tenea[13] apparently struck his contemporaries as so startlingly "naturalistic" that the subsequent legend attributed a superhuman genius to his creator. A constantly closer approach to nature, a perpetual refining of the limit of Distance, yet without overstepping the dividing line of art and nature, has always been the inborn bent of art. To deny this dividing line has occasionally been the failing of naturalism. But no theory of naturalism is complete which does not at the same time allow for the intrinsic idealism of Art: for both are merely degrees in that wide range lying beyond the Distance-limit. To imitate nature so as to trick the spectator into the deception that it is nature which he beholds, is to forsake Art, its anti-realism, its distanced spirituality, and to fall below the limit into sham, sensationalism or platitude.

But what, in the theory of antinomy of Distance, requires explanation is the existence of an

---

[9] The Abbé Jean Baptiste Dubos was one of the first critics in the eighteenth century to propose a thoroughly subjective theory of taste.

[10] Gotthold Ephraim Lessing (1729–1781) was a German philosopher, literary critic, and dramatist. His critical work *Laocöon* examined the differences between classical and modern sculpture and distinguished between the effects of poetry and painting.

[11] Edmund Burke (1729–1797) was the author of a *Philosophical Enquiry into the Origin of Our Ideas of the Sublime and Beautiful* (1756).

[12] James McNeill Whistler (1834–1903) was an American painter who worked primarily in London. He advocated art as an arrangement of light, form, and color.

[13] The Apollo of Tenea is a sixth-century B.C.E. representation of the god. It is in the archaic style that poses the figure with one foot slightly advanced in a style influenced by ancient Egypt.

idealistic, highly distanced Art. There are numerous reasons to account for it; indeed in so complex a phenomenon as Art, single causes can be pronounced almost *a priori* to be false. Foremost among such causes which have contributed to the formation of an idealistic Art appears to stand the subordination of Art to some extraneous purpose of an impressive, exceptional character. Such a subordination has consisted—at various epochs of Art history—in the use to which Art was put to subserve commemorative, hieratic, generally religious, royal or patriotic functions. The object to be commemorated had to stand out from among other still existing objects or persons; the thing or the being to be worshipped had to be distinguished as markedly as possible from profaner objects of reverence and had to be invested with an air of sanctity by a removal from its ordinary context of occurrence. Nothing could have assisted more powerfully the introduction of a high Distance than this attempt to differentiate objects of common experience in order to fit them for their exalted position. Curious, unusual things of nature met this tendency half-way and easily assumed divine rank; but others had to be distanced by an exaggeration of their size, by extraordinary attributes, by strange combinations of human and animal forms, by special insistence upon particular characteristics, or by the careful removal of all noticeably individualistic and concrete features. Nothing could be more striking than the contrast, for example, in Egyptian Art between the monumental, stereotyped effigies of the Pharaohs, and the startlingly realistic rendering of domestic scenes and of ordinary mortals, such as "the Scribe" or "the Village Sheikh." Equally noteworthy is the exceeding artificiality of Russian ikon-painting with its prescribed attributes, expressions, and gestures. Even Greek dramatic practice appears to have aimed, for similar purposes and in marked contrast to our stage-habits, at an increase rather than at a decrease of Distance.[14] Otherwise Greek Art, even of a religious type, is remarkable for its *low* Distance

value; and it speaks highly for the aesthetic capacities of the Greeks that the degree of realism which they ventured to impart to the representations of their gods, while humanizing them, did not, at least at first, impair the reverence of their feelings towards them. But apart from such special causes, idealistic Art of great Distance has appeared at intervals, for apparently no other reason than that the great Distance was felt to be essential to its art-character. What is noteworthy and runs counter to many accepted ideas is that such periods were usually epochs of a low level of general culture. These were times, which like childhood, required the marvelous, the extraordinary, to satisfy their artistic longings, and neither realized nor cared for the poetic or artistic qualities of ordinary things. They were frequently times in which the mass of the people were plunged in ignorance and buried under a load of misery, and in which even the small educated class sought rather amusement or a pastime in Art; or they were epochs of strong practical common sense too much concerned with the rough-and-tumble of life to have any sense of its aesthetic charms. Art was to them what melodrama is to a section of the public at the present time, and its wide Distance was the safeguard of its artistic character. The flowering periods of Art have, on the contrary, always borne the evidence of a narrow Distance. Greek Art, as just mentioned, was realistic to an extent which we, spoilt as we are by modern developments, can grasp with difficulty, but which the contrast with its oriental contemporaries sufficiently proves. During the Augustan period[15]—which Art historians at last are coming to regard no longer as merely "degenerated" Greek Art—Roman Art achieved its greatest triumphs in an almost naturalistic portrait-sculpture. In the Renaissance we need only think of the realism of portraiture, sometimes amounting almost to cynicism, of the *desinvolture*[16] with which the mistresses of popes and dukes were

---

[14] Greek drama used masks for the actors, for example.

[15] The Augustan period is named for Caesar Augustus (63 B.C.E.– 14 C.E.). Greek art was greatly admired and copied during the period.

[16] *Desinvolture* means "gracefulness, ease."

posed as madonnas, saints and goddesses apparently without any detriment to the aesthetic appeal of the works, and of the remarkable interpenetration of Art with the most ordinary routine of life, in order to realize the scarcely perceptible dividing line between the sphere of Art and the realm of practical existence. In a sense, the assertion that idealistic Art marks periods of a generally low and narrowly restricted culture is the converse to the oft-repeated statement that the flowering periods of Art coincide with epochs of decadence: for this so-called decadence represents indeed in certain respects a process of disintegration, politically, racially, often nationally, but a disruption necessary to the formation of larger social units and to the breakdown of outgrown national restrictions. For this very reason it has usually also been the sign of the growth of personal independence and of an expansion of individual culture.

To proceed to some more special points illustrating the distanced and therefore anti-realistic character of art: both in subject-matter and in the form of presentation Art has always safeguarded its distanced view. Fanciful, even fantastic, subjects have from time immemorial been the accredited material of Art. No doubt things, as well as our view of them, have changed in the course of time: *Polyphemus*[17] and *Lotus-Eaters*[18] for the Greeks, the *Venusberg* or the *Magnetic Mountain*[19] for the Middle Ages were less incredible, more realistic than to us. But *Peter Pan* or *L'Oiseau Bleu*[20] still appeal at the present day in spite of the prevailing note of realism of our time. "Probability" and "improbability" in Art are not to be measured by their correspondence (or lack of it) with actual experience. To do so had involved the theories of the fifteenth to the eighteenth centuries in endless contradictions. It is rather a matter of *consistency* of Distance. The note of realism, set by a work as a whole, determines *intrinsically* the greater or smaller degree of fancy which it permits; and consequently we feel the loss of Peter Pan's shadow to be infinitely more probable than some trifling improbability which shocks our sense of proportion in a naturalistic work. No doubt also, fairy-tales, fairy-plays, stories of strange adventures were primarily invented to satisfy the craving of curiosity, the desire for the marvelous, the shudder of the unwonted and the longing for imaginary experiences. But by their mere eccentricity in regard to the normal facts of experience they cannot have failed to arouse a strong feeling of Distance.

Again, certain conventional subjects taken from mythical and legendary traditions, at first closely connected with the concrete, practical, life of a devout public, have gradually, by the mere force of convention as much as by their inherent anti-realism, acquired Distance for us today. Our view of Greek mythological sculpture, of early Christian saints and martyrs must be considerably distanced, compared with that of the Greek and medieval worshipper. It is in part the result of lapse of time, but in part also a real change of attitude. Already the outlook of the Imperial Roman had altered, and Pausanias[21] shows a curious dualism of standpoint, declaring the Athene Lemnia[22] to be the supreme achievement of Phidias's genius, and gazing awe-struck upon the roughly hewn tree-trunk representing some primitive Apollo. Our understanding of Greek tragedy suffers admittedly under our inability to revert to the point of view for which it was originally written. Even the tragedies of Racine[23] de-

---

[17] Polyphemus was the one-eyed monster who ate the men of Odysseus.

[18] The lotus-eaters were a legendary people who subsisted on the lotus flower, which made them forget their own country.

[19] Venusberg and the magnetic mountain are magical mountains of medieval legend.

[20] *Peter Pan* is the play by James Barrie (1860–1937) about a magical land where no one grows past childhood. *L'Oiseau Bleu* (The Blue Bird) is a fable by the Belgian author Maurice Maeterlinck about freedom from death.

---

[21] Pausanias was a second-century B.C.E. traveler and geographer who describes many of the places and sights of Greece.

[22] Phidias (c. 500–432 B.C.E.) was one of the greatest sculptors of classical Athens. The statue of Athena at Lemnos was one of his early works.

[23] Jean Racine (1639–1699) was a French dramatist. His tragedies follow a classical style based on rules derived from Aristotle.

mand an imaginative effort to put ourselves back into the courtly atmosphere of red-heeled, powdered ceremony. Provided the Distance is not too wide, the result of its intervention has everywhere been to enhance the art-character of such works and to lower their original ethical and social force of appeal. Thus in the central dome of the Church (Sta Maria dei Miracoli) at Saronno[24] are depicted the heavenly hosts in ascending ties, crowned by the benevolent figure of the Divine Father, bending from the window of heaven to bestow His blessing upon the assembled community. The mere realism of foreshortening and of the boldest vertical perspective may well have made the naive Christian of the sixteenth century conscious of the Divine Presence—but for us it has become a work of Art.

The unusual, exceptional, has found its especial home in tragedy. It has always—except in highly distanced tragedy—been a popular objection to it that "there is enough sadness in life without going to the theater for it." Already Aristotle appears to have met with this view among his contemporaries clamoring for "happy endings."[25] Yet tragedy is not sad; if it were, there would indeed be little sense in its existence. For the tragic is just in so far different from the merely sad, as it is distanced; and it is largely the exceptional which produces the Distance of tragedy; exceptional situations, exceptional characters, exceptional destinies and conduct. Not of course, characters merely cranky, eccentric, pathological. The exceptional element in tragic figures—that which makes them so utterly different from characters we meet with in ordinary experience—is a consistency of direction, a fervor of ideality, a persistence and driving-force which is far above the capacities of average men. The tragic of tragedy would, transposed into ordinary life, in nine cases out of ten, end in drama, in comedy, even in farce, for lack of steadfastness, for fear of conventions, for the dread of "scenes," for a hundred-

and-one petty faithlessnesses towards a belief or an ideal: even if for none of these, it would end in a compromise simply because man forgets and time heals. (The famous "unity of time," so senseless as a "canon," is all the same often an indispensable condition of tragedy.[26] For in many a tragedy the catastrophe would be even intrinsically impossible, if fatality did not overtake the hero with that rush which gives no time to forget and none to heal. It is in cases such as these that criticism has often blamed the work for "improbability," the old confusion between Art and nature—forgetting that the death of the hero is the convention of the artform, as much as grouping in a picture is such a convention and that probability is not the correspondence with average experience, but consistency of Distance.) Again, the sympathy which aches with the sadness of tragedy is another such confusion, the underdistancing of tragedy's appeal. Tragedy trembles always on the knife-edge of a *personal* reaction, and sympathy which finds relief in tears tends almost always towards a loss of Distance. Such a loss naturally renders tragedy unpleasant to a degree: it becomes sad, dismal, harrowing, depressing. But real tragedy (melodrama has a very strong tendency to speculate upon sympathy), truly appreciated is not sad. "The pity of it—oh, the pity of it," that essence of all genuine tragedy is not the pity of mild, regretful sympathy. It is a chaos of tearless, bitter bewilderment, of upsurging revolt and rapturous awe before the ruthless and inscrutable fate; it is the homage to the great and exceptional in the man who in a last effort of spiritual tension can rise to confront blind, crowning Necessity even in his crushing defeat.

As I explained earlier, the form of presentation sometimes endangers the maintenance of Distance, but it more frequently acts as a considerable support. Thus the bodily vehicle of *drama*

---

[24] Saronno is in Italy.
[25] In the *Poetics,* Aristotle praises Euripides for avoiding the catastrophe.

[26] The unity of time was a neoclassical rule supposedly derived from Aristotle in the seventeenth century that the action in a play should not exceed either the actual time of the performance or twenty-four hours. It was never adhered to by the great dramatists.

is the chief factor of risk to Distance. But, as if to counterbalance a confusion with nature, other features of stage-presentation exercise an opposite influence. Such are the general theatrical *milieu,* the shape and arrangement of the stage, the artificial lighting, the costumes, *mise-en-scene*[27] and make-up, even the language, especially verse. Modern reforms of staging, aiming primarily at the removal of artistic incongruities between excessive decoration and the living figures of the actors and at the production of a more homogeneous stage-picture, inevitably work also towards a greater emphasis and homogeneity of Distance. The history of staging and dramaturgy is closely bound up with the evolution of Distance, and its fluctuations lie at the bottom not only of the greater part of all the talk and writing about "dramatic probability" and the Aristotelian "unities," but also of "theatrical illusion." In *sculpture,* one distancing factor of presentment is its lack of color. The aesthetic, or rather inaesthetic, effect of realistic coloring is in no way touched by the controversial question of its use historically; its attempted resuscitation, such as by Klinger,[28] seems only to confirm its disadvantages. The distancing use even of pedestals, although originally no doubt serving other purposes, is evident to anyone who has experienced the oppressively crowded sensation of moving in a room among life-sized statues placed directly upon the floor. The circumstance that the space of statuary is the same space as ours (in distinction to relief sculpture or painting, for instance) renders a distancing by pedestals, i.e. a removal from our spatial context, imperative. (An instance which might be adduced to disprove this point only shows its correctness on closer inspection: for it was on purpose and with the intention of removing Distance, that Rodin[29] originally intended his

Citoyens de Calais to be placed, without pedestals, upon the market-place of that town.) Probably the framing of *pictures* might be shown to serve a similar purpose—though paintings have intrinsically a much greater Distance—because neither their space (perspective and imaginary space) not their lighting coincides with our (actual) space or light, and the usual reduction in scale of the represented objects prevents a feeling of undue proximity. Besides, painting always retains to some extent a two-dimensional character, and this character supplies *eo ipso* a Distance. Nevertheless, life-size pictures, especially if they possess strong relief, and their light happens to coincide with the actual lighting, can occasionally produce the impression of actual presence which is a far from pleasant, though fortunately only a passing, illusion. For decorative purposes, in pictorial renderings of vistas, garden-perspectives and architectural extensions, the removal of Distance has often been consciously striven after, whether with aesthetically satisfactory results is much disputed.

A general help towards Distance (and therewith an anti-realistic feature) is to be found in the unification of "presentment" of all art-objects. By unification of presentment are meant such qualities as symmetry, opposition, proportion, balance, rhythmical distribution of parts, light-arrangements, in fact all so-called "format" features, "composition" in the widest sense. Unquestionably, Distance is not the only, nor even the principal function of composition; it serves to render our grasp of the presentation easier and to increase its intelligibility. It may even in itself constitute the principal aesthetic feature of the object, as in linear complexes or patterns, partly also in architectural designs. Yet, its distancing effect can hardly be underrated. For, every kind of visibly intentional arrangement or unification must, by the mere fact of its presence, enforce Distance, by distinguishing the object from the confused, disjointed and scattered forms of actual experience. This function can be gauged in a typical form in cases where composition produces an exceptionally marked impression of artificiality

---

[27] *Mise-en-scene* means "direction."

[28] Max Klinger (1857–1920) was a German sculptor and painter. Classical sculpture was painted, probably quite garishly. Klinger produced a painted statue of Beethoven.

[29] Auguste Rodin (1840–1917) was a French monumental sculptor. His *Burghers of Calais* depicts the scene in which the leading burghers surrendered themselves to the English to save the city.

(not in the bad sense of that term, but the sense in which all art is artificial); and it is a natural corollary to the differences of Distance in different arts and of different subjects, that the arts and subjects vary in the degree of artificiality which they can bear. It is this sense of artificial finish which is the source of so much of that elaborate charm of Byzantine work,[30] of Mohammedan decoration, of the hieratic stiffness of so many primitive madonnas and saints. In general the emphasis of composition and technical finish increases with the Distance of the subject matter: heroic conceptions lend themselves better to verse than to prose; monumental statues require a more general treatment, more elaboration of setting and artificiality of pose than impressionistic statuettes like those of Troubetzkoi;[31] an ecclesiastic subject is painted with a degree of symmetrical arrangement which would be ridiculous in a Dutch interior, and a naturalistic drama carefully avoids the tableau impression characteristic of mystery play. In a similar manner the variations of Distance in the arts go hand in hand with a visibly greater predominance of composition and "formal" elements, reaching a climax in architecture and music. It is again a matter of "consistency of Distance." At the same time, while from the point of view of the artist this is undoubtedly the case, from the point of view of the public the emphasis of composition and technical finish appears frequently to relieve the impression of highly distanced subjects by *diminishing the Distance of the whole.* The spectator has a tendency to see in composition and finish merely evidence of the artist's "cleverness," of his mastery over his material. Manual dexterity is an enviable thing to possess in everyone's experience, and naturally appeals to the public *practically,* thereby putting it into a directly personal relation to things which

intrinsically have very little personal appeal for it. It is true that this function of composition is hardly an aesthetic one: for the admiration of mere technical cleverness is not an artistic enjoyment, but by a fortunate chance it has saved from oblivion and entire loss, among much rubbish, also much genuine Art, which otherwise would have completely lost contact with our life.

5. This discussion, necessarily sketchy and incomplete, may have helped to illustrate the sense in which, I suggested, Distance appears as a fundamental principle to which such antitheses as idealism and realism are reducible. The difference between "idealistic" and "realistic" Art is not a clear-cut dividing-line between the art-practice described by these terms, but is a difference of degree in the Distance-limit which they presuppose on the part both of the artist and of the public. A similar reconciliation seems to me possible between the opposites "sensual" and "spiritual," "individual" and " typical." That the appeal of Art is sensuous, even sensual, must be taken as an indisputable fact. Puritanism will never be persuaded, and rightly so, that this is not the case. The sensuousness of Art is a natural implication of the "antinomy of Distance," and will appear again in another connection. The point of importance here is that the whole sensual side of Art is purified, spiritualized, "filtered' as I expressed it earlier, by Distance. The most sensual appeal becomes the translucent veil of an underlying spirituality, once the grossly personal and practical elements have been removed from it. And—a matter of special emphasis here—*this spiritual aspect of the appeal is the more penetrating, the more personal and direct its sensual appeal would have been* BUT FOR THE PRESENCE OF DISTANCE. For the artist, to trust in this delicate transmutation is a natural act of faith which the Puritan hesitates to venture upon: which of the two, one asks, is the greater idealist?

6. The same argument applies to the contradictory epithets "individual" and "typical." A discussion in support of the fundamental individualism of Art lies outside the scope of this essay. Every artist has taken it for granted. Besides it is

---

[30] Byzantine art covers a period of more than 1200 years from about 300 C.E. to the fall of Constantinople in 1453. It is predominantly a religious art with a rigorously developed symbolism.

[31] Paul Troubetskoy (1866–1938) was an Italian sculptor who worked in Europe and the United States. He is particularly known for his statuettes.

rather in the sense of "concrete" or "individual-ized," that it is usually opposed to "typical." On the other hand, "typical," in the sense of "ab-stract," is as diametrically opposed to the whole nature of Art, as individualism is characteristic of it. It is in the sense of "generalized" as a "gen-eral human element" that it is claimed as a nec-essary ingredient in Art. This antithesis is again one which naturally and without mutual sacrifice finds room within the conception of Distance. Historically the "typical" has had the effect of counteracting *under*-distancing as much as the "individual" has opposed over-distancing. Natu-rally the two ingredients have constantly varied in the history of Art; they represent, in fact, two sets of conditions to which Art has invariably been subject: the personal and the social factors. It is Distance which on one side prevents the empty-ing of Art of its concreteness and the develop-ment of the typical into abstractness; which, on the other, suppresses the directly personal ele-ment of its individualism; thus reducing the an-titheses to the peaceful interplay of these two fac-tors. It is just this interplay which constitutes the "antinomy of Distance."

Study Questions

1. Distinguish physical and temporal dis-tance from psychical distance.
2. How is psychical distance related to our ordinary outlook?
3. In what sense is psychical distance objective?
4. In what sense is psychical distance subjective?
5. Give Bullough's argument that psychical distance is both personal and impersonal.

6. What is the antinomy of distance?
7. How does psychical distance vary?
8. Describe *idealistic* art.
9. Describe *naturalistic* art.
10. What does it mean to say that art is anti-realistic?
11. The best way to understand Bullough's points is through examples from your own experience:
    a. Give examples of distanced art.
    b. Give examples where it would be very difficult to distance art.
    c. Give examples of under-distanced art works.
    d. Give examples of under-distanced appreciation.
    e. Give examples of over-distanced art works.
    f. Give examples of over-distanced appreciation.
12. Describe from your own experience a situation that was both distanced and not distanced.
13. Can you "put out of gear" the experience of reading this text? How?
14. How do Bullough's concepts apply to the different art forms of literature, music, and painting?
15. What cultural factors influence your abil-ity to distance properly?
16. If distancing depends on cultural factors, can something be art at one time and not be art later?
17. Can something be art for one person and not be art for someone else at the same time? What would be the consequences of using "art" in this way?

Clive Bell

$\cdot$ $\cdot$ $\cdot$ $\cdot$ $\cdot$ $\cdot$ $\cdot$ $\cdot$ $\cdot$

CLIVE BELL (1881–1964) came from a well-to-do family lacking in social preten-sions. His life cannot be separated from the circle of friends and artists we know as Bloomsbury, which included Lytton Strachey, Thoby Stephen, and Leonard Woolf. The nucleus of this group formed at Cambridge, where they were students to-gether. An older generation of Cambridge intellectuals, including Bertrand Russell and G. E. Moore, exerted a strong influence upon them. Woolf, Stephen, Strachey, and a few other undergraduates belonged to a club they formed that met in Bell's rooms at midnight and went by the name of the Midnight Club. In some ways Bell was the odd man out in this circle. He liked hunting and prior to Cambridge had nothing like the intellectual background of the others. He was rejected for membership in the Apostles, the secret society of intellectuals to which Lytton Strachey and Leonard Woolf, Ber-trand Russell, and Maynard Keynes all belonged. Yet Bell responded to their influence and became an integral part of their circle.

Bloomsbury takes its name from the area around Bloomsbury Square in central Lon-don. The circle of friends and intellectuals to which that name now refers was never a formal group. It began when, after the death of Sir Leslie Stephen in 1904, Stephen's daughters Vanessa and Virginia and their brothers Adrian and Thoby moved to the area, and it was built up around the Cambridge group of friends who continued to meet in London. Clive Bell married Vanessa in 1907; later, Leonard Woolf married Virginia. Thoby died in 1906, but the original group included Maynard Keynes and Duncan Grant. All except Bell were artists or intellectuals of considerable note. Lytton Strachey was a biographer; Duncan Grant and Vanessa Bell were painters; Virginia Woolf be-came one of the leading novelists of the century; and Maynard Keynes was its leading economist. Over the years, others became closely associated with the original circle, in-cluding E. M. Forster, Desmond McCarthy, and Roger Fry, as well as the overlapping circle of Lady Ottoline Morrell. Bloomsbury was marked by two qualities: its reputation for unconventional views and the genuine brilliance of its leading members. Lytton Strachey was lionized for his writing but stigmatized for his open homosexuality. All held more or less "free" views of sexuality from the standpoint of Edwardian England. They were pacifists in an age of patriotism and empire. But if they were unconven-tional, they were also productive.

Bell's place in this circle was guaranteed by his marriage to Vanessa, and he shared in the sexual freedom of the group. He flirted with Virginia at the time that Vanessa had their first child and had other affairs. Vanessa in her turn had affairs with Roger Fry and Duncan Grant. In other respects, Bell had more difficulty finding his niche. The influence of Roger Fry, who was fifteen years older, was decisive. Fry was a painter and an established art critic when he was introduced into the Bloomsbury circle. Bell had already spent time in Paris where he was drawn to the artists, including Picasso and Derain, who were the avant garde of the day. Fry began to promote these artists as "postimpressionists" in a series of exhibitions in England, and Bell found his calling as the advocate of postimpressionist art. Many of the original ideas came from Fry, but Bell gave them shape and became their popular advocate. His combination of theory, critical acuteness, and ability to transcend Bloomsbury's limited circle made Bell the art critic/theoretician of the group. Bloomsbury could be devastating about those outside its circle and catty within it. Fry wrote in a review of Bell's first book that "[Clive] entered the holy of holies of culture in knickerbockers with a big walking-stick in his hand."[1] But Bell belonged, and he gave voice to a form of aesthetic theory that combined aesthetic experience with formalist criticism and a fervor for art that verged on religion. The group survived World War I and continued to be influential up to the beginning of World War II, by which time the social and cultural intimacy it nurtured were no longer possible.

◆   ◆   ◆   ◆   ◆   ◆

Clive Bell was not a philosopher, and his attempt to formulate an aesthetic theory is sometimes more passionate than logical. He was an active promoter of modern art, particularly the art of Cezanne, and his critical views are often perceptive. He brought a formidable sensibility and enthusiasm to the formulation of the aesthetic precepts that he incorporated into his criticism.

For Bell, everything begins with sensibility. Intellect uninformed by sensibility can have nothing to do with art. The data from which a critic must begin a discussion of art are emotional. On that basis, Bell identified two questions. First, he asks about the nature of the aesthetic emotion. Second, he asks what quality is common to all objects that provoke that emotion. Bell did not question the claim that an aesthetic emotion exists or that it, and it alone, is what art is about. If pressed, he could only appeal directly to an immediate experience for the existence of this emotion. He frankly admits that the foundation of aesthetics is subjective. Its twin elements are the personal experience of a peculiar emotion.

Once one grants that starting point, Bell builds another assumption into his aesthetic. Like most nineteenth-century aestheticians, Bell was an essentialist. Essentialism about some object means that defining characteristics are required to apply a name to that object. Bell believed that the existence of an aesthetic emotion implies an essential quality in all objects that produces the emotion. Possession of that essential quality justifies calling an object *art*. Bell is careful to structure his argument so that his claim that only personal experience counts as evidence does not contradict his claim that an essential quality is common to all such experience. Different observers may disagree about which objects have the quality in question, but, Bell argued, they will find that

---

[1] Quoted by David Gadd, *The Loving Friends* (New York: Harcourt Brace Jovanovich, 1974), p. 112.

everyone agrees that when they have the experience, it is produced by the essential quality. In other words, we may disagree about whether a quality is present in some object without disagreeing that it is the essential quality. A number of philosophers have pointed out a logical flaw in this way of arguing. If I claim to have an aesthetic experience that lacks the essential quality Bell identifies, Bell can simply deny either that it is an aesthetic experience or that the essential quality is really present. But a claim that is not subject to empirical falsification is not an empirical claim. It is a disguised definition. Bell's essential quality would then just mean "whatever causes the aesthetic emotion." As definitions, "the aesthetic quality is whatever causes the aesthetic emotion" and "the aesthetic emotion is the emotion produced by aesthetic qualities" do not get us very far. Even if one acknowledges this problem, Bell's basic claim remains clear: art produces an emotional response, and that response has an essential correlate in some qualities of objects which provoke it.

As a critic, Bell was a formalist. In the visual arts, he reduces form to line, color, shape, and their spatial relations. At the same time, Bell claimed that only personal experience counts aesthetically. The combination of these two positions led him to identify what he called "significant form" as the essential aesthetic quality. A precise definition of *significant form* proves elusive. Bell obviously means by significant form combinations of the formal elements available to perception—line, color, shape, and so on in the visual arts—but what makes them significant can only be felt, not described, so a definition says only that significant form is form productive of the aesthetic emotion which leaves the same problem we had in defining the emotion itself. However, Bell's intent is not simply to define but to present significant form critically. The role of the critic in Bell's aesthetic is positive, but a critic is limited to a persuasive task. Critics cannot tell anyone what to feel; they can only try to show what is there so that viewers feel it for themselves. Significant form should be understood in this sense. It is not a formal definition so much as a label for those elements that formalist critics can get perceptive viewers to see.

Bell's formalism led him to some strong claims about where significant form will appear. Bell distinguished two classes of emotions. The first includes emotions that respond to everyday things and events. These are the emotions of life. They include love and hate, desires and antipathies, boredom and intellectual interest. The second is more difficult to describe because it is the aesthetic emotion. It is a response to form itself, apart from any interest in what the form represents. Thus the basic emotional distinction divides emotions between those that are responses to representations and those that are produced independently of representation. Emotions from representations are emotions of life; emotions from form are aesthetic emotions and are "significant" for that reason. Bell went so far as to describe aesthetic emotions as a form of ecstasy since they have no practical application to life.

The strength of Bell's argument rests on the formal insight that his critical perceptiveness produces. He relates many of the common ideas in modern aesthetics—aesthetic emotion, disinterested involvement, pure feeling—directly to a critical practice and critical skills. Even if some of Bell's claims are excessive or logically flawed, he gives a set of directions for how to approach visual art in order to have the experience that he takes as aesthetic. Bell's approach to aesthetic theory has a critical efficacy that continues to make it interesting.

Bell's theory of significant form has a number of difficulties about it. First, as an essential quality, significant form does not seem to extend to literary arts. His aesthetic theory is directed almost exclusively toward visual form. Second, because it is based on immediate subjective responses, it is also an affective theory as Bell initially formulated it. It applies only to the relation between a spectator and a work of art. Aesthetic emotion produced independently of any object (perhaps by appropriate brain stimulation) would be just as effective. Significant form is only a means to an emotional end. Only the effect counts in the end; significant form might be only an accidental relation. Third, Bell maintained that natural beauty produces a different emotional response; art does not produce beauty but aesthetic emotion. Finally, Bell's reliance on significant form does not account for how art comes to be formed. The role of the artist is mysterious. However, Bell provided a way to extend the aesthetics of significant form to include other forms and provide a role for the artist. He called this his metaphysical hypothesis.

Artists, Bell suggests, are fundamentally interested in the *expression* of the significant form that they feel. The expression of an emotion is not the same thing as having the emotion. To express emotion reverses the process. Form produced the emotion; now, having the emotion, an artist gives it form. This operation is different from having the emotion in the first place. Artists are expressers of emotion, not consumers of form. Yet they can express only what their imaginations conceive. Expression provides a potential bridge between art and nature. Artists discover form in life and nature. But since only form produces aesthetic emotion, life and nature are left behind in the production of art. While "beauty" is so loaded with connotations of life and nature that Bell abandons it, significant form can be found virtually anywhere. Thus an artist *may* turn to nature or life and find significant form, which leads to an emotion, which leads to expression, which appears as significant form in art.

Aesthetic expression must be an end in itself and not a means to some other emotional outlet. If it is, Bell is prepared to hazard a metaphysical guess that "ultimate reality" is the cause of significant form. Significant form implies a mind, a creative force, he believes. Neither imitations nor merely natural objects exhibit significant form because they lack a creative mind as their cause. If significant form leads back to a creative force, art puts a viewer in touch with reality directly. While Bell understands significant form in visual terms, it could be defined by this metaphysical link to reality. So, although Bell does not speculate in this direction, significant form in literature might be an expression of the same ultimate reality. Its nonaesthetic counterpart would be a focus on the plot and events that conveyed life emotions.

Bell links aesthetic emotions to religious experience. They have a similar significance, and they lift a sensitive person into an ecstatic state beyond the normal limits of life. Bell combined formalism with emotionalism critically. His theory of the aesthetic shows a similar emotional elevation of form to a passionate independence of its own. Bell believes all true art provokes an aesthetic emotion when it is given a chance. If true art does not produce aesthetic emotion, other, more commonplace emotions have interfered and blocked out the aesthetic feeling. Aesthetic emotion is valuable. Indeed, it is more valuable than any other end accessible to human beings. Thus art replaces religion as a source of ultimate value and reality. Bell believed in art, though he was careful to admit that his belief was only a faith that goes beyond the aesthetic argument.

From *Art*

I. The Aesthetic Hypothesis

It is improbable that more nonsense has been written about aesthetics than about anything else: the literature of the subject is not large enough for that. It is certain, however, that about no subject with which I am acquainted has so little been said that is at all to the purpose. The explanation is discoverable. He who would elaborate a plausible theory of aesthetics must possess two qualities—artistic sensibility and a turn for clear thinking. Without sensibility a man can have no aesthetic experience, and, obviously, theories not based on broad and deep aesthetic experience are worthless. Only those for whom art is a constant source of passionate emotion can possess the data from which profitable theories may be deduced; but to deduce profitable theories even from accurate data involves a certain amount of brain-work, and, unfortunately, robust intellects and delicate sensibilities are not inseparable. As often as not, the hardest thinkers have had no aesthetic experience whatever. I have a friend blessed with an intellect as keen as a drill, who, though he takes an interest in aesthetics, has never during a life of almost forty years been guilty of an aesthetic emotion. So, having no faculty for distinguishing a work of art from a handsaw, he is apt to rear up a pyramid of irrefragable argument on the hypothesis that a handsaw is a work of art. This defect robs his perspicuous and subtle reasoning of much of its value; for it has ever been a maxim that faultless logic can win but little credit for conclusions that are based on premises notoriously false. Every cloud, however, has its silver lining, and this insensibility, though unlucky in that it makes my friend incapable of choosing a sound basis for his argument, mercifully blinds him to the absurdity of his conclusions while leaving him in full enjoyment of his masterly dialectic. People who set out from the hypothesis that Sir Edwin Landseer[2] was the finest painter that ever lived will feel no uneasiness about an aesthetic which proves that Giotto[3] was the worst. So, my friend, when he arrives very logically at the conclusion that a work of art should be small or round or smooth, or that to appreciate fully a picture you should pace smartly before it or set it spinning like a top, cannot guess why I ask him whether he has lately been to Cambridge, a place he sometimes visits.

On the other hand, people who respond immediately and surely to works of art, though, in my judgment, more enviable than men of massive intellect but slight sensibility, are often quite as incapable of talking sense about aesthetics. Their heads are not always very clear. They possess the data on which any system must be based; but, generally, they want the power that draws correct inferences from true data. Having received aesthetic emotions from works of art, they are in a position to seek out the quality common to all that have moved them, but, in fact, they do nothing of the sort. I do not blame them. Why should they bother to examine their feelings when for them to feel is enough? Why should they stop to think when they are not very good at thinking? Why should they hunt for a common quality in all objects that move then in a particular way when they can linger over the many delicious and peculiar charms of each as it comes? So, if they write criticism and call it aesthetics, if they

---

[2] Edwin Landseer (1802–1873) was an extremely popular naturalistic English painter of grandiloquent animals and sentimental scenes. His work is a perfect example of the kind of painting that Bell rejects as art.

[3] Giotto (c. 1266–1337) was a Florentine painter whose work marks a turning point in Western art history. He abandoned the Gothic and Byzantine styles of earlier painters; his work lacks the elaborate perspective of Renaissance styles and looks deceptively simple. He was associated with the Franciscan order, for whom he painted a number of frescos.

imagine that they are talking about Art when they are talking about particular works of art or even about the technique of painting, if loving particular works they find tedious the consideration of art in general, perhaps they have chosen the better part. If they are not curious about the nature of their emotion, nor about the quality common to all objects that provoke it, they have my sympathy, and, as what they say is often charming and suggestive, my admiration too. Only let no one suppose that what they write and talk is aesthetics; it is criticism, or just "shop."

The starting-point for all systems of aesthetics must be the personal experience of a peculiar emotion. The objects that provoke this emotion we call works of art. All sensitive people agree that there is a peculiar emotion provoked by works of visual art, and that this emotion is provoked by every kind of visual art, by pictures, sculptures, buildings, pots, carvings, textiles, etc., etc., is not disputed, I think, by anyone capable of feeling it. This emotion is called the aesthetic emotion; and if we can discover some quality common and peculiar to all the objects that provoke it, we shall have solved what I take to be the central problem of aesthetics. We shall have discovered the essential quality in a work of art, the quality that distinguishes works of art from all other classes of objects.

For either all works of visual art have some common quality, or when we speak of "works of art" we gibber. Everyone speaks of "art," making a mental classification by which he distinguishes the class "works of art" from all other classes. What is the justification of this classification? What is the quality common and peculiar to all members of this class? Whatever it be, no doubt it is often found in company with other qualities; but they are adventitious—it is essential. There must be some one quality without which a work of art cannot exist; possessing which, in the least degree, no work is altogether worthless. What is this quality? What quality is shared by all objects that provoke our aesthetic emotions? What quality is common to Sta. Sophia and the windows at Chartres, Mexican sculpture, a Persian bowl, Chi-

nese carpets, Giotto's frescoes at Padua, and the masterpieces of Poussin, Piero della Francesca, and Cezanne?[4] Only one answer seems possible —significant form. In each, lines and colors combined in a particular way, certain forms and relations of forms, stir our aesthetic emotions. These relations and combinations of lines and colors, these aesthetically moving forms, I call "Significant Form"; and "Significant Form" is the one quality common to all works of visual art.

At this point it may be objected that I am making aesthetics a purely subjective business, since my only data are personal experiences of a particular emotion. It will be said that the objects that provoke this emotion vary with each individual, and that therefore a system of aesthetics can have no objective validity. It must be replied that any system of aesthetics which pretends to be based on some objective truth is so palpably ridiculous as not to be worth discussing. We have no other means of recognizing a work of art than our feeling for it. The objects that provoke aesthetic emotion vary with each individual. Aesthetic judgments are, as the saying goes, matters of taste; and about tastes, as everyone is proud to admit, there is no disputing. A good critic may be able to make me see in a picture that had left me cold things that I had overlooked, till at last, receiving the aesthetic emotion, I recognize it as a work of art. To be continually pointing out those parts, the sum, or rather the combination, of which unite to produce significant form, is the function of criticism. But it is useless for a critic to tell me that something is a work of art; he must make me feel it for myself. This he can do only

---

[4]Sta. (Santa) Sophia is the great Byzantine church/mosque in Istanbul/Constantinople. Originally it was a Christian church built in the sixth century. Later it became a mosque, and it is now a museum. The stained glass windows at the Chartres Cathedral are considered masterpieces of medieval glass. Persian glass has a special quality that may result from having been buried. Giotto's frescoes were painted for the Arena Chapel in Padua. Nicolas Poussin (1594–1665) was the great master of French neoclassical style. Piero della Francesca (1420–1492) was an Italian Renaissance master. Paul Cezanne (1839–1906) transformed modern art by flattening the picture plane, removing realistic perspective.

by making me see; he must get at my emotions through my eyes. Unless he can make me see something that moves me, he cannot force my emotions. I have no right to consider anything a work of art to which I cannot react emotionally; and I have no right to look for the essential quality in anything that I have not *felt* to be a work of art. The critic can affect my aesthetic theories only by affecting my aesthetic experience. All systems of aesthetics must be based on personal experience—that is to say, they must be subjective.

Yet, though all aesthetic theories must be based on aesthetic judgments, and ultimately all aesthetic judgments must be matters of personal taste, it would be rash to assert that no theory of aesthetics can have general validity. For, though A, B, C, D are the works that move me, and A, D, E, F the works that move you, it may well be that x is the only quality believed by either of us to be common to all the works in his list. We may all agree about aesthetics, and yet differ about particular works of art. We may differ as to the presence or absence of the quality x. My immediate object will be to show that significant form is the only quality common and peculiar to all the works of visual art that move me; and I will ask those whose aesthetic experiences does not tally with mine to see whether this quality is not also, in their judgment, common to all works that move them, and whether they can discover any other quality of which the same can be said.

Also at this point a query arises, irrelevant indeed, but hardly to be suppressed: "Why are we so profoundly moved by forms related in a particular way?" The question is extremely interesting, but irrelevant to aesthetics. In pure aesthetics we have only to consider our emotion and its object: for the purposes of aesthetics we have no right, neither is there any necessity, to pry behind the object into the state of mind of him who made it. Later, I shall attempt to answer the question; for by so doing I may be able to develop my theory of the relation of art to life. I shall not, however, be under the delusion that I am rounding off my theory of aesthetics. For a discussion of aesthetics, it need be agreed only that forms arranged and combined according to certain unknown and mysterious laws do move us in a particular way, and that it is the business of an artist so to combine and arrange them that they shall move us in a particular way, and that it is the business of an artist so to combine and arrange them that they shall move us. These moving combinations and arrangements I have called, for the sake of convenience and for a reason that will appear later, "Significant Form."

A third interruption has to be met.

"Are you forgetting about color?" someone inquires. Certainly not; my term "significant form" included combinations of lines and of colors. The distinction between form and color is an unreal one; you cannot conceive a colorless line or a colorless space; neither can you conceive a formless relation of colors. In a black and white drawing the spaces are all white and all are bounded by black lines; in most oil paints the spaces are multi-colored and so are the boundaries; you cannot imagine a boundary line without any content, or a content without a boundary line. Therefore, when I speak of significant form, I mean a combination of lines and colors (counting white and black as colors) that moves me aesthetically.

Some people may be surprised at my not having called this "beauty." Of course, to those who define beauty as "combinations of lines and colors that provoke aesthetic emotion," I willingly concede the right of substituting their word for mine. But most of us, however strict we may be, are apt to apply the epithet "beautiful" to objects that do not provoke that peculiar emotion produced by works of art. Everyone, I suspect, has called a butterfly or a flower beautiful. Does anyone feel the same kind of emotion for a butterfly or a flower that he feels for a cathedral or a picture? Surely, it is not what I call a aesthetic emotion that most of us feel, generally, for natural beauty. I shall suggest, later, that some people may, occasionally, see in nature what we see in art, and feel for her an aesthetic emotion; but I am satisfied that, as a rule, most people feel a very different kind of emotion for birds and flowers and the wings of butterflies from that which they feel for pictures, pots, temples and statues. Why these beautiful things do not move us as works of art move is another, and not an aesthetic, question. For our immediate purpose we have to discover only what quality is common to objects that do move us as works of art. In the last part of this chapter, when I try to answer the question—"Why are we so profoundly moved by some combinations of lines and colors?" I shall hope to offer an acceptable explanation of why we are less profoundly moved by others.

Since we call a quality that does not raise the characteristic aesthetic emotion "Beauty," it would be misleading to call by the same name the quality that does. To make "beauty" the object of the aesthetic emotion, we must give to the word an over-strict and unfamiliar definition. Everyone sometimes uses "beauty" in an unaesthetic sense; most people habitually do so. To everyone, except perhaps here and there an occasional aesthete, the commonest sense of the word is unaesthetic. Of its grosser abuse, patent in our chatter about "beautiful huntin'" and "beautiful shootin'," I need not take account; it would be open to the precious to reply that they never do so abuse it. Besides, here there is no danger of confusion between the aesthetic and the non-aesthetic use; but when we speak of a beautiful woman there is. When an ordinary man speaks of a beautiful woman he certainly does not mean only that she moves him aesthetically; but when an artist calls a withered old hag beautiful he may sometimes mean what he means when he calls a battered torso beautiful. The ordinary man, if he be also a man of taste, will call the battered torso beautiful, but he will not call a withered hag beautiful because, in the matter of women, it is not to the aesthetic quality that the hag may possess, but to some other quality that he assigns the epithet. Indeed, most of us never dream of going for aesthetic emotions to human beings, from whom we ask something very different. This "something," when we find it in a young woman, we are apt to call "beauty." We live in a nice age. With the man-in-the-street "beautiful" is more often than not synonymous with "desirable"; the word does not necessarily connote any aesthetic reaction whatever, and I am tempted to believe that in the minds of many the sexual flavor of the word is stronger than the aesthetic and sensual beauty is not in their case so great as might be supposed. Perhaps there is none; for perhaps they have never had an aesthetic emotion to confuse with their other emotions. The art that they call "beautiful" is generally closely related to the women. A beautiful picture is a photograph of a pretty girl; beautiful music, the music that provokes emotions similar to those provoked by young ladies in musical farces; and beautiful poetry, the poetry that recalls the same emotions felt, twenty years earlier, for the rector's daughter. Clearly the word "beauty" is used to connote the objects of quite distinguishable emotions, and that is a reason for not employing a term which would land me inevitably in confusions and misunderstandings with my readers.

On the other hand, with those who judge it more exact to call these combinations and arrangements of form that provoke our aesthetic emotions, not "significant form," but "significant relations of form," and then try to make the best of two worlds, the aesthetic and the metaphysical, by calling these relations "rhythm," I have no quarrel whatever. Having made it clear that by "significant form" I mean arrangements and combinations that move us in a particular way, I willingly join hands with those who prefer to give a different name to the same thing.

The hypothesis that significant form is the essential quality in a work of art has at least one merit denied to many more famous and more striking—it does help to explain things. We are all familiar with pictures that interest us and excite our admiration, but do not move us as works of art. To this class belongs what I call "Descriptive Painting"—that is, painting in which forms are used not as objects of emotion, but as means of suggesting emotion or conveying information. Portraits of psychological and historical value, topographical works, pictures that tell stories and suggest situations, illustrations of all sorts, belong to this class. That we all recognize the distinction is clear, for who has not said that such and such a drawing was excellent as illustration, but as a work of art worthless? Of course many descriptive pictures possess, amongst other qualities, formal significance, and are therefore works of art: but many more do not. They interest us; they may move us too in a hundred different ways, but they do not move us aesthetically. According to my hypothesis they are not works of art. They leave untouched our aesthetic emotions because it is not their forms but the ideas or information suggested or conveyed by their forms that affect us. . . .

Let no one imagine that representation is bad in itself; a realistic form may be as significant, in its place as part of the design, as an abstract. But if a representative form has value, it is as form, not as representation. The representative element in a work of art may or may not be harmful; always it is irrelevant. For, to appreciate a work of art we need bring with us nothing from life, no knowledge of its ideas and affairs, no familiarity with its emotions. Art transports us from the world of man's activity to a world of aesthetic exaltation. For a moment we are shut off from human interests; our anticipations and memories are arrested; we are lifted above the stream of life. The pure mathematician rapt in his studies knows a state of mind which I take to be similar, if not identical. He feels an emotion for his speculations which arises from no perceived relation between them and the lives of men, but springs, inhuman or super-human, and from the heart of an abstract science. I wonder, sometimes, whether the appreciators of art and of mathematical solutions are not even more closely allied. Before we feel an aesthetic emotion for a combination of forms, do we not perceive intellectually the rightness and necessity of the combination? If we do, it would explain the fact that passing rapidly through a room we recognize a picture to be good, although we cannot say that it has provoked much emotion. We seem to have recognized intellectually the rightness of its forms without staying to fix our attention, and collect, as it were, their emotional significance. If this were so, it would be permissible to inquire whether it was the forms themselves or our perception of their rightness and necessity that caused aesthetic emotion. But I do not think I need linger to discuss the matter here. I have been inquiring why certain combinations of forms move us; I should not have traveled by other roads had I enquired, instead, why certain combinations are perceived to be right and necessary, and why our perception of their rightness and necessity is moving. What I have to say is this: the rapt philosopher, and he who contemplates a work of art, inhabit a world with an intense and peculiar significance of its own; that significance is unrelated to the significance of life. In this world the emotions of life find no place. It is a world with emotions of its own.

To appreciate a work of art we need bring with us nothing but a sense of form and color and a knowledge of three-dimensional space. That bit of knowledge, I admit, is essential to the appreciation of many great works, since many of the most moving forms ever created are in three dimensions. To see a cube or a rhomboid as a flat pattern is to lower its significance, and a sense of three-dimensional space is essential to the full appreciation of most architectural forms. Pictures which would be insignificant if we saw them as flat patterns are profoundly moving because, in fact, we see them as related planes. If the representation of three-dimensional space is to be called "representation," then I agree that there is one kind of representation which is not irrelevant. Also, I agree that along with our feeling for line and color we must bring with us our knowledge of space if we are to make the most of every kind of form. Nevertheless, there are magnificent designs to an appreciation of which this knowledge is not necessary: so, though it is not irrelevant to the appreciation of all. What we must say is that the representation of three-dimensional space is neither irrelevant nor essential to all art, and that every other sort of representation is irrelevant.

That there is an irrelevant representative or descriptive element in many great works of art is not in the least surprising. Why it is not surprising I shall try to show elsewhere. Representation is not of necessity baneful, and highly realistic forms may be extremely significant. Very often, however, representation is a sign of weakness in an artist. A painter too feeble to create forms that provoke more than a little aesthetic emotion will try to eke that little out by suggesting the emotions of life. To evoke the emotions of life he must use representation. Thus a man will pain an execution, and, fearing to miss with his first barrel of significant form, will try to hit with his second by raising an emotion of fear or pity. But if in the artist an inclination to play upon the emotions of life is often the sign of a flickering inspiration, in the spectator a tendency to seek, behind form, the emotions of life is a sign of defective sensibility always. It means that his aesthetic emotions are weak or, at any rate, imperfect. Before a work of art people who feel little or no emotion for pure form find themselves at a loss. They are deaf men at a concert. They know that they are in the presence of something great, but they lack the power of apprehending it. They know that they ought to feel for it a tremendous emotion, but it happens that the particular kind of emotion it can raise is one that they can feel hardly or not at all. And so they read into the forms of the work those facts and ideas for which they are capable of feeling emotion, and feel for them the emotions that they can feel—the ordinary emotions of life. When confronted by a picture, instinctively they refer back its forms to the world from which they came. They treat created form as though it were imitated form, a picture as though it were a photograph. Instead of going out on the stream of art into a new world of aesthetic experience, they turn a sharp corner and come straight home to the world of human interests. For them the significance of a work of art depends on what they bring to it; no new thing is added to their lives, only the old material is stirred. A good work of visual art carries a person who is capable of appreciating it out of life into ecstasy: to use art as a means to the emotions of life is to use a telescope for reading the news. You will notice that people who cannot feel pure aesthetic emotions remember pictures by their subjects; whereas people who can, as often as not, have no idea what the subject of a picture is. They have never noticed the presentative element, and so when they discuss pictures they talk about the shapes of forms and the relations and quantities of colors. Often they can tell by the quality of a single line whether or no a man is a good artist. They are concerned only with lines and colors, their relations and quantities and qualities; but from these they win an emotion more profound and far more sublime than any that can be given by the description of facts and ideas.

This last sentence has a very confident ring—over-confident, some may think. Perhaps I shall be able to justify it, and make my meaning clearer too, if I give an account of my own feelings about music. I am not really musical. I do not understand music well. I find musical form exceedingly difficult to apprehend, and I am sure that the profounder subtleties of harmony and rhythm more often than not escape me. The form of a musical composition must be simple indeed if I am to grasp it honestly. My opinion about music is not worth having. Yet, sometimes, at a concert, though my appreciation of the music is limited and humble, it is pure. Sometimes, though I have a poor understanding, I have a clean palate. Consequently, when I am feeling bright and clear and intent, at the beginning of a concert, for instance, when something that I can grasp is being played, I get from music that pure aesthetic emotion that I get from visual art. It is less intense, and the rapture is evanescent; I understand music too ill for music to transport me far into the world of pure aesthetic ecstasy. But at moments I do appreciate music as pure musical form, as sounds combined according to the laws of a mysterious necessity, as pure art with a tremendous significance of its own and no relation whatever to the significance of life; and in those moments I lose myself in that infinitely sublime state of mind to which pure visual form transports me. How inferior is my normal state of mind at a concert. Tired or perplexed, I let slip my sense of form, my aesthetic emotion collapses, and I begin weaving into the harmonies, that I cannot grasp, the ideas of life. Incapable of feeling the austere emotions of art, I begin to read into the musical forms human emotions of error and mystery, love and hate, and spend the minutes, pleasantly enough in a world of turbid and inferior feeling. At such times, were the grossest pieces of onomatopoeic representation[5]—the song of a bird, the galloping of horses, the cries of children, or the laughing of demons—to be introduced into the symphony, I should not be offended. Very likely I should be pleased; they would afford new points of departure for new trains of romantic feeling or heroic thought. I know very well what has happened. I have been using art as a means to the emotions of life and reading into it the ideas of life. I have been cutting blocks with a razor. I have tumbled from the superb peaks of aesthetic exaltation to the snug foothills of warm humanity. It is a jolly country. No one need be ashamed of enjoying himself there. Only no one who has ever been on the heights can help feeling a little crestfallen in the cozy valleys. And let no one imagine, because he has made merry in the warm tilth and quaint nooks of romance, that he can ever guess at the austere and thrilling raptures of those who have climbed the cold, white peaks of art.

About music most people are as willing to be humble as I am. If they cannot grasp musical form and win from it a pure aesthetic emotion they confess that they understand music imperfectly or not at all. They recognize quite clearly that there is a difference between the feeling of the musician for pure music and that of the cheerful concert-goer for what music suggests. The latter enjoys his own emotions, as he has every right to do, and recognizes their inferiority. Unfortunately, people are apt to be less modest about their powers of appreciating visual art. Everyone is inclined to believe that out of pictures, at any rate, he can get all that there is to be got; everyone is ready to cry "humbug" and "impostor" at those who say that more can be had. The good faith of people who feel pure aesthetic emotions is called in question by those who have never felt

anything of the sort. It is the prevalence of the representative element, I suppose, that makes the man in the street so sure that he knows a good picture when he sees one. For I have noticed that in matters of architecture, potter, textiles, etc., ignorance and ineptitude are more willing to defer to the opinions of those who have been blest with peculiar sensibility. It is a pity that cultivated and intelligent men and women cannot be induced to believe that a great gift of aesthetic appreciation is at least as rare in visual as in musical art. A comparison of my own experience in both has enabled me to discriminate very clearly between pure and impure appreciation. Is it too much to ask that others should be honest about their feelings for pictures as I have been about mine for music? For I am certain that most of those who visit galleries do feel very much what I feel at concerts. They have their moments of pure ecstasy; but the moments are short and unsure. Soon they fall back into the world of human interests and feel emotions, good no doubt, but inferior. I do not dream of saying that what they get from art is bad or nugatory; I say that they do not get the best that art can give. I do not say that they cannot understand art; rather I say that they cannot understand the state of mind of those who understand it best. I do not say that art means nothing or little to them; I say they miss its full significance. I do not suggest for one moment that their appreciation of art is a thing to be ashamed of; the majority of the charming and intelligent people with whom I am acquainted appreciate visual art impurely; and, by the way, the appreciation of almost all great writers has been impure. But provided that there be some fraction of pure aesthetic emotion, even a mixed and minor appreciation of art is, I am sure, one of the most valuable things in the world—so valuable, indeed, that in my giddier moments I have been tempted to believe that art might prove the world's salvation.

Yet, though the echoes and shadows of art enrich the life of the plains, her spirit dwells on the mountains. To him who woos, but woos impurely, she returns enriched what is brought.

---

[5] Onomatopoeic sounds represent by imitation—for example, *bow-wow* for a dog's bark.

Like the sun, she warms the good seed in the good soil and causes it to bring forth good fruit. But only to the perfect lover does she give a new strange gift—a gift beyond all price. Imperfect lovers bring to art and take away the ideas and emotions of their own age and civilization. In twelfth-century Europe a man might have been greatly moved by a Romanesque church[6] and found nothing in a T'ang picture.[7] To a man of a later age Greek sculpture meant much and Mexican nothing, for only to the former could he bring a crowd of associated ideas to be the objects of familiar emotions. But the perfect lover, he who can feel the profound significance of form, is raised above the accidents of time and place. To him the problems of archaeology, history, and hagiography are impertinent. If the forms of a work are significant its provenance is irrelevant. Before the grandeur of those Sumerian figures[8] in the Louvre he is carried on the same flood of emotion to the same aesthetic ecstasy as, more than four thousand years ago, the Chaldean lover was carried.[9] It is the mark of great art that its appeal is universal and eternal. Significant form stands charged with the power to provoke aesthetic emotion in anyone capable of feeling it. The ideas of men go buzz and die like gnats; men change their institutions and their customs as they change their coats; the intellectual triumphs of one age are the follies of another; only great art remains stable and unobscure. Great art remains stable and unobscure because the feelings that it awakens are independent of time and place, because its kingdom is not of this world. To those who have and hold a sense of the significance of form what does it matter whether the forms that

move them were created in Paris the day before yesterday or in Babylon fifty centuries ago? The forms of art are inexhaustible; but all lead by the same road of aesthetic emotion to the same world of aesthetic ecstasy. . . .

II: The Metaphysical Hypothesis

I want now to consider that metaphysical question—"Why do certain arrangements and combinations of form move us so strangely?" For aesthetics it suffices that they do move us; to all further inquisition of the tedious and stupid it can be replied that, however queer these things may be, they are no queerer than anything else in this incredibly queer universe. But to those for whom my theory seems to open a vista of possibilities I willingly offer, for what they are worth, my fancies.

It seems to me possible, though by no means certain, that created form moves us so profoundly because it expresses the emotion of its creator. Perhaps the lines and colors of a work of art convey to us something that the artist felt. If this be so, it will explain that curious but undeniable fact, to which I have already referred, that what I call material beauty (e.g. the wing of a butterfly) does not move most of us in at all the same way as a work of art moves us. It is beautiful form, but it is not significant form. It moves us, but it does not move us aesthetically. It is tempting to explain the difference between "significant form" and "beauty"—that is to say, the difference between form that provokes our aesthetic emotions and form that does not—by saying that significant form conveys to us an emotion felt by its creator and that beauty conveys nothing.

For what, then does the artist feel the emotion that he is supposed to express? Sometimes it certainly comes to him through material beauty. The contemplation of natural objects is often the immediate cause of the artist's emotion. Are we to suppose, then, that the artist feels or sometimes feels, for material beauty what we feel for a work of art? Can it be that sometimes for the artist material beauty is somehow significant—that is, ca-

---

[6] Romanesque architecture, which prevailed from the eleventh to the thirteenth centuries in Europe, produced massive churches with Roman-style rounded arches.

[7] The T'ang dynasty in China lasted from 618 to 906. Its art was noted for sculpture, particularly of horses, and for painting.

[8] Sumerian civilization arose in the third millennium B.C.E. The figures Bell refers to are found in the French museum, the Louvre, in Paris.

[9] Chaldea was the region in southern Mesopotamia that is sometimes taken to include Babylonia.

pable of provoking aesthetic emotion? And if the form that provokes aesthetic emotion be form that expresses something, can it be that material beauty is to him expressive? All these are questions about which I had sooner speculate than dogmatize.

Let us hear what the artists have got to say for themselves. We readily believe them when they tell us that, in fact, they do not create works of art in order to provoke our aesthetic emotions, but because only thus can they materialize a particular kind of feeling. What, precisely, this feeling is they find it hard to say. One account of the matter, given me by a very good artist, is that what he tries to express in a picture is "a passionate apprehension of form." I have set myself to discover what is meant by "a passionate apprehension of form," and, after much talking and more listening, I have arrived at the following result. Occasionally when an artist—a real artist—looks at objects (the contents of a room, for instance) he perceives them as pure forms in certain relations to each other, and feels emotion for them as such. These are his moments of inspiration: follows the desire to express what has been felt. The emotion that artist felt in his moment of inspiration he did not feel for objects seen as means, but for objects seen as pure forms—that is, as ends in themselves. He did not feel emotion for a chair as a means to physical well-being, nor as an object associated with the intimate life of a family, nor as the place where someone sat saying things unforgettable, nor yet as a thing bound to the lives of hundreds of men and women, dead or alive, by a hundred subtle ties; doubtless an artist does often feel emotions such as these for the things that he sees, but in the moment of aesthetic vision he sees objects, not as means shrouded in associations, but as pure forms. It is for, or at any rate through, pure form that he feels his inspired emotion.

Now to see objects as pure forms is to see them as ends in themselves. For though, of course, forms are related to each other as parts of a whole, they are related on terms of equality; they are not a means to anything except emotion. But for ob-

jects seen as ends in themselves, do we not feel a profounder and a more thrilling emotion than ere we felt for them as means? All of us, I imagine, do, from time to time, get a vision of material objects as pure forms. We see things as ends in themselves, that is to say; and at such moments it seems possible, and even probable, that we see them with the eye of an artist. Who has not, once at least in his life, had a sudden vision of landscape as pure form? For once, instead of seeing it as fields and cottages, he has felt it as lines and colors. In that moment has he not won from material beauty a thrill indistinguishable from that which art gives? And, if this be so, is it not clear that he has won from material beauty the thrill that, generally, art alone can give, because he has contrived to see it as a pure formal combination of lines and colors? May we go on to say that, having seen it as pure form, having freed it from all casual and adventitious interest, from all that it may have acquired from its commerce with human beings, from all its significance as a means, he has felt its significance as an end in itself?

What is the significance of anything as an end in itself? What is that which is left when we have stripped a thing of all its associations, of all its significance as a means? What is left to provoke our emotion? What but that which philosophers used to call "the thing in itself" and now call "ultimate reality"? Shall I be altogether fantastic in suggesting, what some of the profoundest thinkers have believed, that the significance of the thing in itself is the significance of Reality? Is it possible that the answer to my question, "Why are we so profoundly moved by certain combinations of lines and colors?" should be, "Because artists can express in combinations of lines and colors an emotion felt for reality which reveals itself through line and color"?

If this suggestion were accepted it would follow that "significant form" was form behind which we catch a sense of ultimate reality. There would be good reason for supposing that the emotions which artists feel in their moments of inspiration, that others feel in the rare moments when they see objects artistically, and that many of us feel when we contemplate works of art, are the same in kind. All would be emotions felt for reality revealing itself through pure form. It is certain that this emotion can be expressed only in pure form. It is certain that most of us can come at it only through pure form. But is pure form the only channel through which anyone can come at this mysterious emotion? That is a disturbing and a most distasteful question, for at this point I thought I saw my way to canceling out the word "reality," and saying that all are emotions felt for pure form which may or may not have something behind it. To me it would be most satisfactory to say that the reason why some forms move us aesthetically, and others do not, is that some have been so purified that we can feel them aesthetically and that others are so clogged with unaesthetic matter (e.g. associations) that only the sensibility of an artist can perceive their pure, formal significance. I should be charmed to believe that it is as certain that everyone must express his sense of it in form. But is that so? What kind of form is that from which the musician draws the emotion that he expresses in abstract harmonies? Whence come the emotions of the architect and the potter? I know that the artist's emotion can be expressed only in form; I know that only by form can my aesthetic emotions be called into play; but can I be sure that it is always by form that an artist's emotion is provoked? Back to reality.

Those who incline to believe that the artist's emotion is felt for reality will readily admit that visual artists—with whom alone we are concerned—come at reality generally through material form. But don't they come at it sometime through imagined form? And ought we not to add that sometimes the sense of reality comes we know not whence? . . .

Certainly, in those moments of exaltation that art can give, it is easy to believe that we have been possessed by an emotion that comes from the world of reality. Those who take this view will have to say that there is in all things the stuff out of which art is made—reality; artists, even, can grasp it only when they have reduced things to

their purest condition of being—to pure form—unless they be of those who come at it mysteriously unaided by externals; only in pure form can a sense of it be expressed. On this hypothesis the peculiarity of the artist would seem to be that he possesses the power of surely and frequently seizing reality (generally behind pure form), and the power of expressing his sense of it, in pure form always. But many people, though they feel the tremendous significance of form, feel also a cautious dislike of big words; and "reality" is a very big one. These prefer to say that what the artist surprises behind form, or seizes by sheer force of imagination, is the all-pervading rhythm that informs all things; and I have said that I will never quarrel with that blessed word "rhythm."

The ultimate object of the artist's emotion will remain for ever uncertain. But, unless we assume at all artists are liars, I think we must suppose that they do feel an emotion which they can express in form—and form alone. . . .

What, then, is the conclusion of the whole matter? No more than this, I think. The contemplation of pure form leads to as state of extraordinary exaltation and complete detachment from the concerns of life: of so much, speaking for myself, I am sure. It is tempting to suppose that the emotion which exalts has been transmitted through the forms we contemplate by the artist who created them. If this be so, the transmitted emotion, whatever it may be, must be of such a kind that it can be expressed in any sort of form—in pictures, sculptures, buildings, pots, textiles, etc., etc. Now the emotion that artists express comes to some of them, so they tell us, from the apprehension of the formal significance of material things; and the formal significance of any material thing is the significance of that thing considered as an end in itself. But if an object considered as an end in itself moves us more profoundly (i.e. has greater significance) than the same object considered as a means to practical ends or as a thing related to human interests—and this undoubtedly is the case—we can only suppose that when we consider anything as an end in itself we become aware of that in it which is of greater moment than any qualities it may have acquired form keeping company with human beings. Instead of recognizing its accidental and conditioned importance, we become aware of its essential reality, of the God in everything, of the universal in the particular, of the all-pervading rhythm. Call it by what name you will, the thing that I am talking about is that which lies behind the appearance of all things—that which gives to all things their individual significance, the thing in itself, the ultimate reality. And if a more or less unconscious apprehension of this latent reality of material things be, indeed, the cause of that strange emotion, a passion to express which is the inspiration of many artists, it seems reasonable to suppose that those who, unaided by material objects, experience the same emotion have come by another road to the same country.

That is the metaphysical hypothesis. Are we to swallow it whole, accept a part of it, or reject it altogether? Each must decide for himself. I insist only on the rightness of my aesthetic hypothesis. And of one other thing am I sure. Be they artists or lovers of art, mystics or mathematicians, those who achieve ecstasy are those who have freed themselves from the arrogance of humanity. He who would feel the significance of art must make himself humble before it. Those who find the chief importance of art or of philosophy in its relation to conduct or its practical utility—those who cannot value things as ends in themselves or, at any rate, as direct means to emotion—will never get from anything the best that it can give. What ever the world of aesthetic contemplation may be, it is not the world of human business and passion; in it the chatter and tumult of material existence is unheard, or heard only as the echo of some more ultimate harmony.

Study Questions

1. What is the necessary condition for aesthetic experience?
2. Is everyone equally able to have aesthetic experiences?
3. Is it possible to know what art is on the basis of someone else's description?
4. What is the common quality that all art possesses?
5. How is significant form recognized? Give examples.
6. Give Bell's argument that the subjective nature of aesthetic experience does not invalidate the claim that there are aesthetic qualities.
7. Can natural objects have significant form?
8. Can representational objects have significant form?
9. What is difference between "emotions of life" and aesthetic emotions?
10. Is representation bad?
11. What is necessary for the appreciation of art?
12. If two people disagree about whether some painting has significant form, how can their disagreement be settled?
13. Why does Bell reject the term *beauty*?
14. What is the difference between Bell's aesthetic hypothesis and his metaphysical hypothesis?
15. What significance does the metaphysical hypothesis assign to the artist?
16. What state results from the contemplation of pure form?
17. Bell is sometimes accused of being elitist. If he is, what is the basis for his elitism? Who are the elite?

Section 3   Passages for Discussion

❖ ❖

We have now reached our definition of beauty, which, in the terms of our successive analysis and narrowing of the conception, is value positive, intrinsic, and objectified. Or, in less technical language, Beauty is pleasure regarded as the quality of a thing.

GEORGE SANTAYANA (1863–1952), *The Sense of Beauty*

Art always aims at what is *individual*. . . . We may, indeed, give general names to these feelings, but they cannot be the same thing in another soul. They are individualized. Thereby, and thereby only, do they belong to art; for generalities, symbols or even types, form the current coin of our daily perception.

HENRI BERGSON (1859–1941), *Laughter*

Suppose a tribe or a nation has won a great victory; "they are feeling big, and they want to make something big," as I have heard an expert say. That, I take it, is the rough account of the beginning of the esthetic attitude. And according to their capacity and their stage of culture, they may make a pile of their enemies' skulls, or they may build the Parthenon. The point of the esthetic attitude lies in the adequate fusion of body and soul, where the soul is a feeling, and the body its expression, without residue on either side.

BERNARD BOSANQUET (1848–1923), *Three Lectures on Aesthetics*

PART THREE

Aesthetics in the Twentieth Century

Aesthetics in the first half of the twentieth century was built on the foundation laid by Kant and developed by various theories of an aesthetic attitude or aesthetic experience. Its fundamental tenets are that the aesthetic is a domain of experience, and its fundamental problems are centered around how that domain is to be marked off and what its properties and role are. The fundamental problem of defining *work of art* is approached in terms of what is understood as the more basic problem of defining aesthetic experience. The positions represented in this anthology by Bullough, Bell, and Croce explore psychological, formal, and epistemological approaches to those fundamental problems. Although they take us up to World War I, they may be regarded as belonging to an extended nineteenth century.

Up to this point, one might expect fairly wide agreement about what are the central positions, the classic essays, or at least representative samples of significant positions. As we move to more recent aesthetic philosophy, however, the status of the discipline and of particular representatives of it becomes less clear. One cannot and should not expect the same kind of agreement among participants in the debates about what is most important. Issues are still very much in contention, and it is the nature of philosophy to move forward (if philosophy does move forward) only after extended discussion and defense of positions. It would be exceedingly presumptuous to select a small number of representative essays from the second half of the twentieth century while the discussion is still ongoing. Nevertheless, I will offer four essays, not as definitive of the state of aesthetics, but as an introduction to the current situation. They represent changes in our basic understanding of what aesthetics is all about and thus alternative possible ways that we may look forward.

♦ ♦ ♦ ♦ ♦ ♦ ♦

Two approaches to identifying aesthetic experience were prominent in the first half of the twentieth century. A number of writers follow the path laid down by Edward Bullough and consider the problem from the standpoint of the observer or audience. On this view, everything is potentially aesthetic, but a special skill is required to achieve the perceptual point of view that provides aesthetic experience. The individual observer is in control. The most common form of theory of this type utilizes concepts of an aesthetic attitude that reach back well into the nineteenth century and perhaps earlier. Initially, an aesthetic attitude was understood simply as descriptive. It marked off the state of the perceptive, cultured members of the audience from those who were more distracted. Lower classes, whose existence was preoccupied with survival, had no time for such aesthetic pursuits. In the work of a number of later theorists, an aesthetic attitude becomes a more active psychological state. In this sense, an aesthetic attitude is cultivated and is productive of aesthetic experience. For example, Virgil Aldrich claims in *Philosophy of Art* that "There is another access to material things—as objective in its own way as the observational is in its way—that the mind may take as prehending subject."[1] By voluntarily choosing this alternative form of perception, the objects "prehended"—which Aldrich describes as an impressionistic way of looking—become aesthetic objects and thus productive of aesthetic experience. Such prehension could apply to any object. The artist cultivates and communicates such an attitude, but everyone can opt for the aesthetic instead of the ordinary mode of perception.

If sensibility is required for aesthetic perception, the aesthetic attitude may not be equally accessible to everyone. This alternative still maintains that aesthetic experience is a product of an attitude, but it locates the production of that experience in the ability to sustain the attitude, a skill either inherited or acquired only by artists and sensitive audiences. The position need not be elitist since sensibility is often found in less educated people whose sensibility has not been overlaid with artificial rules and strictures. Just before the turn of the century, George Santayana claimed in *The Sense of Beauty* that "moments of inspiration are the source of the arts, which have no higher function than to renew them."[2] This recalls the romantic theories that art and aesthetic expression are special forms. The romantic form of an attitude theory remains influential, though it tends to appeal more to artists and aesthetes than to philosophers, who are trained to analyze language and evidence. Elements of many of the classical alternatives persist in attitude theories.

A significant alternative to attitude theories in the twentieth century developed around the work of John Dewey. Dewey's form of pragmatism continued to emphasize experience, so it belongs to the main line of Anglo-American aesthetic thought. But those who followed Dewey's line of thought emphasized a more holistic form of experience. If experience itself is not divided into discrete "moments" of perception, then aesthetic experience is not an attitude that modifies perception of such moments. Instead, aesthetic experience is located in the qualities of experience that are immediately evident when anyone is experiencing the world without theoretical bias. Dewey distinguished between experience and *an* experience.[3] *An* experience is an ordered, emergent phenomenon, and it is always "aesthetic." In many ways, this view serves the same purpose as an attitude theory because it distinguishes aesthetic experience from more ordinary forms, and, like an attitude theory, it allows virtually any object that is experienced to appear in an aesthetic form. However, for Dewey the separation of aesthetic

---

[1] Virgil Aldrich, *The Philosophy of Art* (Englewood Cliffs, NJ: Prentice-Hall, 1963), p. 23.
[2] George Santayana, *The Sense of Beauty* (New York: Dover, 1955 [1896]), p. 262.
[3] John Dewey, *Art as Experience* (New York: Capricorn Books, 1958 [1934]), p. 35.

experience from ordinary experience is only a matter of how experience appears to us. Ordinary experience is unexamined. Aesthetic experience has an immediacy that makes it felt consciously as present. In aesthetic attitude theories, this experience would be private. I would have it by myself and in isolation from my other ways of seeing and thinking. Dewey's approach to aesthetics is more communitarian and less isolating than typical attitude theories. I do not have experiences privately; my experience is always part of some larger whole. My experience is continuous with my past and future and with the experiences of others whom I encounter. Dewey's influence continues to be felt, particularly in aesthetic education.

Anglo-American aesthetics in the first half of the twentieth century remained fundamentally essentialist about the nature of art. Philosophers wanted definitions that would make clear distinctions between art and nonart or aesthetic experience and ordinary experience. Even if the dominant aesthetic theories focused on aesthetic experience and how it might be achieved, those theories still held that art was a unique form that could be defined. The usual way to approach such definitions was to look for some quality or set of qualities that all art had (a necessary condition such that if x is art, x has that quality) and only art had (a sufficient condition such that if x has that quality, then x is art). Necessary and sufficient conditions apply to language; they are conditions for the application of the term art to objects of experience. Thus philosophy of art was closely related to philosophy of language.

The simplest form of definition referred back to the fundamental concept of aesthetic experience: a work of art is any artifact specifically designed to produce aesthetic experience or converted to that use (since utilitarian and religious objects can be art even if they were not designed as art). As a definition, this one is quite vague since it does not specify what aesthetic experience is or how it can be recognized. Philosophers expended considerable ingenuity on attempts to make the definition more descriptive and theoretically significant. Among the more influential attempts were Susanne K. Langer's definition of art as the creation of forms symbolic of human feeling[4] and R. G. Collingwood's adaptation of Croce's idealism into a definition of art as the expression[5] (as opposed to the arousal or betrayal) of emotion. Such definitions embody theory in much the same way that physics embodies theory in its definitions of such concepts as force and energy. Theoretical definitions of this type provide the center for much of the most interesting work in aesthetics during the first half of the century.

Theories of aesthetic experience usually devalue criticism. In some cases, the hostility is open; a critical attitude is felt to interfere with achieving an aesthetic attitude. In other cases, criticism just becomes irrelevant. Since the experience is the important thing, critical judgments are beside the point. Aesthetic experience is most often understood as a pleasant emotion. Critical judgment requires intellectual discrimination. At best, it will be preliminary to the felt emotion; at worst, it will conflict with the emotion by occupying the perceiver in the wrong way. However, in both the visual and literary arts, a powerful formalist criticism developed in the first half of the twentieth century. The watchword of this critical approach was attention to the text or object itself, and it insisted on the priority of internal form over external cultural, historical,

[4] Susanne Langer, *Feeling and Form* (New York: Charles Scribner's Sons, 1953), pp. 59–60.
[5] R. G. Collingwood, *The Principles of Art* (New York: Oxford University Press; Galaxy Books, 1958 [1938]), p. 275.

biographical, and psychological information about the art object or text. So students were taught to look closely at formal details of paintings, for example, and not to make too much of the work as social commentary, biographical information, or something with a religious function. In literature, internal relations of the part to the whole, particularly rhetorical features such as irony and metaphor, were considered more important than the author's intentions or the cultural context of the work.

Formalist criticism provided the basis for an alternative approach to aesthetic theory. In an influential text and a number of essays, Monroe Beardsley proposed to treat aesthetics as a form of *metacriticism*.[6] By this, Beardsley meant that the critical canons of the New Criticism (as the critical movement came to be called when it applied to literature) were themselves aesthetic principles subject to analytical ordering and discipline. The properties of unity and complexity by which the critic is able to assess the structure and value of a text are also the properties that are productive of aesthetic experience, Beardsley argued. The properties being judged critically are perceptual properties in a broad sense of perception that distinguishes perceptual experience from an awareness of the source and end of the object. We can only know about the source and goals of art by thinking about the past and future of its production. We can have a perceptual experience by paying close attention to what is in front of us. Aesthetics, on this understanding, is a modest discipline that aids the critic who in turn aids the audience and the artist in focusing on the perceptual properties. Beardsley's theory follows eighteenth- and nineteenth-century models in many ways, since it still takes aesthetic experience to be an intrinsically valuable and pleasurable emotional form. But Beardsley succeeded in making a place for the intellectual analysis of art that other forms of traditional Anglo-American aesthetics lost.

The fundamental essentialism of Anglo-American aesthetics came under increasing attack after 1950. One part of the attack was a direct criticism of the theoretical definitions philosophers had offered. New art forms arose at a dizzying pace. The avant garde in all its forms shattered any pretensions philosophers had of being able to encompass art within the confines of necessary and sufficient conditions. A second part of the attack was on the nature of theoretical definitions themselves. Unlike their scientific counterparts, theoretical definitions in aesthetics have neither predictive nor constructive value. Increasingly, critical analysis showed them to be concealed forms of persuasion.

A major influence in the turn away from essentialism in aesthetics was the work of Ludwig Wittgenstein.[7] Wittgenstein's work broke down the traditional "philosopher's problems" about the existence of an external world and certainty in knowledge by relocating them in the context of the practical use of language. One consequence of this refocusing of philosophy was to call attention to the way language is used as a more significant clue to its meaning than definitions. The kinds of definitions that earlier aestheticians sought are rare and have only a limited technical use. If we want to understand art, therefore, we must look to the practice of artists and audiences.

---

[6] Monroe Beardsley, *Aesthetics* (New York: Harcourt, Brace & World, 1958), p. 4.

[7] Wittgenstein's most influential work is his *Philosophical Investigations,* trans. G. E. M. Anscombe (New York: Macmillan, 1953). Wittgenstein's ideas on aesthetics come from his students' notes, published in Ludwig Wittgenstein, *Lectures and Conversations on Aesthetics, Psychology, and Religious Belief* (Berkeley: University of California Press, 1972).

Two powerful critiques of traditional aesthetics emerged in the mid-century. Both have their roots in the earlier history of aesthetics and in the practice of art, but they gained new force as experimental forms and philosophical criticism combined to dissolve the established theories. First, it was argued that "taste" concepts are independent of rules.[8] Aesthetic language uses predicates such as *is elegant* and *is graceful.* That language refers directly to perception and experience, making both the critic and the philosopher equally irrelevant. The only function for critics is to point out things that other people might miss. Philosophers of art are limited to removing critical confusions and demolishing exaggerated claims for aesthetic standards. Aesthetic theory is reduced to a kind of therapy for linguistic confusion. Second, some kinds of games do not have fixed rules; they are open to variations and improvisation. Art is like those games. It has a set of common practices, but it also has borderline cases that blur into other practices.[9] Art is orderly, but its rules apply only within a limited sphere located within a larger practice. No sharp boundaries can be drawn around such shifting practices, nor should we want them. Art on this view is an expanding form of life related to culture. This approach has the clear advantage of accounting for the diversity of art forms. It is open and nonjudgmental. But it relinquishes any philosophical basis for judgment and in some writers produces one of the many forms of cultural relativism that characterize much recent philosophy.

More recently, many of the insights of analytical aesthetics have been developed in a new direction. Even if art lacks essential properties, a great deal may be said by way of defining the field. Definitions may specify the kind of properties that depend on how one thing is related to another. The essential properties of being someone's child are genetic; the properties of being a citizen are created by establishing relations that can be granted. Relational properties can identify artistic practice and distinguish it from other practices. Aesthetics done in this way has a close connection with actual artistic and critical practice. For example, the kind of metacriticism advocated by Beardsley has been modified by George Dickie so that not just the critic but the practices of the art world as a whole—artists, critics, and ordinary consumers—define what will be included in aesthetics.[10] Other work along these lines focuses on the constructive role of theory in the production of art and aesthetic response. In a somewhat different vein, Richard Wollheim has emphasized the interaction of art as a form of life with other life forms.[11]

A common thread running through this work is its rejection of the earlier identification of aesthetics as a unique kind of experience.[12] Aesthetics is identified with a practice rather than with theoretically or experientially defined areas of experience. Practices change. They are added to, and they lose some functions. Later readers and viewers may be able to recover earlier forms by learning their "languages," but that does not imply that anyone will be able to adopt the practice in a productive way. Aesthetics understood in this way requires neither systems nor special knowledge, but it does

---

[8] Frank Sibley, "Aesthetic Concepts," *The Philosophical Review* 68 (1959): 421–450.

[9] See, for example, the essay by Morris Weitz on pp. 298–306.

[10] George Dickie, *Aesthetics: An Institutional Analysis* (Ithaca, NY: Cornell University Press, 1975) and *The Art Circle* (New York: Haven, 1984).

[11] Richard Wollheim, *Art and Its Objects* (New York: Harper and Row, 1968).

[12] See the essay by George Dickie on pp. 310–321.

require participation either as an audience or as a producer. Thus, such an aesthetics is antitheoretical in an oddly theoretical way. Theory functions only descriptively, not normatively.

Two other developments along these lines should be noted. A different adaptation of Wittgensteinian themes combined them with the work of the English philosopher J. L. Austin to locate aesthetic practice even more centrally within the context of cultural practice and language.[13] Cultural artifacts such as film both shape culture and are shaped by it. They do not stand apart for inspection by independent audiences but draw us into their own practice. At the same time, they are not independent artifacts but a part of the language of our culture. The aesthetician can only comment on film by viewing film and becoming part of the audience. The language of film and of philosophy overlap in this way of doing aesthetics, and the same must apply by extension to other art forms. Philosophers are not simply audience members. By virtue of their philosophical sophistication, they bring to art questions that other participants only implicitly understand. By being part of the audience, they also change the conditions for art. At its best, this kind of cultural aesthetics produces a dense but engaging encounter with the material of aesthetics. However, it can become introspective in obscure ways.

A divergence between Anglo-American aesthetics and continental European aesthetics becomes marked only in the twentieth century. Clear differences existed earlier. British aesthetics tended to remain closer to its empiricist roots. But such founders of British aesthetics as the Earl of Shaftesbury had a more significant reputation in Germany in the nineteenth century than they retained in England. Parallel developments in idealism on the continent and in Britain after Kant shifted aesthetic preeminence to continental writers.

An important twentieth-century movement in continental aesthetics is Marxism. Twentieth-century Marxism is anti-Hegelian. It arises out of the same historical context as other reactions against Hegelian forms of aesthetics that developed out of the work of the Danish theologian-philosopher Søren Kierkegaard, the materialist philosophy of Ludwig Feuerbach, the Platonic idealism of Arthur Schopenhauer, and Friedrich Nietzsche's radical dialectic. Hegelian aesthetics believed ideas were absolute, real forms. Marxists believed only material forms were real. Hegelian aesthetics saw history as a movement of Absolute spirit. Marxists believed history was moved by economic forces. The influence of Marx also challenged belief in a unique aesthetic experience as one more form of cultural hegemony.[14] Escape into aesthetic pleasure is escape from the reality of economic and material life. Moreover, such escape is at once the privilege of a few and a means of concealing the true conditions of our lives. Like religion, aesthetic experience is a means of controlling a portion of a class that might otherwise be moved to revolution. So Marxism mounted one of the first and most powerful attacks on the basic principles of modern aesthetics. Art was viewed by Marxists as one more part of the struggle to achieve the historical equality toward which we are being drawn inexorably.

---

[13] See, for example, the works of Stanley Cavell, such as *Must We Mean What We Say?* (New York: Charles Scribner's Sons, 1969).

[14] A useful collection of essays from the Marxist perspective can be found in Lee Baxandall, *Radical Perspectives in the Arts* (Baltimore: Penguin Books, 1972).

Marxist aesthetics is not uniformly and drearily political. Aesthetics in this tradition discloses the fundamental ways that political, economic, and cultural conditions are encoded into works of art. Critics as well as artists are a part of this process, and a philosopher of aesthetics is a cultural critic as well. The actual result can take many forms, including psychological criticism and formalism. Some of the most penetrating criticisms of the movements in American abstract art are from a formalist-Marxist perspective.[15] What unites these approaches is their concern that art not be divorced from its cultural roots and that it be defended against the exploitive tendencies of commercial capitalism.[16]

At the beginning of the twentieth century, continental philosophy was shaped by the seminal phenomenological work of Edmund Husserl. Phenomenology is a form of analysis of the "content of consciousness." Since everyone thinks, thought can be analyzed without having to decide questions about what is and is not real. Husserl proposed a method of analysis that he called *reduction,* that has stimulated a school of phenomenological analysis. Husserl had little to say about aesthetics, but several of his followers turned to aesthetics as one area for analysis. The Polish phenomenologist Roman Ingarden is among the most prominent investigators of art and the aesthetic in the phenomenological tradition. He subjected each aspect of literary aesthetics to analysis. Ingarden's approach was to identify and describe each element in the conscious apprehension of a work of literary art. From the side of the subject, he described aesthetic experience. From the side of the object, he described the objective content of aesthetic experience. Neither is merely introspective or subjective; each has formal features that are common to the structure of conscious apprehension.[17] Thus a phenomenological approach to aesthetics shares something with its Kantian heritage. It differs in that it seeks a direct analytical presentation of the structure of aesthetic consciousness rather than the Kantian transcendental, *a priori* structures. Phenomenology also is influential in French philosophy, particularly in the work Mikel Dufrenne.[18]

Equally importantly, phenomenology is developed by two students of Husserl, Martin Heidegger[19] and Jean-Paul Sartre,[20] into competing forms of the movement known as existentialism. Whereas phenomenology claims to be primarily a neutral, analytical movement, existentialism denies that consciousness can be separated from the existence of the person who is conscious. In aesthetics, in one way or another, art and literature are conscious forms that belong to radically historical moments. Aesthetics is neither the distanced, disinterested realm of Kantian aesthetics nor the culturally deterministic element of Marxist aesthetics. Instead, aesthetics is an activity of consciousness. Kierkegaard and Nietzsche are in the background, but for both the Heideggerian and Sartrian forms of existential aesthetics, aesthetic experience, particularly as it is realized through art, is a form of experience that cannot be fixed. Every experience changes with every moment, and memory is nothing more than another present experience that

---

[15] Clement Greenberg, *Art and Culture* (Boston: Beacon Press, 1961).

[16] See, for example, Terry Eagleton, *The Ideology of the Aesthetic* (Oxford: Basil Blackwell, 1991).

[17] Roman Ingarden, *The Literary Work of Art* (Evanston, IL: Northwestern University Press, 1973).

[18] Mikel Dufrenne, *The Phenomenology of Aesthetic Experience* (Evanston, IL: Northwestern University Press, 1973).

[19] See, for example, Martin Heidegger, *The Origin of the Work of Art* (Chicago: University of Chicago Press, 1976). Heidegger's major work is *Being and Time.*

[20] Jean-Paul Sartre, *What Is Literature?* (New York: Philosophical Library, 1949). Sartre's major work is *Being and Nothingness.*

is always changing. Consciousness shapes itself in confrontation with its own contingency. Because both Heidegger and Sartre began as phenomenologists, they produced systematic explanations of how consciousness is located in its own field of awareness that have direct bearing on aesthetics. In their later work, they both moved away from systematic analysis to more evocative and literary forms as the only appropriate philosophical response to the contingency of consciousness. Heidegger found in poetry the form of expression by which "Being" is able to appear in consciousness. Sartre turned to novels and plays to make his philosophy concrete.

A related continental movement, *hermeneutics,* has its roots in the theories of biblical interpretation developed by German theologians going back to the eighteenth century. Hermeneutics emerged in the latter half of the twentieth century as a comprehensive theory of interpretation in the phenomenological-existentialist tradition.[21] The fundamental aesthetic insight of hermeneutics is that any encounter with art must involve a confrontation of a subject and a text in a way that modifies both. When I, as viewer or reader or hearer, encounter an aesthetic object, I bring it into my already structured experience and modify that experience by what I bring into it. The aesthetic object is also modified, however. It is now something that has been interpreted by me, and my interpretation potentially becomes part of it. For example, when a play by Shakespeare is performed, each new performance adds to the meaning of the play by providing a new way that the play has been interpreted. Thus every aesthetic experience is a complex modification of the being of both object and text. Hermeneutics is aware of history as a major part of this encounter; so aesthetic experience is never purely subjective as it is in traditional and existential aesthetics, but it cannot be independent and unique, either. Thus audience and object move in an interpretive circle in which interpretation is constantly changing but is controlled by its past.

Continental aesthetics in the tradition of phenomenological, existential, and hermeneutical theories is quite diverse and flexible in the way it deals with specific art forms. It is open to avant-garde movements, and it is deeply historicist in that history itself is a fundamental context. But even in its beginnings, it remained essentially descriptive. The traditional questions of Anglo-American aesthetics—What is art? and How is aesthetic experience to be identified?—were either bypassed or presumed to have been answered already by Kant. Kant's influence is so strong that everyone has a tendency to take "aesthetic experience" as a given or, alternatively, to look on any theoretical pronouncements about its nature as part of a dead metaphysics. The fluid world of existentialism and hermeneutics denies the possibility of the kind of philosophizing that seeks criteria of identity.

The logical extension of this fluidity is found in the recent turn to a postexistentialist, poststructuralist aesthetics. Existentialism made everything depend on a particular time and a particular place. Structuralism was a way of analyzing cultures that developed in anthropology. No time or place was privileged, so cultures had to be examined by looking at how they structured their activities and relations. Poststructuralists concluded that the observer could not claim to be neutral, so all analysis of culture occurs

---

[21] Hans Georg Gadamer, *The Relevance of the Beautiful and Other Essays* (New York: Cambridge University Press, 1986); Paul Ricoeur, *The Conflict of Interpretations: Essays in Hermeneutics* (Evanston, IL: Northwestern University Press, 1974).

from a shifting, involved point of view. Play has long been an important category in continental aesthetics. Aesthetic experience was understood as free play of the imagination in Kant, and this playfulness was identified as a freedom from the constraints of reality in subsequent neo-Kantian aesthetics. In the poststructuralist aesthetics that developed out of the work of Jacques Derrida[22] play, especially the play of language itself, is the logical outcome of the unavoidable fluidity of the existential encounter of consciousness with its own historical contingency. Aesthetics, in a sense, becomes the detached form of the mind's movement in a world without fixed or absolute forms. Such play is not unmotivated. It remains an intentional act of exploration. But it cannot be restricted to analytical or logical forms because those forms themselves are dissolved in the play of consciousness. If postmodern aesthetics leaves sober philosophical types fuming, so much the better from the point of view of the newly freed aesthetics.

The separation between continental and Anglo-American aesthetics, which was taken for granted for much of the twentieth century, has recently begun to disintegrate. It was always somewhat artificial, given the common roots of aesthetics in the work of Kant and the Romantics. Recent interest in rhetoric, semantics, and historical forms of pragmatism have served to reopen contacts and reintroduce common themes. For example, a writer in the tradition of continental hermeneutics, Paul Ricoeur, draws on analytical philosophy of language in his work on metaphor and the reading of texts. Analytically trained philosophers such as Arthur Danto[23] turn to continental forms of criticism to understand contemporary movements in the arts.

Much recent work focuses directly on cultural phenomena and takes its systematic cue from their concerns. Among the areas of intense interest recently have been environmental aesthetics.[24] The existence of massive art projects in natural settings focuses environmental aesthetics on the role of nature but goes beyond specific works to consider not only their appeal but their sometimes destructive presence. Awareness of the environment and its effects on us returns aesthetics to a sensitivity to nature and our place in it which had been obscured by the emphasis on art. Feminist aesthetics[25] challenges the male-dominated models of art and masculine forms of aesthetic response as well as opening aesthetics to a wider cultural experience. For example, a body of film theory begins with feminist elements in film. It uses psychological insights to distinguish male and female roles. The act of viewing itself has a gender, it is argued. Aesthetics extends those insights to a more comprehensive view of the relation of an audience to a projected image. Cultural studies and the expansion of our understanding of the relations between art and society have opened whole new ranges of texts and deepened our consideration of what is relevant to the formation of aesthetic judgments. The boundaries between art history, music theory, and aesthetics are being crossed in interesting ways. Writers in these areas note that art works create their own context. To

---

[22] Jacques Derrida, *The Truth in Painting* (Chicago: University of Chicago Press, 1987).

[23] See the essay by Arthur Danto on pp. 326–336.

[24] Arnold Berleant, *The Aesthetics of Environment* (Philadelphia: Temple University Press, 1992). Arnold Berleant and Alan Carlson, guest eds., Special Issue: Environmental Aesthetics, *Journal of Aesthetics and Art Criticism* 56, 2 (Spring 1998).

[25] Hilde Hein and Carolyn Korsmeyer, *Aesthetics in Feminist Perspective* (Bloomington: Indiana University Press, 1993); Peggy Zeglin Brand and Carolyn Korsmeyer, guest eds., Special Issue: Feminism and Traditional Aesthetics, *Journal of Aesthetics and Art Criticism* 48, 4 (Fall 1990).

understand such work, an audience must understand the issue and the background upon which their cultural significance rests. Work in these fields proceeds concretely and takes its theoretical cues from the works themselves and from the philosophy which is associated with the movements. In all of these cases, the earlier twentieth-century limitations of the aesthetic to a special realm of contemplation have been left behind. Aesthetics in the Anglo-American tradition has become extremely diverse. Its theoretical shape (if any) remains unclear. Where we will end is not clear, but the journey is likely to stimulate philosophers in ways that we cannot presently anticipate.

In the context of this anthology, it is impossible to represent all of the currents in contemporary aesthetics. They are too diverse, and the process of debate and the inevitable sorting that philosophical debate implies is ongoing. I have chosen, therefore, to look forward from the end of the extended nineteenth century in a very limited way by presenting four influential essays that can be taken as representing turning points in aesthetics in the mid-twentieth century. One, by Walter Benjamin, comes from the Marxist tradition, but it is by no means doctrinaire. It has a strong historical awareness and shares much with hermeneutics in its awareness of the way that culture changes the context in which works of art are available to an audience. The second, by Morris Weitz, was a seminal adaptation of Wittgenstein's insights about language to the problems of aesthetics. The third, by George Dickie, directly confronts the earlier dependence on an aesthetic attitude and argues that such an attitude is itself a "myth"; there is no such thing, and therefore aesthetics must rethink its whole history. Finally, the essay by Arthur Danto combines historical and cultural awareness with the real conditions of what he dubs the "artworld" to reposition aesthetics. No one, including the authors themselves, would maintain that these essays sum up twentieth-century aesthetics. They are, however, ways of opening the door to the contemporary discussion.

Walter Benjamin

$\bullet \quad \bullet \quad \bullet \quad \bullet \quad \bullet \quad \bullet \quad \bullet \quad \bullet \quad \bullet$

WALTER BENJAMIN (1892–1940) was a literary critic and aesthetician associated with what came to be called the Frankfurt school of philosophy. After his doctoral thesis was rejected by the University of Frankfurt, he settled in Berlin, where he wrote criticism. Benjamin fled Germany for Paris when the Nazis came to power in 1933, then tried to escape to Spain when France fell in 1940. He committed suicide to avoid being turned over to the Gestapo.

$\bullet \quad \bullet \quad \bullet \quad \bullet \quad \bullet \quad \bullet$

Walter Benjamin's essay can be regarded as a turning point in the history of aesthetics, not only because of the acuteness of its analysis of a new phase in the history of art, but also because it decisively breaks with the direction that aesthetics had taken at least since the later eighteenth century and the work of Immanuel Kant. Benjamin views art and aesthetics through the lens of history, politics, and economics. He sees art as a part of a larger human world rather than as an autonomous realm of independent value.

Benjamin's overt perspective is that of pre–World War II Marxism. We must be careful not to read our own post-Soviet views of Marxism back onto what Benjamin is saying. Marxism has always had a dual existence—as a political and cultural philosophy and as a quasinationalist political movement in response to western European and American hegemony. As a political and cultural philosophy, Marxism belongs to the tradition of historical analysis that tries to infer larger patterns in the development of society. Its model for thought is the kind of empirical scientific observation that succeeded in the natural sciences, now directed instead toward history and social organizations. It rejects the forms of philosophy of history that looked for some transcendent or ideal overview in favor of a rigorous focus on the material elements of culture. The former are represented in the philosophy of Hegel, who saw history as a movement of "spirit" and viewed cultural manifestations as the product of essentially mental realities. In contrast, Marx and Engels looked to Ludwig Feuerbach, whose materialism was summarized, somewhat misleadingly, in the formula, "We are what we eat": that is, the physical facts of labor and economics take precedence in understanding the movement of history. Marxism shares with its continental opposite, Hegelian idealism, a desire to "read" history as a single movement of forces on the order of the natural forces of science. It differs, however, in seeing that movement as the play not of mental realities and ideas but of the physical and material conditions that are common to and yet divide human beings. Thus *class* as the term is used in Marxism is not simply a social order produced by historical accidents and national differences. It is also an inevitable result of the divisions of labor necessary for the production of goods and services. As long as society is organized along class lines, those divisions must inevitably produce historical tensions that will manifest themselves in economic and cultural phenomena. The role of the Marxist is to analyze those divisions. History itself offers hope for an apocalyptic end to class divisions.

As a political movement, Marxism as we have come to think of it is very different from that kind of analytical philosophy of history and culture. Like most social and political movements, political Marxism seeks to make things happen rather than simply observing and analyzing. In that respect, it has much in common with religious movements. When religion and political theory become wrapped up with national aspirations, the result is no longer philosophy. It becomes a potentially explosive social force in its own right. We can see that effect most clearly now in our own culture, in the fundamentalist religious movements that would transform both society and human nature to their own religious vision. In the 1930s, when Walter Benjamin was writing, Marxism played that role in the aftermath of the cultural and political devastation brought about by World War I. Like the great plagues of the fourteenth and seventeenth centuries, World War I wiped out an economic and political hierarchy that had survived for centuries. Into that chaotic situation, communism in eastern Europe and Russia offered a vision of a new society that could be shaped according to deeply desired ideals. Marxism seemed to offer the philosophical theory to support that political vision in much the same way that biblical literalism offers support for contemporary religious enthusiasm. Benjamin undoubtedly shared some of that vision, and it is reflected in aspects of his essay. It is not, however, the heart of his analysis.

The heart of Benjamin's analysis comes from his understanding of the more basic Marxist insight into the relation of material conditions, economic forces, and the technological possibilities offered by science. Benjamin first observes a basic change in the conditions of productivity that affects not only art but all of society. This change began with the Industrial Revolution and the possibilities opened by the ability to produce by machines large quantities of goods and distribute them widely. That new situation essentially changes the individual production systems based on craftsmanship and guilds. Artists had been members of craft guilds subject to patronage and individual consumers. Now they could become entrepreneurs who could market and distribute their own work. To one who sees art as essentially related to its means of production, that implies that the nature of art itself changes.

The initial change moved art from the largely upper-class arena to a middle-class audience. Plays and novels appealed to a much wider audience than the high art of the Middle Ages and Renaissance, but they still required a level of economic affluence that produced expendable income and leisure for reading and attending plays. More important, they required a level of education that was accessible to the middle class but not yet to the lower working classes, either agricultural or industrial.

Benjamin sees a deeper division, however, than that naive class analysis. He captures it in the division he makes between what he calls "cult art" and mass art. Regardless of which limited audience art presumes, cult art appeals only to a select audience that can access it. Religious art is the paradigm: it means more and something different to those who share the religious vision than to those who are outside that religion. Historically, it is also produced specifically to the conditions set by the religion. The art of courts and of middle class collectors, readers, and playgoers broke away from the strictly religious setting, but it remained a form of cult art because it was produced for and according to the conditions established by certain limited social groups. Thus the initial move from upper-class and religious art to more extensive middle class art does not fundamentally change the nature of art, though it prepared the way by shifting the audience and opening art to a wider public.

The more basic change that Benjamin recognizes came when the means of production themselves changed in such a way that art was no longer limited to an educated elite. The crucial shift, therefore, was to mechanical production. As Benjamin notes, mechanical production goes back to the earliest forms of art in the ability to cast statues, and it develops through graphic reproduction and printing to the modern forms of reproduction based on photography and sound reproduction. Thus, Benjamin does not imply a sharp historical line in the shift to mechanical reproduction. His basic thesis is not simply a historical movement. It is first of all that art has always reflected its means of production. As long as mechanical reproduction was limited, art remained essentially cult art. When mechanical reproduction becomes sufficiently widespread, cult art is replaced by mass art because the nature of art itself will have changed according to the dominant means of producing it.

But a second element in this argument is that with mass art, the distinction between elite groups implied by cult art also disappears. Art in the age of mechanical reproduction appeals directly to its audience. In Benjamin's terminology, it loses its "aura," which we might understand as the identification of the work of art with its historically specific producer and place. The aura of a work assures its authenticity, its uniqueness as a specific object belonging to a specific artist at a specific time and place. To falsify a work of art by forgery or other forms of reproduction destroys its aura and authenticity. But art produced according to the conditions of mechanical reproduction cannot be falsified in that way. It is intended to be detached from its origins and distributed widely to whomever wants it.

Thus, film becomes the focus for Benjamin. Film exists for distribution to thousands of theaters at once. It is open to anyone who enters the theater, and the theater is a place of anonymity. One need not know anyone else in the theater, and the darkness of the projection conditions reinforce that anonymity beyond even what it is in the "legitimate" theater. Class divisions disappear in that setting. The camera replaces the actor and the author as the controlling point of view, and the camera is essentially a mechanical device in spite of what can be done with editing and camera work. Film is a collective enterprise in a way that no previous art has been. Medieval cathedrals were collective projects and architecture has always had a collective aspect, but film appeals to a public directly, and independent of use, in a way that buildings do not. The use of a building dictates to some extent who can fully appreciate it. Film is open, classless, free of cult.

Of course, there are aspects of film that Benjamin recognizes do not fit this picture. In particular, film exploits capital because films have to be financed, and that aspect has become more and more prominent. The actor as star is also a kind of cult figure, so that film persona remains a limiting factor on film. But film still provides the best examples of the full effect of mechanical reproduction at the time that Benjamin was writing. He would undoubtedly be open to extending the analysis to television and directly distributed videotape and CDs that have the potential once again to revise the distribution system. One of the most significant aspects of current artistic production is the development of digital technology that allows photographs to be rearranged so that dead actors appear in contemporary films, and produces such faithful and infinitely reproducible reproductions that existing notions of copyright are becoming obsolete—much to the discomfort of the economic forces that currently control production.

We should read Benjamin's essay not simply as an example of continental Marxist philosophizing and analysis from the 1930s. It represents a significant effort to move aesthetic analysis back into the context of culture, history, and other forms of social philosophy. The analysis is acute and interesting in its own right. But it is even more important in the direction it takes away from what was becoming an increasingly sterile form of aesthetics. Benjamin is a principle figure in Marxist aesthetics. But he is also a major representative of the whole twentieth-century continental philosophical movement that continues to see aesthetics in particular and philosophy in general as historically and culturally founded. One might look to Sartre and Heidegger and to various forms of psychoanalytic criticism for alternate forms of analysis in this tradition, which carries on in more recent structuralist and poststructuralist philosophy.

From *The Work of Art in the Age of Mechanical Reproduction*

Preface

When Marx[1] undertook his critique of the capitalistic mode of production, this mode was in its infancy. Marx directed his efforts in such a way as to give them prognostic value. He went back to the basic conditions underlying capitalistic production and through his presentation showed what could be expected of capitalism in the future. The result was that one could expect it not only to exploit the proletariat with increasing intensity, but ultimately to create conditions which would make it possible to abolish capitalism itself.

The transformation of the superstructure, which takes place far more slowly than that of the substructure, has taken more than half a century to manifest in all areas of culture the change in the conditions of production. Only today can it be indicated what form this has taken. Certain prognostic requirements should be met by these statements. However, theses about the art of the proletariat after its assumption of power or about the art of a classless society would have less bearing on these demands than theses about the developmental tendencies of art under present conditions of production. Their dialectic is no less noticeable in the superstructure than in the economy. It would therefore be wrong to underestimate the value of such theses as a weapon. They brush aside a number of outmoded concepts, such as creativity and genius, eternal value and mystery—concepts whose uncontrolled (and at present almost uncontrollable) application would lead to a processing of data in the Fascist sense. The concepts which are introduced into the theory of art in what follows differ from the more familiar terms in that they are completely useless for the purposes of Fascism.[2] They are, on the other hand, useful for the formulation of revolutionary demands in the politics of art.

I

In principle a work of art has always been reproducible. Man-made artifacts could always be imitated by men. Replicas were made by pupils in practice of their craft, by masters for diffusing their works, and, finally, by third parties in the pursuit of gain. Mechanical reproduction of a work of art, however, represents something new. Historically, it advanced intermittently and in leaps at long intervals, but with accelerated intensity. The Greeks knew only two procedures of technically reproducing works of art: founding and stamping. Bronzes, terra cottas,[3] and coins were the only art works which they could produce in quantity. All others were unique and could not be mechanically reproduced. With the woodcut graphic art became mechanically reproducible for the first time, long before script became reproducible by print. The enormous changes which

---

[1] Karl Marx (1818–1883) was the intellectual founder of communism. Along with Friedrich Engels, he wrote the *Communist Manifesto,* which issued a political call to arms against the prevailing industrial capitalism of the nineteenth century. Marx's major work, *Das Kapital* (Capital), analyzes the class structure and economic imperatives that work through history toward what Marx believed was the inevitable culmination in communism.

[2] The interrelated political movements that developed in Europe between 1919, in the aftermath of World War I, and 1945. Fascism combines nationalism with a mythology of race and ethnic roots to promote the solidarity of a group under a significant leader who is taken to embody the ideology and ideals of the group. Its economic theory is strongly nationalist as well, emphasizing the importance of national industry and a strong military as ways to bind the nation together. Fascism developed grandiose pannationalist ideas of unity that looked back to both Rome and northern European mythology.

[3] Terra cotta is a pottery made from clay that can be fired to a hard finish, in use since at least 3000 B.C.E.

printing, the mechanical reproduction of writing, has brought about in literature are a familiar story. However, within the phenomenon which we are here examining from the perspective of world history, print is merely a special, though particularly important, case. During the Middle Ages engraving and etching were added to the woodcut; at the beginning of the nineteenth century lithography made its appearance.

With lithography the technique of reproduction reached an essentially new stage. This much more direct process was distinguished by the tracing of the design on a stone rather than its incision on a block of wood or its etching on a copperplate and permitted graphic art for the first time to put its products on the market, not only in large numbers as hitherto, but also in daily changing forms. Lithography enabled graphic art to illustrate everyday life, and it began to keep pace with printing. But only a few decades after its invention, lithography was surpassed by photography. For the first time in the process of pictorial reproduction, photography freed the hand of the most important artistic functions which henceforth devolved only upon the eye looking into a lens. Since the eye perceives more swiftly than the hand can draw, the process of pictorial reproduction was accelerated so enormously that it could keep pace with speech. A film operator shooting a scene in the studio captures the images at the speed of an actor's speech. Just as lithography virtually implied the illustrated newspaper, so did photography foreshadow the sound film. The technical reproduction of sound was tackled at the end of the last century. These convergent endeavors made predictable a situation which Paul Valéry[4] pointed up in this sentence: "Just as water, gas, and electricity are brought into our

houses from far off to satisfy our needs in response to a minimal effort, so we shall be supplied with visual or auditory images, which will appear and disappear at a simple movement of the hand, hardly more than a sign." Around 1900 technical reproduction had reached a standard that not only permitted it to reproduce all transmitted works of art and thus to cause the most profound change in their impact upon the public; it also had captured a place of its own among the artistic processes. For the study of this standard nothing is more revealing than the nature of the repercussions that these two different manifestations— the reproduction of works of art and the art of the film—have had on art in its traditional form.

II

Even the most perfect reproduction of a work of art is lacking in one element: its presence in time and space, its unique existence at the place where it happens to be. This unique existence of the work of art determined the history to which it was subject throughout the time of its existence. This includes the changes which it may have suffered in physical condition over the years as well as the various changes in its ownership. The traces of the first can be revealed only by chemical or physical analyses which it is impossible to perform on a reproduction; changes of ownership are subject to a tradition which must be traced from the situation of the original.

The presence of the original is the prerequisite to the concept of authenticity. Chemical analyses of the patina of a bronze can help to establish this, as does the proof that a given manuscript of the Middle Ages stems from an archive of the fifteenth century. The whole sphere of authenticity is outside technical—and, of course, not only technical—reproducibility. Confronted with its manual reproduction, which was usually branded as a forgery, the original preserved all its authority; not so *vis à vis* technical reproduction. The reason is twofold. First, process reproduction is more independent of the original than manual repro-

---

[4] Paul Valéry (1871–1945) was the leading French poet of the first half of the twentieth century. He began under the influence of the symbolists and André Gide, but after the publication of his major poetic work, *La Jeune Parque* (*The Young Fate*), his own intellectual style was recognized. Valéry became one of the leading critics and intellectuals in France, and his opinion was quoted and solicited widely.

duction. For example, in photography, process reproduction can bring out those aspects of the original that are unattainable to the naked eye yet accessible to the lens, which is adjustable and chooses its angle at will. And photographic reproduction, with the aid of certain processes, such as enlargement or slow motion, can capture images which escape natural vision. Secondly, technical reproduction can put the copy of the original into situations which would be out of reach for the original itself. Above all, it enables the original to meet the beholder halfway, be it in the form of a photograph or a phonograph record. The cathedral leaves its locale to be received in the studio of a lover of art; the choral production, performed in an auditorium or in the open air, resounds in the drawing room.

The situations into which the product of mechanical reproduction can be brought may not touch the actual work of art, yet the quality of its presence is always depreciated. This holds not only for the art work but also, for instance, for a landscape which passes in review before the spectator in a movie. In the case of the art object, a most sensitive nucleus—namely, its authenticity—is interfered with whereas no natural object is vulnerable on that score. The authenticity of a thing is the essence of all that is transmissible from its beginning, ranging from its substantive duration to its testimony to the history which it has experienced. Since the historical testimony rests on the authenticity, the former, too, is jeopardized by reproduction when substantive duration ceases to matter. And what is really jeopardized when the historical testimony is affected is the authority of the object.

One might subsume the eliminated element in the term "aura" and go on to say: that which withers in the age of mechanical reproduction is the aura of the work of art. This is a symptomatic process whose significance points beyond the realm of art. One might generalize by saying: the technique of reproduction detaches the reproduced object from the domain of tradition. By making many reproductions it substitutes a plurality of copies for a unique existence. And in permitting the reproduction to meet the beholder or listener in his own particular situation, it reactivates the object reproduced. These two processes lead to a tremendous shattering of tradition which is the obverse of the contemporary crisis and renewal of mankind. Both processes are intimately connected with the contemporary mass movements. Their most powerful agent is the film. Its social significance, particularly in its most positive form, is inconceivable without its destructive, cathartic aspect, that is, the liquidation of the traditional value of the cultural heritage. This phenomenon is most palpable in the great historical films. It extends to ever new positions. In 1927 Abel Gance [5] exclaimed enthusiastically: "Shakespeare, Rembrandt, Beethoven will make films . . . all legends, all mythologies and all myths, all founders of religion, and the very religions . . . await their exposed resurrection, and the heroes crowd each other at the gate." Presumably without intending it, he issued an invitation to a far-reaching liquidation.

III

During long periods of history, the mode of human sense perception changes with humanity's entire mode of existence. The manner in which human sense perception is organized, the medium in which it is accomplished, is determined not only by nature but by historical circumstances as well. The fifth century, with its great shifts of population, saw the birth of the late Roman art industry and the Vienna Genesis, [6] and there developed not only an art different from that of antiquity but also a new kind of perception. The

---

[5] Abel Gance (1889–1981) was a renowned filmmaker whose work extends from the silent period through the mid-1960s. His antiwar films following World War I including *J'accuse* (1919), broke new ground in cinema. He is best known for his early large-scale historical epics.

[6] An illuminated manuscript of the Book of Genesis in the Vienna National Library.

scholars of the Viennese school, Riegl[7] and Wickhoff,[8] who resisted the weight of classical tradition under which these later art forms had been buried, were the first to draw conclusions from them concerning the organization of perception at the time. However far-reaching their insight, these scholars limited themselves to showing the significant, formal hallmark which characterized perception in late Roman times. They did not attempt—and, perhaps, saw no way—to show the social transformations expressed by these changes of perception. The conditions for an analogous insight are more favorable in the present. And if changes in the medium of contemporary perception can be comprehended as decay of the aura, it is possible to show its social causes.

The concept of aura which was proposed above with reference to historical objects may usefully be illustrated with reference to the aura of natural ones. We define the aura of the latter as the unique phenomenon of a distance, however close it may be. If, while resting on a summer afternoon, you follow with your eyes a mountain range on the horizon or a branch which casts its shadow over you, you experience the aura of those mountains, of that branch. This image makes it easy to comprehend the social bases of the contemporary decay of the aura. It rests on two circumstances, both of which are related to the increasing significance of the masses in contemporary life. Namely, the desire of contemporary masses to bring things "closer" spatially and humanly, which is just as ardent as their bent toward overcoming the uniqueness of every reality by accepting its reproduction. Every day the urge grows stronger to get hold of an object at very close range by way of its likeness, its reproduction. Unmistakably, reproduction as offered by picture magazines and newsreels differs from the

image seen by the unarmed eye. Uniqueness and permanence are as closely linked in the latter as are transitoriness and reproducibility in the former. To pry an object from its shell, to destroy its aura, is the mark of a perception whose "sense of the universal equality of things" has increased to such a degree that it extracts it even from a unique object by means of reproduction. Thus is manifested in the field of perception what in the theoretical sphere is noticeable in the increasing importance of statistics. The adjustment of reality to the masses and of the masses to reality is a process of unlimited scope, as much for thinking as for perception.

IV

The uniqueness of a work of art is inseparable from its being imbedded in the fabric of tradition. This tradition itself is thoroughly alive and extremely changeable. An ancient statue of Venus, for example, stood in a different traditional context with the Greeks, who made it an object of veneration, than with the clerics of the Middle Ages, who viewed it as an ominous idol. Both of them, however, were equally confronted with its uniqueness, that is, its aura. Originally the contextual integration of art in tradition found its expression in the cult. We know that the earliest art works originated in the service of a ritual—first the magical, then the religious kind. It is significant that the existence of the work of art with reference to its aura is never entirely separated from its ritual function. In other words, the unique value of the "authentic" work of art has its basis in ritual, the location of its original use value. This ritualistic basis, however remote, is still recognizable as secularized ritual even in the most profane forms of the cult of beauty. The secular cult of beauty, developed during the Renaissance and prevailing for three centuries, clearly showed that ritualistic basis in its decline and the first deep crisis which befell it. With the advent of the first truly revolutionary means of reproduction, photography, simultaneously with the rise of socialism, art sensed the approaching crisis which

---

[7] Alois Riegl (1858–1905) was an Austrian art historian and professor at the University of Vienna whose most important work was *Späterömische Kunstindustrie* [*Late Roman Art Industry*].

[8] Franz Wickhoff (1853–1909) was an Austrian art historian who specialized in early Christian art. His work includes a description of the Vienna Genesis manuscript.

has become evident a century later. At the time, art reacted with the doctrine of *l'art pour l'art*,[9] that is, with a theology of art. This gave rise to what might be called a negative theology in the form of the idea of "pure" art, which not only denied any social function of art but also any categorizing by subject matter. (In poetry, Mallarmé[10] was the first to take this position.)

An analysis of art in the age of mechanical reproduction must do justice to these relationships, for they lead us to an all-important insight: for the first time in world history, mechanical reproduction emancipates the work of art from its parasitical dependence on ritual. To an ever greater degree the work of art reproduced becomes the work of art designed for reproducibility. From a photographic negative, for example, one can make any number of prints; to ask for the "authentic" print makes no sense. But the instant the criterion of authenticity ceases to be applicable to artistic production, the total function of art is reversed. Instead of being based on ritual, it begins to be based on another practice—politics.

V

Works of art are received and valued on different planes. Two polar types stand out: with one, the accent is on the cult value; with the other, on the exhibition value of the work. Artistic production begins with ceremonial objects destined to serve in a cult. One may assume that what mattered was their existence, not their being on view. The elk portrayed by the man of the Stone Age on the walls of his cave was an instrument of magic. He did expose it to his fellow men, but in the main it was meant for the spirits. Today the cult value would seem to demand that the work of art remain hidden. Certain statues of gods are accessible only to the priest in the cella[11]; certain Madonnas remain covered nearly all year round; certain sculptures on medieval cathedrals are invisible to the spectator on ground level. With the emancipation of the various art practices from ritual go increasing opportunities for the exhibition of their products. It is easier to exhibit a portrait bust that can be sent here and there than to exhibit the statue of a divinity that has its fixed place in the interior of a temple. The same holds for the painting as against the mosaic or fresco[12] that preceded it. And even though the public presentability of a mass originally may have been just as great as that of a symphony, the latter originated at the moment when its public presentability promised to surpass that of the mass.

With the different methods of technical reproduction of a work of art, its fitness for exhibition increased to such an extent that the quantitative shift between its two poles turned into a qualitative transformation of its nature. This is comparable to the situation of the work of art in prehistoric times when, by the absolute emphasis on its cult value, it was, first and foremost, an instrument of magic. Only later did it come to be recognized as a work of art. In the same way today, by the absolute emphasis on its exhibition value the work of art becomes a creation with entirely new functions, among which the one we are conscious of, the artistic function, later may be recognized as incidental. This much is certain: today photography and the film are the most serviceable exemplifications of this new function.

VI

In photography, exhibition value begins to displace cult value all along the line. But cult value does not give way without resistance. It retires into an ultimate retrenchment: the human countenance. It is no accident that the portrait was the

---

[9] "Art for art's sake." This slogan is identified with nineteenth-century aesthetes and particularly symbolist poetry.

[10] Stéphan Mallarmé (1842–1898) was a French poet whose work is associated with the symbolist movement in poetry. Sound and even illumination are considered as important as the content of the poems in order to stress the difference between poetry and prose and between art and social content.

[11] The cella is the inner room in a classical temple that usually housed the statue of the god or goddess.

[12] Fresco is the painting technique in which color is laid directly onto damp plaster so that it is absorbed into the surface.

focal point of early photography. The cult of remembrance of loved ones, absent or dead, offers a last refuge for the cult value of the picture. For the last time the aura emanates from the early photographs in the fleeting expression of a human face. This is what constitutes their melancholy, incomparable beauty. But as man withdraws from the photographic image, the exhibition value for the first time shows its superiority to the ritual value. To have pinpointed this new stage constitutes the incomparable significance of Atget,[13] who, around 1900, took photographs of deserted Paris streets. It has quite justly been said of him that he photographed them like scenes of crime. The scene of a crime, too, is deserted; it is photographed for the purpose of establishing evidence. With Atget, photographs become standard evidence for historical occurrences, and acquire a hidden political significance. They demand a specific kind of approach; free-floating contemplation is not appropriate to them. They stir the viewer; he feels challenged by them in a new way. At the same time picture magazines begin to put up signposts for him, right ones or wrong ones, no matter. For the first time, captions have become obligatory. And it is clear that they have an altogether different character than the title of a painting. The directives which the captions give to those looking at pictures in illustrated magazines soon become even more explicit and more imperative in the film where the meaning of each single picture appears to be prescribed by the sequence of all preceding ones. . . .

X

The feeling of strangeness that overcomes the actor before the camera, as Pirandello[14] describes

it, is basically of the same kind as the estrangement felt before one's own image in the mirror. But now the reflected image has become separable, transportable. And where is it transported? Before the public. Never for a moment does the screen actor cease to be conscious of this fact. While facing the camera he knows that ultimately he will face the public, the consumers who constitute the market. This market, where he offers not only his labor but also his whole self, his heart and soul, is beyond his reach. During the shooting he has as little contact with it as any article made in a factory. This may contribute to that oppression, that new anxiety which, according to Pirandello, grips the actor before the camera. The film responds to the shriveling of the aura with an artificial build-up of the "personality" outside the studio. The cult of the movie star, fostered by the money of the film industry, preserves not the unique aura of the person but the "spell of the personality," the phony spell of a commodity. So long as the movie-makers' capital sets the fashion, as a rule no other revolutionary merit can be accredited to today's film than the promotion of a revolutionary criticism of traditional concepts of art. We do not deny that in some cases today's films can also promote revolutionary criticism of social conditions, even of the distribution of property. However, our present study is no more specifically concerned with this than is the film production of Western Europe.

It is inherent in the technique of the film as well as that of sports that everybody who witnesses its accomplishments is somewhat of an expert. This is obvious to anyone listening to a group of newspaper boys leaning on their bicycles and discussing the outcome of a bicycle race. It is not for nothing that newspaper publishers arrange races for their delivery boys. These arouse great interest among the participants, for the victor has an opportunity to rise from delivery boy to professional racer. Similarly, the newsreel offers everyone the opportunity to rise from passerby to movie extra. In this way any man might even find himself part of a work of art, as

---

[13] Eugene Atget (1856–1927) was one of the leaders in establishing photography as an art form. His photographs of Paris and nineteenth-century France are well known.

[14] Luigi Pirandello (1867–1936) was an Italian playwright and novelist. His plays, the best known of which is *Six Characters in Search of an Author,* often posed intellectual puzzles. *Si Gira* (*Turn Around*) is a novel.

witness Vertov's *Three Songs About Lenin*[15] or Iven's *Borinage*.[16] Any man today can lay claim to being filmed. This claim can best be elucidated by a comparative look at the historical situation of contemporary literature.

For centuries a small number of writers were confronted by many thousands of readers. This changed toward the end of the last century. With the increasing extension of the press, which kept placing new political, religious, scientific, professional, and local organs before the readers, an increasing number of readers became writers— at first, occasional ones. It began with the daily press opening to its readers space for "letters to the editor." And today there is hardly a gainfully employed European who could not, in principle, find an opportunity to publish somewhere or other comments on his work, grievances, documentary reports, or that sort of thing. Thus, the distinction between author and public is about to lose its basic character. The difference becomes merely functional; it may vary from case to case. At any moment the reader is ready to turn into a writer. As expert, which he had to become willy-nilly in an extremely specialized work process, even if only in some minor respect, the reader gains access to authorship. In the Soviet Union work itself is given a voice. To present it verbally is part of a man's ability to perform the work. Literary license is now founded on polytechnic rather than specialized training and thus becomes common property.

All this can easily be applied to the film, where transitions that in literature took centuries have come about in a decade. In cinematic practice, particularly in Russia, this change-over has partially become established reality. Some of the players whom we meet in Russian films are not actors in our sense but people who portray *themselves*—and primarily in their own work process. In Western Europe the capitalistic exploitation of the film denies consideration to modern man's legitimate claim to being reproduced. Under these circumstances the film industry is trying hard to spur the interest of the masses through illusion—promoting spectacles and dubious speculations. . . .

XII

Mechanical reproduction of art changes the reaction of the masses toward art. The reactionary attitude toward a Picasso[17] painting changes into the progressive reaction toward a Chaplin[18] movie. The progressive reaction is characterized by the direct, intimate fusion of visual and emotional enjoyment with the orientation of the expert. Such fusion is of great social significance. The greater the decrease in the social significance of an art form, the sharper the distinction between criticism and enjoyment by the public. The conventional is uncritically enjoyed, and the truly new is criticized with aversion. With regard to the screen, the critical and the receptive attitudes of the public coincide. The decisive reason for this is that individual reactions are predetermined by the mass audience response they are about to produce, and this is nowhere more pronounced than in the film. The moment these responses become manifest they control each other. Again, the

---

[15] Dziga Vertov [Vertoff] (1896–1954) was a Russian filmmaker, particularly of documentary films, beginning with films made during the Russian Revolution. He developed a theory of film he called the "film-eye" that opposed theatricalism and used the camera as an "eye" to show real life. *Three Songs About Lenin* (1934) is one of his films.

[16] Joris Iven (1898–1989) was an experimental Dutch filmmaker whose documentaries focused on social issues. Borinage is a coal mining region in Belgium; Iven made a documentary on a coal miners' strike in the region in 1933.

[17] Pablo Picasso (1881–1973) was one of the most prolific and influential twentieth-century artists. With Georges Braque he invented cubism, which broke subject matter into geometric planes, but he was equally influential in other styles, including a simple, almost classical style, collages, and "ready-mades," art works made from ordinary objects.

[18] Charles Chaplin (1889–1979) was one of the leading comic actors and film directors of the silent era, though he continued to make films after sound was introduced. Chaplin's character of the little tramp became synonymous with his silent style.

comparison with painting is fruitful. A painting has always had an excellent chance to be viewed by one person or by a few. The simultaneous contemplation of paintings by a large public, such as developed in the nineteenth century, is an early symptom of the crisis of painting, a crisis which was by no means occasioned exclusively by photography but rather in a relatively independent manner by the appeal of art works to the masses.

Painting simply is in no position to present an object for simultaneous collective experience, as it was possible for architecture all times, for the epic poem in the past, and for the movie today. Although this circumstance in itself should not lead one to conclusions about the social role of painting, it does constitute a serious threat as soon as painting, under special conditions and, as it were, against its nature, is confronted directly by the masses. In the churches and monasteries of the Middle Ages and at the princely courts up to the end of the eighteenth century, a collective reception of paintings did not occur simultaneously, but by graduated and hierarchized mediation. The change that has come about is an expression of the particular conflict in which painting was implicated by the mechanical reproducibility of paintings. Although paintings began to be publicly exhibited in galleries and salons, there was no way for the masses to organize and control themselves in their reception. Thus the same public which responds in a progressive manner toward a grotesque film is bound to respond in a reactionary manner to surrealism.[19]

XIII

The characteristics of the film lie not only in the manner in which man presents himself to mechanical equipment but also in the manner in which, by means of this apparatus, man can represent his environment. A glance at occupational psychology illustrates the testing capacity of the equipment. Psychoanalysis illustrates it in a different perspective. The film has enriched our field of perception with methods which can be illustrated by those of Freudian theory.[20] Fifty years ago, a slip of the tongue passed more or less unnoticed. Only exceptionally may such a slip have revealed dimensions of depth in a conversation which had seemed to be taking its course on the surface. Since the *Psychopathology of Everyday Life*[21] things have changed. This book isolated and made analyzable things which had heretofore floated along unnoticed in the broad stream of perception. For the entire spectrum of optical, and now also acoustical, perception the film has brought about a similar deepening of apperception. It is only an obverse of this fact that behavior items shown in a movie can be analyzed much more precisely and from more points of view than those presented on paintings or on the stage. As compared with painting, filmed behavior lends itself more readily to analysis because of its incomparably more precise statements of the situation. In comparison with the stage scene, the filmed behavior item lends itself more readily to analysis because it can be isolated more easily. This circumstance derives its chief importance from its tendency to promote the mutual penetration of art and science. Actually, of a screened behavior item which is neatly brought out in a

---

[19] Surrealism is the movement in art, poetry, and film that sought to bring the dream world into art. Its images and the logic of its movement are dependent on psychological associations rather than normal cause and effect. It was founded in 1924 by the French poet, André Breton, and flourished in the 1920s and 1930s.

[20] Freudian theory is the psychological theory associated with the work of Sigmund Freud. It locates the motives of many actions at a psychological level beneath our conscious knowledge. Freud developed a method of analysis to reveal those subconscious motivations, many of which are associated with sexual development and repression.

[21] Sigmund Freud (1856–1939), a Viennese physician and the founder of psychoanalysis, began his work with the study of hysteria in women, and his so-called "talking cure" developed into a whole theory of our unconscious life. *The Psychopathology of Everyday Life* extended the theory of psychoanalysis beyond abnormal phenomena to argue that even well-adjusted behavior is often controlled by unconscious motives that exhibit themselves in symbolic form.

certain situation, like a muscle of a body, it is difficult to say which is more fascinating, its artistic value or its value for science. To demonstrate the identity of the artistic and scientific uses of photography which heretofore usually were separated will be one of the revolutionary functions of the film.

By close-ups of the things around us, by focusing on hidden details of familiar objects, by exploring common place milieus under the ingenious guidance of the camera, the film, on the one hand, extends our comprehension of the necessities which rule our lives; on the other hand, it manages to assure us of an immense and unexpected field of action. Our taverns and our metropolitan streets, our offices and furnished rooms, our railroad stations and our factories appeared to have us locked up hopelessly. Then came the film and burst this prison-world asunder by the dynamite of the tenth of a second, so that now, in the midst of its far-flung ruins and debris, we calmly and adventurously go traveling. With the close-up, space expands; with slow motion, movement is extended. The enlargement of a snapshot does not simply render more precise what in any case was visible, though unclear: it reveals entirely new structural formations of the subject. So, too, slow motion not only presents familiar qualities of movement but reveals in them entirely unknown ones "which, far from looking like retarded rapid movements, give the effect of singularly gliding, floating, supernatural motions." Evidently a different nature opens itself to the camera than opens to the naked eye—if only because an unconsciously penetrated space is substituted for a space consciously explored by man. Even if one has a general knowledge of the way people walk, one knows nothing of a person's posture during the fractional second of a stride. The act of reaching for a lighter or a spoon is familiar routine, yet we hardly know what really goes on between hand and metal, not to mention how this fluctuates with our moods. Here the camera intervenes with the resources of its lowerings and liftings, its interruptions and isolations, it extensions and accelerations, its enlargements and reductions. The camera introduces us to unconscious optics as does psychoanalysis to unconscious impulses.

XIV

One of the foremost tasks of art has always been the creation of a demand which could be fully satisfied only later. The history of every art form shows critical epochs in which a certain art form aspires to effects which could be fully obtained only with a changed technical standard, that is to say, in a new art form. The extravagances and crudities of art which thus appear, particularly in the so-called decadent epochs, actually arise from the nucleus of its richest historical energies. In recent years, such barbarisms were abundant in Dadaism.[22] It is only now that its impulse becomes discernible: Dadaism attempted to create by pictorial—and literary—means the effects which the public today seeks in the film.

Every fundamentally new, pioneering creation of demands will carry beyond its goal. Dadaism did so to the extent that it sacrificed the market values which are so characteristic of the film in favor of higher ambitions—though of course it was not conscious of such intentions as here described. The Dadaists attached much less importance to the sales value of their work than to its usefulness for contemplative immersion. The studied degradation of their material was not the least of their means to achieve this uselessness. Their poems are "word salad" containing obscenities and every imaginable waste product of language. The same is true of their paintings, on which they mounted buttons and tickets. What

---

[22] Dada was an avant-garde literary and artistic movement that originated in Zurich around the poet Tristan Tzara in 1916 and was influential until many of its artists shifted to surrealism in 1924. Dada was intentionally outrageous in its desire to shock the art world. Various derivations of the name have been proposed, but essentially dadaism denied any meaning at all in art while also rejecting the affectedness of aestheticism.

they intended and achieved was a relentless destruction of the aura of their creations, which they branded as reproductions with the very means of production. Before a painting of Arp's[23] or a poem by August Stramm[24] it is impossible to take time for contemplation and evaluation as one would before a canvas of Derain's[25] or a poem by Rilke.[26] In the decline of middle-class society, contemplation became a school for asocial behavior; it was countered by distraction as a variant of social conduct. Dadaistic activities actually assured a rather vehement distraction by making works of art the center of scandal. One requirement was foremost: to outrage the public.

From an alluring appearance or persuasive structure of sound the work of art of the Dadaists became an instrument of ballistics. It hit the spectator like a bullet, it happened to him, thus acquiring a tactile quality. It promoted a demand for the film, the distracting element of which is also primarily tactile, being based on changes of place and focus which periodically assail the spectator. Let us compare the screen on which a film unfolds with the canvas of a painting. The painting invites the spectator to contemplation; before it the spectator can abandon himself to his associations. Before the movie frame he cannot do so. No sooner has his eye grasped a scene than it is already changed. It cannot be arrested. Duhamel,[27] who detests the film and knows nothing

of its significance, though something of its structure, notes this circumstance as follows: "I can no longer think what I want to think. My thoughts have been replaced by moving images." The spectator's process of association in view of these images is indeed interrupted by their constant, sudden change. This constitutes the shock effect of the film, which, like all shocks, should be cushioned by heightened presence of mind. By means of its technical structure, the film has taken the physical shock effect out of the wrappers in which Dadaism had, as it were, kept it inside the moral shock effect.

XV

The mass is a matrix from which all traditional behavior toward works of art issues today in a new form. Quantity has been transmuted into quality. The greatly increased mass of participants has produced a change in the mode of participation. The fact that the new mode of participation first appeared in a disreputable form must not confuse the spectator. Yet some people have launched spirited attacks against precisely this superficial aspect. Among these, Duhamel has expressed himself in the most radical manner. What he objects to most is the kind of participation which the movie elicits from the masses. Duhamel calls the movie "a pastime for helots, a diversion for uneducated, wretched, worn out creatures who are consumed by their worries . . . , a spectacle which requires no concentration and presupposes no intelligence . . . . which kindles no light in the heart and awakens no hope other than the ridiculous one of some day becoming a 'star' in Los Angeles." Clearly, this is at bottom the same ancient lament that the masses seek distraction whereas art demands concentration from the spectator. That is a commonplace. The question remains whether it provides a platform for the analysis of the film. A closer look is needed here. Distraction and concentration form polar opposites which may be stated as follows: A man who concentrates before a work of art is absorbed by it. He enters into this work of art the way legend

---

[23] Hans Arp (1887–1966) was a German poet associated with the dadaist movement. His work included collages made from trash.
[24] August Stramm (1874–1915) was a German expressionist poet and playwright. Expressionist poetry sought the expression of feeling by the use of strings of words independent of narrative. Other expressionist poets included Georg Trakl and Franz Werfel.
[25] André Derain (1880–1954) was a French artist temporarily associated with the fauvist movement. His work during that time was characterized by bold, often unrealistic colors vigorously applied. His work gradually became more conservative.
[26] Rainer Maria Rilke (1875–1926) was a German poet. He was closely associated with the circle of artists and writers that formed the avant-garde in Europe before and after World War I.
[27] Georges Duhamel (1884–1966) was a French physician, novelist, and member of the French Academy. His novels deal with the frustrations of life in the first decades of the twentieth century and the futility of war.

tells of the Chinese painter when he viewed his finished painting. In contrast, the distracted mass absorbs the work of art. This is most obvious with regard to buildings. Architecture has always represented the prototype of a work of art the reception of which is consummated by a collectivity in a state of distraction. The laws of its reception are most instructive.

Buildings have been man's companions since primeval times. Many art forms have developed and perished. Tragedy begins with the Greeks, is extinguished with them, and after centuries its "rules" only are revived. The epic poem, which had its origin in the youth of nations, expires in Europe at the end of the Renaissance. Panel painting is a creation of the Middle Ages, and nothing guarantees its uninterrupted existence. But the human need for shelter is lasting. Architecture has never been idle. Its history is more ancient than that of any other art, and its claim to being a living force has significance in every attempt to comprehend the relationship of the masses to art. Buildings are appropriated in a twofold manner: by use and by perception—or rather, by touch and sight. Such appropriation cannot be understood in terms of the attentive concentration of a tourist before a famous building. On the tactile side there is no counterpart to contemplation on the optical side. Tactile appropriation is accomplished not so much by attention as by habit. As regards architecture, habit determines to a large extent even optical reception. The latter, too, occurs much less through rapt attention than by noticing the object in incidental fashion. This mode of appropriation, developed with reference to architecture, in certain circumstances acquires canonical value. For the tasks which face the human apparatus of perception at the turning points of history cannot be solved by optical means, that is, by contemplation, alone. They are mastered gradually by habit, under the guidance of tactile appropriation.

The distracted person, too, can form habits. More, the ability to master certain tasks in a state of distraction proves that their solution has become a matter of habit. Distraction as provided by art presents a covert control of the extent to which new tasks have become soluble by apperception. Since, moreover, individuals are tempted to avoid such tasks, art will tackle the most difficult and most important ones where it is able to mobilize the masses. Today it does so in the film. Reception in a state of distraction, which is increasing noticeably in all fields of art and is symptomatic of profound changes in apperception, finds in the film its true means of exercise. The film with its shock effect meets this mode of reception halfway. The film makes the cult value recede into the background not only by putting the public in the position of the critic, but also by the fact that at the movies this position requires no attention. The public is an examiner, but an absent-minded one. . . .

Study Questions

1. Give examples of nonreproducible and reproducible art.
2. What does Benjamin mean by *authenticity?* Give examples of authentic and inauthentic art.
3. How have changes in historical circumstances changed presentation since Benjamin wrote in 1935?
4. What is the aura of a natural object?
5. What replaces ritual in art? Illustrate with contemporary examples if possible.
6. Give examples of the *exhibition value* and *cult value* of contemporary art.
7. What is the difference between a film actor and a stage actor?
8. What change does Benjamin see in the relation of an author to the public through time?
9. How does mechanical reproduction change the reaction of the "masses" toward art?
10. What is the relation between what a camera films and the unconscious?
11. What is the relation of Dada to film?
12. How is a building received as a work of art?

Morris Weitz

◆ ◆ ◆ ◆ ◆ ◆ ◆ ◆ ◆ ◆

M ORRIS WEITZ (b. 1916) was professor of philosophy at the Ohio State University
and Brandeis University.

◆　◆　◆　◆　◆　◆

The influence of Ludwig Wittgenstein on twentieth-century philosophy would be
difficult to overestimate. Although he published only two books in his lifetime, each
marks a turning point in philosophy and his students have preserved many of his lectures, so that there is an extensive oral tradition that, together with his notes and fragmentary drafts, provides a literature that is still influential. Wittgenstein's first work, the
Tractatus Logico-Philosophicus, was one of the founding works of twentieth-century logical analysis. It incorporates elements of a developing logical calculus with views about
how that calculus constrains what we can meaningfully say. Meaningful language, in
this view, is that which presents a logical picture of states of affairs, and the world is the
sum of the facts expressed or expressible about those states of affairs, and not the sum
of things themselves. What cannot be expressed in the logical pictures we draw with language must remain beyond knowledge; we can only be silent about it. From this seminal work much of analytical philosophy draws its inspiration.

With the completion of the *Tractatus,* Wittgenstein turned away from philosophy,
feeling that he had said all that could be said on the subject. When he returned to philosophy some years later, it was with a new insight that culminated in his *Philosophical
Investigations.* The *Tractatus* was spare, logically precise, and left little for philosophy to
do. The *Philosophical Investigations* concludes that the earlier work is fundamentally mistaken in dismissing all non-logical pictures as meaningless. Instead, Wittgenstein concluded, language has multiple meanings that can only be understood by turning to the
uses to which the language is put. Philosophy then has two tasks. It must elucidate
the uses of language, and it must disclose when those uses are being forgotten because
we are deceived by the form of our language. So, for example, if we speak of the mind
as if it were a thing, then "losing one's mind" would operate on the pattern of losing
one's diary. But if we examine what the expression "losing one's mind" actually does,
we see that it does not describe something lost but a state of confusion. We will no
longer be led to treat mental confusion as a kind of physical loss. The role of philosophy is thus to cure our misconceptions and aid us in understanding what we actually
do with language. Rather than replacing the *Tractatus* view, Wittgenstein includes it as

one small part of a much more extensive view of the potential uses of language. This is a new form of analytical philosophy that can adopt the existing forms of analysis but extend and qualify them in new ways.

Morris Weitz sought to apply Wittgenstein's new insights from *Philosophical Investigations* to the existing state of art. Analysis, which Weitz simply identified as theory, operated within a strictly logical framework. The attempt by analytical philosophers to formulate necessary and sufficient conditions may not have been quite as coextensive with theory as Weitz makes it out to be, but certainly it was central. *Necessary conditions* are those without which one would be mistaken in applying a particular concept. *Sufficient conditions* are those whose presence always makes it correct to use the concept. So if one uses a concept, one is committed to asserting the presence of a certain set of properties (the necessary conditions), and conversely, if one asserts the presence of a certain set of properties, one will always be justified in using the corresponding concept. When one has a set of properties that are both necessary and sufficient for the application of the concept, one has defined its use. Other considerations go into making up a good, or true theory, but Weitz is correct that prior to the insights he derives from Wittgenstein, most theorizing was done in the mode of supplying necessary and sufficient conditions or analyzing claims that were based on the assumed existence of such conditions.

Weitz understands Wittgenstein to have made that kind of analysis impossible. In the spirit of the *Philosophical Investigations,* Weitz argues that it is not just that we do not know what the conditions are for applying the concept of *art* to certain things; we are seriously confused if we look for such conditions. Instead, we should analyze the way that we use the concept of art, and existing theory can be recast as part of that analysis.

Weitz's brief paper leaves many questions unanswered, and students of Wittgenstein have argued that Weitz makes terms like *open concept* and *language game* too simple. Yet Weitz is one of the first to apply those concepts to aesthetics, and he opened the way for much of the analytical aesthetics that has followed. Some have been much more willing to dispense with theory altogether in the arts on the basis of similar arguments. They would hold that not only are our attempts at aesthetic theory confused, they are essentially useless: the invention and criticism of art do not need philosophy at all. Others have taken the basic insight and further distinguished the kind of activities that make up art from other language games and open concepts, maintaining that art, while indefinable, is still distinctive in the way that it provides insights and experiences. These theories claim that art is itself a form of life that has a specific and special cultural role to play. Just as Weitz identified several kinds of art theory, several kinds of Wittgensteinian countertheorizing arose as the *Philosophical Investigations* became more widely discussed.

Weitz's initial attempt is important because it marks a break with logically based analysis. Wittgenstein and his followers were not the only ones, even in the Anglo-American philosophical tradition, to make that break. For example, the English philosopher, J. L. Austin, advanced a different set of arguments about the relation of language and its usage that makes use central, and a form of neo-Kantianism turned to myth and symbols for an alternative. All have in common the conclusion that the kind of precise, quasiscientific definitions that aesthetic theory was built upon are misguided, if not simply wrong. Weitz's attempt, however, remains provocatively simple and straightforward, and it is unquestionably seminal.

The Role of Theory in Aesthetics

THEORY HAS BEEN CENTRAL in aesthetics and is still the preoccupation of the philosophy of art. Its main avowed concern remains the determination of the nature of art which can be formulated into a definition of it. It construes definition as the statement of the necessary and sufficient properties of what is being defined, where the statement purports to be a true or false claim about the essence of art, what characterizes and distinguishes it from everything else. Each of the great theories of art—Formalism, Voluntarism, Emotionalism, Intellectualism, Intuitionism, Organicism[1]—converges on the attempt to state the defining properties of art. Each claims that it is the true theory because it has formulated correctly into a real definition the nature of art; and that the others are false because they have left out some necessary or sufficient property. Many theorists contend that their enterprise is no mere intellectual exercise but an absolute necessity for any understanding of art and our proper evaluation of it. Unless we know what art is, they say, what are its necessary and sufficient properties, we cannot begin to respond to it adequately or to say why one work is good or better than another. Aesthetic theory, thus, is important not only in itself but for the foundations of both appreciation and criticism. Philosophers, critics, and even artists who have written on art, agree that what is primary in aesthetics is a theory about the nature of art.

Is aesthetic theory, in the sense of a true definition or set of necessary and sufficient properties of art, possible? If nothing else does, the history of aesthetics itself should give one enormous pause here. For, in spite of the many theories, we seem no nearer our goal today than we were in Plato's time.[2] Each age, each art-movement, each philosophy of art tries over and over again to establish the stated ideal only to be succeeded by a new or revised theory, rooted, at least in part, in the repudiation of preceding ones. Even today, almost everyone interested in aesthetic matters is still deeply wedded to the hope that the correct theory of art is forthcoming. We need only examine the numerous new books on art in which new definitions are proffered; or, in our own country especially, the basic textbooks and anthologies to recognize how strong the priority of a theory of art is.

In this essay I want to plead for the rejection of this problem. I want to show that theory—in the requisite classical sense—is *never* forthcoming in aesthetics, and that we would do much better as philosophers to supplant the question, "What is the nature of art?" by other questions, the answers to which will provide us with all the understanding of the arts there can be. I want to show that the inadequacies of the theories are not primarily occasioned by any legitimate difficulty such, e.g., as the vast complexity of art, which might be corrected by further probing and research. Their basic inadequacies reside instead in a fundamental misconception of art. Aesthetic theory—all of it—is wrong in principle in thinking that a correct theory is possible because it radically misconstrues the logic of the concept of art. Its main contention that "art" is amenable to real or any kind of true definition is false. Its attempt to discover the necessary and sufficient properties of art is logically misbegotten for the very simple reason that such a set and, consequently, such a formula about it, is never forthcoming. Art, as the logic of the concept shows, has no set of necessary and sufficient properties; hence a theory of it is logically impossible and not merely factually difficult. Aesthetic theory tries to define what cannot be defined in its requisite sense. But in recommending the repudiation of aesthetic theory I shall not argue from this, as too many others have done, that its logical confusions

---

[1] These terms are defined in the text. Their use in this context is peculiar to Weitz.

[2] See the introduction and selection in Part I, pp. 5–19.

render it meaningless or worthless. On the contrary, I wish to reassess its role and its contribution primarily in order to show that it is of the greatest importance to our understanding of the arts.

Let us now survey briefly some of the more famous extant aesthetic theories to see if they do incorporate correct and adequate statements about the nature of art. In each of these theories lies the assumption that it is the true enumeration of the defining properties of art, with the implication that previous theories have stressed wrong definitions. Thus, to begin with, consider a famous version of Formalist theory, that propounded by Bell[3] and Fry.[4] It is true that they speak mostly of painting in their writings but both assert that what they find in that art can be generalized for what is "art" in the others as well. The essence of painting, they maintain, are the plastic elements in relation. Its defining property is significant form, i.e., certain combinations of lines, colors, shapes, volumes—everything on the canvas except the representational elements—which evoke a unique response to such combinations. Painting is definable as plastic organization. The nature of art, what it *really* is, so their theory goes, is a unique combination of certain elements (the specifiable plastic ones) in their relations. Anything which is art is an instance of significant form; and anything which is not art has no such form.

To this the Emotionalist replies that the truly essential property of art has been left out. Tolstoy,[5] Ducasse,[6] or any of the advocates of this theory, find that the requisite defining property is not significant form but rather the expression of emotion in some sensuous public medium. Without projection of emotion into some piece of stone or words or sounds, etc., there can be no art. Art is really such embodiment. It is this that uniquely characterizes art, and any true, real definition of it, contained in some adequate theory of art, must so state it.

The Intuitionist disclaims both emotion and form as defining properties. In Croce's[7] version, for example, art is identified not with some physical, public object but with a specific creative, cognitive, and spiritual art. Art is really a first stage of knowledge in which certain human beings (artists) bring their images and intuitions into lyrical clarification or expression. As such, it is an awareness, non-conceptual in character, of the unique individuality of things; and since it exists below the level of conceptualization or action, it is without scientific or moral content. Croce singles out as the defining essence of art this first stage of spiritual life and advances its identification with art as a philosophically true theory or definition.

The Organicist says to all of this that art is really a class of organic wholes consisting of distinguishable, albeit inseparable, elements in their causally efficacious relations which are presented in some sensuous medium. In A. C. Bradley,[8] in piecemeal versions of it in literary criticism, or in my own generalized adaptation of it in my *Philosophy of the Arts,* what is claimed is that anything which is a work of art is in its nature a unique complex of interrelated parts—in painting, for example, lines, colors, volumes, subjects, etc., all interacting upon one another on a paint surface of some sort. Certainly, at one time at least it seemed to me that this organic theory constituted the one true and real definition of art.

My final example is the most interesting of all, logically speaking. This is the Voluntarist theory of Parker.[9] In his writings on art, Parker persistently

---

[3] See the introduction and selection on pp. 255–269.

[4] Roger Fry (1866–1934) was a painter and art critic. He was somewhat older than other members of the Bloomsbury group that centered around Leonard and Virginia Woolf, but was considered part of the group. Fry was instrumental in introducing postimpressionist painting, particularly the work of Paul Cezanne, into England.

[5] See the introduction and selection on pp. 204–213.

[6] Longtime professor of philosophy at Brown University, C. J. Ducasse's principle work was *The Philosophy of Art* (1929).

[7] See the introduction and selection on pp. 220–236.

[8] A. C. Bradley (1851–1935) was one of the leading British Shakespearean scholars and critics. His critical perspective is both stylistic and psychological.

[9] Dewitt Parker (1885–1949) was professor of philosophy at the University of Michigan. He developed a theory of art as wish

calls into question the traditional simple-minded definitions of aesthetics. "The assumption underlying every philosophy of art is the existence of some common nature present in all the arts."[10] "All the so popular brief definitions of art—'significant form,' 'expression,' 'intuition,' 'objectified pleasure'—are fallacious, either because, while true of art, they are also true of much that is not art, and hence fail to differentiate art from other things; or else because they neglect some essential aspect of art."[11] But instead of inveighing against the attempt at definition of art itself, Parker insists that what is needed is a complex definition rather than a simple one. "The definition of art must therefore be in terms of a complex of characteristics. Failure to recognize this has been the fault of all the well-known definitions."[12] His own version of Voluntarism is the theory that art is essentially three things: embodiment of wishes and desires imaginatively satisfied, language, which characterizes the public medium of art, and harmony, which unifies the language with the layers of imaginative projections. Thus, for Parker, it is a true definition to say of art that it is ". . . the provision of satisfaction through the imagination, social significance, and harmony. I am claiming that nothing except works of art possesses all three of these marks."[13]

Now, all of these sample theories are inadequate in many different ways. Each purports to be a complete statement about the defining features of all works of art and yet each of them leaves out something which the others take to be central. Some are circular, e.g., the Bell-Fry theory of art as significant form which is defined in part in terms of our response to significant form. Some of them, in their search for necessary and sufficient properties, emphasize too few prop-

erties, like (again) the Bell-Fry definition, which leaves out subject-representation in painting, or the Croce theory, which omits inclusion of the very important feature of the public, physical character, say, of architecture. Others are too general and cover objects that are not art as well as works of art. Organicism is surely such a view since it can be applied to *any* causal unity in the natural world as well as to art.[14] Still others rest on dubious principles, e.g., Parker's claim that art embodies imaginative satisfactions, rather than real ones; or Croce's assertion that there is non-conceptual knowledge. Consequently, even if art has one set of necessary and sufficient properties, none of the theories we have noted, or, for that matter, no aesthetic theory yet proposed, has enumerated that set to the satisfaction of all concerned.

Then there is a different sort of difficulty. As real definitions, these theories are supposed to be factual reports on art. If they are, may we not ask, Are they empirical and open to verification or falsification? For example, what would confirm or disconfirm the theory that art is significant form or embodiment of emotion or creative synthesis of images? There does not even seem to be a hint of the kind of evidence which might be forthcoming to test these theories; and indeed one wonders if they are perhaps honorific definitions of "art," that is, proposed redefinitions in terms of some *chosen* conditions for applying the concept of art, and not true or false reports on the essential properties of art at all.

But all these criticisms of traditional aesthetic theories—that they are circular, incomplete, untestable, pseudo-factual, disguised proposals to change the meaning of concept—have been made before. My intention is to go beyond these to make a much more fundamental criticism, namely, that aesthetic theory is a logically vain attempt to define what cannot be defined, to state the necessary and sufficient properties of that which has no necessary and sufficient properties, to con-

---

fulfillment that drew upon psychoanalytical theory. His principle works on aesthetics include *The Analysis of Art* and *The Principles of Aesthetics*.

[10]D. Parker, "The Nature of Art," reprinted in E. Vivas and M. Krieger, *The Problems of Aesthetics* (N.Y., 1953), p. 90. [author's note]

[11]*Ibid.*, pp. 93–94. [author's note]

[12]*Ibid.*, p. 94. [author's note]

[13]*Ibid.*, p. 104. [author's note]

[14]See M. Macdonald's review of my *Philosophy of the Arts, Mind,* Oct. 1951, pp. 561–564, for a brilliant discussion of this objection to the Organic theory. [author's note]

ceive the concept of art as closed when its very use reveals and demands its openness.

The problem with which we must begin is not "What is art?" but "What sort of concept is 'art'?" Indeed, the root problem of philosophy itself is to explain the relation between the employment of certain kinds of concepts and the conditions under which they can be correctly applied. If I may paraphrase Wittgenstein,[15] we must not ask, What is the nature of any philosophical x?, or even, according to the semanticist, What does "x" mean?, a transformation that leads to the disastrous interpretation of "art" as a name for some specifiable class of objects; but rather, What is the use or employment of "x"? What does "x" do in the language? This, I take it, is the initial question, the begin-all if not the end-all of any philosophical problem and solution. Thus, in aesthetics, our first problem is the elucidation of the actual employment of the concept of art, to give a logical description of the actual functioning of the concept, including a description of the conditions under which we correctly use it or its correlates.

My model in this type of logical description or philosophy derives from Wittgenstein. It is also he who, in his refutation of philosophical theorizing in the sense of constructing definitions of philosophical entities, has furnished contemporary aesthetics with a starting point for any future progress. In his new work, *Philosophical Investigations*,[16] Wittgenstein raises as an illustrative question, What is a game? The traditional philosophi-

cal, theoretical answer would be in terms of some exhaustive set of properties common to all games. To this Wittgenstein says, let us consider what we call "games": "I mean board-games, card-games, ball-games, Olympic games, and so on. What is common to them all?—Don't say: 'there *must* be something common, or they would not be called "games"' but *look and see* whether there is anything common to all.—For if you look at them you will not see something that is common to all, but similarities, relationships. and a whole series of them at that. . . .

Card games are like board games in some respects but not in others. Not all games are amusing, nor is there always winning or losing or competition. Some games resemble others in some respects—that is all. What we find are no necessary and sufficient properties, only "a complicated network of similarities overlapping and crisscrossing," such that we can say of games that they form a family with family resemblances and no common trait. If one asks what a game is, we pick out sample games, describe these, and add "This and *similar things* are called 'games.'" This is all we need to say and indeed all any of us knows about games. Knowing what a game is is not knowing some real definition or theory but being able to recognize and explain games and to decide which among imaginary and new examples would or would not be called "games."

The problem of the nature of art is like that of the nature of games, at least in these respects: If we actually look and see what it is that we call "art," we will also find no common properties—only strands of similarities. Knowing what art is is not apprehending some manifest or latent essence but being able to recognize, describe, and explain those things we call "art" in virtue of these similarities.

But the basic resemblance between these concepts is their open texture. In elucidating them, certain (paradigm) cases can be given, about which there can be no question as to their being correctly described as "art" or "game," but no exhaustive set of cases can be given. I can list some cases and some conditions under which I can apply correctly the concept of art but I cannot list

---

[15] Ludwig Wittgenstein (1889–1951) was born into a wealthy Viennese family. His work marks two of the major points in twentieth-century philosophy. First, *Tractatus Logico-Philosophicus,* published at the instigation of Bertrand Russell while Wittgenstein was a prisoner of war of the Italians in 1917, is a major work in both logic and the logically inspired philosophy of the early twentieth century. Later, Wittgenstein came to question the exclusive logical emphasis of his own earlier philosophy and formulated an approach to language and philosophy that linked meaning and linguistic use that he presented both through his lectures at Cambridge and in the only other work that he prepared for publication, his *Philosophical Investigations.*

[16] L. Wittgenstein, *Philosophical Investigations* (Oxford, 1953), tr. E. Anscombe; see esp. Part 1, Sec. 65–75. All quotations are from these sections. [author's note]

all of them, for the all-important reason that unforeseeable or novel conditions are always forthcoming or envisageable.

A concept is open if its conditions of application are emendable and corrigible; i.e., if a situation or case can be imagined or secured which would call for some sort of *decision* on our part to extend the use of the concept to cover this, or to close the concept and invent a new one to deal with the new case and its new property. If necessary and sufficient conditions for the application of a concept can be stated, the concept is a closed one. But this can happen only in logic or mathematics where concepts are constructed and completely defined. It cannot occur with empirically —descriptive and normative concepts unless we arbitrarily close them by stipulating the ranges of their uses.

I can illustrate this open character of "art" best by examples drawn from its sub-concepts. Consider questions like "Is Dos Passos' *U.S.A.* a novel?,"[17] "Is V. Woolf's *To the Lighthouse* a novel?"[18] "Is Joyce's *Finnegan's Wake* a novel?"[19] On the traditional view, these are construed as factual problems to be answered yes or no in accordance with the presence or absence of defin-

ing properties. But certainly this is not how any of these questions is answered. Once it arises, as it has many times in the development of the novel from Richardson[20] to Joyce (e.g., "Is Gide's *The School for Wives* a novel or a diary?"[21]), what is at stake is no factual analysis concerning necessary and sufficient properties but a decision as to whether the work under examination is similar in certain respects to other works, already called "novels," and consequently warrants the extension of the concept to cover the new case. The new work is narrative, fictional, contains character delineation and dialogue but (say) it has no regular time-sequence in the plot or is interspersed with actual newspaper reports. It is like recognized novels, A, B, C . . . , in some respects but not like them in others. But then neither were B and C like A in some respects when it was decided to extend the concept applied to A to B and C. Because work N + 1 (the brand new work) is like A, B, C, . . . N in certain respects—has strands of similarity to them—the concept is extended and a new phase of the novel engendered. "Is N + 1 a novel?," then, is no factual, but rather a decision problem, where the verdict turns on whether or not we enlarge our set of conditions for applying the concept.

What is true of the novel is, I think, true of every sub-concept of art: "tragedy," "comedy," "painting," "opera," etc., of "art" itself. No "Is X a novel, painting, opera, work of art, etc.?" question allows of a definitive answer in the sense of a factual yes or no report. "Is this *collage* a painting or not?" does not rest on any set of necessary and sufficient properties of painting but on whether

---

[17] John Dos Passos (1896–1970) was a novelist whose work chronicled the American experience. His trilogy of novels, *U.S.A.* (1930), deals with the first three decades of the twentieth century and mixes biography, history, and fiction.

[18] Virginia Woolf (1882–1941), together with her husband Leonard, was at the center of the group of intellectuals identified with Bloomsbury in London. Virginia Woolf was one of the leading novelists of the first half of the twentieth century. *To the Lighthouse,* published in 1927, exhibits her stream-of-consciousness technique that produces the narrative from within the consciousness of the principal character rather than as a series of objective events.

[19] James Joyce (1882–1941) was perhaps the most innovative novelist writing in the English language. His novel, *Ulysses,* follows its protagonist around Joyce's native Dublin for a day in a journey that parallels the mythic events of the *Odyssey,* but the novel moves through space and time with such fluidity that one is virtually swallowed up in its language. *Finnegan's Wake* goes even further in dissolving the traditional structure of the novel as a narrative in a linear space/time. It plays on language to such an extent that the novel becomes a linguistic game into which the reader must enter, almost like a puzzle or game to be played with the author.

[20] Samuel Richardson (1689–1761) was one of the inventors of the English novel. He utilized letters to tell the story, focusing on the trials and education of young women (*Pamela, Clarissa*).

[21] André Gide (1869–1951) was a novelist, essayist, and Nobel Prize winner (1947). In many ways he was the leading French intellectual not only of his own generation, but, because of the length of his life, for a subsequent generation as well. Until late in his life, his homosexuality and quest for freedom made him a controversial figure in French intellectual life and limited his success. *The School for Wives* (1929) belongs to the writings that Gide classified as fables and satires and consists of independent stories.

we decide—as we did!—to extend "painting" to cover this case.

"Art," itself, is an open concept. New conditions (cases) have constantly arisen and will undoubtedly constantly arise; new art forms, new movements will emerge, which will demand decisions on the part of those interested, usually professional critics, as to whether the concept should be extended or not. Aestheticians may lay down similarity conditions but never necessary and sufficient ones for the correct application of the concept. With "art" its conditions of application can never be exhaustively enumerated since new cases can always be envisaged or created by artists, or even nature, which would call for a decision on someone's part to extend or to close the old or to invent a new concept. (E.g., "It's not a sculpture, it's a mobile.")

What I am arguing, then, is that the very expansive, adventurous character of art, its ever-present changes and novel creations, makes it logically impossible to ensure any set of defining properties. We can, of course, choose to close the concept. But to do this with "art" or "tragedy" or "portraiture," etc., is ludicrous since it forecloses on the very conditions of creativity in the arts.

Of course there are legitimate and serviceable closed concepts in art. But these are always those whose boundaries of conditions have been drawn for a *special* purpose. Consider the difference, for example, between "tragedy" and "(extant) Greek tragedy." The first is open and must remain so to allow for the possibility of new conditions, e.g., a play in which the hero is not noble or fallen or in which there is no hero but other elements that are like those of plays we already call "tragedy." The second is closed. The plays it can be applied to, the conditions under which it can be correctly used are all in, once the boundary, "Greek," is drawn. Here the critic can work out a theory or real definition in which he lists the common properties at least of the extant Greek tragedies. Aristotle's[22] definition, false as it is as a theory of all

the plays of Aeschylus,[23] Sophocles,[24] and Euripides,[25] since it does not cover some of them,[26] properly called "tragedies," can be interpreted as a real (albeit incorrect) definition of this closed concept; although it can also be, as it unfortunately has been, conceived as a purported real definition of "tragedy," in which case it suffers from the logical mistake of trying to define what cannot be defined—of trying to squeeze what is an open concept into an honorific formula for a closed concept.

What is supremely important, if the critic is not to become muddled, is to get absolutely clear about the way in which he conceives his concepts; otherwise he goes from the problem of trying to define "tragedy," etc., to an arbitrary closing of the concept in terms of certain preferred conditions or characteristics which he sums up in some linguistic recommendation that he mistakenly thinks is a real definition of the open concept. Thus, many critics and aestheticians ask, "What is tragedy?," choose a class of samples for which they may give a true account of its common properties, and then go on to construe this account of the chosen closed class as a true definition or theory of the whole open class of tragedy. This, I think, is the logical mechanism of most of the so-called theories of the sub-concepts of art: "tragedy," "comedy," "novel," etc. In effect, this whole procedure, subtly deceptive as it is, amounts to a transformation of correct criteria for *recognizing* members of certain legitimately closed classes of works of art into recommended criteria for *evaluating* any putative member of the class.

The primary task of aesthetics is not to seek a theory but to elucidate the concept of art.

---

[22] See the introduction and selection in Part I, pp. 20–43.

[23] With Sophocles and Euripides, Aeschylus (525–456 B.C.E.) was one of the three great writers of tragedy whose works survive.
[24] Sophocles (496–406 B.C.E.) was the second of the three great writers of tragedies whose works survive. His *Oedipus Tyrannus* is the prototype for the kind of tragedy Aristotle analyzes and represents the model for classical Greek tragedy.
[25] Euripides (485–406 B.C.E.) was the third of the great Athenian writers of tragedy. His work was considered more "untraditional" than that of Sophocles and Aeschylus.
[26] See H. D. F. Kitto, *Greek Tragedy* (London, 1939), on this point. [author's note]

Specifically, it is to describe the conditions under which we employ the concept correctly. Definition, reconstruction, patterns of analysis are out of place here since they distort and add nothing to our understanding of art. What, then, is the logic of "X is a work of art"?

As we actually use the concept, "Art" is both descriptive (like "chair") and evaluative (like "good"); i.e., we sometimes say, "This is a work of art," to describe something and we sometimes say it to evaluate something. Neither use surprises anyone.

What, first, is the logic of "X is a work of art," when it is a descriptive utterance? What are the conditions under which we would be making such an utterance correctly? There are no necessary and sufficient conditions but there are the strands of similarity conditions, i.e., bundles of properties, none of which need be present but most of which are, when we describe things as works of art. I shall call these the "criteria of recognition" of works of art. All of these have served as the defining criteria of the individual traditional theories of art; so we are already familiar with them. Thus, mostly, when we describe something as a work of art, we do so under the conditions of there being present some sort of artifact, made by human skill, ingenuity, and imagination, which embodies in its sensuous, public medium—stone, wood, sounds, words, etc.—certain distinguishable elements and relations. Special theorists would add conditions like satisfaction of wishes, objectification or expression of emotion, some act of empathy, and so on; but these latter conditions seem to be quite adventitious, present to some but not to other spectators when things are described as works of art. "X is a work of art and contains no emotion, expression, act of empathy, satisfaction, etc.," is perfectly good sense and may frequently be true. "X is a work of art and . . . was made by no one," or ". . . exists only in the mind and not in any publicly observable thing," or ". . . was made by accident when he spilled the paint on the canvas," in each case of which a normal condition is denied, are also sensible and capable of being true in certain cir-

cumstances. None of the criteria of recognition is a defining one, either necessary or sufficient, because we can sometimes assert of something that it is a work of art and go on to deny any one of these conditions, even the one which has traditionally been taken to be basic, namely, that of being an artifact: Consider, "This piece of driftwood is a lovely piece of sculpture." Thus, to say of anything that it is a work of art is to commit oneself to the presence of *some* of these conditions. One would scarcely describe X as a work of art if X were not an artifact, or a collection of elements sensuously presented in a medium, or a product of human skill, and so on. If none of the conditions were present, if there were no criteria present for recognizing something as a work of art, we would not describe it as one. But, even so, no one of these or any collection of them is either necessary or sufficient.

The elucidation of the descriptive use of "Art" creates little difficulty. But the elucidation of the evaluative use does. For many, especially theorists, "This is a work of art" does more than describe; it also praises. Its conditions of utterance, therefore, include certain preferred properties or characteristics of art. I shall call these "criteria of evaluation." Consider a typical example of this evaluative use, the view according to which to say of something that it is a work of art is to imply that it is a *successful* harmonization of elements. Many of the honorific definitions of art and its sub-concepts are of this form. What is at stake here is that "Art" is construed as an evaluative term which is either identified with its criterion or justified in terms of it. "Art" is defined in terms of its evaluative property, e.g., successful harmonization. On such a view, to say "X is a work of art" is (1) to say something which is taken *to mean* "X is a successful harmonization" (e.g., "Art *is* significant form") or (2) to say something praiseworthy *on the basis* of its successful harmonization. Theorists are never clear whether it is (1) or (2) which is being put forward. Most of them, concerned as they are with this evaluative use, formulate (2), i.e., that feature of art that *makes it art* in the praise-sense, and then go on to state

(1), i.e., the definition of "Art" in terms of its art-making feature. And this is clearly to confuse the conditions under which we say something evaluatively with the meaning of what we say. "This is a work of art," said evaluatively, cannot mean "This is a successful harmonization of elements" —except by stipulation—but at most is said in virtue of the art-making property, which is taken as a (the) criterion of "Art," when "Art" is employed to assess. "This is a work of art," used evaluatively, serves to praise and not to affirm the reason why it is said.

The evaluative use of "Art," although distinct from the conditions of its use, relates in a very intimate way to these conditions. For, in every instance of "This is a work of art" (used to praise), what happens is that the criterion of evaluation. (e.g., successful harmonization) for the employment of the concept of art is converted into a criterion of recognition. This is why, on its evaluative use, "This is a work of art" implies "This has P," where "P" is some chosen art-making property. Thus, if one chooses to employ "Art" evaluatively, as many do, so that "This is a work of art and not (aesthetically) good" makes no sense, he uses "Art" in such a way that he refuses to call anything a work of art unless it embodies his criterion of excellence.

There is nothing wrong with the evaluative use; in fact, there is good reason for using "Art" to praise. But what cannot be maintained is that theories of the evaluative use of "Art" are true and real definitions of the necessary and sufficient properties of art. Instead they are honorific definitions, pure and simple, in which "Art" has been redefined in terms of chosen criteria.

But what makes them—these honorific definitions—so supremely valuable is not their disguised linguistic recommendations; rather it is the *debates* over the reasons for changing the criteria of the concept of art which are built into the definitions. In each of the great theories of art, whether correctly understood as honorific definitions or incorrectly accepted as real definitions, what is of the utmost importance are the reasons proffered in the argument for the respective theory, that is, the reasons given for the chosen or preferred criterion of excellence and evaluation. It is this perennial debate over these criteria of evaluation which makes the history of aesthetic theory the important study it is. The value of each of the theories resides in its attempt to state and to justify certain criteria which are either neglected or distorted by previous theories. Look at the Bell-Fry theory again. Of course, "Art is significant form" cannot be accepted as a true, real definition of art; and most certainly it actually functions in their aesthetics as a redefinition of art in terms of the chosen condition of significant form. But what gives it its aesthetic importance is what lies behind the formula: In an age in which literary and representational elements have become paramount in painting, *return* to the plastic ones since these are indigenous to painting. Thus, the role of the theory is not to define anything but to use the definitional form, almost epigrammatically, to pin-point a crucial recommendation to turn our attention once again to the plastic elements in painting.

Once we, as philosophers, understand this distinction between the formula and what lies behind it, it behooves us to deal generously with the traditional theories of art; because incorporated in every one of them is a debate over and argument for emphasizing or centering upon some particular feature of art which has been neglected or perverted. If we take the aesthetic theories literally, as we have seen, they all fail; but if we reconstrue them, in terms of their function and point, as serious and argued-for recommendations to concentrate on certain criteria of excellence in art, we shall see that aesthetic theory is far from worthless. Indeed, it becomes as central as anything in aesthetics, in our understanding of art, for it teaches us what to look for and how to look at it in art. What is central and must be articulated in all the theories are their debates over the reasons for excellence in art—debates over emotional depth, profound truths, natural beauty, exactitude, freshness of treatment, and so on, as criteria of evaluation—the whole of which converges on the perennial problem of what makes a work of art good. To understand the role of aesthetic theory is not to conceive it as definition, logically doomed to failure, but to read it as summaries of seriously made recommendations to attend in certain ways to certain features of art.

Study Questions

1. What is the main concern of theory in the arts?
2. Why, in Weitz's opinion, is all theory of art wrong in principle?
3. Describe and illustrate each of Weitz's types of art theory.
4. In what ways do definitions of art fail?
5. What is the difference between a closed and open concept? Give examples of each.
6. How does the concept of *art* compare to the concept of *game?*
7. When are closed concepts available in art?
8. What should aesthetics do?
9. What is the difference between a descriptive and an evaluative use of a concept?
10. According to Weitz's analysis, can any work of art be wholly different from all preceding works?
11. What is the importance of aesthetic theory?

George Dickie

G EORGE DICKIE (1926–) is professor emeritus of philosophy at the University of
Illinois at Chicago.

♦   ♦   ♦   ♦   ♦   ♦

The criticism of earlier aesthetic theories may take many forms. One might criticize
the formulations of a particular theory, or, as with Morris Weitz, one might criticize the
role of theory itself. George Dickie is doing neither. His approach to arguments about
theories is fairly traditional. He examines cases and definitions, and he considers counterexamples. But he is not simply attacking a particular theory in order to propose an
alternative. In this essay, he proposes no theory of his own. (Dickie does go on to propose an important theory, the "institutional theory of art," in later work.) Yet his quarrel is not with theory as such. Instead, he understands aesthetics to have made a long-
term mistake that has infected virtually all theories since David Hume. Aesthetics is
committed to identifying a kind of aesthetic experience by some criteria, usually in the
form of an aesthetic attitude. However that is done, Dickie believes, it rests on a confusion and mistake. As he says at one point, "an underlying aim of this essay is to suggest the vacuousness of the term 'aesthetic.'" By that he does not mean that there is no
subdiscipline within philosophy that deals with art and natural phenomena related to
art but that the distinctiveness that has been assigned to "aesthetic" experience since
the introduction of the term in the eighteenth century is misleading.

The history of aesthetics is a product of the history of philosophy. The definition of
aesthetic grows out of that history. It is also closely related to the separation of philosophy and psychology. It is still the case that psychology as well as philosophy discusses
the "aesthetic experience." The positions that Dickie attempts to show as misleading and
confused are essentially psychological. They posit states of attention, experience, or
attitude that can be described and enhanced or made more difficult to achieve. Dickie's
strategy is to bring philosophical analysis of conceptual structure to bear on the way
that these experiences are described in order to show that the concepts as presented do
not correspond to the experience that is available to us. Thus he first identifies typical
instances of the concepts: *distance, disinterestedness, transitiveness,* and so on. Then he
looks to see how those concepts are described and what kinds of situations they are
taken to describe. Once he has laid out the concepts for our examination, he then goes

on to cite evidence that shows why the concept, as it is used, is confused. Note that he does not say simply that it is wrong. It is not like saying, "That is not a circle," or even like saying, "One cannot trisect an angle using only a compass and straight edge." It is more like saying, "A person is not a thing" because *person* is a more complex concept than *thing*. We make a different kind of mistake when we call a person a thing than if we call a person a book. It is not that a person is not a thing, but that *person* and *thing* have different, overlapping ranges of reference so that thingness and personhood cannot be understood solely in terms of each other. Similarly, Dickie wants to say that *aesthetic* as it has been used in the history of aesthetics is almost a vacuous term because it does not distinguish a single separate class of experiences.

This kind of philosophical argument is called *conceptual analysis,* and it is the essential technique of analytical philosophy. Dickie does not claim to be the only person to have noted problems with the concept of *the aesthetic*. But his objections are among the clearest and most direct. They amount to arguing that there is simply no psychological state such as the aesthetic attitude presupposes. That does not mean that there are no distinct psychological states. Dickie acknowledges several along the way: intentions, motives, and the like. His argument is that *aesthetic* is not a distinct class in such states because it neither identifies some unique state nor is needed to identify some otherwise undescribable psychological condition. We can do everything that we need to do to describe our attitudes and responses to art or natural phenomena related to art without ever requiring the term *aesthetic*. If Dickie stopped there, he would have presented an interesting and important bit of conceptual analysis.

He does not stop there, however. Dickie goes on to argue that the confusion implicit in all aesthetic attitude theories is positively detrimental to the description of our experience of art and the development of an adequate theory of art. There is both a negative and a positive side to this line of Dickie's argument. Negatively, our reliance on attitude theories causes us to look for things that are not there and separate what we should not separate. We try to find some special state and as a result misapprehend what is before us; it is like looking for the mind inside the skull. And by not being able to achieve the mythical aesthetic state, we separate elements of art and nature that belong together. When we separate morality and art or criticism and art, we lose just those connections that would make the work of art meaningful. At this point, then, Dickie moves beyond diagnosing a conceptual confusion to recommend a regimen that does without the concept of *the aesthetic* for the health of the patient.

Finally, there is an implicit theoretical argument within the kind of conceptual analysis that Dickie practices. He appeals positively to the way that we use concepts and language as the basic authority. We may, of course, stipulate usages if we choose. If we choose to restrict *aesthetic* to "nonmoral" characteristics of a work, so be it. As Dickie says, in this respect, "What we call it doesn't matter." But if one thinks that *aesthetic* is making a real and not just a nominal distinction within the characteristics of a work of art, then one misreads the work. So Dickie is implicitly arguing for a more holistic view of criticism and the perception of art. Such a view is taken to be implicit in language, so language and its use becomes the primary subject for philosophical analysis. A truly psychological analysis would be unlikely to depend on the folk psychology embedded in language. It would require its own technical distinctions and theoretical terminology. Thus Dickie is implicitly accepting the separation between aesthetics as a psychological discipline and philosophy. Since many of the attitude theories that he considers look back to a time before that separation, it is not strange that one would find that they confuse an outmoded psychology with philosophy. That does not make Dickie's warnings any less cogent.

Finally, Dickie's argument represents one more move in the development of twentieth-century aesthetics. Dickie is an excellent reader of eighteenth-century history of aesthetics, and his rejection of aesthetic attitude theories is a part of his understanding of how twentieth-century aesthetics has lost sight of the more integrated theories prior to Kant. He derives this understanding from his conceptual analysis, but one of the consequences of that analysis is that we must look again at how art is related to other aspects of the human understanding. Dickie himself takes that argument in one direction by arguing that the "artworld," the complex of artists, critics, galleries, museums, and appreciators of art, makes possible an intentional stance toward art. It is not a psychological attitude but an institutional enablement that moves some experiences into the artworld. We might compare it to adoption. The artworld takes in all sorts of activities and gives them a home. So aesthetics cannot ignore the influence of the artworld, either historically or theoretically.

The Myth of the Aesthetic Attitude *

SOME RECENT ARTICLES[1] have suggested the unsatisfactoriness of the notion of the aesthetic attitude and it is now time for a fresh look at that encrusted article of faith. This conception has been valuable to aesthetics and criticism in helping wean them from a sole concern with beauty and related notions.[2] However, I shall argue that the aesthetic attitude is a myth and while, as G. Ryle[3] has said, "Myths often do a lot of theoretical good while they are still new,"[4] this particular one is no longer useful and in fact misleads aesthetic theory.

There is a range of theories which differ according to how strongly the aesthetic attitude is characterized. This variation is reflected in the language the theories employ. The strongest variety is Edward Bullough's[5] theory of psychical distance, recently defended by Sheila Dawson.[6] The central technical term of this theory is "distance" used as a verb to denote an action which either constitutes or is necessary for the aesthetic attitude. These theorists use such sentences as "He distanced (or failed to distance) the play." The second variety is widely held but has been defended most vigorously in recent years by Je-rome Stolnitz and Eliseo Vivas. The *central* technical term of this variety is "disinterested"[7] used either as an adverb or as an adjective. This weaker theory speaks not of a special kind of action (distancing) but of an ordinary kind of action (attending) done in a certain way (disinterestedly). These first two versions are perhaps not as different as my classification suggests. However, the language of the two is different enough to justify separate discussions. My discussion of this second variety will for the most part make use of Jerome Stolnitz' book[8] which is a thorough, consistent, and large-scale version of the attitude theory. The weakest version of the attitude theory can be found in Vincent Tomas' statement "If looking at a picture and attending closely to how it looks is not really to be in the aesthetic attitude, then what on earth is?"[9] In the following I shall be concerned with the notion of *aesthetic* attitude and this notion may have little or no connection with the ordinary notion of an *attitude*.

I

Psychical distance, according to Bullough, is a psychological process by virtue of which a person *puts* some object (be it a painting, a play, or a dangerous fog at sea) "out of gear" with the practical interests of the self. Miss Dawson maintains that it is "the beauty of the phenomenon, which

* I wish to thank both Monroe C. Beardsley and Jerome Stolnitz who read earlier drafts of this paper and made many helpful comments. [author's note]

[1] See Marshall Cohen, "Appearance and the Aesthetic Attitude," *Journal of Philosophy*, vol. 56 (1959), p. 926; and Joseph Margolis, "Aesthetic Perception," *Journal of Aesthetics and Art Criticism*, vol. 19 (1960), p. 211. Margolis gives an argument, but it is so compact as to be at best only suggestive. [author's note]

[2] Jerome Stolnitz, "Some Questions Concerning Aesthetic Perception," *Philosophy and Phenomenological Research*, vol. 22 (1961), p. 69. [author's note]

[3] Gilbert Ryle (1900–1976) was a prominent Oxford philosopher of mind and language. His classic work, *The Concept of Mind*, argued that our language misleads us into positing a "ghost in the machine."

[4] *The Concept of Mind* (London, 1949), p. 23. [author's note]

[5] See the introduction and selection on pp. 237–254.

[6] "'Distancing' as an Aesthetic Principle," *Australasian Journal of Philosophy*, vol. 39 (1961), pp. 155–174. [author's note]

[7] "Disinterested" is Stolnitz' term. Vivas uses "intransitive." [author's note]

[8] *Aesthetics and Philosophy of Art Criticism* (Boston, 1960), p. 510. [author's note]

[9] "Aesthetic Vision," *The Philosophical Review*, vol. 68 (1959), p. 63. I shall ignore Tomas' attempt to distinguish between appearance and reality since it seems to confuse rather than clarify aesthetic theory. See F. Sibley, "Aesthetics and the Looks of Things," *Journal of Philosophy*, vol. 56 (1959), pp. 905–915; M. Cohen, *op. cit.*, pp. 915–926; and J. Stolnitz, "Some Questions Concerning Aesthetic Perception," *op. cit.*, pp. 69–87. Tomas discusses only visual art and the aesthetic attitude, but his remarks could be generalized into a comprehensive theory. [author's note]

captures our attention, puts us out of gear with practical life, and forces us, if we are receptive, to view it on the level of aesthetic consciousness."[10]

Later she maintains that some persons (critics, actors, members of an orchestra, and the like) "distance deliberately."[11] Miss Dawson, following Bullough, discusses cases in which people are unable to bring off an act of distancing or are incapable of being induced into a state of being distanced. She uses Bullough's example of the jealous ("under-distanced") husband at a performance of *Othello*[12] who is able to keep his attention on the play because he keeps thinking of his own wife's suspicious behavior. On the other hand, if "we are mainly concerned with the technical details of its [the play's] presentation, then we are said to be over-distanced."[13] There is, then, a species of action—distancing—which may be deliberately done and which initiates a state of consciousness—being distanced.

The question is: Are there actions denoted by "to distance" or states of consciousness denoted by "being distanced"? When the curtain goes up, when we walk up to a painting, or when we look at a sunset are we ever induced into a state of being distanced either by being struck by the beauty of the object or by pulling off an act of distancing? I do not recall committing any such special actions or of being induced into any special state, and I have no reason to suspect that I am atypical in this respect. The distance-theorist may perhaps ask, "But are you not usually oblivious to noises and sights other than those of the play or to the marks on the wall around the painting?" The answer is of course—"Yes." But if "to distance" and "being distanced" simply mean that one's attention is focused, what is the point of introducing new technical terms and speaking as if these terms refer to special kinds of acts and states of consciousness? The distance-theorist might argue further, "But surely you put the play

(painting, sunset) 'out of gear' with your practical interests?" This question seems to me to be a very odd way of asking (by employing the technical metaphor "out of gear") if I attended to the play rather than thought about my wife or wondered how they managed to move the scenery about. Why not ask me straight out if I paid attention? Thus, when Miss Dawson says that the jealous husband under-distanced *Othello* and that the person with a consuming interest in techniques of stagecraft over-distanced the play, these are just technical and misleading ways of describing two different cases of inattention. In both cases something is being attended to, but in neither case is it the action of the play. To introduce the technical terms "distance," "under-distance," and "over-distance" does nothing but send us chasing after phantom acts and states of consciousness.

Miss Dawson's commitment to the theory of distance (as a kind of mental insulation material necessary for a work of art if it is to be enjoyed aesthetically) leads her to draw a conclusion so curious as to throw suspicion on the theory.

> One remembers the horrible loss of distance in *Peter-Pan*[14]—the moment when Peter says "Do you believe in fairies? . . . If you believe, clap your hands!" the moment when most children would like to slink out of the theatre and not a few cry —not because Tinkerbell may die, but because the magic is gone. What, after all, should we feel like if Lear were to leave Cordelia,[15] come to the front of the stage and say, "All the grown-ups who think that she loves me, shout 'Yes'."[16]

It is hard to believe that the responses of any children could be as theory-bound as those Miss Dawson describes. In fact, Peter Pan's request for applause is a dramatic high point to which children respond enthusiastically. The playwright gives the children a momentary chance to become actors in the play. The children do not at that

[10] Dawson, *op. cit.*, p. 158. [author's note]

[11] *Ibid.*, pp. 159–160. [author's note]

[12] Othello is the principal character in Shakespeare's play of that name. Othello's jealousy is exploited by the villain, Iago.

[13] *Ibid.*, p. 159. [author's note]

[14] *Peter Pan* is the children's play by J. M. Barrie (1860–1937) about a magical land where no one grows past childhood.

[15] In Shakespeare's *King Lear,* Cordelia is the only one of Lear's daughters who will not flatter him. As a result, he rejects her and she dies.

[16] Dawson, p. 168. [author's note]

moment lose or snap out of a state of being distanced because they never had or were in any such thing to begin with. The comparison of Peter Pan's appeal to the hypothetical one by Lear is pointless. *Peter Pan* is a magical play in which almost anything can happen, but *King Lear* is a play of a different kind. There are, by the way, many plays in which an actor directly addresses the audience (*Our Town*,[17] *The Marriage Broker*,[18] *A Taste of Honey*,[19] for example) without causing the play to be less valuable. Such plays are unusual, but what is unusual is not necessarily bad; there is no point in trying to lay down rules to which every play must conform independently of the kind of play it is.

It is perhaps worth noting that Susanne Langer reports the reaction she had as a child to this scene in *Peter Pan*.[20] As she remembers it, Peter Pan's appeal shattered the illusion and caused her acute misery. However, she reports that all the other children clapped and laughed and enjoyed themselves.

II

The second way of conceiving of the aesthetic attitude—as the ordinary action of attending done in a certain way (disinterestedly)—is illustrated by the work of Jerome Stolnitz and Eliseo Vivas. Stolnitz defines "aesthetic attitude" as "disinterested and sympathetic attention to and contemplation of any object of awareness whatever, for its own sake alone."[21] Stolnitz defines the main terms of his definition: "disinterested" means "no concern for any ulterior purpose";[22] "sympathetic" means "accept the object on its own terms

to appreciate it";[23] and "contemplation" means "perception directed toward the object in its own right and the spectator is not concerned to analyze it or ask questions about it.[24]

The notion of disinterestedness, which Stolnitz has elsewhere shown[25] to be seminal for modern aesthetic theory, is the key term here. Thus, it is necessary to be clear about the nature of disinterested attention to the various arts. It can make sense to speak, for example, of listening disinterestedly to music only if it makes sense to speak of listening interestedly to music. It would make no sense to speak of walking *fast* unless walking could be done *slowly*. Using Stolnitz' definition of "disinterestedness," the two situations would have to be described as "listening with no ulterior purpose" (disinterestedly) and "listening with an ulterior purpose" (interestedly). Note that what initially appears to be a perceptual distinction—listening in a certain way (interestedly or disinterestedly)—turns out to be a motivational or an intentional distinction—listening for or with a certain purpose. Suppose Jones listens to a piece of music for the purpose of being able to analyze and describe it on an examination the next day and Smith listens to the same music with no such ulterior purpose. There is certainly a difference between the motives and intentions of the two men: Jones has an ulterior purpose and Smith does not, but this does not mean Jones's listening differs from Smith's. It is possible that both men enjoy the music or that both be bored. The attention of either or both may flag and so on. It is important to note that a person's motive or intention is different from his action (Jones's listening to the music, for example). There is only one way to *listen* to (to attend to) music, although the listening may be more or less attentive and there may be a variety of motives, intentions, and rea-

---

[17] *Our Town* is a play by Thornton Wilder (1897–1975). A narrator comes on stage and comments on the action.
[18] *The Marriage Broker* is a play by Tashrak (pseud.) (1872–1926) based on stories of the Shulem, an ultraorthodox Jewish sect.
[19] *A Taste of Honey* is a play by Shelagh Delaney (1939–).
[20] *Feeling and Form* (New York, 1953), p. 318. [author's note]
[21] *Aesthetics and Philosophy of Art Criticism*, pp. 34–35. [author's note]
[22] *Ibid.*, p. 35. [author's note]

[23] *Ibid.*, p. 36. [author's note]
[24] *Ibid.*, p. 38. [author's note]
[25] "On the Origins of 'Aesthetic Disinterestedness'," The *Journal of Aesthetics and Art Criticism*, vol. 20 (1961), pp. 131–143. [author's note]

sons for doing so and a variety of ways of being distracted from the music.

In order to avoid a common mistake of aestheticians—drawing a conclusion about one kind of art and assuming it holds for all the arts—the question of disinterested attention must be considered for arts other than music. How would one look at a painting disinterestedly or interestedly? An example of alleged interested viewing might be the case in which a painting reminds Jones of his grandfather and Jones proceeds to muse about or to regale a companion with tales of his grandfather's pioneer exploits. Such incidents would be characterized by attitude-theorists as examples of using a work of art as a vehicle for associations and so on, i.e., cases of interested attention. But Jones is not looking at (attending to) the painting at all, although he may be facing it with his eyes open. Jones is now musing or attending to the story he is telling, although he had to look at the painting at first to notice that it resembled his grandfather. Jones is not now looking at the painting interestedly, since he is not now looking at (attending to) the painting. Jones's thinking or telling a story about his grandfather is no more a part of the painting than his speculating about the artist's intentions is and, hence, his musing, telling, speculating, and so on cannot properly be described as attending to the painting interestedly. What attitude-aestheticians are calling attention to is the occurrence of irrelevant associations which distract the viewer from the painting or whatever. But distraction is not a special kind of attention, it is a kind of inattention.

Consider now disinterestedness and plays. I shall make use of some interesting examples offered by J. O. Urmson,[26] but I am not claiming that Urmson is an attitude-theorist. Urmson never speaks in his article of aesthetic attitude but rather of aesthetic satisfaction. In addition to aesthetic satisfaction, Urmson mentions economic, moral, personal, and intellectual satisfactions. I think the attitude-theorist would consider these last four kinds of satisfaction as "ulterior purposes" and, hence, cases of interested attention. Urmson considers the case of a man in the audience of a play who is delighted.[27] It is discovered that his delight is *solely* the result of the fact that there is a full house—the man is the impresario of the production. Urmson is right in calling *this* impresario's satisfaction economic rather than aesthetic, although there is a certain oddness about the example as it finds the impresario sitting *in the audience.* However, my concern is not with Urmson's examples as such but with the attitude theory. This impresario is certainly an interested party in the fullest sense of the word, but is his behavior an instance of interested attention as distinct from the supposed disinterested attention of the average citizen who sits beside him? In the situation as described by Urmson it would not make any sense to say that the impresario is attending to the play at all, since his sole concern at the moment is the till. If he can be said to be attending to anything (rather than just thinking about it) it is the size of the house. I do not mean to suggest that an impresario could not attend to his play if he found himself taking up a seat in a full house; I am challenging the sense of disinterested attention. As an example of personal satisfaction Urmson mentions the spectator whose daughter is in the play. Intellectual satisfaction involves the solution of technical problems of plays and moral satisfaction the consideration of the effects of the play on the viewer's conduct. All three of these candidates which the attitude-theorist would propose as cases of interested attention turn out to be just different ways of being distracted from the play and, hence, not cases of interested attention to the play. Of course, there is no reason to think that in any of these cases the distraction or inattention must be total, although it could be. In fact, such inattentions

---

[26] "What Makes a Situation Aesthetic?" in *Philosophy Looks at the Arts,* Joseph Margolis (ed.), (New York, 1962). Reprinted from *Proceedings of the Aristotelian Society,* Supplementary Volume 31 (1957), pp. 75–92. [author's note]

[27] *Ibid.,* p. 15. [author's note]

often occur but are so fleeting that nothing of the play, music, or whatever is missed or lost.

The example of a playwright watching a rehearsal or an out-of-town performance with a view to rewriting the script has been suggested to me as a case in which a spectator is certainly attending to the play (unlike our impresario) and attending in an interested manner. This case is unlike those just discussed but is similar to the earlier case of Jones (not Smith) listening to a particular piece of music. Our playwright—like Jones, who was to be examined on the music—has ulterior motives. Furthermore, the playwright, unlike an ordinary spectator, can change the script after the performance or during a rehearsal. But how is our playwright's *attention* (as distinguished from his motives and intentions) different from that of an ordinary viewer? The playwright might enjoy or be bored by the performance as any spectator might be. The playwright's attention might even flag. In short, the kinds of things which may happen to the playwright's attention are no different from those that may happen to an ordinary spectator, although the two may have quite different motives and intentions.

For the discussion of disinterested-interested reading of literature it is appropriate to turn to the arguments of Eliseo Vivas whose work is largely concerned with literature. Vivas remarks that "By approaching a poem in a nonaesthetic mode it may function as history, as social criticism, as diagnostic evidence of the author's neuroses, and in an indefinite number of other ways." [28] Vivas further notes that according to Plato "the Greeks used Homer as an authority on war and almost anything under the sun," and that a certain poem "can be read as erotic poetry or as an account of a mystical experience." [29] The difference between reading a poem as history or whatever (reading it nonaesthetically) and reading it aesthetically depends on how *we* approach or

read it. A poem "does not come self-labeled," [30] but presumably is a poem only when it is read in a certain way—when it is an object of aesthetic experience. For Vivas, being an aesthetic object means being the object of the aesthetic attitude. He defines the aesthetic experience as "an experience of rapt attention which involves the intransitive apprehension of an object's immanent meanings and values in their full presentational immediacy." [31] Vivas maintains that his definition "helps me understand better what I can and what I cannot do when I read *The Brothers [Karamazov]*" and his definition "forces us to acknowledge that *The Brothers Karamazov* [32] can hardly be read as art. . . ." [33] This acknowledgment means that we probably cannot intransitively apprehend *The Brothers* because of its size and complexity.

"Intransitive" is the key term here and Vivas' meaning must be made clear. A number of passages reveal his meaning but perhaps the following is the best. "Having once seen a hockey game in slow motion, I am prepared to testify that it was an object of pure intransitive experience [attention]—for I was not *interested* in which team won the game and no external factors mingled with my interest in the beautiful rhythmic flow of the slow-moving men." [34] It appears that Vivas' "intransitive attention" has the same meaning as Stolnitz' "disinterested attention," namely, "attending with no ulterior purpose." [35] Thus, the question to ask is "How does one attend to (read) a poem or any literary work transitively?" One can certainly attend to (read) a poem for a variety of dif-

[28] "Contextualism Reconsidered," *The Journal of Aesthetics and Art Criticism*, vol. 18 (1959), pp. 224–225. [author's note]

[29] *Ibid.*, p. 225. [author's note]

[30] *Loc. cit.* [author's note]

[31] *Ibid.*, p. 227. [author's note]

[32] *The Brothers Karamazov* is the novel by Fyodr Dostoevsky (1821–1881) about the relation of three brothers to their domineering father in prerevolutionary Russia.

[33] Vivas, p. 237. [author's note]

[34] *Ibid.*, p. 228. (Italics mine.) [author's note]

[35] Vivas' remark about the improbability of being able to read *The Brothers Karamazov* as art suggests that "intransitive attention" may sometimes mean for him "that which can be attended to at one time" or "that which can be held before the mind at one time." However, this second possible meaning is not one which is relevant here. [author's note]

ferent purposes and because of a variety of different reasons, but can one attend to a poem transitively? I do not think so, but let us consider the examples Vivas offers. He mentions "a type of reader" who uses a poem or parts of a poem as a spring-board for "loose, uncontrolled, relaxed day-dreaming, wool-gathering rambles, free from the contextual control" of the poem.[36] But surely it would be wrong to say such musing is a case of transitively attending to a poem, since it is clearly a case of not attending to a poem. Another supposed way of attending to a poem transitively is by approaching it "as diagnostic evidence of the author's neuroses." Vivas is right if he means that there is no critical point in doing this since it does not throw light on the poem. But this is a case of *using* information gleamed from a poem to make inferences about its author rather than attending to a poem. If anything can be said to be attended to here it is the author's neuroses (at least they are being thought about). This kind of case is perhaps best thought of as a rather special way of getting distracted from a poem. Of course, such "biographical" distractions might be insignificant and momentary enough so as scarcely to distract attention from the poem (a flash of insight or understanding about the poet). On the other hand, such distractions may turn into dissertations and whole careers. Such an interest may lead a reader to concentrate his attention (when he does read a poem) on certain "informational" aspects of a poem and to ignore the remaining aspects. As deplorable as such a sustained practice may be, it is at best a case of attending to certain features of a poem and ignoring others.

Another way that poetry may allegedly be read transitively is by reading it as history. This case is different from the two preceding ones since poetry often contains history (makes historical statements or at least references) but does not (usually) contain statements about the author's neuroses and so on nor does it contain statements about what a reader's free associations are

about (otherwise we would not call them "free associations"). Reading a poem as history suggests that we are attending to (thinking about) historical events by way of attending to a poem—the poem is a time-telescope. Consider the following two sets of lines:

> In fourteen hundred and ninety-two
> Columbus sailed the ocean blue.

> Or like stout Cortez when with eagle eyes
> He star'd at the Pacific—and all his men
> Look'd at each other with a wild surmise—
> Silent, upon a peak in Darien.[37]

Someone might read both of these raptly and not know that they make historical references (inaccurately in one case)—might this be a case of intransitive attention? How would the above reading differ—so far as attention is concerned—from the case of a reader who recognized the historical content of the poetic lines? The two readings do not differ as far as attention is concerned. History is a part of these sets of poetic lines and the two readings differ in that the first fails to take account of an aspect of the poetic lines (its historical content) and the second does not fail to do so. Perhaps by "reading as history" Vivas means "reading *simply* as history." But even this meaning does not mark out a special kind of attention but rather means that only a single aspect of a poem is being noticed and that its rhyme, meter, and so on are ignored. Reading a poem as social criticism can be analyzed in a fashion similar to reading as history. Some poems simply are or contain social criticism, and a complete reading must not fail to notice this fact.

The above cases of alleged interested attending can be sorted out in the following way. Jones listening to the music and our playwright watching the rehearsal are both attending with ulterior

---

[36]Vivas, *op. cit.,* p. 231. [author's note]

[37]The lines are from John Keats's sonnet, "On First Looking into Chapman's Homer." In historical fact it was Balboa, not Cortez, who "stared at the Pacific" from a "peak in Darien," which is the Isthmus of Panama.

motives to a work of art, but there is no reason to suppose that the attention of either is different in kind from that of an ordinary spectator. The reader who reads a poem as history is simply attending to an aspect of a poem. On the other hand, the remaining cases—Jones beside the painting telling of his grandfather, the gloating impresario, daydreaming while "reading" a poem, and so on—are simply cases of not attending to the work of art.

In general, I conclude that "disinterestedness" or "intransitiveness" cannot properly be used to refer to a special kind of attention. "Disinterestedness" is a term which is used to make clear that an action has certain kinds of motives. Hence, we speak of disinterested findings (of boards of inquiry), disinterested verdicts (of judges and juries), and so on. Attending to an object, of course, has its motives but the attending itself is not interested or disinterested according to whether its motives are of the kind which motivate interested or disinterested action (as findings and verdicts might), although the attending may be more or less close.

I have argued that the second way of conceiving the aesthetic attitude is also a myth, or at least that its main content—disinterested attention—is; but I must now try to establish that the view misleads aesthetic theory. I shall argue that the attitude-theorist is incorrect about (1) the way in which he wishes to set the limits of aesthetic relevance; (2) the relation of the critic to a work of art; and (3) the relation of morality to aesthetic value.

Since I shall make use of the treatment of aesthetic relevance in Jerome Stolnitz' book, let me make clear that I am not necessarily denying the relevance of the specific items he cites but disagreeing with his criterion of relevance. His criterion of relevance is derived from his definition of "aesthetic attitude" and is set forth at the very beginning of his book. This procedure leads Monroe Beardsley in his review of the book to remark that Stolnitz' discussion is premature.[38] Beardsley suggests "that relevance cannot be satisfacto-

rily discussed until after a careful treatment of the several arts, their dimensions and capacities."[39]

First, what is meant by "aesthetic relevance"? Stolnitz defines the problem by asking the question: "Is it ever 'relevant' to the aesthetic experience to have thoughts or images or bits of knowledge which are not present within the object itself?"[40] Stolnitz begins by summarizing Bullough's experiment and discussion of single colors and associations[41] Some associations absorb the spectator's attention and distract him from the color and some associations "fuse" with the color. Associations of the latter kind are aesthetic and the former are not. Stolnitz draws the following conclusion about associations:

> If the aesthetic experience is as we have described it, then whether an association is aesthetic depends on whether it is compatible with the attitude of "disinterested attention." If the association reenforces the focusing of attention upon the object, by "fusing" with the object and thereby giving it added "life and significance," it is genuinely aesthetic. If, however, it arrogates attention to itself and away from the object, it undermines the aesthetic attitude.[42]

It is not clear how something could fuse with a single color, but "fusion" is one of those words in aesthetics which is rarely defined. Stolnitz then makes use of a more fruitful example, one from I. A. Richards's *Practical Criticism*.[43] He cites the responses of students to the poem which begins:

> Between the erect and solemn trees
> I will go down upon my knees;
> I shall not find this day
> So meet a place to pray.[44]

---

38 *The Journal of Philosophy*, vol. 57 (1960), p. 624. [author's note]

39 *Loc. cit.* [author's note]

40 *Op. cit.*, p. 53. [author's note]

41 *Ibid.*, p. 54. [author's note]

42 *Ibid.*, pp. 54–55. [author's note]

43 *Ibid.*, pp. 55–56. [author's note]

44 I. A. Richards assembled poems of varying quality and asked students to comment on them without knowing the titles or authors. The student's comments then provided the data for Richards's analysis of critical method in *Practical Criticism*. This poem is titled "The Temple" from *Parentalia and Other Poems* by J. D. C. Pellew.

The image of a rugby forward running arose in the mind of one student-reader on reading the third verse of this poem. A cathedral was suggested to a second reader of the poem. The cathedral image "is congruous with both the verbal meaning of the poem and the emotions and mood which it expresses. It does not divert attention away from the poem."[45] The rugby image is presumably incongruous and diverts attention from the poem.

It is a confusion to take compatibility with disinterested attention as a criterion of relevance. If, as I have tried to show, *disinterested attention* is a confused notion, then it will not do as a satisfactory criterion. Also, when Stolnitz comes to show why the cathedral image is, and the rugby image is not relevant, the criterion he actually uses is *congruousness with the meaning of the poem,* which is quite independent of the notion of disinterestedness. The problem is perhaps best described as the problem of relevance to a poem, or more generally, to a work of art, rather than aesthetic relevance.

A second way in which the attitude theory misleads aesthetics is its contention that a critic's relationship to a work of art is different in kind from the relationship of other persons to the work. H. S. Langfeld in an early statement of this view wrote that we may "slip from the attitude of aesthetic enjoyment to the attitude of the critic." He characterizes the critical attitude as "intellectually occupied in coldly estimating . . . merits" and the aesthetic attitude as responding "emotionally to" a work of art.[46] At the beginning of his book in the discussion of the aesthetic attitude, Stolnitz declares that if a percipient of a work of art "has the purpose of passing judgment upon it, his attitude is not aesthetic."[47] He develops this line at a later stage of his book, arguing that appreciation (perceiving with the aesthetic attitude) and criticism (seeking for reasons to support an evaluation of a work) are (1) distinct and (2) "psychologically opposed to each other."[48] The critical attitude is questioning, analytical, probing for strengths and weakness, and so on. The aesthetic attitude is just the opposite: "It commits our allegiance to the object freely and unquestioningly"; "the spectator 'surrenders' himself to the work of art."[49] "Just because the two attitudes are inimical, whenever criticism obtrudes, it reduces aesthetic interest."[50] Stolnitz does not, of course, argue that criticism is unimportant for appreciation. He maintains criticism plays an important and necessary role in preparing a person to appreciate the nuances, detail, form, and so on of works of art. We are quite right, he says, thus to read and listen perceptively and acutely, but he questions, "Does this mean that we must analyze, measure in terms of value-criteria, etc., *during* the supposedly aesthetic experience?"[51] His answer is "No" and he maintains that criticism must occur "*prior* to the aesthetic encounter,"[52] or it will interfere with appreciation.

How does Stolnitz know that criticism will always interfere with appreciation? His conclusion sounds like one based upon the observations of actual cases, but I do not think it is. I believe it is a logical consequence of his definition of aesthetic attitude in terms of disinterested attention (no ulterior purpose). According to his view, to appreciate an object aesthetically one has to perceive it with no ulterior purpose. But the critic has an ulterior purpose—to analyze and evaluate the object be perceives—hence, in so far as a person functions as a critic he cannot function as an appreciator. But here, as previously, Stolnitz confuses a perceptual distinction with a motivational one. If it were possible to *attend* disinterestedly or interestedly, then perhaps the critic (as percipient) would differ from other percipients. But if my earlier argument about attending is correct, the critic differs from other percipients only in

[45] Richards, p. 56. [author's note]

[46] *The Aesthetic Attitude* (New York, 1920), p. 79. [author's note]

[47] *Op. cit.,* p. 35. [author's note]

[48] *Ibid.,* p. 377. [author's note]

[49] *Ibid.,* pp. 377–378. [author's note]

[50] *Ibid.,* p. 379. [author's note]

[51] *Ibid.,* p. 380. [author's note]

[52] *Loc. cit.* [author's note]

his motives and intentions and not in the way in which he attends to a work of art.

Of course, it might just be a fact that the search for reasons is incompatible with the appreciation of art, but I do not think it is. Several years ago I participated in a series of panel discussions of films. During the showing of each film we were to discuss, I had to take note of various aspects of the film (actor's performance, dramatic development, organization of the screen-plane and screen-space at given moments, and so on) in order later to discuss the films. I believe that this practice not only helped educate me to appreciate subsequent films but that it enhanced the appreciation of the films I was analyzing. I noticed and was able to appreciate things about the films I was watching which ordinarily out of laziness I would not have noticed. I see no reason why the same should not be the case with the professional critic or any critical percipient. If many professional critics seem to appreciate so few works, it is not because they are critics, but perhaps because the percentage of good works of art is fairly small and they suffer from a kind of combat fatigue.

I am unable to see any significant difference between "perceptively and acutely" attending to a work of art (which Stolnitz holds enhances appreciation) and searching for reasons, so far as the experience of a work of art is concerned. If I attend perceptively and acutely, I will have certain standards and/or paradigms in mind (not necessarily consciously) and will be keenly aware of the elements and relations in the work and will evaluate them to some degree. Stolnitz writes as if criticism takes place and then is over and done with, but the search for and finding of reasons (noticing this fits in with that, and so on) is continuous in practiced appreciators. A practiced viewer does not even have to be looking for a reason, he may just notice a line or an area in a painting, for example, and the line or area becomes a reason why he thinks the painting better or worse. A person may be a critic (not necessarily a good one) without meaning to be or without even realizing it.

There is one final line worth pursuing. Stolnitz' remarks suggest that one reason he thinks criticism and appreciation incompatible is that they compete with one another for time (this would be especially bad in the cases of performed works). But seeking and finding reasons (criticism) does not compete for time with appreciation. First, to seek for a reason means to be ready and able to notice something and to be thus ready and able as one attends does not compete for time with the attending. In fact, I should suppose that seeking for reasons, would tend to focus attention more securely on the work of art. Second, finding a reason is an achievement, like winning a race. (It takes time to run a race but not to win it.) Consider the finding of the following reasons. How much time does it take to "see" that a note is off key (or on key)? How long does it take to notice that an actor mispronounces a word (or does it right)? How much time does it take to realize that a character's action does not fit his already established personality? (One is struck by it.) How long does it take to apprehend that a happy ending is out of place? It does not take time to find any of these reasons or reasons in general. Finding a reason is like coming to understand— it is done in a flash. I do not mean to suggest that one cannot be mistaken in finding a reason. What may appear to be a fault or a merit (a found reason) in the middle of a performance (or during one look at a painting and so forth) may turn out to be just the opposite when seen from the perspective of the whole performance (or other looks at the painting).

A third way in which the attitude theory misleads aesthetic theory is its contention that aesthetic value is always independent of morality. This view is perhaps not peculiar to the attitude theory, but it is a logical consequence of the attitude approach. Two quotations from attitude-theorists will establish the drift of their view of morality and aesthetic value.

> We are either concerned with the beauty of the object or with some other value of the same. Just as soon, for example, as ethical considerations occur to our mind, our attitude shifts.[53]

---

[53] H. S. Langfeld, *op. cit.*, p. 73. [author's note]

Any of us might reject a novel because it seems to conflict with our moral beliefs . . . When we do so . . . We have *not* read the book aesthetically, for we have interposed moral . . . responses of our own which are alien to it. This disrupts the aesthetic attitude. We cannot then say that the novel is *aesthetically* bad, for we have not permitted ourselves to consider it aesthetically. To maintain the aesthetic attitude, we must follow the lead of the object and respond in concert with it.[54]

This conception of the aesthetic attitude functions to hold the moral aspects and the *aesthetic* aspects of the work of art firmly apart. Presumably, although it is difficult to see one's way clearly here, the moral aspects of a work of art cannot be an object of aesthetic attention because aesthetic attention is by definition disinterested and the moral aspects are somehow practical (interested). I suspect that there are a number of confusions involved in the assumption of the incompatibility of aesthetic attention and the moral aspects of art, but I shall not attempt to make these clear, since the root of the assumption— disinterested attention—is a confused notion. Some way other than in terms of the aesthetic attitude, then, is needed to discuss the relation of morality and aesthetic value.

David Pole in a recent article[55] has argued that the moral vision which a work of art may embody is *aesthetically* significant. It should perhaps be remarked at this point that not all works of art embody a moral vision and perhaps some kinds of art (music, for example) cannot embody a moral vision, but certainly some novels, some poems, and some films and plays do. I assume it is unnecessary to show how novels and so on have this moral aspect. Pole notes the curious fact that while so many critics approach works of art in "overtly moralistic terms," it is a "philosophical commonplace . . . that the ethical and the aesthetic modes . . . form different categories."[56] I suspect that many philosophers would simply say that these critics are confused about their roles. But Pole assumes that philosophical theory "should take notice of practice"[57] and surely he is right. In agreeing with Pole's assumption I should like to reserve the right to argue in specific cases that a critic may be misguided. This right is especially necessary in a field such as aesthetics because the language and practice of critics is so often burdened with ancient theory. Perhaps all moralistic criticism is wrong but philosophers should not rule it out of order at the very beginning by use of a definition.

Pole thinks that the moral vision presented by a particular work of art will be either true or false (perhaps a mixture of true and false might occur). If a work has a false moral vision, then something "is lacking within the work itself. But to say that is to say that the [work] is internally incoherent; some particular aspect must jar with what— on the strength of the rest—we claim a right to demand. And here the moral fault that we have found will count as an aesthetic fault too."[58] Pole is trying to show that the assessment of the moral vision of a work of art is just a special case of coherence or incoherence, and since everyone would agree that coherence is an aesthetic category, the assessment of the moral vision is an aesthetic assessment.

I think Pole's conclusion is correct but take exception to some of his arguments. First, I am uncertain whether it is proper to speak of a moral vision being true or false, and would want to make a more modest claim—that a moral vision can be judged to be acceptable or unacceptable. (I am not claiming Pole is wrong and my claim is not inconsistent with his.) Second, I do not see that a false (or unacceptable) moral vision makes a work incoherent. I should suppose that to say a work is coherent or incoherent is to speak about how its parts fit together and this involves no reference to something outside the work as the work's truth or falsity does.

---

[54] J. Stolnitz, *op. cit.*, p. 36. [author's note]
[55] "Morality and the Assessment of Literature," *Philosophy*, vol. 37 (1962), pp. 193- 207. [author's note]
[56] *Ibid.*, p. 193. [author's note]

---

[57] *Loc. cit.* [author's note]
[58] *Ibid.*, p. 206. [author's note]

In any event, it seems to me that a faulty moral vision can be shown to be an aesthetic fault independently of Pole's consideration of truth and coherence. As Pole's argument implies, a work's moral vision is a *part* of the work. Thus, any statement—descriptive or evaluative—about the work's moral vision is a statement about the *work;* and any statement about a *work* is a critical statement and, hence, falls within the aesthetic domain. To judge a moral vision to be morally unacceptable is to judge it defective and this amounts to saying that the work of art has a defective part. (Of course, a judgment of the acceptability of a moral vision may be wrong, as a judgment of an action sometimes is, but this fallibility does not make any difference.) Thus, a work's moral vision may be an aesthetic merit or defect just as a work's degree of unity is a merit or defect. But what justifies saying that a moral vision is a part of a work of art? Perhaps "part" is not quite the right word but it serves to make the point clear enough. A novel's moral vision is an essential part of the novel and if it were removed (I am not sure how such surgery could be carried out) the novel would be greatly changed. Anyway, a novel's moral vision is not like its covers or binding. However, someone might still argue that even though a work's moral vision is defective and the moral vision is part of the work, that this defect is not an *aesthetic* defect. How is "aesthetic" being used here? It is being used to segregate certain aspects or parts of works of art such as formal and stylistic aspects from such aspects as a work's moral vision. But it seems to me that the separation is only nominal. "Aesthetic" has been selected as a name for a certain sub-set of characteristics of works of art. I certainly cannot object to such a stipulation, since an underlying aim of this essay is to suggest the vacuousness of the term "aesthetic." My concern at this point is simply to insist that a work's moral vision is a part of the work and that, therefore, a critic can legitimately describe and evaluate it. I would *call* any defect or merit which a critic can legitimately point out an aesthetic defect or merit, but what we call it does not matter.

It would, of course, be a mistake to judge a work solely on the basis of its moral vision (it is only one part). The fact that some critics have judged works of art in this way is perhaps as much responsible as the theory of aesthetic attitude for the attempts to separate morality from the aesthetic. In fact, such criticism is no doubt at least partly responsible for the rise of the notion of the aesthetic attitude.

If the foregoing arguments are correct, the second way of conceiving the aesthetic attitude misleads aesthetic theory in at least three ways.

III

In answer to a hypothetical question about what is seen in viewing a portrait with the aesthetic attitude, Tomas in part responds "If looking at a picture and attending closely to how it looks is not really to be in the aesthetic attitude, then what on earth is?"[59] I shall take this sentence as formulating the weakest version of the aesthetic attitude. (I am ignoring Tomas' distinction between appearance and reality. See footnote 9. My remarks, thus, are not a critique of Tomas' argument; I am simply using one of his sentences.) First, this sentence speaks only of "looking at a picture," but "listening to a piece of music," "watching and listening to a play," and so on could be added easily enough. After thus expanding the sentence, it can be contracted into the general form: "Being in the aesthetic attitude is attending closely to a work of art (or a natural object)."

But the aesthetic attitude ("the hallmark of modern aesthetics") in this formulation is a great letdown—it no longer seems to say anything significant. Nevertheless, this does seem to be all that is left after the aesthetic attitude has been purged of *distancing* and *disinterestedness*. The only thing which prevents the aesthetic attitude from collapsing into simple attention is the qualification *closely*. One may, I suppose, attend to a work of art more or less closely, but this fact

---

[59] Tomas, *op. cit.,* p. 63. [author's note]

does not seem to signify anything very important. When "being in the aesthetic attitude" is equated with "attending (closely)," the equation neither involves any mythical element nor could it possibly mislead aesthetic theory. But if the definition has no vices, it seems to have no virtues either. When the aesthetic attitude finally turns out to be simply attending (closely), the final version should perhaps not be called "the weakest" but rather "the vacuous version" of the aesthetic attitude.

Stolnitz is no doubt historically correct that the notion of the aesthetic attitude has played an important role in the freeing of aesthetic theory from an overweening concern with beauty. It is easy to see how the slogan, "Anything can become an object of the aesthetic attitude," could help accomplish this liberation. It is worth noting, however, that the same goal could have been (and perhaps to some extent was) realized by simply noting that works of art are often ugly or contain ugliness, or have features which are difficult to include within beauty. No doubt, in more recent times people have been encouraged *to take an aesthetic attitude toward a painting* as a way of lowering their prejudices, say, against abstract and non-

objective art. So if the notion of aesthetic attitude has turned out to have no theoretical value for aesthetics, it has had practical value for the appreciation of art in a way similar to that of Clive Bell's[60] suspect notion of significant form.

Study Questions

1. What are the different theories of an aesthetic attitude that Dickie discusses? What do they have in common?
2. What is Dickie's criticism of the concept of *aesthetic disinterestedness*?
3. What are some ways of not paying attention to something?
4. What is Dickie's criticism of the concept of *aesthetic distance*?
5. What does *disinterested* properly refer to?
6. In what ways do attitude theories mislead?
7. How does a critic differ from an ordinary person who appreciates art?
8. What is Dickie's position on the moral vision of art?

---

[60] See the introduction and selection on pp. 255–269.

Arthur Danto

ARTHUR DANTO (1924–) is professor emeritus of philosophy at Columbia University and art critic for *The Nation*.

♦   ♦   ♦   ♦   ♦   ♦

Walter Benjamin represents the materialist inversion of Hegel's dialectical movement of art, transformed by Marx and a knowledge of history in the first half of the twentieth century. Arthur Danto presents a very different sense of the historicity of art and aesthetics. Yet in a way, Danto's rejection of the earlier aesthetics of attitudes and perception is even more radically complete. That aesthetics presumed that art was timelessly present and that aesthetics was a matter of perception—of seeing what was truly to be seen in works of art and nature from an aesthetic perspective. Danto challenges both the timelessness of art and the perceptual nature of aesthetics.

Arthur Danto is an art critic as well as a philosopher of art. He is well aware that much of the visual art of the twentieth century challenges earlier expectations about what art is and what it does. The earliest changes reflected a simple move away from pictorial transparency—the view that in looking at a picture one saw through it to what it was a picture of. Impressionism focused on the "surface" of the picture—the play of light and color rather than the objects and their arrangement that had made up the focus of traditional visual art. But postimpressionism went farther, abandoning perspective and formal verisimilitude. From there, art has exploded into so many forms of abstraction and eccentricity that one would be hard pressed to mention all of them. To some extent, this change in the visual arts has been, as Benjamin emphasized, a result of new technology such as photography and sound reproduction making the earlier functions of visual art and music superfluous. But Danto sees a deeper significance in what we should now be able to recognize in the history of art.

As new art forms appear, not just in the visual arts but across the fields of art in general, we gain a new perspective. What we had taken to be the only available forms and styles of art now become only one part of the larger historical picture. Art has a history, and its history dictates our theoretical understanding. Morris Weitz argued that theory has only a limited role. It misleads us into looking for only one thing and not seeing what is present. The positive role of theory is to help us see. But Danto argues that theory is essential to the very existence of art in the first place. One must be careful, therefore, to understand what the term *theory* refers to. For Danto, theory is the ability to apply predicates correctly. It is thus a linguistic operation, but it assumes a standard independent of language. In science, theory would be determined by its ability to account for all known facts and to assimilate new facts as they become known. But in the human realm, history makes those kinds of facts problematic. Facts are what happens, and they are not repeatedly observable. They are matters of human action and human invention, but action and invention are themselves constrained by what has happened and what possibilities are present. This is not Hegel's single movement; Danto avoids the kind of system building common to nineteenth-century German philosophy. But it is also not the kind of ahistorical theory of science that provided the model for much of twentieth-century philosophy.

One theory may replace another. Danto recognizes two broad categories of theories —imitation theory (IT) and reality theory (RT)—that largely account for the art theories that we have known so far. Reality theories come later, so they subsumes imitation theories as special cases or replace them with different explanations of the same phenomena. A painting that was valued because of what it represented comes to be explained and valued for what it creates. If that movement of theories were all that were at stake, however, we would not have fundamentally changed the role of theory. We would continue to look for definitions, though we would have to include more. Danto recognizes that eventually the definitions become so broad that they become meaningless. Anything and everything becomes art. Brillo boxes are no different from Renaissance masterpieces. So more is at work than one theory replacing another or one kind of theory, however different, replacing another kind of theory.

Theory itself becomes part of the historical explanation according to Danto. A theory is not just a formulation by some philosopher or art critic. Theory is implicit in what we do and say. A theory need not be formally presented in order to be present as long as we use terms consistently. Thus *theory* refers less to paradigms like the theory of relativity—careful formulations that describe a situation—than to the logical notion of a theory as whatever determines the value of terms. It is not that we begin with predicates and when we have observed enough applications of them, we can construct a theory that will show us how the predicates are applied. Instead, we construct a theory that allows us to apply predicates. There is no art independent of art theory. When what Danto calls the Reality Theory of Art (RT) replaces the Imitation Theory of Art (IT), it does not just redescribe known art objects. It adds to what Danto calls a matrix of possible styles that now can be retrospectively applied to earlier objects. Things that were not art are now included in Danto's "artworld" because they are now described by the art-theoretical predicates that history has made available. If this view lacks the sense of a single continuous movement toward an ultimate ideal goal that one finds in Hegel or Marx, it nevertheless understands history as a part of the reality of the artworld.

There would still be a problem for Danto if the effects of theory were simply to modify the possibilities. Once again, everything would potentially become art. Danto is fascinated by examples in which there is no perceptual or physical distinction between objects and yet one is art and another is not. Such examples decisively refute the claims that aesthetics depends on a form of perception, yet they seem to leave no way to make a distinction between art and nonart at all. Danto wants to maintain that distinction, so he must account for the difference in some other way.

His solution is to point once again to the history of the object—not in the sense of its history of production, however, as in Marxism, but its historical place as it now stands. Something is art because it occupies a position in the artworld, and it gains that position by being the subject of existing artworld predicates. Those predicates are made possible by art theories and aesthetic theories. Something is not art simply because an artist makes it or because some critic calls it art. The artist and the critic are themselves enabled by the existence at this time and place of art theories. An artist does not have to be a theoretician. It is enough that in becoming an artist, she or he belongs to a theoretically informed and constituted domain. A critic is not always right in the way she or he applies the predicates. There can be theoretical misunderstandings and misapplications. But art is essentially what the artworld succeeds in including within its scope. Something that at some other time and place would not have been a possibility for art may become a possibility. Something that is perceptually indistinguishable from something else may in fact belong to the artworld.

There are some interesting consequences of Danto's way of saving art theory and formulating his own overarching historical version: something that was not art may become art. This was true according to RT as well since at least some things were moved from museums of anthropology to museums of art. But under Danto's theory, they are not just seen differently; something is discovered about them that was not previously known. Moreover, some things could not be art until the requisite theory is available to disclose their possibilities. Art, therefore, is radically temporal.

It is less clear on Danto's theory whether, once a theory has appeared, its theoretical possibilities are always available. Danto's focus is on the unexpected things that turn up in the artworld. It is also not clear why some things cease to be a part of the artworld, at least as continuing possibilities for artists. Danto might argue that some forms are exhausted once all of the possibilities of the style matrix are explored. That is a problematic claim, however. Why should *original* now be a predicate capable of excluding exhausted forms when for long periods in art history variations on the same theme were desirable? Of course, one might say that still another fugue composed in the style of Bach is art; it is just not very interesting any more. But that seems to subordinate art theory and the artworld to some set of value predicates (*interesting*) that operate independently.

Danto's understanding of the artworld is one instance of a larger movement in aesthetics. Popular culture, historical awareness, and global perspectives have all contributed to qualify the confidence that classical and "high" art are the only aesthetic paradigms. The limitations of traditional Anglo-American analytical philosophy and continental Kantian and idealist traditions are also factors. Danto, in particular, has been associated with both traditions. Aesthetics influenced by Wittgenstein considers something like the artworld when it turns to "forms of life," though the basis is quite different. Similarly, continental aestheticians have moved beyond both the academic idealism of the nineteenth century and the phenomenology and existentialism of the post–World War I era in the direction of *hermeneutics,* which seeks to situate aesthetics in the context of a meeting of the work and audience that modifies both. What is common to all of these new directions is an increasing awareness that aesthetics cannot be isolated from the artworld and that the artworld is more extensive than what was recognized by theories of an aesthetic attitude and the paradigm of the "fine" arts.

One particular aspect of Danto's work needs to be clarified. An argument advanced by George Dickie uses the artworld to propose a different kind of definition of art, one that depends on relational properties rather than essential or perceptual properties. *Relational* properties are those that are acquired by an object as a result of its relation to something else. For example, "being above" is a relational property, as is "being a husband." Dickie first proposed that the artworld could establish a relation by making something a candidate for appreciation. When that proved too broad, he modified the proposal to include an intentional aspect in establishing the relation. In both the earlier and later versions of Dickie's theory, the artworld serves as the defining institution, and the theory has become known as the *institutional theory of art*. It shares with Danto's analysis the idea that the artworld itself is a crucial part of describing something as art. Dickie's institutional theory is quite different, however, in the way that it understands the workings of the artworld. For Danto, the artworld is an historical phenomenon. It changes through time and its workings are exhibited in the descriptive predicates and theories it produces. Art results from the application of those descriptions. For Dickie, the artworld is an institution. It produces art by its activities, and the purpose of aesthetics is to formulate the definitions that that activity supports. Thus Dickie's theory continues to function in the scientific/analytical way, while Danto understands aesthetic theory as the dynamic product of historical forces. While both agree on the importance of the artworld, each assigns it a different role in light of their individual understanding of what aesthetic theory is.

Danto is important because of his sensitivity to the current artworld, his awareness of the movement of history, and his analytical precision. He opens the way to many other ways of "saving" a role for art theory in the latter part of the twentieth century with its open and near chaotic artworld. Danto's paradigm is the visual arts, although he has interesting things to say about the literary side of the artworld elsewhere. His perspective is very open to the avant garde. A question remains, however, whether that openness does justice to the dimension of value implicit in aesthetics. In a memorable essay, Clement Greenberg raised the specter of avant garde art being destroyed by "kitsch," popularized cultural artifacts that are parasitic on real art. It remains to be seen whether the artworld can produce the kind of distinctions that will allow art to escape that fate.

The Artworld

Hamlet: Do you see nothing there?
The Queen: Nothing at all; yet all that is I see.
SHAKESPEARE: *Hamlet, act III, scene iv*

HAMLET [1] AND SOCRATES, [2] though in praise and deprecation respectively, spoke of art as a mirror held up to nature. As with many disagreements in attitude, this one has a factual basis. Socrates saw mirrors as but reflecting what we can already see, so art, insofar as mirrorlike, yields idle accurate duplications of the appearances of things, and is of no cognitive benefit whatever. Hamlet, more acutely, recognized a remarkable feature of reflecting surfaces, namely that they show us what we could not otherwise perceive—our own face and form—and so art, insofar as it is mirrorlike, reveals us to ourselves, and is, even by Socratic criteria, of some cognitive utility after all. As a philosopher, however, I find Socrates' discussion defective on other, perhaps less profound grounds than these. If a mirror-image of *o* is indeed an imitation of *o,* then, if art is imitation, mirror-images are art. But in fact mirroring objects no more is art than returning weapons to a madman is justice; and reference to mirrorings would be just the sly sort of counterinstance we would expect Socrates to bring forward in rebuttal of the theory he instead uses them to illustrate. If that theory requires us to class *these* as art, it thereby shows its inadequacy: "is an imitation" will not do as a sufficient condition for "is art." Yet, perhaps because artists *were* engaged in imitation, in Socrates' time and after, the insufficiency of the theory was not noticed until the invention of photography. Once rejected as a sufficient condition, mimesis was quickly discarded as even a necessary one; and since the achievement of Kandinsky, [3] mimetic features have been relegated to the periphery of critical concern, so much so that some works survive in spite of possessing those virtues, excellence in which was once celebrated as the essence of art, narrowly escaping demotion to mere illustrations.

It is, of course, indispensable in Socratic discussion that all participants be masters of the concept up for analysis, since the aim is to match a real defining expression to a term in active use, and the test for adequacy presumably consists in showing that the former analyzes and applies to all and only those things of which the latter is true. The popular disclaimer notwithstanding, then, Socrates' auditors purportedly knew what art was as well as what they liked; and a theory of art, regarded here as a real definition of 'Art,' is accordingly not to be of great use in helping men to recognize instances of its application. Their antecedent ability to do this is precisely what the adequacy of the theory is to be tested against, the problem being only to make explicit what they already know. It is *our* use of the term that the theory allegedly means to capture, but we are supposed able, in the words of a recent writer, "to separate those objects which are works of art from those which are not, because . . . we know how correctly to use the word 'art' and to apply the phrase 'work of art.'" Theories, on this account, are somewhat like mirror-images on Socrates' account, showing forth what we already know, wordy reflections of the actual linguistic practice we are masters in.

But telling artworks from other things is not so simple a matter, even for native speakers, and these days one might not be aware he was on ar-

---

[1] Shakespeare's play, *Hamlet,* about the Prince of Denmark who must avenge his father against his nature by killing the king, his uncle.

[2] Socrates is the speaker in Plato's *Republic.* See the introduction and selection in Part I, pp. 5–19.

[3] Wassily Kandinsky (1866–1944) was a prominent expressionist painter. His work uses forms, independently of their representational significance, to express aesthetic emotion.

tistic terrain without an artistic theory to tell him so. And part of the reason for this lies in the fact that terrain is constituted artistic in virtue of artistic theories, so that one use of theories, in addition to helping us discriminate art from the rest, consists in making art possible. Glaucon[4] and the others could hardly have known what was art and what not: otherwise they would never have been taken in by mirror-images.

I

Suppose one thinks of the discovery of a whole new class of artworks as something analogous to the discovery of a whole new class of facts anywhere, viz., as something for theoreticians to explain. In science, as elsewhere, we often accommodate new facts to old theories via auxiliary hypotheses, a pardonable enough conservatism when the theory in question is deemed too valuable to be jettisoned all at once. Now the Imitation Theory of Art (IT) is, if one but thinks it through, an exceedingly powerful theory, explaining a great many phenomena connected with the causation and evaluation of artworks, bringing a surprising unity into a complex domain. Moreover, it is a simple matter to shore it up against many purported counterinstances by such auxiliary hypotheses as that the artist who deviates from mimeticity is perverse, inept, or mad. Ineptitude, chicanery, or folly are, in fact, testable predications. Suppose, then, tests reveal that these hypotheses fail to hold, that the theory, now beyond repair, must be replaced. And a new theory is worked out, capturing what it can of the old theory's competence, together with the heretofore recalcitrant facts. One might, thinking along these lines, represent certain episodes in the history of art as not dissimilar to certain episodes in the history of science, where a conceptual revolution is being effected and where refusal

to countenance certain facts, while in part due to prejudice, inertia, and self-interest, is due also to the fact that a well-established, or at least widely credited theory is being threatened in such a way that all coherence goes.

Some such episode transpired with the advent of post-impressionist paintings.[5] In terms of the prevailing artistic theory (IT), it was impossible to accept these as art unless inept art: otherwise they could be discounted as hoaxes, self-advertisements, or the visual counterparts of madmen's ravings. So to get them accepted *as* art, on a footing with the *Transfiguration*[6] (not to speak of a Landseer stag[7]), required not so much a revolution in taste as a theoretical revision of rather considerable proportions, involving not only the artistic enfranchisement of these objects, but an emphasis upon newly significant features of accepted artworks, so that quite different accounts of their status as artworks would now have to be given. As a result of the new theory's acceptance, not only were post-impressionist paintings taken up as art, but numbers of objects (masks, weapons, etc.) were transferred from anthropological museums (and heterogeneous other places) to *musées des beaux arts,* though, as we would expect from the fact that a criterion for the acceptance of a new theory is that it account for whatever the older one did, nothing had to be transferred out of the *musée des beaux arts*—even if there were internal rearrangements as between storage rooms and exhibition space. Countless

---

[4]Glaucon, one of the principal characters in Plato's *Republic,* prompts Socrates to give his theory of poetry as imitation.

[5]In the last decades of the nineteenth century, the postimpressionists rejected impressionism and carried the impressionist emphasis on painting as painted surface rather than transparent representation a step farther by eliminating perspective and emphasizing the picture plane itself. Among the leading postimpressionists were Vincent Van Gogh and Paul Cézanne.

[6]Raphael Sanzio (1483–1520) was one of the major painters of the Italian high Renaissance. His work came to be regarded as the highest point of artistry by his immediate successors. *The Transfiguration* shows Christ being taken up into heaven.

[7]Sir Edwin Landseer (1803–1873) was one of the most prominent Victorian academic painters. His painting of a stag, *The Monarch of the Glen,* has come to epitomize the realistic, sentimental style of Victorian painting.

native speakers hung upon suburban mantel-pieces innumerable replicas of paradigm cases for teaching the expression 'work of art' that would have sent their Edwardian[8] forebears into linguistic apoplexy.

To be sure, I distort by speaking of a theory: historically, there were several, all, interestingly enough, more or less defined in terms of the IT. Art-historical complexities must yield before the exigencies of logical exposition, and I shall speak as though there were one replacing theory, partially compensating for historical falsity by choosing one which was actually enunciated. According to it, the artists in question were to be understood not as unsuccessfully imitating real forms but as successfully creating new ones, quite as real as the forms which the older art had been thought, in its best examples, to be creditably imitating. Art, after all, had long since been thought of as creative (Vasari[9] says that God was the first artist), and the post-impressionists were to be explained as genuinely creative, aiming, in Roger Fry's[10] words, "not at illusion but reality." This theory (RT) furnished a whole new mode of looking at painting, old and new. Indeed, one might almost interpret the crude drawing in Van Gogh[11] and Cézanne,[12] the dislocation of form from contour in Rouault[13] and Dufy,[14] the arbitrary use of color planes in Gauguin[15] and the Fauves,[16] as so many ways of drawing attention to the fact that these were non-imitations, specifically intended not to deceive. Logically, this would be roughly like printing "Not Legal Tender" across a brilliantly counterfeited dollar bill, the resulting object (counterfeit *cum* inscription) rendered incapable of deceiving anyone. It is not an illusory dollar bill, but then, just because it is nonillusory it does not automatically become a real dollar bill either. It rather occupies a freshly opened area between real objects and real facsimiles of real objects: it is a non-facsimile, if one requires a word, and a new contribution to the world. Thus, Van Gogh's *Potato Eaters,* as a consequence of certain unmistakable distortions, turns out to be a non-facsimile of real-life potato eaters; and inasmuch as these are not facsimiles of potato eaters, Van Gogh's picture, as a nonimitation, had as much right to be called a real object as did its putative subjects. By means of this theory (RT), artworks re-entered the thick of things from which Socratic theory (IT) had

[8] The period of the reign of King Edward VII of England (1841–1910), who succeeded his mother, Queen Victoria, in 1901. The period is known for its moral contrast to the strict propriety of the Victorian age.

[9] Giorgio Vasari (1511–1574) was an architect, mannerist painter, and one of the first true art historians. His *Lives of the Most Eminent Painters* provides not only a history of high Renaissance art but insight into the art theory and taste of the Renaissance.

[10] Roger Fry (1866–1934) was a painter and art critic. He was somewhat older than other members of the Bloomsbury group that centered around Leonard and Virginia Woolf, but was considered part of the group. Fry was instrumental in introducing postimpressionist painting, particularly the work of Paul Cezanne, into England.

[11] Vincent Van Gogh (1853–1890) was one of the leading postimpressionist painters. His major work was accomplished between 1880 and his suicide in 1890. It included work such as *The Potato Eaters* that incorporated elements of social criticism.

[12] Paul Cézanne (1839–1906) was the leading painter of the postimpressionist school. His subjects are principally still life and landscape, but his paintings flatten the picture plane and reduce the representational elements even further than impressionism.

[13] Georges Rouault (1871–1958) was a French painter whose free style is influenced both by postimpressionism and the strong colors of the fauvists ("wild beasts"). His subjects include religious images presented within distinct outlines suggestive of stained glass.

[14] Raoul Dufy (1877–1953) was a French painter most often associated with the fauvist movement. He began working in an impressionist style, but went through several style changes before achieving his most important works in the 1920s. His paintings use bright colors, sometimes at odds with what they depict, and bold, sketchy representations.

[15] Paul Gauguin (1848–1903) was a leading postimpressionist painter. He was influenced by Van Gogh, whom he met in 1888. Gauguin's work was rejected in Europe, and he turned his back on European civilization in 1891 when he moved to Tahiti. His mature work uses the bold colors and stylized representations of postimpressionism, but his subjects after his move to Tahiti become increasingly sensuous.

[16] Fauvism was a movement in painting that arose around 1898 and lasted for about ten years. Its principle advocate was Henri Matisse and it included the painters Andre Derain and Raoul Dufy. The fauvist style used direct color, applied vigorously, sometimes straight from the tube.

sought to evict them: if no *more* real than what carpenters wrought, they were at least no *less* real. The Post-Impressionist won a victory in ontology.

It is in terms of RT that we must understand the artworks around us today. Thus Roy Lichtenstein[17] paints comic-strip panels, though ten or twelve feet high. These are reasonably faithful projections onto a gigantesque scale, of the homely frames from the daily tabloid, but it is precisely the scale that counts. A skilled engraver might incise *The Virgin and the Chancellor Rollin*[18] on a pinhead, and it would be recognizable as such to the keen of sight, but an engraving of a Barnett Newman[19] on a similar scale would be a blob, disappearing in the reduction. A *photograph* of a Lichtenstein is indiscernible from a photograph of a counterpart panel from *Steve Canyon;*[20] but the photograph fails to capture the scale, and hence is as inaccurate a reproduction as a black-and-white engraving of Botticelli,[21] scale being essential here as color there. Lichtensteins, then, are not imitations but *new entities,* as giant whelks would be. Jasper Johns,[22] by contrast, paints objects with respect to which questions of scale are irrelevant. Yet his objects cannot be imitations, for they have the remarkable property that any intended copy of a member of this class of objects is automatically a member of the class itself, so that these objects are logically inimitable. Thus, a copy of a numeral just *is* that numeral: a painting of 3 is a 3 made of paint. Johns, in addition, paints targets, flags, and maps. Finally, in what I hope are not unwitting footnotes to Plato,[23] two of our pioneers—Robert Rauschenberg[24] and Claes Oldenburg[25]—have made genuine beds.

Rauschenberg's bed hangs on a wall, and is streaked with some desultory housepaint. Oldenburg's bed is a rhomboid, narrower at one end than the other, with what one might speak of as a built-in perspective: ideal for small bedrooms. As beds, these sell at singularly inflated prices, but one *could* sleep in either of them: Rauschenberg has expressed the fear that someone might just climb into his bed and fall asleep. Imagine, now, a certain Testadura[26]—a plain speaker and noted philistine—who is not aware that these are art, and who takes them to be reality simple and pure. He attributes the paintstreaks on Rauschenberg's bed to the slovenliness of the owner, and the bias in the Oldenburg bed to the ineptitude of the builder or the whimsy, perhaps, of whoever had it "custom-made." These would be mistakes, but mistakes of rather an odd kind, and not terribly different from that made by the stunned birds who pecked the sham grapes of Zeuxis.[27]

---

[17] Roy Lichtenstein (1923–1997) was one of the founders of the pop art movement in New York. Pop art reacted against the esoteric nature of abstract expressionism by adopting objects and images from popular culture and ordinary life. Lichtenstein is best known for adapting comic strips, faithfully reproduced in their graphic style, but transformed by their size.

[18] A painting by the Flemish painter, Jan van Eyck (1395–1441), painted in 1432–35 and now in the Louvre, Paris. Van Eyck's style is detailed and meticulous.

[19] Barnett Newman (1905–1970) was a New York painter best known for large color field canvases of geometrical simplicity and austerity.

[20] Steve Canyon was a character in the popular comic strip of that name, done in a relatively realistic style.

[21] Sandro Botticelli (1445–1510) was one of the greatest of the Renaissance painters in Florence. His style is both sensuous and highly colored.

[22] Jasper Johns (1930–) is an American painter associated principally with the pop art movement. His paintings of flags and numbers present a challenge to the idea that paintings are representations of something else since the paintings themselves are instances of what they depict.

[23] See Plato's reference to a bed as an image in the selection from the *Republic* in Part I, pp. 10–11.

[24] Robert Rauschenberg (1925–) is an American painter associated with the pop art movement. Rauschenberg often uses real objects from ordinary life, transforming them into art by their placement and labeling.

[25] Claes Oldenburg (1929–) is a Swedish-born sculptor and painter who became part of the New York pop art movement. Like others in the movement, Oldenburg makes use of the possibilities of real objects from popular culture and commercial settings.

[26] Danto's made-up name for someone who is a literalist and questions whether the emperor has any clothes on. The name may be adapted from the musical term *tessitura*, which applies to the dominant vocal range, ignoring the extremes.

[27] Zeuxis was a classical Greek painter. One of the legends about him is that one of his paintings was so realistic that real birds tried to peck the painted grapes.

They mistook art for reality, and so has Testadura. But it was meant to *be* reality, according to RT. Can one have mistaken reality for reality? How shall we describe Testadura's error? What, after all, prevents Oldenburg's creation from being a misshapen bed? This is equivalent to asking what makes it art, and with this query we enter a domain of conceptual inquiry where native speakers are poor guides: *they* are lost themselves.

II

To mistake an artwork for a real object is no great feat when an artwork is the real object one mistakes it for. The problem is how to avoid such errors, or to remove them once they are made. The artwork is a bed, and not a bed—illusion; so there is nothing like the traumatic encounter against a flat surface that brought it home to the birds of Zeuxis that they had been duped. Except for the guard cautioning Testadura not to sleep on the artworks, he might never have discovered that this was an artwork and not a bed; and since, after all, one cannot discover that a bed is not a bed, how is Testadura to realize that he has made an error? A certain sort of explanation is required, for the error here is a curiously philosophical one, rather like, if we may assume as correct some well-known views of P. F. Strawson,[28] mistaking a person for a material body when the truth is that a person *is* a material body in the sense that a whole class of predicates, sensibly applicable to material bodies, are sensibly, and by appeal to no different criteria, applicable to persons. So you cannot *discover* that a person is not a material body.

We begin by explaining, perhaps, that the paintstreaks are not to be explained away, that they are *part* of the object, so the object is not a mere bed with—as it happens—streaks of paint spilled over it, but a complex object fabricated out of a bed and some paintstreaks: a paint-bed. Similarly, a person is not a material body with—as it

happens—some thoughts superadded, but is a complex entity made up of a body and some conscious states: a conscious body. Persons, like artworks, must then be taken as irreducible to *parts* of themselves, and are in that sense primitive. Or, more accurately, the paintstreaks are not part of the real object—the bed—which happens to be part of the artwork, but are, *like* the bed, part of the artwork as such. And this might be generalized into a rough characterization of artworks that happen to contain real objects as parts of themselves: not every part of an artwork *A* is part of a real object *R* when *R* is part of *A* and can, moreover, be detached from A and seen *merely* as R. The mistake thus far will have been to mistake *A* for *part* of itself, namely *R*, even though it would not be incorrect to say that *A* is *R*, that the artwork is a bed. It is the 'is' which requires clarification here.

There is an *is* that figures prominently in statements concerning artworks which is not the *is* of either identity or predication; nor is it the *is* of existence, of identification, or some special *is* made up to serve a philosophic end. Nevertheless, it is in common usage, and is readily mastered by children. It is the sense of *is* in accordance with which a child, shown a circle and a triangle and asked which is him and which his sister, will point to the triangle saying "That is me"; or, in response to my question, the person next to me points to the man in purple and says "That one is Lear"; or in the gallery I point, for my companion's benefit, to a spot in the painting before us and say "That white dab is Icarus."[29] We do not mean, in these instances, that whatever is pointed to stands for, or represents, what it is said to be, for the word 'Icarus' stands for or represents Icarus: yet I would not in the same sense

---

[28] Sir Peter Strawson (1919–) is an Oxford philosopher whose work on the mind and language combines logical analysis with the philosophy of language.

[29] Icarus was the son of Daedalus. In the myth, Daedalus invented wings that allowed them to fly, but Icarus ignored his father's warning not to fly too close to the sun. The wax that held the wings together melted, and Icarus plunged into the sea and was killed. *The Fall of Icarus* is a painting by Pieter Bruegel (1525–1569) that depicts the event with Icarus only a tiny speck in the painting, which is taken up largely with a ship sailing by and a plowman who ignores the whole scene. W. H. Auden pointed the contrast in a poem, "Musée des Beaux Arts."

of *is* point to the word and say "That is Icarus." The sentence "That a *is* b" is perfectly compatible with "That a is not b" when the first employs this sense of *is* and the second employs some other, though a and b are used nonambiguously throughout. Often, indeed, the truth of the first *requires* the truth of the second. The first, in fact, is incompatible with "That a is not b" only when the *is* is used nonambiguously throughout. For want of a word I shall designate this the *is* of artistic identification; in each case in which it is used, the *a* stands for some specific physical property of, or physical part of, an object; and, finally, it is a necessary condition for something to be an artwork that some part or property of it be designable by the subject of a sentence that employs this special *is*. It is an *is,* incidentally, which has near-relatives in marginal and mythical pronouncements. (Thus, one *is* Quetzalcoatl;[30] those *are* the Pillars of Hercules.[31])

Let me illustrate. Two painters are asked to decorate the east and west walls of a science library with frescoes[32] to be respectively called *Newton's First Law*[33] and *Newton's Third Law.*[34] These paintings, when finally unveiled, look, scale apart, as follows:

A   B

As objects I shall suppose the works to be indiscernible: a black, horizontal line on a white

---

[30] Quetzalcoatl, the feathered serpent, is one of the major deities of the ancient Mexican pantheon.

[31] The pillars of Hercules marked the western end of the Mediterranean Sea in the classical world. They are usually identified as the Rock of Gibraltar.

[32] Fresco is the painting technique developed during the Renaissance in which paint is applied directly to a damp layer of plaster on a wall. The painter must work fast and accurately because the paint is absorbed into the plaster layer as the plaster dries.

[33] Newton's First Law of Motion states that a body at rest will remain at rest and a body in motion will remain in motion unless acted upon by an outside force.

[34] Newton's Third Law of Motion states that for every action, there is an equal and opposite reaction.

ground, equally large in each dimension and element. *B* explains his work as follows: a mass, pressing downward, is met by a mass pressing upward: the lower mass reacts equally and oppositely to the upper one. *A* explains his work as follows: the line through the space is the path of an isolated particle. The path goes from edge to edge, to give the sense of its *going beyond.* If it ended or began within the space, the line would be curved: and it is parallel to the top and bottom edges, for if it were closer to one than to another, there would have to be a force accounting for it, and this is inconsistent with its being the path of an *isolated* particle.

Much follows from these artistic identifications. To regard the middle line as an edge (mass meeting mass) imposes the need to identify the top and bottom half of the picture as rectangles, and as two distinct parts (not necessarily as two masses, for the line could be the edge of *one* mass jutting up—or down—into empty space). If it is an edge, we cannot thus take the entire area of the painting as a single space: it is rather composed of two forms, or one form and a non-form. We could take the entire area as a single space only by taking the middle horizontal as a *line* which is not an edge. But this almost requires a three-dimensional identification of the whole picture: the area can be a flat surface which the line is *above* (*Jet-flight*), or *below* (*Submarine-path*), or *on* (*Line*), or *in* (*Fissure*), or *through* (*Newton's First Law*)—though in this last case the area is not a flat surface but a transparent cross section of absolute space. We could make all these prepositional qualifications clear by imagining perpendicular cross sections to the picture plane. Then, depending upon the applicable prepositional clause, the area is (artistically) interrupted or not by the horizontal element. If we take the line as *through* space, the edges of the picture are not really the edges of the space: the space goes beyond the picture if the line itself does; and we are in the same space as the line is. As *B,* the edges of the picture can be *part* of the picture in case the masses go right to the edges, so that the edges of the picture are *their* edges. In that case, the vertices of the picture would be the vertices of the masses, except that the masses have four vertices more than the picture itself does: here four vertices would be part of the art work which were not part of the real object. Again, the faces of the masses could be the face of the picture, and in looking at the picture, we are looking at these faces: but *space* has no face, and on the reading of *A* the work has to be read as faceless, and the face of the physical object would not be part of the artwork. Notice here how one artistic identification engenders another artistic identification, and how, consistently with a given identification, we are *required* to give others and *precluded* from still others: indeed, a given identification determines how many elements the work is to contain. These different identifications are incompatible with one another, or generally so, and each might be said to make a different artwork, even though each artwork contains the identical real object as part of itself—or at least parts of the identical real object as parts of itself. There are, of course, senseless identifications: no one could, I think, sensibly read the middle horizontal as *Love's Labours Lost*[35] or *The Ascendancy of St. Erasmus*.[36] Finally, notice how acceptance of one identification rather than another is in effect to exchange one *world* for another. We could, indeed, enter a quiet poetic world by identifying the upper area with a clear and cloudless sky, reflected in the still surface of the water below, whiteness kept from whiteness only by the unreal boundary of the horizon.

And now Testadura, having hovered in the wings throughout this discussion, protests that *all he sees is paint:* a white painted oblong with a black line painted across it. And how right he really is: that is all he sees or that anybody can, we aesthetes included. So, if he asks us to show him what there is further to see, to demonstrate through pointing that this is an artwork (*Sea and Sky*), we cannot comply, for he has overlooked nothing (and it would be absurd to suppose he had, that there was something tiny we could

point to and he, peering closely, say "So it is! A work of art after all!"). We cannot help him until he has mastered the *is of artistic identification* and so *constitutes* it a work of art. If he cannot achieve this, he will never look upon artworks: he will be like a child who sees sticks as sticks.

But what about pure abstractions, say something that looks just like *A* but is entitled No. 7? The 10th Street abstractionist blankly insists[37] that there is nothing here but white paint and black, and none of our literary identifications need apply. What then distinguishes him from Testadura, whose philistine utterances are indiscernible from his? And how can it be an artwork for him and not for Testadura, when they agree that there is nothing that does not meet the eye? The answer, unpopular as it is likely to be to purists of every variety, lies in the fact that this artist has returned to the physicality of paint through an atmosphere compounded of artistic theories and the history of recent and remote painting, elements of which he is trying to refine out of his own work; and as a consequence of this his work belongs in this atmosphere and is part of this history. He has achieved abstraction through rejection of artistic identifications, returning to the real world from which such identifications remove us (he thinks), somewhat in the mode of Ch'ing Yuan,[38] who wrote:

> Before I had studied Zen for thirty years, I saw mountains as mountains and waters as waters. When I arrived at a more intimate knowledge, I came to the point where I saw that mountains are not mountains, and waters are not waters. But

---

[35] Shakespeare's comedy of vows made and broken and remade.
[36] *The Ascendancy of St. Erasmus* is perhaps Nicholas Poussin's (1594–1665) large altarpiece for St. Peter's representing the "Martyrdom of St. Erasmus" (1629).

[37] 10th Street abstractionists are minimalists who are identified by their studio location as opposed to the more "traditional" abstraction shown at such galleries as Peggy Guggenheim's Art of the Century Gallery on 57th Street in New York. The severe black and white palettes of Franz Klein and Ad Reinhardt fit the description given here.
[38] Zen Buddhism was introduced into Japan from China, beginning in the sixth century. Three important sects followed: the Rinzai in the twelfth century, the Soto in the thirteenth, and the Obaku, introduced by the Chinese monk Yin-yüan in the seventeenth century. Zen looks to meditation and enlightenment rather than scripture or works as a way of transcending existence. Danto identifies this passage elsewhere as coming from one of the more radical forms of Zen, the Diamond Sutras.

now that I have got the very substance I am at rest. For it is just that I see mountains once again as mountains, and waters once again as waters.

His identification of what he has made is logically dependent upon the theories and history he rejects. The difference between his utterance and Testadura's "This is black paint and white paint and nothing more," lies in the fact that he is still using the *is* of artistic identification, so that his use of "That black paint is black paint" is not a tautology. Testadura is not at that stage. To see something as art requires something the eye cannot decry—an atmosphere of artistic theory, a knowledge of the history of art: an artworld.

III

Mr. Andy Warhol,[39] the Pop artist,[40] displays facsimiles of Brillo cartons, piled high, in neat stacks, as in the stockroom of the supermarket. They happen to be of wood, painted to look like cardboard, and why not? To paraphrase the critic of the *Times,* if one may make the facsimile of a human being out of bronze, why not the facsimile of a Brillo carton out of plywood? The cost of these boxes happens to be 2×10^3 that of their homely counterparts in real life—a differential hardly ascribable to their advantage in durability. In fact, the Brillo people might, at some slight increase in cost, make their boxes out of plywood without these becoming artworks, and Warhol might make *his* out of cardboard without their ceasing to be art. So we may forget questions of intrinsic value, and ask why the Brillo people cannot manufacture art and why Warhol cannot *but* make artworks. Well, his are made by hand, to be sure. Which is like an insane reversal of Picasso's[41] strategy in pasting the label from a bottle

of Suze[42] onto a drawing, saying as it were that the academic artist, concerned with exact imitation, must always fall short of the real thing: so why not just *use* the real thing? The Pop artist laboriously reproduces machine-made objects by hand, e.g., painting the labels on coffee cans (one can hear the familiar commendation "Entirely made by hand" falling painfully out of the guide's vocabulary when confronted by these objects). But the difference cannot consist in craft: a man who carved pebbles out of stones and carefully constructed a work called *Gravel Pile* might invoke the labor theory of value to account for the price he demands; but the question is, What makes it art? And why need Warhol *make* these things anyway? Why not just scrawl his signature across one? Or crush one up and display it as *Crushed Brillo Box* ("A protest against mechanization . . .") or simply display a Brillo carton as *Uncrushed Brillo Box* ("A bold affirmation of the plastic authenticity of industrial . . .")? Is this man a kind of Midas, turning whatever he touches into the gold of pure art? And the whole world consisting of latent artworks waiting, like the bread and wine of reality, to be transfigured, through some dark mystery, into the indiscernible flesh and blood of the sacrament? Never mind that the Brillo box may not be good, much less great art. The impressive thing is that it is art at all. But if it is, why are not the indiscernible Brillo boxes that are in the stockroom? Or *has* the whole distinction between art and reality broken down?

Suppose a man collects objects (ready-mades), including a Brillo carton; we praise the exhibit for variety, ingenuity, what you will. Next he exhibits nothing but Brillo cartons, and we criticize it as dull, repetitive, self-plagiarizing—or (more profoundly) claim that he is obsessed by regularity and repetition, as in *Marienbad.*[43] Or he piles

---

[39] Andy Warhol (1928–1987) was perhaps the best known of the American pop artists. His use of objects such as Coke bottles and Brillo boxes to construct art works is paradigmatic of pop art.
[40] In reaction against abstraction, pop art turned in the 1950s and 1960s to popular culture and commercial products to demonstrate that art could be both representational and independent of the demands of "high art."
[41] Pablo Picasso (1881–1973) was one of the most prolific and influential twentieth-century artists. With Georges Braque he

invented cubism, which broke subject matter into geometric planes, but he was equally influential in other styles, including a simple, almost classical style, collages, and "ready-mades."
[42] A Swiss liquor.
[43] *Last Year in Marienbad* (1961), a film directed by Alain Resnais (1929–1999), who was a leader in the French New Wave cinema, presents a kind of dreamworld narrative in which events are contradictory and misleading.

them high, leaving a narrow path; we tread our way through the smooth opaque stacks and find it an unsettling experience, and write it up as the closing in of consumer products, confining us as prisoners: or we say he is a modern pyramid builder. True, we don't say these things about the stockboy. But then a stockroom is not an art gallery, and we cannot readily separate the Brillo cartons from the gallery they are in, any more than we can separate the Rauschenberg bed from the paint upon it. Outside the gallery, they are pasteboard cartons. But then, scoured clean of paint, Rauschenberg's bed is a bed, just what it was before it was transformed into art. But then if we think this matter through, we discover that the artist has failed, really and of necessity, to produce a mere real object. He has produced an artwork, his use of real Brillo cartons being but an expansion of the resources available to artists, a contribution to *artists' materials,* as oil paint was, or *tuche.*[44]

What in the end makes the difference between a Brillo box and a work of art consisting of a Brillo box is a certain theory of art. It is the theory that takes it up into the world of art, and keeps it from collapsing into the real object which it is (in a sense of *is* other than that of artistic identification). Of course, without the theory, one is unlikely to see it as art, and in order to see it as part of the artworld, one must have mastered a good deal of artistic theory as well as a considerable amount of the history of recent New York painting. It could not have been art fifty years ago. But then there could not have been, everything being equal, flight insurance in the Middle Ages, or Etruscan[45] typewriter erasers. The world has to be ready for certain things, the artworld no less than the real one. It is the role of artistic theories, these days as always, to make the artworld, and

art, possible. It would, I should think, never have occurred to the painters of Lascaux[46] that they were producing *art* on those walls. Not unless there were neolithic aestheticians.

IV

The artworld stands to the real world in something like the relationship in which the City of God[47] stands to the Earthly City. Certain objects, like certain individuals, enjoy a double citizenship, but there remains, the RT notwithstanding, a fundamental contrast between artworks and real objects. Perhaps this was already dimly sensed by the early framers of the IT who, inchoately realizing the nonreality of art, were perhaps limited only in supposing that the sole way objects had of being other than real is to be sham, so that artworks necessarily had to be imitations of real objects. This was too narrow. So Yeats[48] saw in writing "Once out of nature I shall never take / My bodily form from any natural thing." It is but a matter of choice: and the Brillo box of the artworld may be just the Brillo box of the real one, separated and united by the *is* of artistic identification. But I should like to say some final words about the theories that make artworks possible, and their relationship to one another. In so doing, I shall beg some of the hardest philosophical questions I know.

---

[44] Also spelled *tusche.* A crayon used to draw the pattern in producing silk screen prints and lithographs.

[45] The region of Italy known as Etruria located between the Tiber and Arno Rivers west and south of the Apennines. The Etruscan civilization preceded the rise of Rome, which did not begin until the fifth century B.C.E. Rome assimilated many aspects of Etruscan civilization, but the language itself was completely lost.

[46] A cavern in the Dordogne region of central France that contains extensive examples of prehistoric drawings. It was discovered in 1940.

[47] *The City of God* is the major theological work of St. Augustine of Hippo (354–430). The City of God is contrasted to the Earthly City, which is at once Rome and all earthly existence. Augustine sought to answer the charge that the weakness of Christianity had brought about the barbarian invasions and the sack of Rome in 430 by arguing that the City of God is not identical with the physical city or the material world.

[48] William Butler Yeats (1865–1939) was an Irish poet and Nobel prize winner (1923) whose poetry ranges from Irish mythology to Irish nationalism. Yeats held to a "vision" that led him to construct an elaborate mythology of his own around a spiral (gyre) version of history. His poem, "Sailing to Byzantium" contrasts the permanence of art to the transience of the human body.

I shall now think of pairs of predicates related to each other as "opposites," conceding straight off the vagueness of this *demodé* [49] term. Contradictory predicates are not opposites, since one of each of them must apply to every object in the universe, and neither of a pair of opposites need apply to some objects in the universe. An object must first be of a certain kind before either of a pair of opposites applies to it, and then at most and at least one of the opposites must apply to it. So opposites are not contraries, for contraries may both be false of some objects in the universe, but opposites cannot both be false; for of some objects, neither of a pair of opposites *sensibly* applies, unless the object is of the right sort. Then, if the object is of the required kind, the opposites behave as contradictories. If F and non-F are opposites, an object o must be of a certain kind K before either of these sensibly applies; but if o is a member of K, then o either is F or non-F, to the exclusion of the other. The class of pairs of opposites that sensibly apply to the $(\delta)Ko$ [50] I shall designate as the class of *K-relevant predicates*. And a necessary condition for an object to be of a kind K is that at least one pair of K-relevant opposites be sensibly applicable to it. But, in fact, if an object is of kind K, at least and at most one of each K-relevant pair of opposites applies to it.

I am now interested in the K-relevant predicates for the class K of artworks. And let F and non-F be an opposite pair of such predicates. Now it might happen that, throughout an entire period of time, every artwork is non-F. But since nothing thus far is both an artwork and F, it might never occur to anyone that non-F is an artistically relevant predicate. The non-F-ness of artworks goes unmarked. By contrast, all works up to a given time might be G, it never occurring to anyone until that time that something might both be an artwork and non-G; indeed, it might have been thought that G was a *defining trait* of artworks when in fact something might first have

to be an artwork before G is sensibly predicable of it—in which case non-G might also be predicable of artworks, and G itself then could not have been a defining trait of this class.

Let G be 'is representational' and let F be 'is expressionist.' At a given time, these and their opposites are perhaps the only art-relevant predicates in critical use. Now letting '+' stand for a given predicate P and '−' for its opposite non-P, we may construct a style matrix more or less as follows:

F	G
+	+
+	−
−	+
−	−

The rows determine available styles, given the active critical vocabulary: representational expressionistic (e.g., Fauvism); representational non-expressionistic (Ingres [51]); nonrepresentational expressionistic (Abstract Expressionism [52]); nonrepresentational nonexpressionist (hard-edge abstraction [53]). Plainly, as we add art-relevant predicates, we increase the number of available styles at the rate of 2^n. It is, of course, not easy to see in advance which predicates are going to be added or replaced by their opposites, but suppose an artist determines that H shall henceforth be artistically relevant for his paintings. Then, in fact, both H and non-H become artistically relevant for all painting, and if his is the first and only painting that is H, every other painting in existence becomes non-H, and the entire community of paintings is enriched, together with a doubling of the available style opportunities. It is this retroactive enrichment of the entities in the artworld

---

[49] Whatever is old fashioned.

[50] Logical symbolism for whatever object, o, has the property or attribute, K.

[51] Jean-Auguste Dominique Ingres (1780–1867) was a French painter of neoclassical and romantic subjects. His work belongs to the conservative nineteenth-century French cultural tradition.

[52] The name given to the New York art movement in the 1950s that sought to free painting from the last elements of representationalism.

[53] Hard-edge abstraction is a form of minimalism. It seeks to reduce painting to its geometric essentials by using sharp edges and areas of undifferentiated color.

that makes it possible to discuss Raphael and De Kooning[54] together, or Lichtenstein and Michelangelo.[55] The greater the variety of artistically relevant predicates, the more complex the individual members of the artworld become; and the more one knows of the entire population of the artworld, the richer one's experience with any of its members.

In this regard, notice that, if there are m artistically relevant predicates, there is always a bottom row with m minuses. This row is apt to be occupied by purists. Having scoured their canvasses clear of what they regard as inessential, they credit themselves with having distilled out the essence of art. But this is just their fallacy: exactly as many artistically relevant predicates stand true of their square monochromes as stand true of any member of the Artworld, and they can *exist* as artworks only insofar as "impure" paintings exist. Strictly speaking, a black square by Reinhardt[56] is artistically as rich as Titian's *Sacred and Profane Love*.[57] This explains how less is more.

Fashion, as it happens, favors certain rows of the style matrix: museums, connoisseurs, and others are makeweights in the Artworld. To insist, or seek to, that all artists become representational, perhaps to gain entry into a specially prestigious exhibition, cuts the available style matrix in half: there are then $2^n/2$ ways of satisfying the

requirement, and museums then can exhibit all these "approaches" to the topic they have set. But this is a matter of almost purely sociological interest: one row in the matrix is as legitimate as another. An artistic breakthrough consists, I suppose, in adding the possibility of a column to the matrix. Artists then, with greater or less alacrity, occupy the positions thus opened up: this is a remarkable feature of contemporary art, and for those unfamiliar with the matrix, it is hard, and perhaps impossible, to recognize certain positions as occupied by artworks. Nor would these things be artworks without the theories and the histories of the Artworld.

Brillo boxes enter the artworld with that same tonic incongruity the *commedia dell'arte*[58] characters bring into *Ariadne auf Naxos*.[59] Whatever is the artistically relevant predicate in virtue of which they gain their entry, the rest of the Artworld becomes that much the richer in having the opposite predicate available and applicable to its members. And, to return to the views of Hamlet with which we began this discussion, Brillo boxes may reveal us to ourselves as well as anything might: as a mirror held up to nature, they might serve to catch the conscience of our kings.

Study Questions

1. Why isn't *is an imitation* a sufficient condition for *is art*?
2. How does one theory replace another? Why?
3. How does a Reality Theory win a victory in ontology?

---

[54] Willem De Kooning (1904–1997) was one of the leading painters in the abstract expressionist movement in the 1940s and 1950s, but his "action painting" led him to combine representational and abstract techniques, particularly in a series of paintings after 1950 focused on women that incorporate psychological insight.

[55] Michelangelo Buonarroti (1475–1564) was a sculptor, painter, architect, and poet. Together with Raphael, he was considered the most important of the high Renaissance painters by his contemporaries and immediate followers.

[56] Ad Reinhardt (1913–1967) was an American minimalist painter active in New York. He painted in a number of styles, but by 1950 his work had become increasingly monochromatic until it consisted of nothing but black geometrical shapes.

[57] Titian (1488/90–1576) was a Venetian artist whose portraits, classical paintings, and religious works combine color and movement. Titian is the successor to Raphael as the most popular of the high Renaissance painters.

---

[58] *Commedia dell'arte,* or "comedy of art," was an improvisational theater that developed in Italy in the sixteenth century and flourished through the eighteenth century. It made use of an ensemble of stock characters including Harlequin, Pierrot, and Pantaloon as well as acrobats and comic masks. It is related to the Punch and Judy puppet shows.

[59] The comic opera *Ariadne auf Naxos* (1912) by Richard Strauss (1864–1949) presents the classical legend of Ariadne's desertion by Theseus in the context of a performance of an opera on the subject that is disrupted by its forced combination with the buffoonery of the *commedia dell'arte*.

4. What distinguishes the beds made by Robert Rauschenberg and Claes Oldenburg from beds sold in a furniture store?
5. What three uses of *is* does Danto discuss? Construct a sentence exemplifying each use.
6. How can two perceptually identical objects not be the same?
7. What does one have to do to learn the "id of artistic identification"?
8. Name a pair of terms that are opposites in Danto's sense.
9. What characteristic of opposites prevents everything from being art because of the last row of Danto's matrix?

Passages for Discussion
♦ ♦ ♦ ♦ ♦ ♦ ♦ ♦ ♦ ♦ ♦ ♦ ♦ ♦ ♦

Experience occurs continuously, because the interaction of live creatures and environ-
ing conditions is involved in the very process of living. . . . Oftentimes, however, the
experience had is inchoate. Things are experienced but not in such a way that they are
composed into *an* experience. . . . In contrast with such experience, we have *an* experience when the material experienced runs its course to fulfillment. Then and then only
is it integrated within and demarcated in the general stream of experience from other
experiences. . . . Hence an experience of thinking has its own esthetic quality. It differs from those experiences that are acknowledged to be esthetic, but only in its materials. . . . Nevertheless, the experience itself has a satisfying emotional quality because
it possesses internal integration and fulfillment reached through ordered and organized
movement. This artistic structure may be immediately felt. In so far, it is esthetic. What
is even more important is that not only is this quality a significant motive in undertaking intellectual inquiry and in keeping it honest, but that no intellectual activity is an
integral event (is *an* experience), unless it is rounded out with this quality. Without it,
thinking is inconclusive. In short, esthetic cannot be sharply marked off from intellectual experience since the latter must bear an esthetic stamp to be itself complete.

JOHN DEWEY (1859–1952), *Art as Experience* [1934]

Truth, as the clearing and concealing of what is, happens in being composed, as a poet
composes a poem. All art, as the letting happen of the advent of the truth of what is, is,
as such, essentially poetry. The nature of art, on which both the art work and artist depend, is the setting-itself-into-work of truth. . . . The curious fact here is that the work
in no way affects hitherto existing entities by causal connections. The working of the
work does not consist in the taking effect of a cause. It lies in a change, happening from
out of the work, of the unconcealedness of what is, and this means, of Being.

MARTIN HEIDEGGER (1889–1976), "The Origin of the Work of Art" [1935–36]

The artist proper is a person who, grappling with the problem of expressing a certain
emotion, says, "I want to get this clear." It is no use to him to get something else clear,
however like it this other thing may be. Nothing will serve as a substitute. He does not
want a thing of a certain kind, he wants a certain thing. This is why the kind of person
who takes his literature as psychology, saying "How admirably this writer depicts the
feelings of women, or bus drivers, or homosexuals . . . ," necessarily misunderstands
every real work of art with which he comes into contact, and takes for good art, with
infallible precision, what is not art at all.

R. G. COLLINGWOOD (1889–1943), *The Principles of Art* [1938]

It is remarkable that in real life, when aesthetic judgements are made, aesthetic adjectives such as 'beautiful,' 'fine,' etc., play hardly any role at all. Are aesthetic adjectives
used in a musical criticism? You say: "Look at this transition," or [Rhees] "The passage

here is incoherent." Or you say, in a poetical criticism [Taylor]: "His use of images is precise." The words you use are more akin to 'right' and 'correct' (as these words are used in ordinary speech) than to 'beautiful' and 'lovely.'

LUDWIG WITTGENSTEIN (1889–1951), Lectures on Aesthetics [1938]

The words we call expressions of aesthetic judgement play a very complicated role, but a very definite role, in what we call a culture of a period. To describe their use or to describe what you mean by a cultured taste, you have to describe a culture. What we now call a cultured taste perhaps didn't exist in the Middle Ages. An entirely different game is played in different ages.

LUDWIG WITTGENSTEIN (1889–1951), Lectures on Aesthetics [1938]

I believe the "aesthetic emotion" and the emotional content of a work of art are two very different things; the "aesthetic emotion" springs from an intellectual triumph, from overcoming barriers of word-bound thought and achieving insight into literally "unspeakable" realities; but the emotive content of the work is apt to be much deeper than any intellectual experience, more essential, pre-rational, and vital, something of the life-rhythms we share with all growing, hungering, moving and fearing creatures: the ultimate realities themselves, the central facts of our brief, sentient existence.

SUSANNE LANGER (1895–1985), Philosophy in a New Key [1942]

The design or intention of the author is neither available nor desirable as a standard for judging the success of a work of literary art. . . . One must ask how a critic expects to get an answer to the question about intention. How is he to find out what the poet tried to do? If the poet succeeded in doing it, then the poem itself shows what he was trying to do. And if the poet did not succeed, then the poem is not adequate evidence, and the critic must go outside the poem—for evidence of an intention that did not become effective in the poem.

WILLIAM WIMSATT (1907–1975) and
MONROE BEARDSLEY (1915–1985), "The Intentional Fallacy" [1954]

What I want particularly to emphasize about features which function as conditions for a term is that some group or set of them is sufficient fully to ensure or warrant the application of that term. An individual characterized by some of these features may not yet qualify to be called lazy or intelligent, and so on, beyond all question, but all that is needed is to add some further (indefinite) number of such characterizations and a point is reached where we have enough. There are individuals possessing a number of such features of whom one cannot deny, cannot but admit, that they are intelligent. We have left necessary-and-sufficient conditions behind, but we are still in the realm of sufficient conditions.

But aesthetic concepts are not condition-governed even in this way. There are no sufficient conditions, no non-aesthetic features such that the presence of some set or number of them will beyond question logically justify or warrant the application of an aesthetic term.

FRANK SIBLEY (1923–), "Aesthetic Concepts" [1959]

The work of art says something to the historian: it says something to each person as if it were said especially to him, as something present and contemporaneous. Thus our task is to understand the meaning of what it says and to make it clear to ourselves and others. Even the nonlinguistic work of art, therefore, falls within the province of the proper task of hermeneutics. It must be integrated into the self-understanding of each person. . . . The language of art means the excess of meaning that is present in the work itself.

HANS-GEORG GADAMER (1900–), "Aesthetics and Hermeneutics" [1964]

When I say a form is *imposed,* I obviously do not think of any classical model of causality. The question, so often asked, of knowing if one writes as one speaks or speaks as one writes, if one reads as one writes or conversely, refers in its banality to an historical or prehistoric depth more hidden than is generally suspected. Finally, if one notes that the place of writing is linked, as Rousseau had intuited, to the nature of social space, to the perceptive and dynamic organization of the technical, religious, economic and other such spaces, one realizes the difficulty of a transcendental question on space. A new transcendental aesthetic must let itself be guided not only by mathematical idealities but by the possibility of inscriptions *in general,* not befalling an already constituted space as a contingent accident but producing the spatiality of space. Indeed we say of inscription in general, in order to make it quite clear that it is not simply the notation of a prepared speech representing itself, but inscription within speech and inscription as habitation always already situated. Such a questioning, in spite of its reference to a form of fundamental passivity, ought no longer to call itself a transcendental *aesthetic.*

JACQUES DERRIDA (1930–), *Of Grammatology* [1967]

In the mature expression of Wittgenstein's philosophy, the phrase "form of life" (*Lebensform*) makes a frequent appearance. Art is, in Wittgenstein's sense, a form of life.

The phrase appears as descriptive or invocatory of the total context within which alone language can exist: the complex of habits, experiences, skills, with which language interlocks in that it could not be operated without them and, equally, they cannot be indentified without reference to it.

RICHARD WOLLHEIM (1923–), *Art and Its Objects* [1968]

The definition of aesthetic pleasure as enjoyment of self in the enjoyment of what is other presupposes the primary unity of understanding enjoyment and enjoying understanding and restores the meaning of participation and appropriation which originally characterized German usage. In aesthetic behavior, the subject always enjoys more than itself. It experiences itself as it appropriates an experience of the meaning of world which both its own productive activity and the reception of the experience of others can disclose, and the assent of third parties can confirm. Aesthetic enjoyment that thus occurs in a state of balance between disinterested contemplation and testing participation is a mode of experiencing oneself in a possible being other which the aesthetic attitude opens up.

HANS ROBERT JAUSS, *Aesthetic Experience and Literary Hermeneutics* [1977]

Sources

Aristotle. *Poetics,* trans. Ingram Bywater. Oxford, 1920.

Bell, Clive. *Art.* London, 1913.

St. Bonaventure. *De reductione artium ad theologiam,* trans. Sister Emma Therese Healy. St. Bonaventure, NY: St. Bonaventure College, 1955. Reprinted by permission of the Franciscan Institute.

Benjamin, Walter. "The Work of Art in the Age of Mechanical Reproduction," from *Illuminations.* Copyright © 1955 by Suhrkamp Verlag, Frankfurt a.m., English translation by Harry Zohn copyright © 1968 and renewed 1996 by Harcourt, Inc. Reprinted by permission of Harcourt, Inc.

Bullough, Edward. "'Psychical Distance' as a Factor in Art and an Aesthetic Principle." *British Journal of Psychology* 5 (1912): 87–118. Reprinted by permission of *British Journal of Psychology.*

Croce, Benedetto. *Aesthetic,* trans. Douglas Ainslie. New York: Macmillan, 1909. Reprinted by permission of Farrar, Straus, and Giroux, Inc.

Dante Alighieri. *The Letters of Dante,* trans. Paget Toynbee. Oxford: Oxford University Press, 1966. Reprinted by permission of the Oxford University Press.

Danto, Arthur. "The Artworld," *Journal of Philosophy* 61, 19 (October 15, 1964): 571–584. Reprinted by permission of *Journal of Philosophy* and the Author.

Dickie, George. "The Myth of the Aesthetic Attitude," *American Philosophical Quarterly* 1,1 (1964): 56–66. Reprinted by permission of *American Philosophical Quarterly.*

Hegel, G. W. F. *Philosophy of Mind,* trans. William Wallace. Oxford: Oxford University Press, 1971. Reprinted by permission of Oxford University Press.

Hume, David. *Essays and Treatises on Several Subjects.* London, 1777.

Hutcheson, Francis. *An Inquiry into the Original of Our Ideas of Beauty and Virtue.* London: 1725.

Kant, Immanuel. *Critique of Judgment,* trans. J. H. Bernard. New York: Macmillan, 1914.

Nietzsche, Friedrich. *The Birth of Tragedy* and *The Genealogy of Morals,* trans. Francis Golffing. Copyright © 1956 by Doubleday, a division of Bantam, Doubleday, Dell Publishing Group, Inc. Used by permission of Doubleday, a division of Bantam Doubleday Dell Publishing Group, Inc.

Plato. *The Republic,* trans. Benjamin Jowett. Oxford: Oxford University Press, 1871.

Plotinus. *Ennead VI.1.* trans. Timothy Mahoney and Sherry Blum. Used by permission of the translators.

Ruskin, John. *Modern Painters.* London: Smith, Elder, 1851.

Schopenhauer, Arthur. *The World as Will and Idea,* trans. R. B. Haldane and J. Kemp. New York: Scribner's, 1883.

Tolstoy, Leo N. *What Is Art?* trans. Aylmer Maude. London: W. Scott, 1899.

Weitz, Morris. "The Role of Theory in Aesthetics," *Journal of Aesthetics and Art Criticism,* 15 (1956), 27–35. Used by permission of the *Journal of Aesthetics and Art Criticism.*

The following art work is used by permission of the Kimbell Art Museum, Fort Worth, Texas.

Portrait Head of Marcus Aurelius

Barnabas Altarpiece

Joshua Reynolds, *Lady Frances Warren* (?)

Frederic Leighton, *Miss May Sartoris*

Edvard Munch, *Girls on a Jetty*

Glossary

This glossary is not a substitute for a dictionary. Most of the terms listed here are discussed in more detail in the introductions and the readings. Specific information of a technical or historical nature is provided in the annotations. Specific terms used by a single author in a special sense (e.g., *significant form, psychical distance*) are defined in context; terms are included here that have a wider application. The minimal definitions given are intended as an aid to understanding, not as a substitute for careful reading.

a priori reasoning based on deductions from given premises or definitions. *A priori* reasoning requires no reference to empirical facts.

Academy the school founded by Plato and continued by his disciples to advance his philosophy.

accidents in metaphysics, the superficial differences that any kind of thing can have among its different, individual instances.

act in metaphysics, the actualization of any of the formal properties that make something what it is.

aesthetes those people who have a special devotion to aesthetic feeling for its own sake. Aesthetes represent a special group whose cultural values are centered on feeling.

aesthetic attitude the theory that we can achieve aesthetic experience by adjusting the way that we perceive things.

aesthetics the philosophical discipline that deals with art, beauty, and the human experiences and feelings that produce and respond to art and beauty. The word was first introduced by A. G. Baumgarten in the eighteenth century.

allegory the literary technique of providing multiple symbolic meanings in a single narrative.

anagogical the highest level of allegory, which gives the universal meaning of a symbol.

analytic philosophy the approach to philosophy that holds that the primary function of philosophy is to analyze beliefs, assertions, and claims and the evidence for them. Analytical philosophy as a movement comes to prominence in the twentieth century. It is particularly concerned with the analysis of language.

antinomy the juxtaposition of two opposite and apparently contradictory statements.

apperception consciousness by the mind of its own functions. Among the things that can be perceived are the workings of perception itself.

Aristotelianism the philosophy based on the works of Aristotle. It utilizes categories that are given independently of experience and an analytical method based on a combination of logic and authority.

asceticism self-denial, usually of pleasure. Ascetics distrust the body and its desires.

association of ideas the theory that some ideas give rise to other ideas, either by a physical process or by the formation of mental habits.

avant garde literally, the "advance guard" that goes ahead of an army. The term became attached to self-proclaimed artistic and intellectual innovators in the nineteenth and twentieth centuries.

axiom a rule that is agreed to without further justification. In logic, axioms provide the basic starting point for a logical system.

bourgeois middle class, particularly in the class structure that developed during the nineteenth-century Industrial Revolution. The bourgeois are owners of property and the means of production, depend on the labor of others, but are not themselves at the top of the class structure.

Calvinism the theology of that wing of the Protestant Reformation who follows the doctrine of John Calvin (1509–1564). Calvinists rejected a church structure of bishops and archbishops and emphasized a strict moral code and predestination of the saved and damned.

canticle a main division of a long poem.

categories principles of mental organization. Classical categories are given logically. Modern categories are seen as products of the human mind through which the mind is able to organize its sensory input.

catharsis the emotional or formal resolution of Aristotelian tragedy. The catharsis is both a solving of the problems in terms of the dramatic imagery and an emotional effect on the audience.

chiaroscuro in painting, the use of light and shade to create the effects of depth and contrast.

circumlocution a way of saying indirectly what one does not want to say directly.

cognition conscious, ordered thought. Cognition implies the use of concepts and some ability to abstract from particulars to more general ideas.

comedy a literary genre, not necessarily humorous, distinguished by a resolution that resolves problems by reuniting a community.

common sense the unifying feature of perceptions. In aesthetics, common sense seldom means simply a practical, folk wisdom.

concept a formal or mental construct that organizes ideas. A concept may be thought of as an ideal entity or simply as an abstraction from a number of ideas.

concupiscence lust, or a strong, abnormal desire. Aesthetic feeling must distinguish itself from concupiscence, especially in versions of neo-Platonism.

connoisseur one who, through practice and appreciation, claims a special knowledge of or ability to judge the arts.

corollary a derived condition in mathematics and philosophy. A corollary is strictly implied by a theory, though it may not be stated in the theory.

cosmological proof a proof for the existence of God based on the ordered nature of the cosmos.

cosmos the ordered world. Cosmology seeks to understand the order of the entire universe, all that there is.

counterexamples in philosophy, the technique of refuting a position by providing an example that does not fit the position but would be accepted as relevant.

denouement the ending or resolution of a play or story.

determinism the philosophical theory that all events are uniquely caused by a single set of beginning conditions. Only one outcome is possible, and if we knew all of the initial conditions, we would be able to predict everything that happens.

dialectic literally, argument by a process of opposing ideas. Dialectic is also extended to describe the opposition of realities.

didacticism the theory that a function of art is to teach.

disinterested in morals, directed toward someone else's good; in aesthetics, free from personal considerations. Disinterested does not imply any limit on the intensity of one's attention.

ecstasy being taken out of oneself. In some philosophies, the goal is to achieve such an experience of transcendence.

empiricism the philosophical approach to knowledge that makes individual experience the sole available source of knowledge about the external world. Empiricism becomes the dominant philosophical approach in the eighteenth century.

Enlightenment the literary, philosophical, and theological movement in eighteenth-century Europe and Britain that developed out of the scientific revolution. Enlightenment writers tended to admire scientific advances, to reject supernatural religion, and to stress the potential of humans to solve problems.

ennead any group of nine, especially applied to the way the writings of Plotinus were grouped.

epic the literary form that provides an extended account of some major event in the light of its larger mythological or cultural significance. Epic poetry attempts to represent what is essential to a society.

epistemology the philosophical theories that attempt to characterize knowledge and the conditions of knowing. Epistemology asks what we can know and how we can know it.

esoteric limited to a small circle capable of understanding. A number of philosophers have distinguished between what may be disclosed to the initiated or to believers (the esoteric philosophy) and what may be revealed to everyone.

essence that which defines something. Essentialism in philosophy implies that there are defining characteristics of a thing and that they can be stated in clear, unambiguous terms.

existentialism the twentieth-century philosophical movement that denies the ability to find any essence outside of the momentary existence of an individual consciousness. Existentialism reflects many of the anxieties about the place of the individual in society that already had arisen in the nineteenth century.

faculties in the seventeenth and eighteenth centuries, mental operations were believed to be controlled by faculties—separate psychological abilities that acted on the sense data received from the world.

feudalism a social and political structure organized by rank and personal obligation. In the European Middle Ages, feudalism meant a system of landownership and military obligation based on personal loyalty.

fine arts those art forms that are distinguished in a culture as "higher" arts, as opposed to practical and useful arts. Our system of fine arts—music, sculpture, painting, literature, dance—is a product of the seventeenth and eighteenth centuries.

form in metaphysics, the shaping principle that distinguishes substance from one kind to another.

formalism the theory of art that analyzes works primarily in terms of their form. Formalism contrasts with psychological approaches and with approaches that emphasize the ideas and consequences of a work of art.

hagiography writings about saints, particularly lives of saints and accounts of their miracles. Lives of saints took a fairly standard form.

harmony in classical thought, the mathematical order that underlies the organized world. Harmony is more than just musical order; it is a principle of order, based on mathematical relations, which pervades all of the relations of things.

hedonism the theory that pleasure is the only value that needs no additional justification. Hedonism analyzes all other values in terms of their ability to produce pleasure.

hermeneutics the theory of interpretation, particularly interpretation of texts, broadly conceived. Hermeneutics considers the interaction of the text with its audience as a single complex whole.

hierarchy an arrangement of elements into an ascending order. Hierarchical orders attempt to give everything a fixed place in a single overall order.

hierophant a person who exhibits the sacred, such as a priest. A hierophany is a manifestation of the sacred in the present.

humanism the Renaissance philosophy that emphasized the possibilities and limits of human endeavor. Humanists tended to look back to the ancient world for their models.

hyperbole a figure of speech that makes use of exaggeration and overstatement.

idealism the philosophical theory that takes mental reality as the fundamental reality. Idealism reduces everything else to mental constructs and representations. The material world is an instantiation of ideas.

illumination in medieval philosophy, the means by which some internal principle is known to the mind. Illumination works at all levels, from physical light to the soul's insight into the divine mystery.

imitation literally, making something according to a model already known. In art theory, imitation means more than just copying; it implies a theory in which reality is located in single forms and everything else is derived from those forms.

impressionism the movement in painting that sought to represent visual effects directly. Impressionism is concerned with representing the visual effect and the play of light rather than a polished surface or a transparent image of an object or scene.

incorporeal without a body. Many classical philosophies depended on the existence of an incorporeal reality.

individualism the philosophical view that singles out individual persons as the basic cultural unit. In the classical and medieval worldviews, individuals were subordinate to larger units such as the city, the clan, and the church or religious cult.

innate ideas postulated as ideas that are already in the mind at birth or through a kind of logical or natural memory. Innate ideas do not have to be discovered through experience.

intercalary literally, an extra day or month inserted into a calendar. By extension, any insertion into a literary work, such as an added line, is intercalary.

internal sense a theory that in addition to the five external senses, we have a way of perceiving directly some moral and aesthetic qualities.

introspection the philosophical technique of examining one's own interior consciousness and its contents. Introspection is supposed to have an advantage of immediacy of access because no external transmission of sense data is required.

irony a way of saying something by presenting its opposite. Irony is frequently a matter of tone or style; it suggests that what is said should be taken in the opposite sense.

mannerism in painting, the style that emphasized the individuality of the artist by elaborate use of detail and exaggeration of form. Mannerism is associated with Italian painting in the sixteenth and early seventeenth centuries.

materialism the theory that the mind and ideas are reducible to matter and movement. Materialism opposes idealism.

medieval roughly, the historical period from the breakdown of Roman authority in the West in the fifth century to the rise of the modern worldview in the fifteenth and sixteenth centuries.

metaphor a figure of speech that assigns a new or extended meaning to a term by equating it with something it would not normally describe. Metaphors have the form "*A* is *B*" where *B* would not normally be considered as applying to *A*.

metaphysics the area of philosophy that deals with the kinds and categories of things that make up the world. Metaphysics is concerned with "what there is" in the broadest sense of existence.

meter the arrangement of either stress patterns or voiced length of syllables in poetry.

modernism as an historical period, the term is used to characterize a variety of movements between the seventeenth and twentieth centuries. It is most often applied to the individualistic and optimistic view of human nature, which holds that the human intellect is the measure of all things and can achieve knowledge based on well-established foundations.

Muse literally, the Muses were divine beings who the Greeks believed brought inspiration to humans. They are invoked by poets and other artists in a conventional appeal to be able to create their works.

mythology stories of the gods and the origin of the world at the beginning of time. Mythology now has the connotation of falsehood, but in the classical world of the Mediterranean mythological narratives were perceived as true.

naturalism in painting, the concentration on a realistic depiction of ordinary subjects and life.

neoclassicism the literary and philosophical movement that took as its ideal classical style and values. Neoclassicism tended to be conservative, pessimistic, satiric, and concerned with teaching, particularly moral values.

neo-Kantian the movement in philosophy that applies the work of Kant to language, mythology, and symbolism. Neo-Kantianism views language and symbols as the means by which humans are able to perceive and think.

neo-Platonism the school of philosophy founded by Plotinus. Neo-Platonism claimed to follow and further develop the ideas of Plato. In neo-Platonism, mental reality is basic, and everything is related into a single whole.

nominalism the philosophical theory that the meaning of terms is always given by reference to particular things. For a nominalist, the name of something is assigned more or less arbitrarily; any other name would do as well if the assignment could be made effectively.

objective independent of the thinker or of any mental control.

ode a long lyric poem on a serious subject. Odes do not have any one set structure.

ontological proof a proof of the existence of God based on the meaning of the word *god* itself.

ontology the study of being as such. Ontology attempts to give an account of the meaning of the verb *to be* and its application to what there is.

panegyric a literary form whose primary purpose is praise.

paradigm a model, particularly the first occurrence of something.

paradox an apparent contradiction where two contrary beliefs seem equally obvious and acceptable.

participation the theory, common to Plato and Plotinus, that the mind is joined to higher forms by a direct union.

patronage the practice of support for the arts and artists from institutions and individuals. Prior to our consumer economy, patronage was the primary source of support for the arts.

peripatetics followers of Artistotle and his philosophical successors.

perspective the artistic technique of providing depth to a two-dimensional representation by foreshortening and relative size adjustments.

phenomenology the approach to philosophy that holds that what we are conscious of and the conditions of consciousness can be analyzed independently of their psychological and natural occurrence. Phenomenology has its origin at the beginning of the twentieth century in the work of the German philosopher Edmund Husserl (1859–1938).

phenomenon an occurrence in the world. Phenomena are essentially what happen, independently of what we may think of them or how we may explain them.

pietism the Protestant religious movement, particularly in Germany, that stressed individual religious experience, devotional sincerity, biblical study, and practical as opposed to dogmatic Christianity.

poetics the theory of literary form and practice. Poetics is not limited to poetry as such; it includes drama, fiction, and other literary genres.

polysemy having multiple meanings.

postimpressionism the movement in art that added to the impressionist emphasis on visual effects a flattening of the picture plane and an emphasis on the effects of picture surface as opposed to the subject. The leading postimpressionists were Paul Cézanne (1830–1906) and Vincent Van Gogh (1853–1890).

potency in metaphysics, the potential that any thing has to be other than its immediate form.

proposition a sentence or statement that can be either true or false depending on its form and what it asserts. A proposition is distinguished from the sentence that expresses it. The same proposition may be expressed by many sentences (e.g., in different languages).

protagonist the leading figure in a play around whom the plot revolves.

provenance in art history, the genealogy of a painting. The provenance of a work of art tells when, where, and by whom it was painted and traces its subsequent ownership to guarantee its authenticity.

purgatory in theology, the region occupied by the dead that is neither heaven nor hell. It is possible for some souls to move from purgatory to heaven; pre-Christian souls can occupy purgatory on the basis of their virtue, but they are excluded from heaven because they came before Christ.

rationalism the philosophical approach that sought certainty by confirming what is known by logical methods and abstract standards available to the mind itself. Rationalists held that a perfect science could be formulated and that some ideas did not require direct experience.

Renaissance the period that saw itself as a rebirth of classical style and values. As an historical period, the Renaissance is characterized by a break with medieval communal values and a new emphasis on individual knowledge and experience. The dates of the Renaissance as an historical period vary widely from the fourteenth century in Italy to as late as the seventeenth century in northern Europe.

rhetoric the classical art of speaking. Rhetoric dealt with effective presentation and style. The other elements of the basic classical curriculum included logic—the art of ordering and presenting the argument, and grammar—the art of ordering and presenting the sentences themselves.

romanticism the movement in poetry and philosophy that draws its inspiration from the ability to feel aesthetically and then project that feeling onto life and art.

sacred those parts of reality that come from the gods or belong to a separate realm of reality associated with the origin of the world.

satire a literary genre that holds up some idea or group for examination and ridicule. Satire comes in many forms, but it differs from comedy by being more pointed in its favoring or opposing something.

scholasticism the medieval philosophical method based on setting up opposing positions on a question and then resolving the apparent conflict. More broadly, scholasticism was a method of logical argumentation using syllogisms and based on the precedent of authority.

sensibility the special ability to perceive what is aesthetic, either in art or in nature. Sensibility is more than just perceptual acuteness; it includes a mental ability to appreciate what is perceived.

skepticism the view that knowledge, particularly knowledge of the external world, is impossible. Skeptics deny that we can every really know anything.

solipsism the view that an individual can know only his or her own mind. We have no access to other minds, the solipsist holds.

subjective dependent on the mind or controllable by mental processes.

sublime either an alternative aesthetic form to beauty or a subcategory of beauty. The sublime is characterized by awe approaching fear and an experience of the greatness of what is observed—both physically and emotionally.

substance in metaphysics, the idea that there is an underlying strata of being that is common to all that exists and supports the external differences.

syllogism a form of argument made up of categorical statements arranged in the form of two premises and a conclusion. A syllogism relates three classes by inclusion (all, some) and exclusion (none, not some)—for example, "All P is M," "All M is S," therefore, "All S is P," where S, M, and P are classes of things.

taste in aesthetics, either an additional sense that responds directly to aesthetic properties or a metaphor for a combination of immediate pleasure combined with judgment.

tragedy the literary form that resolves its problems and achieves its effects by a catastrophe or sacrifice of its protagonist.

trompe l'oeil deceiving the eye. A form of painting designed to provide an illusion of reality, usually by the use of perspective and color.

volition voluntary will. Volition implies the ability to act or not to act.

votive a form of worship or offering.

Index